The Self in Context

International Advances in Self Research

Series Editors: Herbert W. Marsh, Australian Catholic University;
Rhonda G. Craven, Australian Catholic University;
Ronnel B. King, The Chinese University of Hong Kong;
Frédéric Guay, Laval University, Quebec;
Theresa Dicke, Australian Catholic University

Maximizing self-concept is recognized as a critical goal in itself and a means to facilitate other desirable outcomes in a diversity of settings. The desire to feel positive about oneself and the benefits of this feeling on choice, planning, persistence, and subsequent accomplishments transcend traditional disciplinary barriers and are central to goals in many social policy areas

"International Advances in Self Research" monograph series publishes scholarly works that primarily focus on self-concept research and pertain to a broad array of self-related constructs and processes including self-esteem, self-efficacy, identity, motivation, anxiety, self-attributions, self-regulated learning, and metacognition. The research focus of the monograph series includes theory underlying these constructs, their measurement, their relation to each other and to other constructs, their enhancement, and their application in research and practice. Chapters address a wide cross-section of settings, participants and research areas. This series has a special interest in self-concept theory and research in settings characterized by diversity, such as special education, linguistic diversity, socioeconomic, and cultural diversity

The book series editors, namely Herbert W. Marsh, Australian Catholic University, Rhonda G. Craven, Australian Catholic University, Ronnel B. King, The Chinese University of Hong Kong, Frédéric Guay, Université Laval, and Theresa Dicke, Australian Catholic University are Executive members of the international Global SELF Research Centre. Under the direction of Herbert W. Marsh, the SELF Research Centre is headquartered at the Institute of Positive Psychology and Education (IPPE), Australian Catholic University. It is a virtual network which currently has 700 members and satellite research centers at leading universities around the world. Its members include many of the world's leading self and identity researchers. The Centre fulfills an important niche both as an international research center of excellence and as the unique center in the world dedicated to self-concept research. The Global SELF Research Centre has organized the Self Biennial International Conferences in Sydney Australia (2000, 2002), Berlin Germany (2004), Ann Arbor USA (2006), United Arab Emirates (2009), Laval Canada (2011), Singapore (2013), Kiel Germany (2015), Melbourne Australia (2017), and Quebec Canada (2022) with leading international scholars in the field of Self as keynote speakers. The next conference will be held in Singapore (November 2025).

OTHER TITLES IN INTERNATIONAL ADVANCES IN SELF RESEARCH SERIES

SELF - A Multidisciplinary Concept
SELF - Driving Positive Psychology and Wellbeing
Self-Concept, Motivation and Identity
Theory Driving Research
Self-Processes, Learning and Enabling Human Potential
New Frontiers for Self Research
International Advances in Self Research – volume 1

The Self in Context

Pathways to Flourishing, Learning, and Well-Being

Edited by

Ronnel B. King

The Chinese University of Hong Kong, Hong Kong

Herbert W. Marsh

Australian Catholic University, Australia

Rhonda G. Craven

Australian Catholic University, Australia

Theresa Dicke

Australian Catholic University, Australia

And

Frédéric Guay

University of Laval, Canada

emerald PUBLISHING

United Kingdom – North America – Japan
India – Malaysia – China

Emerald Publishing Limited, Floor 5, Northspring, 21-23 Wellington Street,
Leeds LS1 4DL

First edition 2026

Printed and bound by CPI Group (UK) Ltd, Croydon, CR0 4YY

British Library Cataloging in Publication Data
A catalog record for this book is available from the British Library

ISBN: 978-1-80686-870-4 (Print hardback)
ISBN: 978-1-80686-872-8 (Print paperback)
ISBN: 978-1-80686-869-8 (PDF)
ISBN: 978-1-80686-871-1 (EPUB)

Typeset by TNQ Tech
Cover design by TNQ Tech

This volume is dedicated to the memory and enduring legacy of Professor Dennis M. McInerney, a pioneer in the study of culture and motivation.

Dennis's groundbreaking work helped reshape our understanding of how culture shapes the self, motivation, and learning. He inspired us to challenge assumptions, embrace cultural nuance, and seek deeper insights into what drives learners across diverse contexts. His commitment to bridging Western theories with nonWestern perspectives opened new frontiers in educational psychology. Beyond his scholarship, Dennis was a generous mentor, a passionate teacher, and a great colleague. He loved life and lived it to the fullest. Beyond his research accomplishments, his legacy is most evident in the lives he has touched, and the new generation of scholars he has generously mentored and supported.

CONTENTS

SECTION 1

THEORETICAL FOUNDATIONS OF THE SELF

SECTION 2

THE SELF AS EMBEDDED IN CULTURE AND CONTEXT

SECTION 3

APPLIED PERSPECTIVES ON SELF RESEARCH

ABOUT THE EDITORS

Professor Ronnel B. King is an Associate Professor in the Faculty of Education, The Chinese University of Hong Kong. He is interested in understanding the factors that underpin motivation, socio-emotional learning, and well-being. He is also keen on leveraging positive psychology/education interventions to enhance these optimal states. He has received numerous awards including the Michael Harris Bond Award for Early Career Contributions to Social Psychology, the Association for Psychological Science Rising Star Award, and the Global SELF Highly Commended Dissertation Award. He is a Top 1% highly cited author according to Clarivate Analytics, among the top 1% most highly cited education researcher in the world both in terms of lifetime citations and recent year citations, and identified as the #1 most productive early career researcher in Asia (Fong et al., 2022).

Professor Herbert W. Marsh is an "ISI highly cited researcher" with 800+ publications, 150,000+ citations, and a Google Scholar H-index = 193. In 2020, and again in 2021, he was recognized as the highest-ranked educational researcher in the world compared to a cohort of 75,000+ educational researchers for both total career and calendar year citations (https://doi.org/10.1371/journal, pbio.3000918). The American Educational Research Association (AERA) awarded him a Career Achievement Award. In 2017, the Australian Psychological Society (APS) awarded him the Distinguished Contribution to Psychological Science Award. He is a Fellow of AERA, Australian Academy of Social Sciences, British Academy of Social Sciences, Society of Multivariate Experimental Psychology, and International Congress of Applied Psychology.

Professor Rhonda G. Craven (PhD, BA (Hons), University Medal, Dip Teach) is the inaugural Director of The Institute for Positive Psychology and Education at the Australian Catholic University. Her published works focus on the structure, measurement, development and enhancement of self-concept; key psycho-social drivers of educational outcomes, wellbeing and life potential; effective methods of teaching Indigenous students and Indigenous Studies in educational settings; and interventions that make a tangible difference in educational settings.

Professor Theresa Dicke is the Educational and Developmental Psychology Program Leader at the Institute for Positive Psychology and Education (IPPE), Australian Catholic University. Her research mainly focuses on resources and their relationship with occupational well-being. She particularly investigates the role of self-beliefs within the stress development or health maintenance process. Having worked at a Department for Instructional Psychology for several years, she is also interested in several constructs related to learning, such as professional knowledge, student attrition, self-regulated learning (strategies), and cognitive load. In her Professorial role at the IPPE, her research is oriented largely around examining self-concept and related constructs.

Professor Frédéric Guay is a professor of Measurement and Evaluation at Université Laval and the chairholder of the Canada research chair on motivation, perseverance, and school success. He holds a PhD in social psychology from the University of Quebec at Montreal. His research, grounded in Self-Determination Theory and Self-Concept Theory, focuses on motivation, academic achievement, and student well-being. He has published extensively in peer-reviewed journals, contributed to book chapters, and presented at international conferences. His work helps shape educational practices and policies, particularly in promoting student engagement and reducing dropout rates. Recognized for his involvement in leading international research networks on motivation, he was elected president of Division 5 (Educational, Instructional, and School Psychology) of the International Association for Applied Psychology in 2014.

ABOUT THE CONTRIBUTORS

Kelly-Ann Allen is an Associate Professor and Educational and Developmental Psychologist at Monash University, and an Honorary Principal Fellow at the Center for Wellbeing Science, University of Melbourne. She is currently the Editor-in-Chief of the *Educational and Developmental Psychologist* and founder and lead director of the Global Belonging Collaborative. A/Prof Allen's mission is to emphasize the importance of belonging in day-to-day life and to understand how it can be enhanced across the lifespan, particularly in educational contexts. Allen is recognised by The Australian as one of Australia's top researchers in belonging and school belonging. In terms of positionality, Allen's personal experiences, as a bi-racial woman of Anglo-Indian/Fijian descent with ancestral ties to indentured labor, displacement, intergenerational abandonment, and family ties to Aboriginal communities, deeply inform her understanding of belonging.

Mimi Bong is a Professor of Educational Psychology and Director of the Brain & Motivation Research Institute (bMRI) at Korea University. She earned her PhD in educational psychology and technology from the University of Southern California in 1995 and was an Associate Professor at the University of South Carolina and Ewha Womans University. Bong studies student motivation with particular emphasis on self-efficacy, achievement goals, and self-regulation. She is also interested in theoretical and empirical comparisons of motivation constructs as well as cross-domain and cross-cultural generalizability of motivational processes. Her work regularly appears in top-tier journals in the field. Bong received the Richard E. Snow Award for Early Contributions in Educational Psychology and is a Fellow of both the American Psychological Association (Division 15) and the American Educational Research Association. She has served as Editor-in-Chief for the Journal of Experimental Education and Associate Editor for the American Educational Research Journal.

Emma L. Bradshaw is Senior Research Fellow and Deputy Director at the Institute for Positive Psychology and Education at Australian Catholic University. A specialist in Self-Determination Theory (SDT), her work focuses on goal contents theory and the role of intrinsic and extrinsic aspirations in shaping well-being, prosocial values, and prosocial striving. Emma applies a range of traditional and advanced quantitative methods to understand the contextual and psychological conditions that support positive development across domains such as parenting, education, and health. She is Review Editor at *Frontiers in Psychology* and Goals and Values Editor for the *Centre for Self-Determination Theory*. Her research has been recognised with the Dennis McInerney SELF PhD Award (2022) and a nomination for the ACU Vice-Chancellor's Award for Excellence During Doctoral Studies.

Julien S. Bureau is a professor of Measurement and Evaluation at Université Laval. He holds a PhD in social psychology from the University of Montreal. His research is grounded in applying Self-Determination Theory to the field of education, emphasizing empirical work using large-scale surveys and experimental designs in the lab. His substantive interests target academic motivation, cheating, student well-being, and educational equity. He also favors working on manuscripts that popularize underexploited or promising quantitative methods. His metaanalytic contributions have provided a clear explanation of antecedents and consequences associated with academic motivation. His teaching focuses on research methodology and the pursuit of equity in assessment.

Li Lian Chua is a Research Fellow at the Physical Education and Sports Science (PESS) in National Institute of Education (Nanyang Technological University). She holds a PhD in Sports and Exercise Psychology from Nanyang Technological University. She was a teacher (1999) and badminton coach (2006) in primary and secondary schools. She was an associate lecturer (2006) at Republic Polytechnic before becoming a research assistant (2008) and part-time lecturer (2021) at Physical Education and Sports Science in National Institute of Education (Nanyang Technological University). She was also a research associate (2023) at Office of Teacher Education in National Institute of Education (Nanyang Technological University). Her research program has been organized by achievement goal theory and self-determination theory. This program has led to publications and book chapters in the educational and sport domains.

William Gilbert is an assistant professor of social psychology at Université du Québec à Rimouski (Quebec, Canada). His research focuses on the individual and social determinants of youth well-being and optimal functioning, particularly during key life transitions. His work examines factors such as self-esteem, self-control, self-determination, achievement goals and emotional competence. He has published extensively on the role of educational contexts in shaping students' academic and psychological outcomes. His research employs longitudinal designs and a combination of variable- and person-centered analyses to better capture the complexity of student experiences and well-being.

Luyang Guo is an Assistant Professor of Educational Testing, Assessment, and Evaluation at the University of Macau. She received her PhD from The Chinese University of Hong Kong and holds two master's degrees from Teachers College, Columbia University. Her research program centers on educational psychology, career development, and school-to-work transitions, with a particular focus on international large-scale assessments and quantitative research methods. Grounded in theoretical frameworks such as the big-fish-little-pond effect, her work examines how personal and contextual factors influence adolescents' career expectations and psychological well-being. Her research has been published in leading journals, including the *Journal of Vocational Behavior* and the *Journal of Youth and Adolescence*. Dr. Guo has also contributed to global education initiatives, serving as an International Quality Control Monitor for the 2023 Trends in International Mathematics and Science Study (TIMSS).

John Hattie is Emeritus Laureate Professor at the Melbourne Graduate School of Education at the University of Melbourne, Chief Academic Advisor for Corwin, i-Ready Technical Advisor, and co-director of the Hattie Family Foundation. His Visible Learning research is based on ¼ billion students and he continues to update this research (with the recent Sequel). He has published and presented over 1,000 papers, 70 books – including 40 on Visible Learning, and supervised 220 theses students.

Kit-Tai Hau is a Research Professor of Educational Psychology at The Chinese University of Hong Kong. A recognized Fellow of both the American Educational Research Association (AERA) and the International Association of Applied Psychology (IAAP), Professor Hau has contributed significantly to educational and curriculum reform through expert panels in mainland China, Macau SAR, Korea, Brunei, and other regions. He formerly served as IAAP President of the Educational, Instructional, and School Psychology Division. Professor Hau has also been a member of numerous advisory groups for the Program for International Student Assessment (PISA), including the Technical Advisory Group (TAG), Questionnaire Expert Group (QEG), Strategic Development Group (SDG), and the Study on Social and Emotional Skills (SSESs), as well as the TIMSS Questionnaire Item Expert Group for the International Association for the

Evaluation of Educational Achievement (IEA). His research interests include academic motivation, international educational comparisons, educational assessment, and psychological well-being.

Dayeon Jeong is a PhD candidate in educational psychology and a graduate research assistant at the Brain & Motivation Research Institute (bMRI) at Korea University. She earned her master's degree in educational psychology from Korea University in 2023 and is currently serving as a student representative at bMRI. Her research interests include learners' achievement goals, growth mindset, self-efficacy, task values, as well as academic and social emotions that motivate learners. She is particularly interested in how motivational constructs interact, how context and culture influence achievement motivation, and how evidence-based interventions can enhance student motivation. Jeong has presented research on the interaction between achievement goals and cognitive load, the contextual and personal precursors of growth mindset and expectancy-value profiles, and the use of technology to enhance the self-efficacy of counselors-in-training.

Ying Hwa Kee is an Associate Professor and currently the Head of the Physical Education and Sports Science Department at NIE. He was the Assistant Dean, Graduate Education (Research) at NIE. Dr. Kee received his doctoral training from National Taiwan Normal University, supported by the Taiwan Scholarship. He holds a MSc in Exercise & Sport Studies from NTU and a Bachelor's degree in Physical and Health Education (B.P.H.E) from the University of Western Australia. As a scholar in sport psychology and motor behavior, his specific research interest lies in the application of mindfulness in human movements and peak performance. His authored work, "Relationships between mindfulness, flow dispositions and mental skills adoption," published in the journal Psychology of Sport & Exercise Science, ranks among the top three most frequently cited articles on mindfulness and sport from 1968 to 2021 (Birrer et al., 2023). His latest research focuses on the effects of mindfulness on complex pattern recognition to enhance performance in sports and human movements. Dr. Kee's teaching expertise includes sport psychology, motor behavior, research methods, sport technology, and systems thinking. He also holds a WSQ Diploma in Adult and Continuing Education (DACE) and has extensive experience in conducting corporate training workshops. Previously serving as Co-Editor for the International Journal of Sport Psychology, Dr. Kee is currently an Associate Editor for the Asian Journal of Sport and Exercise Psychology.

Sungwha Kim earned her PhD in educational psychology from Korea University in 2025. She was a graduate research assistant at the Brain & Motivation Research Institute (bMRI) and previously served as a student representative at bMRI. Her research focuses on academic motivation, particularly in the areas of achievement goals, growth mindset, and self-regulated learning. She is especially interested in distinguishing between different motivational constructs from both theoretical and empirical perspectives, examining the role of sociocultural factors in shaping student motivation, and developing interventions to enhance student motivation in K-12 classrooms. Her work has been published in the Journal of Educational Psychology, Social Psychology of Education, and Theory Into Practice, covering a range of related yet diverse topics such as the effects of different types of achievement goals, the influence of socializers' beliefs on student motivation, and the development and evaluation of intervention programs designed to improve educational outcomes.

Leng Chee Kong holds a PhD from the National Institute of Education, Nanyang Technological University (2020)and was a postdoctoral research fellow at the Motivation in Educational Research Laboratory of the same university (2021–2022). She has variously been a school-teacher, a teacher-educator and an educational researcher. Her research interests center around motivation and mindfulness in learning. She is a strong believer of self-determination as the energizer, driver and staying power in the many things people do. She is curious about the application of Self-Determination Theory in a myriad of settings, such as in K-12 mainstream and special education schools, higher education institutions and mental health institutions. She is particularly interested in exploring the conditions under which self-determined behaviors can be fostered such as through autonomy-supportive instructions or mindfulness practices. She is currently with the Singapore Public Service where she does educational research and conducts courses for teachers.

Gregory Arief D. Liem is an Associate Professor in the Department of Psychology and Child & Human Development at the National Institute of Education, Nanyang Technological University, Singapore. He currently serves as an Associate Editor of *Educational Psychology: An International Journal of Experimental Educational Psychology and Psychology in the Schools,* and sits on the Editorial Boards of several leading journals, including *The Journal of Experimental Education, British Journal of Educational Psychology, Measurement and Evaluation in Counseling and Development,* and *Journal of Psychologists and Counsellors in Schools.* He is also the Editor of the book series *Research on Sociocultural Influences on Learning and Motivation* (Emerald, UK), originally founded by the late Dennis McInerney.

Woon Chia Liu is the Director at the National Institute of Education (NIE), Nanyang Technological University (NTU), the sole teacher education institute in Singapore. She is also a Professor with the Psychology and Child & Human Development Department, and a co-founder of the NIE's Motivation in Educational Research Laboratory (MERL). She is the Immediate Past Dean of Teacher Education at the NIE. During her Deanship, she led her team to develop and implement the NTU-NIE Teaching Scholars Program (TSP), the Bachelor of Arts/Science Double Major Programmes (Academic Discipline and Education) and the 16-month extended Postgraduate Diploma in Education programmes. In addition, she was a key member of the steering committee and a co-chair of the working committee that shaped the Singapore Teaching Practice (STP), which articulates Singapore's vision of learning in the classroom, our beliefs about students as learners, and the teaching practices that support the realisation of this vision. Her research interests include motivation, teacher education, innovative pedagogy, e-portfolio and clinical practice.

Betsy Ng is a researcher and lecturer at the National Institute of Education, Nanyang Technological University, Singapore. Having a strong interest in education, Betsy has an extensive working experience as an education specialist, polytechnic lecturer, editor, and educator in a range of educational settings. She has been actively involved in education research since 2009. Her areas of expertise include motivation and lifelong learning. Her research interests are educational psychology, adult learning, educational neuroscience, and gerontology. To date, she has over 80 peer-reviewed articles and conference paper presentations. She is the lead and sole editor (and author) of four scholarly books. She serves as an invited reviewer for numerous academic journals and conferences such as *Learning and Individual Differences*, *Learning and Motivation*, and *American Educational Research Association*. She is also an invited international editorial panel member for the *Cambridge Journal of Education*.

Seohee Park is a PhD candidate in educational psychology and a graduate research assistant at the Brain & Motivation Research Institute (bMRI) at Korea University. She earned her master's degree in educational psychology from Korea University in 2022 and previously served as a student representative at bMRI. Her research centers on academic motivation, especially achievement goals, self-regulation, and curiosity. She is particularly interested in how motivational constructs interact with cognitive and emotional processes, the influence of sociocultural contexts on students' motivation, and the design and validation of intervention programs aimed at fostering adaptive motivation and learning behaviors in K–12 settings. Her work includes research on the effects of achievement goals on self-control, teacher effects on student motivation across classroom variables, and the longitudinal development of motivational profiles among adolescents.

Reinhard Pekrun is a Professor of Psychology at the University of Essex, United Kingdom, and a Professorial Fellow at the Institute of Positive Psychology and Education, Australian Catholic University, Sydney, Australia. He pioneered research on emotions in education, originated the Control-Value Theory of Achievement Emotions, and authored 27 books and more than 350 articles and chapters. Pekrun is a Web of Science highly cited researcher listed among the top 10 currently most cited educational scientists in the world. Among his numerous awards are the 2015 John G. Diefenbaker Award from the Canada Council, which acknowledges outstanding research accomplishments in the humanities and social sciences, the Sylvia Scribner Award 2017 (American Educational Research Association), the EARLI Oeuvre Award 2017 (European Association for Research on Learning and Instruction), and the Lifetime Achievement Award 2018 of the German Psychological Society.

Johnmarshall Reeve is a Professor in the Institute for Positive Psychology and Education at the Australian Catholic University (since February 2019). Before ACU, Reeve was a professor in both South Korea (Korea University) and the United States (University of Iowa, University of Wisconsin-Milwaukee). His research focuses on all aspects of human motivation and emotion with a special emphasis on teachers' motivating styles, students' engagement, and the neuroscience of intrinsic motivation. For his work on autonomy-supportive teaching, Prof. Reeve received (a) the Thomas N. Urban Research Award for the enhancement of educational practice from the FINE Foundation (2005), (b) the Research Excellence Award from Korea University (2016, 2017), and (c) the Excellence in Research Award from the NASPSPA (2017, 2024). He has published 94 articles in peer-reviewed journals, such as the Journal of Educational Psychology, authored 33 book chapters and 4 books, including Supporting students' motivation and Understanding Motivation and Emotion (8e). Prof. Reeve served as past Editor-in-Chief of the journal *Motivation and Emotion*, and he currently serves on the editorial boards of five journals.

Professor Richard M. Ryan is a clinical psychologist and co-developer of Self-Determination Theory (SDT), a leading theory of human motivation, healthy development, and optimal functioning. With over 500 published scientific papers and books, Professor Ryan is among the most cited and influential researchers in psychology and social sciences today. Reflective of Ryan's influence internationally and across disciplines, he has been recognized as one of the eminent psychologists of the modern era, listed among the "World's Top 20 Scientists" across all fields, and been honored with multiple lifetime achievement awards. Professor Ryan currently holds the positions of Professor at the Institute for Positive Psychology and Education at Australian Catholic University and Distinguished Professor at Ewha Womans University in South Korea.

Ellen A. Skinner is a Professor of Psychology at Portland State University, in Portland, Oregon. As part of Psychology's concentration in Developmental Science and Education, her research explores the development and optimization of students' motivation, coping, and academic identity during middle childhood and early adolescence. She is especially focused on two ingredients that shape motivational resilience: (1) close relationships with teachers, parents, and peers, and (2) academic work that is authentic and intrinsically motivating. Dr Skinner received her PhD in Human Development from Pennsylvania State University in 1981 and then worked at the Max Planck Institute for Human Development and Education in Berlin, Germany, for seven years. She spent four years at University of Rochester with appointments in Psychology and the Graduate School of Education and Human Development, where she worked with the Motivational Research Group, and was tenured before moving to Portland in 1992.

Chee Keng John Wang is the Inaugural E. W. Barker Chair Professor at the Department of Physical Education and Sport Science (PESS), National Institute of Education (NIE), Nanyang Technological University and a full professor at National University of Singapore. He is a British Psychological Society Chartered Psychologist and Associate Fellow and registered with the Health Professions Council of UK as a Sport and Exercise Psychologist. He obtained his PhD from Loughborough University in the United Kingdom in Sport and Exercise Psychology. Dr Wang leads a group of NIE staff in the Motivation in Educational Research Lab (MERL) in NIE. His areas of research include motivational and emotional aspects of sport, physical activity, as well as in academic subject areas. His recent publications have been on sport ability beliefs, achievement goals, intrinsic motivation, emotion, and self-esteem. In addition, he also wrote papers on outdoor education, project work, internet gaming, and problem-based learning.

Michael Witter is Senior Lecturer at Australian Catholic University. He received his PhD through the Science of Learning Research Center at Melbourne University. His research focuses on quality teaching, its multidimensionality and its measurement, including the beliefs of effective teachers. He led the development of and is currently Head of Discipline for an employment-based, equity-driven teacher education program that integrates and applies research-based best practices for promoting quality teaching.

REFERENCES

Birrer, D., Scalvedi, B., & Frings, N. (2023). A bibliometric analysis of mindfulness and acceptance research in sports from 1969 to 2021. *Mindfulness, 14*(5), 1038–1053.

Fong, C. J., Flanigan, A. E., Hogan, E., Brady, A. C., Griffin, M. M., Gonzales, C., García, A. J., Fathi, Z., & Robinson, D. H. (2022). Individual and institutional productivity in educational psychology journals from 2015 to 2021. *Educational Psychology Review, 34*(4), 2379–2403.

SECTION 1

THEORETICAL FOUNDATIONS OF THE SELF

CHAPTER 1

DEVELOPMENT OF THE SELF AS PART OF DYNAMIC SYSTEMS INVOLVING CONTEXT, ACTION, AND OUTCOMES: THE SAMPLE CASE OF MOTIVATIONAL RESILIENCE

Ellen A. Skinner
Portland State University, USA

ABSTRACT

The goal of this chapter is to explore how systems theories of motivation and the self can be used to provide a window on the invisible workings underlying student motivational resilience and vulnerability. The major contribution this chapter attempts to make to these discussions is the idea that the self, along with motivational resilience and vulnerability, cannot be understood by looking at these processes in isolation. Instead, they are better conceptualized as parts of *dynamic systems*, self-systems and motivational systems, that consist of multiple components (including other people, activities, and settings) that work together over time to give rise to the states referred to as motivational resilience as well as the constructions we call "self." To illustrate the utility of

The Self in Context, pages 3–47

Published under exclusive licence by Emerald Publishing Limited
doi:10.1108/978-1-80686-869-820261001

systems conceptualizations, this chapter uses Self-Determination Theory as a springboard to explore the role of key aspects of academic identity and the self in the development of students' motivational resilience. The chapter is organized in three sections. The first briefly explains a systems perspective by laying out the major components of the motivational system. The second section explains how these parts work together to create dynamics that shape the development of both motivational resilience and the self. The third section explores how this view of motivation can be useful not only to researchers, but also to practitioners, parents, and other educational stakeholders whose goals include supporting the academic development and success of children and youth.

Keywords: Motivational resilience; dynamic systems; academic identity; self-determination theory; motivation in education

Teachers, parents, and researchers recognize engaged and motivated students when they see them. No matter their age, these students' energy and enthusiasm spill out into the classroom or home setting. In school, such students come prepared, listen carefully, work industriously, raise their hands, have lots to say to their group members about projects they are working on, follow instructions and take feedback from teachers, can work independently but know when to ask for help, take on challenging assignments, and persevere despite obstacles and setbacks. Researchers have even coined a term for these exuberant behaviors, namely, *motivational resilience*, defined as "patterns of action that allow students to constructively deal with, overcome, recover, and learn from encounters with academic obstacles and failures" (Skinner et al., 2020, p. 290).

Teachers and parents agree that motivational resilience is good for students, and research from a range of areas in education, psychology, and developmental and motivational science backs them up. Largely independent lines of work (on, for example, buoyancy, mastery, engagement and re-engagement, self-regulated learning, academic coping, emotion regulation, tenacity, grit, and productive persistence) converge on their benefits for a range of student outcomes, encompassing not only academic functioning and success but also student well-being and personal growth (Datu & Yuen, 2018; Martin, 2013; Skinner et al., 2020; Wang et al., 2019; Wong et al., 2024). Teachers and parents are also clear on the costs to students who do not manifest these behaviors, a state sometimes referred to as *motivational vulnerability*, which involves a range of disengaged and disaffected actions, like passivity, boredom, frustration, under or overregulation, maladaptive coping, giving up, and burnout (Madigan & Curran, 2021; Skinner et al., 2020). As can be imagined, research also shows that indicators of motivational vulnerability are risk factors for students, foreshadowing potential academic trouble, emotional distress, and eventual dropout (Li & Lerner, 2011; Wang et al., 2019).

Although the experience and importance of motivational resilience are apparent, the causal processes that support it are not. We can agree that we want to help children and adolescents develop a rich and flexible repertoire of tools for dealing productively with everyday academic demands and challenges. However, for the most part, we do not know as much as we would like about how to accomplish this goal—for reasons theoretical, empirical, and practical. Theoretically and empirically, most research relevant to motivational resilience focuses on its markers and outcomes; few studies examine its interpersonal and contextual antecedents, and even fewer its developmental course. Practically, although the manifestations of motivational resilience and vulnerability are actions, and therefore visible to parents, teachers, and peers, their underlying causes are not, leaving caring adults with a clear picture of motivational "symptoms" but little information about how to "diagnose" and "treat" these issues (Furrer et al., 2014).

The primary goal of this chapter is to explain how systems theories of motivation and the self can be used to provide a window on the invisible workings underlying student motivational resilience and vulnerability. And to do so in a way that is useful, not only to researchers but also to practitioners, parents, and other educational stakeholders whose goals include supporting the academic development and success of children and youth. In keeping with the central theme of this volume, the construct of "self" figures prominently (Koenka, 2020). The major contribution this chapter attempts to make to these discussions is the idea that the self, along with motivational resilience and vulnerability, cannot be understood by looking at these processes in isolation. Instead, they are better conceptualized as parts of *dynamic systems,* self-systems and motivational systems, that consist of multiple components (including other people, activities, and settings) that work together over time to give rise to the states referred to as motivational resilience as well as the constructions we call "self."

These systems have both "internal dynamics," in which students' self-systems and motivated actions can create self-amplifying or self-correcting cycles, as well as "external dynamics" in which students' social partners (like teachers, parents, and peers) and educational tasks, along with the forces from local and higher-order settings, shape their motivation and its resilience (Skinner et al., 2020; Skinner & Pitzer, 2012). The motivational system is complex, but if explained clearly, can readily be incorporated into the mental models of the adults who teach and care for children and youth (Grolnick et al., 2024). Such enriched models, which include a central place for interpersonal factors like parenting and teaching, can paint a fuller picture of the development of students' motivation and selves, and thus provide actionable information to those who wish to support them.

To illustrate the utility of systems conceptualizations, this chapter uses Self-Determination Theory (SDT) (Connell & Wellborn, 1991; Ryan & Deci, 2017, 2020) as a springboard to explore the role of key aspects of academic identity and the self in the development of students' motivational resilience. The chapter is organized in three sections. The first briefly explains a systems perspective by laying out the major components of the motivational system, zooming in especially on the parts labeled "self," which play many important roles in its functioning. The second, and longest, section of the chapter explains how these parts work together to create dynamics that shape the development of both motivational resilience and the self. The third section explores how a view of motivation as a dynamic system can be useful in guiding educational practices and interventions.

SYSTEMS PERSPECTIVES ON THE DEVELOPMENT OF MOTIVATION AND THE SELF

A systems perspective starts with a simple premise: The patterns of motivated action we call "motivational resilience" and the constructions we call "self" are not individual attributes that belong to students. Instead, they emerge from complex orchestrations of processes from many levels and time scales, inside and outside the student. Motivational systems comprise integrated wholes, meaning that their corresponding parts work together to create (or sustain or transform) any motivational attribute researchers choose to examine. Systems perspectives offer some tools for thinking about these complex systems. They start by insisting that the many different things that motivational researchers are studying are all part of one larger thing, the motivational system. And the many different features of the self included in these theories are all part of one larger thing, the self-system.

To picture these larger wholes, systems perspectives offer ideas like "structures," "functions," and "dynamics." "Structures" refers to the parts of motivational systems and how they are organized; "functions" to how the parts work together to do things; and "dynamics" to how these two processes, namely, organization (structure) and production (function), simultaneously and cumulatively, lead the system to take on some directionality and to transform (i.e., develop) over time. At their best, systems perspectives can be integrative, organizational, and wholistic, while also being process-oriented, dynamic, and developmental. As can be imagined, there are many systems perspectives. The one utilized in this chapter has its roots in organismic-dialectical (Ryan & Deci, 2017), lifespan developmental (Skinner et al., 2019), and relational developmental systems frameworks (Overton, 2013; Overton & Lerner, 2014).

Organization of Motivational Systems

Organizations of systems are described based on the specification of component parts and their interrelationships. As pictured in Fig. 1.1, most theories of motivation are structured around four key components: context, self, action, and outcomes (Connell & Wellborn, 1991). Designating these as components of motivational systems serves several purposes. First, it underscores the differences between them. Differentiation can be helpful to motivational theories, because it suggests important distinctions between constructs of "self" and those of "motivated action" and "context." Such distinctions may be useful, for example, in conceptualizations of engagement, where features of the self are sometimes incorporated into the action component (Christenson & Reschly, 2022); or in research on sense of belonging, where operationalizations sometimes include features of the

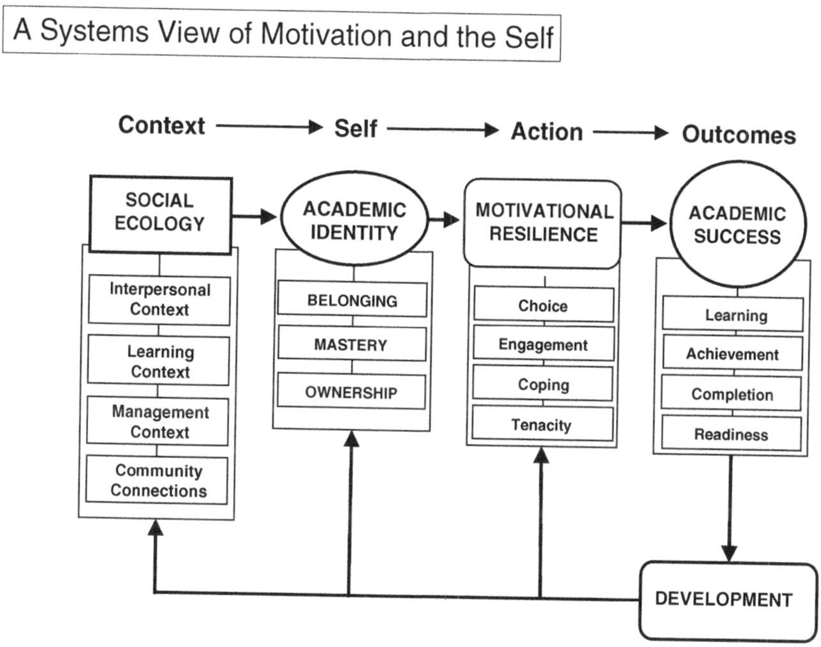

Fig. 1.1. A Schematic of the Structure of Motivational Theories Organized Around Four Components: (1) *Context*, including interpersonal, learning, and management contexts and community connections; (2) *Self* or students' motivationally relevant academic identities made up of self-system processes organized around belonging (relatedness), mastery (competence), and ownership (autonomy); (3) *Action* or students' patterns of motivational resilience, including choice, engagement, coping, and tenacity; and (4) *Outcomes* or important educational and developmental outcomes.

interpersonal context (Koerpershoek et al., 2020). Differentiation among components makes it possible to see how they work together.

Second, identifying higher-order components surfaces commonalities across motivational theories, allowing researchers to collect and integrate constructs that belong to the same component. For example, they can organize multiple aspects of the self under the umbrella of "academic identity." Third, it points the way to research on adjacent topics (like engagement, self-regulation, or coping) that may also be looking at components of motivational systems. This allows cross-fertilization and integration across areas. Finally, specifying core components can highlight gaps in individual motivational theories, which may not incorporate a particular component; as well as complementarities, where another theory may have the potential to fill in that gap. This section explains these four core components and suggests some organization within each.

Action and Its Subcomponents

The heart of motivational theories lies in the *action* component, which includes the patterns of action described previously as characterizing motivated and engaged states. This component is central because it comprises the defining features of motivation (Ryan, 2012), namely, the energy, direction, and persistence of student behavior, affect, and cognition in the educational process. The action component includes subcomponents, like choice (e.g., preference for challenge; Eccles & Wigfield, 2020), ongoing engagement (i.e., enthusiastic participation in learning activities; Wang et al., 2019), adaptive coping (i.e., constructive responses, like self-regulated leaning and adaptive help-seeking, to obstacles and problems; Karabenick & Gonida, 2018; Skinner & Saxton, 2019), and tenacity (i.e., productive persistence or buoyancy; Martin, 2013). All theories of motivation are built around some combination of these markers of motivated and engaged action (Skinner, 2023). For example, expectancy-value theories highlight choice (Eccles & Wigfield, 2020) and social cognitive theories of self-efficacy focus on effort and persistence (Schunk & DiBenedetto, 2020).

Subcomponents of action. Constructs that depict students' goal-directed behaviors and emotions on the plane of action can be collected from theories of motivation, engagement, and regulation. Once they are considered together, some additional organization *within* this component becomes apparent. For example, multiple processes surrounding students' participation in educational tasks, such as effort, initiation, concentration, and enjoyment, can be combined into a higher-order multidimensional subcomponent like engagement (Reeve, 2012; Wang et al., 2019). Or constructs like self-regulated learning, help-seeking, and coping can be combined into a subcomponent that depicts how students regulate their actions in the face of obstacles and setbacks. And constructs like tenacity, perseverance, and productive persistence can be combined into a subcomponent that refers to the durability of action.

Outcomes and Their Subcomponents

Students' motivated actions are important in their own right, but also because of the important *outcomes* they help to generate. In the academic domain, these include positive academic functioning, as seen in actual learning, achievement, and success, as well as processes of well-being and personal development. Decades of naturalistic and experimental research, from preschool to high school and beyond, have documented the important role motivated and engaged actions play in a range of student outcomes (Lei et al., 2018; Wigfield et al., 2015; Wong et al., 2024). Such actions also seem to serve as protective factors against academic problems and risky behaviors that otherwise become more common during early adolescence, like drop-out and delinquency (Li & Lerner, 2011). The clear connections established between actions and outcomes provide the empirical warrant for interventions that target motivation and engagement.

Self and Its Subcomponents

The third component of the motivational system is the "self," and it is the part around which many theories of motivation are organized, as sometimes reflected in their titles—self-determination theory, self-efficacy, mindsets, and so on. For purposes of this chapter, we consider them all facets of an umbrella self-construct called *academic identity*, defined as students' deeply held views of themselves and their potential in relation to the enterprise of education (Skinner, 2023). In the field of motivation, there is no consensus about how the constructs inside this component should be organized. SDT suggests one place to start: Organizing self-systems around themes reflecting the three basic psychological needs (Connell & Wellborn, 1991; Ryan & Deci, 2017; Skinner, 2023; described in more detail below). This would allow self-constructs that convey a sense of relatedness to others (like belonging, connection, and attachment) to be considered parts of the same subcomponent. Likewise, self-constructs that refer to experiences of effectiveness in interactions with the environment, like perceived competence, self-efficacy, expectancies of success, and mastery orientations, could be considered part of the same subcomponent. And a third subcomponent could include self-constructs related to autonomy and ownership, like valuing of schoolwork, feelings of authenticity, and sense of purpose.

Context and Its Subcomponents

The fourth component of motivational systems is the context. Contexts entail the multilevel *social ecologies*, both local and higher order, within which the other components are embedded and within which students' motivation and self are developing (Bronfenbrenner & Morris, 2006; Spencer, 2006; Wang et al., 2019). Motivational theories usually focus on immediate face-to-face social contexts where students spend their time, like home, school, and neighborhoods, and often drill down further into classroom contexts and their qualities (e.g., social relationships, academic work, classroom pedagogical and management practices, peer climate). Contexts are crucial because these are the factors practitioners and interventionists can intentionally change in order to create better conditions for the development of the self and motivational resilience (Eccles & Roeser, 2015; Grolnick et al., 2024; Reeve, Jang, et al., 2022). In motivational theories, as in other areas of psychology, contextual components have received relatively less attention, compared to self and action components (Wentzel & Skinner, 2022). However, theorists have borrowed from ecological and ecocultural systems models to help make these larger contextual factors and their effects visible (e.g., Bronfenbrenner & Morris, 1998; Garcia Coll et al., 1996; Spencer, 2006), In this chapter, we borrow from these models to conceptualize social ecologies of motivational development (e.g., Skinner & Raine, 2022).

Three Systems Insights Into the Developmental Dynamics of the Self and Motivational Resilience

Motivational systems have their parts, like these four components and their subcomponents, also referred to as their *structure*, but even more interesting, they have their *functions*—which describe how the parts work together. Systems perspectives focus especially on *dynamics* or cycles—recursive loops of feedforward and feedback effects (Reeve, 2016). This section explores three ways that a consideration of causal processes (functions) and recursive cycles (dynamics) can contribute to a deeper understanding of the development of the self and motivational resilience. They are all based on the notion that the functioning of such systems involves the participation of these essential components—context, self, action, and outcomes. Hence, in order to understand, study, or optimize any of them (and this chapter focuses on the self and motivational resilience), it is necessary to examine how they work together.

The three ideas laid out below explore: (1) how the internal and external dynamics of motivational resilience make episodes of academic engagement and coping especially important sites of development; (2) how the internal and external dynamics of the self position academic identity as a central (and changing) component of motivational development, including the development of the self; and (3) how local social partners and contexts act as key players in all of these dynamics, as do the larger ecologies in which students' motivation and selves develop.

Developmental Dynamics of Motivational Resilience

A first way systems approaches can be useful is to highlight the functions and dynamics involved in motivated action, and to explain how these processes make episodes of motivational resilience such an important location for growth and development. Functions and dynamics become visible when one examines how the parts of a system work together over time, more specifically, their causal processes. When considering motivational resilience and vulnerability, the key idea is that the subcomponents depicted in Fig. 1.1 are more than just "parts." They can be seen as steps in a time ordered process that create interaction episodes (Skinner et al., 2020). Depending on the academic task, episodes can last minutes (e.g., an in-class exercise), hours (e.g., a group project), or days (e.g., studying for an exam). Since components of motivational resilience and vulnerability are not seen as expressions of stable interindividual differences in fixed student characteristics, systems perspectives would expect that for any given student, episodes could include a variety of changing modes of engaging and stepping back from academic tasks, some of which would be considered adaptive and some not.

Internal Dynamics of Motivational Resilience

Over time, these interactional processes can create dynamics, comprised, for example, of virtuous cycles of preference for challenge, engagement, coping, and tenacity that exercise and consolidate motivational resilience. As pictured in Fig. 1.2, students who prefer challenge are more likely to encounter interesting and demanding educational opportunities, which should promote their enthusiastic participation (or engagement). Highly engaged students, in turn, have energetic resources that support their effort and provide momentum when they encounter academic difficulties or setbacks. The investment and commitment underlying engagement make it more likely that students will draw on adaptive coping strategies—like problem-solving or help-seeking—which allow them to return to the task with new strategies and renewed vigor. These ways of dealing with challenges are more likely to support persistence and (eventually) lead to learning and success on difficult tasks. But even when they don't, students should still be able to discover more about how to effectively engage and self-regulate in the face of academic demands, and so gain renewed confidence and zest for future encounters. Such feedforward and feedback effects can form self-amplifying loops, in which students develop and refine tools for dealing productively with academic challenges.

Motivational Vulnerability. In contrast, also pictured in Fig. 1.2, are processes of motivational vulnerability that likewise contribute to self-amplifying loops, but these inscribe vicious cycles. Here, students who have a habit of avoidance become cut off from opportunities for learning. Their

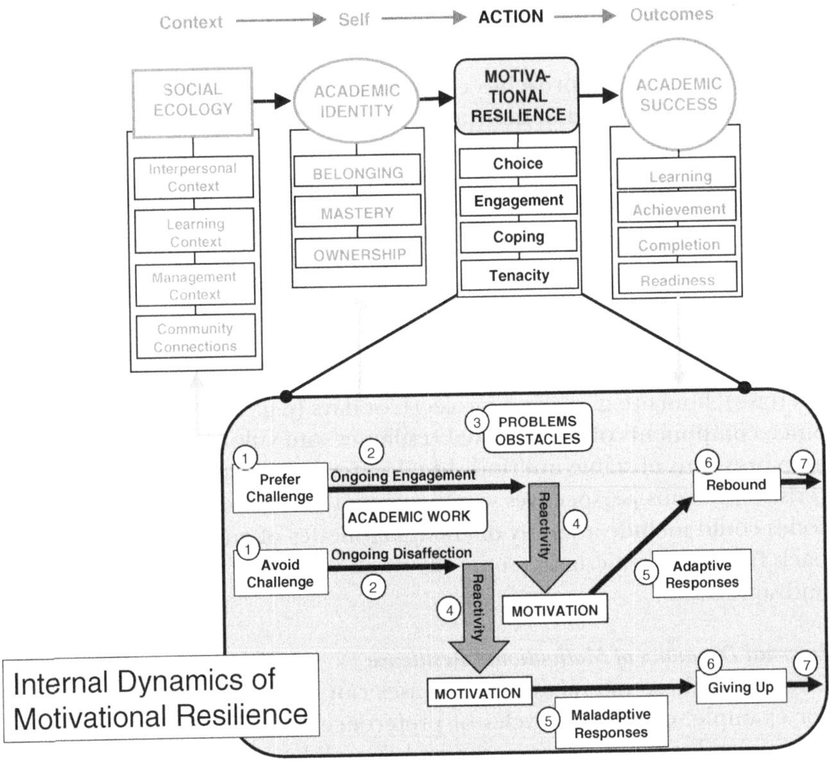

Fig. 1.2. An Episodic Account of Seven Steps in the Internal Dynamics of Motivational Resilience and Vulnerability in Which (1) Students either undertake or avoid challenging academic tasks and then (2) During ongoing engagement and disaffection with academic work, students (3) Encounter problems or obstacles that exert a downward pressure on their motivation, and (4) Generate reactivity. In turn, through (5) a variety of regulatory and motivational processes, students either (6) Rebound and Re-engage in learning activities or withdraw, forfeiting opportunities for learning and satisfaction, which (7) Feeds forward into subsequent episodes of task choice and engagement. *Source:* Adapted from Skinner et al. (2020), with permission.

history of interactions with schoolwork has produced a tendency toward disaffection, which includes passivity, lack of effort, frustration, and other forms of disengaged behaviors and emotions. As can be imagined, disaffection creates a precarity in students' participation, so that when they run into trouble, their motivation can decline sharply, and they are more likely to fall back on forms of coping, like escape and blaming others, that undermine their tenacity and re-engagement. These experiences consolidate students' discouragement and disaffection, and make them more likely to avoid or escape academic challenges in the future. From a systems perspective, these two kinds of dynamics (virtuous and vicious) are a product of different developmental histories and current conditions, and left unchecked, they are likely to lead to different developmental pathways of motivational resilience and vulnerability.

External Dynamics of Motivational Resilience

These recursive cycles can be called *internal dynamics* because they include only processes *inside* motivational resilience (Skinner et al., 2020; Skinner & Pitzer, 2012). However, the larger motivational system also includes processes external to student action, namely, context, self, and outcomes. These components also participate in the cycles just described. Their participation can be called *external dynamics*. As pictured in Fig. 1.3, these are represented as input arrows running from the three components outside of action toward processes of motivational resilience. They include inputs from (1) the social ecology; (2) students' academic identities; and (3)

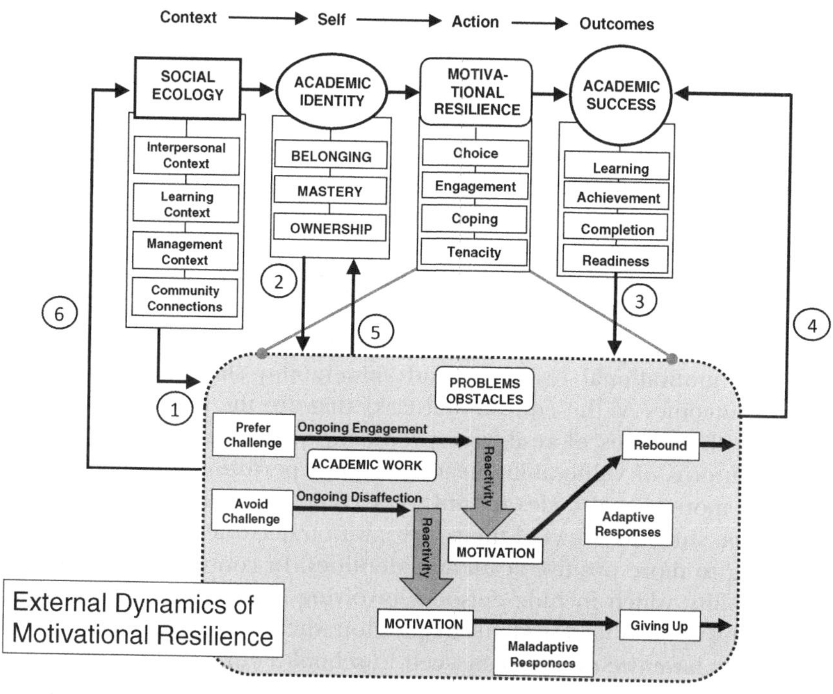

Fig. 1.3. A Model of the External Dynamics of Motivational Resilience, including Contributions From (1) the Social Ecology, including the Interpersonal, Learning, Management, and Community Contexts; (2) Students' Own Academic Identity; and (3) Learning and Performance Outcomes; as Well as Consequences of Motivational Resilience for (4) Subsequent Academic Success; (5) the Development of Academic Identity; and (6) Future Interactions With the Social Context. *Source:* Adapted from Skinner et al. (2020), with permission.

academic outcomes. They are meant to represent, for example, that classroom contexts, including interpersonal relationships, pedagogical practices, learning activities, and management strategies, exert an impact on student engagement, coping, tenacity, and all the other subcomponents of motivational resilience. For example, a close friend or a caring teacher might aid a student enmeshed in vicious cycles of motivational vulnerability by offering strategic help even when the student is too overwhelmed to ask for it. Alternatively, an educational activity that is wildly interesting to a student (e.g., starting a garden as part of science class) may unleash intrinsic motivation powerful enough to fuel high levels of engagement and tenacity.

Similarly, students' academic identities, including their feelings of belonging, competence, and autonomy, can buffer them or render them more susceptible to motivational struggles. Finally, students' actual educational success should also feed back into their ongoing engagement and disaffection, as well as how they deal with and rebound from academic problems. And if the learning garden or friend or teacher can provide sustained support, it may be possible, based on, for example, a change in the student's self-appraisals about their own competence or the value of science, for the functioning of their whole motivational systems to undergo a qualitative shift. Instead of self-amplifying cycles, these could be transformed to compensatory or self-correcting external dynamics, so called because they disrupt or reverse self-sustaining feedback loops.

Consequences of Motivational Resilience. At the same time, as shown in the output arrows in Fig. 1.3, motivational resilience also exerts an impact on the other components of the motivational system, namely (4) academic outcomes; (5) views of the self; and (6) social contexts. Most obviously, episodes of motivational resilience and vulnerability should influence the actual outcomes of the educational tasks that are the focus of these episodes, with patterns of resilience producing more learning and success while patterns of vulnerability lead to poorer performance. At the same time, as motivational cycles unfold, they could also cumulatively have an impact on students' views of themselves, with trajectories of resilience contributing to more positive academic identities. In contrast, trajectories of vulnerability, which include episodes involving disaffection, poor coping, and giving up, may lead students to question whether they belong, are competent, or have the desire to succeed in school. Perhaps surprisingly, episodes of motivational resilience are also hypothesized to feed back into the social context, shaping interpersonal relationships, such as with teachers and peers, as well as learning opportunities and disciplinary encounters. These are described more fully in later sections on the role of the social context in motivational systems.

Intrinsic and Extrinsic Motivation

Underlying episodes of motivational resilience are the sources of motivation that fuel students' action. As described in SDT (Ryan & Deci, 2000; 2020), these entail intrinsic and extrinsic motivation. Systems perspectives argue that both emerge from the whole motivational system. *Intrinsic motivation,* defined as the desire to participate in activities based on the fun, enjoyment, and satisfaction inherent in doing them, is considered to be a crucial facet of the active curious nature of humans. But its expression in the classroom depends on whether that context provides relevant affordances (such as tasks that are inherently fun, interesting, and meaningful) and a teaching style that supports students' autonomy and other psychological needs. So unleashing and channeling intrinsic motivation in school requires the cooperation of the external dynamics of the motivational system. These external dynamics are also implicated in the steady declines found in students' intrinsic motivation for school across their educational careers (Scherrer & Preckel, 2019), in that longitudinal studies indicate that such losses correspond to declines in the satisfaction of psychological needs (Gnambs & Hanfstingl, 2016).

Extrinsic motivation is defined as the participation in activities for which no spontaneous (intrinsic) motivation is available. Hence, task engagement requires regulation, and the quality of that regulation can range from less to more autonomous: (1) *external* regulation involves outside pressure and coercion (e.g., "I do my homework because I will get in trouble if I don't"); (2) *introjected* regulation involves internal pressure and coercion (e.g., "because I will feel bad about myself if I don't"); (3) *identified* regulation involves personal endorsement of the value of a task (e.g., "because learning is personally important to me"); and (4) *integrated* regulation involves the incorporation of task engagement into a student's view of themselves (e.g., "because learning is an important part of who I am as a student") (Ryan & Deci, 2020). The quality of a students' extrinsic motivation is also an emergent property of the entire motivational system. It involves the self, more specifically students' autonomy orientations, and whether the context provides the kind of scaffolding (e.g., structure and autonomy support) that supports more autonomous forms of regulation (Reeve & Cheon, 2021).

These underlying sources of energy, ranging from nonautonomous to autonomous and intrinsic, are essential parts of motivational systems because they infuse the quality of all subcomponents of motivational resilience with joy, enthusiasm, willingness, commitment, and vitality, or with pressure, ambivalence, and resistance (Ryan & Deci, 2017). These qualities, in turn, make a difference to the effects that these motivational processes will have on the other parts of the system, including academic and developmental outcomes. As social partners, like teachers and parents, try to do their part to support students motivated actions in school, systems perspectives encourage them to consider their practices in light of these sometimes invisible dynamics. How adults set up interpersonal relationships, learning activities, disciplinary strategies, and so on, are all colored by the support they provide for autonomous and intrinsic motivation. Hence, they are an inextricable part of the system that gives rise to them. Social partners are also the beneficiaries of students' autonomous, enthusiastic, and intrinsically joyful engagement in educational activities. Together, these self-sustaining, self-amplifying, and self-correcting internal and external dynamics of motivational resilience and vulnerability, along with their effects on student learning, academic identities, and the consolidation of tools for dealing effectively with educational challenges, show why these episodes are a site of great developmental significance for the entire motivational system (Skinner & Pitzer, 2012).

Developmental Dynamics of the Self in Motivational Theories

A second way systems perspectives can be useful is in underscoring the functions and dynamics of the self. The key idea is that the subcomponents of students' academic identities are constructed and reworked based on their participation and experience in academic activities and settings; it is these cycles that shape their development. Moreover, students' self-appraisals are major contributors to how such cycles unfold; hence, students are active participants in shaping their own experience and development. Of all the components of motivational systems, the self operates most fully under the radar, since it is not directly observable by others. Hence, a goal of systems models is to make this component and its functioning more visible, not only to theorists and researchers, but also to educational stakeholders, like teachers and parents.

Developmental History of the Self

In motivational theories, as in the many other areas that feature self-constructs, conceptualizations of the self vary widely. At one end of the continuum are views of the self as a temporary perception or belief, such as an estimate of one's capacity to successfully carry out a specific task at that moment. From this perspective, self-appraisals are temporary installations, fleeting and situation specific. At the other end of the continuum are self-appraisals as traits, anchored in neurophysiology. From this perspective the self is permanent and enduring. In most motivational theories, conceptualizations fall in between these two extremes; self-appraisals are considered more than mere perceptions but less than stable personality traits. Instead, they could be called convictions, belief systems, or internal working models; and multiple sources contribute to their construction and development, as pictured in Fig. 1.4.

Lived experience. First, they are constructed from lived experience. That is, self-appraisals, although often investigated as the first link in chains of motivated behavior, are actually the product of thousands, or even hundreds of thousands, of transactions with the social and physical worlds. Such appraisals have been studied most intently by attachment theorists (Ainsworth, 1979; Bowlby, 1969/1973) who examine the interactions between babies and their caregivers, starting at birth, and trace the cumulative impact of these transactions on the expectations, action tendencies, and (eventually) internal working models infants form about whether the world is safe and responsive, and whether they are worthy of care (Sherman et al., 2015).

Thus, self-appraisals are deeply tethered to infants' and children's direct experience. In fact, they are tethered not only in the cognitive representations typically studied as the self, but also in neurophysiological and reactive action systems designed to deal with danger and threat and to respond to

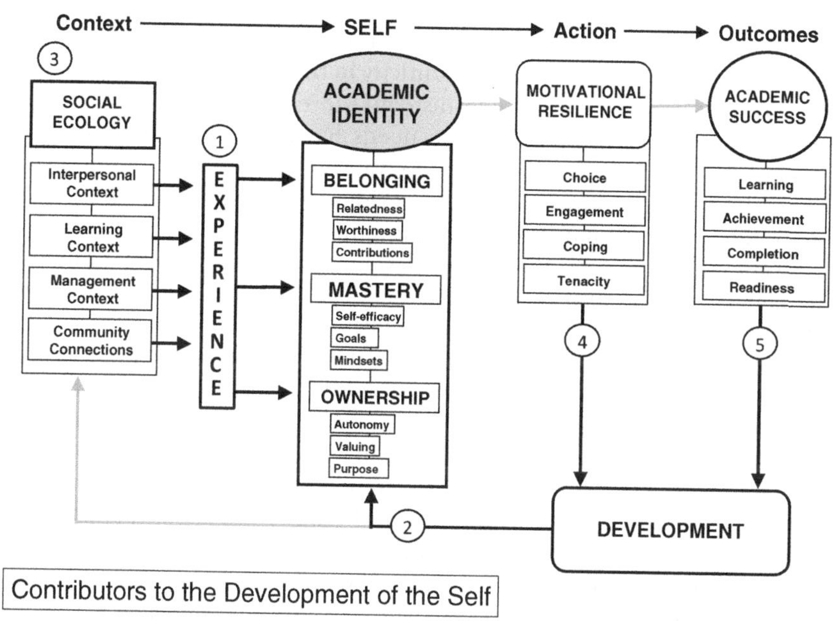

Fig. 1.4. A Systems Perspective on Contributors to Development of the Self, Including (1) The centrality of students' lived experience; (2) The role of the developmental lens student bring to interpreting those experiences; (3) Their ongoing interactions with the social context, including the interpersonal, learning, management, and community contexts; (4) Their own motivated actions; and (5) Their learning and academic outcomes.

opportunities for exploration and novelty (Thompson, 2015). Such neurophysiological and psychological anchoring gives self-appraisals their durability and power. These integrated running totals of experience are not fleeting perceptions; they are better regarded as convictions about "apparent reality" (Fridja, 1988). Although most empirical work on academic motivation starts after students enter formal schooling, it is not lost on researchers or educators that young children's early experiences at home and in preschool have a profound impact on their readiness and success for school, at least partly because of the actions and self-systems to which they contribute.

Fundamental psychological needs. Second, self-appraisals are organized around specific organismic concerns. That is, while young children and then middle-aged children and adolescents attend to and make meaning of their everyday dealings with the physical and social world, they are inherently focused on specific interactions—those with implications for their fundamental psychological needs. SDT posits three basic needs, grounded in evolution, as well as in neurophysiological, psychological, and social processes (Ryan & Deci, 2017). These are the needs for (1) *relatedness*, or the desire for closeness, connection, and belonging; (2) *competence*, or the desire for mastery and effectiveness in interactions with the world; and (3) *autonomy*, or the desire for authenticity in the expression of one's genuine preferences and true self (Vansteenkiste et al., 2020). As befit core organismic concerns, each of these needs has a long history of study in psychological, developmental, and motivational science. For example, the research on attachment mentioned previously converges with SDT on the centrality of the human need for belonging and security that underlies the functioning of the attachment system, as well as the disorganizing neurophysiological and psychological effects if these needs are not met (Arancibia et al., 2023; Granqvist et al., 2017).

In conceptualizations of the self, these three needs can be thought of as crucial nodes around which self-appraisals are organized. As infants (and then children and youth) collect grist for their internal working models, they prioritize and attend to need-relevant interactions. In fact, these kind of transactions are integrated with attentional and emotional systems, which is why they compel attention and trigger emotions (Thompson, 2015). Because of their activating properties, these are sometimes referred to as "hot" interactions. Based on their interactional histories, individuals form convictions about the extent to which needs can be fulfilled in specific relationships and contexts.

Internal working models of relationships with attachment figures are an example of the self-systems formed around the need for relatedness (Sherman et al., 2015). Children's perceptions of control, self-efficacy, and mastery orientations (Elliot & Dweck, 2013) are examples of self-systems formed around the need for competence. Self-regulatory orientations, values, ownership, and sense of purpose are examples of self-systems formed around the need for autonomy (Ryan & Deci, 2017). Hence, self-systems are anchored not only in cumulative lived experience but also in fundamental organismic priorities. This can help to explain why they are so powerful and laden with emotion. Experiences of helplessness (thwarting the need for competence) or of being treated as an outsider (thwarting the need for relatedness) do not just lodge in momentary perceptions or cognitive representations. They are visceral (literally) and can involve overwhelming feelings of despair, shame, fear, or resentment.

Questions in the classroom. Third, the construction and reworking of self-systems continue as children enter and proceed through schooling, where the focus turns toward the meaning they make out of their participation in the educational system. Concerns about the three needs continue to organize students' lived experience and to some extent dictate the "notes" they are taking about their interactions in educational contexts. Some motivational researchers have formulated these concerns as questions students ask themselves as they go about their everyday lives at school (Wigfield et al., 2015). As summarized in Box 1.1, these concerns result in questions

Box 1.1 Three Families Around Which Students' Academic Identities Are Organized

Academic Identity: Students' deeply held views of themselves and their potential to connect to, learn, grow, be themselves, and thrive in school.

1. *Sense of relatedness*: Students' convictions that they are valued and cherished members of a learning community, and that they can make important contributions to the collective.
   - *Belonging*: Are people like me welcome here? Am I safe here? Do I belong?
   - *Self-worth*: Do I deserve love and compassion, even when I feel bad or make mistakes?
   - *Contributions*: Are my strengths and gifts valued and needed?
2. *Perceived competence and mastery*: Confidence that school is organized around individual learning and growth for all students, and that they have the capacity to learn and grow in this place.
   - *Efficacy*: Do I have the capacity to succeed in school?
   - *Growth mindset*: Can I grow and improve my ability?
   - *Mastery goals*: Are we here to learn and grow?
3. *Autonomy and ownership*: Authentic commitment to the educational process; and certainty that participation and success are crucial parts of their identity and long-term purpose.
   - *Value*: Is schoolwork personally important to me?
   - *Authenticity*: Can I be my genuine self here? Explore my own interests and passions?
   - *Purpose*: What are my goals and aspirations? Is school necessary to my larger life project?

Note. Adopted from Skinner, 2023, with permission.

organized around (1) relatedness, such as "Are people like me welcome here? Am I safe here? Do I belong?"; (2) competence, like "Do I have the brains to succeed in school? Are we here to learn and grow?"; and (3) autonomy, like "Can I be my genuine self here? Is this schoolwork personally important to me?".

Such questions offer educational stakeholders a window into the invisible workings of the self, and hence a lens through which to analyze classroom culture and practices. How do the affordances schools provide answer students' questions about their own relatedness, competence, and autonomy (Eccles & Wigfield, 2020; Reeve, Jang, et al., 2022; Skinner, 2023; Wentzel, 2018; Wigfield et al., 2015)? For example, zero tolerance policies and exclusionary discipline practices can send powerful messages about who is welcome in the classroom and worthy of care (Clark-Louque & Sullivan, 2020; Wentzel, 2022). Alternatively, mastery learning, assessment, and grading practices can communicate the message that all students are capable; everyone is expected to learn and succeed (Lalley & Gentile, 2009). Or intrinsically interesting academic activities and opportunities to follow one's own interests can communicate that teachers want learning to be joyful and meaningful (Reeve, Jang, et al., 2022).

Actions and Outcomes. Finally, students' own actions and accomplishments (i.e., outcomes) also provide information in answer to the questions posed by their self-systems. For example, successful learning and performance can strengthen a students' sense of competence and efficacy (Muenks et al., 2018). Since achievement is the coin of the academic realm, success may also convey to the student that they belong at school. In the same vein, students' own industrious engagement and productive persistence can influence their feelings of coping efficacy (competence; Skinner & Saxton, 2019) and ownership (autonomy; Reeve, 2012). From this perspective, it is the whole motivational system—including context (e.g., classroom culture and practices), action (e.g., students' choices, engagement, coping, tenacity), and outcomes (e.g., learning, personal growth)— that generates students' everyday lived experiences. That is, this whole system continuously forms the building blocks students use to construct their self-systems of relatedness, competence, and autonomy, and hence their academic identities.

Self-Appraisals as Participants in Action Episodes

Self-appraisals themselves play an active role in generating the experiences that shape their development. In fact, motivational researchers focus on appraisals, like self-efficacy or autonomy orientations, precisely *because* they are robust predictors of students' motivation, as seen in their impact on engaged and motivated actions or during episodes of motivational resilience. Multiple places in action episodes have been identified where the effects of self-appraisals are especially pronounced. Different theories of motivation hone in on different locations, and systems approaches can integrate them by suggesting that they represent the multiple functions self-appraisals can serve in motivational systems.

Regulatory and Interpretive Functions. Two central functions can be highlighted. An example of their location in action episodes is pictured in Fig. 1.5, illustrated using different motivational theories focused on the self-appraisals organized around the need for competence. The first function can be called a *feedforward regulatory function*, in which self-appraisals help to launch, guide, and sustain actions. For example, research shows that students' perceived control and expectancies of success are robust predictors of their choices, efforts, and engagement in schoolwork (Eccles & Wigfield, 2020; Muenks et al., 2018) as well as their coping with academic difficulties (Skinner & Saxton, 2019). As shown in Fig. 1.5, these self-appraisals influence subsequent action and so feed forward into action sequences, which then contribute to outcomes, like learning and achievement.

In contrast, other theories focus on self-appraisals that operate (i.e., serve their functions) only *after* performances have been enacted and outcomes have been produced. These are evaluative appraisals used to make sense of performance outcomes, and so serve *feedback interpretative functions.* The most well-studied of these are causal attributions (Graham, 2020) in which students make sense of their academic successes and failures by ascribing them to specific causes, like effort, ability, or luck. As depicted in Fig. 1.5, these appraisals feed back into students' subsequent perceptions of competence (e.g., Schmitz & Skinner, 1993). For example, if students ascribe success to high effort, they are more likely to feel efficacious in subsequent encounters than if they attribute it to good luck. These interpretations have their effects on subsequent action by promoting or undermining intervening regulatory self-appraisals. Such interpretative systems, like causal attributions, are powerful because they can take objective performance information (e.g., doing well on an exam) and convert it into evidence of either high or low competence, depending on the causes to which performances are attributed, such as high ability versus an easy task.

Recursive cycles. Because self-appraisals involve both feedforward (regulatory) and feedback (interpretive) functions, the motivational processes depicted in Fig. 1.5 can also be viewed as comprising recursive cycles. For example, researchers interested in learned helplessness have examined students' explanatory styles as risk factors, and found that when students explain negative outcomes (like struggles on an assignment) using causes that are internal, global, and stable (like low ability), they are less likely to initiate action, exert effort, or reengage in challenging academic tasks. These actions can then undermine students' subsequent learning and performance, thus confirming their pessimistic self-appraisals (Buzzai et al., 2021). Without intervention, such self-sustaining dynamics can fuel

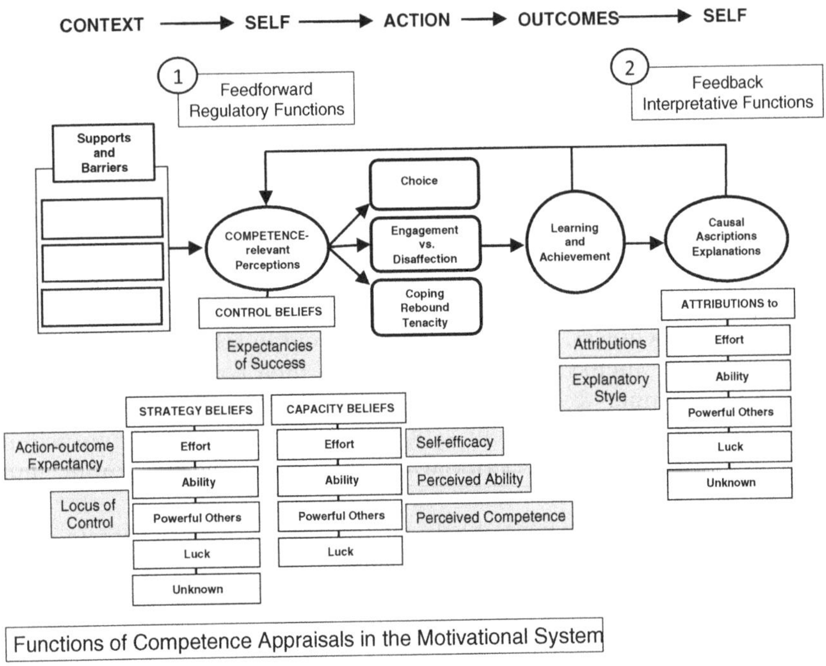

Fig. 1.5. A Depiction of the Self-Systems Organized Around Competence and Perceived Control, Which Can be Differentiated Based on (1) Their feedforward functions in initiating and guiding choice, engagement, coping, and tenacity; and (2) Their feedback effects in interpreting the meaning of academic experiences. Self-systems involved in feedforward effects can be further distinguished based on whether they depict (a) An overall sense of control (e.g., expectancies of success); (b) Strategies that lead to desired outcomes (e.g., locus of control), or (c) Capacities that allow students to enact successful strategies (e.g., self-efficacy or perceived ability). *Source:* Adapted from Skinner (2023), with permission.

downward spirals of catastrophizing, passivity, and giving up, thereby undermining learning and achievement more generally, and forfeiting opportunities to disconfirm and revise these self-appraisals.

Of course, self-appraisals can also participate in virtuous cycles, in which students expect to succeed, and so engage with enthusiasm, strategize, ask for help, and so on—or, in other words show motivational resilience in ways that make learning and achievement more likely. And just as attributions or explanatory styles can discount successful outcomes, more adaptive self-appraisal processes can also buffer students' perceived competence from low objective performance. For example, children can attribute poor performances to lack of effort or bad luck, thus focusing them on strategies and opportunities for doing better during their next encounters with demanding academic tasks (Graham, 2020). From this perspective, students' self-system processes are active agents in the motivational system—by creating feedforward regulatory effects on action, by contributing to performance outcomes, and by interpreting such outcomes during ongoing bouts of academic engagement, they play important roles in generating the very lived experience that shapes them.

Role of the Self in Motivational Systems. These are the internal and external dynamics of the self. Fig. 1.6 summarizes them by depicting seven crucial roles students' academic identities play in the functioning of the motivational system. As can be seen, positive academic identities (in which students feel secure, competent, and take ownership for their participation at school) are strong sources of energy, guidance, and grit (i.e., motivation). Self-systems act (1) as "deciders" that contribute to choices about whether to seek out or take on challenging tasks; (2) as "launch pads" that propel constructive engagement with learning activities; (3) as "guides" that help regulate actions under stress; and (4) as "anchors" that fortify tenacity. Self-systems also serve (5) as "interpreters" that translate the implications of patterns of actions and outcomes for the developing self; (6) as "meaning makers" that make sense of students' lived experience; and (7) as "pathways" or mediators from the actual context to subsequent motivational resilience and outcomes.

Confirming and Disconfirming Experience. One of the more worrisome properties of students' self-system processes stems from how the functioning of these self-action-outcome cycles changes with development. At a very global level, research suggests that as students approach and enter early adolescence, and with the accompanying cognitive shift to formal operations, these systems become less and less open to disconfirming evidence (e.g., Muenks et al., 2018; Skinner & Raine, 2022). There seem to be many mechanisms that contribute to this general trend. For example, young children's appraisals of their capacities are normatively biased toward an optimistic view of their potential to accomplish just about anything (Muenks et al., 2018). However, as they proceed through middle childhood and adolescence, their self-perceptions become more realistic, in that they become more and more calibrated to actual performance in school (Muenks et al., 2018). As can be imagined, this trend is problematic for low performing students. All the internal and external factors that are actually shaping their performances (from neurophysiological contributors to teacher bias) start to become encoded in their self-appraisals as perceived ability. It seems as if this tendency might be an advantage to high performing students, but the perception that one's ability is on the line with every academic performance can actually create a kind of pressure and preoccupation than drains motivational and regulatory resources (Vansteenkiste et al., 2014).

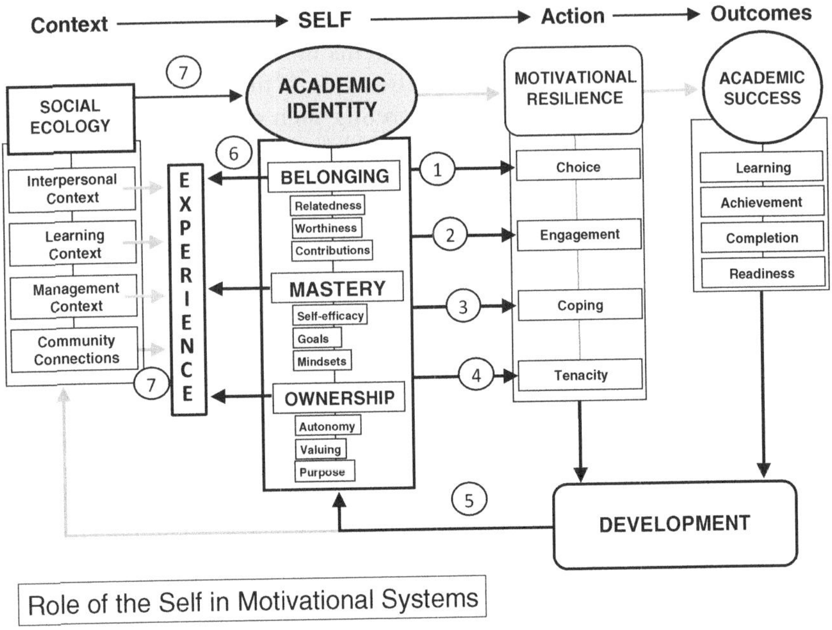

Fig. 1.6. Seven Functions of the Self (Academic Identity) in Motivational Systems: (1) As a "decider" that makes choices about contexts and tasks; (2) As a "launch pad" that propels constructive engagement with learning activities; (3) As a "guide" that helps regulate actions under stress; (4) As an "anchor" that fortifies tenacity; (5) as an "interpreter" that translates the implications of patterns of actions and outcomes for the developing self; (6) As a "meaning maker" that makes sense of students' lived experience; and (7) As a "pathway" or mediator from the actual context to subsequent motivational resilience and outcomes.

A particular turning point during late childhood and early adolescence is tied to cognitive developments across formal operations, specifically, the differentiation of effort from ability (Muenks & Miele, 2017). During early childhood, children's conceptualizations of these causal forces are positively fused, such that young children assume that smarter children try harder, and children who try harder are smarter. However, after older children become capable of differentiating ability from effort, they typically take on the dominant culture's understanding of these two causal forces, as inverse and compensatory, implying that smart children do not need to exert as much effort to succeed, and children who try harder to produce the same performance are not as smart. At this point, self-defeating patterns of action become more common, especially for low performing adolescents—where exerting effort becomes a trap, and it may seem safer not to try at all than to try and fail (Martin, 2007).

Studies of growth versus fixed mindsets, which grew out of the research on students' conceptualizations of ability (Dweck & Yeager, 2019), have documented these patterns most clearly (Burnette et al., 2023). They suggest that the cognitive developments of formal operations only become problematic if (societal or classroom) cultures endorse definitions of ability as a permanent trait, which can be diagnosed via success or failure on academic tasks compared to others. Such fixed mindsets are associated with the motivational vulnerabilities described previously, like avoidance of challenges, lack of effort, poor coping, giving up, and maladaptive attributions. If instead, societies and classrooms endorse a growth mindset, which considers ability to be a limitless resource that can be activated and improved through effort and practice, then students can instead be oriented toward motivational resilience, learning, and development (Bardach et al., 2024; Burnette et al., 2023; Muenks & Miele, 2017).

Social Contexts as Integral to the Development of Motivational Resilience and the Self

A third way systems perspectives can be helpful to the study of motivational resilience and the self is in highlighting the crucial role of social contexts. Theories of motivation agree that interpersonal and contextual factors (e.g., parents, teachers, peers, schoolwork) shape student motivation. However, it is not particularly common to posit that they are all part of motivational systems themselves. As mentioned previously, systems conceptualizations sometimes refer to these as *external* dynamics, in order to distinguish them from the internal dynamics among the self and action components (Skinner et al., 2020). However, by viewing social contexts as parts of the systems that give rise to students' motivated states and self-conceptions, these approaches insist that it is not possible to explain or transform the development of motivation or self without considering the social ecologies that surround and interact with them (Eccles & Roeser, 2015; Kumar et al., 2018; Skinner, Rickert, et al., 2022; Wentzel, 2022; Wigfield et al., 2015).

Complex Microsystems

Local face-to-face social contexts, sometimes called *microsystems* (Bronfenbrenner & Morris, 1998), are important to motivation and the self for many reasons. They contain the social partners (like parents, teachers, friends, and classmates) with whom students interact on a daily basis. They include the educational activities in which students participate as well as the rules, norms, expectations, demands, and scripts that govern how social partners interact with each other and how class is conducted. They involve general climates and cultures, like whether the classroom or school operates as a caring learning community (Battistich et al., 1997). Overall, features of local contexts, like classrooms, can be parsed into multiple layers, including for example (1) the interpersonal context; (2) the learning context; (3) the management and disciplinary context; and (4) community connections (see Box 1.2; see Skinner, Rickert, et al., 2022 for details). These contexts provide the

Box 1.2 Four Functional Contexts in the Complex Microsystem of the Classroom

1. *Interpersonal context*: The quality and closeness of students' interactions and relationships with classroom social partners.
    - Teacher-student interactions and relationships.
    - Interactions and relationships among classmates, friends, and peer group members.
    - Classroom interpersonal climate.
    - Quality of social-emotional behaviors and interactions.
    - Relational attributes like warmth, caring, kindness, structure, autonomy support versus rejection, coldness, neglect, chaos, controllingness, or coercion.
2. *Learning context*: Organization and implementation of processes of learning.
    - Curricula and content of coursework.
    - Nature of academic work: Authentic, relevant, self-selected topics and tasks, passion-projects.
    - Pedagogical strategies: Active learning, coaching, co-teaching.
    - Learning structures: Project-based learning, group learning, cooperative versus competitive.
    - Systems for providing help, scaffolding, and feedback; responses to mistakes and failures; peer feedback.
    - Evaluation and grading practices, and opportunities to redo work: Mastery-grading, individual versus social comparison of performance.
3. *Management and disciplinary context*: Structures and processes for regulating students' participation, behavior, and treatment of others in the classroom.
    - Classroom routines, rituals, norms, rules, sanctions, and punishments.
    - Use of reasoning versus power exertion.
    - Use of natural consequences versus exclusion.
    - Fairness, disciplinary disparities, participatory democracy.
    - Redemption routines and restorative justice practices.
4. *Connections to the community*: Bonds, connections, relevance, engagement, and service to those outside the school building.
    - How/whether the classroom represents and engages the community.
    - Extent to which students and staff represent the cultural, racial, and socioeconomic composition in the neighborhood.
    - Incorporation of families' assets, language, cultural, and historical background in curricula, projects, food, celebrations, and other practices.
    - Community activism and social justice projects within and outside the school.

Note. Adopted from Skinner, Kindermann, et al. (2022), with permission.

motivational affordances with which students interact to generate their lived experiences. As a result, social contexts are always "the other half of the story" in motivational development (Wentzel & Skinner, 2022).

One way to understand how these contextual features (and the interactions in which they participate) influence students' motivation and self-systems is to think of them as "motivational messages." They comprise communications to students in response to the questions prompted by their basic needs (e.g., "Are kids like me welcome here?"). Although, as mentioned previously, students' self-systems play a role in de-coding these communications, contexts are decisive in generating and broadcasting them. For example, as students look around their school, they may see people like themselves in the teachers, staff, and other students; as well as in the curriculum, books, posters on the walls, and guest speakers—or they may not (Gray et al., 2018). Hence, social contexts help create the motivational messages that are incorporated into students' self-systems, and over time, their academic identities. A deeper dive into social contexts and how they function can also reveal whether they contain the motivational nutriments students seek to satisfy their basic needs (Vansteenkiste et al., 2020). Do these contextual affordances support students' autonomy (Reeve, Jang, et al., 2022), provide kindness, care, and respect (Wentzel, 2022), hold high expectations for their performance and scaffold their attempts to learn (Wentzel, 2018)?

Social partners in recursive cycles. Interaction partners, like parents, teachers, and peers, are especially important. Many conceptualizations (Martin & Dowson, 2009) and decades of research (e.g., Kindermann, 2016; Martins et al., 2021; Wentzel, 2016) document what would be called, in systems terms, the *feedforward effects* of parents, teachers, and peers. Such effects encompass the ways these social partners (through, for example, the provision of autonomy support, direct help, or their own enthusiasm) contribute to changes in student's subsequent engagement, motivation, or self-systems. They are called feed *forward,* because social contexts contribute to *future* self-appraisals and motivated action. However, much less attention has been paid to what systems approaches would call their *feedback effects.* Sometimes called "child effects" or "student effects" (to distinguish them from "parent effects" or "teacher effects"), feedback effects comprise all the ways that student characteristics and actions influence the reactions they receive from the social world (Nurmi & Kiuru, 2015).

Feedback effects have been studied most extensively in research on the differential treatment teachers provide based on their expectations for students' academic performance (Rubie-Davies & Hattie, 2024; Wang et al., 2018). In this case, the feedback effects are from student outcomes to social partners' reactions, as represented by the return arrow in Fig. 1.1. Such differential treatment, in which teachers, for example, talk and teach more, and provide more learning opportunities, latitude, and constructive feedback to students they expect to perform well (Wang et al., 2018), contributes to virtuous self-amplifying cycles in which these teacher reactions improve students' subsequent learning and performance. In the same vein, differential treatment of students who are performing poorly (or whom teachers expect to perform poorly) can perpetuate vicious cycles.

Even more interesting, from a motivational perspective, are the feedback arrows from action components to reactions from social partners. In these recursive loops, it is motivated action, or the things students *do*, like their engagement and disaffection (i.e., enthusiasm, effort exertion, boredom, off-task behavior), that attracts teachers' attention and shapes their subsequent reactions. For example, in a study of teacher autonomy support and student engagement during late elementary and early middle school, our research team found that, not only does initial autonomy support predict changes in student engagement over the school year (feedforward effects), but students' initial engagement in turn predicted changes in teacher autonomy support and many of its components (feedback effects; Rickert et al., 2024). In this case, students who were more engaged at the beginning of the year experienced *increases* in the autonomy support provided by their teachers as the year progressed, whereas students evincing lower engagement experienced *decreases.*

It makes sense that the action components of motivational systems are especially likely to elicit differential reactions from teachers—student actions like engagement, adaptive coping (e.g., help-seeking, strategizing), and tenacity, are visible in the classroom and can facilitate or impede ongoing educational activities. As a result, they are observable and salient to teachers, who naturally prefer motivated patterns of action. In recent years, a particularly potent form of student behavior has been identified, called *agentic engagement,* which is defined as "students' constructive contribution into the flow of the instruction they receive" (Tseng & Reeve 2011, p. 258). Examples of such actions include episodes in which students:

> offer input, express a preference, offer a suggestion or contribution, ask a question, communicate what they are thinking and needing, recommend a goal or objective to be pursued, communicate their level of interest, solicit resources or learning opportunities, seek ways to add personal relevance to the lesson, ask for a say in how problems are to be solved, seek clarification, generate options, communicate likes and dislikes,... (Reeve & Tseng, 2011, p. 258)

In experimental and naturalistic studies, these student actions have been shown to "steer" teacher behaviors and classroom interactions in ways that create more motivationally-supportive learning environments for the students who show them, by, for example, eliciting more autonomy support from teachers (Reeve, 2013; Reeve, Jang, et al., 2022). Although it is important to cultivate all manner of student engaged and motivated actions, it may be especially important to intentionally prompt agentic engagement—because it makes more visible students' underlying goals, interests, and understandings of classroom material. Through their agentic engagement, students bring these normally inward-facing features of their motivational systems outward into classroom interactions where they can provide actionable information to teachers.

Feedback Effects involving Social Partners. In discussing the role of social partners in feedback effects, it is important to highlight three points. First, these do not just involve teachers; parents are also differentially responsive to their children's motivated actions. For example, both feedforward and feedback effects have been found in studies examining the transactional effects of parent motivational support and child engagement (Rickert & Skinner, 2023) and academic coping (Raine & Skinner, 2023). In both studies, children who started the school year higher in engagement or adaptive coping (i.e., motivated action) experienced *increases* in parental support over the school year, whereas those initially higher in disengagement or maladaptive ways of coping reported *decreases* in motivational support from their parents.

Second, feedback effects are not limited to adults. Peers also respond differently to engaged versus disaffected students. For example, students who show higher engagement are more likely to be granted entry into peer groups that are also highly engaged, whereas students with lower levels of engagement tend to hang out with peers who are less engaged (Kindermann, 2007). In the same vein, compared to their more engaged classmates, students who are less engaged are more likely to receive support from the members of their peer groups for off-task behavior in the classroom (Sage & Kindermann, 1999). Third, most studies of feedback effects to date suggest self-amplifying dynamics, sometimes referred to as the Matthew effect, in which students already "rich" in engagement and motivation subsequently experience more positive reactions from their social partners and so become motivationally "richer." However, these are not the only dynamics possible. Teachers, parents and even peers could instead provide *compensatory* or *buffering* reactions, in which they respond to students' disaffection, maladaptive coping, or desistence with *increases* in kindness, scaffolding, or other forms of motivational support.

Higher-Order Contextual Systems

Most theories of motivation focus on contextual factors originating in microsystems or local settings, like classrooms, schools, and family homes. Systems approaches, however, as seen in ecological (Spencer, 2006), bioecological (Bronfenbrenner & Morris, 2006), and integrative ecocultural frameworks (Garcia Coll et al., 1996; Suarez Orozco et al., 2018), explicitly emphasize the impact of higher-order contextual forces.

Mesosystem Connections. These include *mesosystems,* or the interconnections and interactions among students' many microsystems (Bronfenbrenner & Morris, 2006; Skinner, Rickert, et al., 2022). These are sometimes called figured worlds (Holland et al., 2001) or multiple worlds (Cooper, 2011; Phelan et al., 1998), to highlight the fact that the microsystems children and youth visit daily, like home and school, have their own microcultures and modes of participation, including, for example, specific expectations, demands, scripts, activities, goals, values, and beliefs. These worlds are not always well-aligned. Sometimes they are congruent or complementary, but sometimes they differ sharply. In terms of schools, which are largely modeled after White middle class European-American norms, disconnects are especially pronounced for children who come from other backgrounds. This can make border crossings challenging or hazardous, and highlights the important role of gatekeepers and brokers, like mentors, older siblings, or cousins (Phelan et al., 1998).

Exosystem Networks. Higher-order contexts also include *exosystems,* defined as settings that do not include the developing student (like their parents' workplace or their teachers' professional development sessions), but nevertheless have an indirect impact on students' microsystems (e.g., when parents bring home stress from work or teachers try out in class what they learned in professional development). A range of exosystems can be identified that shape students' daily experiences in school, at home, and in the neighborhood (Eccles & Roeser, 2015). School boards and superintendents' administrative offices, local police stations and immigration offices, city hall where political decisions are made, grocery chains' deliberations about where to locate food stores, businesses who make hiring or firing decisions—all are outside of students' direct lines of sight, but still have an impact on the microsystems where they live, learn, and work.

The idea of exosystems underscores two important points about motivational systems. First, all the microsystems where students spend their time are shaped by decision-makers and other agents outside the sphere of the local settings typically studied in motivational theories. These higher-order factors become potential targets for intervention and reform that could have powerful downstream effects on the development of students' motivation and selves. Second, all the social partners with whom students interact inside their mesosystems also live in mesosystems of their own, only some of which include the developing student. A focus on exosystem factors allows researchers to step back and consider, for example, the larger social ecologies that shape teachers' classroom behavior, including their home lives, preservice training, and interactions with parents, school leaders, and fellow teachers outside of the classroom.

Such considerations link theories of motivation and the self to larger literatures on teacher stress and burnout (Iancu et al., 2018), as well as teacher thriving and resilience (Hascher & Waber, 2021; Vo & Allen, 2022).

They highlight the day-to-day conditions under which teachers teach, and open up discussion of teachers' lived experiences in schools as well as their own motivational needs (Van den Broeck et al., 2008). Such discussions include issues like a school's social climate, the camaraderie among teachers, parental support, and the quality of school leadership. All of these factors are important in the design of interventions and reforms that do "double duty"—that is, that support teacher motivation, learning, and well-being, so teachers can support these same experiences and outcomes for their students (Reeve, Jang, et al., 2022).

Macrosystem forces. At the highest level of social ecologies are overarching societal and cultural contexts, called *macrosystems* (Bronfenbrenner & Morris, 2006). These include, for example, the educational, legal, economic, political, health care, and immigration systems. Such higher-order sociohistorical systems have an enormous impact on the development of the self and student motivation, both directly and indirectly. This is one of the reasons why sociocultural factors have been of great interest to motivational researchers (e.g., King & McInerney, 2016; Kumar et al., 2018; Liem et al., 2025; Maehr, 1974; Usher, 2018; Wang et al., 2019; Zusho & Kumar, 2018). Among their other functions, macrosystems reify and enforce societally constructed hierarchies that rank order the human worth of specific subgroups, based on artificial categories like race, skin color, ethnicity, gender, sexual orientation, language, (dis)ability, economic status, and so on (Iruka et al., 2022; Spencer, 2006; Suarez Orozco et al., 2018). Hence, these structures create macrosystem *forces* that organize and permeate all the other levels of social ecologies (Vélez-Agosto et al., 2017). To get a sense of the many ways macrosystem forces have an impact on the development of students' academic identities and motivational resilience (see, for example, Skinner & Kindermann, 2025), researchers and interventionists can examine the components of motivational systems—that is, contexts, selves, actions, and outcomes—as pathways through which these forces can enter students lived experiences at school and at home.

Macrosystem Impacts on Contexts. First, contexts. Macrosystem forces create differentially hazardous objective living conditions for students' and the adults who care for and teach them, at all levels of social contexts. For example, they differentially drive risks and resources into stratified mesosystem niches (including schools) occupied by students from specific subgroups. Resistance to such forces also gives rise to *adaptive cultures*, defined as the strengths-based asset rich subcultures created by families and communities who differ from the dominant culture (Garcia Coll et al., 1996; Yosso, 2005). Such adaptive cultures are powerful protective factors for minoritized children and youth, and help to explain why most of them develop along positive lines (Cabrera & Leyendecker, 2017). Schools also have the potential to be(come) adaptive cultures, or what Spencer (2006) calls "pillars of support," that help hold these abrasive forces off children and youth as they develop.

Macrosystem Impacts on Actions and Outcomes. Second, marking the "action" and "outcome" components of motivational systems, systems perspectives would point to episodes of motivational resilience, and especially vulnerability, as one conduit through which macrosystem defaults can enter students' lived experience at school. When students struggle academically, cope poorly, show off-task or disruptive behaviors, or other signs of motivational vulnerability, this can trigger teachers' implicit biases, especially toward students of color and those from other marginalized subgroups (Rubie-Davies & Hattie, 2024; Wang et al., 2018). Such teacher reactions can contribute to more conflictual interactions with students, lower quality teacher-student relationships, and harsher discipline, all of which disproportionally affect Black and other minoritized students (Civitillo et al., 2024; Denessen et al., 2022; Welsh & Little, 2018). Hence, interventions designed to support student motivational resilience can, among other strategies, work with teachers to help them re-interpret the meaning of students' disaffected actions and difficulties learning, thus helping to prevent and reverse vicious cycles that escalate these incidents and contribute to suboptimal educational outcomes.

Macrosystem Impacts on Self. Third, a consideration of the "self" component of motivational systems makes clear that students are always interpreting their experiences, and therefore constructing their academic identities, in the teeth of headwinds created by macrosystem forces. These structures broadcast entrenched myths about the inherent inferiority of subgroups on the lower rungs of societal ladders. Hence, they transmit default messages that tell students who they are and who they can be in school (Clark-Louque & Sullivan, 2020; Nasir et al., 2013). For minoritized children and youth, these motivational messages are often deeply discouraging. When students ask fundamental questions like, "Am I welcome here?" "Am I good enough to succeed?" and "Can I be my authentic self?" (see Box 1.1), the answers at school can easily be read as "No," or at least "The people here don't think so." Schools intent on improvement sometimes employ reflective processes to reconsider whether the messages they send students counteract or reinforce these defaults, for example, through dress codes that make their natural hair a violation, via disciplinary practices that differentially target students of color, by implicitly condoning disparities in achievement and graduation rates, and so on.

Recognition of the power of such macrosystem forces informs researchers and educators that students' academic identities are inextricably intertwined with all the other facets of their intersectional identities, like their racial ethnic, cultural, and gender identities. To counteract societal prejudices and defaults, students need to directly experience school as a place where all aspects of their authentic identities are welcome, treasured, celebrated, needed, and capable of excelling (Gray et al., 2018, 2020, 2022). To counteract the narrow, constrained, and stereotyped identities macrosystem forces often pressure students from specific subgroups to adopt, children and youth need active support in creating counter-narratives that reject and reauthor the storylines of who they are (Nasir et al., 2013). In fact, schools owe students an "expansive self" (Smith et al., 2022). For example, teachers can intentionally and systematically communicate to all students that they are more than their academic performance (sometimes called *broad regard*) and that everyone has the potential for learning, growth, and academic success (sometimes called *inclusive expectations*, Smith et al., 2022). Perhaps schools also owe students a view of the worlds of school and society as "expansive"—with the potential to be very different from what they are today and good for all children and youth (Benjamin, 2016).

IMPLICATIONS FOR PRACTICE

Systems approaches to the development of motivational resilience and academic identities, taken broadly, can also be helpful in providing guidance to practitioners, interventionists, and other educational stakeholders. Box 1.3 lists some of the take home messages about motivation and students' academic identities highlighted in this chapter. For example, systems perspectives remind educators that, whatever else they are trying to accomplish in schools, they are also helping students build an academic identity; that children and youth are paying attention and taking notes; and that students arrive in classrooms with histories and hot convictions about apparent reality. Systems perspectives highlight students' lived experience and encourage educators to remain (or become) curious about students' perspectives, and especially about the messages they themselves and their schools are (intentionally and unintentionally) sending in answer to students' questions about their motivational needs. Teachers and school leaders, like their students, are operating in a complex social ecology that is colored at every turn by harsh societal defaults. But it also has the potential to be colored by the brilliant home and heritage cultures and histories of students and teachers, as well as the strengths and resources active in the local community and beyond (Suarez Orozco et al., 2018). Systems perspectives encourage schools to become havens for students, especially when they struggle, places where they can build tools for motivational resilience and make progress on their growth mindsets, connections to other, and expansive identities.

The biggest contribution of systems perspectives to educational practices is in helping enrich the mental models that educational stakeholders, like parents, teachers, and school leaders, hold about how student motivation works. Hence, this chapter closes by explaining three ways a systems approach can help build out mental models of motivation: (1) it can broaden them, by giving adults to eyes to see student motivational issues as symptoms of problems originating in the larger motivational system; (2) it can deepen them, by helping adults to understand the dynamics that are

Box 1.3 Implications of a Systems Perspective on the Development of Motivation and the Self for Educators and Interventionists

1. An important goal for schools is to nurture students' *motivational resilience*, which includes:
   - enthusiastic engagement in learning activities,
   - constructive coping with obstacles and difficulties,
   - tenacity in the face of challenging tasks, and
   - bouncing back from setbacks and failure.
2. Teachers and parents are interested in motivational resilience for its own sake, but also because it supports student learning, academic success, personal growth, well-being, and enjoyment of school.
3. These kinds of productive engagement, coping, and academic buoyancy are all parts of students' larger *motivational systems*. These systems include, not only patterns of motivational resilience and academic outcomes, but also students' academic identities and their social contexts.
4. *Academic identities* are students' deeply held views of themselves and their potential in relation to the enterprise of education. Strong and positive academic identities are personal resources that students will take with them their whole life long.
5. Student's academic identities *play important roles* in launching and sustaining their motivational resilience. They:
   - guide students' decisions about whether to take on demanding academic tasks,
   - promote or undermine students' constructive engagement,
   - contribute to adaptive and maladaptive ways of coping with academic challenges and problems, and
   - anchor or impede student persistence and re-engagement.
6. Students' academic identities are constructed and reworked based on their *lived experience*, that is, their daily participation in academic activities and settings. This means that students' academic identities and motivational resilience are developing long before students enter a specific teacher's classroom.
7. Students constantly try to make sense of their experiences at school, and these interpretations implicitly guide their decisions about whether to buy in and work hard for a teacher or class. Studies suggest that students' academic identities, motivational resilience and learning depend on the answers they provide to:
   - Questions about themselves
     - ✓ *Belonging*. Am I welcome here? Am I safe here? Do I belong? Do I deserve love and compassion, even when I feel bad or make mistakes?
     - ✓ *Mastery*. Do I have the capacity to succeed in school? Can I grow and improve my ability? Are we here to learn and grow?
     - ✓ *Ownership & commitment*. Is this work meaningful to me and worth my full effort? Can I be my authentic self here? Explore my own interest and passions? Is school necessary to my larger life project?
   - Questions about others
     - ✓ *Caring*. Do people here care about and believe in me? Do they have my back? Do people here think I bring valuable strengths to the table?

(Continued)

Box 1.3 *Implications of a Systems Perspective on the Development of Motivation and the Self for Educators and Interventionists (Continued)*

- ✓ *Scaffolding.* Do these people know their stuff? Are they teaching in a way I can learn? Are they there for me when I need help? Can I count on their support?
- ✓ *Autonomy support.* Do people here respect me, listen to me, and treat me fairly? Do I have a say in what we are doing here? Is my input encouraged?

8. Students' academic identities and motivational resilience are fostered through a *wide variety of activities and channels.* They live in every corner of the classroom, from the classroom climate and relationships between students and their teachers and peers, to the nature of learning activities, to grading and disciplinary practices, to the overall ethos of the school.
9. Students' academic identities are *inextricably intertwined* with other aspects of their identities, like their racial ethnic, cultural, and gender identities. To counteract societal stereotypes and prejudices, students need to directly experience that all of their authentic identities are welcome, treasured, and capable of excelling in school.
10. Students need these messages especially when they *struggle academically or falter behaviorally.* Otherwise, these can trigger a downward spiral. Students need to know that there are second chances and pathways back to success, and that they are encouraged and expected to work hard to get there and make things right.

happening "under the hood," so they can better diagnose the causes of these problems; and (3) it can augment their complexity, by showing adults that the tools they need to "treat" these root causes are everywhere, and once systems are shifted so that virtuous cycles are established, they can become self-sustaining and self-correcting. Although recommendations below are geared toward teachers and parents, systems perspectives insist that schools and the educational system in general also require transformation, so that conditions are in place that enable teachers and parents to successfully engage and sustain these practices (Ryan, 2012).

Student Motivation as a Symptom of Larger Issues with Motivational Systems

First, systems perspectives can help teachers and parents take the motivational issues they see daily in the classroom (or at home) and think about them from a larger perspective. Educators (and sometimes parents) have a front row seat to the actions that comprise motivational struggles, and a primary reason why these actions are so salient is because adults value student behaviors like engagement and tenacity, and know that such actions are a gateway to student learning and academic success. However, like the field of motivation more generally, it is easy to assume that because actions *emerge* from the individual student, all the causes of that action can be found *inside* the student. Systems views insist that the sources of any individual's current motivational state are everywhere and "every-when:" in classroom relationships, tasks, practices, and rules; in students' developmental histories and past experiences; in parenting and teaching practices; in societal messages; in the everlasting intrinsic motivation that is part of every student's phylogenetic make-up; and so on.

From this perspective, the idea of an "unmotivated student" is a myth (Grolnick et al., 2024). To be sure, students present motivational issues (like avoidance, disengagement, maladaptive coping, and giving up), and parents and teachers typically find such encounters to be highly stressful (Turner & Garvis, 2023). However, by taking a systems view, teachers and parents can come to see these issues, not as characteristics of students, but as symptoms of problems in the larger motivational system. Such a perspective may help convert teachers' appraisals of these student behaviors from threats requiring their emotional energy and coping, to signals of unhealthy motivational dynamics, calls for help, and ultimately systems puzzles to be solved. With this mindset, "student motivational issues" can actually be seen as useful because they provide entry points for detecting systems problems and designing interventions. "Fixing" student motivation, just like "fixing" teacher or parent motivation, involves repairing the whole motivational system. For struggling students, this includes responding to "their" problems in ways that create compensatory or buffering dynamics. The goal of motivational practices and interventions becomes clearer (Grolnick et al., 2024; Lazowski & Hulleman, 2016; Reeve, Jang, et al., 2022): to shift this system so that it begins to generate and sustain virtuous cycles on its own.

Differential Diagnosis of the Sources of Motivation Issues

A second way systems perspectives can help parents and educators build out their mental models of motivation is by taking them "under the hood," so they can better understand the dynamics underlying the motivational issues they are seeing. The basic idea is that the motivational struggles visible in students' actions are the "tip of the iceberg," where the iceberg itself entails the complex dynamics active in the larger system. A deeper appreciation of the centrality of students' academic identities may help adults get a better handle on the less visible parts of the system that undergird action. The self-appraisals that comprise students' identities (see Box 1.1) provide a menu of options that can be used to "diagnose" the issues with which they are struggling (Furrer et al., 2014). For example, do students question the value of the schoolwork they are being asked to complete? Do they feel estranged from their teachers and classmates? When they run into challenges, do they have the tools they need to cope productively? As described previously, students construct and rework aspects of their academic identities based on the meaning they make of their lived experience at school. This includes their interactions with other people, academic activities, and teaching and disciplinary practices, as well as their own actions, and learning outcomes (see Fig. 1.4). Hence, self-systems are a repository of information about what is and is not working for students. As a result, they can help pinpoint where and how a student's basic needs are not being met in that class or at school more generally.

Such a possibility may lead parents and teachers to become very curious about students' self-systems, and to view them as "consultants" that can provide crucial information about potential underlying causes. Adults can then consider differential diagnoses and test them by providing students corresponding supports, of the kinds that have been shown to nurture these motivationally-salient needs, such as warm involvement, appropriate structure, and autonomy support (Ahmadi et al., 2023). Educators can also take advantage of the centrality of these self processes by interacting with them directly. They can ask students questions, listen to their opinions and complaints, take their perspectives; they can create activities that surface students' experiences. Teachers can also actively explain their practices to students, being explicit about what they are doing and why they are doing it. To be effective, adults must also ensure that their actual behaviors are congruent with these verbal messages, and that they remain open to flexibly changing their practices so they incorporate student preferences, reactions, and suggestions (Reeve, 2016).

Adults can also take advantage of the interpretative functions of students' self-systems, that is, the way students use them to make sense of their own actions and learning outcomes. For example, conversations about students' ongoing interpretations—like the causes of their successes and failures or the nature of ability—allow those meaning making functions to operate socially as well as internally and psychologically. Discussions with trusted others are a place where attributions and mindsets can be interrogated and revised. They are also a place where classroom practices can be examined and revised, especially ones that teachers discover are sending students the wrong messages, about whether they are welcome, capable, and encouraged to engage with educational activities that are personally meaningful to them. Explicitly working with—talking and listening to—the different facets of students' academic and intersectional identities provide educators and parents with an indirect but powerful entry point to rework their practices in ways that support students' developing identities and so promote their motivational resilience. These pathways may also help to explain the effectiveness of interventions that directly address the questions asked by students' self-systems, like those focused on belonging (Allen et al., 2022), mindsets (Burnette et al., 2023), and the value of schoolwork (Harackiewicz et al., 2016).

Tools for Repairing and Transforming Motivational Systems

Third, systems perspectives give teachers many tools, or better still highlight the many tools teachers already have, for addressing issues that arise in motivational systems. Perhaps most obviously, systems perspectives add complexity to stakeholders' mental models when they highlight the "everywhere-ness" of student motivation. At the same time, systems perspectives also offer tools for dealing with complexity. The most important one is clarity. Given the functions and recursive dynamics of these systems, both the causes and the cures of motivational problems reside in the working together of the parts of these systems. These processes are located and therefore partially visible in students' interactions with their many social partners. Because these interactions are the engines of development (Bronfenbrenner & Morris, 1998), they are also the targets of all educational practices and interventions. All remedies entail shifting the dynamics involved in students' actual lived experiences and their ongoing meaning making.

For educational stakeholders, the proposition that social partners and local settings are crucial parts of motivational systems may seem like a double-edged sword. The "bad news" is that teachers and schools are always parts of students' motivational problems. When adults enact default practices that do not meet students' needs (like high stakes testing or zero tolerance discipline) or when they react negatively to students' substandard performances or motivational struggles, educators can inadvertently escalate vicious cycles that further chip away at students' motivation and views of themselves and schools. As mentioned previously, the handful of studies that have examined these feedback processes to date suggest that teachers typically react to students who show motivational issues by withdrawing their warm support and/or becoming more controlling (e.g., Jang et al., 2016; Skinner & Belmont, 1993). Such reactions are understandable, but they also sustain and amplify cycles in which students already "poor" in motivational resources become "poorer" still.

At the same time, the "good news" represented by the key systems idea that adults (and social partners more generally) are inherently parts of students' motivational systems, is that they are not helpless bystanders to students' motivational struggles. Instead, parents and teachers can leverage their insider status by becoming more intentional and constructive in how they participate. Adults have multiple pathways through which they can support students' active engagement, constructive coping, and tenacity, and by doing so they also strengthen the personal resources, like academic identities, that students will take with them into the future. A consideration of the complex social ecologies of motivation and engagement (Skinner, Kindermann, et al., 2022; Skinner, Rickert, et al., 2022) can also help adults to see the larger stage upon which their interactions with students are taking place. By recognizing the defaults and other forces that fill in the blanks of students' understandings, adults can better appreciate what is at stake, especially as students continue negotiating their intersectional and academic identities, a task that becomes even more salient during adolescence (Velez & Spencer, 2018).

The many moving parts of motivational systems offer educators a menu of options about how to repair and transform them. Interventions can start at many entry points—supporting enthusiastic engagement with project-based learning (Chen & Yang, 2019); scaffolding experiences of competence and tenacity with high teacher expectations (Wang et al., 2018) and mastery grading (Lalley & Gentile, 2009); nurturing belonging by creating a sense of "we-ness" in the classroom and school (Gray et al., 2022); cultivating autonomy with intrinsically motivating learning tasks and opportunities for students to follow their passions (Fredricks et al., 2010); reaching into students' intersectional identities with culturally sustaining pedagogy (Aronson & Laughter, 2016; Kumar et al., 2018); helping students take ownership with restorative disciplinary practices (Lodi et al., 2022); counteracting societal defaults with social justice community initiatives (Lerner et al., 2021).

The guiding principle of systems perspectives is that practices and interventions to improve motivation must tackle the whole system. In fact, educators and interventionists should probably consider *all* the entry points described above in designing their classrooms and programs. The goal is not to find *the* lever or *the* strategy effective in producing higher student motivation. The goal is to create a larger system full of enabling conditions, within which student motivation naturally flourishes (Grolnick et al., 2024; Reeve, 2016; Ryan & Deci, 2017). These systems must be crafted, from many directions, to be good for all students as well as their teachers. They will take culture seriously and they will change or be transformed as students develop, in order to stay culturally- and developmentally-attuned to students' needs. Recognition of the multifaceted participation of social contexts in the systems that shape the development of motivation and the self imposes many responsibilities but also confers many opportunities for the adults who care for and teach children and youth. An appreciation of the larger motivational system, and the recursive dynamics at its heart, can be helpful not only for practice and interventions, but also for future theoretical and empirical work, designed to understand and help students develop strong positive academic identities and robust motivational resilience.

REFERENCES

Ahmadi, A., Noetel, M., Parker, P., Ryan, R. M., Ntoumanis, N., Reeve, J., Beauchamp, M., Dicke, T., Yeung, A., Ahmadi, M., Bartholomew, K., Chiu, T. K. F., Curran, T., Erturan, G., Flunger, B., Frederick, C., Froiland, J. M.,

González-Cutre, D., Haerens, L., ..., & Lonsdale, C. (2023). A classification system for teachers' motivational behaviors recommended in self-determination theory interventions. *Journal of Educational Psychology, 115*(8), 1158–1176. https://doi.org/10.1037/edu0000783

Ainsworth, M. D. S. (1979). Infant-mother attachment. *American Psychologist, 34,* 932–937. https://doi.org/10.1037/0003-066X.34.10.932

Allen, K., Jamshidi, N., Berger, E., Reupert, A., Wurf, G., & May, F. (2022). Impact of school-based interventions for building school belonging in adolescence: A systematic review. *Educational Psychology Review, 34,* 229–257. https://doi.org/10.1007/s10648-021-09621-w

Arancibia, M., Lutz, M., Ardiles, Á., & Fuentes, C. (2023). Neurobiology of disorganized attachment: A review of primary studies on human beings. *Neuroscience Insights, 18,* 26331055221145681.

Aronson, B., & Laughter, J. (2016). The theory and practice of culturally relevant education: A synthesis of research across content areas. *Review of Educational Research, 86*(1), 163–206.

Bardach, L., Bostwick, K. C., Fütterer, T., Kopatz, M., Hobbi, D. M., Klassen, R. M., & Pietschnig, J. (2024). A meta-analysis on teachers' growth mindset. *Educational Psychology Review, 36*(3), 84. https://doi.org/10.1007/s10648-024-09925-7

Battistich, V., Solomon, D., Watson, M., & Schaps, E. (1997). Caring school communities. *Educational Psychologist, 32*(3), 137–151.

Benjamin, R. (2016, June 26-29). *Incubating a better world in the hearts and minds of our students.* Keynote address at the International Society for Technology in Education Conference & Exposition, Denver, CO.

Bowlby, J. (1969/1973). *Attachment and loss* (*Vols. 1 and 2*). Basic Books.

Bronfenbrenner, U., & Morris, P. A. (1998). The ecology of developmental processes. In W. Damon (Series Ed.) & R. M. Lerner (Vol. Ed.), *Handbook of child psychology: Vol. 1. Theoretical models of human development,* (5th ed., pp. 993–1028). John Wiley.

Bronfenbrenner, U., & Morris, P. A. (2006). The bioecological model of human development. In W. Damon (Series Ed.) & R. M. Lerner (Volume Ed.), *Handbook of child psychology: Vol. 1. Theoretical models of human development* (6th ed., pp. 793-828). Wiley. https://doi.org/10.1002/9780470147658.chpsy0114

Burnette, J. L., Billingsley, J., Banks, G. C., Knouse, L. E., Hoyt, C. L., Pollack, J. M., & Simon, S. (2023). A systematic review and meta-analysis of growth mindset interventions: For whom, how, and why might such interventions work? *Psychological Bulletin, 149*(3–4), 174.

Buzzai, C., Sorrenti, L., Tripiciano, F., Orecchio, S., & Filippello, P. (2021). School alienation and academic achievement: The role of learned helplessness and mastery orientation. *School Psychology, 36*(1), 17–23.

Cabrera, N. J., & Leyendecker, B. (Eds.). (2017). *Handbook on positive development of minority children and youth.* Springer.

Chen, C. H., & Yang, Y. C. (2019). Revisiting the effects of project-based learning on students' academic achievement: A meta-analysis investigating moderators. *Educational Research Review, 26,* 71–81.

Christenson, S., & Reschly, A. (Eds.). (2022). *The handbook of research on student engagement.* Springer.

Civitillo, S., Mayer, A. M., & Jugert, P. (2024). A systematic review and meta-analysis of the associations between perceived teacher-based racial–ethnic discrimination and student well-being and academic outcomes. *Journal of Educational Psychology, 116*(5), 719.

Clark-Louque, A., & Sullivan, T. A. (2020). Black girls and school discipline: Shifting from the narrow zone of zero tolerance to a wide region of restorative practices and culturally proficient partnerships. *Journal of Leadership, Equity, and Research, 6*(2), 1–21.

Connell, J. P., & Wellborn, J. G. (1991). Competence, autonomy and relatedness: A motivational analysis of self-system processes. In M. Gunnar & L. A. Sroufe (Eds.), *Minnesota symposium on child psychology*. University of Chicago Press.

Cooper, C. R. (2011). *Bridging multiple worlds: Cultures, identities, and pathways to college*. Oxford University Press.

Datu, J. A. D., & Yuen, M. (2018). Predictors and consequences of academic buoyancy: A review of literature with implications for educational psychological research and practice. *Contemporary School Psychology, 22*(3), 207–212.

Denessen, E., Hornstra, L., van den Bergh, L., & Bijlstra, G. (2022). Implicit measures of teachers' attitudes and stereotypes, and their effects on teacher practice and student outcomes: A review. *Learning and Instruction, 78*, 101437.

Dweck, C. S., & Yeager, D. S. (2019). Mindsets: A view from two eras. *Perspectives on Psychological Science, 14*(3), 481–496. https://doi.org/10.1177/1745691618804166

Eccles, J. S., & Roeser, R. W. (2015). School and community influences on human development. In M. H. Bornstein & M. E. Lamb (Eds.), *Developmental science: An advanced textbook* (7th ed., pp. 645–728). Psychology Press.

Eccles, J. S., & Wigfield, A. (2020). From expectancy-value theory to situated expectancy value theory: A developmental, social cognitive, and sociocultural perspective on motivation. *Contemporary Educational Psychology, 61*, 101859. https://doi.org/10.1016/j.cedpsych.2020.101859

Elliot, A. J. & Dweck, C. S. (Eds.). (2013). *Handbook of competence and motivation*. Guilford Publications.

Fredricks, J. A., Alfeld, C., & Eccles, J. (2010). Developing and fostering passion in academic and nonacademic domains. *Gifted Child Quarterly, 54*(1), 18–30.

Fridja, N. H. (1988). The laws of emotion. *American Psychologist, 43*, 349–358. https://doi.org/10.1037/0003-066X.43.5.349

Furrer, C. J., Skinner, E. A., & Pitzer, J. R. (2014). The influence of teacher and peer relationships on students' classroom engagement and everyday resilience. In D. J. Shernoff & J. Bempechat (Eds.), *National Society for the Study of education yearbook. Engaging youth in schools: Empirically-based models to guide future innovations* (Vol. 113, pp. 101–123). Columbia University: Teachers's College.

Garcia Coll, C., Crnic, K., Lamberty, G., Wasik, B. H., Jenkins, R., Garcia, H. V., & McAdoo, H. P. (1996). An integrative model for the study of developmental competencies of minority children. *Child Development, 67*, 1891–1914.

Gnambs, T., & Hanfstingl, B. (2016). The decline of academic motivation during adolescence: An accelerated longitudinal cohort analysis on the effect of psychological need satisfaction. *Educational Psychology, 36*(9), 1691–1705.

Graham, S. (2020). An attributional theory of motivation. *Contemporary Educational Psychology, 61*, 101861.

Granqvist, P., Sroufe, L. A., Dozier, M., Hesse, E., Steele, M., van Ijzendoorn, M., …, & Duschinsky, R. (2017). Disorganized attachment in infancy: A review of the phenomenon and its implications for clinicians and policy-makers. *Attachment & Human Development, 19*(6), 534–558.

Gray, D. L., Ali, J. N., McElveen, T. L., & Sealy, M. (2022). The cultural significance of "We-ness": Motivationally influential practices rooted in a scholarly agenda on Black education. *Educational Psychology Review, 34*(4), 1985–2013.

Gray, D. L., Hope, E. C., & Byrd, C. M. (2020). Why Black adolescents are vulnerable at school and how schools can provide opportunities to belong to fix it. *Policy Insights from the Behavioral and Brain Sciences, 7*(1), 3–9. https://doi.org/10.1177/2372732219868744

Gray, D. L., Hope, E. C., & Matthews, J. S. (2018). Black and belonging at school: A case for interpersonal, instructional, and institutional opportunity structures. *Educational Psychologist, 53*(2), 97–113.

Grolnick, W. S., Heddy, B. C., & Worrell, F. C. (2024). *Motivation myth busters: Science-based strategies to boost motivation in yourself and others.* American Psychological Association.

Harackiewicz, J. M., Canning, E. A., Tibbetts, Y., Priniski, S. J., & Hyde, J. S. (2016). Closing achievement gaps with a utility-value intervention: Disentangling race and social class. *Journal of Personality and Social Psychology, 111*(5), 745.

Hascher, T., & Waber, J. (2021). Teacher well-being: A systematic review of the research literature from the year 2000–2019. *Educational Research Review, 34,* 100411.

Holland, D., Lachicotte, Jr., W. S., Skinner, D., & Cain, C. (2001). *Identity and agency incultural worlds.* Harvard University Press.

Iancu, A. E., Rusu, A., Măroiu, C., Păcurar, R., & Maricuțoiu, L. P. (2018). The effectiveness of interventions aimed at reducing teacher burnout: A meta-analysis. *Educational Psychology Review, 30,* 373–396.

Iruka, I. U., Gardner-Neblett, N., Telfer, N. A., Ibekwe-Okafor, N., Curenton, S. M., Sims, J., …, & Neblett, E. W. (2022). Effects of racism on child development: Advancing antiracist developmental science. *Annual Review of Developmental Psychology, 4*(1), 109–132.

Jang, H., Kim, E. J., & Reeve, J. (2016). Why students become more engaged or more disengaged during the semester: A self-determination theory dual-process model. *Learning and Instruction, 43,* 27–38.

Karabenick, S. A., & Gonida, E. N. (2018). Academic help seeking as a self-regulated learning strategy: Current issues, future directions. In D. H. Schunk & J. A. Greene (Eds.), *Handbook of self-regulation of learning and performance* (2nd ed., Chapter 27, pp. 421–433). Routledge. .

Kindermann, T. A. (2007). Effects of naturally existing peer groups on changes in academic engagement in a cohort of sixth graders. *Child Development, 78,* 1186–1203. https://doi.org/10.1111/j.1467-8624.2007.01060.x

Kindermann, T. A. (2016). Peer group influences on students' academic motivation. In K. Wentzel & G. Ramani (Eds.), *Handbook of social influences in school contexts: Social-emotional, motivation, and cognitive outcomes* (pp. 31–47). Routledge.

King, R. B., & McInerney, D. M. (2016). Culturalizing motivation research in educational psychology. *British Journal of Educational Psychology, 86*(1), 1–7. https://doi.org/10.1111/bjep.12106

Koenka, A. C. (2020). Academic motivation theories revisited: An interactive dialog between motivation scholars on recent contributions, underexplored issues, and future directions. *Contemporary Educational Psychology*, 101831. https://doi.org/10.1016/j.cedpsych.2019.101831

Korpershoek, H., Canrinus, E. T., Fokkens-Bruinsma, M., & De Boer, H. (2020). The relationships between school belonging and students' motivational, social-emotional, behavioural, and academic outcomes in secondary education: A meta-analytic review. *Research Papers in Education, 35*(6), 641–680.

Kumar, R., Zusho, A., & Bondie, R. (2018). Weaving cultural relevance and achievement motivation into inclusive classroom cultures. *Educational Psychologist, 53*, 78–96.

Lalley, J. P., & Gentile, J. R. (2009). Classroom assessment and grading to assure mastery. *Theory Into Practice, 48*(1), 28–35.

Lazowski, R. A., & Hulleman, C. S. (2016). Motivation interventions in education: A meta-analytic review. *Review of Educational Research, 86*(2), 602–640.

Lei, H., Cui, Y., & Zhou, W. (2018). Relationships between student engagement and academic achievement: A meta-analysis. *Social Behavior and Personality: An International Journal, 46*(3), 517–528.

Lerner, R. M., Lerner, J. V., Murry, V. M., Smith, E. P., Bowers, E. P., Geldhof, G. J., & Buckingham, M. H. (2021). Positive youth development in 2020: Theory, research, programs, and the promotion of social justice. *Journal of Research on Adolescence, 31*(4), 1114–1134.

Li, Y., & Lerner, R. M. (2011). Trajectories of school engagement during adolescence: Implications for grades, depression, delinquency, and substance use. *Developmental Psychology, 47*(1), 233.

Liem, G. A. D., Fredricks, J. A., & Wong, Z. Y. (2025). *Sociocultural perspectives on student engagement: Theory, research, and application*. Vol. 15 of the book series, Research on sociocultural influences on motivation and learning. Emerald Publishing Limited.

Lodi, E., Perrella, L., Lepri, G. L., Scarpa, M. L., & Patrizi, P. (2022). Use of restorative justice and restorative practices at school: A systematic literature review. *International Journal of Environmental Research and Public Health, 19*(1), 96.

Madigan, D. J., & Curran, T. (2021). Does burnout affect academic achievement? A meta-analysis of over 100,000 students. *Educational Psychology Review, 33*, 387–405.

Maehr, M. L. (1974). Culture and achievement motivation. *American Psychologist, 29*, 887–896. https://doi.org/10.1037/h0037521

Martin, A. J. (2007). Examining a multidimensional model of student motivation and engagement using a construct validation approach. *British Journal of Educational Psychology, 77*(2), 413–440.

Martin, A. J. (2013). Academic buoyancy and academic resilience: Exploring "everyday" and "classic" resilience in the face of academic adversity. *School Psychology International, 34*(5), 488–500.

Martin, A. J., & Dowson, M. (2009). Interpersonal relationships, motivation, engagement, and achievement: Yields for theory, current issues, and educational practice. *Review of Educational Research, 79*, 327–365. https://doi.org/10.3102/0034654308325583

Martins, J., Cunha, J., Lopes, S., Moreira, T., & Rosário, P. (2021). School engagement in elementary school: A systematic review of 35 years of research. *Educational Psychology Review.*

Muenks, K., & Miele, D. B. (2017). Students' thinking about effort and ability: The role of developmental, contextual, and individual difference factors. *Review of Educational Research, 87*(4), 707–735.

Muenks, K., Wigfield, A., & Eccles, J. S. (2018). I can do this! The development and calibration of children's expectations for success and competence beliefs. *Developmental Review, 48,* 24–39.

Nasir, N. I. S., Snyder, C. R., Shah, N., & Ross, K. M. (2013). Racial storylines and implications for learning. *Human Development, 55*(5–6), 285–301.

Nurmi, J. E., & Kiuru, N. (2015). Introduction to the special section on student effects on teachers' behaviors and attitudes. *International Journal of Behavioral Development, 39*(5), 389–390.

Overton, W. F. (2013). Relationism and relational developmental systems: A paradigm for developmental science in the post-Cartesian era. *Advances in Child Development and Behavior, 44,* 21–64. JAI.

Overton, W. F., & Lerner, R. M. (2014). Fundamental concepts and methods in developmental science: A relational perspective. *Research in Human Development, 11*(1), 63–73.

Phelan, P., Davidson, A. L., & Yu, H. C. (1998). *Adolescents' worlds: Negotiating family, peers, and school.* Teachers College Press.

Raine, K. E., & Skinner, E. A. (2023). Dynamics of parenting and children's coping: Bidirectional effects between parent motivational support and children's academic coping during late childhood and early adolescence. *International Journal of Behavioral Development, 47*(5), 397–409.

Reeve, J. (2012). A self-determination theory perspective on student engagement. In S. L. Christenson, A. L. Reschly, & C. Wylie (Eds.), *Handbook of research on student engagement* (pp. 149–172). Springer.

Reeve, J. (2013). How students create motivationally supportive learning environments for themselves: The concept of agentic engagement. *Journal of Educational Psychology, 105*(3), 579.

Reeve, J. (2016). Autonomy-supportive teaching: What it is, how to do it. In W. C. Liu, J. C. K. Wang, & R. M. Ryan (Eds.), *Building autonomous learners: Perspectives from research and practice using self-determination theory* (pp. 129–152). Springer Singapore.

Reeve, J., & Cheon, S. H. (2021). Autonomy-supportive teaching: Its malleability, benefits, and potential to improve educational practice. *Educational Psychologist, 56*(1), 54–77.

Reeve, J., Jang, H. R., Shin, S. H., Ahn, J. S., Matos, L., & Gargurevich, R. (2022). When students show some initiative: Two experiments on the benefits of greater agentic engagement. *Learning and Instruction, 80,* 101564.

Reeve, J., Ryan, R. M., Cheon, S. H., Matos, L., & Kaplan, H. (2022). *Supporting students' motivation: Strategies for success.* Routledge.

Reeve, J., & Tseng, M. (2011). Agency as a fourth aspect of student engagement during learning activities. *Contemporary Educational Psychology, 36,* 257–267. https://doi.org/10.1016/j.cedpsych.2011.05.002

Rickert, N. P., Dancis, J., & Skinner, E. A. (2024). Dynamics of teacher autonomy support in early adolescence: Feedforward and feedback effects with students' autonomy, competence, relatedness, and engagement. *European Journal of Psychology of Education, 39*, 2575–2601. https://doi.org/10.1007/s10212-024-00852-3

Rickert, N. P., & Skinner, E. A. (2023). Parent and teacher involvement and adolescent academic engagement: Unique, mediated, and transactional effects. *International Journal of Behavioural Development.* https://doi.org/10.1177/01650254231210561

Rubie-Davies, C. M., & Hattie, J. A. (2024). The powerful impact of teacher expectations: A narrative review. *Journal of the Royal Society of New Zealand, 55*(2), 1–29.

Ryan, R. M. (Ed.). (2012). *The Oxford handbook of human motivation.* Oxford University Press. https://doi.org/10.1093/oxfordhb/9780195399820.001.0001

Ryan, R. M., & Deci, E. L. (2000). Intrinsic and extrinsic motivations: Classic definitions and new directions. *Contemporary Educational Psychology, 25*, 54–67.

Ryan, R. M., & Deci, E. L. (2017). *Self-determination theory: Basic psychological needs in motivation, development, and wellness.* Guilford Press.

Ryan, R. M., & Deci, E. L. (2020). Intrinsic and extrinsic motivation from a self-determination theory perspective: Definitions, theory, practices, and future directions. *Contemporary Educational Psychology*, 101860.

Sage, N. A., & Kindermann, T. A. (1999). Peer networks, behavior contingencies, and children's engagement in the classroom. *Merrill-Palmer Quarterly, 454*, 143–171.

Scherrer, V., & Preckel, F. (2019). Development of motivational variables and self-esteem during the school career: A meta-analysis of longitudinal studies. *Review of Educational Research, 89*(2), 211–258.

Schmitz, B., & Skinner, E. (1993). Perceived control, effort, and academic performance: Interindividual, intraindividual, and multivariate time-series analyses. *Journal of Personality and Social Psychology, 64*(6), 1010–1028.

Schunk, D. H., & DiBenedetto, M. K. (2020). Motivation and social cognitive theory. *Contemporary Educational Psychology, 61*, 101832. https://doi.org/10.1016/j.cedpsych.2019.101832

Sherman, L. J., Rice, K., & Cassidy, J. (2015). Infant capacities related to building internal working models of attachment figures: A theoretical and empirical review. *Developmental Review, 37*, 109–141.

Skinner, E. A. (2023). Four guideposts toward an integrated model of academic motivation: Motivational resilience, academic identity, complex social ecologies, and development. In special issue, "Hybridizing motivational strains: How integrative theoretical models can advance motivation science.". *Educational Psychology Review, 35*(3), 80. https://doi.org/10.1007/s10648-023-09790-w

Skinner, E. A., Graham, J. P., Brule, H., Rickert, N., & Kindermann, T. A. (2020). "I get knocked down but I get up again": Integrative frameworks for studying the development of motivational resilience in school. *International Journal of Behavioral Development, 44*(4), 290–300.

Skinner, E. A., & Kindermann, T. A. (2025). How do macrosystem forces shape the development of student motivation and engagement? Stratified niches, proximal processes, and exosystem entry points. In G. A. D. Liem, J. Fredricks, & W. Z. Yang (Eds.), *Research on sociocultural influences on motivation and learning.* (pp. 31–70). Emerald Publishing Limited.

Skinner, E. A., Kindermann, T. A., & Mashburn, A. J. (2019). *Lifespan developmental systems: Meta-theory, methodology, and the study of applied problems. An advanced textbook.* Routledge.

Skinner, E. A., Kindermann, T. A., Vollet, J. W., & Rickert, N. P. (2022). Complex social ecologies and the development of academic motivation. *Educational Psychology Review, 34,* 2129–2165. https://doi.org/10.1007/s10648-022-09714-0

Skinner, E. A., & Pitzer, J. (2012). Developmental dynamics of engagement, coping, and everyday resilience. In S. Christenson, A. Reschly, & C. Wylie (Eds.), *The handbook of research on student engagement* (pp. 21–45). Springer.

Skinner, E. A., & Raine, K. E. (2022). Unlocking the positive synergy between engagement and motivation. In S. Christenson & A. Reschly (Eds.), *The handbook of research on student engagement* (pp. 25–56). Springer.

Skinner, E. A., Rickert, N. J., Vollet, J. W., & Kindermann, T. A. (2022). The complex social ecology of academic development: A bioecological framework and illustration examining the collective effects of parents, teachers, and peers on student engagement. *Educational Psychologist.* https://doi.org/10.1080/00461520.2022.2038603

Skinner, E. A., & Saxton, E. A. (2019). The development of academic coping in children and youth: A comprehensive review and critique. *Developmental Review, 53,* 100870.

Smith, E. N., Yeager, D. S., Dweck, C. S., & Walton, G. M. (2022). An organizing framework for teaching practices that can "expand" the self and address social identity concerns. *Educational Psychology Review, 34*(4), 2197–2219.

Spencer, M. B. (2006). Phenomenology and ecological systems theory: Development of diverse groups. In W. Damon & R. M. Lerner (Series Eds.) & R. M. Lerner (Volume Ed.), *Handbook of child psychology, Vol. 1: Theoretical models of human development* (6th ed., pp. 829-893). Wiley. https://doi.org/10.1002/9780470147658.chpsy0115

Suárez-Orozco, C., Motti-Stefanidi, F., Marks, A., & Katsiaficas, D. (2018). An integrative risk and resilience model for understanding the adaptation of immigrant-origin children and youth. *American Psychologist, 73*(6), 781–796.

Thompson, R. A. (2015). Relationships, regulation, and early development. In R. M. Lerner (Series Ed.) & M. Lamb (Volume Ed.), *Handbook of child psychology and developmental science: Vol. 3. Socioemotional processes* (7th ed., pp. 201-246). Wiley. https://doi.org/10.1002/9781118963418.childpsy306

Turner, K., & Garvis, S. (2023). Teacher educator wellbeing, stress and burnout: A scoping review. *Education Sciences, 13*(4), 351.

Usher, E. L. (2018). Acknowledging the Whiteness of motivation research: Seeking cultural relevance. *Educational Psychologist, 53*(2), 131–144.

Van den Broeck, A., Vansteenkiste, M., De Witte, H., & Lens, W. (2008). Explaining the relationships between job characteristics, burnout, and engagement: The role of basic psychological need satisfaction. *Work & Stress, 22*(3), 277–294.

Vansteenkiste, M., Lens, W., Elliot, A. J., Soenens, B., & Mouratidis, A. (2014). Moving the achievement goal approach one step forward: Toward a systematic examination of the autonomous and controlled reasons underlying achievement goals. *Educational Psychologist, 49*(3), 153–174.

Vansteenkiste, M., Ryan, R. M., & Soenens, B. (2020). Basic psychological need theory: Advancements, critical themes, and future directions. *Motivation and Emotion, 44,* 1–31. https://doi.org/10.1007/s11031-019-09818-1

Velez, G., & Spencer, M. B. (2018). Phenomenology and intersectionality: Using PVEST as a frame for adolescent identity formation amid intersecting ecological systems of inequality. *New Directions for Child and Adolescent Development, 2018*(161), 75–90.

Vélez-Agosto, N. M., Soto-Crespo, J. G., Vizcarrondo-Oppenheimer, M., Vega-Molina, S., & García Coll, C. (2017). Bronfenbrenner's bioecological theory revision: Moving culture from the macro into the micro. *Perspectives on Psychological Science, 12*(5), 900–910.

Vo, D. T., & Allen, K. A. (2022). A systematic review of school-based positive psychology interventions to foster teacher wellbeing. *Teachers and Teaching, 28*(8), 964–999.

Wang, M.-T., Degol, J. L., & Henry, D. A. (2019). An integrative development-in-sociocultural-context model for children's engagement in learning. *American Psychologist, 74*(9), 1086–1102. https://doi.org/10.1037/amp0000522

Wang, S., Rubie-Davies, C. M., & Meissel, K. (2018). A systematic review of the teacher expectation literature over the past 30 years. *Educational Research and Evaluation, 24*(3–5), 124–179. https://doi.org/10.1080/13803611.2018.1548798

Welsh, R. O., & Little, S. (2018). The school discipline dilemma: A comprehensive review of disparities and alternative approaches. *Review of Educational Research, 88*(5), 752–794.

Wentzel, K. (2016). Teacher-student relationships. In K. R. Wentzel & D. B. Miele (Eds.), *Handbook of motivation in school* (2nd ed., pp. 211–230). NY: Routledge.

Wentzel, K. R. (2018). A competence-in-context approach to understanding motivation at school. In D. McInerney & G. Liem (Eds.), *Big theories revisited* (pp. 193–212). IAP.

Wentzel, K. R. (2022). Does anybody care? Conceptualization and measurement within the contexts of teacher-student and peer relationships. *Educational Psychology Review, 34*(4), 1919–1954.

Wentzel, K. R., & Skinner, E. A. (2022) Co-eds. The other half of the story: The role of social relationships and social contexts in the development of academic motivation. Special Issue in. *Educational Psychology Review,* 1–12.

Wigfield, A., Eccles, J. S., Fredricks, J. A., Simpkins, S., Roeser, R., & Schiefele, U. (2015). Development of achievement motivation and engagement. In R. M. Lerner (Series 7th ed.) & M. Lamb (Vol. 3 Ed.), *Handbook of child psychology and developmental science. Socioemotional processes* (pp. 657-700). John Wiley.

Wong, Z. Y., Liem, G. A. D., Chan, M., & Datu, J. A. D. (2024). Student engagement and its association with academic achievement and subjective well-being: A systematic review and meta-analysis. *Journal of Educational Psychology, 116*(1), 48.

Yosso, T. J. (2005). Whose culture has capital? A critical race theory discussion of community cultural wealth. *Race, Ethnicity and Education, 8*(1), 69–91.

Zusho, A., & Kumar, R. (2018). Introduction to the special issue: Critical reflections and future directions in the study of race, ethnicity, and motivation. *Educational Psychologist, 53*(2), 61–63.

CHAPTER 2

SELF-AS-AGENT: THE WORLD IS WHAT WE MAKE OF IT

Johnmarshall Reeve
Australian Catholic University, Australia

ABSTRACT

For 100+ years, the self has been understood and studied in two ways—the self as object (e.g., self-concept) and the self as action (e.g., agentic self). This chapter focuses on the latter—the self-as-agent, and it uses a self-determination theory framework to do so. The goal of the chapter is to identify the multiple ways in which the self-as-agent creates a motivationally supportive environment for itself (i.e., "The world is what we make it."). The agentic self is fueled by psychological need satisfaction, and it uses this motivational energy to create need-supportive environmental surroundings that can catalyze personal growth and flourishing. To explain what people psychologically "need," I overview the neuroscience of psychological need satisfaction. The chapter also explains three ways the agentic self generates need-supportive surroundings: Receive autonomy support; recruit autonomy support; and give autonomy support. By interacting with the surrounding environment in these ways, the agentic self creates the conditions to be self-determining. The take-home message is this: The self-as-action needs a garden to grow in (autonomy support), but sometimes it needs to create that garden for itself (agentic engagement).

Keywords: Agency; self-determination theory; psychological needs; autonomy support; motivation

---

The Self in Context, pages 49–75

Published under exclusive licence by Emerald Publishing Limited
doi:10.1108/978-1-80686-869-820261002

In the 1997 movie *Contact,* based on Carl Sagan's (1985) book, the young protagonist struggles to navigate the administrative and political obstacles that block her goals and dreams.

Administrator	"I know you must think this is all incredibly unfair. I wish the world was a place where fair was the bottom line and the kind of idealism you showed at the hearing was rewarded and not taken advantage of. Unfortunately, we don't live in that world."
Young Protagonist	"Funny, I always believed that the world is what we make of it."

The young protagonist has goals and dreams. What she lacks is support for those goals and dreams. So, what she decides to do is create a world in which she does receive support for her goals and dreams. But how does she do it? How does anyone do it?

THE SELF IN SELF-DETERMINATION THEORY

For 100+ years, the self has been understood and studied in two ways—the self as object (e.g., self-concept, "the me") and the self as action (e.g., agent, "the I") (Cooley, 1902; Hattie, 1992; James, 1890; McAdams, 1990; Mead, 1934). This chapter focuses on the latter—the self-as-agent, and it uses a self-determination theory (SDT) framework to do so (Deci & Ryan, 1991; Ryan, 1993; Ryan & Deci, 2017).

The self in SDT is not the social-cognitive answer to the age-old questions of, "Who am I?", "Do I have positive qualities?", "How do I compare to others?", and "What is my place in society?" It is not an object to be perceived, evaluated, and labeled via cognitive appraisals and social comparisons. Instead, it is the agent that initiates action (the "I"). In SDT, the self is "action and development from within" (Deci & Ryan, 1991; Ryan, 1993). It is fueled by inherent motivations (e.g., intrinsic motivation, personal causation; deCharms, 1987; Deci & Ryan, 1985) and innate processes (e.g., differentiation, integration, organization; Ryan, 1993). These internal processes energize the self to seek out and volitionally engage its surrounding so to grow, develop, and be well (Deci & Ryan, 1991). Instead of "Who am I?", self-as-agent questions are, "Who can I become?", "What are my interests and goals?", "How do I develop my potential?", and "What makes me happy and fulfilled?"

The self-as-agent is naturally active, because it possesses inherent motivations, such as intrinsic motivation and the psychological needs for autonomy, competence, and relatedness. A psychological need is a desire for a particular type of experience while acting—specifically to feel personal causation while initiating action (autonomy), to feel effectance while interacting with the environment (competence), and to feel valued and closely connected to others during social interaction (relatedness). What SDT research shows is that the satisfaction of these three psychological experiences catalyzes personal growth, social development, and psychological well-being (Ryan & Deci, 2000, 2017; Vansteenkiste et al., 2020).

So, this chapter assumes that (1) the self-as-agent has plenty of motivation and (2) if that motivation is supported then psychological growth and well-being follow. That leaves a key question: How does the self create an environment that will support these growth motivations?

PLAN, PURPOSE, AND STORY OF THE CHAPTER

The chapter's storyline follows the young protagonist's longing to live in a world that supports rather than neglects and thwarts her goals and dreams. Its purpose is to identify how the self-as-agent creates motivationally supportive surroundings for itself.

Albert Bandura first investigated this question in his theory of reciprocal determinism (Bandura, 1978). He showed that both personal factors (e.g., self-efficacy beliefs) and behavioral factors (actions, choices) can change the surrounding environment for the better. For Bandura, an agent is someone who acts on the environment to change it for the better. But, instead of looking at this question from a social-cognitive or a social learning perspective, I will use SDT.

Self-determination theory (SDT; Ryan & Deci, 2000, 2017) is a macrotheory of motivation and wellness. It is rooted in three core assumptions about the nature of motivation and wellness (see Reeve & Jang, 2026). Assumption 1 is that of *intrinsic activity*—namely, that people are naturally active—that everyone possesses inherent strivings toward activity, learning, and personal growth. This assumption leads to SDT's most empirically tested hypothesis—namely, that psychological need satisfaction leads to engagement and flourishing, while psychological need frustration leads to disengagement and suffering.

Assumption 2 is that *growth and flourishing require a supportive environment.* This assumption is nicely illustrated by the classic plant or seed metaphor. Plants thrive and grow with sunshine, water, and nutritious soil, but they suffer and die with pollution, drought, and toxins. The same applies to people. People thrive in psychological need-supporting environments, but they suffer in need-neglecting and need-frustrating environments. This assumption leads to SDT's second most tested hypothesis—namely, that psychological need-supportive environments facilitate flourishing, while need-neglecting and need-frustrating environments lead to suffering.

Assumption 3 is the *person-environment dialectic*—the person acts on and changes the environment, while the environment in turn acts on and changes the person. For instance, the teacher can facilitate or undermine the student's intrinsic motivation (i.e., teacher → student), while the interested or amotivated student can pull autonomy support or interpersonal control from of the teacher (i.e., student → teacher).

When these assumptions and hypotheses are combined, they produce a model like the one in Fig. 2.1. Fig. 2.1 communicates that environmental supports are necessary for psychological need satisfaction to occur (assumption 2), and that once psychological need satisfaction occurs it facilitates flourishing (assumption 1). It further communicates that not only can the environment change the person, but the person can change the environment (assumption 3).

This is a pretty good model, but there is a problem. What if we are not lucky enough to find ourselves surrounded by environmental supports (i.e., by autonomy-supportive teachers, parents, and governments)? What if we look around to see only dream-thwarting administrators? In that case, we need the self-as-agent to capitalize on assumption 3 to transform the opening vignette's "Unfortunately, we don't live in that world" into "The world is what we make of it."

How does one test SDT's assumption 3? Fig. 2.2 summarizes the results of a study by Hye-Ryen Jang and colleagues that tested for reciprocal causation within the person-environment dialect (Jang et al., 2024). It followed the year-long classroom experiences of 2,908 middle and high school Korean students who reported how supportive their teacher was (autonomy support) and how much energy and initiative they had as self-as-agent (agentic engagement) at four points during the academic year. Receiving autonomy support empowered personal agency ($\beta = 0.12$, $p < 0.001$), while agentic engagement recruited greater autonomy support ($\beta = 0.11$, $p < 0.001$). This suggests that these students were able to create a more supportive environment for themselves.

But social systems and interpersonal relationships can be tough minded, inflexible, and authoritarian—dogmatically insisting on compliance. Too often, strong social forces demand that we just shut up and do what we are told. Such "Heavy D" (discipline) attacks and harms the self-as-agent in two ways. First, it suppresses—even turns off—personal motivations. It can bring personal initiative, self-determination, and self-as-agent to a halt. Second, once personal motivations have been turned "off," then these strong and salient social pressures can step in to replace the silenced personal motivations (De Meyer et al., 2016). This is how practically all controlled motivation works—first turn off the self-as-agent and then replace the void it leaves with environmentally contingent incentives, such as money, points, and gold stars, or with pressuring-inducing tactics, such as guilt induction, shaming, and social obligation (Roth et al., 2009).

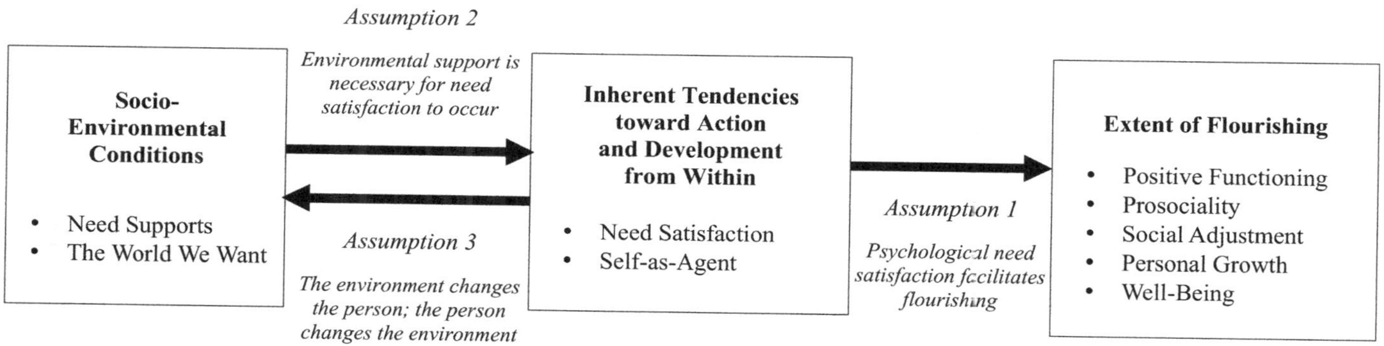

Fig. 2.1. Graphical Representation of the Assumptions and Core Hypotheses Underlying Self-Determination Theory.

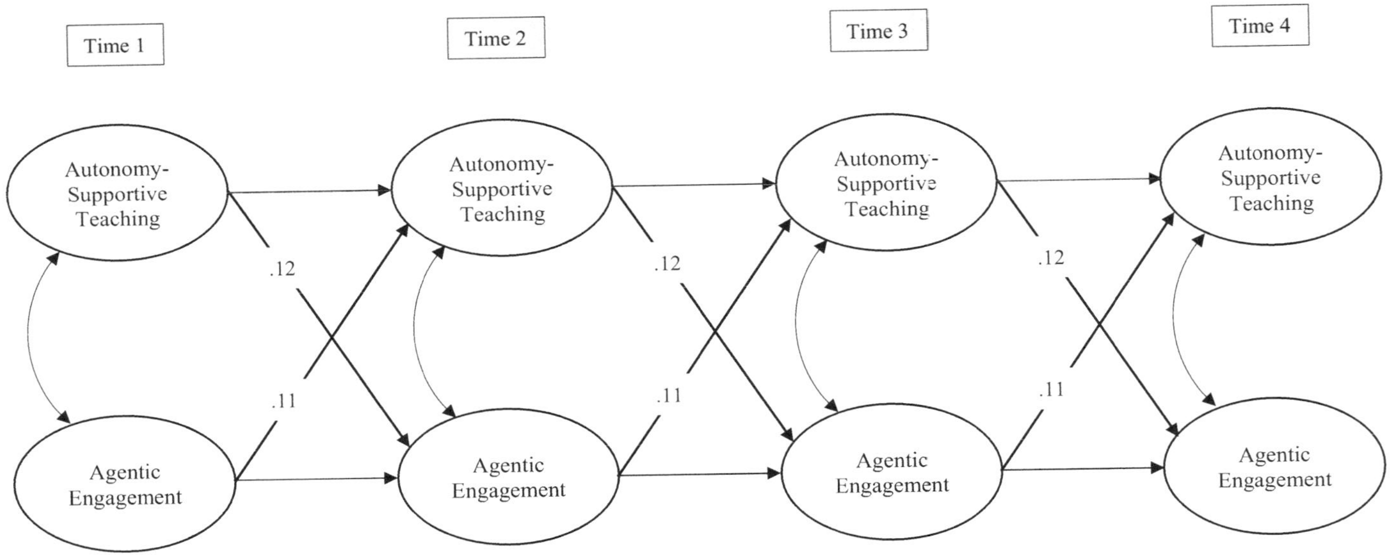

Fig. 2.2. Reciprocal Relations Between Agentic Engagement and Autonomy Support. *Note.* Solid lines represent statistically significant paths, $p < 0.001$. Numbers overlaying the solid lines represent standardized beta weights. The statistical analysis used to test this hypothesized model was a "random intercept—cross-lagged panel model" (RI-CLPM). Data based on Jang et al. (2024).

PSYCHOLOGICAL NEEDS

The most important construct in SDT is the psychological need. But what exactly is a psychological need? What do we "need" psychologically? According to self-determination theory (SDT; Ryan & Deci, 2017), what people need as they interact with the world around them are these three ways of feeling:

- Personal causation while acting (autonomy).
- Effectance during environmental transactions (competence).
- Connection to others in relationships (relatedness).

These needs are so central to SDT and self-as-agent that they need a little more elaboration.

Autonomy is the psychological need to feel personal causation during the initiation and ongoing regulation of one's behavior. Personal causation is feeling *self*-direction and personal endorsement while acting (e.g., "Yes, this is something I freely and wholeheartedly want to do."). It is the essence of *self*-determined action.

Competence is the psychological need to feel effective as one interacts with environmental surroundings, including activities, goal pursuits, and other people. Competence is crucial for personal growth because it fuels to the desire to seek out optimal challenges, take them on, and exert persistent effort and strategic thinking so to improve and gain effectance. It fuels intrinsic motivation (Deci & Ryan, 1980, 1985; White, 1959).

Relatedness is the psychological need to feel socially connected and close to, and accepted and valued by, others. It is the need to belong. It fuels the desire to form close emotional bonds and attachments, and it is fundamental to internalization and adaptive social functioning (Grolnick et al., 1997; Ryan & Deci, 2000).

In the classroom, the satisfaction of these basic psychological needs opens the door to multiples positive student outcomes—such as engagement and flourishing. To summarize this large research literature, Fig. 2.3 graphically identifies many of these education-related benefits.

FEELING AND EXPERIENCING PSYCHOLOGICAL NEED SATISFACTION

I put feelings at the center of psychological need satisfaction. To understand why I do this, I will quickly overview the 15-year neuroscience program of research with Woogul Lee (Lee, 2023; Reeve & Lee, 2019). From the beginning, our goal has always been to find the psychological need within the architecture of the brain.

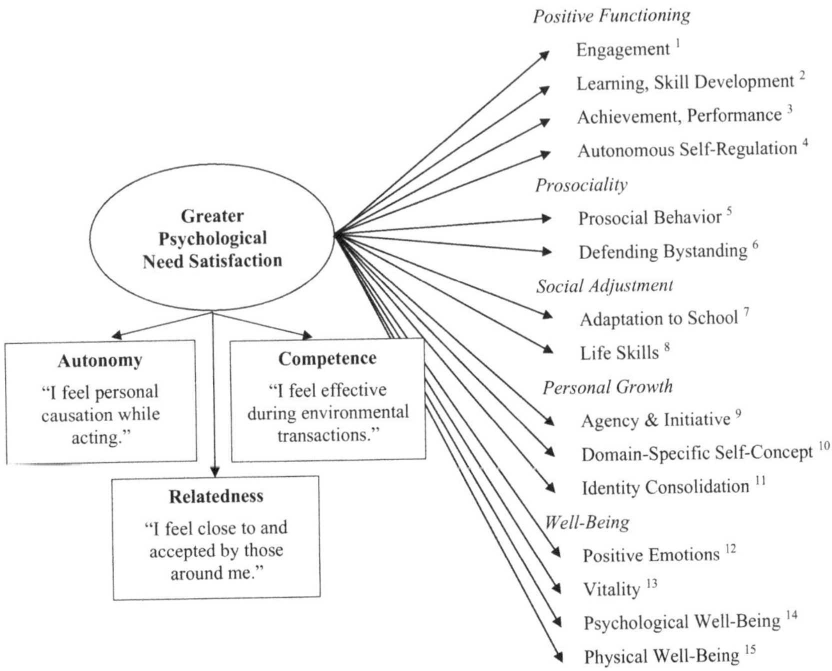

Fig. 2.3. The Benefits of Greater Psychological Need Satisfaction. *Note.* The subscripts 1–14 refer to the journal article that provides the evidence base to support the claim that greater psychological need satisfaction tends to produce that benefit. Those articles are as follows (for the full reference citation, see the Reference section at the end of the chapter): (1) Cheon et al. (2016); (2) Black and Deci (2000); (3) Carmona-Halty et al. (2019); (4) Cheon et al. (2012); (5) Hodge and Gucciardi (2015); (6) Cheon et al. (2023b); (7) Chirkov and Ryan (2001); (8) Cronin et al. (2022); (9) Reeve, Cheon, and Yu (2020); (10) Cheon et al. (2020); (11) Luyckx et al. (2007); (12) Martela and Sheldon (2019); (13) Kasser and Ryan (1993); (14) Sheldon et al. (1996); (15) Reeve and Tseng (2011b).

As our participants lay in a scanner (in an fMRI machine), we observed their brain activations second-by-second while they engaged in activities designed to generate an experience of either autonomy, competence, or intrinsic motivation. Two early findings were that (1) experimentally manipulated experiences of autonomy, competence, and intrinsic motivation were all associated with anterior insular cortex activity (AIC) and (2) the greater the AIC activity, the greater the self-reported feelings of autonomy, competence, and intrinsic motivation (Lee & Reeve, 2013; Lee et al., 2012). In one study, self-reported feelings of autonomy and competence correlated $r = 0.73$ with extent of left AIC activity and $r = 0.79$ with right AIC activity (Lee & Reeve, 2013, see their Fig. 2.6, p. 543).

A third finding was that the anticipation of forthcoming need satisfaction (e.g., during an optimal challenge) generated feelings of interest and AIC activity, while the actual experience of need satisfaction (e.g., successfully solving that optimal challenge) generated feelings of enjoyment and striatum activity (Lee & Reeve, 2017). Finding this, we proposed an intrinsic motivation neural network of bidirectional activity between the AIC and striatum (Lee & Reeve, 2017).

A fourth finding was that while autonomy satisfaction involved AIC and dorsal striatal activity, competence and relatedness satisfaction involved AIC and ventral striatal activity (Reeve & Lee, 2026). This dorsal-ventral distinction is important because ventral striatal activity (e.g., nucleus accumbens) is associated with pleasure, reward, and satisfaction, while dorsal striatal activity (e.g., caudate nucleus) is associated with meaning, purpose, volition, and value-based decision-making. So, fulfilling one's needs for competence and relatedness *feels good and satisfying*, while fulfilling one's need for autonomy *feels right and authentic.*

Fig. 2.4 summarizes what we and others have learned. Fig. 2.4 offers a sagittal view of the brain to illustrate the neuroscience of feeling psychological need satisfaction. Among its many functions, the AIC receives a constant flow of information from and about bodily states. Interoceptive inputs from internal stimuli (i.e., cardiovascular sensations, hormonal fluctuations) and interoceptive inputs from external stimuli (i.e., sight, touch) travel upwards from sensorimotor bodily systems to and through the thalamus to be received and monitored in an automatic and nonconscious way by the posterior insular cortex. As shown by the arrow connecting the posterior and anterior insula, this "state of the body" information is organized in the posterior insula and then relayed to the anterior insula. At this point, the person has a feeling (Craig, 2009; Damasio, 1999). In the anterior insula, this feeling is integrated with social contextual information about what might be causing these bodily states (e.g., social cues, another's tone of voice, nonverbal signals). Now the person has a feeling and an understanding of what might have caused that feeling, such as feeling effective from a job well done, feeling at-risk on a fast-moving motorcycle, or mistrusting a fast-talking salesperson. From the anterior insula, this information is then relayed to multiple parts of the brain, especially to the striatum and prefrontal cortex.

To explain what happens next, Fig. 2.4 shows that the anterior insula sends its feeling-based information to the following:

1. Dorsal striatum. Here people feel autonomy involvement and satisfaction.

2. Ventral striatum. Here people feel competence and relatedness involvement and satisfaction.
3. Prefrontal cortex (multiple areas). Here people gain conscious awareness of the feeling (prefrontal cortex), store and remember it (orbitofrontal cortex), and ready the motor cortex for energized action (supplemental motor cortex).

These events explain how engaging in an activity can generate a feeling of psychological need satisfaction in a bottom-up fashion. That has been the focus of our research group. But others have explained how the self generates psychological need satisfaction in a top-down fashion. As explained by Di Domenico and Ryan (2017, 2023) and as shown by the double-sided arrow in Fig. 2.4, when people experience a self-regulation conflict (e.g., should I work or play? Should I toss this bottle in the trash or walk over to the recycling bin?), the anterior cingulate cortex detects the conflict and recruits the executive functioning of the medial prefrontal cortex to resolve it. Much self-determined decision-making takes place in the medial prefrontal cortex, and this brain area and the anterior insula inform each other reciprocally (see the large two-way arrow). In this way, the self (rather than the activity) generates the experience of psychological need satisfaction.

There is more to the neuroscience of self-determination, intrinsic motivation, and psychological need satisfaction than what appears in Fig. 2.4 (Lee, 2023). But this information is important and relevant to our discussion of self-functioning for two reasons.

We Need to Know What a Psychological Need Is

We have a 100 different AIC-activated feelings—irritation, confusion, awe, suspicion, hesitancy, longing, playful, excited, satisfied, and so on (Reeve, 2025). Three of these are the basis of intrinsic motivation, internalization, and volitional action—namely, the feelings of personal causation, effectance, and closeness. Fifty years of SDT research confirms that these are the psychological nutriments people need to flourish (Vansteenkiste et al., 2020). Autonomy, competence, and relatedness are the energy-mobilizing satisfactions that empower the self-as-agent.

How Can We Create Conditions that Facilitate These Feelings?

Many people are working to answer this question, including us. In the context of education, three direct and person-generated pathways and three

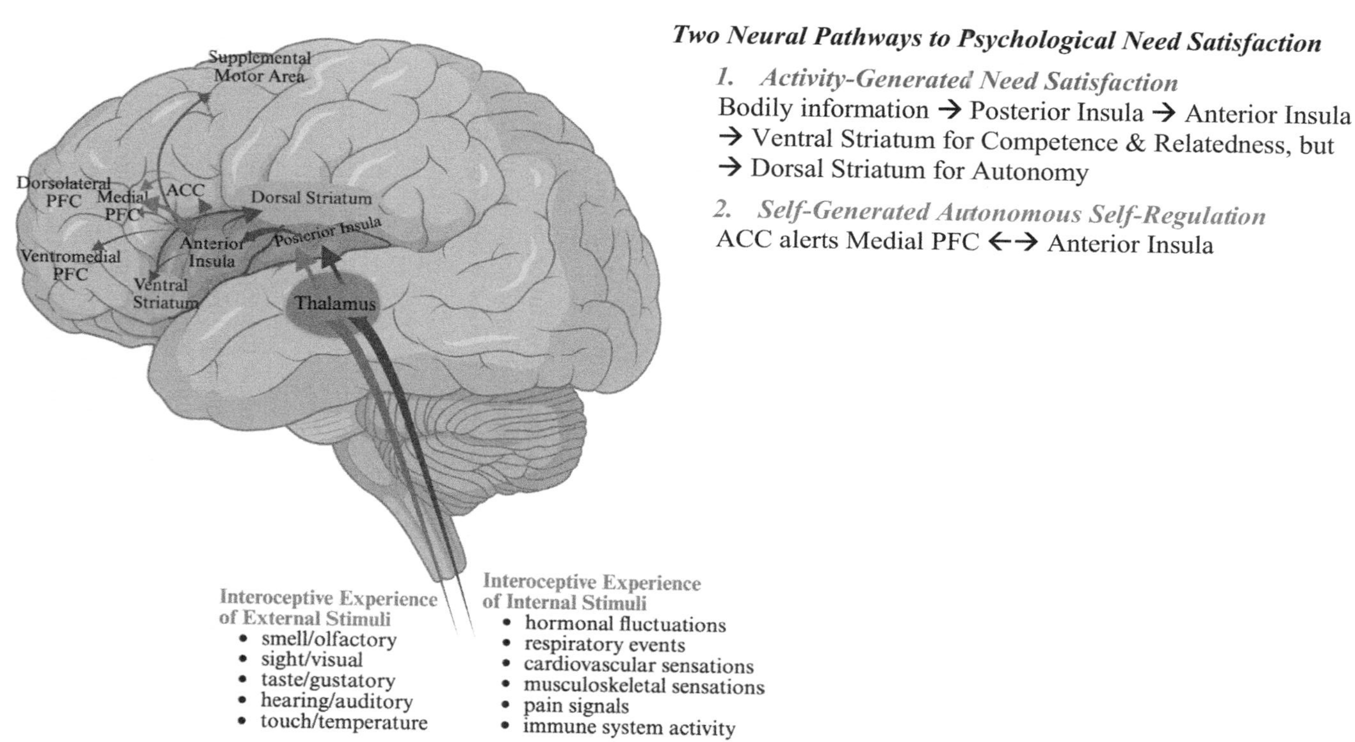

Fig. 2.4. The Neuroscience of the Feeling-Based Experiences Associated With Psychological Need Satisfaction.

indirect and socially initiated pathways to psychological need satisfaction exist. The three direct and person-generated pathways include:

- Engage oneself in an interesting or personally valued activity
- Pursue an intrinsic goal
- Practice need crafting

These are three tried and true (i.e., evidence-based) strategies or pathways to need satisfaction: Engage in interesting (Isen & Reeve, 2005) and personally useful (Vansteenkiste et al., 2018) activities, pursue intrinsic goals (Koestner, 2008), and practice need crafting (Laporte et al., 2021). An interesting activity is any activity that provides an opportunity to experience psychological need satisfaction (Deci, 1992), and a personally valued activity is one that has personal meaning, personal usefulness, or self-relevance (e.g., "I want to revise my paper, because I value good writing—that's who I am"; Vansteenkiste et al., 2018). An intrinsic goal is a pursuit that puts the goal-striver on a journey that offers frequent and recurring opportunities to experience psychological need satisfaction (e.g., as I try to "improve my health", I open up numerous opportunities to feel autonomy, competence, and relatedness along the way; Koestner, 2008). Need crafting is self-initiated action to modify a recurring situation (e.g., at work, studying) to bring it into alignment with one's interests, goals, and psychological needs (e.g., instead of studying alone, the student forms a study group with like-minded and relatedness-supportive classmates, which creates an opportunity to experience relatedness satisfaction; Duchi et al., 2025).

These are all direct pathways to create psychological need satisfaction for oneself, but our research has focused mostly on socially generated pathways, so I will give special attention to these strategies, which are as follows:

- Receive autonomy support
- Recruit autonomy support (i.e., Initiate agentic engagement)
- Give autonomy support

"Receive autonomy support" appears at the top of the list because it is the most studied and empirically validated pathway to psychological need satisfaction. Not all social contexts and interpersonal relationships are autonomy supportive. So, the individual needs intentional action to recruit greater autonomy support, which we study as "agentic engagement." As to the third pathway, I will save "give autonomy support" for the final section, because it is an underappreciated, yet ideal, pathway to "The world is what me make it."

RECEIVE AUTONOMY SUPPORT

Autonomy-supportive teaching (AST) is the instructional effort to identify and support students' psychological needs during instruction, thus helping students willing and proactively engage in classroom learning activities (Aelterman et al., 2019; Patall et al., 2018; Reeve & Cheon, 2021; Reeve, Ryan, et al., 2022). This is the conceptual definition of AST, though I find the diagram in Fig. 2.5 to be more useful when communicating what AST looks like in practice. In one sense, AST is a gestalt experience—my teacher supports me, is on my side, understands me and my concerns. In a workshop to help teachers learn how to become autonomy supportive, we find it helpful to break down this gestalt experience into its three active ingredients: Perspective taking; interest support; and value support. Fig. 2.5 identifies these three essential AST practices.

When teachers participate in our AST workshop, they typically learn AST to a high level (e.g., Cheon et al., 2023a; Reeve & Cheon, 2024; Reeve, Ryan, et al., 2022). They become highly skilled in perspective taking, supporting interest, and supporting value, and they learn how to transform existing controlling teaching practices (e.g., utter directives, use pressuring language) into autonomy-supportive alternatives (e.g., provide explanatory rationales, use invitational language). Postworkshop, the students of these teachers then experience rising levels of psychological need satisfaction (Cheon et al., 2016; 2018a, 2019a) and hence the benefits summarized on the right side of Fig. 2.3. Other research teams have used different workshops to demonstrate similar benefits (Assor et al., 2018; Fin et al., 2019; Huéscar et al., 2020; Tilga et al., 2019).

When teachers participate in an AST workshop, they not only become more able to support students' psychological needs, but they also become more able to create a supportive, closely-knit, peer-to-peer classroom climate (Cheon et al., 2022, 2023a, 2023b, 2024). Classroom climate is a social-ecological concept (Espelage et al., 2003; Hong & Espelage, 2012). In multilevel terms, classroom climate is an L2 effect. It is a group, not an individual L1, phenomenon. AST facilitates the whole class to collectively embrace a more supportive climate or culture (an L2 group effect), one that ideally represents the chapter's subtitle of "The world is what we make it." The emerging egalitarian, cooperative, and closely-knit sense of community promotes students' social flourishing, such as greater prosocial behavior and greater bystander defending and lesser antisocial behavior and lesser bullying (Assor et al., 2018; Cheon et al., 2023a, 2023b; Gest & Rodkin, 2011; Kaplan & Assor, 2012; Roth et al., 2010; Van Ryzin & Roseth, 2018).

AST works really, really well. It produces multiple benefits. But there is a potential problem. To receive autonomy support, one needs to be lucky.

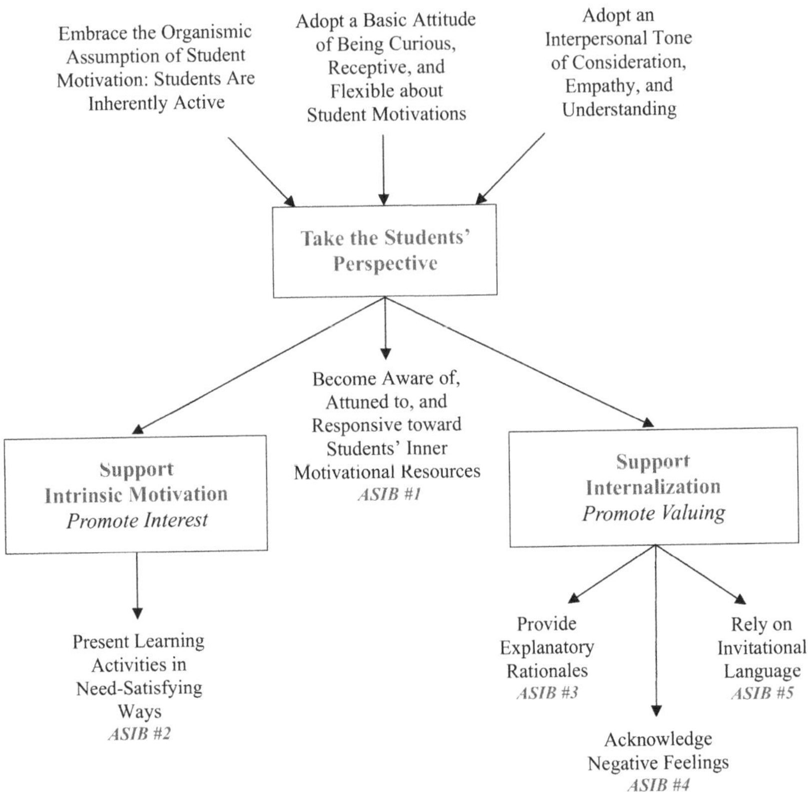

Fig. 2.5. Conceptual Representation of Autonomy-Supportive Teaching Practices. *Note:* ASIB = Autonomy-Supportive Instructional Behavior.

The self needs to find itself in a needs-supportive context with need-supportive relationships. One hopes the teacher, coach, parent, etc. is autonomy supportive. The problem: What if the person is not exposed to autonomy support? What about our young protagonist; what can she do? She is not so lucky. She is stuck with close-minded, need-thwarting administrators. Can she pull greater autonomy support out of her social world? One way to do this is via agentic engagement (recall Fig. 2.2).

RECRUIT AUTONOMY SUPPORT: AGENTIC ENGAGEMENT

An agent acts to change their circumstances for the better (Bandura, 2006, 2018). A nonagent simply accepts their circumstances "as is"—where I live is fine, the courses I am taking are fine, the resources and opportunities afforded me are fine, how my teacher treats me is fine. You get what you get, and you just accept that "This is the world we live in."

Agency is a motivational term—one full of purpose, self-efficacy, and self-determination. Its energizing purpose is to do whatever is necessary to improve, enrich, and personalize one's circumstances, environment, resources, and interpersonal relationships. It is not a protest or complaining; instead, it is a voice—a voice to be heard, appreciated, understood, listened to and, ultimately, supported. When such initiative is successful, agents create new and better opportunities to pursue their interests, satisfy their motivations, develop their skills, and become their desired future self (Patall, 2024; Patall et al., 2022; Reeve, 2013).

Agentic engagement is the personal initiative one undertakes to change their surrounding environment for the better (Patall et al., 2022; Reeve, 2013; Reeve & Tseng, 2011a). It is an action term—one full of seeking, experimenting, communicating, and changing things for the better. Here are some classroom examples (Reeve & Shin, 2020):

- Speak up to let the teacher know what you want, need, and are interested in.
- Ask for a say in what to do and how to do it.
- Express a preference.
- Offer input; make a suggestion.

The primary benefit of agentic engagement is that it recruits greater support from one's interpersonal environment. For instance, students' agentic engagement recruits greater teacher-provided autonomy support, as shown earlier in Fig. 2.2. That is, the more students speak up to express their preferences and let the teacher know what they want and need, the more likely it becomes that the teacher will take their perspective, support their interests, and support their valuing (Matos et al., 2018; Patall et al., 2019; Reeve, 2013; Reeve & Tseng, 2011a; Reeve, Cheon, & Jang, 2020).

Students' agentic engagement also recruits greater peer-based autonomy support (Cheon et al., 2026). Fig. 2.6 shows the findings from a semester-long (18 weeks) longitudinal, classroom-based study in which we assessed students' autonomy need satisfaction at the beginning of the semester (Time 1) and again at the end of the semester (Time 3). As the semester unfolded, we assessed how much students engaged in "teacher-based agentic engagement" ("I let my teacher know what I am interested in.") and "peer-based agentic engagement" ("I let my classmates know what I want and need.") at T1 and again at T2. What we found was that the more autonomously motivated the student was, the more agentically engaged they became toward their teacher ($B = 0.25$, $p < 0.001$) and peers ($B = 0.24$, $p < 0.001$). Further, the more students increased their mid-semester agentic engagement, the more they increased their end-semester autonomy need satisfaction. This greater T3 autonomy need satisfaction effect occurred following both teacher-based ($B = 0.12$,

$p = 0.011$) and peer-based ($B = 0.22$, $p < 0.001$) agentic engagement. These more agentically engaged students were having more motivationally satisfying interactions and relationships with their teacher and peers, compared to their more passive classmates.

In two related experiments, we trained students to display high levels of agentic engagement during an upcoming tutoring session. The students in the experimental group did display more agentic engagement, compared to students in a no-training control group, and they experiencing greater psychological need satisfaction (and task interest) during the tutoring session (Reeve, Jang, et al., 2022). Importantly, they were able to recruit, or bring out, a more autonomy-supportive style from their tutors. These studies are important because they show that agentic engagement can be increased and manipulated to a high level, and its effects on greater AST and psychological need satisfaction are causal. Other research shows that greater agentic engagement enables students to develop course-specific skills, make better grades, and report greater academic and personal growth (Reeve, Cheon, & Jang, 2020, Reeve, Ryan, et al., 2022; Reeve & Tseng, 2011a; Yin et al., 2026).

Overall, agentic engagement is empowering. But it does need a responsive environment. In a motivationally suppressing environment, agentic engagement sometimes just gets the self into a lot of trouble (e.g., the "backfire effect" proposed by Zambrano et al., 2022). Jang and Reeve (2025) used a water faucet metaphor to illustrate how the sociocultural context enables versus restricts agentic engagement and its benefits. Agentic engagement is the flowing water, while sociocultural forces are the handle that opens or closes the flowing water. Need support turns the metaphorical handle to a wide-open position so that agentic engagement flows into high-quality functioning. Need-thwart (e.g., authoritarianism, interpersonal control, high-stakes grading) turns the handle to a closed position (via commands, public shaming, and win-at-all-costs contingencies). In this closed position, the water flow (agentic engagement) dries up. Authoritarian, controlling social forces can be quite harsh and punitive to expressions of agentic engagement (i.e., "Just shut up, and do as you are told—or else!").

The potentially suppressive effect of culture on both autonomy support and agentic engagement raises the question as to whether there might be yet another path to greater psychological need satisfaction. There is, but it is not an obvious one.

GIVING AUTONOMY SUPPORT

Earlier, I emphasized that AST yields two benefits: (1) greater psychological need satisfaction and (2) a more supportive classroom climate. But there is a third benefit. When autonomy supportive, the teacher creates an opportunity to experience their own psychological need satisfaction.

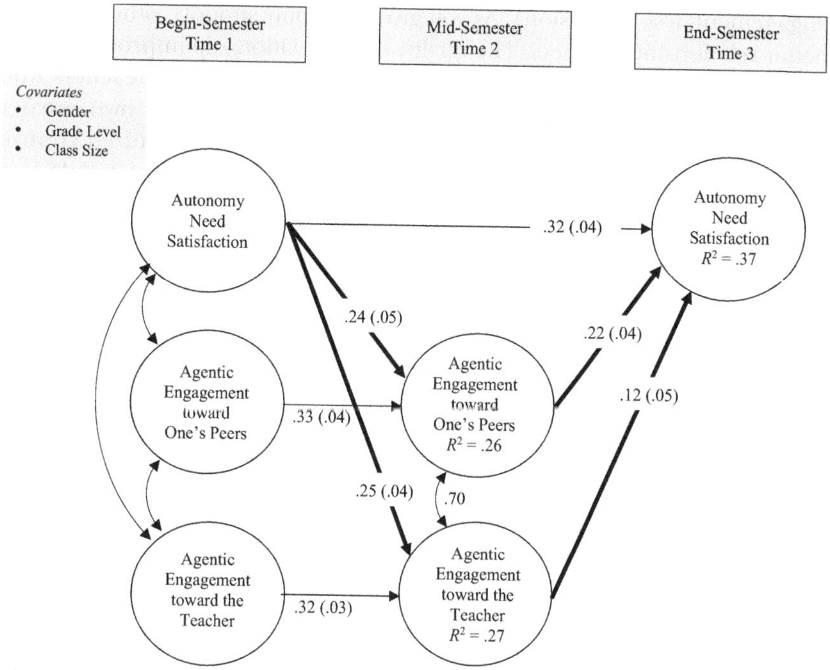

Fig. 2.6. Mid-Semester Gains in Peer-Directed and Teacher-Directed Agentic Engagement Explain End-Semester Gains in Autonomy Psychological Need Satisfaction. *Note.* Thick boldfaced lines represent hypothesized paths, while thin-faced lines represent autoregressive effects. Ovals represent latent variables. Numbers are unstandardized beta weights (with standard errors in parentheses). R^2 = variance explained in that dependent measure. Data based on Cheon et al. (2026).

To explain this, I want to take you back to the original 2006 study conducted by Ed Deci and his colleagues. They wanted to know what made close friends close—what made a relationship a high-quality one? They found that people felt close to those who were autonomy supportive toward them, as you might expect. But, they also found that people felt close when they were the one who gave autonomy support to their partner (e.g., "It is better to give than to receive."). I think this is a very interesting finding.

Something special happens when giving autonomy support. Most researchers suggest a beneficence effect. Beneficence is being generous or doing good (Martela & Ryan, 2015). Autonomy support overlaps with prosocial behavior and doing good (Cheon, Reeve, & Ntoumanis, 2018, Cheon, Reeve, & Ntoumanis, 2019; Gagné, 2003). And helping others is a positive affect, gratitude-inducing, relationship-building thing to do (Bartlett & DeSteno, 2006; Martela & Ryan, 2015; Pavey et al., 2011). But there is more to it than that. Giving autonomy support also improves other people's functioning (e.g., more engagement, less aggression). As you give autonomy support, others become better relationship partners. The quality of the relationship improves.

Inspired by Deci et al.'s finding, we investigated whether teachers who participated in our AST workshop might experience their own greater need satisfaction. They did. We have conducted four randomized control trial (RCT) interventions in which we experimentally manipulated AST to a high level and then assessed for postintervention gains in teachers' psychological need satisfaction, compared to a control group of teachers (Cheon et al., 2014, 2015; Cheon, Reeve, et al., 2018; Jang & Reeve, 2021). We summarize the findings from these four studies in the upper part of Table 2.1. We have also found three correlational studies that assessed both autonomy support given and personal need satisfaction experienced (Aelterman et al., 2019; Deci et al., 2006; Jang et al., 2023). We summarize the findings from these three studies in the lower part of Table 2.1.

As listed in Table 2.1, the average effect size across the four RCT interventions (i.e., experimental studies) was $d_{\text{IPGG-RAW}} = 1.06$ (*range*, 0.55–1.94); and the average effect size across the three correlational studies was $r = 0.29$ (*range*, 0.24 to 0.33). In all 7 studies the relationship between giving autonomy support and experiencing personal psychological need satisfaction was positive, significant, and of a notable effect size.

Two features of "giving autonomy support" are worth emphasizing. First, it is perfectly controllable by the individual. Whether you support, thwart, or are indifferent to other people's psychological needs is pretty much up to you. This makes your own personal need satisfaction controllable. Second, it produces so many benefits—for others, for the social climate, and for the self (Reeve et al., 2023). Together, these features make giving autonomy support a reliable go-to strategy for greater personal need satisfaction and its multiple benefits.

CONCLUSION

The chapter began with a story from a popular book and movie. It now ends the same way.

In the penultimate scene in the final Harry Potter book and movie (Rowling, 2007), with the Elder wand in hand, the young wizard and his two best friends stand together on a war-torn bridge. The Elder wand is the most powerful wand in wizardry, so the young wizard can now be top dog, king, CEO, and 5-star general. He can impose his will on others. But he breaks the wand in two and throws it into the abyss. He walks away, as he would rather "support autonomy than control behavior" (to borrow a favorite phrase from Deci & Ryan, 1987).

The movie does not end there. If you are not going to wield unlimited power, then what are you going to do? What does a lifestyle of "give

TABLE 2.1 Effect Sizes for the Association Between Giving Autonomy Support and the Teacher's Own Experience of Psychological Need Satisfaction: Experimental and Correlational Studies.

Experimental Studies				
Reference	**Journal**	$d_{IPGG\text{-}RAW}$	**p Value**	**Sample**
Cheon et al. (2014)	*Journal of Sport and Exercise Psychology*	1.25	0.001	27 full-time K-12 physical education (PE) teachers
Cheon et al. (2015)	*Psychology of Sport and Exercise*	0.55	0.036	33 head coaches on the Korean national Paralympics team
Cheon, Reeve, Lee, and Lee (2018)	*Teaching and Teacher Education*	0.49	0.010	91 full-time K-12 PE teachers
Jang and Reeve (2021), Study 2	*Learning and Instruction*	1.94	0.001	26 full-time K-12 teachers of multiple subjects

Correlational Studies				
Reference	**Journal**	r	**p Value**	**Sample**
Deci et al. (2006)	*Personality and Social Psychology Bulletin*	0.30	0.001	124 pairs of close friends, university undergraduates
Aelterman et al. (2019)	*Journal of Educational Psychology*	0.24	0.001	795 full-time secondary teachers of multiple subjects
Jang et al. (2023), Study 2	*Physical Education and Sports Pedagogy*	0.33	0.001	134 full-time PE teachers

autonomy support" look like? The final scene is a gentle one. No one yells, threatens, pressures, or tries to dominate and influence. It shows the three protagonists, 19 years later, as parents giving support to their children—to the next generation. The three friends give autonomy support just like they earlier received it in their youth. The credits close, and you know that all will be well in the new and better world they made for themselves.

This was Harry Potter's story—a life surrounded by autonomy-supportive friendships and mentors. But it was not the story of our young protagonist at the start of the chapter. She was alone and surrounded by nonsupportive and harshly need-thwartive relationships. Despite having the proverbial wind in her face, she, as self-as-agent, created her own multiple pathways to need satisfaction and flourishing. She engaged in deeply interesting and personally valued activities, she pursued intrinsic goals, she practiced need crafting, she lived and breathed agentic engagement, and she continually gave autonomy support to those around her. In the end, she walked the talk: "The world is what we make of it."

TAKE HOME MESSAGE

The self-as-action needs a garden to grow in. This is autonomy support. But sometimes it needs to create that garden for itself. This is agentic engagement.

ACKNOWLEDGMENT

Special thanks to Daphne van den Bogaard for her input and reflections on the chapter.

REFERENCES

Aelterman, N., Vansteenkiste, M., Soenens, B., Fontaine, J., Haerens, L., Delrue, J., & Reeve, J. (2019). Toward a fine-grained understanding of the components of need- supportive and need-thwarting teaching: The merits of a gradual approach. *Journal of Educational Psychology, 111,* 497–521. https://doi.org/10.1037/edu0000293

Assor, A., Feinberg, O., Kanat-Maymon, Y., & Kaplan, H. (2018). Reducing violence in non-controlling ways: A change program based on self-determination theory. *The Journal of Experimental Education, 86*(2), 195–213. https://doi.org/10.1080/00220973.2016.1277336

Bandura, A. (1978). The self system in reciprocal determinism. *American Psychologist, 33*(4), 344–358. https://doi.org/10.1037/0003-066X.33.4.344

Bandura, A. (2006). Toward a psychology of human agency. *Perspectives on Psychological Science, 1*, 164–180.

Bandura, A. (2018). Toward a psychology of human agency: Pathways and reflections. *Perspectives on Psychological Science, 13*(2), 130–136.

Bartlett, M. Y., & DeSteno, D. (2006). Gratitude and prosocial behavior: Helping when it costs you. *Psychological Science, 17*, 319–325.

Black, A. E., & Deci, E. L. (2000). The effects of instructors' autonomy support and students' autonomous motivation on learning organic chemistry: A self-determination theory perspective. *Science Education, 84*(6), 740–756.

Carmona-Halty, M., Schaufeli, W. B., Llorens, S., & Salanova, M. (2019). Satisfaction of basic psychological needs leads to better academic performance via increased psychological capital: A three-wave longitudinal study among high school students. *Frontiers in Psychology, 10*, 2113. https://doi.org/10.3389/fpsyg.2019.02113

Cheon, S. H., Reeve, J., Huang, D., Patall, E. A., Im, C.-H., & Kim, U. N. (2026). Greater autonomy need satisfaction with a little help from my friends: A randomized control trial to increase peer-based agentic engagement. *Contemporary Educational Psychology*. https://doi.org/10.1016/j.cedpsych.2026.102447

Cheon, S. H., Reeve, J., Lee, J., & Lee, Y. (2015). Giving and receiving autonomy support in a high-stakes sport context: A field-based experiment during the 2012 London Paralympic Games. *Psychology of Sport and Exercise, 19*, 59–69. https://doi.org/10.1016/j.psychsport.2015.02.007

Cheon, S. H., Reeve, J., Lee, Y., & Lee, J.-W. (2018b). Why autonomy-supportive interventions work: Explaining the professional development of teachers' motivating styles. *Teaching and Teacher Education, 69*, 43–51. https://doi.org/10.1016/j.tate.2017.09.002

Cheon, S. H., Reeve, J., Lee, Y., Ntoumanis, N., Gillet, N., Kim, B. R., & Song, Y.-G (2019a). Expanding autonomy psychological need states from two (satisfaction, frustration) to three (dissatisfaction): A classroom-based intervention study. *Journal of Educational Psychology, 111*(4), 685–702. https://doi.org/10.1037/edu0000306

Cheon, S. H., Reeve, J., & Marsh, H. (2022). Intervention-enabled autonomy-supportive teaching improves the PE classroom climate to reduce antisocial behavior: A cluster randomized control trial. *Psychology of Sport and Exercise, 60*, Article 102174. https://doi.org/10.1016/j.psychsport.2022.102174

Cheon, S. H., Reeve, J., & Marsh, H. (2023a). Autonomy-supportive teaching enhances prosocial and reduces antisocial behavior via classroom climate and psychological needs: A multilevel randomized control intervention. *Journal of Sport & Exercise Psychology, 45*(1), 26–40. https://doi.org/10.1123/jsep.2021-0337

Cheon, S. H., Reeve, J., Marsh, H., & Jang, H.-R. (2023b). Cluster randomized control trial to reduce peer victimization: An autonomy-supportive teaching intervention changes the classroom ethos to support defending bystanders. *American Psychologist, 78*(7), 856–872. https://doi.org/10.1037/amp0001130

Cheon, S. H., Reeve, J., & Moon, I. S. (2012). Experimentally based, longitudinally designed, teacher-focused intervention to help physical education teachers be more autonomy supportive toward their students. *Journal of Sport & Exercise Psychology, 34,* 365–396. https://doi.org/10.1123/jsep.34.3.365

Cheon, S. H., Reeve, J., & Ntoumanis, N. (2018a). A needs-supportive intervention to help PE teachers enhance students' prosocial behavior and diminish anti-social behavior. *Psychology of Sport and Exercise, 35,* 74–88.

Cheon, S. H., Reeve, J., & Ntoumanis, N. (2019b, December). An intervention to help teachers establish a prosocial peer climate in physical education. *Learning and Instruction, 64,* 101223. https://doi.org/10.1016/j.learninstruc.2019.101223

Cheon, S. H., Reeve, J., & Song, Y.-G. (2016). A teacher-focused intervention to decrease PE students' amotivation by increasing need satisfaction and decreasing need frustration. *Journal of Sport & Exercise Psychology, 38,* 217–235. https://doi.org/10.1123/jsep.2015-0236

Cheon, S. H., Reeve, J., & Vansteenkiste, M. (2020). When teachers learn how to provide classroom structure in an autonomy-supportive way: Benefits to teachers and their students. *Teaching and Teacher Education, 90,* 103004. https://doi.org/10.1016/j.tate.2019.103004

Cheon, S. H., Reeve, J., Yoo, K.-E., Song, Y.-G., Ryan, R. M., & Jang, H. (2024). Two randomized control trials to help teachers develop physical education students' course-specific grit-perseverance and mental toughness. *Journal of Sport & Exercise Psychology.* https://doi.org/10.1123/jsep.2024-0102

Cheon, S. H., Reeve, J., Yu, T. H., & Jang, H.-R. (2014). The teacher benefits from giving autonomy support during physical education instruction. *Journal of Sport & Exercise Psychology, 36,* 331–346. https://doi.org/10.1123/jsep.2013-0231

Chirkov, V. I., & Ryan, R. M. (2001). Parent and teacher autonomy-support in Russian and US adolescents: Common effects on well-being and academic motivation. *Journal of Cross-Cultural Psychology, 32*(5), 618–635.

Cooley, C. H. (1902). *Human nature and the social order.* Scribner.

Craig, A. D. (2009). How do you feel—now? The anterior insula and human awareness. *Nature Reviews Neuroscience, 10*(1), 59–70. https://doi.org/10.1038/nrn2555

Cronin, L., Ellison, P., Allen, J., Huntley, E., Johnson, L., Kosteli, M. C., Hollis, A., & Marchant, D. (2022). A self-determination theory based investigation of life skills development in youth sport. *Journal of Sport Sciences, 40*(8), 886–898. https://doi.org/10.1080/02640414.2022.2028507

Damasio, A. (1999). *The feeling of what happens: Body and emotion in the making of consciousness.* Harcourt College Publishers.

deCharms, R. (1987). The burden of motivation. In M. L. Maehr & D. A. Kleiber (Eds.), *Advances in motivation and achievement: Enhancing motivation* (Vol. 5, pp. 1–21). JAI Press.

Deci, E. L. (1992). The relation of interest to the motivation of behavior: A self-determination theory perspective. In K. A. Renninger, S. Hidi, & A. Krapp (Eds.), *The role of interest in learning and development* (pp. 43–70). Lawrence Erlbaum Associates, Inc.

Deci, E. L., La Guardia, J. G., Moller, A. C., Scheiner, M. J., & Ryan, R. M. (2006). On the benefits of giving as well as receiving autonomy support: Mutuality in close friendships. *Personality and Social Psychology Bulletin, 32,* 313–327. https://doi.org/10.1177/0146167205282148

Deci, E. L., & Ryan, R. M. (1980). The empirical exploration of intrinsic motivational processes. In L. Berkowitz (Ed.), *Advances in experimental social psychology* (Vol. *13*, pp. 39–80). Academic Press.

Deci, E. L., & Ryan, R. M. (1985). *Intrinsic motivation and self-determination in human behavior.* Plenum Press.

Deci, E. L., & Ryan, R. M. (1987). The support of autonomy and the control of behavior. *Journal of Personality and Social Psychology, 53*(6), 1024–1037. https://doi.org/10.1037/0022-3514.53.6.1024

Deci, E. L., & Ryan, R. M. (1991). A motivational approach to self: Integration in personality. In R. Dienstbier (Ed.), *Nebraska Symposium on Motivation: Perspectives on motivation* (Vol. *38*, pp. 237–288). University of Nebraska Press.

De Meyer, J., Soenens, B., Aelterman, N., De Bourdeaudhuij, I., & Haerens, L. (2016). The different faces of controlling teaching: Implications of a distinction between externally and internally controlling teaching for students' motivation in physical education. *Physical Education and Sport Pedagogy, 21*(6), 632–652. https://doi.org/10.1080/17408989.2015.1112777

Di Domenico, S. I., & Ryan, R. M. (2017). The emerging neuroscience of intrinsic motivation: A new frontier in self-determination research. *Frontiers in Human Neuroscience, 11*, 145.

Di Domenico, S. I., & Ryan, R. M. (2023). Toward a neurobiology of integrative processes. In R. M. Ryan (Ed.), *The Oxford handbook of self-determination theory* (pp. 292–308). Oxford University Press. https://doi.org/10.1093/oxfordhb/9780197600047.013.14

Duchi, L., Wijnia, L., Loyens, S., & Paas, F. (2025). Redefining education: The role of study crafting in enhancing students' well-being, self-direction, and academic achievement. *Learning and Individual Differences, 118*, 102608. https://doi.org/10.1016/j.lindif.2024.102608

Espelage, D. L., Holt, M. K., & Henkel, R. R. (2003). Examination of peer-group contextual effects on aggression during early adolescence. *Child Development, 74*, 205–220.

Fin, G., Moreno-Murcia, J. A., Leon, J., Baretta, E., & Junior, R. J. N. (2019). Interpersonal autonomy support style and its consequences in physical education classes. *PLoS One, 14*(5), e0216609. https://doi.org/10.1371/journal.pone.0216609

Gagné, M. (2003). The role of autonomy support and autonomy orientation in prosocial behavior engagement. *Motivation and Emotion, 27*(3), 199–223. https://doi.org/10.1023/A:1025007614869

Gest, S. D., & Rodkin, P. C. (2011). Teaching practices and elementary classroom peer ecologies. *Journal of Applied Developmental Psychology, 32*(5), 288–296. https://doi.org/10.1016/j.appdev.2011.02.004

Grolnick, W. S., Deci, E. L., & Ryan, R. M. (1997). Internalization within the family: The self-determination theory perspective. In J. E. Grusec & L. Kuczynski (Eds.), *Parenting and children's internalization of values.* (Chpt. *6*, pp. 135-161). John Wiley & Sons.

Hattie, J. (1992). *Self-concept.* Lawrence Erlbaum Associates, Inc.

Hodge, K., & Gucciardi, D. F. (2015). Antisocial and prosocial behavior in sport: The role of motivational climate, basic psychological needs, and moral disengagement. *Journal of Sport & Exercise Psychology, 37*(3), 257–273.

Hong, J. S., & Espelage, D. L. (2012). A review of research on bullying and peer victimization in school: An ecological system analysis. *Aggression and Violent Behavior, 17*(4), 311–322. https://doi.org/10.1016/j.avb.2012.03.003

Huéscar, E., Moreno-Murcia, J. A., Domenech, J. F., & Núñez, J. L. (2020). Effects of an autonomy-supportive physical activity program for compensatory care students during recess time. *Frontiers in Psychology, 10,* 3091.

Isen, A. M., & Reeve, J. (2005). The influence of positive affect on intrinsic and extrinsic motivation: Facilitating enjoyment of play, responsible work behavior, and self- control. *Motivation and Emotion, 29*(4), 297–325. https://doi.org/10.1007/s11031-006-9019-8

James, W. (1890). *The principles of psychology* (2 vols.). Henry Holt.

Jang, H., & Reeve, J. (2025). Sociocultural forces that encourage and restrict students' agentic engagement. In G. A. D. Liem, J. Fredricks, & Z. Y. Wong (Eds.), *Sociocultural perspectives on student engagement: Theory, research, and application* (Chpt. 9, pp. 261–281). Emerald/Information Age Publishing.

Jang, H.-R., Basarkod, G., Reeve, J., Marsh, H. W., Cheon, S. H., & Guo, J. (2024). Longitudinal reciprocal effects of agentic engagement and autonomy support: Between- and within-person perspectives. *Journal of Educational Psychology, 116*(1), 20–35. https://doi.org/10.1037/edu0000815

Jang, H.-R., Cheon, S. H., Reeve, J., Song, Y.-G., & Lee, Y. (2023). Two ways teachers can develop greater harmonious passion. *Physical Education and Sports Pedagogy*. https://doi.org/10.1080/17408989.2023.2206832

Jang, H.-R., & Reeve, J. (2021). Intrinsic instructional goal adoption increases autonomy- supportive teaching: A randomized control trial and intervention. *Learning and Instruction, 73,* 101415. https://doi.org/10.1016/j.learninstruc.2020.101415

Kaplan, H., & Assor, A. (2012). Enhancing autonomy-supportive I-Thou dialogue in schools: Conceptualization and socio-emotional effects of an intervention program. *Social Psychology of Education, 15*(2), 251–269. https://doi.org/10.1007/s11218-012-9178-2

Kasser, T., & Ryan, R. M. (1993). A dark side of the American dream: Correlates of financial success as a central life aspiration. *Journal of Personality and Social Psychology, 65*(2), 410–422.

Koestner, R. (2008). Reaching one's personal goals: A motivational perspective focused on autonomy. *Canadian Psychology, 49*(1), 60–67.

Laporte, N., Soenens, B., Flamant, N., & Vansteenkiste, M. (2021). The role of daily need crafting in daily fluctuations in adolescents' need-based and affective experiences. *Motivation and Emotion, 46,* 137–149.

Lee, W. (2023). Neuropsychological research in self-determination theory. In R. M. Ryan (Ed.), *The Oxford handbook of self-determination theory* (pp. 258–271). Oxford University Press. https://doi.org/10.1093/oxfordhb/9780197600047.013.12

Lee, W., & Reeve, J. (2013). Self-determined, but not non-self-determined, motivation predicts activations in the anterior insular cortex: An fMRI study of personal agency. *Social Cognitive and Affective Neuroscience, 8,* 538–545. https://doi.org/10.1093/scan/nss029

Lee, W., & Reeve, J. (2017). Identifying the neural substrates of intrinsic motivation during task performance. *Cognitive, Affective, & Behavioral Neuroscience, 17,* 939–953. https://doi.org/10.3758/s13415-017-0524-x

Lee, W., Reeve, J., Xue, Y., & Xiong, J. (2012). Neural differences between intrinsic reasons for doing versus extrinsic reasons for doing: An fMRI study. *Neuroscience Research, 73,* 68–72. https://doi.org/10.1016/j.neures.2012.02.010

Luyckx, K., Soenens, B., Berzonsky, M. D., Smits, I., Goossens, L., & Vansteenkiste, M. (2007). Information-oriented identity processing, identity consolidation, and well-being: The moderating role of autonomy, self-reflection, and self-rumination. *Personality and Individual Differences, 43*(5), 1099–1111. https://doi.org/10.1016/j.paid.2007.03.003

Martela, F., & Ryan, R. M. (2015). The benefits of benevolence: Basic psychological needs, beneficence, and the enhancement of well-being. *Journal of Personality, 84*(6), 750–764. https://doi.org/10.1111/jopy.12215

Martela, F., & Sheldon, K. M. (2019). Clarifying the concept of well-being: Psychological need satisfaction as the common core connecting eudaimonic and subjective well-being. *Review of General Psychology, 23*(4), 458–474.

Matos, L., Reeve, J., Herrera, D., & Claux, M. (2018). Students' agentic engagement predicts longitudinal increases in perceived autonomy-supportive teaching: The squeaky wheel gets the grease. *The Journal of Experimental Education, 86*(4), 579–596. https://doi.org/10.1080/00220973.2018.1448746

McAdams, D. P. (1990). *The person: An introduction to personality psychology.* Harcourt Brace Jovanovich.

Mead, G. H. (1934). *Mind, self, and society.* University of Chicago Press.

Patall, E. A. (2024). Agentic engagement: Transcending passive motivation. *Motivation Science. Motivation Science, 10*(3), 222–233. https://doi.org/10.1037/mot0000332

Patall, E. A., Pituch, K. A., Steingut, R. R., Vasquez, A. C., Yates, N., & Kennedy, A. A. U. (2019). Agency and high school science students' motivation, engagement, and classroom support experiences. *Journal of Applied Developmental Psychology, 62*, 77–92. https://doi.org/10.1016/j.appdev.2019.01.004

Patall, E. A., Steingut, R. R., Vasquez, A. C., Trimble, S. R., Pitch, K. A., & Freeman, J. L. (2018). Daily autonomy supporting or thwarting and students' motivation, engagement, and disaffection in the high school science classroom. *Journal of Educational Psychology, 110*(2), 268–288. https://doi.org/10.1037/edu0000214

Patall, E. A., Zambrano, J., Kennedy, A. A. U., Yates, N., & Vallín, J. A. (2022). Promoting an agentic orientation: An intervention in university psychology and physical science courses. *Journal of Educational Psychology, 114*(2), 368–392. https://doi.org/10.1037/edu0000614

Pavey, P., Greitemeyer, T., & Sparks, P. (2011). Highlighting relatedness promotes prosocial motives and behavior. *Personality and Social Psychology Bulletin, 37*, 905–917.

Reeve, J. (2013). How students create motivationally supportive learning environments for themselves: The concept of agentic engagement. *Journal of Educational Psychology, 105*(3), 579–595. https://doi.org/10.1037/a0032690

Reeve, J. (2025). *Understanding motivation and emotion* (8th ed.). Wiley.

Reeve, J., & Cheon, S. H. (2021). Autonomy-supportive teaching: Its malleability, benefits, and potential to improve educational practice. *Educational Psychologist, 56*(1), 54–77. https://doi.org/10.1080/00461520.2020.1862657

Reeve, J., & Cheon, S. H. (2024). Learning how to become an autonomy-supportive teacher begins with perspective taking: A randomized control trial and model test. *Teaching and Teacher Education, 148*, 104702. https://doi.org/10.1016/j.tate.2024.104702

Reeve, J., Cheon, S. H., & Jang, H. (2020a). How and why students make academic progress: Reconceptualizing the student engagement construct to increase its explanatory power. *Contemporary Educational Psychology, 62*, 101899. https://doi.org/10.1016/j.cedpsych.2020.101899

Reeve, J., Cheon, S. H., & Yu, T. H. (2020b). An autonomy-supportive intervention to develop students' resilience by boosting agentic engagement. *International Journal of Behavioral Development, 44*(4), 325–338.

Reeve, J., & Jang, H. (2026). Self-determination theory. In C. J. Fong, C. S. Ruzek, & A. Zusho (Eds.), *Handbook of school motivation* (3rd ed.). Routledge. (Chapter 6).

Reeve, J., Jang, H.-R., Cheon, S. H., Moss, J. D., Ko, H., & Jang, H. (2023). Extending self-determination theory's dual-process model to a new tripartite model to explain diminished functioning. *Motivation and Emotion, 47*(4), 691–710. https://doi.org/10.1007/s11031-023-10019-0

Reeve, J., Jang, H.-R., Shin, S. H., Ahn, J. S., Matos, L., & Gargurevich, R. (2022c). When students show some initiative: Two experiments on the benefits of greater agentic engagement. *Learning and Instruction, 80*, 1–11. https://doi.org/10.1016/j.learninstruc.2021.101564

Reeve, J., & Lee, W. (2019). A neuroscience perspective on the self-determination theory framework. *Journal of Personality, 87*(1), 102–114. https://doi.org/10.1111/jopy.12390

Reeve, J., & Lee, W. (2026). Autonomy recruits neural support for interest and learning. *Motivation and Emotion. 50*(1), 65–79. https://doi.org/10.1007/s11031-025-10119-z

Reeve, J., Ryan, R. M., Cheon, S. H., Matos, L., & Kaplan, H. (2022a). *Supporting s tudents' motivation: Strategies for success.* Routledge. https://doi.org/10.4324/9781003091738

Reeve, J., & Shin, S. H. (2020). How teachers can support students' agentic engagement. *Theory into Practice, 59*(2), 150–161. https://doi.org/10.1080/00405841.2019.1702451

Reeve, J., & Tseng, C. M. (2011a). Agency as a fourth aspect of students' engagement during learning activities. *Contemporary Educational Psychology, 36*(4), 257–267.

Reeve, J., & Tseng, C.-M. (2011b). Cortisol reactivity to a teacher's motivating style: The biology of being controlled versus supporting autonomy. *Motivation and Emotion, 35*, 63–74. https://doi.org/10.1007/s11031-011-9204-2

Roth, G., Assor, A., Niemiec, C. P., Ryan, R. M., & Deci, E. L. (2009). The emotional and academic consequences of parental conditional regard: Comparing conditional positive regard, conditional negative regard, and autonomy support as parenting practices. *Developmental Psychology, 45*(4), 1119–1142. https://doi.org/10.1037/a0015272

Roth, G., Kanat-Maymon, Y., & Bibi, U. (2010). Prevention of school bullying: The important role of autonomy-supportive teaching and internalization of prosocial values. *British Journal of Educational Psychology, 81*(4), 654–666. https://doi.org/10.1348/2044-8279.002003

Rowling, J. K. (2007). *Harry Potter and the deathly hallows.* Bloomsbury.

Ryan, R. M. (1993). Agency and organization: Intrinsic motivation, autonomy, and the self in psychological development. In J. E. Jacobs (Ed.), *Nebraska Symposium on Motivation: Developmental perspectives on motivation* (Vol. *40*, pp. 1–56). University of Nebraska Press.

Ryan, R. M., & Deci, E. L. (2000). Self-determination theory and the facilitation of intrinsic motivation, social development, and well-being. *American Psychologist, 55*(1), 68–78. https://doi.org/10.1037/0003-066X.55.1.68

Ryan, R. M., & Deci, E. L. (2017). *Self-determination theory: Basic psychological needs in motivation, development, and wellness.* Guilford Press.

Sagan, C. (1985). *Contact.* Simon & Schuster.

Sheldon, K. M., Ryan, R., & Reis, H. T. (1996). What makes for a good day? Competence and autonomy in the day and in the person. *Personality and Social Psychology Bulletin, 22*(12), 1270–1279. https://doi.org/10.1177/01461672962212007

Tilga, H., Hein, V., & Koka, A. (2019). Effects of a web-based intervention for PE teachers on students' perceptions of teacher behaviors, psychological needs, and intrinsic motivation. *Perceptual and Motor Skills, 126*(3), 559–580.

Van Ryzin, M. J., & Roseth, C. J. (2018). Cooperative learning in middle school: A means to improve peer relations and reduce victimization, bullying, and related outcomes. *Journal of Educational Psychology, 110*(8), 1192–1201. https://doi.org/10.1037/edu0000265

Vansteenkiste, M., Aelterman, N., De Muynck, G.-J., Haerens, L., Patall, E., & Reeve, J. (2018). Fostering personal meaning and self-relevance: A self-determination theory perspective on internalization. *The Journal of Experimental Education, 86*(1), 30–49. https://doi.org/10.1080/00220973.2017.1381067

Vansteenkiste, M., Ryan, R. M., & Soenens, B. (2020). Basic psychological need theory: Advancements, critical themes, and future directions. *Motivation and Emotion, 44*(1), 1–31. https://doi.org/10.1007/s11031-019-09818-1

White, R. W. (1959). Motivation reconsidered: The concept of competence. *Psychological Review, 66*(5), 297–333. https://doi.org/10.1037/h0040934

Yin, T., Jang, H., & Reeve, J. (2026). *A critical reexamination of the role of emotion in student engagement and achievement. Manuscript under review.* Hanyang University.

Zambrano, J., Kennedy, A. A. U., Aguilera, C., Yates, N., & Patall, E. A. (2022). Students' beliefs about agentic engagement: A phenomenological study in urban high school physical science and engineering classes. *Journal of Educational Psychology, 114*(5), 1028–1047. https://doi.org/10.1037/edu0000690

CHAPTER 3

CONTROL-VALUE THEORY: A DYNAMIC APPROACH TO SELF, EMOTIONS, AND EMOTION REGULATION

Reinhard Pekrun
University of Essex, UK

ABSTRACT

Across life domains, self-appraisals are critically important to understand the dynamics of emotions. Appraisals of one's competencies, behavioral propensities, past developments, and future prospects shape human emotions, their regulation, and their trajectories over time. In this chapter, I outline how control-value theory (CVT) explains the links between self-appraisals and emotions. More specifically, I focus on developments that transform the original theory into a generalized, dynamic account of self and emotions. In its original version, CVT addressed achievement emotions. The generalized CVT extends the perspective by also considering other types of emotions that are foundational for human development, such as epistemic emotions (e.g., surprise, curiosity, confusion), social emotions (e.g., love, admiration, compassion, contempt, envy), and existential emotions (e.g., hope and fear related to health, life, illness, and death). I first outline how CVT conceptualizes these emotions and how it explains their individual and social origins. Next, I discuss CVT perspectives on how emotions impact essential outcomes, including achievement, well-being, and health, and how emotions, outcomes,

The Self in Context, pages 77–122

Published under exclusive licence by Emerald Publishing Limited
doi:10.1108/978-1-80686-869-820261003

and antecedents are linked by reciprocal causation over different timescales. Based on the CVT model of reciprocal causation, I then propose an expanded conception of emotion regulation. Going beyond traditional accounts, this conception addresses the role of the self as a target of regulation—developing one's competencies, goals, and behavioral dispositions in affectively sound ways is seen as core to healthy emotion regulation. In conclusion, I discuss future directions to further develop CVT and practice to promote emotional flourishing and development.

Keywords: Self-appraisals; control; value; achievement emotions; dynamic systems; emotion regulation

How can we explain human emotions; what are their individual and social origins? How do emotions shape our competencies, well-being, and identity? How can we manage our emotions to flourish and cope with critical life situations? These questions are at the core of the control-value theory (CVT) of emotions. In its original version, CVT addressed one specific group of emotions that is critically important across life domains and cultures today, namely, achievement emotions (Pekrun, 2000, 2006; Pekrun, Marsh, Elliot, et al., 2023; Pekrun & Perry, 2014)—the emotions that are triggered by success and failure and define our achievement strivings in education, work, sports, and beyond. As I will explain below, CVT posits that these emotions are triggered when we feel in control over, or out of control of, achievement situations that are valuable and important to us—meaning that self-appraisals of control and value are at the core of achievement emotions. However, perceptions of control and value are emotionally important not only in achievement situations but across life domains more generally. As such, I have recently revised the theory to also explain other groups of human emotion, such as epistemic, social and health-related emotions (Pekrun, 2021, 2024).

CVT is rooted in different theoretical traditions and integrates assumptions from different scientific disciplines (see Pekrun, 2024, for the history and development of CVT). First, by emphasizing the role of the self and the importance of social factors shaping the self, CVT builds on social-cognitive theories of human agency (e.g., Bandura, 1986; Mischel, 1973; Rotter, 1954). Second, to explain the impact of emotions on learning, behavior, and achievement, CVT draws on principles developed in cognitive science and motivation research (e.g., Marsh, 1987; Mikels & Reuter-Lorenz, 2019; Ryan & Deci, 2017). Third, CVT attends to principles of dynamic systems theory (Sosnowska et al., 2020; von Bertalanffy, 1968)—CVT explains that emotions, their origins and outcomes, and actions to regulate emotions are linked by dynamic, reciprocal relations over time. To understand emotions and support practitioners dealing with emotions,

CVT posits that it is imperative to integrate insights from these different paradigms rather than relying on one single discipline alone.

In this chapter, I provide an overview of CVT's understanding of the nature of human emotions, their origins and effects, as well as ways to regulate them. Throughout the chapter, I provide examples from education—a field that is especially important for our global future. How can we understand and explain students' (and teachers') emotions; how do these emotions impact students' learning and well-being; and what can students and teachers do to regulate emotions such that their power is used to thrive and flourish? I will explain how CVT provides answers to these questions. This includes a review of existing work on CVT, but also new considerations of reciprocal causation linking emotions to their antecedents and outcomes, the dynamics of emotions across different timescales, and ways to regulate emotions.

I first outline how CVT organizes emotions using the dimensions of valence, activation, and object focus (section "Organizing the Diverse World of Emotions"). Next, I discuss how CVT explains the role of the self for the arousal of emotions. I highlight the fundamentally important role of self-appraisals of control and value, outline which control-value appraisals are most relevant, and provide examples of how they generate emotions ("Origins of Emotions: The Role of the Self"). Subsequently, I explain how social environments influence emotions by shaping these appraisals ("The Role of Others and the Social Environment"). I then outline how CVT conceptualizes effects of emotions on learning, achievement, health, and well-being, including both hedonic and eudaimonic facets of well-being ("Impact on Learning, Achievement, Well-Being and Health").

Based on the CVT perspectives on origins and outcomes, I explain how emotions, their outcomes, and their antecedents are reciprocally linked over time, and how these reciprocal links unfold across different timescales and the within- and between-person levels ("Connecting the Dots: Reciprocal Effects Across Timescales and Levels"). Using principles of reciprocal relations, I outline how CVT conceptualizes emotion regulation, emphasizing the role of the self in this process ("Emotion Regulation: The Importance of Self-Development"). In conclusion, I discuss how the theory can be further developed, tested, and used for practice ("Future Directions").

ORGANIZING THE DIVERSE WORLD OF EMOTIONS

Human emotions are complex and multifaceted—they are more than simple, uniform elements of experience. Recall the last time you truly enjoyed studying or working on a project—you may have felt excitement, a sense of mastery, and strong motivation to engage with the task, and your heart may have been pounding with joy when you solved a problem. Similarly, recall the last time you took an important exam—you may have felt nervous, worried about your preparation, and wished to avoid failing the exam; you may have started sweating when thinking about possible failure; and others may have noticed your anxiety when looking into your face. As such, emotions comprise multiple components. Consistent with current conceptions of emotion in affective science (e.g., Scherer & Moors, 2019), CVT considers five components as core to human emotions—affective, cognitive, motivational, physiological, and expressive processes. Not all of these components need to be present in all instances. However, intense emotions typically involve all of them (for implications for assessing emotions, see Pekrun, 2020).

All of these components can take many different forms. For example, emotional cognitions can be directed toward various events. The broad range of contents and combinations of components explains why human emotions show tremendous diversity, as reflected in the large number of emotion terms available in natural languages. Traditionally, researchers have attempted to reduce diversity by considering just one or a few select emotions. For example, achievement motivation researchers have considered four emotions related to success and failure, including hope, fear, pride, and shame (Heckhausen, 1991). In educational research, most scientists have focused on a single emotion, namely, students' achievement anxiety (Zeidner, 2014). CVT contends that this is not sufficient—the world of emotions is broader than that, in education and beyond.

Nevertheless, to better understand emotions, it is important to conceptually organize their diversity. Consistent with traditional two-dimensional models of human affect (e.g., Russell & Barrett, 1999), CVT considers valence and activation as core dimensions of emotions. *Valence* refers to the pleasantness of emotions, making it possible to distinguish between positive (pleasant) emotions such as joy, and negative (unpleasant) emotions like anxiety. *Activation* refers to the physiological arousal or de-arousal that is part of an emotion. Using this dimension, activating emotions, such as excitement or anger, can be distinguished from deactivating emotions that reduce arousal, such as relaxation or boredom.

However, CVT posits that these two dimensions are not sufficient to describe the world of emotions. A third dimension is equally important to understand emotions—namely, their *object focus* (see the glossary of CVT terms in the Appendix). Emotions can be directed toward different objects, broadly defined (events, people, situations, material objects, ideas, etc.). In line with philosophical conceptions of emotions (see Montague, 2009; Scarantino & de Sousa, 2018), CVT considers object focus a critically important feature of emotions. In contrast to valence and activation, however, object focus cannot be conceptualized as a single quantitative dimension. Rather, object focus relates to qualitatively different categories of objects. There may be as many important categories of object focus as there are objects that are important to individuals. Categories explicitly considered in the recent generalized version of CVT (Pekrun, 2024) include achievement emotions; epistemic emotions related to the quality of information (specifically, cognitive incongruity prompting surprise, curiosity, or confusion); social emotions; and existential and health-related emotions. Examples of further important categories are aesthetic emotions (Menninghaus et al., 2019), emotions related to our natural environment, political emotions, and religious emotions.

In addition to the type of object, the temporal relation between the person and the object at the time of the emotional experience is important to understand object focus. Objects of emotions can be located in the present, future, or past. As such, it is possible to distinguish between concurrent emotions that occur parallel to an ongoing action or event, prospective (i.e., anticipatory) emotions related to future actions and events, and retrospective emotions related to past actions and events. For example, hope for success is a prospective, future-oriented emotion; the enjoyment of current work on a project is a concurrent emotion; pride about success is a retrospective emotion.

Valence, activation, and object focus are conceptually independent dimensions. As such, any combination is possible. For any type of object, related emotions can be positive or negative, and they can be activating or deactivating. For example, health-related emotions can be positive-activating (e.g., hope for recovery from an illness), positive-deactivating (e.g., contentment after exercise), negative-activating (e.g., fear of contracting a disease), or negative-deactivating (e.g., hopelessness upon diagnosis with a terminal disease). Combining valence, activation, and object focus renders three-dimensional taxonomies of emotions (Table 3.1; Pekrun, 2021, 2024; Pekrun, Marsh, Elliot, et al., 2023). Alternatively, to the extent that type of object and temporal relation can be considered separate dimensions, in addition to valence and activation, it may be possible to derive four-dimensional conceptions for some categories of emotions (H. W. Marsh, personal communication, January 15, 2025).

Using object focus, we can differentiate between emotions not only across categories of emotions but also within categories. Achievement emotions are an example. In the three-dimensional taxonomy of these emotions that is part of CVT (Pekrun, Marsh, Elliot, et al., 2023), we distinguish between emotions related to achievement activities, such as enjoyment of learning and boredom (activity emotions), and emotions related to the success and failure outcomes of these activities, such as hope for success and anxiety related to failure (outcome emotions). For both activity emotions and outcome emotions, the taxonomy distinguishes between prospective, concurrent, and retrospective emotions. However, all six resulting combinations may not be equally important. Prospective outcome emotions, retrospective outcome emotions, and concurrent activity emotions may occur most frequently in achievement settings.

TABLE 3.1 Three-Dimensional Taxonomy of Emotions: Examples.

	Positive[a]		Negative[b]	
Object Focus	**Activating**	**Deactivating**	**Activating**	**Deactivating**
Achievement				
Activity	Enjoyment, excitement	Relaxation	Anger, frustration	Boredom
Outcome/prospective	Hope	Assurance	Anxiety	Hopelessness
Outcome/retrospective	Joy, pride, gratitude	Relief, contentment	Shame, guilt, anger	Disappointment, sadness
Epistemic				
Incongruity of information	Surprise,[c] curiosity,[d] delight	Contentment	Confusion, frustration	Boredom
Social				
Self-related	Pride	Satisfaction (with self)	Shame, guilt	Dissatisfaction (with self)
Other-related	Love, gratitude, admiration, compassion	Sympathy	Hate, anger, contempt, envy	Antipathy
Existential				
Health, life, disease, death	Happiness (health)	Relief (recovery)	Anxiety (disease, death)	Hopelessness (disease, death)

[a]Positive = pleasant emotion.

[b]Negative = unpleasant emotion.

[c]Alternatively, surprise can be neutral or negative (Pekrun, Vogl, et al., 2017).

[d]Alternatively, curiosity has been described as unpleasant.

Combined with valence and activation, considering these three types of object focus renders the taxonomy of achievement emotions depicted in Table 3.1. Extending previous conceptions, the taxonomy not only organizes these emotions but also facilitates conceptualizing emotions that have not been previously considered. An example is assurance, defined as a pleasant, relaxed state of being confident about attaining success (Pekrun, Marsh, Elliot, et al., 2023). Similarly, structures of epistemic, social, or health-related emotions can be organized using three-dimensional conceptions (Pekrun, 2021, 2024).

INDIVIDUAL ORIGINS OF EMOTIONS: THE ROLE OF THE SELF

Appraisals of Control and Value

CVT contends that self-related appraisals are fundamentally important for understanding human emotions. Two types of appraisals are deemed especially important: perceptions of control over one's activities and their outcomes, and perceptions of the value (importance) of these activities and outcomes.

Perceived Control

Across disciplines, "control" is generally defined as A (a human or nonhuman agent) influencing B (an event, process, object, or outcome). Using this definition, CVT conceptualizes three types of control appraisals related to current and future activities (see Fig. 3.1): Expectancies being able to produce an action (action-control expectancies); expectancies that the action will generate a desired outcome or prevent an undesired outcome (action-outcome expectancies); and expectancies that the situation will generate or prevent the outcome, without one's actions (situation-outcome expectancies).

To explain, *action-control expectancies* are beliefs about one's ability to perform a specific action, such as when a student believes they can focus on doing their homework in mathematics this afternoon. Action-control expectancy is related to Bandura's (1977) notion of self-efficacy expectation, defined as "the conviction that one can successfully execute the behavior" (Bandura, 1977, p. 193). However, the term action-control expectancy is broader; it does not narrow the concept down to the *successful* execution of an action. A student can have control over working on a math problem until they find a solution, but this does not imply that the solution is correct. By introducing the term action-control expectancy (Pekrun, 1988, 1993), I aimed to avoid the ambiguities inherent in the self-efficacy construct, which does not clearly distinguish between action and success.

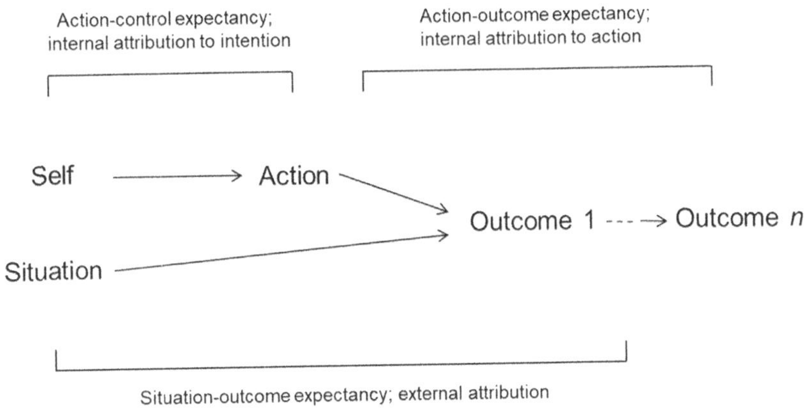

Fig. 3.1. Causal Expectancies and Attributions.

Action-outcome expectancies are beliefs that specific actions will lead to certain outcomes, such as the student doing math homework expecting to receive positive feedback from their teacher the following day. In these expectancies, actions exert control over outcomes. Finally, *situation-outcome expectancies* are beliefs that situational factors or other people generate outcomes, such as a student believing they will receive positive feedback from a teacher regardless of their achievement. The overall expectancy of the outcome is thought to be a joint function of these different expectancies—the outcome seems likely when both action-control and action-outcome expectancy are high, or when the situation is expected to produce the outcome.

Often, positive action-control expectancies are combined with positive action-outcome expectancies, such as when a student believes they can prepare for an exam and that this effort will yield a good grade. However, the two expectancies can also diverge. For example, as a computer engineer, I can be confident that I can develop some software (a positive action-control expectancy), but I can doubt whether customers will buy it. Conversely, I can be convinced that a good software solution will sell well, but I can doubt my ability to develop it. Positive expectations to achieve outcomes through one's own actions require that both expectancies are positive.

In addition, CVT considers retrospective *causal attributions* of actions and outcomes that have already occurred. These attributions can involve the same cause-and-effect relations as expectancies, albeit in a retrospective manner. Specifically, these appraisals comprise attributions of existing actions to one's goals and intentions, as well as attributions of existing outcomes to one's actions or external situational factors (Fig. 3.1). For example, investing effort in doing math homework can be attributed to one's goal of learning math. From the perspective of self-determination theory, such an attribution would indicate autonomous motivation (Ryan & Deci, 2017). Alternatively, the investment of effort can be attributed to the pressure exerted by parents and teachers, indicating controlled motivation. Similarly, outcomes can be attributed to one's own actions or external factors, allowing for the distinction of internal and external attributions of outcomes (Weiner, 1985).

Perceived Value

CVT distinguishes between positive and negative values of actions and outcomes, as well as their intrinsic and extrinsic value (see Pekrun, 2024). *Positive and negative value* denotes direction (positive vs. negative) combined with magnitude (high vs. low importance). For example, a high positive value of success implies that success is desirable and important. A low positive value implies that success is desirable, albeit not particularly important. A high negative value of failure indicates that failure is undesirable and that it is important to avoid it. A low negative value also indicates that failure is undesirable, although it does not matter too much.

Given these definitions, value can be conceived as a bipolar dimension, ranging from high positive to high negative. On this dimension, zero means that the action or outcome does not matter. This dimensional conception is consistent with concepts of value used in behavioral economics, which consider the positive value of assets and the negative value of debts and costs (e.g., Kahneman & Tversky, 1979). Defining value this way makes emotion theory conceptually compatible with theories of value and decision-making in economics.

Intrinsic value of an action means it is perceived as desirable or undesirable for its own sake, regardless of any outcomes. For example, studying can be intrinsically valuable when the material is deemed interesting (positive intrinsic value). Alternatively, studying can be intrinsically undesirable when the effort is experienced as aversive (negative intrinsic value). Intrinsic value of an outcome means that the outcome is desirable or undesirable for its own sake, regardless of any further outcomes it may generate. For instance, success may be valuable in itself, regardless of downstream financial benefits.

Extrinsic value implies that the action or outcome is desirable or undesirable because it generates (further) positive or negative outcomes. As such, extrinsic value depicts the instrumental functions of actions and outcomes. For example, studying can have positive extrinsic value by yielding good grades. At the same time, studying can have negative extrinsic value by reducing opportunities to engage in other actions, such as meeting friends.

Defined this way, perceived control and perceived value integrate various concepts of appraisals that have been considered separate dimensions in previous appraisal theories of emotions, such as power, coping potential, and agency (control), as well as goal congruency, motive consistency, and pleasantness (value; see Scherer et al., 2001). As such, CVT contributes to making appraisal accounts of emotions more parsimonious. Nevertheless, it is important to consider that there are appraisal dimensions beyond control and value that play a role in specific categories of emotions. For example, appraisals of cognitive incongruity are important for epistemic emotions, in addition to control and value (see below).

In the following, I outline how control and value generate different types of emotions, according to CVT. To explain these CVT propositions, I focus on the three groups of emotions targeted in Pekrun, Marsh, Elliot et al.'s (2023) taxonomy of achievement emotions discussed earlier: prospective outcome emotions, retrospective outcome emotions, and concurrent activity emotions. I also highlight that other appraisals can play a role as well, and that emotion generation by appraisals is not always a conscious, reflective process.

Prospective Outcome Emotions

CVT posits that emotions related to future events are generated by expectancies, combined with perceptions of value. For example, hope for success on an exam is prompted when a student is optimistic about the likelihood of success, and when the success is important to the student—a combination of positive action-control expectancy, positive action-outcome expectancy, and positive value. If the student is very confident about attaining success (i.e., when the subjective likelihood of success is close to 100%), hope transforms into anticipatory joy. Conversely, when expectancies for successful preparation and performance are reduced, fear of failure may be prompted, provided that it is important to avoid failure (meaning that failure has a negative value). When the subjective likelihood of success on an important exam is reduced to zero and failure is expected to be certain, hope and anxiety may be replaced by hopelessness. Empirical findings support these propositions (see Pekrun, Marsh, Elliot, et al., 2023).

A possible flow of appraisals generating emotions related to failure on an upcoming exam is depicted in Fig. 3.2, starting with situation-outcome expectancy ("would I fail the exam if I don't prepare?) and an evaluation of importance ("does it matter if I fail?") up to action-control-expectancy ("will I be able to prepare?") and action-control expectancy ("will my preparation prevent failure?"). Depending on the combination of these appraisals, different emotions are generated. If I believe that the exam is important, that failure is certain if I do not prepare, and that I can prevent failure through preparing, I may feel anticipatory relief. In contrast, if I am certain this will not be possible, I feel hopeless; and if I am uncertain, I feel anxious about the outcome.

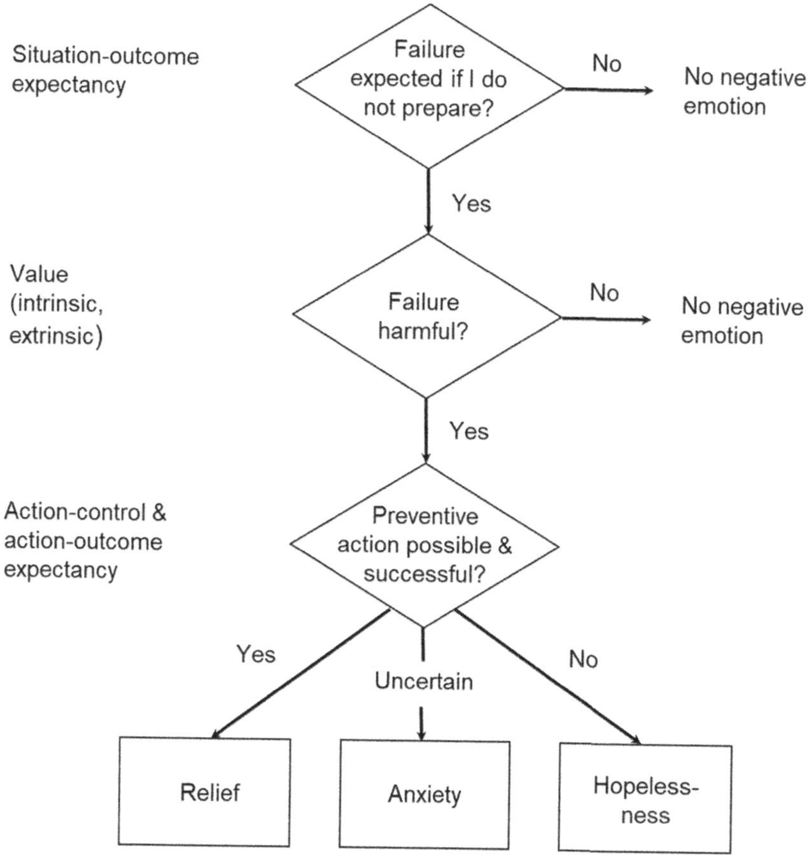

Fig. 3.2. Possible Sequence of Appraisals and Emotions Before an Exam. Source: Adapted from Pekrun (2006).

There are two important implications of these propositions and the extant empirical evidence. First, in contrast to anticipatory joy and hopelessness based on subjective certainty about the future, both hope and anxiety result from uncertainty. The focus is on the uncertain prospect of positive events in hope, and on the uncertain prospect of negative events in fear and anxiety. As such, uncertainty can trigger both hope and fear, and one's emotional state can oscillate between these two emotions depending on the focus of attention on positive versus negative prospects. Second, value is indispensable for prospective emotions to arise. Value amplifies all these emotions. Without value, we would not care and remain emotionally neutral about the future. Methodologically, both expectancy and value being required amounts to an interaction between the two appraisals.

Research has confirmed that control and value appraisals interact in generating emotions (e.g., Putwain et al., 2018; Shao et al., 2020).

Retrospective Outcome Emotions

These emotions function similarly to prospective emotions, with expectancies of future events replaced by memories and causal attributions of past events. As for prospective emotions, value is indispensable for retrospective emotions to be prompted, in addition to attributions. However, there is one important difference between prospective and retrospective emotions. Typically, the future is not fully predictable, meaning that uncertainty plays a major role in prospective emotions. In contrast, the past has happened, which implies that past events are typically certain events. Accordingly, uncertainty-related feelings play a lesser role in retrospective emotions, except when the past still needs to be discovered.

CVT posits that joy, sadness, and frustration about past events are prompted by memories of these events, combined with appraisals of value (to explain, past events can be just a few seconds ago—joy about a good grade on an exam can arise immediately after the grade has been communicated). Further cognitive elaboration in terms of reflecting on causes and control is not needed for these control-independent emotions (see Weiner, 1985). In contrast, control-dependent emotions are shaped by causal attributions of the event, in addition to perceptions of value. Among different dimensions of causal attributions as addressed in Weiner's (1985) attributional theory, the perceived controllability of the event by oneself (internal attributions of control) or by external factors (external attributions of control) is especially important from the perspective of CVT. If positive outcomes are attributed to one's actions and intentions, pride can result; if negative outcomes are attributed this way, shame and guilt can follow. If positive outcomes are attributed to the actions of other individuals, meaning that others were in control, gratitude can be prompted. If negative outcomes are due to the actions of another person, anger can be elicited, on condition that the other person was in control over the action and its outcome (if you find out that somebody has accidentally rather than intentionally stamped on your foot on a crowded bus, your anger may be dampened).

Concurrent Activity Emotions

For emotions related to a current activity, action-control expectancies are thought to be critical, along with perceptions of the value of the activity. Enjoyment is generated by positive action-control expectancies, combined with perceptions of intrinsic value in terms of interest in the activity or other intrinsically rewarding features of the activity, such as the experience of flow. For example, students may enjoy learning if they (a) feel competent to master the material, and (b) the material is sufficiently interesting for them. If students lack competence or do not care about the material, learning will not be enjoyable. If there are obstacles that hinder the successful performance of the action, anger can be prompted.

Similar to outcome emotions, activity emotions are generally boosted by perceptions of value. However, there is one important exception—boredom. Boredom is prompted when value and meaning are lacking. Lack of value can generate boredom during an activity, regardless of one's control over performing it. Nevertheless, control also plays a critical role—both very high and very low control can reduce value and meaning. For example, if academic tasks are too easy for a student, it is of little value to perform them, and boredom can arise. Conversely, if tasks are too difficult, they may also lack meaning, such as a lecture a student does not understand—which can also result in boredom.

As such, extending traditional conceptions of boredom being due to lack of challenge (Csikszentmihalyi, 2000), CVT contends that boredom can arise in response to both task demands that are too low relative to one's competencies (underchallenge) and task demands that exceed competencies (overchallenge). Whereas earlier studies on boredom in classroom and work settings found that boredom was due to underchallenge implied by monotonous routine tasks, current research shows that boredom due to overchallenge may be no less important. For example, boredom in secondary school and university students typically shows negative correlations with perceived academic control, implying that boredom is linked to overchallenge in many students (see Pekrun & Goetz, 2024a, for a summary of evidence).

Other Appraisals and Automatic Emotion Elicitation

CVT contends that perceptions of control and value play a critical role in all major types of human emotions. However, there are two caveats to this statement. First, additional appraisals are important for specific groups of emotions (Pekrun, 2021, 2024). An example is epistemic emotions, which are triggered by appraisals of cognitive incongruity in addition to control and value. Prime epistemic emotions are surprise, curiosity, and confusion. Surprise is prompted by an incongruity between prior expectations and current information; curiosity by an incongruity between current and desired knowledge; and confusion by incongruity in current information (contradictions, inconsistencies, etc.). Whereas surprise may be independent from control-value appraisals (for a discussion, see Neta & Kim, 2023; Reisenzein et al., 2019), curiosity and confusion additionally depend on control and value (see Pekrun, 2024). For example, curiosity is aroused if the lacking knowledge is desired, which implies value; and it is maintained only if there is hope that the gap between current and desired knowledge can be closed, which implies control.

Second, appraisals of control and value do not need to be processed each time an emotion is generated. With recurring emotion generation in a given type of situation, the generation process can become habitual. During this process, appraisals become stored in association with situation perception and the emotion in emotion-generating schemata. Based on these schemata, perceptions can automatically trigger the emotion, without prior activation of appraisals. Whenever the situation changes and existing schemata are challenged, appraisals may need to be revised and come into play again. Such a revision of emotion schemata is one primary aim of psychological therapy and an important way to self-regulate emotions, as discussed in the section on emotion regulation.

SOCIAL ORIGINS: THE ROLE OF OTHERS AND THE SOCIAL ENVIRONMENT

Human emotions develop in interaction with significant others and the social environment. Others and the environment can influence our emotions through various mechanisms. For example, emotions can be directly transferred when others display emotions in facial, postural, or vocal expression, and when we immediately mimic these emotions—an automatic, nonreflective process ("emotional contagion"; Frenzel et al., 2024; Hatfield et al., 1994). For any lasting development of emotions, however, the influence of others on emotion-generating thoughts and beliefs is more important. As such, consistent with principles of social-cognitive theories, CVT posits that the influence of social and cultural factors on emotions is mediated by appraisals, including perceptions of control and value. As explained above, control-value appraisals are considered proximal antecedents of emotions; any more distal antecedents exert an influence by shaping these appraisals (Fig. 3.3). This view implies that all factors that impact these appraisals can influence one's emotions.

Social factors are organized in different layers—from immediate social environments, such as the classroom, workplace, family, and neighborhood, to broader institutional, economic, and sociocultural contexts (Bronfenbrenner, 1979; Pekrun, 2018). For changing emotions, shaping the immediate environment in affectively sound ways is especially important. From a CVT perspective, the following factors in social environments and the broader institutional and socio-cultural context are critical for shaping control-value appraisals and resulting emotions.

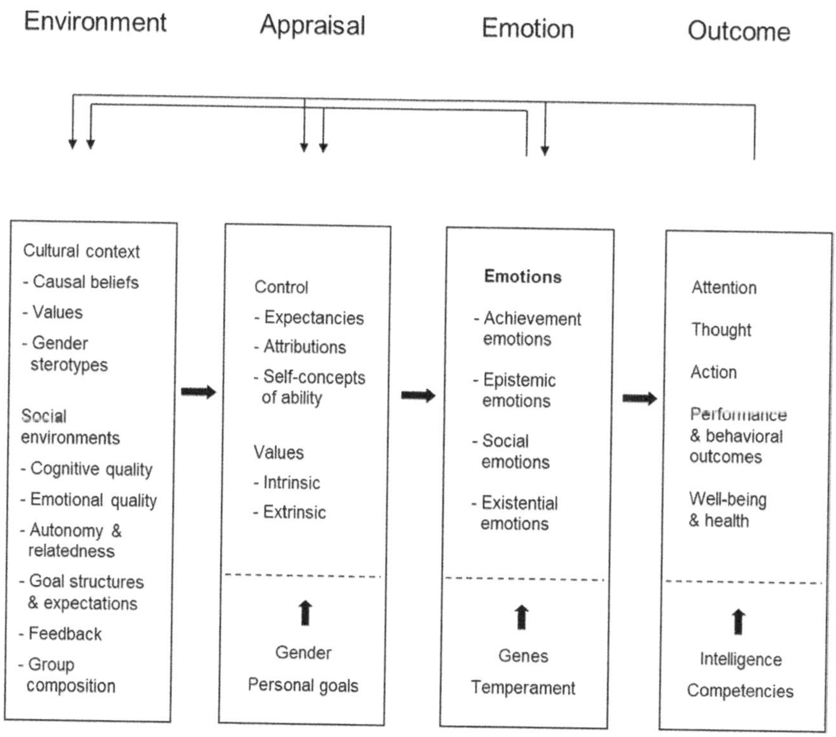

Fig. 3.3. CVT: Basic Propositions.

Immediate Social Environments

Cognitive Quality

Cognitive dimensions of the environment are particularly important for achievement-related and epistemic emotions. Three relevant factors are structure and clarity, the match between task demands and individual competencies, and the stimulation of cognitive incongruity. Well-structured materials, transparent instructions, and high-quality explanations support problem-solving and the development of competencies, thereby facilitating perceptions of control and positive emotions such as enjoyment of learning, and reducing negative emotions like test anxiety. Empirical studies have found that clarity of classroom instruction contributes to students' positive achievement emotions (e.g., Pekrun, Marsh, Elliot, et al., 2023), and that unclear instructions and lack of transparency of the demands of exams exacerbate students' anxiety (Zeidner, 1998, 2014).

The match between cognitive demands and competencies defines the difficulty of tasks. Demands that exceed competencies imply that tasks are overly difficult (overchallenge); demands that are very low relative to competencies imply that tasks are too easy (underchallenge). Tasks that are perceived as easy can support competence appraisals and control. Given the link between control and positive emotions, it would be plausible to assume that easy tasks promote enjoyment. However, any positive effect of this type can be undermined by the boredom generated by underchallenge. As such, even though controllable, tasks that are too easy may be emotionally detrimental.

Cognitive incongruity is essential for stimulating epistemic emotions like surprise, curiosity, and confusion. Given the knowledge-generating quality of these emotions, teachers and parents should promote productive variants of curiosity and confusion by supporting students in detecting incongruity. One possibility is to provide cognitive problems that are difficult to solve, such that students experience emotion-generating failure, and then scaffolding ways to resolve cognitive incongruity and successfully manage task completion (see Kapur, 2024).

Emotional Quality

The emotions conveyed by others can be contagious. If others laugh, it is easier for us to laugh; if others cry, we may also be prone to cry. As noted, emotional contagion is an immediate, automatic process; within seconds, we can mimic the emotions displayed by others. In our research, we found that emotional contagion plays a major role in the interaction between teachers and students (Frenzel et al., 2024). Specifically, our research has shown that students can immediately take up the enjoyment displayed by teachers. If teachers enjoy teaching and display their enthusiasm, students are more likely to enjoy classroom instruction as well. However, the spark of enthusiasm and excitement can also be transferred from students to teachers—students who display enjoyment and engagement make teaching rewarding and stimulate enjoyment in teachers. As such, teachers' and students' enjoyment can be reciprocally related over time (Frenzel et al., 2018).

However, the effects of emotional contagion may be short-lived. To survive the moment, perceptions of the emotions displayed by others, and one's own emotions, need to be transferred into beliefs about the value of the emotion-generating objects or events, such as the learning materials at school. In other words, the emotions of others can have lasting effects when interpreted as signaling value. Positive emotions can signal positive value, such as teachers' enjoyment of teaching math signaling that math can be interesting. Negative emotions can signal negative value, like boredom displayed by peers during a lecture signaling that the material is not interesting. Through these value appraisals, the emotions displayed by others can facilitate the development of positive and negative emotions.

Autonomy and Relatedness

The cognitive quality of environments, as addressed above, is suited to satisfy needs for competence and resulting appraisals of competence and the value of mastery. In addition, environments differ in the extent to which they satisfy needs for autonomy and social relatedness. Based on self-determination theory, autonomy can be defined as congruency between actions and one's identity, goals, and intentions (Ryan & Deci, 2017). From a CVT perspective, features of the environment that promote or undermine autonomy do not only satisfy or frustrate needs for autonomy. They also facilitate related control-value appraisals and the emotions resulting from these appraisals. For example, if students' sense of autonomy is supported by providing them with a choice among tasks or opportunities to self-generate tasks, their sense of control and perceptions of value can be enhanced. However, one boundary condition is that students have sufficient competencies to self-regulate and make appropriate choices. If these competencies are lacking, choice can undermine rather than promote a sense of competence.

Similarly, if the environment promotes social relatedness, the development of social competencies and values can be promoted, leading to positive perceptions of social competence and value. These perceptions, in turn, can boost social emotions such as love and compassion. In education, pedagogical formats that include teamwork and cooperative learning can support students in developing friendships, competencies to engage in collaborative work, and the resulting control-value appraisals and positive social emotions.

Goal Structures and Expectations

Goals and expectations conveyed by others can influence appraisals of value. For example, if teachers and parents expect students to outperform their peers, students may adopt performance goals (i.e., goals to outperform others or not to perform worse than others; Elliot et al., 2011). In this way, the perceived value of normative achievement can be enhanced. In contrast, if the importance of learning and mastery is emphasized, students may adopt mastery goals (i.e., goals to master tasks and to acquire competencies, or to avoid losing competencies). In this way, perceptions of the value of mastery are facilitated. Through these value appraisals, normative expectations and goals can increase students' outcome emotions related to success and failure, and mastery-oriented expectations and goals can promote their activity emotions, such as enjoyment of learning (Bross et al., 2024).

The level of significant others' expectations can influence perceptions of competence and control. Expectations that are lower than a student's competencies can signal that teachers and parents do not trust that the student is competent, thus potentially undermining perceived control and exacerbating negative emotions. However, overly high expectations from others can also signal that competence is not sufficient, which can also result in a perceived lack of control and negative emotions. By implication, both overly low and excessively high expectations could be detrimental emotionally, whereas expectations that meet students' competencies can be beneficial. Empirical research has yet to test these possible curvilinear relations between social expectations and students' control appraisals and emotions (see also Marsh, Pekrun, et al., 2023; Murayama et al., 2016).

Feedback and Future Opportunities

Feedback about accomplishments and behavior can impact control perceptions and resulting emotions. In the education domain, feedback about performance as provided by grades, test scores, and verbal teacher comments is especially relevant. Research has shown that positive feedback signaling success increases positive emotions and reduces negative emotions; negative feedback has the opposite effects (Pekrun et al., 2017; Pekrun, Marsh, Suessenbach, et al., 2023). In line with CVT, these effects have been found to be mediated by control appraisals (Forsblom et al., 2022).

In addition, the consequences of performance assessments and feedback are relevant. The stakes are especially high if future educational and occupational opportunities are made contingent on individual performance. Control perceptions may be undermined, and the perceived importance of achieving success and avoiding failure may be exacerbated under these conditions. Given these effects on appraisals, high-stakes testing can boost positive emotions in those who succeed, but inevitably exacerbates negative emotions like test anxiety in students who are prone to failure. From an educational policy and practice perspective, CVT implies that high-stakes testing should be avoided or minimized wherever possible, given its dire emotional consequences.

Composition of Groups

All social factors discussed so far depend on the emotion-generating actions of others. However, beyond action, the mere presence of others can also shape our emotions. From a CVT perspective, one important mechanism transforming our perceptions of others into emotions is social comparison. Upward social comparison can reduce our self-confidence to achieve at a similar level; downward social comparison can boost our confidence and perceptions of control.

Based on these assumptions, H. Marsh and I have developed a model on the emotional effects of the ability composition of groups (Pekrun et al., 2019). This model integrates propositions from CVT and Marsh's big-fish-little-pond effect (BFLPE) model (Marsh, 1987; Marsh et al., 2020). The

BFLPE model and related evidence show that membership in a high-ability group reduces individuals' self-concept of ability, because opportunities to experience success relative to others are reduced, all else being equal. In contrast, membership in a low-ability group increases self-concept. By implication, being a member of a high-ability group, such as a classroom of gifted students, can reduce positive and increase negative emotions. In contrast, being a member of a low-ability group can benefit emotional well-being. We have called this effect the happy-fish-little-pond effect (HFLPE)—all else being equal, you may be happier in a small pond of peers who achieve at moderate levels, as compared with being surrounded by top performers.

In sum, from a CVT perspective, environments are emotionally beneficial if they provide high cognitive and emotional quality, support needs for autonomy and relatedness, convey challenging but attainable expectations that focus on mastery, deliver feedback that improves confidence and does not derail future opportunities, and are composed in a way that prevents unhealthy social comparison. Across domains, policymakers and practitioners would be well advised to attend to these principles (see also Linnenbrink-Garcia et al., 2016; Pekrun, 2014).

The Role of Institutional, Political, Economic, and Socio-Cultural Contexts

Immediate social environments—referred to as "microsystems" in Bronfenbrenner's (1979) social-ecological model—are embedded in broader institutional, economic, political, and socio-cultural contexts. For example, in education, classrooms are embedded within schools, and schools are embedded within neighborhoods and shaped by educational policies. Across these contexts, it follows from CVT that any factors that impact control and value appraisals also influence resulting emotions, similar to the impact of immediate social environments. Importantly, the influence of institutional and socio-cultural factors can take direct or indirect forms. For example, cultural beliefs about the importance of achievement can directly influence individuals' achievement emotions when endorsed by the individual. In contrast, the influence of policymakers is typically indirect, mediated by defining legal and administrative procedures that shape institutions, which, in turn, provide the immediate social environments that shape emotions.

Institutions, Economy, and Political Context

Institutions like schools, organizations, and companies provide rules and opportunities that promote or constrain the practices shaping control and value that I discussed above. For example, schools and universities provide teachers with opportunities to improve the cognitive quality of instruction, define assessment practices and standards for evaluating achievement that shape goal structures, and practice allocations of teachers and students which define group compositions and the resulting compositional effects. To the extent that schools promote emotionally positive practices, they can foster a positive emotional climate within classrooms and the whole school, according to CVT. In contrast, schools that do not deliver high-quality instruction, promote overly competitive goal structures, and derail students' sense of autonomy may undermine the emotional climate, with detrimental consequences for social interaction (e.g., bullying; Marsh, Pekrun, et al., 2023), achievement, and well-being of both students and teachers.

Institutions, in turn, depend on the *economic and political systems* in which they are embedded. For schools, critical factors are the education of teachers which makes it possible to recruit teachers that are able to provide affectively sound instruction; the national and regional economic situation that promotes or constraints recruitment (e.g., via teacher salaries) and building high-quality institutional infrastructures; and educational policy-making that defines curricula, assessment practices (e.g., high-stakes testing), and the structure of students' educational careers (e.g., in terms of tracking and retention policies).

Cultural Beliefs

Beyond the features of institutions and systems within society, culturally shared beliefs are critically important for shaping individuals' control and value appraisals, according to CVT (see Pekrun, 2018, for theory and related evidence). Cultural beliefs influencing control appraisals refer to the causal relations between goals, actions, and outcomes (*causal beliefs*; Fig. 3.3). For example, cultures that emphasize the link between individual effort and success are likely to boost internal attributions of achievement and related emotions, such as self-centered pride and shame based on individual (rather than collective) accomplishments. Cultural beliefs that impact values refer to the intrinsic and instrumental importance of actions and outcomes (*value beliefs*). For example, cultures differ in the importance they place on achievement and the attainment of long-term goals, denoted as 'long-term orientation' in Hofstede's (2011) classification of values.

A special case of culturally formed control-value beliefs is *stereotypes* based on gender, race, ethnicity, or socio-economic status. For example, traditionally, females have been perceived as less competent in mathematics and related STEM (*s*cience, *t*echnology, *e*ngineering, *m*athematics) fields than males. Related to this belief, learning mathematics was considered less important for females. These stereotypes help explain related differences in emotions. For example, to the extent that girls endorse these stereotypes and integrate them into their self-concepts, they may experience less control and positive value in mathematics, even if their performance equals that of boys. Accordingly, girls have been shown to experience more negative emotions in math, such as math anxiety, and less positive emotions than boys, despite similar performance (e.g., Frenzel et al., 2007).

However, caution should be exercised in interpreting differences in cultural beliefs across countries and groups of individuals. The existing evidence suggests that differences in beliefs can be substantially larger within countries than between countries (e.g., OECD, 2017). Especially for achievement-related beliefs, between-country differences may be shrinking today due to the globalization of economies, which may drive the adoption of common standards of economic and educational achievement. Similarly, differences between genders in control-value beliefs and resulting emotions are typically much smaller than differences between individuals of the same gender (e.g., Hart & Ganley, 2019).

Impact on Learning, Performance, Well-Being, and Health

In the previous sections, I have outlined how emotions are generated by individual and social factors, according to CVT. However, knowledge about origins does not answer the question of whether emotions matter. Are emotions sufficiently important to warrant attention and the investment of time and money to conduct empirical studies? Alternatively, are emotions just epiphenomena of existing achievements, having little influence beyond being pleasant or unpleasant? In the following, I discuss how CVT addresses these questions. Specifically, I consider possible effects of emotions on learning and performance, as well as their impact on well-being and health.

Learning and Performance

According to CVT, emotions matter. They are prime drivers of learning, behavior, and achievement, according to the cognitive-motivational model of emotion effects that is part of the theory. However, as argued in this model, the effects of emotions are not direct but rather mediated by various cognitive and motivational processes (Pekrun, 2006; Pekrun & Linnenbrink-Garcia, 2022). Given the multiplicity of these processes, the effects of emotions on learning and achievement are inevitably complex. To understand them, it is essential to consider both the defining features of emotions and their influence on cognition and motivation.

Traditionally, experimental research on mood and emotions has only distinguished between positive and negative emotions, without further differentiating between emotions within these categories. Findings of this research have suggested that positive mood is detrimental by biasing judgment and fostering illusory expectations, and that negative mood is detrimental by depleting cognitive resources and distracting attention (Aspinwall, 1998; Ellis & Ashbrook, 1988). However, from a CVT perspective, activation and object focus are also critically important. Considering all three dimensions renders a more nuanced and less pessimistic perspective on the impact of emotions.

In terms of cognition and motivation influenced by emotion, four especially important processes are the following. First, emotions impact the availability of *cognitive resources* in working memory. Emotions direct our attention toward the object of emotion. By implication, emotions can distract attention from the current task. This is true not only for negative emotions but also for positive emotions (Meinhardt & Pekrun, 2003; Mikels & Reuter-Lorenz, 2019). For example, if a student is excited about the dinner with a new friend planned for the evening, attention to classroom instruction may be diminished. Generally, by consuming attention, all incidental emotions (i.e., emotions unrelated to the current task) can undermine cognitive performance on difficult or complex tasks that require cognitive resources. However, there is one important exception: If positive emotions are directed toward the task itself, attention is focused on task performance.

As such, positive task-related emotions can boost performance by allocating cognitive resources to task completion rather than thinking about other, task-irrelevant matters. Due to positive effects on attention, students who enjoy studying perform better. Importantly, these positive effects require that the task is the object of positive emotion. For teachers, simply generating a positive mood in the class may not be sufficient and even be detrimental if students' attention is distracted.

Second, emotions affect *intrinsic and extrinsic motivation*. Positive activating emotions are thought to enhance motivation. More specifically, positive activating emotions that are task-related, such as enjoyment of learning, promote intrinsic motivation to perform the task. Positive activating emotions related to outcomes, such as hope for success, can facilitate extrinsic task motivation. The opposite pattern of effects is expected for negative deactivating emotions, like boredom and hopelessness. These emotions generally undermine motivation, both intrinsic and extrinsic. Bored students are motivated to leave the situation and do something else rather than engage in studying.

Positive deactivating emotions like relaxation and relief, and negative activating emotions like anger and anxiety, can have more variable effects on motivation. For example, test anxiety can reduce students' interest and intrinsic motivation, but it can also prompt strong motivation to invest effort to avoid failure. It depends on the individual balance of these negative and positive effects if anxiety boosts or undermines students' overall motivation to learn (see Pekrun et al., 2002, for an empirical example).

Third, emotions impact *modes of thinking and memory retrieval.* Positive emotions are known to foster flexible, creative, and holistic thinking styles and widespread activation of materials stored in long-term memory. In contrast, negative emotions can promote more rigid, analytical, and detail-oriented thinking and memory retrieval. As explained by mood-as-information approaches (Schwarz & Clore, 2003) and Fredrickson's (2001) broaden-and-build theory, positive emotions signal that everything is well, making it possible to creatively explore new horizons. In contrast, negative emotions signal threat and potential problems, suggesting it is wise to be more cautious cognitively. Accordingly, it depends on task demands if positive or negative emotions are more helpful in terms of emotion-contingent styles of thinking—for creative tasks, positive emotions are typically more beneficial; for evaluative tasks, the cautious, critical style of thinking promoted by negative emotions can be helpful. In a recent study with university students enrolled in mathematics programs, we found support for these propositions. Generating mathematical ideas about a geometrical figure was easier after induction of enjoyment, as compared with an anxious or neutral state. In contrast, evaluating existing ideas was enhanced after inducing an anxious mood (Schubert, Ufer, & Pekrun, 2025).

Finally, the cognitive-motivational model posits that emotions' impact on cognitive flexibility has consequences for *self-regulation versus external regulation* of learning and behavior. Positive emotions can promote the flexible setting of goals, planning, monitoring of actions, and evaluating outcomes that is core to self-regulation. In contrast, when in an anxious state of mind, we may resort to more cautious styles of regulation, such as letting our actions be guided by teachers, parents, or supervisors (for supporting evidence, see, e.g., Pekrun, Marsh, Elliot, et al., 2023).

The overall effects of emotions on performance depend on the interplay between these mechanisms and their interaction with task demands. *Positive activating* emotions like enjoyment may typically exert positive effects, especially when they are task-related. *Negative deactivating* emotions like boredom and hopelessness have detrimental effects; these emotions deplete cognitive resources, undermine any task-related motivation, and lead to superficial information processing. The effects of *deactivating positive* emotions like relaxation and relief, and *negative activating* emotions like anger and anxiety, are more complex. For example, the negative effects of anxiety and shame on cognitive resources, intrinsic motivation, and creative thinking may be counterbalanced by positive effects on extrinsic motivation and evaluative thinking. Similarly, the effects of activating negative epistemic emotions like confusion need not be adverse—confusion can motivate us to work on cognitive problems as long as we maintain optimism that we will eventually resolve the problem.

Well-Being and Health

An important message following from the above analysis of emotion effects, and related empirical evidence, is that the world of emotions is *not black and white* from a functional perspective. Pleasant emotions are not always beneficial, and unpleasant emotions are not always detrimental. This view has important consequences for an adequate definition of psychological well-being. Well-being is often defined as maximizing positive affect and minimizing negative affect. For example, the Oxford English Dictionary (2024) depicts well-being as „the state of being healthy, happy, or prosperous." Such a definition suggests that positive emotion is core to well-being, in addition to health and prosperity. However, this view is limited to *hedonic* well-being and disregards the positive functions of negative (unpleasant) emotions.

In contrast, from the perspective of *eudaimonic* well-being as advocated by philosophers in Aristotle's tradition (Kraut, 2022), it is essential to strike a balance between positive and negative emotions that helps fulfill one's mission and behave in alignment with one's goals and identity. To this end, negative emotions like frustration and confusion, and even anger, anxiety, or boredom, may sometimes be helpful. For example, in education, it may be beneficial to endure the boredom and frustration that come with studying complex and tedious materials, and to use the motivational energy of anxiety when facing evaluative situations like tests and exams. For achieving long-term goals, such an approach may be more adaptive than trying to eliminate negative emotions at all costs.

Nevertheless, it is important to note that excessive negative emotions, such as excessive test anxiety, are typically detrimental. Excessive negative emotions are not only detrimental to goal attainment, but they can also harm physical health. Regarding emotions in educational settings, research has shown that test anxiety can undermine students' health by compromising immune system functioning and sleep (see, e.g., Segerstrom & Miller, 2004). For achievement emotions other than anxiety, evidence is scarce. In a recent study of university students' health (Pekrun, Marsh, Elliot, et al., 2023, Study 3), we investigated links between achievement emotions and students' health problems, including psychosomatic symptoms such as headaches, stomach problems, dizziness, cardiovascular symptoms, back problems, and reduced sleep quality. The findings show that these problems were closely linked to students' negative achievement emotions, especially their anxiety, shame, and hopelessness. Positive emotions, as well as anger and boredom, did not show a substantial relation with these problems. From a CVT perspective, anxiety, shame, and hopelessness involve a lack of control, with stressful uncertainty added in the case of anxiety. As such, the findings suggest that *low-control emotions* are detrimental to physical health, at least in terms of everyday psychosomatic problems.

CONNECTING THE DOTS: RECIPROCAL EFFECTS ACROSS TIMESCALES AND LEVELS

Reciprocal Effects

As explained above, individual and social antecedents influence emotions, and emotions, in turn, impact outcomes. However, outcomes are expected to reciprocally impact emotions and their antecedents (Fig. 3.3). For example, academic success and failure can alter students' appraisals and emotions, and they can prompt responses from parents and teachers. By implication, emotions, their outcomes, and their antecedents can be linked by reciprocal effects over time. These reciprocal effects can take the form of both positive and negative feedback loops. Generally, a positive feedback loop implies that some variable A has a positive effect on another variable B, and B has a positive reciprocal effect on A. Alternatively, a positive feedback loop can imply that A has a negative effect on B, and B has a negative effect on A (this loop is also called positive because the product of two negative coefficients is positive). In contrast, a negative feedback loop implies that the effects linking A and B take opposite signs. In a negative feedback loop, A has a positive effect on B and B has a negative effect on A; or A has a negative effect on B, and B has a positive effect on A.

Adopting perspectives from dynamic systems theories, positive feedback loops generate and amplify variables over time. For example, a student's success on the first major exam at university can prompt enjoyment, which, in turn, drives motivation to invest effort and increases the likelihood of success on subsequent exams. Further success can amplify the student's enjoyment, which can further boost the motivation to learn. Similarly, failure on an exam can trigger fear of failure on the next exam, and this fear can prompt worries and avoidance motivation that reduce subsequent performance. Reduced performance can further exacerbate fear and anxiety, which can contribute to repeated failure on subsequent exams. As such, positive feedback loops can amount to either virtuous or vicious cycles of emotions, outcomes, and antecedents.

In contrast, negative feedback loops serve to stabilize systems, maintain the current state, and prevent amplification of the variables involved. For example, instead of demotivating a fearful student, anxiety generated by failure can motivate the student to invest effort, as argued earlier, and effort can reduce the likelihood of further failure. In this case, failure has a positive effect on anxiety, but anxiety has a negative effect on failure, thus preventing anxiety from being exacerbated and performance from further deteriorating. Negative feedback loops can also play a role in positive emotions. Success can prompt joy, but joy can be interpreted as a signal that sufficient effort was invested, thus reducing subsequent effort and performance. Similarly, emotions and social antecedents can be linked by negative feedback loops, such as when anxiety motivates students to seek support, and support keeps anxiety at bay.

The Role of Time

The effects linking emotions, outcomes, and antecedents take time. Some unfold within fractions of seconds, whereas others require weeks, months, or years to develop fully. As such, the generation of emotions can also unfold over different timescales, from micro-level (seconds, minutes, and hours) to meso-level (days, weeks, and months) and macro-level (years) development (Hamaker et al., 2015). Notably, whereas some effects linking emotions to other variables may take the same form across timescales, others may vary depending on the timescale. As a general rule, it seems reasonable to assume that effects based on unitary, basic mechanisms of psychological functioning take the same form across timescales. In contrast, complex effects arising from the interplay of multiple mechanisms can exhibit more variation.

From a CVT perspective, the effects of control and value on emotions represent basic functional relations that should be uniform across various timeframes. For example, reduced control and uncertainty can prompt anxiety within seconds. Similarly, they are expected to generate habitual anxiety occurring over months and years if they are stored as lasting control beliefs in long-term memory that are activated in many situations. In contrast, the effects of emotions on outcomes, such as performance, depend on the complex interplay of various cognitive and motivational mechanisms, as argued earlier. These mechanisms can operate in different ways across different timescales, making it possible that their interactions and the overall effects of emotions also vary.

For example, achievement emotions such as joy related to success or anxiety related to failure may have different effects on current task performance versus long-term achievement outcomes. As noted, it could be that joy after success leads to short-term relaxation and a reduction in effort, but fuels motivation to strive for further success over a longer period. Conversely, anxiety could have short-term booster effects driven by the impact of anxiety on effort investment, but long-term erosion effects due to anxiety depleting motivational and physical resources.

If effects vary according to timeframe, feedback loops could also change. One possibility is that initial positive feedback loops later transform into negative feedback loops stabilizing the emotions and related variables. For example, initial positive feedback loops of achievement and anxiety (failure prompting anxiety, and anxiety leading to failure) could later turn negative, with failure still prompting anxiety, but anxiety signaling that effort is needed. If resources are not depleted, this could lead to subsequent investment of effort, improvement of performance, and avoidance of repeated failure.

Similarly, initial negative feedback loops could evolve into positive feedback loops over time. For example, adolescents' depression can initially prompt parents' support, and support can reduce depression (a negative feedback loop). Later, parents may be exhausted and respond negatively, implying that their child's depressive episodes reduce support, although support still alleviates the depression (a positive feedback loop including two negative effects; see also Boele et al., 2022).

Furthermore, it is sensible to assume that repeated interactions between situations, appraisals, and emotions generate cognitive emotion schemata over meso- and macro-timescales. When momentary (i.e., micro-timescale) sequences of situational perceptions, appraisals, and emotions recur repeatedly (on meso- and macro-timescales), schemata can be formed that integrate representations of situation, appraisals, and emotions, as argued earlier. Once such a schema is activated in a subsequent situation, perceptions of the situation can immediately trigger the schema-defined set of appraisals and emotions.

As such, emotion schemata can shape micro-timescale interactions between the variables in subsequent cycles. To the extent that these schemata represent trait emotions, it follows that state and trait emotions are linked by bottom-up and top-down processes that unfold on different timescales: Appraisal-emotion linkages need to be repeated over time to crystallize in long-term situation-appraisal-emotion schemata. These schemata, however, can lead to the generation of situation-contingent state emotions within seconds.

Dynamics Across the Within- and Between-Person Levels

An important corollary of the above view is that within-person and between-person relations of situations, appraisals, and emotions should exhibit equivalence, provided that there are no additional factors (e.g., genetic dispositions) that drive one of the two types of relations in the opposite direction. To explain, within-person relations refer to associations among variables across different occasions for each individual, such as different time points in longitudinal studies. These relations answer the question: Is an individual's fluctuation in one variable related to fluctuation in the other variable over time? For example, does a student's achievement vary with their enjoyment, such that they show better achievement when they enjoy learning? Between-person relations refer to associations across different individuals. These relations address the question: Do individuals who score high on one variable also score high on the other variable? For example, do students who enjoy learning show higher achievement than students who do not enjoy learning?

From a statistical perspective, within-person and between-person covariation between variables are independent, except if specific conditions hold (i.e., ergodicity; Voelkle et al., 2014). It has, therefore, been argued that within- and between-person relations among variables can diverge widely (see Hamaker, 2023; Murayama et al., 2017). An example cited by Schmitz and Skinner (1993) is the relation between sleep duration and the frequency of migraine headaches: Within individuals, the relation is negative (short sleep precipitates headaches); between persons, the relation is positive (individuals who sleep longer suffer more from these headaches). Obviously, interpreting the between-person association as indicating within-person effects would be misleading. Furthermore, such an interpretation would suggest practical solutions that would not work, namely, shortening one's sleep rather than getting sufficient sleep.

However, if within-person effects lead to the establishment of individual schemata and between-person differences that are congruent with these effects, within- and between-person relations can be equivalent. In our research on achievement and epistemic emotions, we found support for this claim. In several studies, the links between appraisals and emotions, and the links between emotions and achievement-related outcomes, were surprisingly similar across the within-person and between-person levels. For example, using dynamic structural equation modeling, Pekrun, Marsh, Elliot et al. (2023) found that perceived control and positive value related positively to positive achievement emotions, and negatively to negative achievement emotions, in both within- and between-person analysis.

In the experimental studies reported by Vogl et al. (2020), participants' surprise, curiosity, and confusion about answers to trivia questions positively predicted their motivation to explore the correct answers from both within- and between-person perspectives. Pekrun, Marsh, Suessenbach et al. (2023) showed that students' positive math emotions had positive effects on their math performance, and negative emotions had adverse effects, using a within-person causal modeling approach (Hamaker et al.'s, 2015, random-intercept cross-lagged panel model), similar to Pekrun et al.'s (2017) findings using classic between-person modeling with the same dataset.

EMOTION REGULATION: THE IMPORTANCE OF SELF-DEVELOPMENT

The CVT perspective on reciprocal effects has important implications for the regulation of emotions. Given reciprocal links, emotions can be regulated by changing not only their presumed antecedents but also their outcomes. Over time, outcomes influence subsequent emotions. As such, outcomes can become antecedents, and influencing outcomes can impact emotions. This view makes it possible to amend current conceptions of emotion regulation by an important family of regulatory strategies neglected in existing research: The development of competencies that make it possible to achieve emotionally positive outcomes.

In the original CVT of achievement emotions (Pekrun, 2006), competence-oriented regulation was considered one of several families of emotion regulation strategies, in addition to strategies that target the situation (selecting and modifying situations to influence emotions), one's cognitions (attention and appraisal), and the emotional response itself (directly targeting components of the emotion, such as arousal or expression; Gross, 2015). However, competencies and other personal attributes, such as one's interests, are critical for other emotions as well. Generally, changing oneself is one way to change one's emotions.

In addition to the target of regulation, the intended direction of regulation is important to understand emotion regulation. Across disciplines, the term regulation is used to denote the mechanisms by which an organism or technical device maintains or changes its current state in accordance with a given goal or rule (see, e.g., Merriam-Webster, 2024). Using this definition, emotion regulation can imply either maintaining an emotion or changing it. Change can imply either increasing (upregulating) the frequency or intensity of an emotion or decreasing (downregulating) it. The existing literature on emotion regulation has focused on changing emotions by up- or downregulating them (see Gross & Brett, 2024). I propose that maintaining emotions is an equally important direction of regulation.

Influencing any of the different targets of emotion regulation can lead to upregulating, downregulating, or maintaining an emotion. As such, target and direction are conceptually independent dimensions of emotion regulation. Considering both the five targets discussed below and the three possible directions renders a 5 × 3 taxonomy of regulatory strategies (Table 3.2). In the following, I discuss both dimensions. I specifically highlight the target and the direction that were neglected in the literature, namely, personal competencies as a target and maintaining an emotion as a direction.

Targets of Emotion Regulation

Emotions can be influenced by changing any of the components of emotion-generating processes. A classic view implies that situational events trigger emotions, and that this process is mediated by appraisals of the situation (Scherer & Moors, 2019). This view makes it possible to consider regulatory

TABLE 3.2 Two-Dimensional Taxonomy of Emotion Regulation: Examples.

	Target				
Direction	***Person***	***Situation***	***Perception***	***Cognition***	***Emotion***
Up-regulating	Competencies to generate the emotion	Approaching situations that generate the emotion	Focusing attention	Positive reappraisal to increase positive emotion	Expression; increasing arousal
Maintaining	Competencies to maintain the emotion	Shaping situations to maintain the emotion	Keeping attention	Maintaining current appraisals	Acceptance
Down-regulating	Competencies to avoid or reduce the emotion	Avoiding situations that generate the emotion	Distracting attention	Distancing; positive reappraisal to decrease negative emotion	Suppression; reducing arousal

Note: The table lists examples, not a complete set of strategies. For instance, negative reappraisal to generate negative emotions or reduce positive emotions is not listed.

actions that target the situation, cognitive appraisals, and the emotional response itself (Gross, 2015). The situation-appraisal-emotion model of emotion generation is consistent with neo-behaviorist views on behavior, such as the S-O-R (stimulus-organism-response) model (see Kanfer, 1971; Woodworth, 1921). However, it does not sufficiently consider the role of the person (i.e., the self). The person (the "organism") serves as a mediator explaining the influence of situational stimuli but does not figure as an independent actor in this type of model. In contrast, personality and social psychologists have posited early on that person and situation are equally important for explaining behavior (see Lewin, 1936; Sherman et al., 2015), and that their interaction is critical for understanding human action.

From this perspective, it is time to bring the person back into models of emotion generation and emotion regulation. As argued, for example, in Lazarus's transactional model of coping with stress, it is the interaction of individual propensities and situational demands that determines possibilities to cope and resulting emotions. In principle, the person and the situation have the same rank in causing thought and action. However, from the perspective of self-research, it may even make sense to give the person precedence—at least given sufficient competencies and a mature developmental status, it is we who select and shape situations in the first place rather than being subjected to situations that are imposed on us. Such a view would be consistent with self-determination theory perspectives on autonomous motivation and regulation (Ryan & Deci, 2017). Adopting this view, it is sensible to position the person as the starting point in the emotion-generating process (Fig. 3.4). It is the (mature) person who selects and shapes their situation, deploys attention, develops thoughts about the situation, and responds emotionally.

Person-oriented regulation of emotions implies changing (or maintaining) personal competencies and attributes, such as expertise in a given field or one's profile of interests (for empirical evidence, see Stockinger et al., 2025). As noted, competencies and interests are relevant not only to achievement emotions but to other groups of emotions as well. For example, social competencies are foundational for initiating and maintaining social relationships and all the social emotions that are generated by these relationships. Similarly, health-related competencies and interests guide health behavior and health-related emotions, and competencies in music or the performing arts are critical for experiencing aesthetic emotions (Menninghaus et al., 2019).

Competencies are fundamentally important not only for shaping situations and actions in emotionally adaptive ways but are also foundational for directly targeting the emotional response. Competencies to process emotions and modulate their component processes—traditionally summarized using the term "emotional intelligence" (Matthews et al., 2002)—directly influence possibilities to regulate one's emotional responses.

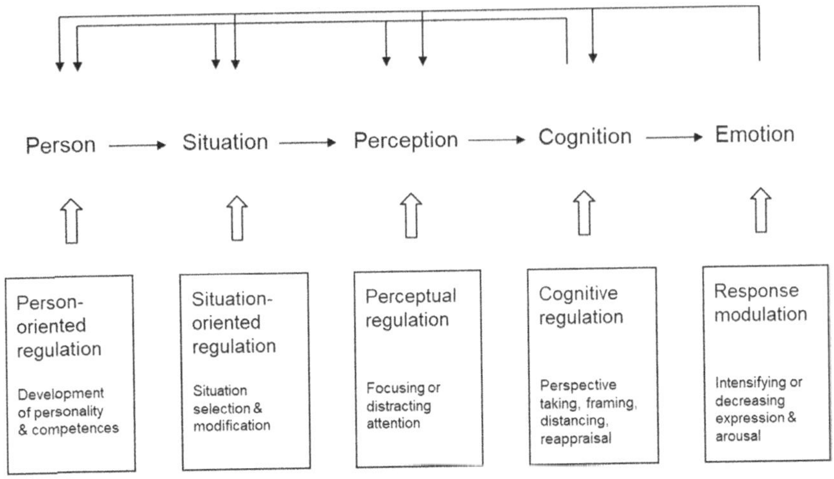

Fig. 3.4. CVT Model of Emotion Regulation.

As part of one's personality, emotion-generating competencies and attributes can last over time. However, competencies can also be developed in the moment in response to current situational demands, and they can be rapidly lost again if they are no longer needed. For example, knowledge of travel routes or restaurants in a foreign city may be needed to navigate that city in emotionally beneficial ways, but may be forgotten later when it was just a single trip. Similarly, students may develop emotion-enhancing competencies in academic subjects when striving to master exams, but lose them after the exam if they are not interested in the subject. As such, competencies and interests can be trait- or state-like, similar to emotion-generating situations that can be durable or temporary.

Alternatively, emotion regulation can address the situation, perceptions of the situation (specifically, attention), thoughts about the situation (e.g., perspective taking, appraisals), and the emotion itself, as argued in Gross's (2015) process model of emotion regulation (Fig. 3.4). In contrast to person development, regulatory strategies targeting these components of the emotion-generating process have been extensively investigated during the past two decades (Gross & Ford, 2024).

For all these regulatory possibilities, it is essential to consider principles of reciprocal causation, as illustrated in Fig. 3.4. For example, regulating emotions by building competencies not only changes one's profile of competencies, but it can also change the situation as well as one's attention and thoughts about the situation. Similarly, directly changing component processes of the emotion (e.g., facial expression) can not only alter the emotion but also influence the environment, such as teachers' expression of emotion influencing their students' emotions, as outlined earlier.

Direction of Emotion Regulation

As noted, emotion regulation can imply upregulating, downregulating, or maintaining an emotion. Using Gross's (2015) distinction between response-focused and antecedent-focused regulation, two variants of such a process need to be distinguished. If the emotion has already been generated, regulation implies changing or maintaining the existing emotion. If the emotion has not yet been generated, regulation targets the antecedents of emotion, which presupposes reflective awareness of the emotions that the antecedents are likely to generate. In this case, anticipated emotions are regulated, rather than existing emotions.

Regulation can imply changing existing or anticipated emotions, but it can also consist of attempts to maintain an existing emotion, or to ensure that the situation is maintained such that an upcoming emotion unfolds as anticipated. As with up- and downregulation, for eudaimonic well-being, it may not only be important to maintain positive emotions but sometimes also to maintain negative emotions.

Maintaining emotions is not guaranteed by just doing nothing. Rather, maintaining emotions can be an effortful process. Imagine you are in a positive mood on a Sunday morning, anticipating joyful activities with the family—maintaining that mood may be quite a task when children complain, unwanted visitors arrive at the doorstep, or the car engine fails to start. As such, maintaining an emotion can be a costly process, similar to up- or downregulating the emotion.

Maintaining emotions presupposes that accepting them as they are is a valuable goal. Reflective awareness and acceptance of emotions are core to mindfulness, and they are a core requirement for emotional integration as conceptualized in self-determination theory. Emotional integration has been defined as being aware and interested in one's emotions, exploring them, and using them as a guide for action (Roth et al., 2019; Ryan et al., 2006). While emotional integration includes more than regulating the emotion, maintaining and accepting the emotion (at least for a while) is needed to explore and use it. However, acceptance can also lead to subsequent attempts to change the emotion. Acceptance and awareness enable exploration, and exploration can motivate regulatory thoughts and actions, including all the strategies that can be used to change emotions. For example, momentary acceptance of anxiety before an exam can motivate a student to explore the sources of anxiety, leading to the insight that it is caused by incorrect perceptions of the demands of the exam—which can motivate reappraisal of the situation and lead to a reduction of the anxiety.

Importantly, it is possible and often beneficial to accept not only positive emotions but also negative emotions. Negative emotions are no less important as information and a guide for action than positive emotions. As such, as argued earlier, both positive and negative emotions can be part of eudaimonic well-being. Consistent with this view, and with the self-determination theory perspective on emotional integration (Ryan & Deci, 2017; Ryan et al., 2006), acceptance is critical to eudaimonic well-being. Nevertheless, there are limits to the positive functions of acceptance. If excessive, both positive and negative emotions can be detrimental. This may be especially true for negative emotions. In the first place, negative emotions signal that something is going wrong, and they can be detrimental to performance and health as discussed earlier. As such, it is often important to change the situation and downregulate negative emotions rather than just accept them.

FUTURE DIRECTIONS

Since its inception, CVT has developed into a mature theory that has found broad empirical support. Nevertheless, further development is needed, both in refining the theory and in gathering longitudinal and causal evidence. The following three lines of further advancing CVT may be most important (for a more complete treatment, see Pekrun, 2024).

Formalizing Emotion Theory

Theoretical propositions vary in their specificity and explanatory strength. Low explanatory strength of a proposition implies that it holds in many cases, and that only a few possible cases would not be consistent with the proposition. Conversely, high explanatory strength implies that only a few cases would be consistent with the proposition, whereas many cases would disconfirm it. As such, low explanatory strength implies low falsifiability, and high explanatory strength implies high falsifiability.

An example of low strength would be the statement that variable A relates to variable B. Psychological variables never show true zero relations ("The point-null hypothesis H0 is, in psychology, [quasi-] always false"; Meehl, 1967, p. 10). Relations can be non-significant from a statistical inference perspective, but this does not mean they are truly zero. As such, it may be impossible to falsify this kind of proposition, except if some non-zero threshold is specified to decide whether it is disconfirmed. An example in emotion science would be the statement that emotions and appraisals are related—a truism with zero or low falsifiability, depending on the threshold used to define disconfirmation.

Propositions that A has a causal influence on B are stronger—there may be more cases that disconfirm the proposition, such as B influencing A rather than vice versa. If the direction of the effect is specified, stating that A has a positive (or negative) causal influence on B, then explanatory strength and falsifiability increase, because even more possible cases are excluded. An example would be the proposition that high perceived control has positive effects on positive emotions and adverse effects on negative emotions. In this proposition, the direction of the effect is specified. However, the form of the function is left open—any monotonically positive or negative relation would be consistent with the proposition. As such, explanatory strength and falsifiability are still limited.

To further increase strength, it is necessary to specify the functional form of the effect, beyond stating that it is positive or negative. For example, it could be specified that the effect is linear, or that it takes a specific curvilinear form. Statements of this type can be formalized using the language of mathematics (Robinaugh et al., 2021). Emotion theories have not yet reached this level of precision and explanatory strength, except for a few recent computational models of epistemic emotions (surprise, Modirshanechi et al., 2022; curiosity, Dubey & Griffiths, 2020).

CVT includes propositions on non-linear relations. An example is the hypothesis that the effects of perceived control on boredom follow a U-shaped curvilinear function (boredom induced by over- and underchallenge but not by optimal challenge; Pekrun & Goetz, 2024a). Another example is the proposition that lack of control and negative expectancies increase anxiety except for very high levels of certainty about failure, where anxiety is replaced by hopelessness. However, even for these propositions, open questions remain. For example, are very low subjective probabilities of an adverse event sufficient to generate anxiety or are higher probabilities needed? To answer these questions and further specify propositions on appraisals and emotions, it may be helpful to formalize propositions and transform CVT into a computational theory of emotions.

Emotions Across Individuals, Contexts, and Time

CVT proposes that the objects of emotions, their frequency, and their process parameters (e.g., intensity, duration) can vary across individuals, settings, sociocultural contexts, and time. Nevertheless, the basic mechanisms linking emotions to their antecedents and outcomes are considered universal. I have proposed to call the combination of these two principles the "relative universality" of emotions (Pekrun, 2006, 2024). Claims of the universality of mechanisms are not unique to CVT; they are typical for most theories of psychological processes, including theories of self, motivation, and emotion (e.g., self-concept theory, Marsh et al., 2019; self-determination theory, Vansteenkiste et al., 2020). For CVT propositions on universality, there is rich evidence that links between control-value appraisals and emotions, and between emotions and achievement outcomes, indeed show generalizability (see Pekrun & Goetz, 2024b).

As argued earlier, variation of more complex relations is thought to be due to variation in the interplay of basic mechanisms. However, more work is needed on two critically important issues. First, what exactly are the basic mechanisms of emotion for which it is sensible to assume universality? From a CVT perspective, this is clear for the impact of control and value appraisals on emotions—the theory proposes that these relations hold universally. It is less clear for the influence of emotions on outcomes. For example, it seems straightforward to assume that task-irrelevant emotions reduce working memory resources needed for task performance. However, which of the various types of resources (Mikels & Reuter-Lorenz, 2019) and related executive functions are affected by emotions, and in what ways? Similarly, how do emotions affect the various components of motivation (goals, wishes, intentions, etc.; Pekrun, 2023) that should be considered to understand the effects of emotions on intrinsic and extrinsic motivation? As such, work is needed to clarify the level of granularity of cognitive and motivational processes that needs to be considered to define basic mechanisms of the effects of emotions.

Second, theory and evidence are needed to understand how the interplay of basic mechanisms varies across individuals, contexts, and time. For example, any effects of test anxiety on intrinsic and extrinsic motivation before an exam can be balanced in different ways across students and time—but who exactly benefits from the resulting balance, and under what conditions is students' overall motivation to prepare influenced positively? How do different strategies for regulating emotions interact in different individuals and cultural contexts? After critical life transitions such as entering university or a new career, when and how do initially positive feedback loops of emotions develop into negative feedback loops (see the earlier discussion of the role of time)? Answers to these questions require theoretical modeling and empirical investigation of the role of individual differences, situational differences, and time in relations between emotions, antecedents, and outcomes.

Intervention and Practice

CVT implies that changing appraisals, and the situational and personal circumstances that shape appraisals, is a primary way to change emotions. Specifically, it follows from the theory that three strategies to modify appraisals should be beneficial for strengthening adaptive emotions and preventing or reducing maladaptive emotions. First, it should be beneficial to modify perceptions of control, especially when they are unrealistically negative, such as when students do not believe in their abilities despite being well-prepared for an exam. Second, to promote adaptive positive emotions, it would be helpful to increase the positive value of activities and outcomes. It may be especially promising to promote the intrinsic value of activities, such as the interest value of studying. Intrinsic value not only promotes positive activity emotions but also intrinsic motivation (autonomous motivation from the perspective of self-determination theory; Ryan & Deci, 2017). Third, to reduce maladaptive negative emotions, it is useful to reduce excessive perceptions of the negative value of activities and outcomes. For example, intense test anxiety can be caused by beliefs that failure on an upcoming exam implies being worthless as a person, and that second chances do not exist, thus exacerbating the importance of the exam. Reducing these beliefs would be a primary way to reduce excessive test anxiety.

Changing appraisals in this way can help different groups of individuals who are at risk emotionally, including those who lack control, lack positive value, or suffer from excessive negative value perceptions. In the education domain, existing interventions typically either target control appraisals or positive value appraisals. Examples of the former group of interventions are attributional retraining (Perry et al., 2014) and growth mindset interventions (Burnette et al., 2023). An example of positive value treatment is utility value interventions (Hulleman & Harackiewicz, 2021).

To address all three groups of problems, we developed a control-value intervention that combines components of attributional retraining, growth mindset interventions, and utility value interventions. Following established procedures for these interventions, the control-value intervention comprises psychoeducation, exercises, and the use of tools to modify control appraisals and promote positive value perceptions. In addition, the intervention includes a new component aiming to reduce excessive beliefs about the negative value of failure. In this component, participants receive psychoeducation about the detrimental impact of excessive achievement value on decision-making and emotional well-being, including scenarios describing single cases and instruction about the importance of second chances and alternative careers. In addition, they take related quizzes, reflect on their own value appraisals, and are provided with tools to recognize and regulate their value appraisals in achievement situations.

The control-value intervention was included in a broader set of interventions aiming to support young people (aged 16–22 years) in promoting well-being and preventing mental health problems (*Assessing and Enhancing Emotional Competence for Well-Being in the Young*, ECoWeB; see Watkins et al., 2024). ECoWeB followed a personalized approach to offer each participant a combination of two app-based interventions. For example, the control-value intervention could be combined with emotional knowledge training or a rumination intervention. As such, while the findings attest to the feasibility of an app-based control-value intervention, the project did not yield evidence of the effectiveness of this intervention specifically. It is a task for future studies to investigate the specific benefits of control-value interventions simultaneously targeting control, positive value, and negative value.

Beyond individual intervention, CVT has been used to derive recommendations about how to shape settings to benefit emotional well-being (e.g., Linnenbrink-Garcia et al., 2016; Pekrun, 2014). Following the principles explained in the section on the social origins of emotions, important strategies include increasing the cognitive and emotional quality of environments, promoting autonomy and basic need satisfaction, implementing mastery-oriented goal structures and expectations, providing feedback that promotes development and avoids negative future contingencies, and attending to the composition of groups. Research has documented the importance of these factors for performance and emotional well-being. However, as yet the available studies have focused on investigating the relevance of these factors in existing environments, such as the learning environments in classrooms at school. In addition, we need emotion-focused intervention research that is designed to change environments. Collaborating with policymakers and practitioners, this research should aim to redesign the control-value structures of environments and investigate the benefits of such change to promote emotional flourishing, development, and health.

REFERENCES

Aspinwall, L. G. (1998). Rethinking the role of positive affect in self-regulation. *Motivation and Emotion, 22*(1), 1–32. https://doi.org/10.1023/A:1023080224401

Bandura, A. (1977). Self-efficacy: Toward a unifying theory of behavioral change. *Psychological Review, 84*(2), 191–215. https://doi.org/10.1037/0033-295X.84.2.191

Bandura, A. (1986). *Social foundations of thought and action: A social cognitive theory.* Prentice-Hall.

Boele, S., Nelemans, S. A., Denissen, J. J. A., Prinzie, P., Bülow, A., & Keijsers, L. (2022). Testing transactional processes between parental support and adolescent depressive symptoms: From a daily to a biennial timescale. *Development and Psychopathology, 35*(4), 656–1670. https://doi.org/10.1017/S0954579422000360

Bronfenbrenner, U. (1979). *The ecology of human development.* Harvard University Press.

Bross, T., Nett, U. E., & Daumiller, M. (2024). Interrelations among achievement goals and achievement emotions: A meta-analytic examination. *Educational Psychology Review, 36*, 98. https://doi.org/10.1007/s10648-024-09931-9

Burnette, J. L., Billingsley, J., Banks, G. C., Knouse, L. E., Hoyt, C. L., Pollack, J. M., & Simon, S. (2023). A systematic review and meta-analysis of growth mindset interventions: For whom, how, and why might such interventions work? *Psychological Bulletin, 149*(3–4), 174–205. https://doi.org/10.1037/bul0000368

Csikszentmihalyi, M. (2000). *Beyond boredom and anxiety.* Jossey-Bass.

Dubey, R., & Griffiths, T. L. (2020). Reconciling novelty and complexity through a rational analysis of curiosity. *Psychological Review, 127*(3), 455–476. https://doi.org/10.1037/rev0000175

Elliot, A. J., Murayama, K., & Pekrun, R. (2011). A 3 x 2 achievement goal model. *Journal of Educational Psychology, 103*(3), 632–648. https://doi.org/10.1037/a0023952

Ellis, H. C., & Ashbrook, P. W. (1988). Resource allocation model of the effects of depressed mood on states on memory. In K. Fiedler & J. Forgas (Eds.), *Affect, cognition and social behavior* (pp. 25–43). Hogrefe

Forsblom, L., Pekrun, R., Loderer, K., & Peixoto, F. (2022). Cognitive appraisals, achievement emotions, and students' math achievement: A longitudinal analysis. *Journal of Educational Psychology, 114*(2), 346–367. https://doi.org/10.1037/edu0000671

Fredrickson, B. L. (2001). The role of positive emotions in positive psychology: The broaden-and-build theory of positive emotions. *American Psychologist, 56*(3), 218–226. https://doi.org/10.1037/0003-066X.56.3.218

Frenzel, A. C., Becker-Kurz, B., Pekrun, R., Goetz, T., & Lüdtke, O. (2018). Emotion transmission in the classroom revisited: A reciprocal effects model of teacher and student enjoyment. *Journal of Educational Psychology, 110*(5), 628–639. https://doi.org/10.1037/edu0000228

Frenzel, A. C., Dindar, M., Pekrun, R., Reck, C., & Marx, A. K. G. (2024). Joy is reciprocally transmitted between teachers and students: Evidence on facial mimicry in the classroom. *Learning and Instruction, 91,* Article 101896. https://doi.org/10.1016/j.learninstruc.2024.101896

Frenzel, A. C., Pekrun, R., & Goetz, T. (2007). Girls and mathematics – a "hopeless" issue? A control-value approach to gender differences in emotions towards mathematics. *European Journal of Psychology of Education, 22*(4), 497–514. https://doi.org/10.1007/BF03173468

Gross, J. J. (2015). Emotion regulation: Current status and future prospects. *Psychological Inquiry, 26*(1), 1–26. https://doi.org/10.1080/1047840X.2014.940781

Gross, J. J. & Brett, B. Q. (Eds.) (2024), *Handbook of emotion regulation* (3rd ed.). The Guilford Press.

Hamaker, E. L. (2023). The within-between dispute in cross-lagged panel research and how to move forward. *Methods, 31*(1), 56–76. https://doi.org/10.1037/met0000600

Hamaker, E. L., Kuiper, R. M., & Grasman, R. P. P. P. (2015). A critique of the cross-lagged panel model. *Psychological Methods, 20*(1), 102–116. https://doi.org/10.1037/a0038889

Hart, S. A., & Ganley, C. M. (2019). The nature of math anxiety in adults: Prevalence and correlates. *Journal of Numerical Cognition, 5*(2), 122–139. https://doi.org/10.5964/jnc.v5i2.195

Hatfield, E., Cacioppo, J. T., & Rapson, R. L. (1994). *Emotional contagion.* Cambridge University Press.

Heckhausen, H. (1991). *Motivation and action.* Springer.

Hofstede, G. (2011). Dimensionalizing cultures: The Hofstede model in context. *Online Readings in Psychology and Culture, 2*(1). https://doi.org/10.9707/2307-0919.1014

Hulleman, C. S., & Harackiewicz, J. M. (2021). The utility-value intervention. In G. M. Walton & A. J. Crum (Eds.), *Handbook of wise interventions: How social psychology can help people change* (pp. 100–125). The Guilford Press.

Kahneman, D., & Tversky, A. (1979). Prospect theory: An analysis of decision under risk. *Econometrica, 47*(2), 263–292. https://doi.org/10.2307/1914185

Kanfer, F. H. (1971). The maintenance of behavior by self-generated stimuli and reinforcement. In A. Jacobs & L. B. Sachs (Eds.), *The psychology of private events* (pp. 39–59). Academic Press.

Kapur, M. (2024). *Productive failure: Unlocking deeper learning through the science of failing.* Wiley. https://doi.org/10.1002/9781394308712

Kraut, R. (2022). Aristotle's ethics. In E. N. Zalta & U. Nodelman (Eds.), *The Stanford encyclopedia of philosophy (Fall 2022 edition).* https://plato.stanford.edu/archives/fall2022/entries/aristotle-ethics/

Lewin, K. (1936). *Principles of topological psychology.* McGraw-Hill. https://doi.org/10.1037/10019-000

Linnenbrink-Garcia, L., Pekrun, R., & Patall, E. A. (2016). Adaptive motivation and emotion in education: Research and principles for instructional design. *Policy Insights from the Behavioral and Brain Sciences, 3*(2), 228–236. https://doi.org/10.1177/2372732216644450

Marsh, H. W. (1987). The big-fish-little-pond effect on academic self-concept. *Journal of Educational Psychology, 79*(3), 280–295. https://doi.org/10.1037/0022-0663.79.3.280

Marsh, H. W., Parker, P. D., Guo, J., Pekrun, R., & Basarkod, G. (2020). Psychological comparison processes and self-concept in relation to five distinct frame-of-reference effects: Pan-human cross-cultural generalizability over 68 countries. *European Journal of Personality, 34*(2), 180–202. https://doi.org/10.1002/per.2232

Marsh, H. W., Parker, P. D., & Pekrun, R. (2019). Three paradoxical effects on academic self-concept across countries, schools, and students: Frame-of-reference as a unifying theoretical explanation. *European Psychologist, 24*(3), 231–242. https://doi.org/10.1027/1016-9040/a000332

Marsh, H. W., Pekrun, R., Guo, J., Hattie, J., & Eyal, K. (2023). Too much of a good thing might be bad: The double-edged sword of parental aspirations and the adverse effects of aspiration-expectation gaps. *Educational Psychology Review, 35*, 49. Article number. https://doi.org/10.1007/s10648-023-09768-8

Marsh, H. W., Reeve, J., Guo, J., Pekrun, R., Parada, R. H., Parker, P. D., Basarkod, G., Craven, R., Jang, H.-R., Dicke, T., Ciarrochi, J., Sahdra, B., Devine, E. K., & Cheon, S. H. (2023). Overcoming limitations in peer victimization research that impede successful intervention. *Perspectives on Psychological Science, 18*(4), 812–828.

Matthews, G., Zeidner, M., & Roberts, R. D. (2002). *Emotional intelligence: Science and myth.* The MIT Press.

Meehl, P. E. (1967). Theory-testing in psychology and physics: A methodological paradox. *Philosophy of Science, 34*(2), 103–115. https://doi.org/10.1086/288135

Meinhardt, J., & Pekrun, R. (2003). Attentional resource allocation to emotional events: An ERP study. *Cognition & Emotion, 17*(3), 477–500. https://doi.org/10.1080/02699930244000039

Menninghaus, W., Wagner, V., Wassiliwizky, E., Schindler, I., Hanich, J., Jacobsen, T., & Koelsch, S. (2019). What are aesthetic emotions? *Psychological Review, 126*(2), 171–195. https://doi.org/10.1037/rev0000135

Merriam-Webster. (2024). *Regulation.* Merriam-Webster Dictionary. https://www.merriam-webster.com/dictionary/regulation. Accessed on Dec 5, 2024.

Mikels, J. A., & Reuter-Lorenz, P. A. (2019). Affective working memory: An integrative psychological construct. *Perspectives on Psychological Science, 14*(4), 543–559. https://doi.org/10.1177/1745691619837597

Mischel, W. (1973). Toward a cognitive social learning reconceptualization of personality. *Psychological Review, 80*(4), 252–283. https://doi.org/10.1037/h0035002

Modirshanechi, A., Brea, J., & Gerstner, W. (2022). A taxonomy of surprise definitions. *Journal of Mathematical Psychology, 110,* Article 102712. https://doi.org/10.1016/j.jmp.2022.102712

Montague, M. (2009). The logic, intentionality, and phenomenology of emotion. *Philosophical Studies, 145*(2), 171–192. https://doi.org/10.1007/s11098-008-9218-0

Murayama, K., Goetz, T., Malmberg, L.-E., Pekrun, R., Tanaka, A., & Martin, A. J. (2017). Within-person analysis in educational psychology: Importance and illustrations. In D. W. Putwain & K. Smart (Eds.), *British Journal of Educational Psychology Monograph Series II: Psychological aspects of education – current trends: The role of competence beliefs in teaching and learning* (pp. 71–87). Wiley.

Murayama, K., Pekrun, R., Suzuki, M., Marsh, H. W., & Lichtenfeld, S. (2016). Don't aim too high for your kids: Parental over-aspiration undermines students' learning in mathematics. *Journal of Personality and Social Psychology, 111*(5), 166–179. https://doi.org/10.1037/pspp0000079

Neta, M., & Kim, M. J. (2023). Surprise as an emotion: A response to Ortony. *Perspectives on Psychological Science, 18*(4), 854–862. https://doi.org/10.1177/17456916221132789

OECD [Organization for Economic Cooperation and Development]. (2017). *PISA 2015 results (volume 3): Students' well-being.* OECD Publishing. https://doi.org/10.1787/9789264273856-en

Oxford English Dictionary, s.v. (2024, September). *well-being (n.).* https://doi.org/10.1093/OED/7175092406

Pekrun, R. (1988). *Emotion, Motivation und Persönlichkeit* (*Emotion, motivation, and personality*). Psychologie Verlags Union.

Pekrun, R. (1993). Facets of students' academic motivation: A longitudinal expectancy-value approach. In M. Maehr & P. Pintrich (Eds.), *Advances in motivation and achievement* (Vol. 8, pp. 139–189. JAI Press.

Pekrun, R. (2000). A social cognitive, control-value theory of achievement emotions. In J. Heckhausen (Ed.), *Motivational psychology of human development* (pp. 143–163). Elsevier Science.

Pekrun, R. (2006). The control-value theory of achievement emotions: Assumptions, corollaries, and implications for educational research and practice. *Educational Psychology Review, 18*(4), 315–341. https://doi.org/10.1007/s10648-006-9029-9

Pekrun, R. (2014). *Emotions and learning (educational practices series,* (Vol. 24). International Academy of Education (IAE) and International Bureau of Education (IBE) of the United Nations Educational, Scientific and Cultural Organization (UNESCO). http://www.iaoed.org/downloads/edu-practices_24_eng.pdf

Pekrun, R. (2018). Control-value theory: A social-cognitive approach to achievement emotions. In G. A. D. Liem & D. M. McInerney (Eds.), *Big theories revisited 2: A volume of research on sociocultural influences on motivation and learning* (pp. 162–190). Information Age Publishing.

Pekrun, R. (2020). Self-report is indispensable to assess students' learning. *Frontline Learning Research, 8*(3), 185–193. https://doi.org/10.14786/flr.v8i3.637

Pekrun, R. (2021). Self-appraisals and emotions: A generalized control-value approach. In T. Dicke, F. Guay, H. W. Marsh, R. G. Craven, & D. M. McInerney (Eds.), *Self – a multidisciplinary concept* (pp. 1–30). Information Age Publishing.

Pekrun, R. (2023). Dissecting the elephant: Cognition, emotion, and motivation as distinct but intertwined entities. In M. Bong, J. Reeve, & S. Kim (Eds.), *Motivation science: Controversies and insights* (pp. 227–231). Oxford University Press. https://doi.org/10.1093/oso/9780197662359.003.0038

Pekrun, R. (2024). Control-value theory: From achievement emotion to a general theory of human emotions. *Educational Psychology Review, 36,* Article 83. https://doi.org/10.1007/s10648-024-09909-7

Pekrun, R., & Goetz, T. (2024a). Boredom: A control-value theory approach. In M. Bieleke, W. Wolff, & C. Martarelli (Eds.), *The Routledge international handbook of boredom* (pp. 74–89). Routledge.

Pekrun, R., & Goetz, T. (2024b). How universal are academic emotions? A control-value theory perspective. In G. Hagenauer, R. Lazarides, & H. Järvenoja (Eds.), *Motivation and emotion in learning and teaching across educational contexts: Theoretical and methodological perspectives and empirical insights* (pp. 85–99). Taylor & Francis.

Pekrun, R., Goetz, T., Titz, W., & Perry, R. P. (2002). Academic emotions in students' self-regulated learning and achievement: A program of qualitative and quantitative research. *Educational Psychologist, 37*(2), 91–105. https://doi.org/10.1207/S15326985EP3702_4

Pekrun, R., Lichtenfeld, S., Marsh, H. W., Murayama, K., & Goetz, T. (2017). Achievement emotions and academic performance: Longitudinal models of reciprocal effects. *Child Development, 88*(5), 1653–1670. https://doi.org/10.1111/cdev.12704

Pekrun, R., & Linnenbrink-Garcia, L. (2022). Academic emotions and student engagement. In A. L. Reschly & S. L. Christenson (Eds.), *The handbook of research on student engagement* (2nd ed., pp. 109–132). Springer.

Pekrun, R., Marsh, H. W., Elliot, A. J., Stockinger, K., Perry, R. P., Vogl, E., Goetz, T., van Tilburg, W. A. P., Lüdtke, O., & Vispoel, W. P. (2023). A three-dimensional taxonomy of achievement emotions. *Journal of Personality and Social Psychology, 124*(1), 145–178. https://doi.org/10.1037/pspp0000448

Pekrun, R., Marsh, H. W., Suessenbach, F., Frenzel, A. C., & Goetz, T. (2023). School grades and students' emotions: Longitudinal models of within-person reciprocal effects. *Learning and Instruction, 83,* Article 101626. https://doi.org/10.1016/j.learninstruc.2022.101626

Pekrun, R., Murayama, K., Marsh, H. W., Goetz, T., & Frenzel, A. C. (2019). Happy fish in little ponds: Testing a reference group model of achievement and emotion. *Journal of Personality and Social Psychology, 117*(1), 166–185. https://doi.org/10.1037/pspp0000230

Pekrun, R., & Perry, R. P. (2014). Control-value theory of achievement emotions. In R. Pekrun & L. Linnenbrink-Garcia (Eds.), *International handbook of emotions in education* (pp. 120–141). Taylor & Francis.

Perry, R. P., Chipperfield, J. G., Hladkyj, S., Pekrun, R., & Hamm, J. M. (2014). Attribution-based treatment interventions in some achievement settings. In S. Karabenick & T. C. Urdan (Eds.), *Advances in motivation and achievement* (Vol. 18, pp. 1–35). Emerald. https://doi.org/10.1108/s0749-742320140000018000

Putwain, D. W., Pekrun, R., Nicholson, L. J., Symes, W., Becker, S., & Marsh, H. W. (2018). Control-value appraisals, enjoyment, and boredom in mathematics: A longitudinal latent interaction analysis. *American Educational Research Journal, 55*(6), 1339–1368. https://doi.org/10.3102/0002831218786689

Reisenzein, R., Horstmann, G., & Schützwohl, A. (2019). The cognitive-evolutionary model of surprise: A review of the evidence. *Topics in Cognitive Science, 11*, 50–74. https://doi.org/10.1111/tops.12292

Robinaugh, D. J., Haslbeck, J. M. B., Ryan, O., Fried, E. I., & Waldorp, L. J. (2021). Invisible hands and fine calipers: A call to use formal theory as a toolkit for theory construction. *Perspectives on Psychological Science, 16*(4), 725–743. https://doi.org/10.1177/1745691620974697

Roth, G., Vansteenkiste, M., & Ryan, R. M. (2019). Integrative emotion regulation: Process and development from a self-determination theory perspective. *Development and Psychopathology, 31*(3), 945–956. https://doi.org/10.1017/S0954579419000403

Rotter, J. B. (1954). *Social learning and clinical psychology*. Prentice-Hall. https://doi.org/10.1037/10788-000

Russell, J. A., & Barrett, L. F. (1999). Core affect, prototypical emotional episodes, and other things called emotion: Dissecting the elephant. *Journal of Personality and Social Psychology, 76*(5), 805–819. https://doi.org/10.1037/0022-3514.76.5.805

Ryan, R. M., & Deci, E. L. (2017). *Self-determination theory: Basic psychological needs in motivation, development, and wellness*. The Guilford Press. https://doi.org/10.1521/978.14625/28806

Ryan, R. M., Deci, E. L., Grolnick, W. S., & La Guardia, J. G. (2006). The significance of autonomy and autonomy support in psychological development and psychopathology. In D. Cicchetti & D. Cohen (Eds.), *Developmental psychopathology: Vol. 1. Theory and methods* (2nd ed., pp. 295–849). Wiley.

Scarantino, A., & de Sousa, R. (2018). Emotion. In N. Zalta (Ed.), *The Stanford encyclopedia of philosophy (Winter 2018 Edition)*. https://plato.stanford.edu/archives/win2018/entries/emotion/

Scherer, K. R., & Moors, A. (2019). The emotion process: Event appraisal and component differentiation. *Annual Review of Psychology, 7*, 719–745. https://doi.org/10.1146/annurev-psych-122216-011854

Scherer, K. R., Schorr, A., & Johnstone, T. (Eds.) (2001), *Appraisal processes in emotion: Theory, methods, research*. Oxford University Press.

Schmitz, B., & Skinner, E. (1993). Perceived control, effort, and academic performance: Interindividual, intraindividual, and multivariate time-series analyses. *Journal of Personality and Social Psychology, 64*(6), 1010–1028. https://doi.org/10.1037/0022-3514.64.6.1010

Schubert, S., Ufer, S., & Pekrun, R. (2025). *Both positive and negative emotions can boost mathematical reasoning.* Manuscript in preparation.

Schwarz, N., & Clore, G. L. (2003). Mood as information: 20 years later. *Psychological Inquiry, 14*(3–4), 296–303. https://doi.org/10.1207/S15327965PLI1403&4_20

Segerstrom, S. C., & Miller, G. E. (2004). Psychological stress and the human immune system: A meta-analytic study of 30 years of inquiry. *Psychological Bulletin, 130*(4), 601–630. https://doi.org/10.1037/0033-2909.130.4.601

Shao, K., Pekrun, R., Marsh, H. W., & Loderer, K. (2020). Control-value appraisals, achievement emotions, and foreign language performance: A latent interaction analysis. *Learning and Instruction, 69,* 101356. Article. https://doi.org/10.1016/j.learninstruc.2020.101356

Sherman, R. A., Rauthmann, J. F., Brown, N. A., Serfass, D. G., & Jones, A. B. (2015). The independent effects of personality and situations on real-time expressions of behavior and emotion. *Journal of Personality and Social Psychology, 109*(5), 872–888. https://doi.org/10.1037/pspp0000036

Sosnowska, J., Kuppens, P., De Fruyt, F., & Hofmans, J. (2020). New directions in the conceptualization and assessment of personality—A dynamic systems approach. *European Journal of Personality, 34*(6), 988–998. https://doi.org/10.1002/per.2233

Stockinger, K., Dresel, M., Marsh, H. W., & Pekrun, R. (2025). Strategies for regulating achievement emotions: Conceptualization and relations with university students' emotions, well-being, and health. *Learning and Instruction, 98,* Article 102089. https://doi.org/10.1016/j.learninstruc.2025.102089

Vansteenkiste, M., Ryan, R. M., & Soenens, B. (2020). Basic psychological need theory: Advancements, critical themes, and future directions. *Motivation and Emotion, 44,* 1–31. https://doi.org/10.1007/s11031-019-09818-1

Voelkle, M. C., Brose, A., Schmiedek, F., & Lindenberger, U. (2014). Towards a unified framework for the study of between-person and within-person structures: Building a bridge between two research paradigms. *Multivariate Behavioral Research, 49,* 193–213. https://doi.org/10.1080/00273171.2014.889593

Vogl, E., Pekrun, R., Murayama, K., & Loderer, K. (2020). Surprised–curious–confused: Epistemic emotions and knowledge exploration. *Emotion, 20*(4), 625–641. https://doi.org/10.1037/emo0000578

von Bertalanffy, L. (1968). *General systems theory. Foundations, development, applications.* George Braziller.

Watkins, E. R., Warren, F. C., Newbold, A., Taylor, R. S., Hulme, C., Cranston, T., Aas, B., Bear, H., Botella, C., Burkhardt, F., Ehring, T., Fazel, M., Fontaine, J. R. J., Frost, M., Garcia-Palacios, A., Greimel, E., Hoessle, C., Hovasapian, A., Huyghe, V. E. I., … Voss, M. (2024). Emotional competence self-help mobile app versus cognitive-behavioural self-help app versus self-monitoring app to promote wellbeing in healthy young adults (ECoWeB PROMOTE): An international parallel randomised controlled trial. *The Lancet Digital Health, 6*(12), e904–e913. https://doi.org/10.1016/S2589-7500(24)00149-3

Weiner, B. (1985). An attributional theory of achievement motivation and emotion. *Psychological Review, 92*(4), 548–573.

Woodworth, R. S. (1921). *Psychology: A study of mental life.* Henry Holt. https://doi.org/10.1037/13976-000

Zeidner, M. (1998). *Test anxiety: The state of the art.* Plenum.

Zeidner, M. (2014). Anxiety in education. In R. Pekrun & L. Linnenbrink-Garcia (Eds.), *International handbook of emotions in education* (pp. 265–288). Taylor & Francis.

APPENDIX: GLOSSARY OF BASIC CVT TERMS.

Term	Explanation
Dimensions of Emotions	
Valence	Pleasantness; positive = pleasant, negative = unpleasant
Activation	Physiological arousal (activating vs. deactivating)
Object focus	Relation of emotion with object, defined by type of object and temporal relation with object
Object	Real or fictitious phenomenon an emotion can relate to (event, situation, activity, person, material object, idea)
Temporal relation	Prospective (immediate or distant future); concurrent (simultaneous); retrospective (immediate or distant past)
Categories of emotions	
Achievement emotions	Related to activities and outcomes judged by competence standards of quality
Epistemic emotions	Related to knowledge generation
Social emotions	Related to other individuals (other-related) or socially defined aspects of self (self-related)
Existential emotions	Related to health, life, illness, death
Appraisals	
Action-control expectancy	Expectancy to be able to execute an action
Action-outcome expectancy	Expectancy that the action will cause an outcome
Situation-outcome expectancy	Expectancy that the situation will cause an outcome
Causal attribution	Attribution of actions and outcomes to causes

Term	Explanation
Internal causal attribution	Attribution of outcomes to one's own action, or action to one's own intention
External causal attribution	Attribution of actions and outcomes to situation
Value	Desirability; positive = desirable, negative = undesirable
Intrinsic value	Action/outcome is desirable or undesirable for its own sake
Extrinsic value	Action/outcome is desirable or undesirable due to its consequences
Mechanisms mediating emotion effects	
Cognitive resources	Resources of working memory; attention
Intrinsic motivation	Motivation to perform action for its own sake
Extrinsic motivation	Motivation to perform action in order to attain outcomes
Self-regulation	Oneself defines goals, strategies, monitoring, and evaluation of actions
External regulation	Others define goals, strategies, monitoring, and evaluation of actions
Emotion regulation	
Person-oriented regulation	Developing one's competencies and personality
Situation-oriented regulation	Selecting and modifying situations
Perceptual regulation	Focusing or distracting attention
Cognitive regulation	Changing appraisals and cognitive perspectives
Response modulation	Changing arousal and expression

CHAPTER 4

ACHIEVEMENT GOALS REVISITED: A SELF-BASED PERSPECTIVE

Mimi Bong
Korea University, South Korea

Seohee Park
Korea University, South Korea

Dayeon Jeong
Korea University, South Korea

Sungwha Kim
Korea University, South Korea

ABSTRACT

Achievement goal theory has evolved over time, with different views about what the construct represents. Initially referred to as *goal orientation*, it was defined as the underlying reasons for engaging in achievement behavior and seen as a cognitive framework that individuals use to interpret and respond to achievement-related information. This definition was criticized for mixing up the reasons underlying achievement behavior and the aims individuals strive to attain. Also, mastery goal orientations focusing on learning and growth did not always predict better performance, while performance goal orientations

The Self in Context, pages 123–154

Published under exclusive licence by Emerald Publishing Limited
doi:10.1108/978-1-80686-869-820261004

focusing on demonstrating ability and outperforming others often led to higher anxiety but better performance. This ambiguity prompted researchers to redefine *achievement goals* solely as the aim of achieving competence. Despite this attempt for clarification, controversies persisted, and new questions arose regarding the motivational properties of these competence-driven aims. Some researchers proposed *goal complexes* in response, combining both the reasons for and the aims of achievement behavior back together. However, it remains unclear whether this effort can resolve existing issues or reinvigorate research on achievement goals. We argue that the problem may stem from the neglect of self-evaluation motives—internal reasons for behaving in specific ways and seeking particular types of information. We propose that incorporating these motives into the theory could provide fresh insights into understanding why and how different achievement goals influence learning and performance.

Keywords: Achievement goals; goal orientations; self-motives; goal complexes; self-processes

The definition of achievement goals has undergone several transformations since the construct made its debut. The original conceptualization emphasized the interpretive role of what was then called *goal orientations,* by defining them as a general cognitive framework used to construe and react to achievement-relevant information (Dweck & Leggett, 1988). This definition was criticized for lacking conceptual precision by intermixing the "reasons" and "aims" of achievement behaviors (Elliot, 1999). The failure of mastery goal orientations to consistently predict better performance, and the perplexing effects of performance goal orientations to predict both higher anxiety and better performance, were attributed to this definitional ambiguity.

Several attempts have been made to address this situation, primarily by reconceptualizing the construct. Performance goals have been bifurcated into performance-approach and performance-avoidance goals (Elliot & Harackiewicz, 1996), followed by a similar dichotomization of mastery goals (Elliot & McGregor, 2001). In addition, *achievement goals* have been redefined solely as the "aims" of competence-oriented behaviors, explicitly excluding their underlying reasons (Elliot & Thrash, 2001). Unfortunately, these revisions have only been partially successful in resolving the controversies. Separating performance-avoidance goals from performance-approach goals has not eliminated the mixed effects of performance-approach goals, leading to a further distinction between ability validation (or appearance) and normative competence (or competition) performance-approach goals (Grant & Dweck, 2003; Hulleman et al., 2010; Urdan & Mestas, 2006). Achievement goals, defined as competence-driven aims, have thus raised new questions about their motivational properties, as the construct has lost its initial appeal of explaining and predicting individuals' responses to failures and setbacks.

More recently, some researchers have proposed a new concept called *goal complexes* by essentially merging the reasons and the aims back together (Elliot & Sommet, 2023; Vansteenkiste et al., 2010, 2014). However, it remains unclear where this effort is headed or whether it can address existing issues and revitalize research on achievement goals. We contend that at least part of this lamentable state of affairs stems from the neglect of self-motives. In this chapter, we briefly summarize the evolution of achievement theory and research, along with its key findings, and propose a framework to integrate self-processes into the understanding of achievement goal effects.

INTUITIVE APPEAL OF THE EARLY CONCEPTUALIZATION OF ACHIEVEMENT GOALS

Goal Orientations as Underlying Causes of Motivational Patterns

Before the advent of the concept called goal orientation, *goals* typically specify what individuals seek to accomplish. Locke and Latham (2002) stated, "A goal is the object or aim of an action... to attain a specific standard of proficiency, usually within a specified time limit" (p. 705). The extensive body of literature on goal-setting is based on this definition of goals as key drivers of motivation, central to the conscious regulation of action. According to goal-setting theory, performance improves linearly with the increasing difficulty of the goals that individuals set for themselves or are assigned by others. Major mechanisms underlying goal-setting effects include focused attention to relevant actions, effective planning, automatic application of knowledge, greater effort expenditure, and prolonged persistence. These mediating processes are presumed to be facilitated by the direction offered and the satisfaction derived from successful goal attainment. Therefore, goals function as both guides for action and standards for evaluating the quality of performance.

Whereas goal-setting theory was proposed to explain variations in the level of performance, achievement goal theory was developed to account for two major response patterns toward failure: mastery-oriented and helpless responses (Dweck & Leggett, 1988). Rather than delineating the function and properties of discrete individual goals, the *goal orientation model* proposes two broad categories of goals. They are thought to represent the ultimate purpose or reason underlying individuals' achievement behaviors and to emanate from different implicit theories. Individuals who believe ability is malleable tend to be oriented toward *learning goals* and strive to develop their ability by learning from failures, whereas those who view ability as fixed are oriented toward *performance goals* and are concerned about documenting their ability by avoiding failures. Several features of this original conceptualization enabled achievement goal theory to gain immediate and widespread popularity.

Addressing a Key Question in Motivation

Understanding why and how individuals behave in achievement contexts is central to all motivation theories. Early research on achievement motivation theory by Atkinson (1964) provided a foundation for explaining behavior by showing that individuals differ in their levels of desire for excellence across achievement contexts. This foundational theory inspired the development of more focused theories that integrated both cognitive and emotional elements of goal-directed behavior. Brophy (2004) described how achievement motivation theory evolved into a family of theories, each emphasizing different aspects of broader themes. These include Dweck's (1986) implicit theories of intelligence, Weiner's (1979) attribution theory regarding success and failure, and Bandura's (1977) self-efficacy theory concerning perceptions of efficacy for attaining a desired outcome. These theories have all been applied to explore motivational differences in achievement settings.

Achievement goal theory not only explains differences in achievement and performance levels but also describes qualitative differences in the achievement process, such as the effort and strategies employed, preference for challenging tasks, anxiety levels, responses to setbacks, and depth of academic engagement. The theory has garnered significant attention in academic settings because it addresses the core question in achievement motivation: Why do individuals behave the way they do when faced with achievement tasks? The distinct motivational characteristics of each achievement goal illustrate major patterns of achievement behaviors and how individuals' perceptions of ability connect to their motivation.

Linking Children's Lay Theories to Their Goal Orientations

The implicit theories of intelligence suggest that children's tacit beliefs about the nature of ability influence their goal preferences in learning situations. They originated from Dweck's (1975) observations of children exhibiting drastically different reactions to failure. Some children displayed heightened negative emotional responses and sought to avoid subsequent tasks, leading to deteriorated performance. In contrast, other children showed resilience, demonstrating a desire to retry tasks, employing enhanced strategies, and investing greater effort after experiencing failure. Interviews revealed that these differing responses were associated with contrasting views about the nature of ability. This indicated that beliefs about ability affect attributions for failure, purposes of achievement pursuit, and subsequent behaviors.

Children who adhere to the *entity theory* believe that intelligence or ability is largely fixed and determined at birth, with little capacity for change despite effort. Conversely, those who adhere to the *incremental theory* view ability as malleable and capable of improvement through effort and new learning experiences. Dweck and her colleagues explored the relationship between children's implicit theories of intelligence and their goal orientations (Dweck & Elliott, 1983; Elliott & Dweck, 1988). They discovered that children who subscribe to the entity theory are oriented toward performance and more prone to feelings of helplessness when experiencing difficulties. In contrast, those who hold an incremental theory are oriented toward mastery and responding to setbacks in a more constructive manner.

Explaining the Decline in Children's Motivation Over Time

Studies have also shown that children typically exhibit high levels of motivation when they first enter school, but this motivation tends to wane as they progress through grades. This decline sparked scholarly interest, with Nicholls (1978) taking a leading role in investigating its causes. According to Nicholls, younger children believe that effort leads to ability, essentially equating effort with ability. However, as they grow, they begin to think that ability and effort are inversely related. In other words, they come to believe that achieving the same result requires less effort from individuals with higher ability but greater effort from those with lower ability. Consequently, children's understanding of the relationship between ability and effort influences the goals they pursue and their definitions of success in given situations. Dweck's implicit theories of intelligence align with Nicholls' (1984) findings. While younger children are more likely to believe that ability can improve through effort (aligning with the incremental theory), older children increasingly adopt the entity theory. This is consistent with the development of the inverse relationship between ability and effort suggested by Nicholls, further reinforcing the validity of Dweck's (1986) implicit theories and, more generally, goal orientation theory.

Empirical Legacy of Achievement Goal Research

Despite criticisms regarding the ambiguity of construct definitions and the resulting lack of consistency in empirical evidence, the early achievement goal orientation theory made significant contributions to understanding motivational phenomena. In particular, it excelled in predicting contrasting responses to failure and subsequent motivation, as well as the construal and willingness to pursue challenging tasks compared to other motivation constructs.

Coping With Failures and Setbacks

Through a substantial body of empirical findings that support its foundational principles (e.g., Elliott & Dweck, 1988; Graham & Golan, 1991; Grant & Dweck, 2003; Wolters et al., 1996), goal orientation theory has demonstrated its utility as a powerful framework for understanding students' motivation and behavioral patterns. Studies have confirmed that, whereas mastery goals produce positive outcomes, performance goals often lead to negative outcomes. Notably, evidence from this line of research suggests that the unique effects of mastery and performance goals become most evident during difficulties or setbacks (Chung et al., 2020; Elliott & Dweck, 1988; Grant & Dweck, 2003). Students' achievement goals, together with their implicit beliefs about the nature of ability, form a cognitive framework that guides how they understand and interpret achievement-related cues and respond to setbacks or failures (Dweck & Leggett, 1988; Kaplan & Maehr, 2007).

For mastery goal-oriented students who believe in the malleable nature of ability, performance outcomes are not viewed as fixed measures of their abilities. They perceive setbacks and failures as temporary obstacles that can be overcome through effort and the use of effective strategies, rather than as permanent deficits in their abilities. To these students, setbacks highlight areas for growth and improvement, serving as valuable opportunities to learn rather than threats to their self-worth. These cognitions help mastery goal-oriented students cope with setbacks in an adaptive and constructive manner. For instance, students with mastery goals often attribute failures to insufficient effort (Elliott & Dweck, 1988; Grant & Dweck, 2003). They are also less likely to experience anxiety in challenging situations; instead, they exhibit positive affect and sustained interest (Chung et al., 2020; Elliott & Dweck, 1988). With their primary focus on learning and personal growth, these students actively seek help from others when needed (Butler & Neuman, 1995; Ryan & Pintrich, 1997), employ effective and deep processing strategies (Grant & Dweck, 2003; Nolen, 1988; Stipek & Kowalski, 1989), and persevere through difficulties (Chung et al., 2020; Grant & Dweck, 2003).

In contrast, performance goals mainly operate under the belief that ability is inherent and fixed in nature (Dweck & Leggett, 1988). Students with performance goals thus perceive performance outcomes as a direct reflection of their unchangeable abilities. Successes are interpreted as validation of their competence, whereas failures and setbacks are seen as evidence of their permanent inadequacy. Consequently, these students show adaptive patterns when their competence is high or when they encounter no significant challenges. However, when faced with difficulties, they display maladaptive motivational and behavioral tendencies (Elliott & Dweck, 1988; Grant & Dweck, 2003). For example, they often blame their low abilities for their failures (Ames & Archer, 1988; Elliott & Dweck, 1988). They also exhibit heightened anxiety, a quick loss of interest (Chung et al., 2020;

Dykman, 1998), and reluctance to seek help (Butler & Neuman, 1995), due to the fear of exposing their incompetence. They often rely on ineffective surface processing strategies such as rote memorization, which may help them temporarily preserve their self-image, but do little to support meaningful learning (Elliott & Dweck, 1988; Meece et al., 1988; Nolen, 1988). Believing that their inadequacies are fundamental and there is nothing much they can do to change them, they withdraw their effort prematurely (Grant & Dweck, 2003).

The distinctive effects of mastery and performance goals in challenging situations are well illustrated in the seminal experiment by Elliott and Dweck (1988). They manipulated both achievement goal orientations (mastery vs. performance) and the perceived level of ability (high vs. low) among fifth-grade students; they then observed students' responses to continuous failure feedback in terms of their attributions, positive and negative affect, and strategy use. Key findings include significant differences in the frequency of ability attributions between low- and high-ability groups within the performance goal condition, but not in the mastery goal condition. Many performance goal-oriented students in the low-ability group attributed their failures to uncontrollable causes such as a lack of ability, and none attributed their failures to a lack of effort. Affective responses followed a similar pattern. Although neither the low- nor the high-ability group expressed negative affect in response to continuous failure feedback under the mastery-goal condition, the low-ability group was more likely to express negative affect compared to the high-ability group under the performance-goal condition. In addition, when mastery goals were highlighted, no differences emerged between the low- and high-ability groups in the effectiveness of strategies. When performance goals were emphasized, strategy effectiveness tended to worsen for low-ability students but to improve for high-ability students.

The differing effects of mastery (learning) and performance goals were echoed by Grant and Dweck (2003). They explored how different goal orientations influenced various cognitive, emotional, and behavioral coping in response to a hypothetical failure scenario (Study 4) and real-life challenges in a demanding college course (Study 5). Their results revealed that learning goals were linked to mastery-oriented behaviors, whereas performance goals were associated with a helpless response pattern. Students with learning goals viewed failure as a result of insufficient effort, maintained their interest, persisted, and sustained their performance. In contrast, students with performance goals attributed their failure to a lack of ability, lost interest, and withdrew from the task.

Willingness to Reengage and Embrace Challenges

In addition to shaping how students cope with failures, mastery goals and performance goals also create differences in how learners reengage with tasks following failure. Chung et al. (2020) examined how experimentally manipulated mastery and performance goals influence students' reengagement intentions after experiencing difficulties. Compared to students in the mastery-goal condition, a significantly fewer number of students in the performance-goal condition chose to reengage with the task. Performance goal-oriented students would have been less willing to return to activities where they previously failed and exposed their incompetence, to avoid further damage to their self-esteem. Quite the contrary, mastery goal-oriented students would have been more eager to reengage with the same tasks, driven by the belief that overcoming these challenges will contribute to their growth.

Such behavioral patterns are also evident in task-choice behaviors, particularly in students' tendency to seek challenges. Students with performance goals, compared to those with mastery goals, often prioritize protecting their self-image over learning, leading them to avoid challenges (Ames & Archer, 1988; Lee & Kim, 2014; Shim & Ryan, 2005). After experiencing setbacks and failures that reveal what they believe to be permanent ineptitude, it becomes important for them to further validate their competence. Consequently, they avoid situations that might expose their perceived deficiencies, even at the cost of valuable learning opportunities. By contrast, mastery goal-oriented students focus on their personal growth and skill development, which motivates them to embrace challenges as essential gateways for improving their abilities.

For instance, Shim and Ryan (2005) investigated the longitudinal relationship between students' achievement goals measured at the beginning of the semester, and their preference for avoiding challenging work assessed immediately after receiving grades. Their findings revealed that mastery goals were not a significant predictor of challenge avoidance, regardless of students' grades. Performance-approach goals, however, showed a distinct pattern. While these goals did not significantly predict challenge avoidance for students with high grades, they were significantly and positively associated with challenge avoidance among students with lower grades. This finding indicates that students pursuing performance goals tend to avoid challenging tasks after setbacks, which sacrifices opportunities for learning and development. This pattern is especially pronounced when low grades intensify feelings of inadequacy. Differences in re-engagement and task-choice behaviors thus underscore the harmful nature of performance goals.

ENHANCING PRECISION OR OVER-NARROWING THE CONSTRUCT DEFINITION?

As discussed above, earlier research on achievement goal orientation established its strength in explaining students' cognitive, affective, and behavioral responses in achievement-related contexts, particularly under ego-threatening or taxing conditions. Nonetheless, contrary to the originally hypothesized helpless patterns associated with performance goals, findings increasingly showed that performance goals were not always detrimental (e.g., Bouffard et al., 1995; Harackiewicz & Elliot, 1993; Harackiewicz et al., 1997). For example, performance goals were more beneficial than mastery goals for the course grades of college students and did not negatively predict interest or positively correlate with test anxiety (Harackiewicz et al., 1997). These findings compelled revisions to the original achievement goal theory.

Incorporating the Approach-Avoidance Distinction

In the mid-1990s, achievement goal theory underwent a notable development. The distinction between approach-avoidance orientations was integrated into the conceptualization of performance goals. Approach and avoidance motivation had been contrasted in the classic achievement motivation literature (Atkinson, 1957; McClelland, 1951), which was also reflected in earlier writings about achievement goals (e.g., Nicholls, 1984). Based on the literature, Elliot and his colleagues (e.g., Elliot & Church, 1997; Elliot & Harackiewicz, 1996), as well as other researchers at that time (Middleton & Midgley, 1997; Skaalvik, 1997; Vandewalle, 1997), argued for the need to bring the avoidance-related aspects of performance goals back into achievement goal theory.

Performance-Approach Goals Versus Performance-Avoidance Goals

Individuals endorsing *performance-approach goals* operate to demonstrate their superior competence to that of others, whereas those with *performance-avoidance goals* function to prevent negative evaluation of their competence compared to others (Elliot & Harackiewicz, 1996). By partitioning the performance goal construct into the opposite motivational directions, the detrimental effects of performance goals are specifically linked to performance-avoidance goals (Elliot & Church, 1997; Elliot & Harackiewicz, 1996). The nuanced understanding of performance goals was expected to improve the precision of achievement goal theory.

Elliot and Harackiewicz (1996) conducted experiments to show that performance-avoidance goals indeed yield maladaptive effects on intrinsic motivation compared to the approach counterpart. Two experiments demonstrated that performance-avoidance goals decreased the time spent on the task and enjoyment of the task through reduced task involvement. These experimental findings were further extended into college students' achievement goals in a psychology course (Elliot & Church, 1997). In addition to proving once again that performance-avoidance goals negatively predict, while mastery goals positively predict, students' intrinsic motivation, the goals' relationships with antecedents and consequences were tested. Both mastery goals and performance-approach goals were characterized by high achievement motivation and competence expectancy, suggesting the common approach basis of both goals. However, performance-approach goals were also defined by fear of failure, thus showing similarity with performance-avoidance goals that were predicted by low competence expectancy and high fear of failure. For intrinsic motivation, mastery goals were beneficial, but performance-avoidance goals were not. For graded performance, performance-approach and performance-avoidance goals were, respectively, a positive and a negative predictor, whereas mastery goals did not show any predictive power. In short, performance-approach goals shared antecedents and outcomes with both mastery goals and performance-avoidance goals.

This trichotomous conceptualization received much attention from achievement goal researchers. Metaanalytical investigations have constantly documented the divergent effects of performance-approach and performance-avoidance goals. Rawsthorne and Elliot's (1999) early meta-analysis on experiments regarding the relationship between achievement goals and intrinsic motivation revealed that applying the approach-avoidance distinction helped clarify the performance goals' predictive relationships with intrinsic motivation: Only performance-avoidance goals showed a clear undermining effect, unlike performance-approach goals. Other meta-analyses have also highlighted the detrimental role of performance-avoidance goals, such as their positive associations with negative emotions and internalizing problems, negative or null associations with positive emotions and achievement, in contrast to the rather adaptive roles of performance-approach goals and/or mastery goals (Bross et al., 2024; Diaconu-Gherasim et al., 2024; Huang, 2011; Hulleman et al., 2010).

Mastery-Approach Goals Versus Mastery-Avoidance Goals

As demonstrated by the meta-analyses, the introduction of the approach-avoidance distinction into performance goals enhanced the precision of the theory. The trichotomous model proved more effective than the dichotomous model in predicting and explaining outcomes. However, applying the approach-avoidance distinction to mastery goals has been less successful. *Mastery-avoidance goals*, defined as the goal to prevent losing knowledge or skills, were proposed to be another important component of achievement goals at the start of the 2000s (Elliot, 1999; Elliot & McGregor, 2001). Nevertheless, the 2 × 2 model, including both mastery and performance goals in approach and avoidance forms, did not receive as much theoretical and empirical support as the trichotomous model. Mastery-avoidance goals were criticized for their empirical overlap with both mastery-approach and performance-avoidance goals (Bong, 2009), for their absence in young students' instant repertoire of their achievement goals, which questions the goals' psychological validity (Lee & Bong, 2016), and for the metaanalytically unverifiable factor structure of the 2 × 2 framework that contains mastery-avoidance goals (Strunk et al., 2020).

Normative Versus Appearance Performance Goals

Furthermore, despite the benefits that the trichotomous framework brought to literature, the theory still had room for gaining greater accuracy because weak and inconsistent predictive power had been observed for performance-approach goals (e.g., Huang, 2011; Rawsthorne & Elliot, 1999). To resolve this issue, Hulleman et al. (2010) examined the heterogeneity in the definitions and measurements of performance-approach goals in extant research. Their meta-analysis indicated that the predictive relationship of performance-approach goals with academic performance depends on the content of the items used to measure the goal. *Normative performance-approach goals* with which learners strive to outperform others were positively connected to performance ($\hat{r}$ = 0.14). However, *appearance* and *evaluative performance-approach goals* with which learners engage in achievement behaviors to appear able in front of others—a construct close to the original conceptualization of performance goals—displayed a negative association with performance ($\hat{r}$ = −0.14). Senko and Dawson's (2017) meta-analysis further supported that normative and appearance performance-approach goals have discrete explanatory power, thus suggesting that the trichotomous achievement goal framework requires further revisions despite its theoretical contributions.

Redefining the Construct as Aims at the Expense of Its Unique Explanatory Power

Another significant theoretical transition is the shift in defining achievement goals from broad cognitive orientations or schemas to specific aims. The initial theories, such as the "goal orientation" framework, conceptualized achievement goals as underlying *reasons* for engaging in achievement tasks (Dweck, 1986; Nicholls, 1984). These reasons operate as motivational schemas and often involve motives such as personal growth or competence validation. With the introduction of the trichotomous achievement goal framework, however, Elliot and his colleagues (Elliot, 1999; Elliot & Thrash, 2001) proposed the "goal standard" model in which achievement goals were defined simply as specific *aims*, separate from the underlying reasons behind them. The researchers argue that this definition clarifies the goal construct by decoupling the motivational source (reason) from the directional guide (aim). Unlike reasons, which provide the psychological impetus for action, aims refer to the end-states or outcomes individuals intend to attain by engaging in achievement behaviors.

This revised approach to the construct shifted the focus explicitly to the pursuit of competence, as indicated by competence evaluation standards, in defining achievement goals (Elliot & McGregor, 2001). These standards are classified into three categories: absolute standards, which involve meeting the inherent requirements of a task such as mastering the material; intrapersonal standards, which focus on comparing one's current performance to past achievements or personal growth potential; and normative standards, which emphasize social comparative superiority and the desire to outperform others. While absolute and intrapersonal standards overlap conceptually due to their shared emphasis on competence improvement and task mastery, normative standards are distinct in their focus on interpersonal competition. Thus, mastery goals are associated with absolute and intrapersonal standards, while performance goals are linked to normative standards. Under this definition, performance-approach goals are characterized by the aim to outperform others (Elliot & Church, 1997; Elliot & McGregor, 2001). Notably, striving for self-presentation or the validation of competence is excluded altogether from the definition of achievement goals. Rather, these concerns are now considered part of the reasons for adopting performance goals, which may vary—to demonstrate competence to others, to enjoy a challenge, or to gain social approval (Elliot & McGregor, 2001).

Diminished Predictive Utility of the Newly Defined Performance Goal

Despite contributing to the conceptual clarity of the construct, redefining achievement goals as specific aims rather than broad orientations has raised debates about its potential to weaken the explanatory power of the original theory, particularly regarding performance-approach goals (Chung & Bong, 2017; Grant & Dweck, 2003; Senko & Tropiano, 2016; Urdan & Kaplan, 2020). Specifically, the goal standard model diminished the focus on the essence of competence validation in performance-approach goals. As discussed above, performance-approach goals are redefined as normative aims to outperform others, reflecting an interpersonal standard of competence. This change situates the concern for appearance and competence validation not as a distinct goal but as one of the many potential reasons for pursuing normative aims. However, such conceptualization risks curtailing the unique predictive power of performance goals, which have historically been associated with maladaptive achievement behaviors.

For example, Senko and Tropiano (2016) found that appearance goals (i.e., striving to demonstrate one's ability) positively predicted undesirable behaviors such as self-handicapping and help avoidance, while having no significant relationship with positive outcomes such as self-efficacy and interest. In contrast, normative goals predicted higher self-efficacy and showed no significant effects on maladaptive behaviors. These findings are generally consistent with those of Hulleman et al. (2010) and indicate that the distinct motivational processes underlying appearance goals may play a more central role than normative aims in contributing to negative achievement patterns. The exclusive focus on the end-states of achievement behaviors and the resultant conceptualization of performance goals as normative aims may obscure the unique explanatory utility that performance goals once offered in understanding detrimental motivational responses in achievement settings.

Achievement Goal Complexes: Reintegrating Reasons and Aims

As an alternative framework for understanding achievement goals, the *goal complex model* has garnered significant attention in recent years (Vansteenkiste et al., 2010, 2014). Whereas the *goal standard model* separates aims and reasons and focuses solely on aims, the goal complex model integrates aims and reasons into a single composite construct called an *achievement goal complex*. By distinguishing the *what* of goal pursuit (the standard or aim) from the *why* (the reasons for pursuing it), this model seeks to account for the interplay between the two dimensions in influencing behavior and outcomes.

The early goal complex model incorporates self-determination theory to explain why individuals pursue specific goals, distinguishing primarily between autonomous reasons and controlled reasons (Deci & Ryan, 2000). Autonomous reasons involve pursuing goals because they are enjoyable or personally meaningful, while controlled reasons stem from external pressures such as the desire to gain rewards or avoid guilt. The goal complex model explains that these reasons underlying goal pursuit may shape the effects of the goal complex, leading to varying outcomes. For instance, students pursuing a normative goal for autonomous reasons could experience heightened self-efficacy and interest, whereas those pursuing the same normative goal but driven by controlling reasons might display undesirable patterns such as self-handicapping or help-avoidance (Senko & Tropiano, 2016).

While this approach acknowledges the interplay between aims and reasons, a key limitation of the goal complex model is its failure to provide a clear answer to the nature of performance goals. Since its inception, achievement goal theory has gained prominence for highlighting the detrimental effects of performance goals on students' functioning, especially in the face of setbacks. According to the goal complex model, the effects of performance goals can differ widely, depending on the specific combination of aims and reasons. The same performance goal could lead to varying outcomes, contingent upon the reasons for pursuing that goal. This reasoning raises the question of whether the model is falsifiable, as any outcome—whether it aligns with or diverges from previous findings—can simply be attributed to different underlying reasons.

Consequences of Shifting Focus Away From the Self and Its Associated Implications for Ability

As outlined above, recent models of achievement goals have considered normative strivings as the central aspect of performance goals. The ability validation component in performance goals, once regarded as fundamental to achievement goal theory, has been de-emphasized (Elliot & Thrash, 2001). This shift in focus has come at a cost—it has diverted attention away from the self within achievement goal theory.

De-emphasizing the role of the self risks losing the explanatory power of achievement goals, particularly in illuminating one's responses to setbacks, a key strength of the original achievement goal orientation theory. Early research highlights that the type of achievement goals students pursue determines their reactions to failure (Elliott & Dweck, 1988; Grant & Dweck, 2003). Students with mastery goals remain resilient when experiencing difficulties, whereas those with performance goals, particularly the ones focused on demonstrating ability rather than improving it, succumb to challenges. The relative vulnerability of learners who adopt ability goals stems from how setbacks and obstacles are interpreted in relation to the self and its competence. For those with ability validation goals, failures are more likely to be perceived as reflections of their intelligence and ability. Failures and difficulties thus present direct threats to their sense of the self (Chung & Bong, 2017), triggering distinct maladaptive responses aimed at avoiding further damage to their self-worth, such as avoidance of help-seeking (Butler & Neuman, 1995) and reluctance to engage in challenging tasks subsequently (Ames & Archer, 1988; Lee & Kim, 2014).

Models that place normative striving at the core of performance goals do not report these distinct patterns. Learners who pursue normative forms of performance goals are not inherently vulnerable to failures or setbacks because impediments are not as directly tied to their self-worth and personal identity as they are to ability goals (Chung et al., 2020; McGregor & Elliot, 2002). Some findings even suggest that individuals with normative goals may function better under challenging situations. Senko et al. (2013) demonstrated that students who were instructed to adopt a performance goal of doing better than others performed better when the task was framed as challenging rather than simple (Study 1) and that the positive relationship between normative performance-approach goals and course grades was stronger in difficult courses (Study 2).

Within the research adopting normative performance goals, undesirable motivational and behavioral outcomes have been attributed largely to avoidance motives, hence performance-avoidance goals (Elliot & Church, 1997; Elliot & McGregor, 2001). However, maladaptive responses to obstacles and challenges may be better understood as stemming from the desire to preserve a positive self-image and protect self-worth, rather than merely to avoid normative inferiority (Chung et al., 2020; Elliott & Dweck, 1988).

Taken together, these findings underscore the importance of reinstating self-related processes as a core component of achievement goal theory, emphasizing their critical role in shaping motivation and goal pursuit. By re-integrating the self as a central feature of achievement goal processes, we can more comprehensively explain the diverse ways achievement goals influence student outcomes, particularly in challenging situations. The following section elaborates on the significance of re-centering self-related processes within achievement goal theory.

SELF-MOTIVES DRIVING ACHIEVEMENT GOALS

Although achievement goals have rarely been associated with self-evaluation motives (cf. Elliot et al., 2000; O'Keefe, 2013), the operation of different achievement goals may be driven by the factors that stimulate self-evaluation. Self-evaluation motives refer to the underlying psychological drives that steer self-evaluation and information processing to develop the sense of self (Sedikides & Strube, 1995, 1997). We argue that self-evaluation motives may provide deeper insights into the processes and effects of achievement goals.

Individuals almost always engage in self-evaluation, judging the diverse aspects of their subjective and socially constructed self-concepts (Sedikides & Strube, 1995). Striving toward better self-understanding is essential for individuals because it leads to better outcomes such as greater control, better predictability and coping, and more effective self-regulation. Self-evaluation processes help one to form a more sophisticated self-concept (Sedikides & Strube, 1995; Taylor et al., 1995). Especially in achievement-related situations, self-reflection on one's current state plays a critical role in initiating goal-directed behavior and self-regulated learning. The specific motive that drives this evaluative process determines the direction and form of subsequent behavior (Sedikides & Strube, 1997).

Of the diverse motives that propel self-evaluation, three prominent self-motives highlighted in the social psychological literature appear to be integral to the adoption and operation of achievement goals; they include self-enhancement, self-assessment, and self-improvement motives.[1] *Self-enhancement motives* are rooted in the assumption that self-protection and the desire to feel good about oneself are inherent aspects of human nature. These motives drive individuals to raise their self-esteem by maintaining a positive self-view and avoiding negative self-perceptions. Self-evaluation motivated by self-enhancement often accompanies selective filtering and interpreting of information in ways that favor the self. *Self-assessment motives* compel individuals to seek an accurate understanding of themselves, driving them to pursue stimuli that diminish uncertainty about the self. Self-evaluation motivated by self-assessment thus maximizes individuals' preference toward highly diagnostic information. Finally, *self-improvement motives* encourage individuals to actively engage in developing and enhancing specific aspects of themselves, going beyond merely maintaining a positive self-perception. The major function of self-improvement motives is to foster positive and long-term growth in one's skills and personality traits. Self-evaluation motivated by self-improvement guides individuals to detect helpful information from their own failures and from individuals with superior performance (for review, see Sedikides & Strube, 1997; Taylor et al., 1995).

According to Sedikides and Strube's (1997) self-evaluation model, different motives both compete and integrate to shape distinct tendencies in information-seeking, information-interpretation, and subsequent action. More importantly, certain motives become more prevalent in the given situation depending on factors such as individual differences, availability of information about the self, and the importance of the attribute under consideration. For example, when the self-attribute under evaluation is deemed unmodifiable but important, the need for accurate self-assessment would diminish. Whereas highly diagnostic tasks tend to trigger self-assessment motives, context-embedded threats against the self may instead instigate self-enhancing processes even when the task is informative about one's attribute.

Self-evaluation motives have also been suggested to play an important role within mindset meaning systems. Based on empirical findings on how individuals with either a fixed or a growth mindset function, O'Keefe (2013) linked self-improvement motives to a growth mindset and mastery goals, and self-enhancement motives to a fixed mindset and performance goals. His research illustrates how a different mindset makes certain self-evaluation motives more or less prevalent in the given circumstances to result in the adoption of a particular achievement goal. Understanding personal and contextual moderators of self-evaluation processes may thus help us gain further knowledge on how self-motives underlie the operation of achievement goals and manifest in different coping patterns in certain situations.

In the following section, we further elaborate on conceptual connections between self-evaluation motives and achievement goals to present a more nuanced understanding of different achievement goals. Relationships between self-motives and achievement goals are discussed based on theoretical assumptions and empirical evidence, followed by tentative hypotheses regarding the pattern of their interaction. It should be noted that we do not assume a strict one-to-one correspondence between a self-motive and an achievement goal, as multiple self-evaluation motives usually function hand-in-hand (Sedikides & Strube, 1997). Instead, we aim to illustrate how consideration of fundamental self-motives contributes to our understanding of the function and effects of achievement goals.

Self-Improvement and Self-Assessment Motives as Drivers of Mastery Goals

Mastery goals and self-improvement motives share an emphasis on personal growth and the development of competence. Their apparent alignment can be traced to the common underlying belief that one's abilities and traits are malleable and can improve through effort and perseverance (Dweck & Leggett, 1988; Nussbaum & Dweck, 2008; O'Keefe, 2013). Achievement goal research has highlighted that an incremental theory of intelligence promotes the pursuit of mastery goals because it encourages individuals to view challenges and setbacks as opportunities for new learning (Dweck & Leggett, 1988). Similarly, the self-improvement motive is tied to the perception that one's traits are modifiable, thus particularly prevailing among incremental theorists (Nussbaum & Dweck, 2008; O'Keefe, 2013; Trope et al., 2003). Individuals driven by self-improvement motives are armed with a strong sense of control over their personal development, treating obstacles and negative feedback as opportunities for remediation and growth.

The characteristics exhibited by individuals with self-improvement motives thus overlap with the tendencies commonly observed in individuals pursuing mastery goals. Grounded in incremental beliefs and a sense of internal controllability, students driven by mastery goals often demonstrate a willingness to re-attempt tasks after failure and actively seek opportunities to further refine their skills (Chung et al., 2020; Grant & Dweck, 2003). Similar to mastery goals, self-improvement motives have been shown to play an essential role in guiding how individuals process self-relevant information, particularly in response to negative feedback. For example, Trope et al. (2003) showed that individuals were more likely to seek negative feedback when they perceived their weaknesses as controllable or changeable. This relationship was mediated by the perceived informational value of negative feedback, reflecting the operation of self-improvement motives, as individuals prioritize information that highlights areas for improvement, even when it is emotionally aversive. The alignment between mastery goals and self-improvement motives is thus evident in their shared roles in promoting resilience and constructive engagement with negative feedback.

Green et al.'s (2009) Experiment 1 provides further evidence for this conjecture. Participants were either primed with self-improvement motives or not (i.e., control condition). Because the self-protection motive is the default mechanism for processing feedback, individuals tend to process negative, and thus self-threatening, feedback in a superficial manner, exhibiting a phenomenon known as "mnemic neglect." When mnemic neglect occurs, threatening feedback is selectively forgotten to protect one's central self-conceptions. Whereas participants in the control condition indeed showed this mnemic neglect by recalling positive feedback significantly more than negative feedback, those primed with self-improvement motives recalled both types of feedback to similar degrees. This finding indicates that self-improvement motives override self-protection motives, enabling individuals to process not only the positive but also the negative and threatening feedback constructively, even when the feedback challenges their self-worth. Just as mastery goals encourage individuals to embrace setbacks as opportunities for growth, self-improvement motives seem to foster a similar adaptive response to negative feedback, suggesting that these motives may guide individuals toward adopting mastery goals.

Personal growth is facilitated by an accurate diagnosis of one's competence, which serves as an instructive tool (Butler, 2000). The process of endorsing mastery goals, therefore, may also involve self-assessment motives. Self-assessment motives can manifest in two ways. First, students with mastery goals engage in self-assessment while using self-referential standards to appraise competence (Dweck & Leggett, 1988; Elliot & McGregor, 2001). Through intrapersonal and temporal evaluations, comparing one's present performance with their past performance on a given achievement task, learners strive for competence development. Second, mastery goals can facilitate social comparison not to outperform others but to learn and improve (Butler, 2000; Darnon et al., 2010; Régner et al., 2007). Such use of social comparison is regarded as a constructive metacognitive tool for learning that represents self-assessment motives, driven by the desire to objectively evaluate one's abilities and promote growth. Taken together, considering mastery goals as guided by growth-oriented self-motives, such as self-improvement and self-assessment motives, enriches our understanding of the adaptive nature of mastery goal orientation.

Self-Enhancement Motives and Contingent Self-Worth as Drivers of Ability Goals

Ability goals are closely tied to self-enhancement motives, as demonstrating positive outcomes and showcasing high competence lie at the heart of these goals. Although all achievement goals are intertwined with the universal tendency to pursue self-positivity (Sedikides & Strube, 1997; Taylor et al., 1995), self-enhancement motives are particularly relevant to ability goals as they encourage individuals to publicly demonstrate a positive self-image. Self-enhancement motives are assumed to be adaptive because they help individuals maintain a favorable view of themselves and protect their self-worth (Sedikides & Strube, 1997). The supportive nature of the self-enhancement motive aligns with the finding that ability goals are not necessarily harmful when prior performance is high—a condition in which a positive self-perception is naturally maintained (Grant & Dweck, 2003, Study 5).

However, when confronted with ego threats, neither self-enhancement motives nor ability goals effectively support genuine learning and growth. The self-enhancement motive shares a constellation of defensive reactions to threats with ability goals, including self-handicapping, reduced effort, and diminished focus on tasks when one experiences failure (O'Keefe, 2013). In particular, self-handicapping, an apparent behavioral manifestation of the self-enhancement motive to preserve positive self-views (Sedikides & Gregg, 2008; Sedikides & Strube, 1997), is a notable characteristic associated with ability goals. Students self-handicap to enhance their self-image when they are conscious about the public presentation of their ability (Shepperd & Arkin, 1989). Such defensive reactions to threats do not support further growth, which sharply contrasts with the motivational foundation of mastery goals discussed earlier.

Self-enhancement motives become stronger when individuals experience self-worth threats (Brown, 2012) and may turn into an even more defensive form of self-protection motives. While drawing a clear line between self-enhancement and self-protection can be challenging, self-enhancement generally refers to exaggerating one's contributions to positive outcomes in order to present oneself more favorably, whereas self-protection involves denying responsibility for negative outcomes to shield oneself from negative judgments. Self-protection is triggered when the threat to one's positive self-image intensifies, or when the ideal self feels unattainably distant from the current unsatisfactory self. This process distorts cognition to prevent a negative self-view from emerging (Alicke & Sedikides, 2009).

A recent neuro-experimental study by Shin et al. (2025) illustrates this point. The researchers compared the brain activation pattern during working memory and self-control tasks between two groups of participants. One group was instructed to prove their cognitive ability to an expert by performing well, thus manipulated to adopt an ability goal; the other group was told to outperform an ostensible competitor who was a confederate, thus guided to pursue a normative goal. Both groups then received bogus failure feedback. Pursuing ability goals and failing on tasks activated the precuneus, a brain region that processes information about the self. Furthermore, its activation was correlated with higher ratings of self-esteem but only in the ability goal condition. Presumably, participants with ability goals experienced a greater threat to their self-esteem from the failure feedback and engaged in self-protection by evaluating themselves more positively than warranted. This distortion was not observed among participants with normative goals.

By considering other self-related psychological constructs, such as the entity theory of intelligence and the contingency of self-worth on academic competence, together with the motives to save the positivity of the self, we can better understand the mechanism underlying ability goal-induced detriments under challenge. Since its theoretical inception, the ability-validation goal was conceptualized to be stemming out of the entity theory of intelligence (Dweck & Leggett, 1988). Students pursuing ability goals tend to believe intelligence, the attribute of which they want to retain positivity, is definitive rather than suggestive. Under this belief, performance failure directly denotes inadequate academic competence, and it would activate a greater degree of self-protection and avoidance of challenges.

The situation worsens when one's evaluation of self-worth is heavily tied to their academic competence, which they perceive as fixed and unchangeable. Contingency of self-worth refers to placing a high value on a specific domain so that one's successful engagement in it determines the perception of self-worth (Crocker & Wolfe, 2001). Because self-enhancement and self-protection motives often outweigh successful self-regulation or long-term growth, contingency of self-worth frequently leads to less focused task engagement. Moreover, it can cause significant damage to self-esteem when individuals fail in domains they deem important, inducing a collapse of their overall self-worth. The maladaptive impact of contingent self-worth becomes more pronounced during difficult tasks, leading individuals to abandon perseverance and resort to self-handicapping behaviors (Crocker et al., 2006).

For learners who endorse ability goals, who strive to demonstrate their ability in front of others and have it validated by receiving positive approval, the negative effect of contingent self-worth would prevail even more strongly. The disadvantages associated with ability-validation goals, therefore, can be traced back to their self-centered nature, intertwined with the contingency of self-worth and self-enhancement motives.

Self-Assessment and Self-Enhancement Motives as Drivers of Normative Goals

Conceptualization of normative goals may accommodate the coexistence of multiple self-motives in achievement contexts. This perspective aligns with Elliot's (1999), Elliot and Thrash's (2001) proposal of the goal standard framework, where he explicitly argued that the reasons underlying normative goals can vary. For instance, the desire to outperform others may originate from a need to assess one's competence objectively using normative benchmarks or from a need to demonstrate and validate one's abilities to others (Elliot & McGregor, 2001).

One prominent self-motive associated with normative goals would be self-assessment, given that pursuing normative goals requires individuals to evaluate their competence by comparing their performance with that of others. Butler (2000) showed that performance goals stimulate social comparison in an attempt to assess one's level of competence relative to others. Later, Elliot et al. (2018) demonstrated that both dispositional competitiveness and perceptions of a competitive environment are key predictors of normative goals, both of which accentuate social comparison and foster a heightened concern for one's competence compared to others. Adoption of normative goals, therefore, may arise from a strong desire to accurately assess one's competence.

Self-assessment motives in the pursuit of normative goals can play an informative role without necessarily exerting the definitive or threatening impact on self-worth that self-enhancement motives often have in ability-focused goals. Bounoua et al. (2012) found that students with normative goals tend to engage in upward social comparisons, comparing themselves to superior peers, when seeking information about their abilities. Upward comparisons can provide insights into how to improve current competencies and boost an aspiration for future success, as long as individuals believe in the possibility of change in their status (Lockwood & Kunda, 1997; Suls et al., 2002). Such positive role of self-assessment and upward comparison may explain why normative goals are not as strongly associated with maladaptive motivational patterns as ability goals (Chung et al., 2020; Grant & Dweck, 2003; Hulleman et al., 2010).

In social competition, success or failure depends not only on one's own ability but also on the opponents' performance or other situational factors. Excelling over or falling behind others does not necessarily imply a perpetual and absolute indicator of one's ability because outcomes can also be influenced by a host of other external factors. Given the fluid nature of interpersonal normative contexts, individuals may recognize a possibility to change their outcomes through effort or situational adjustments. This would be especially true when accompanied by the belief that increased effort can lead to future success (Noel et al., 1987), even if this belief is grounded in extrinsic motivation, such as to win and defeat others rather than intrinsic ones, such as for one's learning and development. In these cases, losing in a competition might be interpreted as a temporary setback that offers an understanding of one's current status and helps guide remedial actions for further improvement.

The other prominent self-mechanism associated with normative goals appears to be self-enhancement motives. Outperforming or surpassing others naturally enhances one's positive self-view. More importantly, while self-assessment motives often prompt the pursuit of normative goals and seeking informative feedback that helps diagnose one's standing, the dynamics may shift in the context of repeated failures or perceived threats to self-worth. When individuals perceive normative rankings as changing rather than fixed and see the possibility of improving their statuses through additional effort, self-assessment motives will remain the dominant self-evaluation motive. However, under conditions of repeated failures or seemingly insurmountable challenges, self-enhancement and self-protection motives are likely to emerge, as individuals prioritize preserving and safeguarding a positive self-image.

Prior research on self-evaluation motives partly supports this speculation. For example, Brown (1990, Experiment 2) found that, after experiencing success, individuals were more likely to seek additional information about their abilities. However, after failure, the desire for further evaluation decreased, particularly when feedback validity was high. These results suggest that, in the face of failure, the desire to maintain positive perceptions of the self likely outweighs the need for accurate self-assessment. Similarly, Sachs (1982) demonstrated that threats to self-concept reduced self-assessment motives. Relevant evidence from achievement goal research comes from Chung et al. (2020, Study 3). Compared to Studies 1 and 2, Study 3 adjusted the difficulty level of the experimental task to increase the perceived challenge. When the level of challenge substantially increased, the anxiety level of normative-goal students, which was significantly lower than that of ability-goal students in Studies 1 and 2, rose to a level comparable to that of ability-goal students. These findings suggest that the relative activation of self-assessment and self-enhancement motives during the pursuit of normative goals may be influenced by the experience of success and failure, as well as whether individuals attribute these outcomes to controllable factors.

The Self and Goal Processes in Achievement Contexts: Present Hypotheses

In this section, we summarize and extend our proposed approach by introducing our hypothesized model and suggesting directions for future research. We again emphasize that our framework does not suggest a direct one-on-one relationship between self-evaluation motives and achievement goals, nor do we argue that self-motives replace achievement goals. Rather, we propose that certain self-evaluation motives, activated by a combination of personal and contextual factors (Sedikides & Strube, 1995), facilitate the adoption of a specific achievement goal. Potential factors that "trigger" a particular self-motive can be broadly categorized into individual differences (e.g., growth vs. fixed mindset, perceived competence for a given task), task characteristics (e.g., task difficulty and diagnosticity, implications of task success and failure for one's ability), and achievement contexts (e.g., evaluation criteria introduced to students, social comparison and competition in the learning environment). While everyone possesses multiple self-evaluation motives, the prominence of specific motives, we conjecture, plays a critical role in determining which achievement goal individuals are more likely to endorse in the given circumstances. The hypothesized connections between triggers, self-motives, and achievement goals are depicted in Fig. 4.1.

Based on Fig. 4.1, we now illustrate our tentative hypotheses regarding how self-motives could function as drivers of achievement goals through examples. We believe self-improvement motives may serve as a key driver of mastery goals because both share an emphasis on learning and task mastery (Nussbaum & Dweck, 2008; O'Keefe, 2013; Sedikides & Strube, 1997). The purpose of self-improvement motives is to attain personal growth, which necessitates an accurate understanding of oneself as a prerequisite. The desire to accurately evaluate one's own competence and make informed adjustments to learning is represented by self-assessment motives. Under the dominant activation of self-improvement motives, self-assessment motives may also be stimulated and support the adoption of mastery goals (Butler, 2000). A student with a growth mindset (*individual difference*) facing a challenging task would believe that her competence can be developed through effort (Dweck & Leggett, 1988; Nussbaum & Dweck, 2008). This belief would prompt self-improvement motives to become predominant, even when the task is difficult (*task characteristic*) (O'Keefe, 2013). The

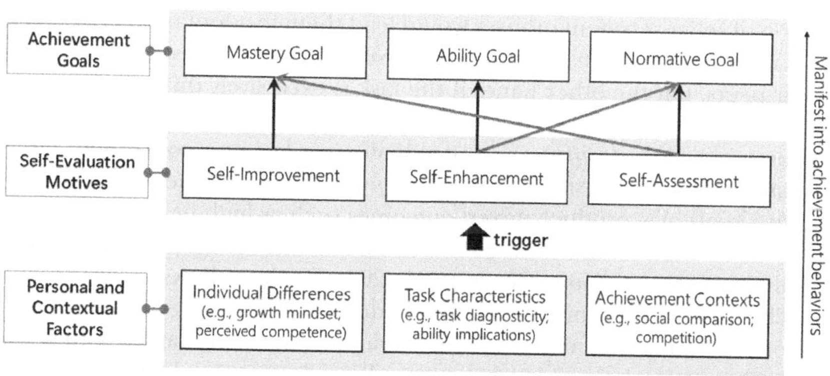

Fig. 4.1. Operation of the Self and Goal Processes Under Achievement Context.

tendency to act on self-improvement motives would be further reinforced in a learning environment that emphasizes intrapersonal and temporal evaluation rather than interpersonal or comparative assessments (*achievement context*) (Meece et al., 2006). Under these circumstances, learners with strong self-improvement motives would likely be drawn to mastery goals.

Self-enhancement motives, particularly when tied to contingent self-worth, may result in the adoption of ability goals. When individuals' self-worth is closely linked to their academic performance, self-enhancement motives may drive them to seek external validation of their abilities and avoid failure at all costs (Brown, 2012; Crocker et al., 2006). We assume this self-enhancement—ability validation association would become stronger, especially when individuals experience repeated failures or believe that improvement through effort is unattainable. Consider a student with a fixed mindset (*individual difference*) performing a difficult task reflecting one's ability (*task characteristic*), where test scores are made public (*achievement context*). Self-enhancement motives, rather than self-improvement or self-assessment motives, are likely to be activated because one's self-concept is at stake and there is a strong need to preserve a positive self-view (Nussbaum & Dweck, 2008; O'Keefe, 2013). As a consequence, learners would pursue ability goals and seek to demonstrate their competence.

We hypothesized that the adoption of normative goals may be influenced by both self-assessment and self-enhancement motives. The desire to compare oneself against others aligns with self-assessment motives, particularly in competitive environments where relative superiority is rewarded. For example, a highly competitive environment with a normative grading system (*achievement context*) would simultaneously elicit both self-enhancement and self-assessment motives. On the one hand, if perceived competence is high (*individual difference*), students would want to obtain information that can help them form a more accurate evaluation of their own academic competence (Bounoua et al., 2012; Lockwood & Kunda, 1997). The strong activation of self-assessment motives would lead them to adopt normative goals, striving to outperform others and assessing their relative standing among their peers. On the other hand, if the task is excessively difficult (*task characteristic*) and perceived competence decreases upon experiencing repeated failures (*individual difference*), individuals may become concerned about enhancing their self-esteem as well. When this happens, the pursuit of normative goals may produce mixed outcomes such as high performance coupled with high anxiety as both self-assessment and self-enhancement motives are in operation (Chung et al., 2020; Senko & Dawson, 2017).

The hypotheses generated above are derived from our review of relevant theories and the available yet limited evidence in the literature. Our ideas regarding the relationships between self-motives and achievement goals currently stay at the conceptual level, and more empirical research is required to test the proposed relationships. Investigations can start establishing if self-improvement, self-enhancement, and self-assessment motives under achievement contexts indeed predict the adoption of, respectively, mastery goals, ability goals, and normative goals. Another important avenue for future research involves examining the role of personal and contextual factors in the activation of each self-evaluation motive and subsequently the pursuit of achievement goals via self-motives. For instance, the hypothesized mitigating role of a growth mindset is of special interest. Studies could explore whether individuals with a growth mindset, compared to those with a fixed mindset, continue to act on self-improvement motives even in failure situations and maintain their mastery goals. Conversely, one can test if individuals who possess a fixed mindset prioritize self-enhancement in achievement situations and adopt ability validation goals to protect their self-worth.

It would also be interesting to investigate whether the activation of self-enhancement motives weakens the influence of self-assessment motives among students pursuing normative goals. Potential moderators, such as a fixed mindset, the ability implications of the task, repeated failures, or some combination of these factors, warrant consideration in this analysis. Finally, longitudinal studies could explore whether and how the activation patterns of self-motives evolve in response to salient personal and contextual factors, as well as their impact on achievement goal processing.

CONCLUSION

Achievement goal theories and research have undergone significant transformations since their inception. Some of these changes have been valuable in clarifying ambiguous findings and improving our understanding of the distinctive role played by each achievement goal. However, in the pursuit of greater theoretical precision, the empirical legacy of the original achievement goal orientation tradition has been overlooked, and the unique explanatory power of achievement goals has been diminished. We attribute this unfortunate state of affairs to the neglect of self-processes as key psychological mechanisms underlying achievement goal effects and propose a conceptual framework that integrates various self-motives into the understanding of these effects. While we acknowledge that our arguments are still largely speculative, we hope the theoretical connections and empirical findings presented in this chapter underscore the need to reconsider self-processes within the framework of achievement goal theory. We believe that examining the role of self-evaluation motives could revitalize achievement goal research, offering a more nuanced approach to understanding how motivation shapes performance and development.

ACKNOWLEDGEMENT

This work was supported by the Humanities and Social Sciences Institute Support Program through the Ministry of Education of the Republic of Korea and the National Research Foundation of Korea (NRF-2023S1A5C2A02095547) awarded to Mimi Bong.

NOTE

1. Scholars typically discuss four self-evaluation motives, including self-verification motives. Self-verification motives represent individuals' desire to confirm their known attributes, either positive or negative, to maintain stability in their self-views. These motives are presumed to operate when one is highly certain about an attribute and additional diagnostic information is unnecessary (Sedikides & Strube, 1997). Although supported well in the existing literature, they do not offer direct implications for the achievement goal processes and are hence excluded from the present discussion.

REFERENCES

Alicke, M. D., & Sedikides, C. (2009). Self-enhancement and self-protection: What they are and what they do. *European Review of Social Psychology*, *20*(1), 1–48. https://doi.org/10.1080/10463280802613866

Ames, C., & Archer, J. (1988). Achievement goals in the classroom: Students' learning strategies and motivation processes. *Journal of Educational Psychology*, *80*(3), 260–267. https://doi.org/10.1037/0022-0663.80.3.260

Atkinson, J. W. (1957). Motivational determinants of risk-taking behavior. *Psychological Review*, *64*(6), 359–372. https://doi.org/10.1037/h0043445

Atkinson, J. W. (1964). *An introduction to motivation*. D. Van Nostrand.

Bandura, A. (1977). Self-efficacy: Toward a unifying theory of behavioral change. *Psychological Review*, *84*(2), 191–215.

Bong, M. (2009). Age-related differences in achievement goal differentiation. *Journal of Educational Psychology*, *101*(4), 879–896. https://doi.org/10.1037/a0015945

Bouffard, T., Boisvert, J., Vezeau, C., & Larouche, C. (1995). The impact of goal orientation on self-regulation and performance among college students. *British Journal of Educational Psychology*, *65*(3), 317–329. https://doi.org/10.1111/j.2044-8279.1995.tb01152.x

Bounoua, L., Cury, F., Regner, I., Huguet, P., Barron, K. E., & Elliot, A. J. (2012). Motivated use of information about others: Linking the 2 × 2 achievement goal model to social comparison propensities and processes. *British Journal of Social Psychology*, *51*(4), 626–641. https://doi.org/10.1111/j.2044-8309.2011.02027.x

Brophy, J. (2004). *Motivating students to learn* (2nd ed.). Lawrence Erlbaum, Associates, Inc., Publishers.

Bross, T., Nett, U. E., & Daumiller, M. (2024). Interrelations among achievement goals and achievement emotions: A meta-analytic examination. *Educational Psychology Review, 36,* Article 98. https://doi.org/10.1007/s10648-024-09931-9

Brown, J. D. (1990). Evaluating one's abilities: Shortcuts and stumbling blocks on the road to self-knowledge. *Journal of Experimental Social Psychology, 26*(2), 149–167. https://doi.org/10.1016/0022-1031(90)90073-U

Brown, J. D. (2012). Understanding the better than average effect: Motives (still) matter. *Personality and Social Psychology Bulletin, 38*(2), 209–219. https://doi.org/10.1177/0146167211432763

Butler, R. (2000). Making judgments about ability: The role of implicit theories of ability in moderating inferences from temporal and social comparison information. *Journal of Personality and Social Psychology, 78*(5), 965–978. https://doi.org/10.1037/0022-3514.78.5.965

Butler, R., & Neuman, O. (1995). Effects of task and ego achievement goals on help-seeking behaviors and attitudes. *Journal of Educational Psychology, 87*(2), 261–271. https://doi.org/10.1037/0022-0663.87.2.261

Chung, Y., & Bong, M. (2017). Striving to validate competence versus striving to attain normative superiority: Two distinct motivational processes with different implications for the self. In F. Guay, H. Marsh, R. Craven, & D. McInerney (Eds.), *Self: Driving positive psychology and wellbeing* (pp. 27–49). Information Age.

Chung, Y., Bong, M., & Kim, S.-i. (2020). Performing under challenge: The differing effects of ability and normative performance goals. *Journal of Educational Psychology, 112*(4), 823–840. https://doi.org/10.1037/edu0000393

Crocker, J., Brook, A. T., Niiya, Y., & Villacorta, M. (2006). The pursuit of self-esteem: Contingencies of self-worth and self-regulation. *Journal of Personality, 74*(6), 1749–1772. https://doi.org/10.1111/j.1467-6494.2006.00427.x

Crocker, J., & Wolfe, C. T. (2001). Contingencies of self-worth. *Psychological Review, 108*(3), 593–623. https://doi.org/10.1037/0033-295X.108.3.593

Darnon, C., Dompnier, B., Gilliéron, O., & Butera, F. (2010). The interplay of mastery and performance goals in social comparison: A multiple-goal perspective. *Journal of Educational Psychology, 102*(1), 212. https://doi.org/10.1037/a0018161

Deci, E. L., & Ryan, R. M. (2000). The "what" and "why" of goal pursuits: Human needs and the self-determination of behavior. *Psychological Inquiry, 11*(4), 227–268. https://doi.org/10.1207/S15327965PLI1104_01

Diaconu-Gherasim, L. R., Elliot, A. J., Zancu, A. S., Brumariu, L. E., Măirean, C., Opariuc-Dan, C., & Crumpei-Tanasă, I. (2024). A meta-analysis of the relations between achievement goals and internalizing problems. *Educational Psychology Review, 36,* Article 109. https://doi.org/10.1007/s10648-024-09943-5

Dweck, C. S. (1975). The role of expectations and attributions in the alleviation of learned helplessness. *Journal of Personality and Social Psychology, 31*(4), 674–685.

Dweck, C. S. (1986). Motivational processes affecting learning. *American Psychologist, 41*(10), 1040–1048. https://doi.org/10.1037/0003-066X.41.10.1040

Dweck, C. S., & Elliott, E. S. (1983). Achievement motivation. In P. H. Mussen & E. M. Hetherington (Eds.), *Handbook of child psychology* (Vol. *4*, pp. 643–691). Wiley.

Dweck, C. S., & Leggett, E. L. (1988). A social-cognitive approach to motivation and personality. *Psychological Review, 95*(2), 256–273. https://doi.org/10.1037/0033-295X.95.2.256

Dykman, B. M. (1998). Integrating cognitive and motivational factors in depression: Initial tests of a goal-orientation approach. *Journal of Personality and Social Psychology, 74*(1), 139–158. https://doi.org/10.1037/0022-3514.74.1.139

Elliot, A. J. (1999). Approach and avoidance motivation and achievement goals. *Educational Psychologist, 34*(3), 169–189. https://doi.org/10.1207/s15326985ep3403_3

Elliot, A. J., & Church, M. A. (1997). A hierarchical model of approach and avoidance achievement motivation. *Journal of Personality and Social Psychology, 72*(1), 218–232. https://doi.org/10.1037/0022-3514.72.1.218

Elliot, A. J., Faler, J., McGregor, H. A., Campbell, W. K., Sedikides, C., & Harackiewicz, J. M. (2000). Competence valuation as a strategic intrinsic motivation process. *Personality and Social Psychology Bulletin, 26*(7), 780–794. https://doi.org/10.1177/0146167200269004

Elliot, A. J., & Harackiewicz, J. M. (1996). Approach and avoidance achievement goals and intrinsic motivation: A mediational analysis. *Journal of Personality and Social Psychology, 70*(3), 461–475. https://doi.org/10.1037/0022-3514.70.3.461

Elliot, A. J., Jury, M., & Murayama, K. (2018). Trait and perceived environmental competitiveness in achievement situations. *Journal of Personality, 86*(3), 353–367. https://doi.org/10.1111/jopy.12320

Elliot, A. J., & McGregor, H. A. (2001). A 2 × 2 achievement goal framework. *Journal of Personality and Social Psychology, 80*(3), 501–519. https://doi.org/10.1037/0022-3514.80.3.501

Elliot, A. J., & Sommet, N. (2023). Integration in the achievement motivation literature and the hierarchical model of achievement motivation. *Educational Psychology Review, 35*, Article 77. https://doi.org/10.1007/s10648-023-09785-7

Elliot, A. J., & Thrash, T. M. (2001). Achievement goals and the hierarchical model of achievement motivation. *Educational Psychology Review, 13*, 139–156. https://doi.org/10.1023/A:1009057102306

Elliott, E. S., & Dweck, C. S. (1988). Goals: An approach to motivation and achievement. *Journal of Personality and Social Psychology, 54*(1), 5–12. https://doi.org/10.1037/0022-3514.54.1.5

Graham, S., & Golan, S. (1991). Motivational influences on cognition: Task involvement, ego involvement, and depth of information processing. *Journal of Educational Psychology, 83*(2), 187–194. https://doi.org/10.1037/0022-0663.83.2.187

Grant, H., & Dweck, C. S. (2003). Clarifying achievement goals and their impact. *Journal of Personality and Social Psychology, 85*(3), 541–553. https://doi.org/10.1037/0022-3514.85.3.541

Green, J. D., Sedikides, C., Pinter, B., & Van Tongeren, D. R. (2009). Two sides to self-protection: Self-improvement strivings and feedback from close relationships eliminate mnemic neglect. *Self and Identity, 8*(2–3), 233–250. https://doi.org/10.1080/15298860802505145

Harackiewicz, J. M., Barron, K. E., Carter, S. M., Lehto, A. T., & Elliot, A. J. (1997). Predictors and consequences of achievement goals in the college classroom: Maintaining interest and making the grade. *Journal of Personality and Social Psychology, 73*(6), 1284–1295. https://doi.org/10.1037/0022-3514.73.6.1284

Harackiewicz, J. M., & Elliot, A. J. (1993). Achievement goals and intrinsic motivation. *Journal of Personality and Social Psychology, 65*(5), 904–915. https://doi.org/10.1037/0022-3514.65.5.904

Huang, C. (2011). Achievement goals and achievement emotions: A meta-analysis. *Educational Psychology Review, 23,* 359–388. https://doi.org/10.1007/s10648-011-9155-x

Hulleman, C. S., Schrager, S. M., Bodmann, S. M., & Harackiewicz, J. M. (2010). A meta-analytic review of achievement goal measures: Different labels for the same constructs or different constructs with similar labels? *Psychological Bulletin, 136*(3), 422–449. https://doi.org/10.1037/a0018947

Kaplan, A., & Maehr, M. L. (2007). The contributions and prospects of goal orientation theory. *Educational Psychology Review, 19*(2), 141–184. https://doi.org/10.1007/s10648-006-9012-5

Lee, M., & Bong, M. (2016). In their own words: Reasons underlying the achievement striving of students in schools. *Journal of Educational Psychology, 108*(2), 274–294. https://doi.org/10.1037/edu0000048

Lee, W., & Kim, S.-i. (2014). Effects of achievement goals on challenge seeking and feedback processing: Behavioral and fMRI evidence. *PLoS One, 9*(9), Article e107254. Article. https://doi.org/10.1371/journal.pone.0107254

Locke, E. A., & Latham, G. P. (2002). Building a practically useful theory of goal setting and task motivation: A 35-year odyssey. *American Psychologist, 57*(9), 705–717.

Lockwood, P., & Kunda, Z. (1997). Superstars and me: Predicting the impact of role models on the self. *Journal of Personality and Social Psychology, 73*(1), 91–103. https://doi.org/10.1037/0022-3514.73.1.91

McClelland, D. C. (1951). Measuring motivation in phantasy: The achievement motive. In H. Guetzkow (Ed.), *Groups, leadership and men: Research in human relations* (pp. 191–205). Carnegie Press.

McGregor, H. A., & Elliot, A. J. (2002). Achievement goals as predictors of achievement-relevant processes prior to task engagement. *Journal of Educational Psychology, 94*(2), 381–395. https://doi.org/10.1037/0022-0663.94.2.381

Meece, J. L., Anderman, E. M., & Anderman, L. H. (2006). Classroom goal structure, student motivation, and academic achievement. *Annual Review of Psychology, 57*(1), 487–503. https://doi.org/10.1146/annurev.psych.56.091103.070258

Meece, J. L., Blumenfeld, P. C., & Hoyle, R. H. (1988). Students' goal orientations and cognitive engagement in classroom activities. *Journal of Educational Psychology, 80*(4), 514–523. https://doi.org/10.1037/0022-0663.80.4.514

Middleton, M. J., & Midgley, C. (1997). Avoiding the demonstration of lack of ability: An underexplored aspect of goal theory. *Journal of Educational Psychology, 89*(4), 710–718. https://doi.org/10.1037/0022-0663.89.4.710

Nicholls, J. G. (1978). The development of the concept of effort and ability, perception of own attainment, and the understanding that difficult tasks require more ability. *Child Development, 49*(3), 800–814.

Nicholls, J. G. (1984). Achievement motivation: Conceptions of ability, subjective experience, task choice, and performance. *Psychological Review, 91*(3), 328–346. https://doi.org/10.1037/0033-295X.91.3.328

Noel, J. G., Forsyth, D. R., & Kelley, K. N. (1987). Improving the performance of failing students by overcoming their self-serving attributional biases. *Basic and Applied Social Psychology, 8*(1–2), 151–162. https://doi.org/10.1080/01973533.1987.9645882

Nolen, S. B. (1988). Reasons for studying: Motivational orientations and study strategies. *Cognition and Instruction, 5*(4), 269–287. https://doi.org/10.1207/s1532690xci0504_2

Nussbaum, A. D., & Dweck, C. S. (2008). Defensiveness versus remediation: Self-theories and modes of self-esteem maintenance. *Personality and Social Psychology Bulletin, 34*(5), 599–612. https://doi.org/10.1177/0146167207312960

O'Keefe, P. A. (2013). Mindsets and self-evaluation: How beliefs about intelligence can create a preference for growth over defensiveness. In S. B. Kaufman (Ed.), *The complexity of greatness: Beyond talent or practice* (pp. 119–134). Oxford University Press.

Rawsthorne, L. J., & Elliot, A. J. (1999). Achievement goals and intrinsic motivation: A meta-analytic review. *Personality and Social Psychology Review, 3*(4), 326–344. https://doi.org/10.1207/s15327957pspr0304_3

Régner, I., Escribe, C., & Dupeyrat, C. (2007). Evidence of social comparison in mastery goals in natural academic settings. *Journal of Educational Psychology, 99*(3), 575. https://doi.org/10.1037/0022-0663.99.3.575

Ryan, A. M., & Pintrich, P. R. (1997). "Should I ask for help?" The role of motivation and attitudes in adolescents' help seeking in math class. *Journal of Educational Psychology, 89*(2), 329–341. https://doi.org/10.1037/0022-0663.89.2.329

Sachs, P. R. (1982). Avoidance of diagnostic information in self-evaluation of ability. *Personality and Social Psychology Bulletin, 8*(2), 242–246. https://doi.org/10.1177/0146167282082010

Sedikides, C., & Gregg, A. P. (2008). Self-enhancement: Food for thought. *Perspectives on Psychological Science, 3*(2), 102–116. https://doi.org/10.1111/j.1745-6916.2008.00068.x

Sedikides, C., & Strube, M. J. (1995). The multiply motivated self. *Personality and Social Psychology Bulletin, 21*(12), 1330–1335. https://doi.org/10.1177/01461672952112010

Sedikides, C., & Strube, M. J. (1997). Self-evaluation: To thine own self be good, to thine own self be sure, to thine own self be true, and to thine own self be better. *Advances in Experimental Social Psychology, 29*, 209–269. https://doi.org/10.1016/S0065-2601(08)60018-0

Senko, C., Durik, A. M., Patel, L., Lovejoy, C. M., & Valentiner, D. (2013). Performance-approach goal effects on achievement under low versus high challenge conditions. *Learning and Instruction, 23*, 60–68. https://doi.org/10.1016/j.learninstruc.2012.05.006

Senko, C., & Dawson, B. (2017). Performance-approach goal effects depend on how they are defined: Meta-analytic evidence from multiple educational outcomes. *Journal of Educational Psychology, 109*(4), 574–598. https://doi.org/10.1037/edu0000160

Senko, C., & Tropiano, K. L. (2016). Comparing three models of achievement goals: Goal orientations, goal standards, and goal complexes. *Journal of Educational Psychology, 108*(8), 1178–1192. https://doi.org/10.1037/edu0000114

Shepperd, J. A., & Arkin, R. M. (1989). Self-handicapping: The moderating roles of public self-consciousness and task importance. *Personality and Social Psychology Bulletin, 15*(2), 252–265. https://doi.org/10.1177/0146167289152012

Shim, S., & Ryan, A. (2005). Changes in self-efficacy, challenge avoidance, and intrinsic value in response to grades: The role of achievement goals. *The Journal of Experimental Education, 73*(4), 333–349. https://doi.org/10.3200/JEXE.73.4.333-349

Shin, D. D., Kim, S., Park, S., Jeong, D., Park, Y., Kim, S.-I., & Bong, M. (2025). *Unveiling the performance-oriented brains: Striving to prove versus outshine* Manuscript in preparation. Department of Education, Korea University.

Skaalvik, E. M. (1997). Self-enhancing and self-defeating ego orientation: Relations with task and avoidance orientation, achievement, self-perceptions, and anxiety. *Journal of Educational Psychology, 89*(1), 71–81. https://doi.org/10.1037/0022-0663.89.1.71

Stipek, D. J., & Kowalski, P. S. (1989). Learned helplessness in task-orienting versus performance-orienting testing conditions. *Journal of Educational Psychology, 81*(3), 384–391. https://doi.org/10.1037/0022-0663.81.3.384

Strunk, K. K., Lester, W. S., Lane, F. C., Hoover, P. D., & Betties, J. S. (2020). Testing the mastery-avoidance construct in achievement goal theory: A meta-analytic confirmatory factor analysis (MA-CFA) of two achievement goals scales. *Educational Psychology, 41*(4), 383–400. https://doi.org/10.1080/01443410.2020.1824268

Suls, J., Martin, R., & Wheeler, L. (2002). Social comparison: Why, with whom, and with what effect? *Current Directions in Psychological Science, 11*(5), 159–163. https://doi.org/10.1111/1467-8721.00191

Taylor, S. E., Neter, E., & Wayment, H. A. (1995). Self-evaluation processes. *Personality and Social Psychology Bulletin, 21*(12), 1278–1287. https://doi.org/10.1177/01461672952112005

Trope, Y., Gervey, B., & Bolger, N. (2003). The role of perceived control in overcoming defensive self-evaluation. *Journal of Experimental Social Psychology, 39*(5), 407–419. https://doi.org/10.1016/S0022-1031(03)00035-0

Urdan, T., & Kaplan, A. (2020). The origins, evolution, and future directions of achievement goal theory. *Contemporary Educational Psychology, 61*, Article 101862. https://doi.org/10.1016/j.cedpsych.2020.101862

Urdan, T., & Mestas, M. (2006). The goals behind performance goals. *Journal of Educational Psychology, 98*(2), 354–365. https://doi.org/10.1037/0022-0663.98.2.354

Vandewalle, D. (1997). Development and validation of a work domain goal orientation instrument. *Educational and Psychological Measurement, 57*(6), 995–1015. https://doi.org/10.1177/0013164497057006009

Vansteenkiste, M., Lens, W., Elliot, A. J., Soenens, B., & Mouratidis, A. (2014). Moving the achievement goal approach one step forward: Toward a systematic examination of the autonomous and controlled reasons underlying achievement goals. *Educational Psychologist, 49*, 153–174. https://doi.org/10.1080/00461520.2014.928598

Vansteenkiste, M., Mouratidis, A., & Lens, W. (2010). Detaching reasons from aims: Fair play and well-being in soccer as a function of pursuing performance-approach goals for autonomous or controlling reasons. *Journal of Sport & Exercise Psychology, 32*(2), 217–242. https://doi.org/10.1123/jsep.32.2.217

Weiner, B. (1979). A theory of motivation for some classroom experiences. *Journal of Educational Psychology, 71,* 3–25.

Wolters, C. W., Yu, S., & Pintrich, P. R. (1996). The relation between goal orientation and students' motivational beliefs and self-regulated learning. *Learning and Individual Differences, 8*(3), 211–238. https://doi.org/10.1016/S1041-6080(96)90015-1

CHAPTER 5

AUTONOMY DEEPLY CONSIDERED

Emma L. Bradshaw
Australian Catholic University, Australia

Richard M. Ryan
Australian Catholic University, Australia
Ewha Womans University, South Korea

ABSTRACT

According to *self-determination theory* (SDT; Ryan & Deci, 2017), the satisfaction of humans' basic psychological needs for autonomy, competence, and relatedness fundamentally undergirds optimal motivation, wellbeing, and personal growth. Of these, autonomy holds a uniquely significant place in the theory. Autonomy functions not only as a fundamental psychological need but also a defining characteristic of the most optimal forms of motivation and behavioral regulation. Empirically, autonomy has been measured using behavioral, neurologic, and phenomenological indicators, yet because of its psychological salience it can often be effectively assessed with just a few self-report items, although such measures cannot capture the full breadth of the construct as conceptualized in the theory. Accordingly, we tease apart different aspects of autonomy and differentiate autonomy from commonly conflated constructs such as freedom, independence, "free will," and individualism. We discuss how capacities for autonomy develop in pace with demands of socialization, as well as the interpersonal processes that support this. Finally, we outline evidence that individual autonomy is impacted not

The Self in Context, pages 155–180

doi:10.1108/978-1-80686-869-820261005

only by intra- and interpersonal processes, but also by group and societal factors. We conclude by discussing future directions in research on autonomy.

Keywords: Autonomy; self-determination theory; internalization; authenticity; autonomy support

Given the name of *self-determination theory* (SDT; Ryan & Deci, 2017) it should come as no surprise that *autonomy*—a term often thought synonymous with self-determination—is a fundamental aspect of the theory. The concept of autonomy refers to self-regulation or self-governance. When acting autonomously an individual behaves willingly and there is a self-endorsement of one's actions and life projects. Along with this comes a sense of responsibility, since these actions are "one's own." When fully autonomous the person is "whole heartedly" behind what they are doing and experiences their actions as congruent and authentic. Understood in this way, the concept of autonomy is readily recognized, and experiences regarding autonomy are central to people's sense of thriving and vitality. Opposing autonomy is heteronomy, the sense of feeling controlled. Heteronomy can lead to feelings of alienation and depletion, and often to disengagement. People everywhere can suffer from such external control, whether in school, work, or close relationships, and often strive to resist it.

Given its phenomenal salience and functional importance, it seems paradoxical that of the three basic psychological needs specified within SDT—autonomy, competence, and relatedness—autonomy has been the most hotly debated (Ryan & Deci, 2006). Past misconceptions and simplifications have led to confusion about what autonomy truly entails, especially within the context of psychological research. Autonomy has been erroneously conflated with independence, individualism, and even antideterministic free will (e.g., Iyengar & DeVoe, 2003; Markus & Kitayama, 1991). It has also been oversimplified to experiences like freedom or choice (Iyengar & Lepper, 1999). Accordingly, in this chapter we explore this cornerstone construct of SDT and its more nuanced aspects.

Both basic and applied psychological literature contain extensive empirical evidence of the critical importance of autonomy satisfaction and autonomy support to people's motivation, wellness, and integrity. Several meta-analyses (e.g., Bradshaw, Duineveld, et al., 2024; Slemp et al., 2024; Van den Broeck et al., 2016; Vasquez et al., 2016) and a metareview (Ryan et al., 2022) have comprehensively covered that territory. Rather than reiterate this large evidence base, herein we offer a more conceptual discussion of autonomy, teasing out its various aspects and clarifying misconceptions. We hope to speak to the complexity and critical value of this basic psychological need, because "when accurately defined, [autonomy] is essential to the full functioning and mental health of individuals and optimal functioning of organizations and cultures" (Ryan & Deci, 2006, p. 1559).

A BRIEF OVERVIEW OF SDT AND THE AUTONOMY CONTINUUM

SDT is a long-standing theory of human motivation, development, and wellness that has found application across many fields (Ryan & Deci, 2017). The theory builds on the organismic assumption that humans are inherently growth-oriented, interested, and integrative. When healthy, humans actively assimilate new experiences in both their physical and social environments and integrate these into functional knowledge and self-regulations. Yet these inherent integrative tendencies depend to a great extent on people experiencing support for and satisfaction of their basic psychological needs. Need-supportive social environments are those that provide support for autonomy (vs a sense of being controlled), effectance and competence (vs nonoptimal challenges or discouragement), and a sense of relatedness and belonging (vs exclusion or alienation). Environments and experiences with these qualities will lead to motivation and engagement of higher quality, and greater wellbeing and internal coherence.

The empirical roots of SDT began with the study of *intrinsic motivation* and its dynamics (Deci & Ryan, 1980). This was an apt beginning because intrinsic motivation, defined as doing an activity for its inherent satisfactions, is an archetypically autonomous form of motivation. When people are intrinsically motivated, they are interested and find enjoyment in what they are doing, and thus are acting with a high degree of volition and willingness.

Intrinsic motivation is contrasted with the broad category of extrinsic motivation, defined as the doing of an activity for instrumental reasons. Extrinsic motivations vary in their *relative autonomy*, and SDT specifies a taxonomy of extrinsic motivations that lie along a continuum from external regulation (being controlled by external rewards or punishments) to identification/integration (doing an activity because it is personally perceived as of value or merit). Between these extremes lie various forms of introjection, in which behavior is sustained via internal pressures like guilt and shame avoidance (negative introjection) or the pursuit of pride and ego enhancements (positive introjection).

In SDT, the process of integrating external demands and values is called *internalization* (Ryan & Deci, 2017). When fully internalized a person identifies with their motives and values seeing them as their own. Many actions and behaviors might start out fully externally regulated (e.g., directed by others) yet subsequently be assimilated as useful to the self (e.g., brushing teeth, see Chandler & Connell, 1987). Yet SDT's motivational taxonomy is *not* a developmental continuum, as new behaviors may be initiated at any point on this taxonomy and move either toward or away from integration. For example, a student might start a new course with interest (intrinsic motivation) and a sense of value (identification), only to have that autonomous motivational configuration undermined and supplanted by external regulation because of a controlling classroom environment.

Within SDT more well internalized, or autonomous, forms of motivation are expected to foster higher quality engagement (Ng et al., 2012; Tang et al., 2020), greater productivity and enjoyment at work (Van den Broeck et al., 2016), and better school performance (Vasquez et al., 2016). Greater autonomy also characterizes healthier relationships (Patrick et al., 2007) and predicts better mental health and wellbeing (Reis et al., 2000; Stanley et al., 2021), among other benefits. Conversely, more controlled motivational regulations are associated with suboptimal functioning, including lower quality engagement and performance, and more negative experience (Bartholomew et al., 2011; Donald et al., 2021; Ryan et al., 2016).

There is considerable empirical support for SDT's continuum—or taxonomy—of motivational regulations. For example, SDT's motivational taxonomy as it applies in the academic domain was examined in a recent meta-analysis by Howard et al. (2021). Drawing from 344 samples, they compiled the associations between the different types of motivation in SDT's taxonomy and 26 different school related outcomes, including indicators of performance, well-being, and persistence. Results both supported the continuum model and showed that intrinsic motivation was positively related to student success and well-being, whereas identified regulation was particularly important for persistence. Introjected regulation was positively related to persistence and performance goals, but also positively related with indicators of ill-being. External regulation was not predictive of performance or persistence but was related to lower well-being. Finally, amotivation was associated with poor school outcomes, lower persistence and greater ill-being.

Similarly, many studies have investigated autonomy need satisfaction—as distinct from autonomous motivation—as a predictor of outcomes. Autonomy satisfaction reflects the feeling that underpins more autonomous forms of motivation, which is that one has a strong sense of volition and agency in the important areas of their life (Ryan & Deci, 2017). Here again, meta-analytic evidence supports the positive effects of autonomy satisfaction, and the negative effects of autonomy frustration as expected within SDT (e.g., see King et al., 2024; Slemp et al., 2018, 2024).

Such results from research on the SDT motivational taxonomy and autonomy need satisfaction confirm that motivations and life conditions characterized by greater autonomy produce myriad benefits relative to more controlled motives and more externally driven, heteronomous ways of living. Insofar as an individual experiences autonomy, their wellbeing and vitality are enhanced. Deprivation of autonomy, in contrast, predicts poorer functioning and ill-being, and if severe or chronic, results in maladaptation and psychopathology (Ryan et al., 2016). Autonomy is thus essential to wellness and healthy development, making it a truly basic psychological need. So, let us move closer to what autonomy entails.

CLARIFYING THE DEFINITION: WHAT AUTONOMY IS

As SDT researchers we are frequently tasked with communicating this "essence" of the theory with people outside of SDT or even beyond psychology and academia. At the SDT Conference in Egmond aan Zee in 2019, one conversation turned to how each scholar tackles the task of describing autonomy to those who ask. Some described autonomy as the capacity for true self-regulation, others emphasized the importance of feeling like "the author" or "in the driver's seat" of one's life. Still others offered a more philosophical summary of autonomy as representing the self-endorsement of one's actions and life projects. However people chose to explain the concept of autonomy and its importance, there was strong recognition that these experiences regarding autonomy were essential to thriving.

Within the formal SDT literature, autonomy is also variously described. Vansteenkiste et al. (2023) defined autonomy as "volition, willingness, and authenticity, [as well as] integrity" (p. 85). Ryan and Deci (2020) described it as "a sense of initiative and ownership in one's actions" (p. 1), Deci and Ryan (1985) referred to autonomy as "self-organization" (p. 27), and Ryan (1991) described it as "a process of 'self-rule'," "being an origin," and having "a sense of freedom, identity, responsibility, and control" (p. 209). All these definitions are accurate and together speak to the breadth of autonomy as conceptualized within SDT. These definitions show that autonomy is represented by an interplay of concepts including self-organization, self-regulation, volition, authenticity, responsibility, and integrity. An exploration of these aspects will provide a fuller portrait of the multifaceted nature of autonomy within the theory.

Theoretical Background

The concept of autonomy as used in SDT emerges from an organismic perspective (Ryan, 1995) in which living beings, when healthy and vital, are seen as actively moving toward self-regulation and integrity. In nature we typically find organisms moving away from, or actively resisting, heteronomous control or being externally entrained. This does not mean they are never fooled, hijacked, or compromised by outer forces. It means that capacities for autonomy and self-organization represent a generally adaptive propensity, one that is evident in many species (Waller, 1998).

Humans have, however, a unique capacity for, and set of challenges to, autonomy and self-organization stemming from their capacities for self-consciousness. Serious treatments of human autonomy in philosophy thus often begin with Kant's (2017) recognition that because we can have a transcendent awareness of our own interests, valuations, and investments, we have a capacity to endorse or reject them. This gives us a capacity for choice unavailable to other animals. Yet this capacity is not always, and in fact normatively is not, fully realized by individuals.

Building on this Kantian tradition, phenomenological philosophers applying the methods of Husserl (2001) explored these capacities for transcendence and choice, including authors such as Pfander (1967) and Ricoeur (1966). These phenomenological perspectives (reviewed elsewhere, e.g., Ryan & Deci, 2017) converge in understanding autonomy as reflecting the self-endorsement of one's values, behaviors, and life projects. They also suggest that autonomous actions can be initiated by either external or internal prompts or pressures and yet can still be autonomous to the extent that one concurs with, or willingly agrees to, these prompts or inputs. Similarly, analytic philosophers such as Frankfurt (1971, 2018) consider autonomy to entail a reflective endorsement of one's actions, and doing so affords the ability to choose and potentially act on one's interests, preferences, and values.

Feminist analytic philosophers coined the term *relational autonomy* (Mackenzie & Stoljar, 2000) in an approach that resonates with SDT's views and findings. These authors recognize that autonomy, a sense of volition and willingness, can include preferences for interdependent functioning and interpersonal caring, as well as for independence and self-direction (Friedman, 2014). Oshana (2014) positions this as "taking seriously [that] any woman's autonomy involves honoring her interdependent, social personality" (p. 154). We simply add that this would be true for people of all gender identifications. Choice and liberty, that is, do not inherently entail separateness or independence, and in fact rarely do. Insofar as autonomy is about pursuing what matters and what one values, caring for others is commonly autonomously motivated, and satisfies multiple needs, a point upon which we will later elaborate.

INTEGRITY AND AUTONOMY

Autonomy is more than simply doing what one "wants" and it is not defined by an action being self-initiated (Ryan & Deci, 2000). Much of what adults (in particular) do is a function of an external input or demand of some kind.

We might cook nutritious meals when we would strongly prefer doughnuts, take our kids to soccer practice instead of relaxing after work, or pitch in for a volunteer effort instead of enjoying a leisure activity. Even leisure activities like a family holiday or attending a get together can be shaped by social norms or expectations. However, autonomy is still very much achievable because it is not defined by an absence of external influences but rather by the effective integration of these influences into one's values and aims (see also Tiberius, 2018).

Drawing on an example above, one could provide healthy meals not just out of obligation, but because of earnestly believing in the importance of nutrition. In this case, external influences become internalized and self-organized such that they are aligned with personal values. Self-organization is therefore a dynamic process of internalization that allows individuals to navigate an often demanding world without losing their sense of agency, as they balance social responsibilities with personal meaning. Ineffective self-organization—a disintegrated, introjected, or compartmentalized incorporation of external regulations—may result in people feeling alienated or internally conflicted. This underscores the importance of self-organization and integration as drivers of the psychological coherence that typifies experiencing and acting with autonomy (Weinstein et al., 2012).

Volition and Willingness

Another key characteristic of autonomy is volition—the experience of acting with a sense of willingness and self-endorsement (Ryan & Deci, 2017). It is the subjective experience of endorsing one's actions that accompanies behaviors that have been effectively internalized. Volitional acts feel born from or supported by one's interests and values, rather than from external or internal pressures. The inner sense of willingness distinguishes autonomous acts not only from controlled ones, but also from those that are merely reactive or nonconformist (e.g., Koestner & Losier, 1996). Reactive and rebellious actions may often be "self-initiated" but are not autonomous unless aligned with and integrated such that they can be reflectively self-endorsed.

Authenticity

Acting autonomously requires that people have access to their genuine inner experiences—their desires, beliefs, and values. Alignment between one's actions and one's integrated values and sensibilities is often described as *authenticity*, which Wild (1965) defined as being: a) typified by authorship—fully "owning" one's behavior; and b) characterized by genuineness or reality-based engagement with one's circumstances. This perspective is consistent with contemporary definitions of authenticity as the free expression of feelings, thoughts, and behaviors that are congruent with one's inner experiences (Kernis & Goldman, 2006). Based on these definitions, authenticity is clearly a critical aspect of autonomy. Authenticity ensures that self-awareness guides action, rather than external control, image management, or the rebellion that can sometimes drive other forms of nonconformity. Without authenticity, any apparent "autonomy" would be only superficial, resulting in actions that feel hollow or contrived. In this way, authenticity reflects the integrity of autonomous functioning, which supports a meaningful, responsible, and honest engagement with life.

The authenticity aspect of autonomy may partly explain why *mindfulness* has been shown to predict more autonomous forms of motivation (Donald et al., 2020; Ryan et al., 2021). True authenticity requires relentless interest in one's own existence (Ryan & Ryan, 2026), and mindfulness is defined as an open and receptive awareness of the present moment (Brown & Ryan, 2003). Thus, a mindful orientation could pave the way toward experiences of authenticity and autonomous self-regulation. Mindfulness cultivates the open stance necessary for individuals to better perceive their internal conditions—such as urges, feelings, and values—and external influences—such as social pressures, temptations, or conflicts—without defensiveness or distortion. This heightened awareness can enable people to identify more self-congruent forms of action, as they become conscious not only of what they genuinely value but also of the nature and source of the motivations affecting their behavior. As a result, mindfulness is clearly a potent facilitator of autonomy, fostering a clearer, more authentic sense of self (Ryan et al., 2021).

The authenticity aspect of autonomy may speak, in part, to why some young people struggle to feel genuinely autonomous (Soenens & Vansteenkiste, 2005). Adolescence is typified by significant self-discovery, during which individuals' identities are developing and unfolding, and they are learning to distinguish actions motivated by internal values from those driven by external pressures (Erikson, 1968). During this time, they may find it difficult to discern whether their behaviors are driven by authentic self-expression, the influence of social expectations, or reactive opposition to authority. This is one reason why autonomy support is so important for children and adolescents (Bradshaw, Duineveld, et al., 2024; Deci & Ryan, 1987; Vasquez et al., 2016). Opportunities to explore values, beliefs, and desires in the context of nonjudgmental guidance rather than rigid control can help young people—and, indeed, everyone—to recognize the authentic origins of their behaviors. In this sense, authenticity acts as both a foundation of and a guide for autonomy, enabling individuals to distinguish genuinely self-endorsed actions from those that reflect external demands, pressures to conform, or illusions.

Responsibility and Ethical Consideration

Another important, and perhaps underemphasized, characteristic of autonomy is an interplay between responsibility, integrity, and ethical reasoning. Responsibility, in this context, means taking ownership of one's behavior. To do so, in an integrated way, is to make choices that align with abiding values and with a larger ethical framework, even in the face of outside pressure, or the temptation to compromise. As previously discussed, SDT's definition of autonomy involves making decisions that would stand up to open consideration and evaluative reflection in their full form, which encompasses assessing the implications of these choices for others and society at large (Ryan & Deci, 2017).

The fact that responsibility, integrity, and ethical consideration are fundamental to the definition of autonomy highlights that autonomy is not solely about pursuing personal desires but also about recognizing and honoring our interdependence with, and accountability to, others. Without responsibility and integrity, autonomy is incomplete and may resemble mere independence or, in some cases, unintegrated selfishness. Someone could, for example, choose to ignore a safety protocol in the workplace because they feel it is inconvenient, or they are overconfident. Insofar as that choice, even though self-originating, lacks regard for or ignores consideration of the reasons for the protocol, it is not fully autonomous as defined in the theory. True autonomy requires that actions are aligned not only with personal values but also openly consider real-world consequences. Controlled motives are in contrast often characterized by compartmentalizing or avoiding awareness of competing concerns, including the perspectives and/or welfare of others.

CLARIFYING THE DEFINITION II: WHAT AUTONOMY IS NOT

While our primary aim is to offer a deep consideration of what autonomy means within SDT, equally relevant to that description is recognition of what autonomy is not. Definitional confusion has led to several misconceptions about autonomy, several of which we will address here.

Autonomy Is Not Antithetical to Relatedness

Historically, some perspectives have suggested that autonomy and relatedness are antithetical, arguing that people's autonomy necessitates a separation or "individuation" from close others (Blos, 1967; Iyengar & DeVoe, 2003), or is in some ways opposed to interdependence (Iyengar & DeVoe, 2003). On the contrary, SDT holds that autonomy is not only compatible with relatedness but, in fact, interactive with and deeply complementary to it (Ryan, 1991), a point we discussed earlier as reflected in contemporary feminist philosophies of autonomy.

To illustrate their complementarity, there are few contexts more poignant than the parent-child dyad. Throughout early development, parents support autonomy through their responsiveness, empathy, and provision of opportunities for the child to initiate and make age-appropriate choices. Of course, the shape and forms of parental autonomy support evolves as children and young adults become increasingly self-directed and competent in multiple domains. However, this shift does not require a reduction in emotional connectedness (Ryan, 1991). Instead, effective parental autonomy support requires providing the necessary space and structure for children to safely explore their interests and make choices, with acceptance for their experiences and challenges. Allowing a teenager to decide how to allocate their time between schoolwork, hobbies, and social activities, would be a show of respect for their autonomy. More than just an act of generosity, that permission tells the teen they have useful and novel insight into how they spend their time, and that you trust their inner sense and so should they. Thus, by genuinely supporting autonomy, the parent also communicates trust, consideration, and recognition of the value of their child's perspective, which all builds relatedness.

When autonomy is supported, relatedness becomes a source of genuine emotional connection and trust. However, when relatedness is offered without autonomy support, the emotional connection can become superficial and coercive. Parents who offer warmth and affection alongside rigid control over their child's decisions create an environment in which affection is designed to enforce or reward compliance rather than fostering genuine connection. In such scenarios, the child may outwardly appear loved and supported, but internally, they lack a true sense of autonomy, which can erode trust and emotional bonds as well as lead to self-doubt and insecurity (Ryan & Lynch, 1989).

The interplay between autonomy and relatedness is also evident to and important within close adult relationships. *Relationship motivation theory*—the most recently formulated of SDT's six mini-theories—holds that high quality relationships cannot be effectively maintained through relatedness alone (Deci & Ryan, 2014). Intimate relationships require a mutual regard for each partner's autonomy—an appreciation of their perspective, volition, and ability to both select and endorse behavior. In autonomy-supportive relationships, both partners are able to articulate their preferences, pursue personal interests, and respond authentically rather than through obligation or fear of reprisal or loss of regard, which builds deeper understanding, trust, and emotional security. There is also evidence that the benefits of autonomy-support in romantic relationships are dynamic and reciprocal. When one supports the autonomy of the other, the other experiences increased need satisfaction, but one's own needs are also more satisfied, suggesting that mutuality of autonomy support constitutes a strong ideal in relationships (Weinstein & Ryan, 2010).

Autonomy Is Not Independence

Another misconception is that autonomy and independence are equivalent. Yet within SDT independence is quite distinct from autonomy. *Independence* is defined as not relying on others for help, resources, or guidance. An individual can autonomously choose to depend on and accept guidance from others, and in so doing, fully endorse their choice. In fact, people tend to rely more on those from whom they receive autonomy support (Bradshaw, Anderson, et al., 2024; Ryan & Lynch, 1989). In the same vein, independence is often not indicative of autonomy. Someone might be forced to be independent ("thrown in to the deep end") when they feel unprepared and thus be heteronomously independent. Put another way, the opposite of independence is dependence, but dependence is not always lacking in autonomy, and independence sometimes is.

Beyond these definitional distinctions, autonomy and independence differ considerably in how they relate to important outcomes. Independence support can be a component of effective socialization when it is willfully sought, autonomy-supportively provided, and developmentally appropriate. Independence support can be beneficial to the parent-child dyad (Gibler et al., 2018), in the workplace (Gatti et al., 2019), in relationships (Hodges et al., 1999), and beyond (Alonso-Sardón et al., 2019; Nagumey et al., 2004). Yet, because independence needs to be supported with sensitivity to context and individual needs, some studies have shown that the link between, for example, emotional independence from parents and adolescent functioning is negative (Beyers & Goossens, 1999), which can lead to greater feelings of insecurity toward parents (Ryan & Lynch, 1989).

In contrast, autonomy has been meta-analytically shown to be beneficial across a wide variety of outcomes including well-being in children (Bradshaw, Duineveld, et al., 2024) and adults (Yu et al., 2018), athletic motivation and performance (Mossman et al., 2024), prosocial behavior (Donald et al., 2021), and care settings (Bradshaw, Anderson, et al., 2024). Notably, such positive outcomes appear to be universal, with meta-analyses typically finding that the benefits of autonomy support are not moderated by age, sex, or cultural region (e.g., Bradshaw, Duineveld, et al., 2024; Slemp et al., 2024; Yu et al., 2018).

Autonomy Is Not Freedom, or "Free Will"

Freedom

In SDT autonomy concerns volition and willingness to act. In contrast, freedom means not having constraints or restrictions. Freedom can facilitate autonomy when it affords opportunities to choose valued activities or goals. This is why giving people choices can often stimulate their intrinsic motivation and energies—particularly if the choices provided are meaningful and relevant. However, merely being released from constraints, or even having choices, does not ensure autonomy. Autonomy depends on having a self-endorsed goal or purpose, and merely removing constraints may not supply that. For example, taking away all rules in a classroom will not likely foster autonomous behaviors—instead it may produce chaos and anxiety for many. Similarly, meaningless or trivial choices that do not conduce to greater behavioral fit or preferences will not necessarily yield more autonomy.

Free Will

A related idea sometimes associated with autonomy is "free will." As Ryan and Deci (2006) describe, free will is often a "straw man" construct in which people are said to not be determined by prior events or causes. SDT does not see this as characterizing autonomy, which itself is lawfully related to contextual conditions, and often prompted by external influences with which one concurs (or does not). Indeed, both autonomous motivations and controlled motivations have prior influences, and both require specific neurological supports to occur, a point we shall elaborate below. Thus, autonomy does not require a concept of free will as so defined, and sees instead autonomy as a natural and functional process characterizing healthy self-regulation.

Autonomy Is Not an Individualistic Construct

The question of generalizability is at the heart of the next misconception about autonomy and its value; the belief that autonomy is an individualistic construct not important within collectivist, and particularly, East-Asian cultures (Iyengar & DeVoe, 2003; Markus & Kitayama, 1991). It is intentional that the topic of individualism follows discussion about the conflation of autonomy with independence, because that lack of distinction largely underpins the seemingly persistent (e.g., De Leersnyder et al., 2015) notion that autonomy is less valuable to people from collectivistic countries and cultures than those from individualistic countries and cultures.

Markus and Kitayama (1991) posited that "autonomy [is] secondary to, and constrained by, the primary task of interdependence" in many non-Western cultures. However, this perspective does not consider that autonomy may be expressed differently across cultural contexts. In collectivistic cultures, autonomy intertwines with relational harmony and interdependence, rather than standing in opposition to them. People from collectivistic cultures may genuinely internalize and integrate the norms and beliefs of their family or group and thus autonomously place the interests of their group ahead of self-interests (as might people from any culture). Such integration would demonstrate that autonomy not only coexists with but also benefits relational interdependence, challenging the stereotype of autonomy as purely individualistic.

Yu et al. (2018) tested the claim that autonomy is less relevant to wellbeing in East Asian countries and cultures, focusing specifically on a meta-analysis of the associations between autonomy and wellbeing including correlations reported in the US versus East Asia. The average association between autonomy and wellbeing was strongly positive ($r = 0.46$, $p < 0.001$), and the magnitude of the association did not differ by region, supporting the universal relevance of autonomy to wellbeing. Similarly, Bradshaw, Duineveld, et al. (2024) meta-analyzed the links between parental autonomy support and child well-being and assessed the extent to which region, degree of national individualism, and degree of cultural hierarchy moderated the association. The strong, positive effect ($r = 0.30$, $p < 0.001$) was found to be consistent (i.e., not moderated) across each of these variables. King et al. (2024) extracted data from studies comprising over a half million participants across 70 countries and diverse cultural, economic, and political settings, and concluded that need-supportive teaching—including autonomy-supportive teaching—was generally associated with better well-being across contexts. They concluded that their findings supported SDT's universalist perspective on basic needs (see also Slemp et al., 2024).

Such findings speak to the claim that autonomy is a universal need that transcends cultural boundaries, thus debunking the myth of its individualistic nature. Understanding how autonomy manifests within different cultural frameworks enriches our comprehension of its role in human wellbeing and allows us to appreciate the versatile ways autonomy supports personal and collective growth, regardless of cultural orientation.

AUTONOMY SUPPORT AND THE FOSTERING OF AGENCY

Clearly, understanding this encompassing definition of autonomy is essential for accurately studying it, discussing it, and recognizing when you are experiencing it (or not). Equally important is understanding how to support the autonomy of others (and how others can support yours) across a variety of real-world settings. Autonomy support involves specific behaviors and attitudes from others—such as parents, teachers, coaches, employers, and peers—that encourage the above-described sense of volition, authenticity, self-direction, and responsibility (Ryan & Deci, 2017). Those who successfully convey autonomy support to others do several essential things.

First, they take in the other's perspective with openness and genuine receptivity. In the workplace a leader might simply ask, "How is it going?" and then deeply listen, clarifying and showing empathy for the employee's response, and perhaps following through with relevant actions. Reeve and

Cheon (2024) have even argued that perspective taking—really taking interest in and caring about the experience of the other—is the foundational skill of autonomy support.

Second, people provide autonomy support by offering a meaningful rationale when making a request or setting a limit. The provision of a meaningful rationale is a vital aspect of autonomy support and yet is often misapplied. For example, schoolteachers are often tasked with teaching material designed to help students pass standardized tests or demonstrate required knowledge. These benchmarks mean little to many students. To set tasks while supporting students' autonomy—and thus support more enjoyment and engagement—teachers could instead explain how the topic relates to their personal interests or what skills will be developed. By framing tasks in ways that resonate personally, teachers help learners to find meaning in what they do and thus be more able to be autonomously engaged (Ahmadi et al., 2023).

Third, autonomy-supportive people and environments encourage people to self-initiate and make nonarbitrary choices. This means providing opportunities for individuals to take initiative and make decisions they care about. In the context of sports coaching, for example, a coach might invite athletes to set their own performance goals or allow them to guide their own development outside of specified training periods. By allowing the athletes to lead their development and serving more of a guidance role, the coach fosters the athletes' sense of ownership and accountability (Mageau & Vallerand, 2003). This approach not only enhances the athletes' engagement but also promotes their development of self-regulation and decision-making skills.

Finally, the provision of autonomy support depends on the minimization of controlling language and pressure (Ryan & Deci, 2017). Controlling language involves directives that pressure individuals to think, feel, or behave in specific ways, through the use of guilt, shame, or external rewards. A friend might pressure one to act by suggesting that "if you care about me at all, you will do as I ask." Messages like this are designed—consciously or not—to induce introjects and they therefore undermine the other person's sense of autonomy and ability to choose willingly. Friends can still ask for help without thwarting autonomy, though. One might instead ask, "I could really use some help moving this weekend; if you're able to come, I'd appreciate it." The latter phrasing respects the other's autonomy by allowing them to choose, based on the extent to which they (a) can and (b) have internalized the value of helping friends when they need it.

Evidence for the positive effects of autonomy support exists within multiple domains. When managers (Slemp et al., 2018), coaches (Mossman et al., 2024), clinicians (Bradshaw, Anderson, et al., 2024; Zuroff et al., 2012), teachers (Mammadov & Schroeder, 2023) and parents (Bradshaw,

Duineveld, et al., 2024) use more autonomy-supportive strategies to motivate others, they more effectively foster higher quality motivation, better performance, and enhanced wellness. Of these many domains, early childhood and adolescent environments—including the home and in school—play an important role in developing and supporting children's experiences of autonomy and shaping their well-being and optimal motivation over the long term.

EARLY EXPERIENCES IN THE DEVELOPMENT OF AUTONOMY AND SELF-REGULATION

Experiences of autonomy support are vital throughout the lifespan, though during childhood and adolescence they are especially formative. Carlson (2023) argued that by reflecting children's experience and giving them "a sense of choice in how to act, think, and feel" we can greatly enhance early developments in executive functioning. That is, by providing children with autonomy support, parents, teachers, and other proximal caregivers help build their capacities for effective self-regulation and thus autonomy. In support of this view, Bindman et al. (2015) examined the relations between autonomy-supportive parenting and children's subsequent achievement as mediated by executive functions. Their longitudinal analyses revealed that mothers' autonomy support over the first three years of life predicted greater executive functions (e.g., delay of gratification, directed attention, impulse inhibition) during the year prior to kindergarten and subsequent achievement in elementary and high school, even controlling for warmth, cognitive stimulation, child temperament, and other relevant variables.

In educational settings, these developmental gains can be extended. Reeve and Cheon (2021) show that when teachers are trained in autonomy-supportive practices—such as acknowledging students' feelings and seeking their input—students experience gains in self-regulation as well as improved task persistence. Similarly, Mammadov and Schroeder's (2023) recent meta-analysis showed that teacher autonomy support is associated with gains in academic performance and student engagement, as well as student well-being from primary right through to secondary school. Evidently, teachers and the classroom environment can strengthen students' development from more external guidance to effective self-direction via the provision of autonomy support. Together with parents and caregivers, the gradual process strengthens children's self-governance abilities which creates a foundation for future well-being and improved academic and social results.

SOCIETAL AUTONOMY SUPPORT

The capacity for autonomy does not occur in a societal vacuum. Just as there are schools, workplaces, teams, and families that are more supportive of autonomy than others, we can also evaluate societal forms—cultures, governments, and societies—in terms of the degree to which they support autonomy versus engender heteronomy. In fact, this has been the focus of much social theory. For example, philosophers such as Nussbaum (2011), Sen (2005), and Rawls (1971/2009) have posited that societies can support autonomy and justice by providing citizens with certain resources, capabilities, and rights that allow them to pursue what matters to them.

Recent work in SDT has been directly exploring these formulations. For example, Bradshaw et al. (2025) presented three studies examining Nussbaum's (2011) conception of societal *capabilities* and how these relate to citizens' well-being and ill-being via basic psychological needs. They specifically assessed links from freedom of expression to need satisfaction and freedom from discrimination to lower need frustration as differential pathways to wellness outcomes. The findings underscored the importance of societal conditions on people's autonomy and basic psychological needs, and thus their capacity to flourish. Similarly, Bradshaw, DeHaan, et al. (2024) examined how access to the social determinants of health—things like access to housing, nutritious food, and health care—might influence people's basic psychological need satisfactions, including autonomy. Findings show that access to these basic resources is associated with enhanced functioning and greater autonomy. Finally, in a third prong of this research, Bradshaw et al. (2021) validated an assessment of *primary goods*, which represent the basic societal rights and resources that are proposed as the bases for social justice in the well-known work of Rawls (1971/2009). Here again, it was found that in social contexts where people perceived they had better access to primary goods they had more autonomy and basic psychological need satisfaction, and in turn evidence of greater flourishing. Together such studies show that autonomy support is not just something that happens at an interpersonal level, but also can be leveraged by institutional, cultural, and governmental influences, thus having a pervasive effect on societal autonomy and health. Illustrating this, Martela et al. (2023) showed across 27 European countries that well-being was uniformly and robustly predicted by greater autonomy and need satisfaction.

It is thus the case that environments vary in autonomy support, and impact people's thriving accordingly. SDT studies social environments ranging from the proximal (e.g., parents and children; managers and workers, etc.) to the institutional (e.g., school or organizational conditions and policies) to the pervasive (e.g., cultures and political regimes). But across these levels of analysis the focus is on the functional impact of environmental features in supporting or thwarting of basic psychological needs, including autonomy.

FUTURE DIRECTIONS IN RESEARCH ON AUTONOMY

The Black Box of Integration

As we have emphasized, experiences of autonomy support and satisfaction are vital because they underpin the process of integration, and acting with autonomy requires an inner sense of integration (Ryan & Deci, 2017), so in theory autonomy and integration are reciprocally linked. However, evidence for the autonomy-integration dynamic is scarce. This scarcity is because integration cannot, in our view, be effectively measured by self-report. Like autonomy, integration is a complex experience and process, involving the assimilation of external and sometimes conflicting inputs, and the absence of defensiveness and compartmentalization. If someone is defensive or compartmentalizing, they are unlikely to say so on a self-report measure. So, how to measure it then? Answering this question represents a major opportunity in the future of SDT. One possibility could involve the use of psychophysiological measures such as heart rate variability or cortisol levels. These variables could serve as objective indicators of integration by assessing physiological responses to stress and conflict, thereby reflecting the presence or absence of compartmentalization and defensiveness. Another approach is to use neurological studies of differential processing of inputs to differentiate autonomous from controlled processes, examples of which we shall describe below. Finally, longitudinal studies are also essential, as they can track the development of integration over time, revealing how sustained autonomy support contributes to the assimilation of diverse experiences and greater internal consistency.

Measurement of Autonomy

Much like the operationalization of integration, an important part of meaningfully understanding autonomy and its role in our lives hinges on its effective measurement. The most used measure of basic psychological needs uses four items to index each need satisfaction and each need frustration (Chen et al., 2015). More recently, Martela and Ryan (2024) have even validated single items to measure each need, which offer considerable practical utility, especially for use in large, national and multinational data collections for which brevity is essential. Although these streamlined measures facilitate efficient data collection, they potentially obscure the construct's complexity. This conceptual reduction can lead to more simplified definitions and interpretations, potentially overlooking the subtle and nuanced dimensions and facets of autonomy. So, although brief measures enhance practicality and certainly have their place, they necessitate careful application to ensure that the multifaceted nature of autonomy continues to be adequately quantified, studied, and discussed. It is incumbent upon SDT researchers to continue studying the diverse aspects of autonomy alongside the practical use of concise self-report measures. This balanced approach will hopefully ensure that even with the use of brief tools, the rich and complex qualities of autonomy remain acknowledged and understood.

In this regard a recent study by Di Domenico et al. (2024) is illustrative. These researchers assembled more than 1,000 items from the diverse universe of measures tapping motivation. Using a "bass-ackwards" method to derive facets of motivation, they identified 28 common motives. Then using multidimensional scaling, they modeled these facets alongside SDT's motivational taxonomy. Results suggested that most all motivational constructs can be positioned along the continuum of autonomy suggesting that the concept of autonomy has relevance to all types of motives, influencing their relations with outcomes.

Neuropsychology of Autonomy: An Emerging Area

There is a burgeoning area of research on the neuropsychological underpinnings of autonomous functioning (see reviews by Di Domenico & Ryan, 2023; Lee, 2023). Specific neuropsychological processes underlying both intrinsic motivation and autonomous self-regulation are being uncovered. For example, research on intrinsic motivation suggests a prominent role of the anterior insula, a brain region important in self-initiative and choice, as well as striatal activations associated with rewarding experiences (Lee, 2023). Beyond intrinsic motivation, autonomy also involves making decisions and choices aligned with the self. Studies by Di Domenico et al. (2013; 2016) show that persons higher in general need satisfaction, including autonomy, when making difficult preference decisions, were more prone to activations in the medial prefrontal cortex, suggesting richer processing of self-related information in the face of decisional conflicts. In related findings, Legault and Inzlicht (2013) found that higher autonomy predicted greater sensitivity to self-regulation failures, also pointing to the adaptive nature of higher autonomy.

These and other studies show promise, but at this point SDT researchers are just beginning to get a picture of the mechanistic underpinnings of both autonomous and controlled forms of motivation. We do not believe this will be a simple picture because there are different forms of autonomous motivation (e.g., intrinsic and identified motives), multiple brain networks involved in each, as well as some equifinality in terms of how autonomous and controlled goal-directed behavior can be accomplished. But the iterative study of psychological, behavioral, and neuropsychological processes will help further define the characteristics and conditions for autonomous functioning and the adaptive outcomes associated with it.

SOCIO-CULTURAL PERSPECTIVES

Another area ripe for exploration is how socio-cultural dimensions bear on the expression of autonomy. As we have outlined here, questions about the universal importance of the satisfaction (and nonfrustration) of SDT's basic psychological needs have largely been addressed, with multiple meta-analyses in different domains suggesting that autonomy is essential to all people, everywhere. But we understand that autonomy can manifest differently depending on cultural norms, institutional practices, and other setting features. A deeper exploration of those variations would be a valuable expansion of the theory. Cross-cultural investigations with longitudinal and, potentially, qualitative methodologies stand to deepen our understanding of how people address and express their need for autonomy. In addition, research is currently looking at how variations not only in culture, but also political forms, influences autonomy. For instance, Waterschoot and Ryan (2025) recently reported that to the extent democratic regimes foster greater wellness in citizens, this is substantially mediated by the experience of autonomy they engender.

It is also important in this context to reiterate that autonomy concerns the opportunity to pursue what matters to the individual. Socio-cultural contexts lead to a diversity of values and preferences, some of which are more easily integrated than others because some norms and institutional structures and features differentially influence the internalization process. Societal gender norms can inform people's identity and role choices, which can shape how they navigate personal aspirations within cultural norms. Similarly, educational systems that emphasize achievement can foster competence, but may shape how people pursue learning and creativity too. Socio-cultural contexts also provide variations in the obstacles, affordances, and resources they present to people's free pursuit of what matters to them. Systems of government that permit participation and free expression foster people's explicit engagement, whereas people within authoritarian regimes may have to develop more subtle adaptive strategies for pursuing personal interests and values. As outlined in SDT then, both cultural contents and political processes will influence the autonomy and thriving of populations, highlighting why this is an area in need of ever more study.

CONCLUSION

Autonomy is not about unabated freedom or the provision of arbitrary choices, nor merely the absence of external control. It is also deeply multifaceted. The various aspects of autonomy—self-organization, volition, authenticity, responsibility, integrity, choice, and freedom—are interconnected. They collectively contribute to a holistic understanding of what it means to act autonomously and to feel autonomous. Self-organization and internalization help us integrate external influences meaningfully. Volition and authenticity mean our actions are self-endorsed and aligned within the self. Responsibility and integrity embed ethical considerations into autonomous actions, and choice and freedom provide the context in which autonomy can often be more readily exercised. The interconnectedness of the various aspects of autonomy shows it is not a simple concept but a dynamic process involving multiple phenomenal and functional aspects of self-organization that support personal growth, psychological well-being, and social harmony.

Support for and satisfaction of this conception of autonomy has implications throughout the life span as it fuels self-regulation, executive functioning, and our integrative capacities. Over time people who experience consistent autonomy support learn to navigate complex choices, reconcile internal and external demands and become the authors of their own lives. Whether in family, academic, professional, or personal life, autonomy paves the way toward engagement, creativity, and a more authentic connection to one's goals and aspirations. It shapes how people approach challenges, learn from setbacks and find sustainable sources of motivation that contribute to long term well-being. It is therefore critical to strive for and maintain autonomy support across social, institutional, and cultural contexts. By understanding the characteristics and the features of conditions that support autonomy, we are better able to foster deeper engagement, richer relationships, and more ethical and responsible participation in the world. Through acting with autonomy, we do not merely choose our actions; we meaningfully define who we are, how we relate to others, and what we value, and therefore can foster both personal growth and collective flourishing.

REFERENCES

Ahmadi, A., Noetel, M., Parker, P., Ryan, R. M., Ntoumanis, N., Reeve, J., … Lonsdale, C. (2023). A classification system for teachers' motivational behaviors recommended in self-determination theory interventions. *Journal of Educational Psychology, 115*(8), 1158–1176. https://doi.org/10.1037/edu0000783

Alonso-Sardón, M., Iglesias-de-Sena, H., Fernández-Martín, L. C., & Mirón-Canelo, J. A. (2019). Do health and social support and personal autonomy have an influence on the health-related quality of life of individuals with intellectual disability? *BMC Health Services Research, 19*, 1–10. https://doi.org/10.1186/s12913-018-3856-5

Bartholomew, K. J., Ntoumanis, N., Ryan, R. M., Bosch, J. A., & Thøgersen-Ntoumani, C. (2011). Self-determination theory and diminished functioning: The role of interpersonal control and psychological need thwarting. *Personality and Social Psychology Bulletin, 37*(11), 1459–1473. https://doi.org/10.1177/0146167211413125

Beyers, W., & Goossens, L. (1999). Emotional autonomy, psychosocial adjustment and parenting: Interactions, moderating and mediating effects. *Journal of Adolescence, 22*(6), 753–769. https://doi.org/10.1006/jado.1999.0268

Bindman, S. W., Pomerantz, E. M., & Roisman, G. I. (2015). Do children's executive functions account for associations between early autonomy-supportive parenting and achievement through high school? *Journal of Educational Psychology, 107*(3), 756–770. https://doi.org/10.1037/edu0000017

Blos, P. (1967). The second individuation process of adolescence. *Psychoanalytic Study of the Child, 22*(1), 162–186. https://doi.org/10.1080/00797308.1967.11822595

Bradshaw, E. L., Anderson, J. R., Banday, M. A., Basarkod, G., Daliri-Ngametua, R., Ferber, K. A., Henry, D., & Ryan, R. M. (2024a). A quantitative meta-analysis and qualitative meta-synthesis of aged care residents' experiences of autonomy, being controlled, and optimal functioning. *The Gerontologist, 64*(5), gnad135. https://doi.org/10.1093/geront/gnad135

Bradshaw, E. L., DeHaan, C. R., Neufeld, A., Diaz-Castillo, S., & Ryan, R. M. (2024b). *A self-determination theory approach to the social determinants of health and psychological well-being.* Australian Catholic University. [Unpublished manuscript].

Bradshaw, E. L., DeHaan, C. R., Parker, P. D., Curren, R., Di Domenico, S. I., & Ryan, R. (2021). The perceived conditions for living well: Positive perceptions of primary goods linked with basic psychological needs and wellness. *The Journal of Positive Psychology, 18*(1), 44–60. https://doi.org/10.1080/17439760.2021.1991446

Bradshaw, E. L., Duineveld, J. J., Conigrave, J. H., Steward, B. A., Ferber, K. A., Joussemet, M., Parker, P. D., & Ryan, R. M. (2024c). Disentangling autonomy-supportive and psychologically controlling parenting: A meta-analysis of self-determination theory's dual process model across cultures. *American Psychologist.* https://doi.org/10.1037/amp0001389

Bradshaw, E. L., Ferber, K. A., DeHaan, C. R., & Ryan, R. M. (2025). Fundamental freedoms and optimal functioning: Nussbaum's capabilities predict wellness in a dual process model via basic psychological need satisfaction and frustration. *Motivation and Emotion,* 1–19.

Brown, K. W., & Ryan, R. M. (2003). The benefits of being present: Mindfulness and its role in psychological well-being. *Journal of Personality and Social Psychology, 84*(4), 822–848. https://doi.org/10.1037/0022-3514.84.4.822

Carlson, S. M. (2023). Let me choose: The role of choice in the development of executive function skills. *Current Directions in Psychological Science, 32*(3), 220–227. https://doi.org/10.1177/09637214231159052

Chandler, C. L., & Connell, J. P. (1987). Children's intrinsic, extrinsic and internalized motivation: A developmental study of children's reasons for liked and disliked behaviours. *British Journal of Developmental Psychology, 5*(4), 357–365. https://doi.org/10.1111/j.2044-835X.1987.tb01072.x

Chen, B., Vansteenkiste, M., Beyers, W., Boone, L., Deci, E. L., Van der Kaap-Deeder, J., Duriez, B., Lens, W., Matos, L., Mouratidis, A., Ryan, R. M., Sheldon, K. M., Soenens, B., Van Petegem, S., & Verstuyf, J. (2015). Basic psychological need satisfaction, need frustration, and need strength across four cultures. *Motivation and Emotion, 39*(2), 216–236. https://doi.org/10.1007/s11031-014-9450-1

Deci, E. L., & Ryan, R. M. (1980). The empirical exploration of intrinsic motivational processes. *Advances in Experimental Social Psychology, 13*, 39–80. https://doi.org/10.1016/S0065-2601(08)60130-6

Deci, E. L., & Ryan, R. M. (1985). *Intrinsic motivation and self-determination in human behavior*. Springer Science & Business Media.

Deci, E. L., & Ryan, R. M. (1987). The support of autonomy and the control of behavior. *Journal of Personality and Social Psychology, 53*(6), 1024–1037. https://doi.org/10.1037/0022-3514.53.6.1024

Deci, E. L., & Ryan, R. M. (2014). Autonomy and need satisfaction in close relationships: Relationships motivation theory. In N. Weinstein (Ed.), *Human motivation and interpersonal relationships: Theory, research, and applications* (pp. 53–73). Springer. https://doi.org/10.1007/978-94-017-8542-6_3

De Leersnyder, J., Kim, H., & Mesquita, B. (2015). Feeling right is feeling good: Psychological well-being and emotional fit with culture in autonomy-versus relatedness-promoting situations. *Frontiers in Psychology, 6*. https://doi.org/10.3389/fpsyg.2015.00630

Di Domenico, S. I., Fournier, M. A., Ayaz, H., & Ruocco, A. C. (2013). In search of integrative processes: Basic psychological need satisfaction predicts medial prefrontal activation during decisional conflict. *Journal of Experimental Psychology: General, 142*(3), 967–978. https://doi.org/10.1037/a0030257

Di Domenico, S. I., Le, A., Liu, Y., Ayaz, H., & Fournier, M. A. (2016). Basic psychological needs and neurophysiological responsiveness to decisional conflict: An event-related potential study of integrative self processes. *Cognitive, Affective, & Behavioral Neuroscience, 16*, 848–865. https://doi.org/10.3758/s13415-016-0436-1

Di Domenico, S. I., & Ryan, R. M. (2023). Toward a neurobiology of integrative processes. In R. M. Ryan (Ed.), *The Oxford handbook of self-determination theory* (pp. 292–308). Oxford University Press.

Di Domenico, S. I., Ryan, R. M., Duineveld, J. J., Bradshaw, E. L., Parker, P., & Steward, B. A. (2024). Exploring facets of student motivation using a Bass Ackward strategy and the conceptual lens of self-determination theory. *Contemporary Educational Psychology, 79*, 102321. https://doi.org/10.1016/j.cedpsych.2024.102321

Donald, J. N., Bradshaw, E. L., Conigrave, J. H., Parker, P. D., Byatt, L. L., Noetel, M., & Ryan, R. M. (2021). Paths to the light and dark sides of human nature: A meta-analytic review of the prosocial benefits of autonomy and the antisocial costs of control. *Psychological Bulletin, 147*(9), 921–946. https://doi.org/10.1037/bul0000338

Donald, J. N., Bradshaw, E. L., Ryan, R. M., Basarkod, G., Ciarrochi, J., Duineveld, J. J., Guo, J., & Sahdra, B. K. (2020). Mindfulness and its association with varied types of motivation: A systematic review and meta-analysis using self-determination theory. *Personality and Social Psychology Bulletin, 46*(7), 1121–1138. https://doi.org/10.1177/0146167219896136

Erikson, E. H. (1968). *Identity: Youth and crisis* (Vol. *68*). Norton.

Frankfurt, H. G. (1971). Freedom of the will and the concept of a person. *The Journal of Philosophy, 68*(1), 5–20. https://doi.org/10.2307/2024717

Frankfurt, H. (2018). Freedom of the will and the concept of a Person. In L. Ekstrom (Ed.), *Agency and responsiblity* (pp. 77–91). Routledge.

Friedman, M. (2014). Relational autonomy and independence. In A. Veltman & M. Piper (Eds.), *Autonomy, oppression, and gender* (pp. 42–60). Oxford Academic. https://doi.org/10.1093/acprof:oso/9780199969104.003.0003

Gatti, P., Bligh, M. C., & Cortese, C. G. (2019). When a leader job resource can be ambivalent or even destructive: Independence at work as a double-edged sword. *PLoS One, 14*(5), e0217482. https://doi.org/10.1371/journal.pone.0217482

Gibler, R. C., Kalomiris, A. E., & Kiel, E. J. (2018). Paternal anxiety in relation to toddler anxiety: The mediating role of maternal behavior. *Child Psychiatry and Human Development, 49*, 512–522. https://doi.org/10.1007/s10578-017-0771-7

Hodges, E. V., Finnegan, R. A., & Perry, D. G. (1999). Skewed autonomy–relatedness in preadolescents' conceptions of their relationships with mother, father, and best friend. *Developmental Psychology, 35*(3), 737–748. https://doi.org/10.1037/0012-1649.35.3.737

Howard, J. L., Bureau, J., Guay, F., Chong, J. X., & Ryan, R. M. (2021). Student motivation and associated outcomes: A meta-analysis from self-determination theory. *Perspectives on Psychological Science, 16*(6), 1300–1323.

Husserl, E. (2001). *Phenomenology and the foundations of the sciences* (Vol. *1*). Springer Science & Business Media.

Iyengar, S. S., & Lepper, M. R. (1999). Rethinking the value of choice: A cultural perspective on intrinsic motivation. *Journal of Personality and Social Psychology, 76*(3), 349–366. https://doi.org/10.1037/0022-3514.76.3.349

Kant, I. (2017). *Kant: The metaphysics of morals.* Cambridge University Press.

Kernis, M. H., & Goldman, B. M. (2006). A multicomponent conceptualization of authenticity: Theory and research. *Advances in Experimental Social Psychology, 38*, 283–357. https://doi.org/10.1016/S0065-2601(06)38006-9

King, R. B., Haw, J. Y., & Wang, Y. (2024). Need-support facilitates well-being across cultural, economic, and political contexts: A self-determination theory perspective. *Learning and Instruction, 93.* https://doi.org/10.1016/j.learninstruc.2024.101978

Koestner, R., & Losier, G. F. (1996). Distinguishing reactive versus reflective autonomy. *Journal of Personality, 64*(2), 465–494. https://doi.org/10.1111/j.1467-6494.1996.tb00518.x

Lee, W. (2023). Neuropsychological research in self-determination theory. In R. M. Ryan (Ed.), *The Oxford handbook of self-determination theory* (pp. 258–271).

Legault, L., & Inzlicht, M. (2013). Self-determination, self-regulation, and the brain: Utonomy improves performance by enhancing neuroaffective responsiveness to self-regulation failure. *Journal of Personality and Social Psychology, 105*(1), 123–138. https://doi.org/10.1037/a0030426

Mackenzie, C., & Stoljar, N. (2000). *Relational autonomy: Feminist perspectives on automony, agency, and the social self.* Oxford University Press.

Mageau, G. A., & Vallerand, R. J. (2003). The coach–athlete relationship: A motivational model. *Journal of Sports Science, 21*(11), 883–904. https://doi.org/10.1080/0264041031000140374

Mammadov, S., & Schroeder, K. (2023). A meta-analytic review of the relationships between autonomy support and positive learning outcomes. *Contemporary Educational Psychology, 75*, 102235. https://doi.org/10.1016/j.cedpsych.2023.102235

Markus, H. R., & Kitayama, S. (1991). Culture and the self: Implications for cognition, emotion, and motivation. *Psychological Review, 98*(2), 224–253. https://doi.org/10.1037/0033-295X.98.2.224

Martela, F., Lehmus-Sun, A., Parker, P. D., Pessi, A. B., & Ryan, R. M. (2023). Needs and well-being across Europe: Basic psychological needs are closely connected with well-being, meaning, and symptoms of depression in 27 European countries. *Social Psychological and Personality Science, 14*(5), 501–514. https://doi.org/10.1177/19485506221113678

Martela, F., & Ryan, R. M. (2024). Assessing autonomy, competence, and relatedness briefly: Validating single-item scales for basic psychological need satisfaction. *European Journal of Psychological Assessment.* https://doi.org/10.1027/1015-5759/a000846

Mossman, L. H., Slemp, G. R., Lewis, K. J., Colla, R. H., & O'Halloran, P. (2024). Autonomy support in sport and exercise settings: A systematic review and meta-analysis. *International Review of Sport and Exercise Psychology, 17*(1), 540–563. https://doi.org/10.1080/1750984X.2022.2031252

Nagurney, A. J., Reich, J. W., & Newsom, J. (2004). Gender moderates the effects of independence and dependence desires during the social support process. *Psychology and Aging, 19*(1), 215–218. https://doi.org/10.1037/0882-7974.19.1.215

Ng, J. Y., Ntoumanis, N., Thøgersen-Ntoumani, C., Deci, E. L., Ryan, R. M., Duda, J. L., & Williams, G. C. (2012). Self-determination theory applied to health contexts: A meta-analysis. *Perspectives on Psychological Science, 7*(4), 325–340. https://doi.org/10.1177/1745691612447309

Nussbaum, M. C. (2011). *Creating capabilities: The human development approach.* Harvard University Press.

Oshana, M. (2014). A commitment to autonomy is a commitment to feminism. In A. Veltman & M. Piper (Eds.), *Autonomy, oppression, and gender* (pp. 141–160). https://doi.org/10.1093/acprof:oso/9780199969104.003.0007

Patrick, H., Knee, C. R., Canevello, A., & Lonsbary, C. (2007). The role of need fulfillment in relationship functioning and well-being: A self-determination theory perspective. *Journal of Personality and Social Psychology, 92*(3), 434–457. https://doi.org/10.1037/0022-3514.92.3.434

Pfander, A. (1967). *Phenomenology of willing and motivation* H. Spiegelberg, Translator. Northwestern University Press. Original work published 1908.

Rawls, J. (1971/2009). *A theory of justice.* Harvard University Press.

Reeve, J., & Cheon, S. H. (2021). Autonomy-supportive teaching: Its malleability, benefits, and potential to improve educational practice. *Educational Psychologist, 56*(1), 54–77. https://doi.org/10.1080/00461520.2020.1862657

Reeve, J., & Cheon, S. H. (2024). Learning how to become an autonomy-supportive teacher begins with perspective taking: A randomized control trial and model test. *Teaching and Teacher Education, 148,* 104702. https://doi.org/10.1016/j.tate.2024.104702

Reis, H. T., Sheldon, K. M., Gable, S. L., Roscoe, J., & Ryan, R. M. (2000). Daily well-being: The role of autonomy, competence, and relatedness. *Personality and Social Psychology Bulletin, 26*(4), 419–435.

Ricoeur, P. (1966). *Freedom and nature: The voluntary and the involuntary.* Northwestern University Press.

Ryan, R. M. (1991). The nature of the self in autonomy and relatedness. In J. Strauss (Ed.), *The self: Interdisciplinary approaches* (pp. 208–238). Springer.

Ryan, R. M. (1995). Psychological needs and the facilitation of integrative processes. *Journal of Personality, 63*(3), 397–427. https://doi.org/10.1111/j.1467-6494.1995.tb00501.x

Ryan, R. M., & Deci, E. L. (2000). Self-determination theory and the facilitation of intrinsic motivation, social development, and well-being. *American Psychologist, 55*(1), 68–78. https://doi.org/10.1037/0003-066X.55.1.68

Ryan, R. M., & Deci, E. L. (2006). Self-regulation and the problem of human autonomy: Does psychology need choice, self-determination, and will? *Journal of Personality, 74*(6), 1557–1586. https://doi.org/10.1111/j.1467-6494.2006.00420.x

Ryan, R. M., & Deci, E. L. (2017). *Self-determination theory: Basic psychological needs in motivation, development, and wellness.* Guilford Press.

Ryan, R. M., & Deci, E. L. (2020). Intrinsic and extrinsic motivation from a self-determination theory perspective: Definitions, theory, practices, and future directions. *Contemporary Educational Psychology, 61,* 101860. https://doi.org/10.1016/j.cedpsych.2020.101860

Ryan, R. M., Deci, E. L., & Vansteenkiste, M. (2016). Autonomy and autonomy disturbances in self-development and psychopathology: Research on motivation, attachment, and clinical process. *Development and Psychopathology, 1,* 385–438. https://doi.org/10.1002/9781119125556.devpsy109

Ryan, R. M., Donald, J. N., & Bradshaw, E. L. (2021). Mindfulness and motivation: A process view using self-determination theory. *Current Directions in Psychological Science, 30*(4), 300–306. https://doi.org/10.1177/09637214211009511

Ryan, R. M., Duineveld, J. J., Di Domenico, S. I., Ryan, W. S., Steward, B. A., & Bradshaw, E. L. (2022). We know this much is (meta-analytically) true: A meta-review of meta-analytic findings evaluating self-determination theory. *Psychological Bulletin, 148*(11–12), 813–842. https://doi.org/10.1037/bul0000385

Ryan, R. M., & Lynch, J. H. (1989). Emotional autonomy versus detachment: Revisiting the vicissitudes of adolescence and young adulthood. *Child Development, 60*(2), 340–356. https://doi.org/10.2307/1130981

Ryan, R. M., & Ryan, W. S. (2026). from authenticity to I-thou relationships. In K. E. Vail, D. R. Van Tongeren, R. J. Schlegel, J. Greenberg, L. A. King, & R. M. Ryan (Eds.), *Handbook of the science of existential psychology* (pp. 279–293). Guildford Publications.

Sen, A. K. (2005). Human rights and capabilities. *Journal of Human Development, 6*(2), 151–166. https://doi.org/10.1080/14649880500120491

Slemp, G. R., Field, J. G., Ryan, R. M., Forner, V. W., Van den Broeck, A., & Lewis, K. J. (2024). Interpersonal supports for basic psychological needs and their relations with motivation, well-being, and performance: A meta-analysis. *Journal of Personality and Social Psychology, 127*(5), 1012–1037. https://doi.org/10.1037/pspi0000459

Slemp, G. R., Kern, M. L., Patrick, K. J., & Ryan, R. M. (2018). Leader autonomy support in the workplace: A meta-analytic review. *Motivation and Emotion, 42*(5), 706–724. https://doi.org/10.1007/s11031-018-9698-y

Soenens, B., & Vansteenkiste, M. (2005). Antecedents and outcomes of self-determination in 3 life domains: The role of parents' and teachers' autonomy support. *Journal of Youth and Adolescence, 34,* 589–604. https://doi.org/10.1007/s10964-005-8948-y

Stanley, P. J., Schutte, N. S., & Phillips, W. J. (2021). A meta-analytic investigation of the relationship between basic psychological need satisfaction and affect. *Journal of Positive School Psychology, 5*(1), 1–16. https://hdl.handle.net/1959.11/29530

Tang, M., Wang, D., & Guerrien, A. (2020). A systematic review and meta-analysis on basic psychological need satisfaction, motivation, and well-being in later life: Contributions of self-determination theory. *PsyCh Journal, 9*(1), 5–33. https://doi.org/10.1002/pchj.293

Tiberius, V. (2018). *Well-being as value fulfillment: How we can help each other live well.* Oxford.

Van den Broeck, A., Ferris, D. L., Chang, C.-H., & Rosen, C. C. (2016). A review of self-determination theory's basic psychological needs at work. *Journal of Management, 42*(5), 1195–1229. https://doi.org/10.1177/0149206316632058

Vansteenkiste, M., Soenens, B., & Ryan, R. M. (2023). Basic psychological needs theory: A conceptual and empirical review of key criteria. In R. M. Ryan (Ed.), *The Oxford handbook of self-determination theory* (pp. 84–123).

Vasquez, A. C., Patall, E. A., Fong, C. J., Corrigan, A. S., & Pine, L. (2016). Parent autonomy support, academic achievement, and psychosocial functioning: A meta-analysis of research. *Educational Psychology Review, 28*, 605–644. https://doi.org/10.1007/s10648-015-9329-z

Waller, B. N. (1998). *The natural selection of autonomy: Redefining competence and femininity.* SUNY Press.

Waterschoot, J., & Ryan, R. M. (2025). *The impact of democracy on people's well-being through enhanced autonomy: Findings from three cross-national surveys.* (manuscript under review).

Weinstein, N., Przybylski, A. K., & Ryan, R. M. (2012). The index of autonomous functioning: Development of a scale of human autonomy. *Journal of Research in Personality, 46*(4), 397–413. https://doi.org/10.1016/j.jrp.2012.03.007

Weinstein, N., & Ryan, R. M. (2010). When helping helps: Autonomous motivation for prosocial behavior and its influence on well-being for the helper and recipient. *Journal of Personality and Social Psychology, 98*(2), 222–244. https://doi.org/10.1037/a0016984

Wild, J. (1965). Authentic existence: A new approach to. *Selected Studies in Phenomenology and Existential Philosophy, 1*, 59–77. https://doi.org/10.5840/sspep196514

Yu, S., Levesque-Bristol, C., & Maeda, Y. (2018). General need for autonomy and subjective well-being: A meta-analysis of studies in the US and East Asia. *Journal of Happiness Studies, 19*, 1863–1882.

Zuroff, D. C., Koestner, R., Moskowitz, D. S., McBride, C., & Bagby, R. M. (2012). Therapist's autonomy support and patient's self-criticism predict motivation during brief treatments for depression. *Journal of Social and Clinical Psychology, 31*(9), 903–932. https://doi.org/10.1521/jscp.2012.31.9.903

SECTION 2

THE SELF AS EMBEDDED IN CULTURE AND CONTEXT

CHAPTER 6

INTERDEPENDENT SELF-DETERMINED MOTIVATION: A COMPLEMENTARY—YET OFTEN OVERLOOKED—MODEL OF SELF AND AGENCY ACROSS WEIRD AND RELATE CULTURES

Gregory Arief D. Liem
Nanyang Technological University, Singapore

ABSTRACT

Students' academic motivation is rooted in their self and occurs in a particular sociocultural context. The academic motivation literature has been replete with the work that revolves around the concept of self-determination and personal causation. This view of motivation is predominantly built on the independent models of the self and agency that are more pervasive among individuals in culturally individualistic and Western, Educated, Industrialized, Rich, Democratic or WEIRD societies. Individuals in nonWEIRD cultures, however, would internalize, ascribe to, and make collective goals, relational

The Self in Context, pages 183–223

Published under exclusive licence by Emerald Publishing Limited
doi:10.1108/978-1-80686-869-820261006

values, and group preferences as key constituents of their self. Thus, students in the more collectivistic and nonWEIRD traditions tend to adopt what I call the interdependent self-determined motivation. Like its independent self-determined counterpart, the interdependent self-determined motivation promises an equally powerful way of explaining student motivation. Aligned with the recent call for considering both intrapersonal and interpersonal roots and processes of motivation to arrive at a more holistic understanding of human motivation, the current focus on the interdependent ways of being, doing, and becoming builds a more culturally comprehensive and responsive science of student motivation and provides a culturally diversified educational psychology toolkit that benefits our understanding of student motivation across cultural boundaries. Implications for theorizing, research, and practice of the synergistic integration of the independent and interdependent models of student motivation are drawn and discussed.

Keywords: Interdependent self; self determined motivation; introjected regulation; intrapersonal–interpersonal motivation; cultural models of agency

Jenny and Jun-mi—both pseudonyms—are in their final year of high school, preparing for university entrance examinations. First, let's meet Jenny.

> Jenny—a Year-12 student in Sydney—is determined to excel, not just for the grades, but for the deep sense of worth and purpose they give her. She believes in her ability to succeed, and every A fills her with pride, affirming that she is on the right path. Yet, one bad grade stings with shame, making her question whether she has the ability to do well. Her dream of becoming a doctor fuels her passion for Biology and Chemistry, where she immerses herself in every concept, fascinated by the science behind medicine. She devours medical documentaries, reads about groundbreaking treatments, and envisions herself in a white coat, saving lives. While her parents hope she will follow a different path and become a psychologist, Jenny is firm in her conviction—this is her life, and she wants to make her own choices. She clings to the belief that if you find your passion, success will follow—a mantra she encountered in the motivational books she read early in life. The challenge of mastering difficult concepts and the satisfaction of proving herself keep her motivated. As she sits at her desk, reviewing her notes one last time, she reminds herself: her future is in her hands, and she is ready to shape it. No matter the path she chooses, she knows her parents are proud of her.

Now, let's turn to Jun-mi.

> Jun-mi—a Grade-12 student in Seoul—is determined to succeed, not just for herself, but to make her family proud. She isn't the most confident student in her class and often wonders if she is truly capable. Yet, she believes that with hard work, she can achieve her dreams. Every A fills her with pride, affirming

> that she is meeting her parents' expectations and upholding the family's honor. But a bad grade feels like more than just disappointment—it brings shame, making her question if she has done enough and whether she has let her family down. She also carries the weight of guilt, knowing how much her parents have sacrificed for her education. Her dream of becoming a doctor is shaped by their hopes, even though, deep down, she longs to be a psychologist. Still, she dedicates herself to Biology and Chemistry, knowing her success is not hers alone—it belongs to her family. The expectations are heavy, but they give her purpose. Late at night, she studies anatomy diagrams, reminding herself of a saying she learned early in life: "Even a dog can recite poetry after three years of schooling"—with enough effort, anything is possible. As she reviews her notes one last time, she reassures herself: her future is not just hers—it is a promise she must fulfill for those who believe in her. As much as she worries, she knows her parents are proud of her.

To an outsider unfamiliar with cultural perspectives on motivation, Jenny and Jun-mi might appear nearly identical despite their geographical distance. Both are diligent, hardworking high school seniors who push themselves to excel, driven by a deep sense of purpose. They are fully committed to their studies, particularly in Biology and Chemistry, knowing these subjects are key to their shared dream of becoming doctors. Their emotional responses to achievement mirror each other—every A fills them with pride, reinforcing their commitment, while a bad grade sparks self-doubt and disappointment. Late into the night, both immerse themselves in their studies, each propelled by an unwavering sense of responsibility. Their perseverance, ambition, and relentless pursuit of excellence unite them in their journey toward a future in medicine.

A closer look, however, reveals two distinct stories. Jenny pursues her goals with a strong sense of personal agency, driven by her own aspirations rather than external pressure. She values learning as essential to her dream of becoming a doctor, and her confidence—reinforced by past successes—fuels her determination. Setbacks do not discourage her; instead, they push her to reflect and work harder. She sees achievement as a product of her own abilities, maintaining a strong sense of control over her academic outcomes. Even in the face of parental expectations, she asserts her independence, believing that passion and perseverance lead to success. Fully owning her ambitions, she embraces challenges and sees effort as the key to realizing her potential.

Jun-mi's motivation, in contrast, is shaped by a deep sense of responsibility to her family. She works hard not only for herself but also to bring honor to her parents, taking pride in meeting their expectations. While she sometimes questions her abilities, she believes that effort is the key to success and approaches her studies with diligence and discipline. For her, achievement is not just a personal accomplishment but a shared family success, reinforcing her strong connection to those who have supported her. Though she carries the weight of expectations, she finds meaning in striving toward a goal that aligns with her family's hopes. While her path is guided more by duty than personal passion—at least initially—she remains committed to excelling, knowing that her hard work will contribute to a future that brings fulfillment to both herself and her loved ones.

Whose motivation is more authentic, agentic, and autonomous? Jenny studies hard to realize her potential and pursue her dream, while Jun-mi is equally diligent, driven by a strong sense of duty to her family. Both students find meaning in academic achievement—Jenny views it as a path to personal fulfillment and self-actualization, whereas Jun-mi sees it as a way to bring pride to her family and honor their sacrifices. Although the outcome they strive for is identical (academic success and becoming a doctor) and their behaviors are similar (studying late into the night), their motivations differ in origin and orientation. Yet, both are deeply meaningful and propel them toward success. From the perspective of contemporary motivation theories that emphasize personal agency and self-determination, Jenny exemplifies the ideal student: self-directed, intrinsically motivated, and in control of her success. In contrast, Jun-mi may be seen as less ideal, as her motivation is shaped more by family obligation than individual choice. These theories often imply that Jenny's motivation is more authentic, agentic, and autonomous. However, while such frameworks offer valuable insights into students like Jenny, they provide only a partial understanding of students like Jun-mi, whose motivation is embedded in relational contexts and shaped by cultural expectations of duty and interdependence.

Importantly, this is not to suggest that all students in Sydney are like Jenny or that all students in Seoul are like Jun-mi. Indeed, there is a bit of Jenny and a bit of Jun-mi in every student—or, more broadly, in each of us, regardless of our cultural backgrounds. These illustrations are intended not to stereotype students by cultural background (e.g., Western vs. Eastern) or to impose rigid dichotomies (e.g., individualistic vs. collectivistic). Rather, they serve to illuminate how students who pursue similar academic goals and exhibit comparable achievement behaviors may nevertheless be motivated by fundamentally different selves and forms of agency. Recognizing this diversity in motivation challenges us to broaden our theoretical frameworks to more fully account for culturally embedded sources of meaning and drive.

Beyond Jun-mi, a growing body of research shows that students from collectivistic, particularly East Asian, backgrounds often prioritize fulfilling familial expectations over, or as much as, pursuing personal interests (Fu & Markus, 2014; Iyengar & Lepper, 1999)—a practice that, through an individualistic lens, may be mistakenly viewed as a lack of autonomy. Similarly, deferring to authority figures such as parents or teachers, and making academic decisions based on social obligations rather than personal passions, is often misread as diminished personal agency (Li et al., 2021; Wang & Miller,

2020). Moreover, placing greater value on family reputation or group harmony over individual distinction may be perceived as conformist or unambitious, when in fact it reflects a culturally grounded ethic of social interdependence and collective responsibility (Buchtel et al., 2018; Hwang, 2012).

To broaden the behavioral science toolkit and develop a more comprehensive understanding of student achievement motivation and behavior across contexts, a culturally responsive framework is essential—one that also reflects the lived experiences of students from interdependent, collectivistic societies. Building on earlier efforts (e.g., Boekaerts, 1998; King et al., 2018; Kumar & Maehr, 2007; Pajares, 2007), this chapter advances an interpersonal theory of academic motivation by proposing an interdependent-self perspective on student agency and motivated action (see also Liem, 2026). It argues that incorporating an interdependence-oriented lens enriches the study of student motivation by complementing—and not replacing—prevailing independence-centric models. The chapter unfolds in five sections. The first reviews the current state of student motivation research. The second highlights the distinction between intrapersonal and interpersonal perspectives on student motivation. The third examines how sociocultural contexts shape self-concept, agency, and motivation. The fourth demonstrates how an interdependent perspective can clarify and extend existing motivational theories when applied to students with interdependent backgrounds. The final section discusses the theoretical, empirical, and practical implications of integrating both independent and interdependent perspectives into student motivation research and educational practice.

PREMISES AND PITFALLS IN THE CURRENT STUDENT MOTIVATION LITERATURE

The study of student achievement motivation examines the psychological processes that drive students toward educational goals (Covington, 1998; Liem & Senko, 2022; Schunk et al., 2014; Wigfield et al., 2021). Over the past five decades, scholars have developed various theories to explain what fuels student achievement motivation. Some of the most influential focus on causal attributions (Weiner & Kukla, 1970), self-worth (Covington & Beery, 1976), self-efficacy (Bandura, 1977), expectancy-value beliefs (Eccles-Parsons, 1983), achievement goals (Dweck, 1986; Elliot, 1999; Nicholls, 1989), self-determination (Deci & Ryan, 1985), ability mindsets (Dweck, 2006), and achievement emotions (Pekrun, 2006). While each theory emphasizes distinct self-related constructs and processes (Covington, 2000; Wigfield et al., 2021), they share a fundamental premise that motivation is largely shaped by internal factors such as individual abilities, goals, values, preferences, mindsets, and attitudes. These intrapersonal attributes—the "force within" or what Plaut and Markus (2005) call the "inside story"—are considered central to students' agency and their achievement motivation, behavior, and outcomes.

Despite decades of research, student motivation theories remain largely focused on intrapersonal determinants, overlooking the social and cultural contexts in which motivation develops. Wentzel and Skinner (2022) argue that this *intrapersonal* emphasis captures only "one half of the story," urging greater attention to "the other missing half"—*interpersonal* forces, including sociocultural influences, that shape motivation. While many theories acknowledge the role of social agents in student motivation (Martin & Dowson, 2009; Wentzel, 2021), they primarily frame them as contextual factors that promote motivational belief formation (e.g., expectancy-value beliefs, achievement goals) or as facilitate self-systems (e.g., relatedness, competence, autonomy). Attribution Theory (Weiner, 2000, 2008), for example, stands out by explicitly differentiating these intrapersonal-interpersonal perspectives, explaining how students' causal beliefs (e.g., effort, ability) drive their motivation while recognizing how adults shape it through their interpretations and responses to student performance. However, this theory still considers others as socializers of causal beliefs (Liem, 2026). Similarly, Self-Determination Theory (Ryan & Deci, 2020) acknowledges social agents as sources of autonomy, relatedness, and competence support (Connell & Wellborn, 1991). Yet, it classifies interpersonal motives—such as seeking approval or fulfilling social expectations—as controlling and less adaptive as they do not stem from personal values, goals, or intrinsic interests (but cf. autonomous interdependence, Deci & Ryan, 1991).

Concerns about the dominance of the intrapersonal perspective in motivation research are not new. Scholars such as Maehr (1974), Waterman (1981), and Spence (1985) have long critiqued mainstream motivation theories for being rooted in the values and worldviews of people in individualistic—or what is now termed WEIRD (Western, Educated, Industrialized, Rich, and Democratic)—societies (Henrich, 2020; Markus, 2016; Usher, 2018), primarily referring to countries in Western Europe, North America, and Oceania. These theories assume that individuals hold an independent view of selfhood, portraying individuals as unique and autonomous agents whose motivation is driven by personal goals, values, and interests (Markus & Kitayama, 1991; Miller et al., 2017; Plaut & Markus, 2005). While this intrapersonal framework and its specific motivation theories have yielded valuable insights and shown strong cross-cultural relevance (e.g., King et al., 2024; Liem & Elliot, 2018; Sheldon et al., 2017; Vansteenkiste et al., 2005; Weiner, 2008), their universal application risks misinterpretation. Taking the "right" cultural standpoint to understand student motivation is crucial, as applying a mismatched lens risks misinterpreting students as "irrational, deficient, or even immoral" (Markus, 2016, p. 161). Thus, a paradigm shift is needed—one that incorporates social, cultural, and historical influences (Miller et al., 2017; Plaut & Markus, 2005). This shift aligns with an interdependent-self model, which foregrounds relational autonomy, shared agency, and social obligations as core motivational forces (Cross et al., 2010; Kitayama & Uchida, 2005; Markus & Kitayama, 1991, 1994, 2010). From this perspective, motivation is not solely an individual pursuit but is also deeply embedded in relationships, social expectations, and cultural norms.

Indeed, a growing body of research has now highlighted that students pursue achievement not only for personal growth and self-authenticity but also for interpersonal reasons such as social acceptance, approval, and affiliation (e.g., Dowson & McInerney, 2003; Hwang, 2012; Leary & Gabriel, 2022; Liem, 2025; Liem & Fredricks, 2025; Liem & Senko, 2022; Markus, 2016; Miller et al., 2017; Senko et al., 2023; Urdan & Maehr, 1995). For example, mastery goals—traditionally linked to self-development motives—and performance goals—often associated with self-enhancement and self-protection motives (Dweck, 1986; Nicholls, 1989)—can also serve social utility or desirability purposes (e.g., Dompnier et al., 2015). Similarly, in addition to self-oriented determinants (e.g., personal control and task value; Pekrun, 2006), achievement emotions may also be socially grounded. Pride reinforces social standing and approval, guilt signals a threat to social acceptance, and shame arises from failing others' expectations (Gruenewald et al., 2007). Thus, while motivation is often framed in intrapersonal terms, many achievement behaviors are deeply rooted in interpersonal dynamics. Expanding the focus beyond traditional intrapersonal motives to include interpersonal influences is crucial for a more comprehensive understanding of student motivation.

INTRAPERSONAL AND INTERPERSONAL FOUNDATIONS OF STUDENT ACHIEVEMENT MOTIVATION

The preceding section has highlighted a clear parallel: intrapersonal perspectives on motivation align closely with independence-centric views of the self, whereas interpersonal perspectives on motivation resonate more strongly with interdependence-centric views of the self. Accordingly, both mainstream educational psychology and cross-cultural scholarship acknowledge the need to advance an interpersonal theory of student motivation to complement its intrapersonal counterpart. The distinction between intrapersonal and interpersonal foundations of motivation has deep and long historical roots. For instance, James (1890) distinguished between *spiritual self-seeking*, grounded in autonomy and personal values, and *social self-seeking*, centered on gaining acceptance, validation, and recognition from others. This conceptual divide has persisted across subsequent theories. Heider (1958) differentiated between *personal intentionality* (internal agency) and *impersonal causation* (external forces), while Rotter (1966) contrasted *internal* and *external attributions* for success and failure. de Charms (1968) introduced the idea of *origins*, who act with agency, versus *pawns*, whose behavior is externally controlled. Similarly, Maslow (1954, 1971) followed this broad framework, distinguishing *self-esteem* from *esteem conferred by others*, and later contrasting *self-actualization* (personal growth) with *self-transcendence* (altruism and connectedness). Contemporary theories reinforce this distinction too. Ford (1992) contrasts *individual-oriented goals* (e.g., self-determination, self-evaluation) with *other-oriented goals* (e.g., belongingness, social responsibility); Schwartz (1992) differentiates values promoting independence and autonomy (*openness to change*) from those emphasizing social welfare, tradition, and conformity (*self-transcendence* and *conservation*); and Higgins (1987) distinguishes the *ideal self* (personal aspirations) from the *ought self* (duties and obligations shaped by social expectations). This enduring self-social dichotomy underscores the dynamic interplay between self-directed and socially anchored agency in shaping motivated behavior.

To clarify their differences, I propose an organizing framework distinguishing intrapersonal and interpersonal sources of motivation underlying actions and outcomes, building upon classic (e.g., de Charms, 1968; James, 1890) and contemporary (e.g., Higgins, 1987; Leary et al., 2015) models of self, agency, and motivation. The intrapersonal basis of academic motivation refers to motives closely tied to students' intrapsychic attributes and unique characteristics, such as their personal abilities, goals, aspirations, and values. This form of motivation originates from self-oriented motives, including the pursuit of self-authenticity and autonomy (or the avoidance of inauthenticity and external control), self-improvement (or the avoidance of failure), self-worth regulation (e.g., self-enhancement or self-protection), self-verification and cognitive consistency (or the avoidance of inconsistency), as well as mastery and understanding (or the avoidance of incompetence and confusion) (Higgins & Pittman, 2007; Hoyle et al., 1999; Leary et al., 2015; Reiss, 2004). These motives constitute the foundation of many major motivation theories, such as self-determination, self-worth, achievement goal, attribution, expectancy-value, intrinsic motivation, and mastery orientation (see Schunk et al., 2014; Wigfield et al., 2021). In contrast, the interpersonal basis of academic motivation stems from students' relationships with significant others (e.g., parents, teachers, peers) or their in-groups (e.g., family, ethnic communities, ancestral heritage). This form of motivation originates from social motives, such as the pursuit of social approval, belonging, and recognition, or avoiding interpersonal rejection, exclusion, and disapproval. These interpersonal motives are reflected in a growing body of research on social belonging, acceptance, validation, approval, and status (Baumeister & Leary, 1995; Dowson & McInerney, 2003; Hwang, 2012; Leary & Gabriel, 2022; Liem &

Fredricks, 2025; Liem & Senko, 2022; Miller et al., 2017; Urdan & Maehr, 1995).

As graphically illustrated in Fig. 6.1, the framework distinguishes between intrapersonal and interpersonal foundations of motivation along two distinct but complementary dimensions: *origin* and *orientation.* Origin refers to the broad psychological source or basis of motivation—whether *intrapersonal,* rooted in students' general tendencies to regulate their internal cognitive and affective states (e.g., the needs to maintain coherence, competence, or emotional equilibrium, along with corresponding avoidance motives), or *interpersonal,* grounded in characteristics of students' interpersonal relationships and their general tendencies to manage these relationships (e.g., the needs to secure group belonging or to obtain social resources and rewards, along with corresponding avoidance motives). Although all motives ultimately reside within the individual and involve intrapsychic processes, the critical distinction lies in whether they are *self-originated* (personally generated) or *socially-originated* (shaped by social interactions and expectations) (Leary et al., 2015).

Orientation refers to the more specific end states or concrete goals that individuals seek to attain or avoid as expressions of their underlying intrapersonal or interpersonal motives. These end states may involve *self-oriented* goals (e.g., achieving cognitive consistency regarding competence, maintaining self-esteem, or avoiding shame) or *socially-oriented* goals (e.g., gaining peer recognition, strengthening family acceptance, or avoiding exclusion from one's in-group). Orientation is more concrete than origin because it typically involves the regulation of specific internal attributes (e.g., self-worth, perceived ability, attitudes in the case of self-oriented goals) or the pursuit of outcomes tied to specific social referents (e.g., parents, teachers, peers in the case of socially oriented goals).

Distinguishing origin from orientation is important because it separates the source of motivation (*why it arises*) from its goal content (*what it seeks to achieve*)—two pivotal components for understanding how motivation both *energizes* and *directs* behavior (Elliot & Sommet, 2023; Liem & Senko, 2022). This distinction also clarifies how broad intrapersonal or interpersonal motives can manifest in different end states, including cross-over cases where self-focused motives are pursued through social goals, and vice versa. For instance, when the origin of motivation is intrapersonal, it may naturally be oriented toward self-focused end states. A student who feels an internal need to maintain competence may study hard for an exam to prove to themselves that they can master difficult concepts, thereby protecting their self-esteem. At the same time, motives with intrapersonal origins can also be oriented toward socially-focused end states. In this case, the same desire for self-esteem regulation might be expressed through the pursuit of social recognition—for example, a student working diligently not only to

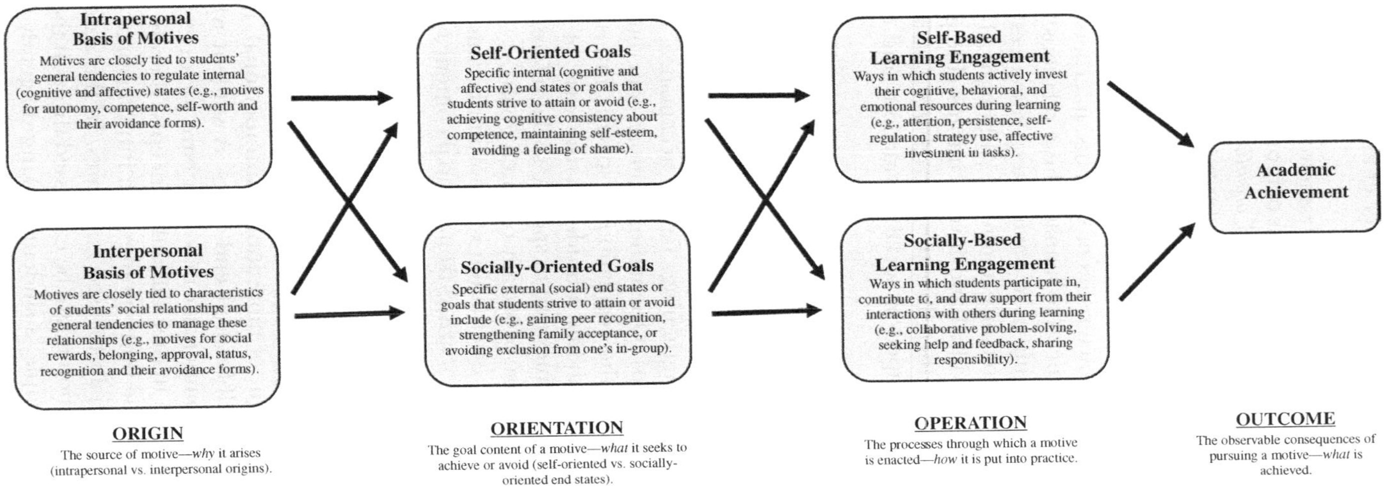

Fig. 6.1. Directional Flow From Motivational Origin (Intrapersonal or Interpersonal) to Motivational Orientation (Desired End States to Attain or Avoid), to Operation (Achievement Related Processes), and Culminating in Outcomes (Achievement): A Motivational Process Model.

feel capable but also to gain praise from teachers or peers. Conversely, when the origin of motivation is interpersonal, it may naturally align with socially-focused end states. A student motivated by the need to belong or to maintain harmony with others may work hard in group projects to gain peer acceptance and avoid rejection, thereby strengthening social bonds. Yet, motives with interpersonal origins can also be oriented toward self-focused end states. For example, a student who strives to excel academically in order to meet family expectations may come to interpret success as personal validation, using achievement as a way of maintaining self-worth. These examples underscore that the pathways from origin to orientation are not rigidly bound but fluid and interwoven, highlighting the analytical value of distinguishing between the two. Without this distinction, researchers risk conflating why motivation arises with what specific outcomes it aims to achieve, thereby obscuring the complex interplay between psychological sources and their contextual expressions.

Regardless of their origins and orientations, motives in the context of achievement motivation are typically expressed and end states pursued through institutionally valued forms of success—forms that function less as ends in themselves than as means of fulfilling deeper motivational desires shaped by intrapersonal and interpersonal sources. In students' academic and social lives, and in student motivation research more specifically, academic achievement is commonly regarded as the primary outcome through which intrapersonal and interpersonal motives are realized and their corresponding self- and socially-oriented end states attained or avoided. Equally important, however, are the achievement-related processes—such as task analysis, goal setting, sustained effort, and collaborative participation—which function as the operational mechanisms that translate underlying motives and goals into meaningful outcomes. These processes can be expressed through self-based learning engagement, such as sustained attention, persistence, and self-regulation in managing one's own learning, or through socially-based learning engagement, such as coordinating with peers, seeking help and feedback, or contributing to group problem-solving. Distinguishing between self- and socially-based forms of engagement highlights that achievement is not merely an individual pursuit but is often enacted within relational and collaborative contexts. Taken together, this framework underscores the need to attend not only to the personal and social origins of the achievement processes and outcomes that students pursue, but also to the ways in which achievement serves as a conduit for fulfilling broader intrapersonal and interpersonal motivational imperatives.

Fig. 6.1 also depicts the proposed motivational sequence, beginning with origin, which refers to the underlying source of a student's motivation—either intrapersonal (i.e., the broad desire for managing internal—cognitive and affective—states) or interpersonal (e.g., the broad desire for obtaining external—social—rewards, resources, and reactions from others). This origin gives rise to a specific motivational orientation or direction—the particular end states or goals—the student seeks to attain or avoid (e.g., maintaining self-esteem as an example of a self-oriented goal or gaining peer recognition as an example of a socially-oriented goal). These orientations then shape the operation—the achievement-related-processes (e.g., affective, behavioral, and cognitive strategies associated with self-based and socially-based learning engagement) through which the intrapersonal and interpersonal foundations of motivation are operationally enacted. Finally, these processes culminate in observable outcomes, such as academic achievement, which serve as a means to attain or avoid the student's ultimate or superordinate self- or socially oriented goals (e.g., to maintain self-esteem or avoid shame, to gain peer approval or avoid rejection) and express their underlying intrapersonal or interpersonal motives. This directional flow from origin to orientation to operation to outcome highlights how internal-personal and external-social sources of motivation are transformed into purposeful action and achievement. It should be noted that although the discussion so far may give the impression that intrapersonal and interpersonal motives are separate, the intention is not to dichotomize them; in reality, these motives are often intertwined and operate in tandem and dynamic combination.

Let us revisit Jenny and Jun-mi, the two students introduced at the beginning of this chapter. Jenny's motivation reflects an intrapersonal origin—her drive stems from a desire to affirm her self-worth and maintain a strong sense of personal purpose. Her motivational orientation is self-focused: she seeks internal consistency and pride by mastering subjects that align with her passion and her goal of becoming a doctor. She engages in operations such as immersing herself in textbooks, watching medical documentaries, and organizing her notes—behaviors that directly support her success in Biology and Chemistry. For Jenny, academic achievement is not merely an end in itself but a pathway to realizing the person she aspires to become. In contrast, Jun-mi's motivation reflects an interpersonal origin, grounded in her relationships and her desire to honor her family's expectations. Her motivational orientation is socially focused: she strives to make her parents proud and to avoid disappointing them. This leads her to engage in operations such as late-night studying and meticulous review of anatomy diagrams—behaviors aligned with her parents' hopes. For Jun-mi, academic achievement does not simply signify personal success; it serves as an expression of devotion and gratitude toward her family. These contrasting examples show that students may pursue similar academic outcomes while differing in their motivational origins, orientations, and operations. They underscore the importance of looking beyond what students strive to achieve to also consider why they pursue their goals and how their motivations are shaped—recognizing that achievement often carries deeper personal and social meanings.

To clarify, the issue is not whether students' achievement motivation is shaped by either personal characteristics or social relationships—both intrapersonal and interpersonal motives play a role, and neither should be dismissed. Nor is the focus on the general role of intrapsychic processes in thought, emotion, and behavior, as these are fundamental to all psychological phenomena. Even behaviors driven by interpersonal motives—such as seeking social approval or fulfilling social obligations—are ultimately mediated by internal processes occurring within the individual. Rather, the problem lies in the longstanding history and tendency of educational psychology—and psychology as a discipline—in prioritizing intrapersonal over interpersonal motives when explaining motivation and achievement (for reviews and discussions, see Leary et al., 2015; Markus, 2016; Plaut & Markus, 2005; Wentzel & Skinner, 2022). As noted, this bias reflects the individualistic and independence-centric values that have historically shaped motivation science (Maehr, 1974; Spence, 1985; Waterman, 1981), conducted with participants from, and by researchers in, WEIRD contexts (Henrich, 2020; Markus, 2016), leading to an underrepresentation of interpersonal motives in achievement motivation theories (cf. Urdan & Maehr, 1995).

Another issue concerns the frequent blurring and misattribution of the origins and orientations of achievement processes and outcomes, as both intrapersonal and interpersonal motives can be served by the same outcomes (e.g., academic achievement) and can be pursued through either self-directed or socially-directed goals and processes—or both (Leary et al., 2015; Liem & Senko, 2022). In their pure forms, intrapersonal motives are satisfied through self-directed cognitive-affective processes and the attainment of intrapersonal end states, whereas interpersonal motives are expressed through social processes and the attainment of interpersonal end states. Wentzel (1999) illustrates this well by showing that self-oriented motives (e.g., striving for understanding) are often enacted through self-directed behaviors, while relationally-oriented motives (e.g., seeking group belonging) tend to be pursued through social behaviors. Yet, these pathways are not mutually exclusive: self-directed processes can serve social motives (e.g., studying hard to gain teacher approval), just as socially-directed processes can facilitate self-oriented motives (e.g., collaborating to enhance learning and mastery). Both types of processes contribute to intrapersonal (e.g., mastery, understanding) and interpersonal (e.g., peer acceptance, social connection) outcomes, which in turn support academic achievement. Thus, achievement behaviors (i.e., the operation) alone do not reveal a student's ultimate motive, as the same action may originate from either an intrapersonal or interpersonal motivational source, or both (Leary et al., 2015). The key distinction lies not in the behavior itself, but in whether the underlying motive is primarily oriented toward self- or socially-focused end states.

Most importantly, theories that explain behavior as oriented toward interpersonal end states (e.g., approval, duty) differ fundamentally from those that frame it as driven by intrapersonal end states (e.g., self-pride) (Leary et al., 2015; Markus, 2016; Weiner, 2008). These distinct motivational orientations not only shape behavior but also offer different psychological frameworks and meaning systems for individuals. For instance, a student studying to protect their self-worth or avoid personal shame is motivated in fundamentally different ways than one studying to bring honor to their family or avoid disappointing them. These underlying motives and their associated end states shape how individuals interpret their efforts, successes, and failures—affecting emotional responses, persistence, and engagement. The key question, then, is whether students' achievement behaviors are primarily driven by intrapersonal or interpersonal motives, and whether they are predominantly directed toward self-focused or socially-focused end states.

This distinction is especially critical for understanding students with predominantly interdependent self-concepts, for whom traditional, individualism-oriented theories may offer an incomplete account for academic motivation. To address this gap, this chapter introduces an interdependent-self perspective as a conceptual framework and a promising way for developing an interpersonal theory of student motivation. The first step to this end is to review the distinction between independent and interdependent selves and their psychosocial implications. This is the focus of the next section.

INDEPENDENCE AND INTERDEPENDENCE: CULTURAL MODELS OF SELF AND AGENCY

Sociocultural contexts—shaped by historical, philosophical, political, economic, and ecological forces—deeply shape how individuals develop, adapt, and make meaning of their lives (Bronfenbrenner, 1994; Hamamura et al., 2018; Inglehart & Baker, 2000). These contexts provide shared cultural templates comprising concepts, values, narratives, and behavioral patterns that influence how people think, feel, and act. They play a central role in shaping self-concepts (self-construals), cognition, emotion, and motivation (Cross & Gore, 2012; Cross et al., 2010; Markus & Kitayama, 1991, 1994, 2010). Through processes of enculturation, individuals construct a sense of self in relation to others and to society, and this self-construals in turn shapes their agency—the capacity to act with intention and purpose in ways that are personally or socially meaningful (Markus & Kitayama, 1991, 1994, 2010). As such, what it means to be an authentic, capable, or moral person varies across cultures, giving rise to culturally specific models of self and agency. These cultural models serve at least three critical functions:

they help people make sense of personhood (knowledge), guide daily actions (behavior), and shape emotional life (feeling) in ways that are socially and culturally coherent (Cross & Gore, 2012).

One of the most widely used frameworks for capturing sociocultural variation in self-construal is the distinction between independent and interdependent models of self and agency (Cross & Gore, 2012; Markus & Kitayama, 1991, 1994, 2010; Triandis, 1995; Vignoles et al., 2016). These models are not abstract theories but deeply embedded cultural schemas that shape how individuals understand identity, define success, and evaluate motivation. Jenny and Jun-mi offer compelling illustrations of these cultural dynamics in action. While both girls are equally committed to academic success and aspire to become doctors, their motivations are shaped by different cultural models of self and agency. Jenny, growing up in an independent cultural context, is motivated by personal aspirations and a sense of authenticity. Jun-mi, in contrast, is motivated by her role in the family and the responsibilities she feels toward others—a hallmark of interdependent selfhood.

Independent Contexts

In independent and individualistic societies—particularly those referred to as WEIRD—cultural ideals or mandates emphasize autonomy, self-expression, and personal achievement. Institutional structures such as education systems, economic policies, and legal frameworks are designed to support individual rights, self-direction, and upward mobility. Within these contexts, identity is understood as stable and anchored in personal traits and choices. Success is internally driven, attributed to one's own efforts, initiative, and ability to pursue self-defined goals. While traditions may still hold value, they are often seen as adaptable, evolving to align with personal growth and societal change (Henrich, 2020; Oishi, 2014; Thomas & Markus, 2023; Triandis, 1995).

Individuals in individualistic settings tend to see themselves as independent agents with a unique set of characteristics, distinct and separate from others and relatively unbound by relational or contextual constraints (Cross & Gore, 2012; Markus & Kitayama, 1991, 1994, 2010). As Jenny's story illustrates, her motivation stems from a deep sense of personal purpose and a belief in the importance of aligning her choices with her authentic interests—specifically, her passion for medical science and her dream of becoming a doctor. Her self-concept is built around internal values and long-term aspirations, reinforced by the motivational literature she engaged with. In independent contexts, the most meaningful actions are those that reflect personal agency, self-consistency, and internal conviction (Leary et al., 2015). External pressures, including well-meaning parental guidance or family expectations, are often viewed as constraints on authenticity (cf. Deci & Ryan, 1991).

A "morally good" person is one who acts with self-direction, remains true to personal values, and pursues individual goals with integrity. Personal fulfillment arises from achieving self-defined aspirations, not from conforming to external expectations. Thus, the rationale for action often follows the logic: "I do that because I want to, because it matters to me, and because it expresses who I am," emphasizing the belief that meaningful action is rooted in internal authenticity and personal agency (Markus, 2016). Jenny's mindset—"I must succeed because this is my dream and passion"—illustrates how motivation is guided by internal convictions and the pursuit of self-congruent goals. This reflects a person-centric model of attitude and behavior, where motivation and value systems are regulated by internal standards and a desire for self-actualization, coherence, and autonomy (Riemer et al., 2014).

Interdependent Contexts

In interdependent, collectivistic, or what may be referred to in this chapter as RELATE (Relational, Embedded, Long-term, Ancestral, Traditional, Eastern) societies, cultural values emphasize group harmony, role-based duty, and social responsibility.[1] Institutional and familial structures promote cohesion, respect for hierarchy, and the prioritization of collective well-being over individual desires. In such contexts, identity is viewed as fluid and socially defined—shaped through interpersonal relationships, shared roles, and communal expectations. Fulfillment is achieved not through standing out, but through belonging and contributing to the group (Cross & Gore, 2012; Hwang, 2012; Markus & Kitayama, 2010; Schwartz, 2006; Triandis, 1995).[2]

People in collectivistic environments perceive themselves as interdependent agents—members of a larger social fabric whose actions are deeply responsive to the needs and expectations of others. As seen in Jun-mi's experience, her motivation to succeed is shaped by the weight of familial hope and her desire to honor her parents' sacrifices. Although she also aspires to be a doctor, her aspiration is closely tied to collective values and shared purpose. Her achievement is meaningful not merely as personal success, but as a fulfillment of familial duty. In interdependent contexts, autonomy is not absent but expressed relationally—through commitment to others and alignment with social norms—and this form of relational autonomy is not at odds with personal autonomy (Helwig, 2006; Markus, 2016; Miller et al., 2017).

A "morally good" person is one who honors relationships, respects social hierarchy, and contributes to group harmony. Personal fulfillment arises from fulfilling responsibilities, not asserting uniqueness. Thus, the rationale for action often follows the logic: "I do that because I should, because it is expected of me, and because it is what people do," underscoring the belief that action derives its meaning from its social embeddedness (Markus, 2016). Jun-mi's mindset—"I must succeed because others believe in me"—reflects how motivation is deeply shaped by relational obligations and social norms. This represents a normative-contextual model of attitude and behavior, in which motivation and value systems are regulated by context-sensitive expectations and the desire to maintain harmony with others (Riemer et al., 2014).

Clarifying Cultural Models of Self and Agency

Since its initial articulation, Markus and Kitayama's (1991) self-construal theory has undergone necessary refinements (see Smith et al., 2013 for an excellent overview). While independence and interdependence are often associated with particular societies, these tendencies are not orthogonal, mutually exclusive, or fixed. Individuals across all cultures express both, though one orientation may be more salient depending on developmental history and contextual cues (Kagitçibasi, 2005; Markus & Kitayama, 2010). Students like Jenny and Jun-mi may also embody both orientations at different points, depending on the social context or life domain. Research on situational priming demonstrates that both independent and interdependent selves can be activated dynamically based on environmental triggers (Oyserman, 2016). This "working self-concept" (Markus & Cross, 1990) at any given moment reflects the subset of one's identity most relevant to a specific context or goal.

Furthermore, cultural groups are not homogeneous. Even within WEIRD societies, significant within-culture variation exists based on socioeconomic status, gender, and community norms (Cross et al., 2010). Similarly, individuals in RELATE societies may also pursue personal goals and express personally autonomous preferences, albeit often within relationally defined boundaries. Importantly, autonomy and interdependence are not opposites. Personal agency can coexist with social obligation, and autonomy can be exercised in the service of others (Chirkov et al., 2003; Kagitçibasi, 2005; Markus & Kitayama, 2010).

In summary, cultural models of self and agency—independent and interdependent—provide powerful insights into how students like Jenny and Jun-mi pursue their educational goals. These models shape the kinds of motives that feel authentic, the sources of validation students seek, and the meanings they attach to achievement. While these models are widely utilized in social and developmental psychology, they remain underexplored in educational psychology. Table 6.1 synthesizes psychosocial implications of these models to guide future research in student motivation and offers a conceptual foundation for hypothesizing how selves influence motivational processes across and within contexts.

TABLE 6.1 Differences in Psychosocial Tendencies Often Linked to Independent and Interdependent Self and Agency.

	Psychosocial Tendencies Linked to Independent Models of Self and Agency	Psychosocial Tendencies Linked to Interdependent Models of Self and Agency
View of the self	A person is an autonomous, free, bounded, and relationally independent entity, separate from others and social contexts.	A person is a relationally connected entity whose self is primarily defined by relationships with close others (e.g., family).
Defining elements of the self	The self is primarily defined by the person's unique and idiosyncratic attributes (e.g., personal needs, attitudes, goals, values).	The self is primarily defined by the person's role in social contexts (e.g., a student, a child, a family member, an ethnic community).
Drivers of actions	Personal agency, coming from within the person, arising from internal attributes (motives, thoughts, and feelings).	Relational agency, arising from the person's responsiveness and attunement to social contexts (norms and expectations).
Sociocultural norms	Loose, norms are not strongly endorsed and individual deviance is tolerated and even encouraged.	Tight, norms are more strongly enforced and individual deviance is less tolerated and even penalized.
Goal priorities	Personal goals over collective or socially shared goals.	Collective or socially shared goals over personal goals.
Key psychological processes	Self-expression, self-validation, self-clarification, self-consistency, self-enhancement.	Social compliance, social concern, social contribution, social adjustment, social compromise.
Ideal behavior	Acting autonomously, feeling in control and self-determined, free from others' influence.	Maintaining relationships, being responsive to and accommodative of the needs of others.

Source: See Cross et al. (2010), Gelfand et al. (2011), Kitayama et al. (2022), Kitayama and Uchida (2005), Krys et al. (2025), Markus (2016), Markus and Kitayama (1991, 2010), and Thomas and Markus (2023).

AN INTERDEPENDENT-SELF PERSPECTIVE ON SELF-DETERMINATION THEORY: RECONSIDERING INTROJECTED REGULATION

Understanding student motivation through the lens of the interdependent self requires a shift from viewing selfhood as defined by individual traits and personal uniqueness—as emphasized in independence-centric theories—to recognizing relationships as central and integral to the construction of self (Markus & Cross, 1990). This relational perspective highlights that identity, agency, and motivation are shaped not only by internal attributes but also by one's embeddedness in social relationships and collective responsibilities. As such, from an interdependent-self standpoint, "I" becomes "we," "my" becomes "our," and "me" becomes "us" (Gore & Cross, 2006; Rudy et al., 2007). In this regard, Self-Determination Theory (Ryan & Deci, 2003, 2017, 2020) offers a compelling framework to apply this interdependence-centric model. While rooted in WEIRD contexts that emphasize autonomy and self-direction, it posits the self as the source of motivation, making it well-suited for examining how behavioral regulation emerges from within. Further, it accommodates a socially- and culturally-constituted self, opening space to reinterpret motivation as also arising from relational commitments and collective values.

At the core of Self-Determination Theory is the concept of internalization—the process by which individuals absorb values and regulations from their social environment and transform them into self-endorsed commitments (Ryan & Deci, 2017). The theory outlines a continuum of motivation that varies in autonomy, from *amotivation* (lack of intention) to *intrinsic motivation* (engaging in activities for their inherent interest and challenge), the most autonomous form of motivation. Between these endpoints lie four types of extrinsic motivation. At the least autonomous end is *external regulation,* driven by rewards or punishments, followed by *introjected regulation,* which involves partially internalized motives such as striving for approval or avoiding rejection. Though introjection has a more internal locus of causality than external regulation, both are still forms of *controlling motivation.* In contrast, *identified regulation* reflects a personal valuing of the goal, and *integrated regulation* occurs when the goal aligns fully with one's sense of self. However, because the boundary between identified and integrated regulation is often unclear, research commonly emphasizes identified regulation and intrinsic motivation as the most reliable indicators of *autonomous motivation* (Howard et al., 2017).

Jenny's and Jun-mi's motivations can be meaningfully situated along the self-determination continuum, revealing distinct pathways toward the same academic goal. Jenny, with a stronger independent view of self, is primarily driven by intrapersonal motives: her aspiration to become a doctor reflects a desire for personal fulfillment, self-worth, and autonomy. In contrast,

Jun-mi, shaped by a stronger interdependent sense of self, is motivated largely by interpersonal commitments, though intrapersonal motives may also be present. Her academic goal is deeply rooted in her family's expectations and sacrifices. From the Self-Determination Theory standpoint, Jun-mi's motivation would be classified as introjected regulation, as it is driven by internal pressure to meet social expectations and norms. While Jun-mi's motivation may not be "self-determined" in the individualistic sense, is it less authentic, effective, and meaningful than Jenny's? This question invites us to reconsider the concept of introjection and to rethink the assumptions in Self-Determination Theory—and other dominant motivational theories—by recognizing that authenticity and agency can take culturally diverse forms.

DIMENSIONS OF INTROJECTED REGULATION

Within Self-Determination Theory, introjection is understood as a controlled form of motivation driven by partially internalized expectations and both self- and socially-imposed pressures. Individuals regulated by introjection strive to maintain self-worth and gain social approval, often experiencing pride when they succeed and guilt or shame when they fall short. This form of regulation can be unpacked across three intertwined dimensions: self-social orientation, approach-avoidance motivation, and pleasant-unpleasant emotions. The *self-social orientation* of introjection distinguishes between striving to affirm self-worth (self-oriented) and seeking approval from others (socially-oriented). Jenny, with a more independent self-construal, may feel pressure to prove her competence to herself, reflecting a primarily self-focused form of introjection. Jun-mi, grounded in an interdependent self-construal, may be more attuned to social expectations—studying hard to meet her family's hopes and avoid letting them down. However, her motivation is not exclusively socially oriented; she may also internalize these expectations as part of her own self-concept, striving to feel worthy in light of her family's sacrifices.

The *approach-avoidance dimension* differentiates between striving for approval (approach) and avoiding rejection or disapproval (avoidance). Both students can experience both orientations, but the way these motives operate may differ. Jenny might pursue academic success to feel validated by meeting her own standards (approach), while separately fearing personal failure (avoidance). For Jun-mi, however, approach and avoidance are more deeply intertwined: her drive to seek her parents' approval (approach) is inseparable from her fear of disappointing them (avoidance). Her motivation reflects a simultaneous pull toward recognition and a push away from relational rejection—both rooted in her interdependent self and her sense of responsibility to significant others.

The *emotional valence dimension* reflects how introjection can elicit both pleasant and unpleasant emotions—pride when expectations are met, and guilt or shame when they are not. Jenny's emotional responses are primarily internally anchored: she feels pride when she meets her own standards and shame when she falls short of them. Jun-mi, in contrast, experiences emotion in a more relational context. Her pride comes not only from academic success, but from fulfilling her family's hopes and honoring their sacrifices. Similarly, her guilt and shame is not just self-directed, but also reflects a sense of having let her family down—a perceived failure to uphold relational duties and expectations.

Together, while both Jenny and Jun-mi can experience introjection across all three dimensions, the degree, balance, and meaning of these experiences differ. Jenny's experiences of introjection may be more compartmentalized—driven by personal standards of excellence and internal benchmarks of success—aligning with a culturally independent sense of self that emphasizes individual agency. For Jun-mi, self- and socially-oriented motives, approach and avoidance tendencies, and positive and negative emotions are often intertwined, reflecting a culturally embedded sense of self shaped by relational obligations. Disentangling these dimensions—and interpreting them in light of students' self—offers a more nuanced understanding of introjection and further insights on this regulation.

When Can Introjection Be Beneficial?

Emerging research affirms the value of unpacking the dimensions of introjection to better understand diverse motivational experiences. Assor et al. (2009), studying students in Israel and Belgium, distinguished between introjected approach (striving for pride) and introjected avoidance (avoiding shame), finding the former more beneficial for well-being, though still less adaptive than identified regulation. Sheldon et al. (2017) reported similar results. Bieg et al. (2024) extended this work with German and Austrian university students, further differentiating introjection along two axes: affective valence (pleasant vs unpleasant) and referential focus (self vs others). Only self-approach-pleasant introjection—striving to feel proud of oneself—was positively associated with subjective vitality; all other forms, including socially-oriented and avoidance-based motives, were negatively associated. Together, these findings underscore the relative benefits of self-focused pride and the potential costs of social and avoidance-based introjection in WEIRD cultural contexts.

Yet, a growing body of research suggests that socially-oriented—and even avoidance-oriented—introjection can serve an adaptive function in interdependent contexts. Senko et al. (2023) found that although autonomous motivation predicted positive outcomes for both US and Thai students, controlling motivation, including introjection, was not necessarily detrimental for Thai students. In fact, others' pride and shame—a socially-oriented form of introjection—were nearly as beneficial as autonomous motivation in promoting persistence, collaboration, and emotional resilience, effects not observed among US students. These findings align with earlier studies: Iyengar and Lepper (1999) showed that Asian American children were more motivated when their mothers chose tasks, while European American children preferred self-choice. Similarly, Fu and Markus (2014) found that maternal pressure, when framed as shared responsibility, enhanced motivation in Asian American students but undermined it for European Americans (see also Chua, 2011 on "tiger parenting"). While these findings collectively suggest that externally mediated motivation can effectively support task engagement when aligned with interdependent values, how might we explain the apparent benefits of socially-grounded introjection in interdependent contexts?

From an independent-self perspective, identified regulation reflects autonomous motivation driven by personally meaningful, self-endorsed goals (e.g., "because it is important to me"). In contrast, introjected regulation involves controlling motivation, rooted in internal pressure to feel pride or avoid guilt and shame, often contingent on social approval (e.g., "so I'll feel proud of myself" or "so others will think well of me"). For example, Jenny aspires to study medicine because she values helping others and sees it as a path to personal growth—demonstrating identified regulation. Yet, at times, she is also driven by a need to prove her worth to herself or others (parents, teachers, peers), such as earning praise or avoiding disapproval, reflecting introjected regulation.

In contrast, from an interdependent-self perspective, the sense of "we-ness" in regulation reframes social introjection not as coercive, but as a meaningful and agentic form of motivation—deeply embedded in relational obligations and shared purpose. Within this view, identified regulation extends beyond personal values to encompass goals that are relationally shared with significant others (e.g., "because it is important for us as a family"; Rudy et al., 2007). For students like Jun-mi, academic goals are not chosen in isolation but pursued collectively, with success representing not only personal achievement but also the fulfillment of familial aspirations. Further, as these goals are often pursued in a socially shared manner, Jun-mi's emotional investment is also collective. What she seeks to attain or avoid is not just personal pride or guilt, but collectively experienced pride and the avoidance of shared shame or disappointment.

In this context, Jun-mi's desire to make her family proud and avoid letting them down are not experienced as external demands, but as emotionally meaningful expressions of shared values. Thus, an interdependent form of introjection—when tied to family and other significant others in one's in-groups—functions not as a controlling force, but as an emotional extension of identified motivation. Thus, in interdependent contexts, emotions typically associated with introjection—pride, guilt, and shame—can serve as integral components of interdependently autonomous motivation. Rather than signaling control, they reflect a deep commitment to relational harmony and collective purpose (Chao, 1994). While acknowledging the potential effects of anticipated emotions, there is a need to unpack them and clarify their role in motivational processes. Let's begin with pride.

Potential Benefits of Pride

Within Self-Determination Theory, personal pride is the pleasant emotion most commonly associated with introjection, traditionally classified as a controlling form of motivation due to its reliance on perceived social approval. However, growing evidence suggests that pursuing pride for self-validation (e.g., "because I want to feel proud of myself") is consistently linked to adaptive academic and well-being outcomes (Assor et al., 2009; Bieg et al., 2024), and may even operate as a form of autonomous motivation (Senko & Tropiano, 2016; Senko et al., 2023). Although this challenges the theory's conventional classification of introjection, it aligns with the distinction between *authentic pride*—rooted in effort, mastery, and meaningful goal pursuit—and *hubristic pride*, which reflects inflated self-importance and is linked to narcissism and maladaptive outcomes (Tracy & Robins, 2007). When pride arises from genuine engagement with valued challenges, it functions more like autonomous motivation than a controlling force (Senko & Tropiano, 2016). Further, from an independent-self perspective, pride is often tied to ability-based attributions: success is seen as a reflection of one's personal competence, capacity, and internal standards (Choi et al., 1999; Plaut & Markus, 2005; Weiner, 2008). This is exemplified by students like Jenny, who strive to realize their potential and pursue personally meaningful goals with a strong sense of self-direction and belief in their own abilities. Fig. 6.2a illustrates.

By the same logic, the desire to make significant others proud (e.g., "because I want to make my parents proud") can have adaptive effects, particularly when rooted in authentic pride—not as a means of gaining approval or status, but as a sincere expression of relational commitment to meaningful achievement. Furthermore, from an interdependent-self perspective, pride stems not only from personal success but from fulfilling the aspirations of one's in-group—involving the student and their family—through the pursuit of consensually valued goals (e.g., "because accomplishing our goals would make us—my family and me—proud"; cf. Gore & Cross, 2006; Rudy et al., 2007). Pride here is often attributed to sustained effort, perseverance, and honoring relational obligations (Choi et al., 1999; Plaut & Markus, 2005; Weiner, 2008). Such success frequently evokes a sense of collectively shared pride, where the emotional reward is distributed across the group rather than experienced individually, affirming the importance of collective effort and mutual support. Achievement, in this context, is not experienced as external pressure but as an affirmation of shared identity and responsibility. Thus, students like Jun-mi are not driven by passive compliance but by a purposeful and emotionally resonant commitment to honoring family sacrifices and advancing a shared vision of success—an autonomous engagement with interdependent values rather than a reaction to external demands. Fig. 6.2b illustrates.

Together, existing theory and findings support the adaptive role of pride—whether self- or socially oriented—when it reflects authentic engagement with meaningful goals. Perhaps, this also underscores the need for Self-Determination Theory to more clearly distinguish authentic from hubristic pride, and to consider the former as a potential component of autonomous motivation within both independent and interdependent frameworks.

Potential Differences in the Effects of Shame and Guilt

Building on the adaptive potential of pride, it is important to distinguish between shame and guilt, particularly through the lens of independent versus interdependent selves. Although both may follow failure, Attribution Theory (Weiner, 2000, 2008) suggests that shame typically stems from perceived low ability, while guilt arises from insufficient effort (see also Leary et al., 2015). Yet, most Self-Determination Theory research has emphasized shame as the dominant affective marker of introjection—whether in isolation (e.g., Senko et al., 2023), as a generalized negative emotion (Ryan & Connell, 1989), or combined with guilt (Bieg et al., 2024; Sheldon et al., 2017). This focus apparently reflects the independent-centric assumptions of mainstream motivational theories, in which personal competence and ability are central to self-worth (Assor et al., 2009; Covington, 1998; Nicholls, 1989). In such contexts, failure is often attributed to internal, uncontrollable factors like low ability, which elicits shame more than guilt (Pekrun, 2006; Weiner, 2008). Parents and teachers—who tend to favor ability-based over situational attributions (Choi et al., 1999; Plaut & Markus, 2005)—may respond with sympathy or pity, redirecting students toward tasks they are "good at" rather than encouraging persistence on the tasks that students are "weaker at." As a result, students like Jenny, when feeling ashamed for not meeting internal standards, may avoid challenging tasks to protect their self-worth—ultimately limiting growth in areas of perceived weakness (Weiner, 2000, 2008). Fig. 6.2a illustrates.

In contrast, the interdependent-self perspective emphasizes relational agency, social acceptance, and the pursuit of collective goals. Academic success contributes not only to the student's pride but also to that of their

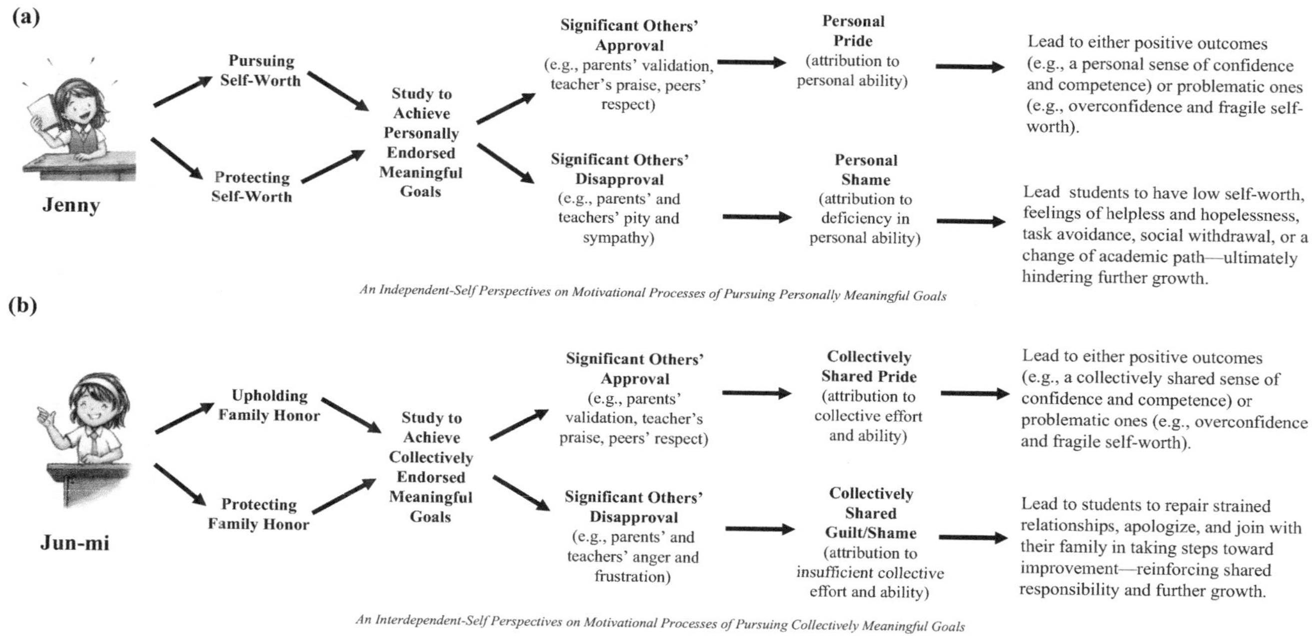

Fig. 6.2. Schematic Representations of Student Motivational Processes Through the Lens of the Independent Self (Jenny) and Interdependent Self (Jun mi).

in-group—particularly the family—while failure can elicit collectively experienced shame (a loss of face) or guilt (a sense of having let others down). These responses are consistent with attribution models that link guilt to controllable factors, such as low effort (Pekrun, 2006; Weiner, 2008). In such contexts, teachers and parents often emphasize effort-based attributions—internal yet controllable—and may react to failure with frustration or disappointment rather than sympathy, signaling that both the student and significant others could have done more. These reactions do not necessarily imply rejection, but rather reflect ongoing investment rooted in the cultural imperative to preserve family honor and group harmony. Fig. 6.2b illustrates.

As such, for students like Jun-mi, failure may signal personal inadequacy, but more profoundly, it evokes a deep sense of relational accountability—a feeling that she has not worked hard enough to honor her parents' sacrifices (Chao, 1994; Chua, 2011). Importantly, this emotional burden is not hers alone. Her parents may also experience guilt or shame, believing that they too have fallen short in supporting her. In this way, failure becomes a shared emotional experience, reflecting the interdependence of responsibility within close relationships. This collectively held guilt and shame can strengthen the family's commitment to Jun-mi's academic journey, reinforcing mutual motivation to persist and improve.

It is important to note that while significant others, particularly parents, are often viewed in independent contexts as external social referents—from whom students seek validation and approval, and thus as sources of introjected regulation—in interdependent cultural contexts, parents are experienced as integral to the student's self-concept. Thus, from an interdependent-self perspective, close others such as parents are not external agents but constitutive of the self. As a result, striving to meet parental expectations may reflect not externally imposed pressure, but rather a self-relevant and emotionally meaningful commitment. Consequently, when interpreting introjected regulation through this lens, it is more appropriate to associate true introjection with motivation influenced by out-group members (e.g., family friends, distant relatives, or peers from another class or school)—individuals who lie outside the student's core self. From this standpoint, only motivation driven by concerns about how one is perceived by out-groups would qualify as controlling. In contrast, striving to meet the expectations of close others may function more like autonomous motivation, even if it appears introjected from the perspective of independence-oriented Self-Determination Theory.

Together, such intrapersonal–interpersonal dynamics help explain why parental support predicts achievement more strongly than personal passion among East Asian students, whereas the opposite holds true in Western contexts (Li et al., 2021). In interdependent cultural settings, academic goals are often shaped by relational expectations and family obligations, making students more motivated by the desire to meet others' standards than to pursue personal interests. These dynamics also shed light on findings that perceived task usefulness predicts performance for East Asian—but not Western—students with low intrinsic motivation (Liu et al., 2023). When students view a task as instrumentally valuable for fulfilling future roles or family expectations, they remain engaged even in the absence of inherent interest—reflecting a means-to-an-end orientation rooted in social responsibility. Furthermore, they clarify why East Asian students, despite reporting lower self-efficacy than their Western peers, consistently excel in international assessments while exhibiting higher levels of fear of failure, self-doubt, and guilt-proneness (J. Lee, 2009; Stankov, 2010). These emotional responses reflect a heightened sense of relational accountability—a belief that academic failure is not only a personal shortcoming, but also a failure to meet the expectations of significant others.

Notes on Interdependent Self-Determined Motivation

The preceding discussion has underscored that, when viewed from an interdependent-self model, introjected regulation is not necessarily detrimental. Perhaps this helps explain why Howard et al.'s (2021) metaanalysis found that introjection's links to adaptive and maladaptive outcomes were evenly split, with roughly a 50% likelihood of either. The idea of what I call *interdependent self-determined motivation* is not entirely new. Deci and Ryan (1991) themselves coined the term *autonomous interdependence* to signal the possibility that self-determination can be relational in nature, expressed through commitments to significant others and alignment with shared values (see also *relational autonomy*, Gore & Cross, 2006; Helwig, 2006; Kagitçibasi, 2005). This early insight suggested that autonomy and relatedness need not be in opposition but could coexist as complementary aspects of motivated action. Yet, this line of thinking has rarely been taken up in the student motivation literature, where autonomy has typically been conceptualized in individualistic terms. By revisiting the construct of introjection from an interdependent-self perspective, my argument extends Deci and Ryan's foundational recognition of relational autonomy to demonstrate when and how socially grounded forms of introjection may function as adaptive and agentic sources of motivation.

ADVANCING AN INTERPERSONAL PERSPECTIVE OF STUDENT MOTIVATION THROUGH THE LENS OF THE INTERDEPENDENT SELF: IMPLICATIONS FOR THEORY, RESEARCH, AND PRACTICE

Most leading models of academic motivation emphasize internal traits and individual agency as the core drivers of engagement and persistence. This intrapersonal focus, rooted in the values of individualistic societies, has contributed to the development of robust theories that prioritize autonomy, self-determination, and personal achievement (Plaut & Markus, 2005; Spence, 1985; Wentzel & Skinner, 2022). While these models offer substantial insight for Jenny's motivation, they may only partially explain motivation in contexts like those of Jun-mi, whose striving is deeply shaped by familial obligation and shared aspirations. This chapter presents the interdependent-self perspective as a way to address this conceptual gap and develop a fuller, more culturally inclusive interpersonal theory of motivation. This section examines the theoretical, research, and practical implications of adopting an interdependent approach to student motivation and its integration with the independent perspective.

Integrating an Interdependent-Self Perspective into Motivation Models

Jenny's motivation illustrates what current theories like Self-Determination Theory do well: she is driven by her personal values and passions, motivated by a desire for self-fulfillment and internal coherence. For her, autonomy is self-determination. In contrast, Jun-mi's efforts—though equally intense—are directed toward meeting her family's expectations and upholding their sacrifices. Self-Determination Theory traditionally classifies this form of motivation as introjected and controlling. However, through an interdependent-self lens, Jun-mi's motivation is experienced as autonomous because it aligns with shared values and relational commitments (cf. autonomous interdependence, Deci & Ryan, 1991). To advance motivational theory, this relational understanding of autonomy should be better integrated into other self-relevant models. For instance, Situated Expectancy-Value Theory's main constructs of personal value, identity, and utility (Eccles & Wigfield, 2020) could be reconceptualized to include shared utility (e.g., "this major is useful for our family's financial well-being") or relational value (e.g., "this subject is important for our family's future").

Considering Both Intrapersonal and Interpersonal Views of Student Motivation

Jenny and Jun-mi highlight how achievement behaviors may look similar but stem from different sources of motivation—personal passion versus social duty. A comprehensive theory must account for both. While many models acknowledge social agents, they often position them as socializers of motivational beliefs or social influencers of self-systems. As noted earlier, Attribution Theory (Weiner, 2008) is one exception, distinguishing interpersonal from intrapersonal influences. However, even this theory tends to frame others' reactions (e.g., disappointment, sympathy) as shaping internal beliefs about effort or ability. By contrast, the interdependent-self framework proposed here situates the social world at the center of motivational experience. As seen in Jun-mi's story, others are not merely observers—they are woven into the student's goals, sense of purpose, and regulation of effort. This perspective offers a unified language for interpreting diverse motivational pathways across contexts.

Measuring Interdependence in Motivation Research

To better capture the motivational diversity of students like Jun-mi, future research must refine how it conceptualizes and measures interdependence. Students act in response to different levels of agency: *personal* ("this matters to me"), *relational* ("this matters to my mother and me"), or *collective* ("this matters to my family, school, or community and me"). While Jenny's motivation is personally anchored, Jun-mi's is embedded in relational or collective identities. It is important to distinguish relational interdependence, grounded in close, dyadic emotionally significant relationships (e.g., parents, siblings), from collective interdependence, which reflects a sense of duty to broader in-groups (e.g., extended family, school, cultural community) (Brewer & Chen, 2007). Although both forms involve interdependence, they differ in emotional proximity and the scale of social influence. Clarifying these distinctions will enable researchers to better examine how different sources of agency shape behavioral regulation, and to more precisely test motivational pathways across sociocultural contexts.

Incorporating Both Independence- and Interdependence-Oriented Motivation in Research

It is not enough to examine motivation solely through the lens of autonomy versus control. Jenny and Jun-mi remind us that both personal and social motives can be powerful drivers—and that similar academic outcomes can stem from different motivational frameworks. Too often, empirical support for autonomous motivation is used to confirm theory without testing alternative pathways (Leary & Gabriel, 2022; Leary et al., 2015). But in contexts like Jun-mi's, social expectations and family pride can drive adaptive behavior, even when not "self-chosen" in the conventional sense. Rather than framing independence and interdependence as competing forces, researchers should ask: Under what conditions does each matter? How do they interact? A single-minded emphasis on self-autonomy and personal agency may obscure the role of social meaning in sustaining motivation.

Focusing on Intersubjective Perceptions of Cultural Norms

Jun-mi's behavior is shaped not just by her parents' explicit wishes but by her beliefs about what is expected of her—what "students like us" do. These intersubjective perceptions—what students believe other students in their culture value—often guide behavior more powerfully than personal beliefs (Chiu et al., 2010). In RELATE contexts, where harmony and obligation are central, these perceived norms can function as motivational blueprints. For Jenny, cultural norms around personal choice and passion likely reinforce her belief that she is doing the "right" thing by choosing her own path. In contrast, Jun-mi derives her sense of "rightness" from fulfilling obligations. Motivation research should incorporate such intersubjective beliefs—what students think others expect—as core explanatory variables, especially in collectivist cultures.

Expanding the Scope of Motivational Processes and Outcomes

Motivation research has traditionally focused on constructs like self-efficacy, self-regulated learning, and personal achievement. Jenny embodies these ideals: she monitors her learning, seeks mastery, and connects academic success to her future identity. But Jun-mi's motivation includes collaborative study, learning for the sake of family honor, and contributing to shared welfare. These are not well captured by current research. To truly understand student motivation, researchers should examine socially-based learning engagement, shared goal-setting, and communal forms of efficacy (Vauras & Volet, 2013; Yu & Yang, 1994). Similarly, outcome measures should expand to include contributions to family success or community development—outcomes that carry deep meaning in interdependent settings.

Tailoring Interventions to Motivational Orientation

Understanding students' motivational orientation prevents misinterpretation and misunderstanding (Markus & Conner, 2014). Encouraging Jenny to follow her passions resonates with her worldview, but urging Jun-mi to assert independence could undermine her engagement. Misaligned interventions—such as promoting individual goal setting in collectivist settings—may fall flat or even backfire (Markus, 2016). Instead, culturally sensitive interventions should affirm existing motivations while equipping students to manage their potential downsides. For Jenny, that might mean learning to collaborate without losing her sense of self-agency. For Jun-mi, it could involve strategies for coping with pressure and guilt, while maintaining her commitment to her family. Interventions should foster cultural congruence, but also personal reflection and metamotivational regulation, as highlighted next.

Helping Students Reflect on What Drives Them

Whether driven by autonomy or obligation, students benefit from understanding the sources of their motivation. Jenny's story shows how personal goals can foster direction and resilience, but also vulnerability to perfectionism or self-judgment. Jun-mi's experience reveals how relational motives can sustain persistence, but also invite pressure and fear of failure. Helping students recognize these patterns through metamotivation—reflecting on why they strive and how it affects them—can support more adaptive self-regulation (Miele & Scholer, 2018). Motivational interventions that guide students to reflect on their dominant motivational sources—and explore both their strengths and risks—can empower them to stay engaged while protecting their well-being. Whether a student draws strength from personal identity or collective belonging, such awareness is key to sustaining meaningful learning and achievement.

CONCLUSION

The sociocultural models of self and agency—independent and interdependent—offer a more comprehensive understanding of student motivation by accounting for both personal attributes and social relationships as motivational drivers. Jenny and Jun-mi's stories illustrate this distinction. Jenny's motivation reflects an independent-self model typical of individualistic, WEIRD societies. She is guided by personal aspirations, a desire for self-expression, and the belief that success follows passion. In contrast, Jun-mi embodies the interdependent self commonly nurtured in collectivistic, RELATE contexts. Her academic efforts are shaped by familial expectations, relational obligations, and a strong sense of shared purpose. Both students are academically committed and deeply engaged, yet their motivations stem from different cultural models of self and carry distinct meanings. This framework lays a strong foundation for advancing an interpersonal theory of student motivation—one that recognizes how social roles, collective values, and relational expectations shape why and how students strive.

Emerging research grounded in RELATE contexts supports the interdependent-self perspective, showing that motivations arising from connection, duty, and reciprocity can be just as powerful—and sometimes more adaptive—than motivations rooted in the independent-self perspective. Jun-mi's experience reveals how striving to honor others or avoid letting them down can sustain meaningful engagement, particularly when such motives are deeply relational. At the same time, Jenny's story highlights the importance of personal autonomy and internal coherence. Honoring this duality does not undermine individual agency. Instead, it calls for a more inclusive and culturally attuned view—one that bridges both independence- and interdependence-oriented motivations.

Importantly, there is often a bit of Jenny and more of Jun-mi—or a bit of Jun-mi and more of Jenny—in each student. These models are not mutually exclusive, but coexist in dynamic ways across individuals and contexts. Recognizing that student motivation is both personally constructed and socially embedded expands how we understand achievement. This view paves the way for more balanced theories, research agendas, and educational practices—ones that reflect the diversity of motivational landscapes in which students like Jenny and Jun-mi live, learn, and thrive. This recognition of both difference and shared humanity is something Dennis McInerney exemplified so well. He had a remarkable ability to see others clearly, to value cultural nuance while remaining unassuming, grounded, and deeply respectful in his interactions across cultures. That is what we strive to become—not only as scholars, but as individuals. Thank you, Dennis!

ACKNOWLEDGMENTS

I am deeply grateful to Paulus Hidajat Prasetya and Avi Kaplan for their invaluable insights and generous intellectual companionship. The hours of discussion we shared—marked by critical questions, thoughtful reflections, and conceptual clarity—have significantly shaped the development of this manuscript. The limitations, however, are mine.

NOTES

1. The RELATE framework encapsulates a distinct yet interrelated set of core values, worldviews, norms, and practices that differentiate East Asian cultural orientations from those of WEIRD societies (Henrich, 2020; see; Krys et al., 2025). At its core, *Relational* emphasizes the deeply interconnected nature of individuals in these contexts, where identity is shaped through close, reciprocal relationships. Social life is structured around social roles, positions, and duties, with harmony prioritized within families, in-groups, and society (Markus & Kitayama, 1991; Triandis, 1995). These relationships are collectively *Embedded*, shaped by historical, cultural, and communal ties that interweave personal and collective identities. Meaning in life comes from maintaining social cohesion, upholding traditions, and contributing to shared

goals (Schwartz, 2006; Triandis, 1995). *Long-term orientation* reflects perseverance, future planning, and enduring goals, prioritizing long-term societal and familial success over immediate gratification (Chinese Culture Connection, 1987). This culture-level orientation is markedly linked to international differences in academic achievement, particularly in mathematics, where sustained effort and delayed rewards are understood as contributors of student performance (Minkov & Hofstede, 2012). An *Ancestral* perspective guides reverence for past generations and their wisdom shapes current efforts and motivations. This guidance reinforces a strong sense of identity, continuity, and connection across time (Ebrey, 2014; Sung, 2001). The commitment to the past extends to the focus on *Tradition,* where customs and long-established norms provide stability, preserving cultural heritage while allowing for adaptive change. Finally, the framework reflects East Asian philosophies rooted in Confucianism, emphasizing self-cultivation, lifelong learning, filial piety, obedience, respect for elders including teachers, and family loyalty (Huang & Chang, 2017; Hwang, 2012; W. O. Lee, 1996). Together, the RELATE framework focuses on Confucian Heritage Cultures (CHC), including China, Hong Kong, Japan, Macao, Singapore, South Korea, and Taiwan (W. O. Lee, 1996), offering a meaningful counterpart to WEIRD paradigms.

2. In this chapter, the RELATE framework focuses specifically on East Asian societies rather than adopting a broader Eastern or pan-Asian lens for two important reasons. First, although collectivist and interdependent orientations are found across many global regions, they manifest in culturally distinct ways—for instance, through conflict avoidance in East Asia, in-group loyalty in Arab societies, and argumentative engagement in South Asia (Kitayama et al., 2022). Using broad classifications such as "Eastern," "Asian," or "collectivist" risks generalizing over these important differences. A region-specific focus on East Asia, therefore, allows for a more precise and culturally grounded exploration of motivational processes (Vignoles et al., 2016). Second, the foundational independence–interdependence framework proposed by Markus and Kitayama (1991) was originally developed through comparisons between the United States and East Asian societies. Since then, a substantial body of empirical and theoretical work has emerged, especially in the contexts of Japan, South Korea, and China (Krys et al., 2025). This accumulated scholarship offers a robust platform for extending theory, including the present development of RELATE, and enables a deeper, more nuanced understanding of cultural alternatives to WEIRD frameworks (cf. Tweed & Lehman, 2002). While East Asia serves as the focus here, future research should broaden the scope to include other regions within Asia or beyond, to further enrich cross-cultural perspectives on student motivation (see e.g., Kitayama & Salvador, 2024).

REFERENCES

Assor, A., Vansteenkiste, M., & Kaplan, A. (2009). Identified versus introjected approach and introjected avoidance motivations in school and in sports: The limited benefits of self-worth strivings. *Journal of Educational Psychology, 101*(2), 482–497. https://doi.org/10.1037/a0014236

Bandura, A. (1977). Self-efficacy: Toward a unifying theory of behavioral change. *Psychological Review, 84*(2), 191–215. https://doi.org/10.1037/0033-295X.84.2.191

Baumeister, R. F., & Leary, M. R. (1995). The need to belong: Desire for interpersonal attachments as a fundamental human motivation. *Psychological Bulletin, 117*(3), 497–529. https://doi.org/10.1037/0033-2909.117.3.497

Bieg, S., Thomas, A. E., Spreitzer, C., & Müller, F. H. (2024). Exploring the complexity of introjected regulation in self-determination theory. *International Journal of Teaching and Learning Sciences*, 103. Article IJTLS-103.

Boekaerts, M. (1998). Do culturally rooted self-construals affect students' conceptualization of control over. *Educational Psychologist, 33*(2–3), 87–108. https://doi.org/10.1080/00461520.1998.9653293

Brewer, M. B., & Chen, Y.-R. (2007). Where (who) are collectives in collectivism? Toward conceptual clarification of individualism and collectivism. *Psychological Review, 114*(1), 133–151. https://doi.org/10.1037/0033-295X.114.1.133

Bronfenbrenner, U. (1994). Ecological models of human development. In T. Husén & T. N. Postlethwaite (Eds.), *The international encyclopedia of education* (2nd ed., Vol. *3*, pp. 1643–1647). Pergamon Press.

Buchtel, E. E., Ng, L. C. Y., Norenzayan, A., Heine, S. J., Biesanz, J. C., Chen, S. X., Bond, M. H., Peng, Q., & Su, Y. (2018). A sense of obligation: Cultural differences in the experience of obligation. *Personality and Social Psychology Bulletin, 44*(11), 1545–1566. https://doi.org/10.1177/0146167218769610

Chao, R. K. (1994). Beyond parental control and authoritarian parenting style: Understanding Chinese parenting through the cultural notion of training. *Child Development, 65*(4), 1111–1119. https://doi.org/10.2307/1131308

Chinese Culture Connection. (1987). Chinese values and the search for culture-free dimensions of culture. *Journal of Cross-Cultural Psychology, 18*(2), 143–164. https://doi.org/10.1177/0022002187018002002

Chirkov, V., Ryan, R. M., Kim, Y., & Kaplan, U. (2003). Differentiating autonomy from individualism and independence: A self-determination theory perspective on internalization of cultural orientations and well-being. *Journal of Personality and Social Psychology, 84*(1), 97–110. https://doi.org/10.1037/0022-3514.84.1.97

Chiu, C.-Y., Gelfand, M. J., Yamagishi, T., Shteynberg, G., & Wan, C. (2010). Intersubjective culture: The role of intersubjective perceptions in cross-cultural research. *Perspectives on Psychological Science, 5*(4), 482–493. https://doi.org/10.1177/1745691610375562

Choi, I., Nisbett, R. E., & Norenzayan, A. (1999). Causal attribution across cultures: Variation and universality. *Psychological Bulletin, 125*(1), 47–63. https://doi.org/10.1037/0033-2909.125.1.47

Chua, A. (2011). *Battle hymn of the tiger mother.* Penguin Press.

Connell, J. P., & Wellborn, J. G. (1991). Competence, autonomy, and relatedness: A motivational analysis of self-system processes. In M. R. Gunnar & L. A. Sroufe (Eds.), *Self processes and development* (pp. 43–77). Lawrence Erlbaum Associates, Inc.

Covington, M. V. (1998). *The will to learn.* Cambridge University Press.

Covington, M. V. (2000). Goal theory, motivation, and school achievement: An integrative review. *Annual Review of Psychology, 51,* 171–200. https://doi.org/10.1146/annurev.psych.51.1.171

Covington, M. V., & Beery, R. G. (1976). *Self-worth and school learning.* Holt, Rinehart & Winston.

Cross, S. E., & Gore, J. S. (2012). Cultural models of the self. In M. R. Leary & J. P. Tangney (Eds.), *Handbook of self and identity* (2nd ed., pp. 587–614). The Guilford Press.

Cross, S. E., Hardin, E. E., & Gercek-Swing, B. (2010). The what, how, why, and where of self-construal. *Personality and Social Psychology Review, 15*(2), 142–179. https://doi.org/10.1177/1088868310373752

de Charms, R. (1968). *Personal causation: The internal affective determinants of behavior.* Academic Press.

Deci, E. L., & Ryan, R. M. (1985). *Intrinsic motivation and self-determination in human behavior.* Springer Science.

Deci, E. L., & Ryan, R. M. (1991). A motivational approach to self: Integration in personality. In R. A. Dienstbier (Ed.), *Nebraska symposium on motivation: Perspectives on motivation* (pp. 237–288). University of Nebraska Press.

Dompnier, B., Darnon, C., Meier, E., Brandner, C., Smeding, A., & Butera, F. (2015). Improving low achievers' academic performance at university by changing the social value of mastery goals. *American Educational Research Journal, 52*(4), 720–749. https://doi.org/10.3102/0002831215585137

Dowson, M., & McInerney, D. M. (2003). What do students say about their motivational goals? Towards a more complex and dynamic perspective on student motivation. *Contemporary Educational Psychology, 28*(1), 91–113. https://doi.org/10.1016/S0361-476X(02)00010-3

Dweck, C. S. (1986). Motivational processes affecting learning. *American Psychologist, 41*(10), 1040–1048. https://doi.org/10.1037/0003-066X.41.10.1040

Dweck, C. S. (2006). *Mindset: The new psychology of success.* Random House.

Ebrey, P. (2014). The Chinese family and the spread of Confucian values. In F. Rozman (Ed.), *The East Asian region* (pp. 45–83). Princeton University Press.

Eccles, J. S., & Wigfield, A. (2020). From expectancy-value theory to situated expectancy-value theory: A developmental, social cognitive, and sociocultural perspective on motivation. *Contemporary Educational Psychology, 61,* 101859. https://doi.org/10.1016/j.cedpsych.2020.101859

Eccles-Parson, J. S. (1983). Expectancies, values and academic behaviors. In J. T. Spence (Ed.), *Achievement and achievement motives: Psychological and sociological approaches* (pp. 75–146). Freeman.

Elliot, A. J. (1999). Approach and avoidance motivation and achievement goals. *Educational Psychologist, 34*(3), 169–189. https://doi.org/10.1207/s15326985ep3403_3

Elliot, A. J., & Sommet, N. (2023). Integration in the achievement motivation literature and the hierarchical model of achievement motivation. *Educational Psychology Review, 35*(3), 77. https://doi.org/10.1007/s10648-023-09785-7

Ford, M. E. (1992). *Motivating humans: Goals, emotions, and personal agency beliefs.* Sage.

Fu, A. S., & Markus, H. R. (2014). My mother and me: Why tiger mothers motivate Asian Americans but not European Americans. *Personality and Social Psychology Bulletin, 40*(6), 739–749. https://doi.org/10.1177/0146167214524992

Gelfand, M. J., Raver, J. L., Nishii, L., Leslie, L. M., Lun, J., Lim, B. C., Duan, L., Almaliach, J., Ang, S., Arnadottir, J., Aycan, Z., Boehnke, K., Boski, P., Cabecinhas, R., Chan, D., Chhokar, J., D'Amato, A., Ferrer, M., Fischlmayr, I. C., … Yamaguchi, S. (2011). Differences between tight and loose cultures: A 33-nation study. *Science, 332*(6033), 1100–1104. https://doi.org/10.1126/science.1197754

Gore, J. S., & Cross, S. E. (2006). Pursuing goals for us: Relationally autonomous reasons in long-term goal pursuit. *Journal of Personality and Social Psychology, 90*(5), 848–861. https://doi.org/10.1037/0022-3514.90.5.848

Gruenewald, T. L., Dickerson, S. S., & Kemeny, M. E. (2007). A social function for the self-conscious emotions: Social self-preservation theory. In J. Tracy, R. Robins, & J. Tangney (Eds.), *Self-conscious emotions* (2nd ed., pp. 68–87). Guilford Press.

Hamamura, T., Bettache, K., & Xu, Y. (2018). Individualism and collectivism. In V. Zeigler-Hill & T. K. Shackelford (Eds.), *The SAGE handbook of personality and individual differences: Origins of personality and individual differences* (pp. 365–382). Sage. https://doi.org/10.4135/9781526451200.n20

Heider, F. (1958). *The psychology of interpersonal relations.* Wiley.

Helwig, C. C. (2006). The development of personal autonomy throughout cultures. *Cognitive Development, 21*(4), 458–473. https://doi.org/10.1016/j.cogdev.2006.06.009

Henrich, J. (2020). *The WEIRDest people in the world: How the West became psychologically peculiar and particularly prosperous.* Farrar, Straus and Giroux.

Higgins, E. T. (1987). Self-discrepancy: A theory relating self and affect. *Psychological Review, 94*(3), 319–340. https://doi.org/10.1037/0033-295X.94.3.319

Higgins, E. T., & Pittman, T. S. (2007). Motivation. In D. T. Gilbert, S. T. Fiske, & G. Lindzey (Eds.), *The handbook of social psychology* (5th ed., Vol. *1*, pp. 361–432). Hill.

Howard, J. L., Bureau, J., Guay, F., Chong, J. X. Y., & Ryan, R. M. (2021). Student motivation and associated outcomes: A meta-analysis from self-determination theory. *Perspectives on Psychological Science, 16*(6), 1300–1323. https://doi.org/10.1177/1745691620966789

Howard, J. L., Gagné, M., & Bureau, J. S. (2017). Testing a continuum structure of self-determined motivation: A meta-analysis. *Psychological Bulletin, 143*(12), 1346–1377. https://doi.org/10.1037/bul0000125

Hoyle, R. H., Kernis, M. H., Leary, M. R., & Baldwin, M. W. (1999). *Selfhood: Identity, esteem, regulation.* Westview Press.

Huang, M.-H., & Chang, S.-H. (2017). Similarities and differences in East Asian Confucian culture: A comparative analysis. *The Journal of Multicultural Society,* 7(2), 1–40. https://doi.org/10.15685/omnes.2017.01.7.2.1

Hwang, K. K. (2012). *Foundations of Chinese psychology: Confucian social relations.* Springer.

Inglehart, R., & Baker, W. E. (2000). Modernization, cultural change, and the persistence of traditional values. *American Sociological Review, 65*(1), 19–51. https://doi.org/10.2307/2657288

Iyengar, S. S., & Lepper, M. R. (1999). Rethinking the value of choice: A cultural perspective on intrinsic motivation. *Journal of Personality and Social Psychology, 76*(3), 349–366. https://doi.org/10.1037/0022-3514.76.3.349

James, W. (1890). *The principles of psychology* (Vol. *1*). Henry Holt and Company.

Kagitçibasi, C. (2005). Autonomy and relatedness in cultural context: Implications for self and family. *Journal of Cross-Cultural Psychology, 36*(4), 403–422. https://doi.org/10.1177/0022022105275959

King, R. B., Haw, J. Y., & Wang, Y. (2024). Need-support facilitates well-being across cultural, economic, and political contexts: A self-determination theory perspective. *Learning and Instruction, 93,* 101978. https://doi.org/10.1016/j.learninstruc.2024.101978

King, R. B., McInerney, D. M., & Pitliya, R. J. (2018). Envisioning a culturally imaginative educational psychology. *Educational Psychology Review, 30*(3), 1031–1065. https://doi.org/10.1007/s10648-018-9440-z

Kitayama, S., & Salvador, C. E. (2024). Cultural psychology: Beyond East and West. *Annual Review of Psychology, 75,* 495–526. https://doi.org/10.1146/annurev-psych-021723-063333

Kitayama, S., Salvador, C. E., Nanakdewa, K., Rossmaier, A., San Martin, A., & Savani, K. (2022). Varieties of interdependence and the emergence of the Modern West: Toward the globalizing of psychology. *American Psychologist, 77*(9), 991–1006. https://doi.org/10.1037/amp0001073

Kitayama, S., & Uchida, Y. (2005). Interdependent agency: An alternative system for action. In R. M. Sorrentino, D. Cohen, J. M. Olson, & M. P. Zanna (Eds.), *Cultural and social behavior: The Ontario symposium* (Vol. *10,* pp. 137–164). Lawrence Erlbaum.

Krys, K., de Almeida, I., Wasiel, A., & Vignoles, V. L. (2025). WEIRD–Confucian comparisons: Ongoing cultural biases in psychology's evidence base and some recommendations for improving global representation. *American Psychologist, 80*(2), 247–263. https://doi.org/10.1037/amp0001298

Kumar, R., & Maehr, M. L. (2007). Cultural interpretations of achievement motivation: A situated perspective. In F. Salili & R. Hoosain (Eds.), *Culture, motivation, and learning: A multicultural perspective* (pp. 43–66). Information Age Publishing.

Leary, M. R., & Gabriel, S. (2022). The relentless pursuit of acceptance and belonging. *Advances in Motivation Science, 9,* 135–178. https://doi.org/10.1016/bs.adms.2021.12.001

Leary, M. R., Raimi, K. T., Jongman-Sereno, K. P., & Diebels, K. J. (2015). Distinguishing intrapsychic from interpersonal motives in psychological theory and research. *Perspectives on Psychological Science, 10*(4), 497–517. https://doi.org/10.1177/1745691615583132

Lee, J. (2009). Universals and specifics of math self-concept, math self-efficacy, and math anxiety across 41 PISA 2003 participating countries. *Learning and Individual Differences, 19*(3), 355–365. https://doi.org/10.1016/j.lindif.2008.10.009

Lee, W. O. (1996). The cultural context for Chinese learners: Conceptions of learning in the Confucian tradition. In D. A. Watkins & J. B. Biggs (Eds.), *The Chinese learner: Cultural, psychological and contextual influences, The comparative education research centre* (pp. 25–41). University of Hong Kong.

Li, X., Han, M., Cohen, G. L., & Markus, H. R. (2021). Passion matters but not equally everywhere: Predicting achievement from interest, enjoyment, and efficacy in 59 societies. *PNAS, 118*(11), e2016964118. https://doi.org/10.1073/pnas.2016964118

Liem, G. A. D. (2025). Teacher role in student engagement: The classic, the current, and the cultural. In G. A. D. Liem, J. A. Fredricks, & Z. Y. Wong (Eds.), *Sociocultural perspectives on student engagement: Theory, research, and practice* (pp. 373–407). Emerald.

Liem, G. A. D. (2026). Toward an interpersonal theory of academic motivation: Rethinking student agency through an interdependent-self lens. *Educational Psychology Review, 38*(21). https://doi.org/10.1007/s10648-026-10122-x

Liem, G. A. D., & Elliot, A. J. (2018). Sociocultural influences on achievement goal adoption and regulation: A goal complex perspective. In G. A. D. Liem & D. M. McInerney (Eds.), *Big theories revisited 2* (pp. 41–67). Information Age Publishing.

Liem, G. A. D., & Fredricks, J. A. (2025). Groups, goals, and growth: How peer acceptance shapes student development in co-curricular activities. *British Journal of Educational Psychology, 95*(4), 431–455. https://doi.org/10.1111/bjep.12753

Liem, G. A. D., & Senko, C. (2022). Goal complexes: A new approach to studying the coordination, consequences, and social contexts of pursuing multiple goals. *Educational Psychology Review, 34*(4), 2167–2195. https://doi.org/10.1007/s10648-022-09701-5

Liu, W., Hofmann, W., Buchtel, E. E., & Chen, L. (2023). Would emphasizing the instrumental value of learning help unmotivated students? Large-scale cross-cultural comparisons. *Personality and Individual Differences, 203*, 112037. https://doi.org/10.1016/j.paid.2022.112037

Maehr, M. L. (1974). Culture and achievement motivation. *American Psychologist, 29*(12), 887–896. https://doi.org/10.1037/h0037521

Markus, H., & Cross, S. (1990). The interpersonal self. In L. A. Pervin (Ed.), *Handbook of personality: Theory and research* (pp. 576–608). The Guilford Press.

Markus, H. R. (2016). What moves people to action? Culture and motivation. *Current Opinion in Psychology, 8*, 161–166. https://doi.org/10.1016/j.copsyc.2015.10.028

Markus, H. R., & Conner, A. C. (2014). *Clash! How to thrive in a multicultural world.* Hudson Street Press.

Markus, H. R., & Kitayama, S. (1991). Culture and the self: Implications for cognition, emotion, and motivation. *Psychological Review, 98*(2), 224–253. https://doi.org/10.1037/0033-295X.98.2.224

Markus, H. R., & Kitayama, S. (1994). The cultural shaping of emotion: A conceptual framework. In S. Kitayama & H. R. Markus (Eds.), *Emotion and culture: Empirical studies of mutual influence* (pp. 339–351). American Psychological Association. https://doi.org/10.1037/10152-020

Markus, H. R., & Kitayama, S. (2010). Cultures and selves: A cycle of mutual constitution. *Perspectives on Psychological Science, 5*(4), 420–430. https://doi.org/10.1177/1745691610375557

Martin, A. J., & Dowson, M. (2009). Interpersonal relationships, motivation, engagement, and achievement: Yields for theory, current issues, and educational practice. *Review of Educational Research, 79*(1), 327–365. https://doi.org/10.3102/0034654308325583

Maslow, A. H. (1954). *Motivation and personality.* Harper & Row.

Maslow, A. H. (1971). *The farther reaches of human nature.* Viking Press.

Miele, D. B., & Scholer, A. A. (2018). The role of metamotivational monitoring in motivation regulation. *Educational Psychologist, 53*(1), 1–21. https://doi.org/10.1080/00461520.2017.1371601

Miller, J. G., Goyal, N., & Wice, M. (2017). A cultural psychology of agency: Morality, motivation, and reciprocity. *Perspectives on Psychological Science, 12*(5), 867–875. https://doi.org/10.1177/1745691617706099

Minkov, M., & Hofstede, G. (2012). Hofstede's fifth dimension: New evidence from the world values survey. *Journal of Cross-Cultural Psychology, 43*(1), 3–14. https://doi.org/10.1177/0022022110388567

Nicholls, J. G. (1989). *The competitive ethos and democratic education.* Harvard Univ. Press.

Oishi, S. (2014). Socioecological psychology. *Annual Review of Psychology, 65*, 581–609. https://doi.org/10.1146/annurev-psych-030413-152156

Oyserman, D. (2016). What does a priming perspective reveal about culture: Culture-as-situated cognition. *Current Opinion in Psychology, 12*, 94–99. https://doi.org/10.1016/j.copsyc.2016.10.002

Pajares, F. (2007). Culturalizing educational psychology. In F. Salili & R. Hoosain (Eds.), *Culture, motivation, and learning: A multicultural perspective* (pp. 19–42). Information Age Publishing.

Pekrun, R. (2006). The control-value theory of achievement emotions: Assumptions, corollaries, and implications for educational research and practice. *Educational Psychology Review, 18*(4), 315–341. https://doi.org/10.1007/s10648-006-9029-9

Plaut, V. C., & Markus, H. R. (2005). The "inside" story: A cultural-historical analysis of being smart and motivated—American style. In A. J. Elliot & C. S. Dweck (Eds.), *Handbook of competence and motivation* (pp. 457–488). The Guilford Press.

Reiss, S. (2004). Multifaceted nature of intrinsic motivation: The theory of 16 basic desires. *Review of General Psychology, 8*(3), 179–193. https://doi.org/10.1037/1089-2680.8.3.179

Riemer, H., Shavitt, S., Koo, M., & Markus, H. R. (2014). Preferences don't have to be personal: Expanding attitude theorizing with a cross-cultural perspective. *Psychological Review, 121*(4), 619–648. https://doi.org/10.1037/a0037666

Rotter, J. B. (1966). Generalized expectancies for internal versus external control of reinforcement. *Psychological Monographs: General and Applied, 80*(1), 1–28. https://doi.org/10.1037/h0092976

Rudy, D., Sheldon, K. M., Awong, T., & Tan, H. H. (2007). Autonomy, culture, and well-being: The benefits of inclusive autonomy. *Journal of Research in Personality, 41*(5), 983–1007. https://doi.org/10.1016/j.jrp.2006.11.004

Ryan, R. M., & Connell, J. P. (1989). Perceived locus of causality and internalization: Examining reasons for acting in two domains. *Journal of Personality and Social Psychology, 57*(5), 749–761. https://doi.org/10.1037/0022-3514.57.5.749

Ryan, R. M., & Deci, E. L. (2003). On assimilating identities to the self: A self-determination theory perspective on internalization and integrity within cultures. In M. R. Leary & J. P. Tangney (Eds.), *Handbook of self and identity* (pp. 253–272). The Guilford Press.

Ryan, R. M., & Deci, E. L. (2017). *Self-determination theory: Basic psychological needs in motivation, development, and wellness.* The Guilford Press.

Ryan, R. M., & Deci, E. L. (2020). Intrinsic and extrinsic motivation from a self-determination theory perspective: Definitions, theory, practices, and future directions. *Contemporary Educational Psychology, 61*, Article 101860. https://doi.org/10.1016/j.cedpsych.2020.101860

Schunk, D. H., Meece, J. L., & Pintrich, P. R. (2014). *Motivation in education: Theory research and applications* (4th ed.). Pearson.

Schwartz, S. H. (1992). Universals in the content and structure of values: Theoretical advances and empirical tests in 20 countries. *Advances in Experimental Social Psychology, 25*, 1–65. https://doi.org/10.1016/S0065-2601(08)60281-6

Schwartz, S. H. (2006). A theory of cultural value orientations: Explication and applications. *Comparative Sociology, 5*(2–3), 137–182. https://doi.org/10.1163/156913306778667357

Senko, C., Liem, G. A. D., Lerdpornkulrat, T., & Poondej, C. (2023). Why do students strive to outperform classmates? Unpacking their reasons for pursuing performance goals. *Contemporary Educational Psychology, 73,* 1–18. https://doi.org/10.1016/j.cedpsych.2023.102178

Senko, C., & Tropiano, K. L. (2016). Comparing three models of achievement goals: Goal orientations, goal standards, and goal complexes. *Journal of Educational Psychology, 108*(8), 1178–1192. https://doi.org/10.1037/edu0000114

Sheldon, K. M., Osin, E. N., Gordeeva, T. O., Suchkov, D. D., & Sychev, O. A. (2017). Evaluating the dimensionality of self-determination theory's relative autonomy continuum. *Personality and Social Psychology Bulletin, 43*(9), 1215–1238. https://doi.org/10.1177/0146167217711915

Smith, P. B., Fischer, R., Vignoles, V. L., & Bond, M. H. (2013). *Understanding social psychology across cultures: Engaging with others in a changing world* (2nd ed.). Sage Publications.

Spence, J. T. (1985). Achievement American style: The rewards and costs of individualism. *American Psychologist, 40*(12), 1285–1295. https://doi.org/10.1037/0003-066X.40.12.1285

Stankov, L. (2010). Unforgiving Confucian culture: A breeding ground for high academic achievement, test anxiety and self-doubt? *Learning and Individual Differences, 20*(6), 555–563. https://doi.org/10.1016/j.lindif.2010.05.003

Sung, K.-t. (2001). Elder respect: Exploration of ideals and forms in East Asia. *Journal of Aging Studies, 15*(1), 13–26. https://doi.org/10.1016/S0890-4065(00)00014-1

Thomas, C. C., & Markus, H. R. (2023). Enculturating the science of international development: Beyond the WEIRD independent paradigm. *Journal of Cross-Cultural Psychology, 54*(2), 195–214. https://doi.org/10.1177/00220221221128211

Tracy, J. L., & Robins, R. W. (2007). The psychological structure of pride: A tale of two facets. *Journal of Personality and Social Psychology, 92*(3), 506–525. https://doi.org/10.1037/0022-3514.92.3.506

Triandis, H. C. (1995). *Individualism & collectivism.* Westview Press.

Tweed, R. G., & Lehman, D. R. (2002). Learning considered within a cultural context: Confucian and Socratic approaches. *American Psychologist, 57*(2), 89–99. https://doi.org/10.1037/0003-066X.57.2.89

Urdan, T. C., & Maehr, M. L. (1995). Beyond a two-goal theory of motivation and achievement: A case for social goals. *Review of Educational Research, 65*(3), 213–243. https://www.jstor.org/stable/1170683

Usher, E. L. (2018). Acknowledging the Whiteness of motivation research: Seeking cultural relevance. *Educational Psychologist, 53*(2), 131–144. https://doi.org/10.1080/00461520.2018.1442220

Vansteenkiste, M., Zhou, M., Lens, W., & Soenens, B. (2005). Experiences of autonomy and control among Chinese learners: Vitalizing or immobilizing? *Journal of Educational Psychology, 97*(3), 468–483. https://doi.org/10.1037/0022-0663.97.3.468

Vauras, M., & Volet, S. (Eds.). (2013). *Interpersonal regulation of learning and motivation*. Routledge.

Vignoles, V. L., Owe, E., Becker, M., Smith, P. B., Easterbrook, M. J., Brown, R., González, R., Didier, N., Carrasco, D., Cadena, M. P., Lay, S., Schwartz, S. J., Des Rosiers, S. E., Villamar, J. A., Gavreliuc, A., Zinkeng, M., Kreuzbauer, R., Baguma, P., Martin, M., … Bond, M. H. (2016). Beyond the 'east–west' dichotomy: Global variation in cultural models of selfhood. *Journal of Experimental Psychology: Genera, 145*(8), 966–1000. https://doi.org/10.1037/xge0000175

Wang, Z., & Miller, J. G. (2020). Cost and family obligation in everyday sacrifice to parents among European American and Chinese emerging adults. *Cross-Cultural Research: The Journal of Comparative Social Science, 54*(2–3), 156–179. https://doi.org/10.1177/1069397119863422

Waterman, A. S. (1981). Individualism and interdependence. *American Psychologist, 36*(7), 762–773. https://doi.org/10.1037/0003-066X.36.7.762

Weiner, B. (2000). Intrapersonal and interpersonal theories of motivation from an attributional perspective. *Educational Psychology Review, 12*(1), 1–14. https://doi.org/10.1023/A:1009017532121

Weiner, B. (2008). An attribution theorist addresses the co-existence of theoretical generality and cultural specificity. In R. M. Sorrentino & S. Yamaguchi (Eds.), *Handbook of motivation and cognition across cultures* (pp. 143–160). Academic Press.

Weiner, B., & Kukla, A. (1970). An attributional analysis of achievement motivation. *Journal of Personality and Social Psychology, 15*(1), 1–20. https://doi.org/10.1037/h0029211

Wentzel, K. R. (1999). Social-motivational processes and interpersonal relationships: Implications for understanding motivation at school. *Journal of Educational Psychology, 91*(1), 76–97. https://doi.org/10.1037/0022-0663.91.1.76

Wentzel, K. R. (2021). Motivational decision-making in achievement settings: A competence-in-context approach. In A. J. Elliot (Ed.), *Advances in motivation science* (pp. 245–284). Elsevier Academic Press. https://doi.org/10.1016/bs.adms.2020.06.002

Wentzel, K., & Skinner, E. (2022). The other half of the story: The role of social relationships and social contexts in the development of academic motivation. *Educational Psychology Review, 34*(4), 1865–1876. https://doi.org/10.1007/s10648-022-09713-1

Wigfield, A., Muenks, K., & Eccles, J. S. (2021). Achievement motivation: What we know and where we are going. *Annual Review of Developmental Psychology, 3*, 87–111. https://doi.org/10.1146/annurev-devpsych-050720-103500

Yu, A. B., & Yang, K. S. (1994). The nature of achievement motivation in collectivist societies. In U. Kim, H. C. Triandis, C. Kagitcibasi, S. C. Choi, & G. Yoon (Eds.), *Individualism and collectivism: Theory, method, and applications* (pp. 239–250). Sage.

CHAPTER 7

GLOBAL BELONGING: FROM CONFLICT AND EXCLUSION TO UNTAPPED POTENTIAL

Kelly-Ann Allen[†]
Monash University, Australia

ABSTRACT

This chapter presents a critical review of belonging research, positing that the pursuit of belonging, while a fundamental human need, embodies complexities that profoundly influence the self. By integrating interdisciplinary perspectives, the chapter explores the intricate interplay between individual and collective identities in the context of belonging. This approach incorporates both etic (universal) and emic (culturally specific) perspectives on belonging through two parts. The first section in the chapter entitled, *The Dark Side of Belonging: Exclusion and division* explores the inherent tensions within the construct of belonging. This section examines how belonging can be weaponized, considers the psychological impact of exclusion, explores geopolitical divisions and antisocial behavior, and scrutinizes how social categorizations and identity while creating opportunities for belonging, can concurrently create exclusion, othering, and ostracism. The second section, *The Light Side of*

[†]https://orcid.org/0000-0002-6813-0034

The Self in Context, pages 225–258

Published under exclusive licence by Emerald Publishing Limited
doi:10.1108/978-1-80686-869-820261007

Belonging: A path to flourishing, proposes an expansive and globalized conceptualization of belonging, drawing inspiration from the Overview Effect observed in space psychology. It posits that cultivating a sense of global belonging and shared humanity can transcend the limitations of traditional categorizations of in-groups/out-groups dynamics. This section explores how this broadened sense of belonging might influence individual behavior and perceptions in the face of global challenges, such as geopolitical divisions and climate destruction, potentially fostering a more collective and flourishing global community. By examining belonging through an overview lens, the chapter contributes to the volume's mission of exploring the self in context, specifically a global belonging context.

Keywords: Global belonging; self; geopolitics; thriving communities; climate change

If we could look from above at our world of eight billion people, we might see something as complex as a sprawling ant colony, humans building infrastructure and working collectively, constructing, innovating, surviving and, most of all, *belonging*. But do we, as individuals, truly appreciate this sense of togetherness? Despite our vaunted cognitive abilities, we humans are often caught up in our own stories, oblivious to our place within a larger system (Som, 2019). There are parallels in how our brains unconsciously filter out familiar obstructions, like specks on a windscreen or a nose intruding into our field of vision (Kreitz et al., 2015). This perceptual quirk generally serves us well. If we stopped to fully engage with the enormity of the universe and our smallness within it, could we still find meaning in life and the sense of purpose that drives us to continue pursuing it? Maybe we sometimes need to overlook the bigger picture and focus on the self. Or do we then ignore the delicate ecosystem that sustains us, creating havoc in the world through wars, famine and climate destruction (Ripple et al., 2020)?

The human tendency to focus on and find comfort in the self, a construct that shapes how we live and exist as individuals within our families, networks, friendship groups, workplaces, and society, helps us to navigate and build a sense of meaning in our lives, serving as an important lens through which experiences of belonging are perceived and interpreted (Baumeister & Leary, 1995; Yuval-Davis, 2006). Individualistic perspectives of the self are reinforced in psychology. For example, the *spotlight effect* is a term used by psychological researchers to describe how individuals overestimate the extent to which their actions and appearance are noticed by others (Gilovich et al., 2000). Psychological interventions like Cognitive Behavior Therapy have thrived because of a focus on internal cognition (Beck, 2011). The origins of many psychological constructs and observations like empathy, compassion, happiness, motivation, and self-efficacy emerged from our sense of self, as they are deeply rooted in subjective experience (Harter, 2006). Often, it is not until many years later that collective versions of the constructs are studied. This has been observed in research on *collective self-efficacy* (Butel & Braun, 2019) and Gross National Happiness (Ura et al., 2012). Then there are neologisms like *main character energy* and *sonder*, created to remind us that others also live their lives as the main characters in their own stories, immersed in the self.

Without the concept of self, the ability to distinguish and articulate the significance of our own experiences and thoughts relative to those of others would be severely diminished, potentially rendering human existence an undifferentiated mass of uniformity. The concept of belonging could lose its psychological significance, becoming a mere observation of physical proximity or categorization, akin to noticing that pencils belong in a pencil case or that rubbish is found in a bin. Disciplines such as sociology, organisational psychology, and *systems thinking* have helped progress Westernized psychological theories toward understanding the influence of the system (or systems) on the individual and how systems can oppress, marginalize, and challenge belonging (Allen, Kern, et al., 2021; Brewer, 2007; Yuval-Davis, 2006). Therefore, a comprehensive understanding of belonging must incorporate emic and etic perspectives. The emic perspective provides an insider's view, representing the internal subjective experiences and meanings attributed to belonging. In contrast, the etic perspective offers an external, comparative approach that allows for *big-picture,* systemic, and cross-cultural understandings. These perspectives enable a balanced exploration of how belonging is constructed and experienced across individual and collective contexts (Anthias, 2006; Yuval-Davis, 2006).

At the same time, the construct of belonging emerges as being both essential and problematic when we consider an individual within a global context. While it fulfills the pursuit of a fundamental human drive at an individual level (Baumeister & Leary, 1995), it also presents a diabolical challenge at a global level. The mechanisms that foster belonging, such as cultural identity, group affiliation, and social identity, may also be seen to inadvertently lead to divisions and exclusion in-groups, communities, societies, and even countries. This paradox becomes evident when examining persistent issues such as widespread loneliness, social marginalization (Lim et al., 2021), geopolitical conflict, food insecurity, and environmental destruction on a global scale. Perhaps there is a critical gap in understanding: *How can individual needs for belonging be reconciled with the need for global cooperation?* This question gains urgency as we face unprecedented global challenges that require collective action and a shared sense of responsibility. The chapter structures the discussion of belonging in two parts. First, it investigates *The dark side of belonging: exclusion and division,* examining how belonging can be weaponized, the psychological impact of exclusion, the role of geopolitical divisions and antisocial behavior, and how social categorizations and identities can create both belonging and barriers that lead to exclusion, othering, and ostracism. The second part, *The Light Side of Belonging: A path to flourishing*, proposes an expanded conceptualization of belonging. Drawing inspiration from the *Overview Effect* observed in space, the latter part of the chapter explores how cultivating a sense of global belonging might influence individual behavior and self-perception in the face of global challenges. Through an *overview lens*, belonging is examined (and imagined) in relation to the self within a global or even planetary context. This chapter explores whether the Overview Effect can offer a meaningful lens for considering a global perspective on belonging. Can a global sense of belonging address our intrinsic need to belong and the urgent demands of our shared planet to foster a flourishing future?

THE FUNDAMENTAL HUMAN NEED TO BELONG

While contemporary researchers often credit Baumeister and Leary (1995) with popularizing the construct of belonging, its intellectual roots extend far beyond modern scholarship. This is easily overlooked in an academic landscape that increasingly favors recent citations. For belonging research, the tendency to neglect earlier works risks leaving the field languishing, especially when the construct has deep historical roots. For example, presocratic philosophers like Thales and Heraclitus explored fundamental questions of existence, change, and continuity, directly informing the understanding of belonging and its dynamic nature (Kirk et al., 1983). Protagoras, a Sophist, introduced the idea that truth is subjective, emphasizing that perceptions of social connection and belonging are not always based on fact (Guthrie, 1971). Aristotle's view of humans as social animals aligns with modern thinking about belonging, underscoring the importance of social connections for fulfilling lives (Aristotle, 30 B.C.E/trans. Jowett, 2009). In the Hellenistic period, the Stoics and Epicureans focused on how individuals could live harmoniously within communities, highlighting the balance between the self and the collective, with Epicureans in particular, emphasizing the role of friendships (Rist, 2010; Sandbach, 1989). This emphasis on harmony within social structures is also reflected in Eastern traditions, such as Confucianism, which underscored the value of social cohesion across cultures (Yao, 2012). Although this is a necessarily brief and selective overview, these examples from earlier traditions create a foundation for how belonging is understood today.

The Australian Indigenous population, with over 80,000 years of passed-down knowledge, also offers profound evidence of the significance of belonging long before it gained prominence in the West in the 90s. Rooted in a deep connection to land, the spiritual connection to country challenges Western perspectives that often frame belonging as primarily a social phenomenon (see Allen et al., 2022). While Baumeister and Leary (1995) define belonging as a fundamental human motivation toward forming and maintaining positive interpersonal relationships, Moreton-Robinson (2015) suggests that Indigenous belonging is ontological, based on a deep spiritual and relational connection to the land. This challenges colonial framings of land as property and taxonomies of belonging based on possession or ownership. She also argues that this connection to land is central to Indigenous sovereignty, opposing the doctrine of terra nullius, which claimed the land was unoccupied before British colonization. The land remains unceded.

While much scholarly work centers on interpersonal belonging and the importance of connections with others, it is essential to acknowledge that belonging can extend to broader domains, encompassing place (Allen, Kern, et al., 2021; Mohseni et al., 2024) ideas, cultures, memories, and even abstract concepts (e.g., May, 2017). It is important to recognize that the socio-political belonging Moreton-Robinson describes is rooted in Indigenous sovereignty. While it shares commonalities with the emotional or relational sense of belonging discussed in this Chapter, Moreton-Robinson frames belonging within the context of power dynamics and colonial histories. Further adding to the complexity of belonging from a cross-cultural, or etic, perspective is the variation in how belonging is perceived, understood, operationalized, and expressed across different languages and cultures (Abubakar et al., 2016; Cortina et al., 2017; Markus & Kitayama, 1991). Moreton-Robinson's (2015) work is a reminder that nothing is apolitical, including belonging, which can also serve as a tangible and political term when concerned with possession and sovereignty, particularly in the context of Indigenous relationships to land. Such differences show that belonging is shaped by cultural context and histories of power and dispossession. Even the literal meaning of the word belonging itself varies across languages, further illustrating the diverse ways it is conceptualized and enacted (Allen, 2023).

Some disciplines might also question whether belonging is an exclusively human experience. For instance, there is biological evidence for the importance of social bonds across various species, with primatology documenting affiliative behaviors and complex social structures in primates and ethology documenting social behaviors in animals, such as herd behaviors in sheep or flocking patterns in birds (Farine & Whitehead, 2015; Silk & House, 2016). These animal observations are more than just charming analogies for belonging (e.g., Brooks, 2011; Riesman et al., 1950). Given we are animals ourselves, they suggest that the drive to belong is ingrained in the biology we share with other animal species.

Speculation that the need to belong is in our DNA (e.g., Allen, Kern, et al., 2021; Carr et al., 2019) is usually framed by the premise that our ancient ancestors relied on social bonds for safety, protection, access to resources, and social cohesion, all of which increased their chances of survival (Page et al., 2017). Certainly, contemporary research points to modern-day survival advantages of belonging (see Holt-Lunstad et al., 2015), with growing evidence from the emerging field of social genomics (Slavich & Cole, 2013). Social isolation, therefore, would have had dire consequences in ancestral environments, reinforcing the idea that the drive to belong has a biological benefit (Holt-Lunstad et al., 2015).

Twin studies offer another compelling perspective on whether belonging is rooted in biology or shaped by experience. Despite sharing identical genetic material, twins often report divergent experiences of belonging, influenced by the environments they grow up in. As Oikkonen (2018) discusses, while genetics may lay the foundation for certain social behaviors, the expression of belonging is far from predetermined. Instead, it emerges through the complex interplay of biology and the distinct social, cultural, and relational contexts that shape individual lives. In this way, twin studies highlight the fluidity of belonging and show that while biology provides the groundwork, a sense of belonging is ultimately forged through personal and collective experiences that differ even among genetically identical people. The putative truth of the claim that the "need to belong is in our DNA" requires further research (Sack, 2016, paragraph 1).

A futuristic contribution to belonging research may come from quantum physics. The observation of quantum entanglement, where particles remain connected regardless of distance (Potter & Simmons, 2021), raises questions about analogous processes in human connections, especially in relationships with close bonds, such as between parents and children. Imagine if quantum effects like entanglement were active within biological systems. This speculative idea could explain how humans maintain deep emotional bonds across vast distances and time, even without physical contact, opening new avenues for understanding our connections. It could also describe feelings of longing to belong or explain rising rates of loneliness, as we are living farther apart and becoming more independent with each generation, especially in the West. Anecdotal stories tell of people reunited, like the Chicago man who ate at a bakery for over a decade, which felt like home, only to discover that the owner was his birth mother (Land, 2024) or of twins separated at birth. However, the lack of empirical evidence to demonstrate that these occurrences are more than just coincidences (Tancredy & Fraley, 2006) shows that quantum entanglement is likely a better metaphor than an explanation for deep human bonds.

While diverse disciplinary perspectives enrich our understanding of belonging, arguably the most impactful and practical insights emerge from those with lived experience, those whom researchers call stakeholders, or more fittingly right holders, as described by Hare (2023), reflecting everyone's right to feel they belong. Stakeholder perspectives provide invaluable insights into the practical applications and the personal ways individuals define and experience belonging in various contexts. We have learned through stakeholders that young children can find belonging in familiar and safe environments and relationships, particularly through unstructured play (Hudson et al., 2025). As children grow into adolescence, their sense of belonging becomes more complex but continues to be tied to safety, autonomy, and relationships, especially those with parents and teachers (Allen, Berger, et al., 2023; Allen, Mulholland, et al., 2025). Belonging for university students is often shaped by their experiences during transition (orientation), their ability to feel like they can be themselves, and their relationships with peers and faculty staff (Allen, Crawford, et al., 2025; Crawford et al., 2024). Safety continues to be central, while the ways belonging is considered varies by enrollment stage and status, with alumni continuing to feel a sense of belonging. These evolving perspectives drawn directly from stakeholders show how the need to belong is universal and highly contextual, changing across the lifespan. Given the contextual nature of belonging, stakeholders provide insights reflecting their sensitivity to environmental and ecological factors as well as individual difference. It is worth noting that academic writing often positions scholars as detached observers of belonging, but we are also stakeholders shaped by the experiences of (or not) belonging.

Various determinants and predictors shape the experience of belonging. It has been argued that this is particularly so for marginalized groups who have historically been excluded or considered not to belong (Faircloth & Hamm, 2005; Faircloth et al., 2021). Race, socioeconomic status, gender, and disability often influence how individuals perceive their place within social, educational, or professional contexts (Blanchett, 2006; Carter, 2016; Espinosa et al., 2019; Scottham et al., 2008). However, research has shown that individuals and communities who have experienced exclusion can and do experience belonging when intentional structural and cultural changes are implemented within educational environments (e.g., Cortina et al., 2017; Gopalan & Brady, 2020; Gray et al., 2018, 2024; Harrison & McLean, 2017; Sánchez et al., 2005). Interestingly, shared experiences of exclusion can foster strong bonds within groups and communities, leading to enhanced resilience and creating a sense of unity. For instance, studies on students from racial minority backgrounds demonstrate that fostering inclusive environments and supportive peer relationships significantly enhances their sense of belonging (Walton & Cohen, 2007, 2011). Furthermore, research on LGBTQ+ individuals highlights that access to safe and affirming spaces is a key predictor of belonging, as seen in environments that actively support identity expression (Day et al., 2019; Heck et al., 2014; Snapp et al., 2015; Woodford et al., 2018). These findings suggest that individuals from groups who have historically faced systemic exclusion can and do experience belonging, often challenging long-held assumptions, when provided meaningful opportunities to belong.

These observations parallel *Heisenberg's uncertainty principle* in many ways (Oxford University Press, n.d.). "The uncertainty principle describes an imprecision in nature resulting in a limit to what we can know about the behavior of quantum particles and, hence the smallest scales of nature" (Eastwood, 2017, p. 335). Nature is imprecise and limited by operational possibilities (Busch et al., 2007). The closer we come to understanding something like belonging—whether through theory, research, frameworks or the voices of people—the less we understand as we discover complexities and contradictions. We know that the experience of belonging can vary significantly. One individual may feel a sense of belonging in a context, while another does not. Similarly, one group may experience belonging, while another group with the same identity may feel excluded. In one way, belonging has been found to foster wellbeing, togetherness, social support, and mental and physical benefits (Allen, Greenwood, et al., 2024; Cook et al., 2012; Walton & Cohen, 2011), yet in other ways, it has been linked to exclusion, division, conflict, manipulation and even abuse. The remainder of this chapter will explore the dark and light sides of this dialectical nature of belonging.

THE DARK SIDE OF BELONGING: EXCLUSION AND DIVISION

Before entering the dark side of belonging, we must first appreciate how important belonging is for our mental health and wellbeing and understand the true implications of its absence.

The Importance of Belonging

Belonging is strongly linked with wellbeing and mental health and a buffer against loneliness, depression, and psychological distress (Allen et al., 2018; Allen, Greenwood, et al., 2024; Arslan et al., 2020). Extensive research demonstrates that when individuals experience a strong sense of belonging, their mental health outcomes are significantly improved (Arslan, 2021; Shochet et al., 2011). Conversely, the absence or denial of belonging can lead to severe emotional and psychological consequences (Dutcher et al., 2022).

One of the most extensively researched areas concerning belonging and mental health is within educational settings, where a sense of school belonging has been consistently linked to positive socioemotional outcomes. Alternatively, its absence correlates powerfully with depression (Parr et al., 2020). Palikara et al. (2021) examined the mediating role of school belonging in the relationship between socioemotional wellbeing and loneliness in primary school children. Their findings indicated that children who felt a strong sense of belonging to school were less likely to experience loneliness and more likely to report higher levels of socioemotional wellbeing. This relationship extends beyond childhood. Allen et al. (2018) found that school belonging is positively associated with mental health outcomes, such as increased happiness, self-esteem, and psychological adjustment, while a lack of belonging is correlated with mental health problems, including depression, anxiety, and emotional distress. One of the most fascinating implications, however, is that the effects of belonging during adolescence—a time often considered critical for developing a sense of belonging and particularly sensitive to experiences of exclusion—are linked to adult mental health outcomes up until middle age (Allen, Greenwood, et al., 2024; Allen, Mulholland, et al., 2025; Steiner et al., 2019). Early life experiences that challenge belonging, such as neglect, parental withdrawal, and disorganised attachment—often described as early childhood trauma—may lead to lifelong mental health challenges, even before children are fully aware of these experiences. While the evidence surrounding the impact of belonging from birth is still developing, there are indications that early social bonds may profoundly affect a person's psychological trajectory.

With the well-established links between mental health and belonging, adding systemic exclusion and discrimination to the equation only seems to exacerbate problems. Racism and exclusion reported by Asian Australian populations during the COVID-19 pandemic found a strong correlation between experiences of online racism and feelings of nonbelonging, which were associated with poor mental health outcomes, including anxiety and depression (Kamp et al., 2022). Transgender youth, who often face cisnormativity and transphobia in both public and private spheres (i.e., messages that they do not belong), were found to be more vulnerable to mental health issues such as depression, anxiety, and suicidality (Connolly et al., 2016; Toomey et al., 2018). Alternatively, Gotfredsen and Linander (2023) found that when transgender youth had access to safe and inclusive leisure spaces, there was a direct benefit for their mental health outcomes.

Other evidence for the importance of belonging for mental health comes from the benefits reported. Berry and Hou (2021) found that immigrants who felt a strong sense of belonging to their heritage culture and the broader Canadian society reported higher life satisfaction and better mental health outcomes. Conversely, those who struggled to reconcile these dual identities or felt excluded from either group experienced higher levels of psychological distress. Similarly, Caxaj and Gill (2017) found that the interplay of cultural identity and belonging was critical for the wellbeing of people of the rural Indian Canadian diaspora (people of Indian heritage who live in rural areas of Canada). Feelings of exclusion and marginalization—within their communities and from broader society—were linked to social isolation, anxiety, and depression. These studies do not represent the experiences of all marginalized groups, an important point that will be discussed further, but they emphasize the critical role of belonging and why humans consider it so important.

However, it is not just about mental health; a lack of belonging has also been found to have severe effects on physical health, with research linking social isolation to higher risks of heart attack, stroke, and impaired immune functioning (Cacioppo et al., 2015; Holt-Lunstad et al., 2017). Moreover, ostracism and social rejection can be as painful as physical injury (see Williams & Nida, 2016). Studies show that the emotional pain from being excluded triggers the same neural pathways as those activated by physical pain, such as breaking an arm (Eisenberger et al., 2003).

In total, not belonging is profoundly painful and detrimental to both mental and physical health (Baumeister & Leary, 1995), leaving it ripe for exploitation by others.

THE WEAPONISATION OF BELONGING

An obvious dark side of the power of belonging lies in the fact that humans can weaponize it—using exclusion for bullying, pain, and torture. Drabman and Spitalnik (1973) showed that removing individuals from the social environment, such as isolating children in educational settings, is an effective form of behavior control, which is possible because it denies children the fundamental human need for belonging. This practice has continued for decades and remains debated, yet it is widely used in many contemporary homes and school contexts (Xu et al., 2024). Isolation is more than just the separation of individuals—it is a clear and tangible signal that the isolated do not belong, even when temporary. For instance, a parent or educator removing a child from a space says through their actions that you do not belong in this space at this time. However, such exclusion as a form of punishment is not straightforward. The reason for the exclusion, particularly the intention of the excluder, is important. Boccadoro et al. (2021) described altruistic and retaliatory punishments as ways to correct behavior and reinforce social norms. A parent or educator may have no choice but to exclude a child temporarily if they pose a risk to themselves or others. Similarly, adults are excluded from the community when they commit crimes or endanger societal safety. The key point is that intent is not always malicious. Altruistic punishment aims to uphold integrity, while retaliatory punishment, driven by spite, pushes perpetrators further away. For example, Piggy in Lord of the Flies is excluded for his physical differences. As the hostility grows, this exclusion becomes retaliatory (Golding, 1954). While intent is an important factor, altruistic and retaliatory exclusion conveys to everyone concerned that belonging is conditional and that the same mechanisms that create belonging can also remove it (Boccadoro et al., 2021). As emphasized in the previous section, the personal cost of this exclusion makes it more powerful.

NOT EVERYONE CAN BELONG

The fact that not everyone can belong is an uncomfortable truth that exists (philosophically or perhaps politically) light years away from the inclusive policies, visions, and missions of most educational contexts. A school may have rules for belonging and inclusion, you can't say you can't play (Paley, 1992) while being situated in a country that prohibits certain groups from fully participating in society based on their nationality, religion, or legal status (United Nations High Commissioner for Refugees [UNHCR], 2015). The concept of belonging becomes more complex and fraught when considering geopolitics, migration, and forced displacement (Yuval-Davis, 2006). For many individuals, particularly refugees and immigrants, belonging is not just an unmet need but an ongoing struggle against exclusion and marginalization that may be so pervasive it persists throughout an individual's entire life (Ager & Strang, 2008). As geopolitical conflicts, migration crises, and nationalistic policies intensify, the truth emerges that not everyone can, or is allowed to, belong.

This selective nature of belonging in a global society is undeniable for refugees and immigrants who may flee war, persecution, or poverty to find themselves in spaces where their belonging is disrupted (Koser, 2007). The displacement from conflicts in Syria, Afghanistan, and Gaza has left millions without a home or a country (UNHCR, 2020). Refugees and immigrants in their new or host countries may never feel fully accepted in their new countries or be able to return to their countries of origin. If they are accepted, it can take time, sometimes decades, to feel they belong (Ager & Strang, 2008).

In regions marked by war and conflict, the drive to belong can also fuel violence. In Eastern Ukraine, people are mobilized to defend their country, not solely based on politics or nationalism but through their attachment and sense of belonging to their homeland (Aliyev, 2020). This deep-seated connection to one's place can lead people to engage in actions far removed from their typical daily behaviors, moral standards, or usual treatment of others. This impact can persist long after the conflict itself. For instance, in post-apartheid South Africa, the state continued to marginalize African immigrants (i.e., immigrants from other African countries, such as Zimbabwe, Mozambique, and Somalia), contributing to continued outbreaks of xenophobic violence over time (Bank, 2019). While belonging can bring people together, it can also create divisions and conflict that can ripple far beyond political events (Hogg, 2016). Conflicts and violence of this nature could arise from individuals who feel a strong sense of belonging rather than those who lack it, as one might assume. This dynamic is observed through research on school bullying, where both the perpetrator and the victim may struggle with belonging, suggesting that the need to belong can manifest in harmful behaviors irrespective of whether the need is being met (Arslan, 2022).

Geopolitical conflicts, wars, natural disasters, and shifting political climates are constant reminders that belonging is often fragile and is subject to forces beyond individual control. Events like hurricanes or typhoons can displace entire communities, while political movements and crises reshape social landscapes, reordering who is considered to belong. For example, Ahmed (2019) examined how British Pakistani Kashmiri Muslims experienced heightened exclusion during the war on terror, as counterterrorism policies reframed citizenship and threatened the legal rights of specific populations, particularly Muslims, effectively criminalizing their identities and alienating them from the broader community. Similarly, Gibian (2012) described post-Civil War American society, where individuals who deviated from the "national imaginary," such as immigrants and refugees, were often excluded and branded as men without a country, perceived as threats to national security and economic stability (p. 37). These examples reveal how legislation and policy can become barriers to belonging. Similar dynamics were at play in former Prime Minister John Howard's Australia. The Be alert, not alarmed campaign encouraged vigilance that disproportionately targeted specific communities, leading many Australians of diverse backgrounds to feel alienated and surveilled rather than secure (Cherney & Murphy, 2016). These cases show that while belonging is universally valued, it is not universally granted, and its disruption can result from complex sociopolitical systems and decisions.

UNDERGROUND BELONGING

In certain contexts, and at a civil level, the need to belong can fuel destructive behaviors, drawing people into harmful groups like gangs and cults (Allen, Morris, et al., 2023). These groups can exploit belonging to entrench members, promoting violence, aggression and coercion. For example, gangs may emerge as a response to exclusion, providing members with identity, social connection, common interests, or a shared purpose, often when more prosocial or normed opportunities to belong are not available, however, membership may lead to antisocial or aggressive behavior (Goldman & Hogg, 2016).

History has shown us that ostracizing or rejecting individuals from society due to their physical traits or behaviors can also lead to tragic outcomes, such as school shootings or gun violence. Martin Bryant was widely reported to have experienced longstanding social isolation and bullying before he murdered 35 people in Port Arthur (Sutton, 2021). The Port Arthur massacre illustrates how a lack of belonging may drive individuals toward mass violence, and the 2024 Bondi Junction attack in Sydney shows a similar pattern where the perpetrator, who killed six people at a shopping centre, had been homeless and socially isolated in the months leading up to the attack (O'Sullivan, 2026). Criminal gangs can also lead to violence and offer others a sense of belonging that was otherwise unmet. Social Identity Theory explains how group affiliations shape self-concept, reinforcing ingroup loyalty and hostility toward perceived outsiders (Tajfel & Turner, 1979). Matusitz and Repass (2009) argue that gangs exploit this loyalty by casting outsiders, rival groups, and authorities as adversaries. In Nigeria, university-based gang cults use religious and ethnic divides to reinforce cohesion, often through violent acts like arson and intimidation, showing how belonging can be weaponized for social harm.

Violence can be central to gang membership, as seen in initiation rituals. Murer and Schwarze (2022) note that gang initiations go beyond brutality; they solidify bonds through shared violence, isolating members from mainstream society. In Mexican narcocultos, violence is further ritualized, with acts of torture and beheadings used to solidify cartel control and build identity. Bunker et al. (2010) describe these acts as practical and symbolic displays, often involving figures like Santa Muerte to create a quasispiritual form of cartel belonging.

Like gangs, cults can also manipulate belonging, targeting isolated individuals seeking meaning. Harris et al. (2018) note that cults form cohesive social units where members' identities are subordinated to a group ideology, fostering an *us* versus *them* mentality to strengthen solidarity and reinforce the group's aims and norms. This psychological coercion has been known to use rituals, as seen in groups like the Mafia, which employ shared meals and communal living to simulate loyalty and family bonds. Such shared acts can reinforce group identity, heighten the perceived value of membership, and impose substantial costs on disloyalty, consequently isolating members from broader society. The process of leaving such groups can be challenging, although possible (Harris et al., 2018). Berger et al. (2017) identify stages of desistance among gang members, showing the psychological impact of breaking away from the relationships forged. The triggering events that lead members to consider leaving, such as personal victimisation or disillusionment, may challenge their sense of belonging. Paradoxically, the promise of belonging that draws individuals into these groups often becomes a trap. Metcalf (2012) illustrates this in gang memoirs, such as Sanyika Shakur's *Monster*, showing how gang life imposes identity at the cost of freedom. As such, belonging to gangs or cults has significant consequences, where members become entrenched in cycles of violence and crime with limited exit routes.

Sorority groups serve as another example of the dark facet of belonging, where the desire for acceptance can push individuals toward risky, even harmful, behaviors. Hazing rituals associated with university fraternities and sororities impose social and physical trials that exploit members' need for connection. The tragic case of Chun (Michael) Deng, who died in a hazing ritual for the Pi Delta Psi fraternity, shows how these rituals can weaponize belonging to enforce loyalty and result in dire consequences (Shapiro, 2023). Research highlights the prevalence of binge drinking, risky sexual behaviors, and coercion within fraternity/sorority settings (Ragsdale et al., 2011). While the promise of camaraderie may be attractive to members, initiations involving psychologically and physically taxing activities, framing belonging as high stakes rather than high support can lead to unsafe environments and harmful behaviors. Ragsdale et al. (2011) found that fraternity members who frequently binge drank were more likely to engage in physical fights and unprotected sex, while sorority members were found to report greater risks of sexual victimisation, injury, and driving under the influence.

Gangs, cults, and sororities aside, the discomfort of not belonging can be so strong that even otherwise average individuals will compromise their values to avoid it. Fabbri and Carbonara (2017) illustrated this with a study in which participants acted as third-party punishers in a modified dictator game, penalizing dictators who unfairly took tokens from others. When participants were then shown their peers' responses, many adjusted their punishment decisions to align with the group, even at a personal loss. This behavior demonstrates how the fear of exclusion may push people to adapt their choices, often at the expense of personal values or autonomy. The need for acceptance frequently drives individuals to suppress their identities, adopt behaviors they would otherwise avoid, or conform to norms they privately disagree with. Conformity, however, operates as a double-edged sword. Some people find belonging through conformity, while others who cannot or will not conform face exclusion. Thus, the same social norms that foster belonging for some create barriers for others, reinforcing divides between those who belong and those who do not.

OTHERING AND BELONGING

At the core of identity lies a complex entanglement with belonging, revealing a darker side where the need to define *us* versus *them* can foster exclusion and marginalization. Scholars examining the intersection of identity and belonging are increasingly aware of how identities, whether based on race, gender, culture, or socioeconomic status, often emerge within, and sometimes against, established social structures that reinforce separation (Anthias, 2018; Collins et al., 2021; Tatum, 2017). Identity groups can offer community and support, yet they also serve to delineate boundaries, enabling stereotypes and oppressive systems that sustain inequality. The Indian diaspora in Fiji is a case in point. Indians were initially brought to the country as indentured labourers in the early 1900s; thereafter, their Fijian-born descendants were denied recognition as Fijian (V. Mishra, personal communication, November 20, 2024), tarred with this pejorative label. Under certain governments, they were excluded from the education and healthcare opportunities available to native-born Fijians, emphasizing how belonging, when tied to rigid identity categories, can deepen social divides (Prasad, 2006).

In contrast, identity can also positively benefit individuals and communities in terms of belonging. Representation and awareness of identities have enabled groups and communities to coalesce and articulate their specific needs, providing a platform to advocate for recognition and resources (Rong et al., 2023). In Fiji, this has meant educational and political advancements resulting from identity awareness (Prasad, 2006). In terms of gender identity, increased visibility has allowed younger generations to identify as gay, lesbian, or bisexual much earlier than was possible in previous generations (Bishop et al., 2024; Russell & Fish, 2019). Moreover, transgender individuals have gained earlier access to interventions, facilitating personal alignment with their gender identity (Puckett et al., 2022). This visibility has also opened opportunities for pioneering individuals to challenge systems that previously oppressed particular groups. In the context of gender and sport, for instance, female rugby players have challenged traditional femininity norms by participating in a hypermasculine sport while simultaneously navigating societal expectations by reinforcing heteronormative identities (Ezzell, 2009). This is an example of defensive othering, where socially perceived marginalized individuals distinguish themselves from others within their group, reinforcing dominant group norms to gain acceptance. Taken together, this highlights the complexities of identity formation, where belonging is sought by resisting dominant narratives and distancing the self from navigating negative attitudes and stigma (Ezzell, 2009).

While identities create avenues for belonging, they can also magnify othering by creating more varied ways to exclude and marginalize others. Tensions have surfaced within communities previously perceived as unified, where intersectional factors such as socioeconomic status or cultural background have strained a once-shared identity. Jensen (2011) examines this among young ethnic minority men in Denmark, highlighting the influence of media portrayals. He identifies varied responses, including capitalisation on their position as "the other" and refusing the imposed identities (Jensen, 2011). Furthermore, deliberate forms of othering, where groups exclude others to affirm their identity, have further enabled subgroup cohesion. For instance, Gormally (2019) discusses how male youth gang members in Scotland leveraged racial othering against Roma migrants to reinforce their sense of belonging. These young men, marginalized by broader social systems, found a sense of power through exclusion, showing how marginalized groups may, in turn, marginalize others to assert identity.

While othering is often seen negatively, it can also serve as a tool for empowerment. Muftee and León Rosales (2022) examine how racialized women artists in Sweden use art to challenge their marginalization, creating spaces to express their unique identities and confront societal narratives that seek to define them. These artists draw strength from their shared experience of exclusion, using it to shape identities that resist the dominant social order.

Othering can also be wielded for strategic purposes. Self-othering is employed as a political tactic within some right-wing discourse, where right-wing leaders may construct narratives of exclusion and victimhood to solidify group identity and distinguish themselves from a perceived leftist elite (Orkibi, 2022). This tactic shows how those in power can frame themselves as marginalized to strengthen group cohesion. Identity construction, therefore, is not solely based on personal experiences of marginalization but can also be used as a deliberate strategy to assert dominance and maintain control over others (Modood & Thompson, 2021).

For marginalized groups, balancing belonging with experiences of othering can be challenging. Indian communities, for instance, face obstacles tied to their distinct skin color. Similarly, African immigrants[1] in Australia, as shown by Udah and Singh (2019), encounter racialized exclusion that restricts their social mobility and shapes their identity in response to this exclusion. Song (2023) highlights how women from marginalized backgrounds navigate complex intersections of gender, religion, and nationality, dealing with patriarchal norms within their communities while also facing racial and cultural othering in their host countries. These examples underscore the dual burden for those managing intersecting identities in often unwelcoming spaces.

Belonging and identity are constantly evolving concepts. For example, the term Asperger's was widely used and embraced by many individuals within the neurodivergent community until it was subsumed under the broader umbrella of autism spectrum disorders in the Diagnostic Statistics Manual (DSM-5). This amendment to diagnostic criteria influenced how many individuals identified, demonstrating how an identity can be created and taken away (American Psychiatric Association, 2013).

While each person uniquely holds multiple identities, intersectionality illuminates the intricate nuances within these overlapping social categories (Crenshaw, 1989). Although othering, often seen as the darker side of belonging, can be divisive, it may also foster belonging within subgroups, driving collective change (Modood & Thompson, 2021). Our understanding of identity is in a state of continuous evolution. The struggle to belong and navigate multiple social categories is not the dark side of belonging but does appear in ways that are complex and require consideration.

BELONGING AND ITS PARADOXES

The darker sides of belonging, seen in gangs, crime, and exclusion, can foster both trauma and a sense of community for perpetrators and victims. This creates a paradox. The belonging-trauma paradox (Allen, Counted, et al., 2026) captures this complex relationship. As described previously, belonging can become a source of trauma in environments where it is built through exclusion, coercion, or violence. However, trauma can also create belonging, especially when individuals form tight-knit communities out of shared hardship, adversity, or experiences. Survivors of traumatic events, like natural disasters or violence, often find solidarity in collective suffering. Conversely, this paradox emerges in contexts like hazing rituals or peer pressure, where the desire to belong draws individuals into harmful or traumatizing situations. The belonging-trauma paradox emphasizes the dual nature of belonging, where belonging can act as a force for healing and connection but also inflict harm, especially for those marginalized or excluded from mainstream groups (Allen, Counted, et al., 2026).

THE LIGHT SIDE OF BELONGING

If we were to observe humanity from space, the presence of gangs, cults, and individual identities might appear inconsequential as we hasten away from Earth. In the same way that we do not speculate about the identities or the romantic lives of ants, our own affiliations and identities may seem trivial at such a scale. This section adopts a broader perspective, exploring a lighter side of belonging. It does not necessarily explore the benefits of belonging, already well established in the literature (Allen, 2020; Lambert et al., 2013; Walton & Brady, 2020) but considers its potential to address large-scale challenges.

Before this can occur, we need to reconceptualize belonging, taking it beyond something individuals strive to achieve and seeing it as a shared reality that permeates boundaries. This shift requires us to look beyond the self, including personal identities and goals, and expand our view to encompass a collective, global conceptualization of belonging. Perhaps the most effective way to embrace this perspective is to imagine ourselves from a distance, from space.

Early astronauts Yuri Gagarin and Alan Shepard were among the first to witness Earth from above, describing its beauty and the profound realisation of our planet's fragility (White, 2014). Others who followed also reported a deep sense of transformation, seeing geopolitical borders as arbitrary and recognizing the importance of a healthy and thriving planet over national or political interests (Som, 2019; Yaden et al., 2016). This cognitive shift, termed the Overview Effect by Frank White in 1987 based on his interviews with astronauts, describes the awareness that emerges from viewing Earth as a shared home. Space exploration has allowed many astronauts to encounter the Earth in ways that challenge their traditional understandings of shared humanity (Weibel, 2020; Yaden et al., 2016). Observing Earth from a distance has been described as evoking a sense of awe and wonder, challenging personal beliefs about culture and religion (Yaden et al., 2016). Even awe (in its own right) can challenge existing perceptions about self-concept and personal identity by prompting profound alterations in self-awareness and identification, leading individuals to experience a sense of unity with others and a broader understanding of their place in the world (Keltner & Haidt, 2003; Yaden et al., 2016). Astronauts who experience the Overview Effect describe it as a profound emotional experience that is life-changing and transformative in the way it reshapes their worldview and influences their actions long after they return (Kanas, 2020; Yaden et al., 2016). Could a sense of belonging to something greater, a sense of global belonging inspired by the Overview Effect, trigger a renewed commitment to causes beyond the self, such as environmental stewardship and social responsibility? Global belonging could be imagined as a broad and unbounded form of belonging that transcends individual, local, and national identities and recognizes humanity as interconnected and beyond the boundaries of geography, culture, or social categorizations alone. Could such a shift in perspective bridge cultural, national, and religious divides, promoting global cooperation and empathy? Could a simple shift in perspective help us tackle issues like war and famine to create truly thriving global communities?

Using the Overview Effect to examine a global belonging perspective, the following section will explore a zoomed-out perspective to offer an alternative view of the self within the vastness of the universe, examining the global challenges tied to belonging covered in the previous section, such as geopolitical divisions, antisocial behavior, and othering.

EVIDENCE FOR THE OVERVIEW EFFECT

Research evidence shows that the Overview Effect serves as a catalyst for positive psychological transformation (Voski, 2020; Yaden et al., 2016), fostering outcomes such as an increased sense of environmental responsibility (Ihle et al., 2006), heightened interconnectedness with others (Yaden et al.,

2016), and other benefits including enhanced wellbeing, increased altruism, improved emotional resilience, and greater engagement in pro-environmental behaviors (Kanas, 2020; White, 2014; Yaden et al., 2016). Yaden et al. (2016) describe the experience of witnessing Earth from a unique perspective to be related to *broaden and build theory*. Broaden and build refers to how positive emotions can build our social resources and ability to cope and create a broadening of attention (Fredrickson, 2001). Research evidence further supports this, indicating that the Overview Effect promotes shifts in self-perception and values and a deeper appreciation for human life (Yaden et al., 2016).

Ihle et al. (2006) observed that astronauts often return from space with increased positive psychological outcomes, including an "appreciation for the fragility of Earth"—a heightened sense of global responsibility, greater involvement in environmental issues, and increased engagement in activities that support environmental sustainability (p. 100). Similarly, Voski (2020) demonstrated increased awareness of humans' ecological impact after experiencing the Overview Effect, noting that astronauts also frequently report an acute awareness of Earth's fragility, increased awareness of existing environmental degradation, a sense of urgency related to climate emergencies, and changed environmental attitudes and behaviors. Further research by Kanas (2020) supports these findings, linking the Overview Effect to a better understanding of the unity of humankind. Thus, the Overview Effect emerges as a powerful motivator for ecological and social responsibility, with significant psychological impacts.

SIMULATING AWE AND POTENTIAL FOR GLOBAL BELONGING

If the Overview Effect is to be harnessed for its related benefits and to examine global belonging in the future, its inaccessibility to the general population remains a barrier. However, virtual reality (VR) simulations offer a promising solution for the wider public, including educational contexts (Loy et al., 2024; Stepanova et al., 2019; van Limpt-Broers et al., 2024). Loy et al. (2024) demonstrated that a VR simulation of Earth viewed from space could also evoke feelings of awe, significantly impacting participants' global self-investment. Participants reported shifts in perspective akin to those described by astronauts, illustrating that VR may be an effective medium for engendering the Overview Effect.

Awe could be particularly relevant to global belonging because it encourages a shift in perception beyond the individual to a broader awareness of something greater than the self—such as, in the case of the overview effect, the planet—where experiencing awe may disrupt self-focused cognition, fostering a more collective mindset that is central to the idea of global belonging. Loy et al. (2024) also examined the link between the Overview Effect and pro-environmental actions, finding that while VR did not directly increase participants' willingness to support the Paris Climate Agreement, it indirectly fostered this behavior by creating feelings of awe. Their results point to the importance of awe as a catalyst for environmental action, suggesting that awe-inducing experiences like the Overview Effect could inspire collectively motivated behaviors to protect the planet.

van Limpt-Broers et al. (2024) provide further evidence for the potential to simulate the Overview Effect, investigating neurophysiological markers of the Overview Effect using VR simulations combined with electroencephalography technology. Their study revealed that participants exposed to Earth-viewing experiences in VR exhibited decreased activity in the beta and gamma frequency bands during moments of awe, suggesting a relaxation of typical cognitive patterns and an increased openness to new perspectives. Other evidence for this comes from Gallagher et al. (2014), who also revealed reductions in theta and beta brainwave activity when viewing Earth from space, indicating changes in cognitive processing. The evidence for reduced brain activity corresponds with astronauts' accounts of the Overview Effect as a transformative experience, characterized by a fading of everyday concerns and a profound sense of interconnectedness.

These findings show the potential for VR to be used as an educational and psychological tool to promote an immersive Overview Effect experience, which has not been replicable in all previous studies utilizing static images or less immersive media (see van Limpt-Broers et al., 2024). By accurately recreating visual and emotional experiences akin to space travel, VR simulations may facilitate the psychological benefits associated with the Overview Effect. Although it is important to note that awe-inducing experiences do not need to be limited to VR, it is worth considering the impact of other potential awe-inducing interventions through creative arts, music, storytelling, and outdoor experiences. However, more research is needed to fully explore different approaches, including VR, and their potential to build a sense of global belonging.

LIMITATIONS OF THE OVERVIEW EFFECT

While accessibility presents obvious barriers to experiencing the Overview Effect, other important limitations warrant consideration. White's (1987) interviews show that an individual's background, context, and existing worldviews may influence their Overview experience. That is, the foundation from which the experience emerges. An example of this could be considered through an Australian Indigenous peoples lens, where deep connections to land and kinship are central to culture through sophisticated knowledge systems. "Zooming out" may not be the only path forward –

to truly understand, we must also "zoom in" to understand the foundation of people's beliefs and the effects on their perceptions of, and actions in the world (J. Phillips, personal communication, December 2024). This also brings forward another potential limitation. With the emphasis on individual transformation, the Overview Effect could work against its aim of building collective appreciation and global belonging. Future Overview Effect research and applications must grapple with how to achieve meaningful individual relevance while maintaining its core insights about humanity's relationship with Earth.

ADVANCING BELONGING THEORY AND RESEARCH, IMPACTS AND IMPLICATIONS

The Overview Effect provides a potential direction for future research by offering a pathway to explore elements of the dark side of belonging discussed in this chapter, such as geopolitical divisions, antisocial behavior, and the process of othering - some of the most collective and pervasive problems of our time. A shift toward a global perspective may improve attitudes and behaviors related to our shared responsibilities, foster an appreciation of the collective, and promote global wellbeing and a perspective that extends beyond the self. Specifically, the sense of awe associated with the Overview Effect and linked to enhanced empathy (Voski, 2020; Yaden et al., 2016) may have implications for mitigating antisocial tendencies. It could encourage individuals to view others, especially those from different backgrounds, through a more inclusive lens (Yaden et al., 2016) or to adopt a position that focuses on our commonality, most importantly, the fact that we are all human. It may be worth asking: could the Overview Effect inspire greater social cohesion and collaboration by fostering collective commitments to issues like the climate emergency? Research shows that astronauts often report adopting pro-environmental behaviors and advocacy following their space experiences (Voski, 2020), but more is needed.

It is also worth considering whether the Overview Effect has the potential to change understandings of social identity or group dynamics to push the boundaries of what we consider to be true belonging. Could a global identity that transcends current distinctions challenge longstanding notions of in-groups and out-groups deeply entrenched in 20th-century psychological theories, a period rife with structural racism, classism, and sexism? Early theories and frameworks in psychology at the time reflected a society defined by division and hierarchy. Subsequent research has mostly built on these theories. But could (or should) we hold these theories further to account and speculate whether they perpetuate the view that belonging is inherently exclusive? What if these foundational theories have subtly prescribed norms that we have accepted as reality, thereby unwittingly perpetuating them?

As society has evolved, so too have ideas of inclusion. Many visible signs of inequities are challenged (though some remain deeply entrenched). Have our psychological models, theories, and frameworks, which have remained largely unchanged, kept up with our evolving understandings of inclusion?

Future researchers and theory builders could reimagine global identity as a form of global belonging—not to replace notions of individual or group identity but to expand them. This shift may represent the next phase in the evolution of belonging, inclusion, and identity research, aligned with increasing commitments and interests in building thriving and flourishing communities. Such a possibility moves beyond traditional identity theories, opening doors to explore the self within a reconceptualized form of belonging. Here, global belonging prevails over division, differences, and distinctions. These ideas may seem aspirational, but they are congruent with emerging research that shows what is needed for communities to flourish (Goodman et al., 2022).

Viewing global or community flourishing as a collective goal is not a new concept. Many cultures, including Australian Indigenous cultures, have long upheld community wellbeing, where the flourishing of each individual is inseparable from that of the group. In these communities, if one member struggles, for example, with mental illness, the wellness of the entire community is affected. In fact, Indigenous languages describing mental illness are claimed not to have existed prior to invasion. These perspectives align with many traditional and historical collectivist ideals worldwide. Future research may return to these earlier ways of thinking.

Positioning existing psychological theory within an Overview Effect lens reveals new possibilities for understanding belonging. Take, Allen, Kern, et al.'s (2021) belonging framework, which integrates competencies, opportunities, motivations, and perceptions within cultural and temporal systems as predominant determinants for belonging. While this system acknowledges the influence of social and cultural environments, it stops short of addressing the larger global, universal context. This limitation raises a critical question: If belonging is a fundamental human need, what happens when the environment to which one belongs—the planet itself—is threatened? As climate crises accelerate, displacing populations and disrupting ecosystems, we confront a scenario where physical belonging may become more and more at risk. In such a future, the absence of a healthy, inhabitable planet would leave humanity with nothing physical to belong to.

By reimagining Allen, Kern, et al.'s (2021) framework from an expanded, zoomed-out perspective, we might re-examine belonging to incorporate aspects of a global belonging where opportunities also include opportunities to engage in pro-environmental behaviors or initiatives that foster connection or belonging to Earth as a collective home. Perceptions could encompass the viewing of oneself as part of a larger system or adopting a collectivist mindset. Motivations could be expanded to include collective goals and a shared drive to support global wellbeing. In this expanded view, competencies would also emphasize abilities tied to sustainable living, global cooperation, and environmental consciousness.

This reconceptualized framework would incorporate a global overview perspective to remind us that belonging operates on both emic and etic levels and that personal experiences and global dimensions of belonging are essential when considering flourishing communities and a sustainable future.

Throughout the literature, belonging has been explored primarily at the individual level. The emphasis is on focusing on the self through individual differences and personal perspectives positioned within a broader system, mostly encompassing local or immediate contexts. A global belonging perspective zooms out a step further. However, moving toward such a perspective to tackle global challenges will take time (if it happens at all). Cultivating a global sense of belonging would acknowledge that belonging is not just an individual human right and need but a collective one. Advancing the idea of global belonging through further research and theoretical development could contribute to self-psychology, where many other individualistic constructs benefit from a broader perspective.

Educational Settings

As we plant the seeds to explore the construct of global belonging, its potential implications for educational settings warrant careful consideration. While it would be premature to make specific recommendations, this emerging concept raises important questions about how educational institutions might evolve to meet global challenges. Further theoretical development and research are needed before considering practical applications. This includes work on how to define and operationalize global belonging in educational contexts, and careful examination of potential benefits and risks, particularly in terms of cultural relevance and universal applicability. Important considerations include how such an expanded view of belonging might interact with existing educational approaches, and what unintended consequences might arise. As we move forward in exploring these possibilities, close interdisciplinary and research-practice collaboration between researchers, educators, and the community will be essential. This emerging area of study reminds us that while global belonging holds promise, its development must be approached thoughtfully and carefully as we understand this construct more fully.

CONCLUSION

A sense of belonging, particularly when viewed through a zoomed-out Overview Effect, opens the potential for new directions in psychology and related fields. A broader perspective positions belonging as a personal and cultural pursuit but adds a rarely explored global dimension. By shifting the focus from the self to a collective, approaches like the Overview Effect have the potential to consider a global belonging perspective positioned to tackle pressing global issues such as geopolitical conflicts, antisocial behaviors, and societal divides. It seems that the more we understand about belonging, the less we know, but we are also on the precipice of unlocking new understandings about our planet that are yet to be discovered. How will animal communication or potential life on other planets inform our sense of belonging? In the words of Madonna, "Life is a mystery," but we should challenge the idea that we must stand alone. Perhaps the true evolution of belonging research lies in recognizing that even when we stand alone (as our self), we remain undeniably, unavoidably, and inextricably linked to one another and our shared planet.

NOTE

1. In the study, participants came from a range of African regions, including Nigeria, Ghana, Sierra Leone, and Liberia (West Africa); Uganda and Tanzania (East Africa); Rwanda and Congo (Central Africa); Somalia, Eritrea, Sudan, and South Sudan (Northeast Africa); and Zimbabwe and Botswana (Southern Africa) (Udah & Singh, 2019).

REFERENCES

Abubakar, A., van de Vijver, F. J. R., Alonso-Arbiol, I., Suryani, A. O., Pandia, W. S., Handani, P., Arasa, J., Mazrui, L., & Murugumi, M. (2016). Assessing sense of school belonging across cultural contexts using the PSSM: Measurement and functional invariance. *Journal of Psychoeducational Assessment, 34*(4), 380–388. https://doi.org/10.1177/0734282915607161

Ager, A., & Strang, A. (2008). Understanding integration: A conceptual framework. *Journal of Refugee Studies, 21*(2), 166–191. https://doi.org/10.1093/jrs/fen016

Ahmed, S. (2019). British Muslims perceptions of social cohesion: From multiculturalism to community cohesion and the 'war on terror'. *Crime, Law and Social Change, 71,* 581–595. https://doi.org/10.1007/s10611-018-9804-9

Aliyev, H. (2020). When neighborhood goes to war: Exploring the effect of belonging on violent mobilisation in Ukraine. *Eurasian Geography and Economics, 62*(1), 21–45. https://doi.org/10.1080/15387216.2020.1756366

Allen, K.-A. (2020). *The psychology of belonging* (1st ed.). Routledge. https://doi.org/10.4324/9780429327681

Allen, K.-A. (2023, July 7). What "Belonging" means around the globe. In *Psychology Today. Belonging in translation: A linguistic journey.* https://www.psychologytoday.com/au/blog/sense-of-belonging/202307/what-belonging-means-around-the-globe

Allen, K.-A., Berger, E., Reupert, A., Grove, C., May, F., Patlamazoglou, L., Gamble, N., Wurf, G., & Warton, W. (2023). Student-identified practices for improving belonging in Australian Secondary Schools: Moving beyond COVID-19. *School Mental Health 15*, 927–939. https://doi.org/10.1007/s12310-023-09596-9

Allen, K.-A., Counted, V., Bozorg, B., Crosby, S., Crawford, J., & Slaten, C. D. (2026). *Unseen intersections of trauma and belonging: The good, the bad, and the belonging-trauma paradox on university students.* In J. Lynch, A. Padmanabhanunni, & E. Berger (Eds.), *Handbook of trauma-informed approaches in higher education.* Bloomsbury Publishing.

Allen, K.-A., Crawford, J., Sanders, T., Bozorg, B., & Saunders, C. (2025). Belonging beyond crisis: Predictors are stable in higher education, despite a pandemic. Higher Education. https://doi.org/10.1007/s10734-025-01549-2

Allen, K.-A., Gray, D. L., Baumeister, R. F., & Leary, M. R. (2022). The need to belong. A deep dive into the origins, implications, and future of a foundational construct. *Educational Psychology Review, 34*(2), 1133–1156. https://doi.org/10.1007/s10648-021-09633-6

Allen, K. A., Greenwood, C. J., Berger, E., Patlamazoglou, L., Reupert, A., Wurf, G., May, F., O'Connor, M., Sanson, A., Olsson, C. A., & Letcher, P. (2024). Adolescent school belonging and mental health outcomes in young adulthood: Findings from a multi-wave prospective cohort study. *School Mental Health, 16*(1), 149–160. https://doi.org/10.1007/s12310-023-09626-6

Allen, K. A., Greenwood, C. J., Berger, E., Reupert, A., Wurf, G., Rajendran, N., Warton, W., O'Connor, M., Sanson, A., Olsson, C. A., & Letcher, P. (2025). Adolescent school belonging and substance use in young adulthood: Findings from a multi-wave prospective cohort study. *International Journal of Mental Health and Addiction.* https://doi.org/10.1007/s11469-024-01427-5

Allen, K. A., Jamshidi, N., Berger, E., Reupert, A., Wurf, G., & May, F. (2021). Impact of school-based interventions for building school belonging in adolescence: A systematic review. *Educational Psychology Review, 33*(1), 1–34. https://doi.org/10.1007/s10648-021-09621-w

Allen, K.-A., Kern, M. L., Rozek, C. S., McInerney, D. M., & Slavich, G. M. (2021). Belonging: A review of conceptual issues, an integrative framework, and directions for future research. *Australian Journal of Psychology, 73*(1), 87–102. https://doi.org/10.1080/00049530.2021.1883409

Allen, K. A., Morris, Z. A., Kern, M. L., Boyle, C., & McGlinchey, C. (2023). The need to belong: The appeal, benefits and dangers of QAnon and similar groups. In M. K. Miller (Ed.), *The social science of QAnon: A new social and political phenomenon* (pp. 176–191). Cambridge University Press. ISBN: 9781316511534, 9781009055024 (Print), eISBN: 9781009052061.

Allen, K., Kern, M. L., Vella-Brodrick, D., Hattie, J., & Waters, L. (2018). What schools need to know about fostering school belonging. A meta-analysis. *Educational Psychology Review, 30*(1), 1–34. https://doi.org/10.1007/s10648-016-9389-8

Allen, K.-A., Mulholland, N., Berger, E., Warton, W., Pitehnoee, M. R., & Reupert, A. (2025). Defining school belonging. A cross-cultural investigation of student-led conceptualisations. *European Journal of Education.* https://doi.org/10.1111/ejed.70290

American Psychiatric Association. (2013). *Diagnostic and statistical manual of mental disorders* (5th ed.). American Psychiatric Publishing, Inc. https://doi.org/10.1176/appi.books.9780890425596

Anthias, F. (2006). Belongings in a globalising and unequal world: Rethinking translocations. In N. Yuval-Davis, K. Kannabiran, & U. Vieten (Eds.), *The situated politics of belonging* (pp. 17–31). Sage.

Anthias, F. (2018). Identity and belonging: Conceptualizations and reframings through a translocational lens. In K. Davis, H. Ghorashi, & P. Smets (Eds.), *Contested belonging: Spaces, practices, biographies* (pp. 137–159). Emerald Publishing Limited. https://doi.org/10.1108/978-1-78743-206-220181007

Aristotle. (2009). *Politics* (B. Jowett, Trans.). Batoche Books. (Original work published 350 BCE).

Arslan, G. (2021). School belongingness, well-being, and mental health among adolescents. Exploring the role of loneliness. *Australian Journal of Psychology, 73*(1), 70–80. https://doi.org/10.1080/00049530.2021.1904499

Arslan, G. (2022). School bullying and youth internalizing and externalizing behaviors: Do school belonging and school achievement matter? *International Journal of Mental Health and Addiction, 20*, 2460–2477. https://doi.org/10.1007/s11469-021-00526-x

Arslan, G., Allen, K.-A., & Ryan, T. (2020). Exploring the impacts of school belonging on youth wellbeing and mental health among Turkish adolescents. *Child Indicators Research, 13*(5), 1619–1635. https://doi.org/10.1007/s12187-020-09721-z

Bank, L. J. (2019). Migrancy, war and belonging: The cultural politics of African nationalism at Marikana. *Transformation: Critical Perspectives on Southern Africa, 100*, 1–26. https://doi.org/10.1353/trn.2019.0020

Baumeister, R. F., & Leary, M. R. (1995). The need to belong: Desire for interpersonal attachments as a fundamental human motivation. *Psychological Bulletin, 117*(3), 497–529. https://doi.org/10.1037/0033-2909.117.3.497

Beck, A. T. (2011). *Cognitive therapy: Basics and beyond* (2nd ed.). Guilford Press.

Berger, R., Abu-Raiya, H., Heineberg, Y., & Zimbardo, P. (2017). The process of desistance among core ex-gang members. *American Journal of Orthopsychiatry, 87*(4), 487–502. https://doi.org/10.1037/ort0000196

Berry, J. W., & Hou, F. (2021). Immigrant acculturation and wellbeing across generations and settlement contexts in Canada. *International Review of Psychiatry, 33*(1–2), 140–153. https://doi.org/10.1080/09540261.2020.1750801

Bishop, M. D., Fish, J. N., & Russell, S. T. (2024). The developmental collision hypothesis: An empirical test with three generations of sexual minority youth. *Journal of Youth and Adolescence*, 1–15.

Blanchett, W. J. (2006). Disproportionate representation of African American students in special education: Acknowledging the role of white privilege and racism. *Educational Researcher, 35*(6), 24–28. https://doi.org/10.3102/0013189X035006024

Boccadoro, S., Wagels, L., Puiu, A. A., Votinov, M., Weidler, C., Veselinovic, T., Demko, Z., Raine, A., & Neuner, I. (2021). A meta-analysis on shared and distinct neural correlates of the decision-making underlying altruistic and retaliatory punishment. *Human Brain Mapping, 42*(17), 5547–5562. https://doi.org/10.1002/hbm.25635

Brewer, M. B. (2007). The importance of being we: Human nature and intergroup relations. *American Psychologist, 62*(8), 728–738. https://doi.org/10.1037/0003-066X.62.8.728

Brooks, D. (2011). *The social animal: The hidden sources of love, character, and achievement.* Random House.

Bunker, P. L., Campbell, L. J., & Bunker, R. J. (2010). Torture, beheadings, and narcocultos. *Small Wars and Insurgencies, 21*(1), 145–178. https://doi.org/10.1080/09592310903561668

Busch, P., Heinonen, T., & Lahti, P. (2007). Heisenberg's uncertainty principle. *Physics Reports, 452*(6), 155–176. https://doi.org/10.1016/j.physrep.2007.05.006

Butel, J., & Braun, K. L. (2019). The role of collective efficacy in reducing health disparities: A systematic review. *Family & Community Health, 42*(1), 8–19. https://doi.org/10.1097/FCH.0000000000000206

Cacioppo, J. T., Cacioppo, S., Capitanio, J. P., & Cole, S. W. (2015). The neuroendocrinology of social isolation. *Annual Review of Psychology, 66,* 733–767. https://doi.org/10.1146/annurev-psych-010814-015240

Carr, E. W., Reece, A., Kellerman, G. R., & Robichaux, A. (2019). The value of belonging at work. *Harvard Business Review.* https://hbr.org/2019/12/the-value-of-belonging-at-work

Carter, P. L. (2016). Educational equality is a multifaceted issue: Why we must understand the school's sociocultural context for student achievement. *RSF: The Russell Sage Foundation Journal of the Social Sciences, 2*(5), 142–163. https://doi.org/10.7758/rsf.2016.2.5.07

Caxaj, C. S., & Gill, N. K. (2017). Belonging and mental wellbeing among a rural Indian-Canadian Diaspora: Navigating tensions in "finding a space of our own". *Qualitative Health Research, 27*(8), 1119–1132. https://doi.org/10.1177/1049732316648129

Cherney, A., & Murphy, K. (2016). Being a 'suspect community' in a post 9/11 world – The impact of the war on terror on Muslim communities in Australia. *Australian and New Zealand Journal of Criminology, 49*(4), 480–496. https://doi.org/10.1177/0004865815585392

Collins, P. H., da Silva, E. C. G., Ergun, E., Furseth, I., Bond, K. D., & Martínez-Palacios, J. (2021). Intersectionality as critical social theory: Intersectionality as critical social theory. Patricia Hill Collins, Duke University Press, 2019. *Contemporary Political Theory, 20*(3), 690–725. https://doi.org/10.1057/s41296-021-00490-0

Connolly, M. D., Zervos, M. J., Barone, C. J., Johnson, C. C., & Joseph, C. L. M. (2016). The mental health of transgender youth: Advances in understanding. *Journal of Adolescent Health, 59*(5), 489–495. https://doi.org/10.1016/j.jadohealth.2016.06.012

Cook, J. E., Purdie-Vaughns, V., Garcia, J., & Cohen, G. L. (2012). Chronic threat and contingent belonging: Protective benefits of values affirmation on identity development. *Journal of Personality and Social Psychology, 102*(3), 479–496. https://doi.org/10.1037/a0026312

Cortina, K. S., Arel, S., & Smith-Darden, J. P. (2017). School belonging in different cultures: The effects of individualism and power distance. *Frontiers in Education, 2,* 56. https://doi.org/10.3389/feduc.2017.00056

Crawford, J., Allen, K. A., Sanders, T., Baumeister, R., Parker, P., Saunders, C., & Tice, D. (2024). Sense of belonging in higher education students: An Australian longitudinal study from 2013 to 2019. *Studies in Higher Education.* https://doi.org/10.1080/03075079.2023.2238006

Crenshaw, K. (1989). Demarginalising the intersection of race and sex: A Black feminist critique of antidiscrimination doctrine, feminist theory and antiracist politics. *University of Chicago Legal Forum, 1*, 139–167.

Day, J. K., Ioverno, S., & Russell, S. T. (2019). Safe and supportive schools for LGBT youth: Addressing educational inequities through inclusive policies and practices. *Journal of School Psychology, 74*, 29–43. https://doi.org/10.1016/j.jsp.2019.05.007

Drabman, R., & Spitalnik, R. (1973). Social isolation as a punishment procedure. A controlled study. *Journal of Experimental Child Psychology, 16*(2), 236–249. https://doi.org/10.1016/0022-0965(73)90164-1

Dutcher, J. M., Lederman, J., Jain, M., Price, S., Kumar, A., Villalba, D. K., Tumminia, M. J., Doryab, A., Creswell, K. G., Riskin, E., Sefdigar, Y., Seo, W., Mankoff, J., Cohen, S., Dey, A., & Creswell, J. D. (2022). Lack of belonging predicts depressive symptomatology in college students. *Psychological Science, 33*(7), 1048–1067. https://doi.org/10.1177/09567976211073135

Eastwood, M. A. (2017). Heisenberg's uncertainty principle. *QJM: An International Journal of Medicine, 110*(5), 335–336. https://doi.org/10.1093/qjmed/hcw193

Eisenberger, N. I., Lieberman, M. D., & Williams, K. D. (2003). Does rejection hurt? An fMRI study of social exclusion. *Science, 302*(5643), 290–292. https://doi.org/10.1126/science.1089134

Espinosa, L. L., Turk, J. M., Taylor, M., & Chessman, H. M. (2019, September 24). *Race and ethnicity in higher education: A status report.* American Council on Education. https://www.equityinhighered.org/resources/report-downloads/race-and-ethnicity-in-higher-education-a-status-report/

Ezzell, M. B. (2009). "Barbie Dolls" on the pitch: Identity work, defensive othering, and inequality in women's rugby. *Social Problems, 56*(1), 111–131. https://doi.org/10.1525/sp.2009.56.1.111

Fabbri, M., & Carbonara, E. (2017). Social influence on third-party punishment: An experiment. *Journal of Economic Psychology, 62*, 204–230. https://doi.org/10.1016/j.joep.2017.07.003

Faircloth, B. S., Gonzalez, L. M., & Ramos, K. (Eds.). (2021). *Resisting barriers to belonging: Conceptual critique and critical applications.* Lexington Books.

Faircloth, B. S., & Hamm, J. V. (2005). Sense of belonging among high school students representing 4 ethnic groups. *Journal of Youth and Adolescence, 34*(4), 293–309. https://doi.org/10.1007/s10964-005-5752-7

Farine, D. R., & Whitehead, H. (2015). Constructing, conducting and interpreting animal social network analysis. *Journal of Animal Ecology, 84*(5), 1144–1163. https://doi.org/10.1111/1365-2656.12418

Fredrickson, B. L. (2001). The role of positive emo- tions in positive psychology. The broaden-and- build theory of positive emotions. *American Psychologist, 56*, 218–226. https://doi.org/10.1037/0003-066X.56.3.218

Gallagher, S., Reinerman-Jones, L., Sollins, B., & Janz, B. (2014). Using a simulated environment to investigate experiences reported during space travel. *Theoretical Issues in Ergonomics Science, 15*(4), 376–394. https://doi.org/10.1080/1463922X.2013.869370

Gibian, P. (2012). "The Man Without a Country" and America's post-war crisis of national belonging. *Canadian Review of American Studies, 42*(1), 36–48. https://doi.org/10.1353/crv.2012.0007

Gilovich, T., Medvec, V. H., & Savitsky, K. (2000). The spotlight effect in social judgment: An egocentric bias in estimates of the salience of one's own behavior. *Journal of Personality and Social Psychology, 78*(2), 508–518. https://doi.org/10.1037//0022-3514.78.2.211

Golding, W. (1954). *Lord of the flies.* Faber and Faber.

Goldman, L., & Hogg, M. A. (2016). Going to extremes for one's group: The role of prototypicality and group acceptance. *Journal of Applied Social Psychology, 46*(9), 544–553. https://doi.org/10.1111/jasp.12382

Goodman, M., Theron, L., Seidel, S., Elliott, A., Raimer-Goodman, L., Keiser, P., Gitari, S., & Gatwiri, C. (2022). Flourishing communities: A new model to promote sustainable community leadership and transformation in semi-rural Kenya. *Journal of Community & Applied Social Psychology*. Advance online publication. https://doi.org/10.1002/casp.2665

Gopalan, M., & Brady, S. T. (2020). College students' sense of belonging: A national perspective. *Educational Researcher, 49*(2), 134–137. https://doi.org/10.3102/0013189X19897622

Gormally, S. (2019). "It's Not Being Racist, but …": A Youth Gang and the Creation of Belonging Based on "Othering". *Boyhood Studies, 12*(2), 70+. https://link.gale.com/apps/doc/A672509545/AONE?u=anon%7Ed68ad65f&sid=googleScholar&xid=6bf17bd0

Gotfredsen, A. C., & Linander, I. (2023). Young trans people's experiences of leisure and mental health. Belonging, creativity, and navigation. *Wellbeing, Space and Society, 4,* 100139. https://doi.org/10.1016/j.wss.2023.100139

Gray, D. L., Harris-Thomas, B., Ali, J. N., Cummings, T. N., McElveen, T. L., & Jones, T. R. (2024). Urban middle schoolers' opportunities to belong predict fluctuations in their engagement across the school day. *Urban Education, 59*(9), 2583–2618. https://doi.org/10.1177/00420859221117682

Gray, D. L., Hope, E. C., & Byrd, C. M. (2018). Black and belonging at school: A case for interpersonal, instructional, and institutional opportunity structures. *Educational Psychologist, 53*(2), 97–113. https://doi.org/10.1080/00461520.2017.1421466

Guthrie, W. K. C. (1971). *The sophists.* Cambridge University Press.

Hare, J. (2023, August 17). Excellence and equity, connecting for equity and community. In *South Australian Secondary Principals Association (SASPA), SA Secondary Principals' Association (SASPA) Conference keynote presentation.* YouTube. Video. https://www.youtube.com/watch?v=tveaTRi7cRU

Harris, K. J., Gringart, E., & Drake, D. (2018). Leaving ideological groups behind: A model of disengagement. *Behavioral Sciences of Terrorism and Political Aggression, 10*(2), 91–109. https://doi.org/10.1080/19434472.2017.1299782

Harrison, N., & McLean, R. (2017). Getting yourself out of the way: Aboriginal people listening and belonging in the city. *Geographical Research, 55*(4), 359–368. https://doi.org/10.1111/1745-5871.12238

Harter, S. (2006). The self. In N. Eisenberg, W. Damon, & R. M. Lerner (Eds.), *Handbook of child psychology: Social, emotional, and personality development* (6th ed., pp. 505–570). John Wiley & Sons, Inc.

Heck, N. C., Lindquist, L. M., Machek, G. R., & Cochran, B. N. (2014). School belonging, school victimization, and the mental health of LGBT young adults: Implications for school psychologists. *School Psychology Forum: Research in Practice, 8*(1), 28–37.

Hogg, M. A. (2016). Social identity theory. In S. McKeown, R. Haji, & N. Ferguson (Eds.), *Understanding peace and conflict through social identity theory: Contemporary global perspectives* (pp. 3–17). Springer International Publishing. https://doi.org/10.1007/978-3-319-29869-6_1

Holt-Lunstad, J., Robles, T. F., & Sbarra, D. A. (2017). Advancing social connection as a public health priority in the United States. *American Psychologist, 72*(6), 517–530. https://doi.org/10.1037/amp0000103

Holt-Lunstad, J., Smith, T. B., Baker, M., Harris, T., & Stephenson, D. (2015). Loneliness and social isolation as risk factors for mortality: A meta-analytic review. *Perspectives on Psychological Science, 10*(2), 227–237. https://doi.org/10.1177/1745691614568352

Hudson, C., Allen, K.-A., & Bozorg, B. (2025). Starting school in Australia. What gives young children a sense of school belonging? *Early Childhood Education Journal*, 1–18. https://doi.org/10.1007/s10643-025-01979-8

Ihle, E. C., Ritsher, J. B., & Kanas, N. (2006). Positive psychological outcomes of spaceflight: An empirical study. *Aviation Space & Environmental Medicine, 77*, 93–101.

Jensen, S. Q. (2011). Othering, identity formation, and agency. *Qualitative Studies, 2*(2), 63–78. https://doi.org/10.7146/qs.v2i2.5510

Kamp, A., Denson, N., Sharples, R., & Atie, R. (2022). Asian australians' experiences of online racism during the COVID-19 pandemic. *Social Sciences, 11*, 227. https://doi.org/10.3390/socsci11050227

Kanas, N. (2020). Spirituality, humanism, and the overview effect during manned space missions. *Acta Astronautica, 166*, 525–528. https://doi.org/10.1016/j.actaastro.2018.08.004

Keltner, D., & Haidt, J. (2003). Approaching awe, a moral, spiritual, and aesthetic emotion. *Cognition and Emotion, 17*(2), 297–314. https://doi.org/10.1080/02699930302297

Kirk, G. S., Raven, J. E., & Schofield, M. (1983). *The presocratic philosophers: A critical history with a selection of texts.* Cambridge University Press.

Koser, K. (2007). Refugees, transnationalism, and the state. *Journal of Ethnic and Migration Studies, 33*(2), 233–254. https://doi.org/10.1080/13691830601154195

Kreitz, C., Furley, P., Memmert, D., & Simons, D. J. (2015). Inattentional blindness and individual differences in cognitive abilities. *PLoS One, 10*(8), e0134675. https://doi.org/10.1371/journal.pone.0134675

Lambert, N. M., Stillman, T. F., Hicks, J. A., Kamble, S., Baumeister, R. F., & Fincham, F. D. (2013). To belong is to matter: Sense of belonging enhances meaning in life. *Personality and Social Psychology Bulletin, 39*(11), 1418–1427. https://doi.org/10.1177/0146167213499186

Land, O. (2024, November 14). Chicago man discovers owner of his favorite bakery is his birth mother. *New York Post.* https://nypost.com/2024/11/14/us-news/chicago-man-discovers-owner-of-his-favorite-bakery-is-his-birth-mother/

Lim, M. H., Allen, K. A., Furlong, M. J., Craig, H., & Smith, D. C. (2021). Introducing a dual continuum model of belonging and loneliness. *Australian Journal of Psychology, 73*(1), 81–86. https://doi.org/10.1080/00049530.2021.1883411

Loy, L. S., Steppler, K., Kliachko, I., Kuhlmann, J., Menzel, C., Schick, O., & Reese, G. (2024). A virtually-induced overview effect? How seeing the world from above through a simulated space tour is related to awe, global identity and pro-environmental behaviour. *Journal of Environmental Psychology, 99*, 102428. https://doi.org/10.1016/j.jenvp.2024.102428

Markus, H. R., & Kitayama, S. (1991). Culture and the self: Implications for cognition, emotion, and motivation. *Psychological Review, 98*(2), 224–253.

Matusitz, J., & Repass, M. (2009). Gangs in Nigeria: An updated examination. *Crime, Law and Social Change, 52*(5), 495–511. https://doi.org/10.1007/s10611-009-9208-y

May, V. (2017). Belonging from afar: Nostalgia, time and memory. *The Sociological Review, 65*(2), 401–415. https://doi.org/10.1111/1467-954X.12402

Metcalf, J. (2012). Reviewing "monsters": The press reception and media constructions of contemporary street gang memoirs. *Crime, Media, Culture, 8*(3), 333–353. https://doi.org/10.1177/1741659012443228

Modood, T., & Thompson, S. (2021). Othering, alienation and establishment. *Political Studies, 70*(3), 786–803. https://doi.org/10.1177/0032321720986698

Mohseni, H., Silvennoinen, J., & Kujala, T. (2024). Place-belongingness in real-life contexts: A review of practical meanings, contributing factors, and evaluation methods. *Geojournal, 89*, 187. https://doi.org/10.1007/s10708-024-11173-9

Moreton-Robinson, A. (2015). I still call Australia home. In *The White possessive*. University of Minnesota Press. https://doi.org/10.5749/minnesota/9780816692149.003.0001

Muftee, M., & León Rosales, R. (2022). 'We just want to make art' – Women with experiences of racial othering reflect on art, activism and representation. *European Journal of Women's Studies, 29*(4), 559–576. https://doi.org/10.1177/13505068221127127

Murer, J. S., & Schwarze, T. (2022). Social rituals of pain: The socio-symbolic meaning of violence in gang initiations. *International Journal of Politics, Culture, and Society, 35*(1), 95–110. https://doi.org/10.1007/s10767-020-09392-2

O'Sullivan, T. (2026). Inquest into the deaths at Westfield Bondi Junction (Findings Report). Coroners Court of New South Wales. https://coroners.nsw.gov.au/documents/bondi-junction-inquest/findings/Inquest_into_the_deaths_at_Westfield_Bondi_Junction_Volume_1.pdf

Oikkonen, V. (2018). *Population genetics and belonging: A cultural analysis of genetic ancestry*. Palgrave Macmillan. https://doi.org/10.1007/978-3-319-62881-3

Orkibi, E. (2022). Self-othering to power: Vilification, ridicule and moral claims in the Israeli right 'underdog' discourse. *Journal of Multicultural Discourses, 17*(2), 158–172. https://doi.org/10.1080/17447143.2022.2079649

Oxford University Press. (n.d. November, 24). *Heisenberg uncertainty principle*. Oxford Reference. https://www.oxfordreference.com/display/10.1093/oi/authority.20110803110605504

Page, A. E., Chaudhary, N., Viguier, S., Dyble, M., Thompson, J., Smith, D., Salali, G. D., Mace, R., & Migliano, A. B. (2017). Hunter-gatherer social networks and reproductive success. *Scientific Reports, 7*(1), 1153. Article. https://doi.org/10.1038/s41598-017-01310-5

Paley, V. G. (1992). *You can't say you can't play*. Harvard University Press.

Palikara, O., Castro-Kemp, S., Gaona, C., & Eirinaki, V. (2021). The mediating role of school belonging in the relationship between socioemotional well-being and loneliness in primary school age children. *Australian Journal of Psychology, 73*(1), 24–34. https://doi.org/10.1080/00049530.2021.1882270

Parr, E. J., Shochet, I. M., Cockshaw, W. D., & Kelly, R. L. (2020). General belonging is a key predictor of adolescent depressive symptoms and partially mediates school belonging. *School Mental Health, 12*, 626–637. https://doi.org/10.1007/s12310-020-09371-0

Potter, K. S., & Simmons, J. H. (2021). Optical properties of insulators—Materials, devices, and applications. In K. S. Potter & J. H. Simmons (Eds.), *Optical materials* (2nd ed., pp. 173–228). Elsevier. https://doi.org/10.1016/B978-0-12-818642-8.00004-1

Prasad, U. (2006). *I remember Mai Fiji.* Dr Umanand Prasad.

Puckett, J. A., Tornello, S., Mustanski, B., & Newcomb, M. E. (2022). Gender variations, generational effects, and mental health of transgender people in relation to timing and status of gender identity milestones. *Psychology of Sexual Orientation and Gender Diversity, 9*(2), 165–178. https://doi.org/10.1037/sgd0000391

Ragsdale, K., Porter, J. R., Mathews, R., White, A., Gore-Felton, C., & McGarvey, E. L. (2011). "Liquor before beer, you're in the clear": Binge drinking and other risk behaviours among fraternity/sorority members and their non-Greek peers. *Journal of Substance Use, 17*(4), 323–339. https://doi.org/10.3109/14659891.2011.583312

Riesman, D., Glazer, N., & Denney, R. (1950). *The lonely crowd: A study of the changing American character.* Yale University Press.

Ripple, W. J., Wolf, C., Newsome, T. M., Barnard, P., & Moomaw, W. R. (2020). World scientists' warning of a climate emergency. *BioScience, 70*(1), 8–12. https://doi.org/10.1093/biosci/biz088

Rist, J. M. (2010). *Epicurus: An introduction.* Cambridge University Press.

Rong, T., Ristevski, E., & Carroll, M. (2023). Exploring community engagement in place-based approaches in areas of poor health and disadvantage: A scoping review. *Health & Place, 81*, 103026. https://doi.org/10.1016/j.healthplace.2023.103026

Russell, S. T., & Fish, J. N. (2019). Sexual minority youth, social change, and health: A developmental collision. *Research in Human Development, 16*(1), 5–20. https://doi.org/10.1080/15427609.2018.1537772

Sack, D. (2016, October 17). *8 ways to stop worrying about what other people think. Where science meets the steps.* https://www.psychologytoday.com/blog/where-science-meets-the-steps/201610/8-ways-to-stop-worrying-about-what-other-people-think

Sánchez, B., Colón, Y., & Esparza, P. (2005). The role of sense of school belonging and gender in the academic adjustment of Latino adolescents. *Journal of Youth and Adolescence, 34*, 619–628. https://doi.org/10.1007/s10964-005-8950-4

Sandbach, F. H. (1989). *The stoics.* Chatto & Windus.

Scottham, K. M., Sellers, R. M., & Nguyen, H. X. (2008). A measure of racial identity in African American adolescents: The development of the Multidimensional Inventory of Black Identity–Teen. *Cultural Diversity and Ethnic Minority Psychology, 14*(4), 297–306. https://doi.org/10.1037/1099-9809.14.4.297

Shapiro, E. (2023, January 12). The hazing death of Baruch fraternity pledge Michael Deng was 'an active cover-up', prosecutor says. *ABC News.* https://abcnews.go.com/US/hazing-death-baruch-fraternity-pledge-michael-deng-active/story?id=96365470

Shochet, I. M., Smith, C. L., Furlong, M. J., & Homel, R. (2011). A prospective study investigating the impact of school belonging factors on negative affect in adolescents. *Journal of Clinical Child & Adolescent Psychology, 40*(4), 586–595. https://doi.org/10.1080/15374416.2011.581616

Silk, J. B., & House, B. R. (2016). The evolution of altruistic social preferences in human groups. *Philosophical Transactions of the Royal Society B, 371*(1687). https://doi.org/10.1098/rstb.2015.0097

Slavich, G. M., & Cole, S. W. (2013). The emerging field of human social genomics. *Clinical Psychological Science, 1*(3), 331–348. https://doi.org/10.1177/2167702613478594

Snapp, S. D., Burdge, H., Licona, A. C., Moody, R. L., & Russell, S. T. (2015). Students' perspectives on LGBTQ-inclusive curriculum. *Equity & Excellence in Education, 48*(2), 249–265. https://doi.org/10.1080/10665684.2015.1025614

Som, S. M. (2019). Common identity as a step to civilisation longevity. *Futures, 106*, 37–43. https://doi.org/10.1016/j.futures.2018.08.002

Song, J. (2023). Contesting and negotiating othering from within: A Saudi Arabian female student's gendered experiences in the U.S. *Journal of Language, Identity and Education.* https://doi.org/10.1080/15348458.2019.1654386

Stepanova, E. R., Quesnel, D., & Riecke, B. E. (2019). Understanding AWE: Can a virtual journey, inspired by the overview effect, lead to an increased sense of interconnectedness? *Frontiers in Digital Humanities, 6*, 1–21. https://doi.org/10.3389/fdigh.2019.00009

Steiner, R. J., Sheremenko, G., Lesesne, C., Dittus, P. J., Sieving, R. E., & Ethier, K. A. (2019). Adolescent connectedness and adult health outcomes. *Pediatrics, 144*(1), e20183766. https://doi.org/10.1542/peds.2018-3766

Sutton, C. (2021). *Life of Bryant: Killer's bizarre existence before he murdered 35 in Port Arthur massacre.* National Crime. https://www.news.com.au/national/crime/life-of-bryant-killers-bizarre-existence-before-he-murdered-35-in-port-arthur-massacre/news-story/7d0f846e758877f801d23ff34064a9bc

Tajfel, H., & Turner, J. C. (1979). An integrative theory of intergroup conflict. In W. G. Austin & S. Worchel (Eds.), *The social psychology of intergroup relations* (pp. 33–47). Brooks/Cole.

Tancredy, C. M., & Fraley, R. C. (2006). The nature of adult twin relationships: An attachment-theoretical perspective. *Journal of Personality and Social Psychology, 90*(1), 78–93. https://doi.org/10.1037/0022-3514.90.1.78

Tatum, B. D. (2017). *Why are all the Black kids sitting together in the cafeteria? And other conversations about race* (2nd ed.). Basic Books.

Toomey, R. B., Syvertsen, A. K., & Shramko, M. (2018). Transgender adolescent suicide behavior. *Pediatrics, 142*(4). https://doi.org/10.1542/peds.2017-4218

Udah, H., & Singh, P. (2019). Identity, othering and belonging: Toward an understanding of difference and the experiences of African immigrants to Australia. *Social Identities, 25*(6), 843–859. https://doi.org/10.1080/13504630.2018.1564268

United Nations High Commissioner for Refugees. (2015, August 24). *"Global trends: Forced displacement in 2015".* UNHCR. https://www.unhcr.org/statistics/unhcrstats/576408cd7/unhcr-global-trends-2015.html

United Nations High Commissioner for Refugees. (2020, August 24). *"Global trends: Forced displacement in 2020".* UNHCR. https://www.unhcr.org/media/global-trends-forced-displacement-2020

Ura, K., Alkire, S., & Zangmo, T. (2012). Case study: Bhutan gross national happiness and the GNH index. In J. F. Helliwell, R. Layard, & J. Sachs (Eds.), *World happiness report* (pp. 108-148). The Earth Institute, Columbia University. http://www.earth.columbia.edu/sitefiles/file/Sachs%20Writing/2012/World%20Happiness%20Report.pdf

van Limpt-Broers, H. A. T., Postma, M., van Weelden, E., Kroes, M. C. W., Brouwer, A.-M., Perugia, G., Pratiwi, A. B., Gong, Q., Louwerse, M. M., & Brinkman, W.-P. (2024). Neurophysiological evidence for the overview effect. A virtual reality journey into space. *Virtual Reality, 28*, 140. https://doi.org/10.1007/s10055-024-01035-7

Voski, A. (2020). The ecological significance of the overview effect: Environmental attitudes and behaviours in astronauts. *Journal of Environmental Psychology, 70*, 101454. https://doi.org/10.1016/j.jenvp.2020.101454

Walton, G. M., & Brady, S. T. (2020). The many questions of belonging. In A. J. Elliot (Ed.), *Advances in motivation science* (Vol. 7, pp. 1–40). Elsevier. https://www.guilford.com/excerpts/elliot3.pdf?t=1

Walton, G. M., & Cohen, G. L. (2007). A question of belonging: Race, social fit, and achievement. *Journal of Personality and Social Psychology, 92*(1), 82–96. https://doi.org/10.1037/0022-3514.92.1.82

Walton, G. M., & Cohen, G. L. (2011). A brief social-belonging intervention improves academic and health outcomes of minority students. *Science, 331*(6023), 1447–1451. https://doi.org/10.1126/science.1198364

Weibel, D. L. (2020). The overview effect and the ultraview effect: How extreme experiences in/of outer space influence religious beliefs in astronauts. *Religions, 11*(8), 418. https://doi.org/10.3390/rel11080418

White, F. (1987). *The overview effect. Space exploration and human evolution.* Houghton Mifflin.

White, F. (2014). *The overview effect: Space exploration and human evolution* (3rd ed.). American Institute of Aeronautics and Astronautics.

Williams, K. D. & Nida, S. A. (Eds.). (2016). *Ostracism, exclusion, and rejection* (1st ed.). Routledge. https://doi.org/10.4324/9781315308470

Woodford, M. R., Kulick, A., Garvey, J. C., Sinco, B. R., & Hong, J. S. (2018). LGBTQ policies and resources on campus and the experiences and psychological well-being of sexual minority college students: Advancing research on structural inclusion. *Psychology of Sexual Orientation and Gender Diversity, 5*(4), 445–456. https://doi.org/10.1037/sgd0000289

Xu, J., Tully, L. A., & Dadds, M. R. (2024). Generation time-out grows up: Young adults' reports about childhood time-out use and their mental health, attachment, and emotion regulation. *European Child & Adolescent Psychiatry, 33*, 3471–3479. https://doi.org/10.1007/s00787-024-02408-8

Yaden, D. B., Iwry, J., Slack, K. J., Eichstaedt, J. C., Zhao, Y., Vaillant, G. E., & Newberg, A. B. (2016). The overview effect: Awe and self-transcendent experience in space flight. *Psychology of Consciousness: Theory, Research, and Practice, 3*(1), 1–11. https://doi.org/10.1037/cns0000086

Yao, X. (2012). *An introduction to Confucianism.* Cambridge University Press.

Yuval-Davis, N. (2006). Belonging and the politics of belonging. *Patterns of Prejudice, 40*(3), 197–214. https://doi.org/10.1080/00313220600769331

CHAPTER 8

SOCIAL GOALS: RETROSPECT AND PROSPECT

Ronnel B. King
The Chinese University of Hong Kong, Hong Kong

ABSTRACT

Past studies on goals have mostly focused on achievement goals, with social goals receiving relatively less attention. This chapter aims to look back at past research on social goals and map out future developments. More specifically, the aims of this chapter were to: (1) survey the various research traditions on social goals, (2) proffer a working definition of social goals, (3) develop a conceptual framework that elucidates the antecedents, consequences, and moderators of social goals, (4) map out directions for future research, and (5) suggest practical implications of social goal research. Three distinct research traditions on social goals–goal content, social-academic, and social achievement goal approaches were reviewed. We identified a range of individual and context factors that could serve as possible antecedents of social goals and elucidated how social goals could influence both academic and nonacademic outcomes. The chapter ends with key questions that await further research.

Keywords: Social goals; achievement goals; social achievement goal; social-academic goals; student motivation

---

The Self in Context, pages 259–298

Published under exclusive licence by Emerald Publishing Limited
doi:10.1108/978-1-80686-869-820261008

INTRODUCTION

In school, students do not just pursue academic goals but also different types of social goals. For example, some students might be interested in helping their friends (prosocial goal), while other students are more concerned with gaining the approval of their teachers (social approval goal). Still others might be focused on how they can appear cool and impress their friends (social demonstration approach goal). Students pursuing these distinct social goals will also experience different cognitive and motivational outcomes (Wentzel, 2021).

Social goals are closely linked with student engagement, learning, and well-being (Goagoses & Eilts, 2024; Hofverberg et al., 2024; Kim et al., 2021; King, 2016; King & McInerney, 2019b; King, McInerney, & Watkins, 2012; Senko et al., 2023; Shim et al., 2024; Wentzel, 2021). However, we know relatively little about social goals compared to the more commonly examined achievement goals. The social goal literature is characterized by three key challenges. First, different researchers usually study social goals within their own theoretical framework with little attempt to synthesize across frameworks. This has resulted in a literature that is difficult to summarize. While a multiplicity of theoretical positions is not necessarily a problem, and most topics that receive vigorous research attention may in fact be characterized by disagreements among various theorists, it might also be important to get an overview of the field and explore points of convergence and divergence across these frameworks.

Second, there is a lack of a precise definition, as social goals are considered "fuzzy but powerful constructs" (Pintrich, 1994, p. 139). Researchers adopt different definitions of social goals, which makes theoretical integration more challenging. Third, social goals are relatively undertheorized. Hence, there is still a lot of ground to be covered in terms of exploring its antecedents, consequences, and potential moderators. Exploring more deeply the nomological network of social goals might be a fruitful research agenda given the ubiquity of social goals in the school context.

This chapter discusses past research on social goals (retrospect) and maps out future developments (prospect). It is divided into four major parts. First, we describe the various conceptualizations of social goals. Second, we propose our own working definition of social goals and critiqued the various social goal research traditions in light of our working definition. Third, we proffer a tentative conceptual framework to identify the antecedents, consequences, and moderators of social goals. Last, we mapped out directions for future research and outlined some practical implications.

WHY SOCIAL GOALS?

Motivation is inherently goal-directed (Austin & Vancouver, 1996; Elliot & Sommet, 2023). Within the educational context, research on goals has mostly focused on achievement goals, which focus mostly on academic competence

(Elliot & Murayama, 2008; Liem & Elliot, 2018). Although there has been an increasing number of studies that call for greater awareness of the social aspects of schooling (e.g., Senko et al., 2023), education is not just about academic competence. Another critical goal of education is the development of social competence as evinced by positive interpersonal interactions, cooperation, and respect for others (Wentzel, 2021). Government policies have also strongly emphasized the development of social responsibility and social competence as explicit goals of the educational enterprise (OECD, 2023).

Aside from the importance of the social aspects of schooling, there are other theoretical and practical reasons for examining social goals. From a theoretical standpoint, numerous studies have demonstrated that students endorse a variety of social goals and often value them highly (Bernardo, 2008; Bernardo et al., 2008; Dawes, 2017; King & McInerney, 2019b; Trinidad et al., 2023). These social goals have been found to account for a meaningful portion of variance in important academic and psychological outcomes, even after controlling for the effects of more widely studied achievement goals (e.g., Bardach et al., 2023; Chang & Wong, 2008; King, McInerney, & Watkins, 2012, 2013; Liem, 2016; Shim, Cho, & Wang, 2013, Shim, Wang, et al., 2013; Wentzel, 2021). In some instances, social goals emerge as even stronger predictors of outcomes than achievement goals themselves (Bernardo, 2008; King, 2016; King, McInerney, & Watkins, 2012; Liem, 2016). These findings underscore the unique and incremental predictive power of social goals in understanding student motivation and well-being.

As a testament to their practical utility, social goals have been used to predict a diverse range of outcomes such as academic achievement, behaviors in school, social relationships, effort and motivation, self-regulated learning, emotions, and socio-emotional well-being among others (King et al., 2024; Shim et al., 2024; Wentzel, 2021). Practitioners who want to solve pragmatic issues related to students' ill-being, problem behaviors, and low levels of achievement would probably gain more tools to address these seemingly intractable problems through understanding students' social goals. Taken together, social goals have key theoretical and practical value. Investigations of school motivation that focus exclusively on competence-related constructs present a one-dimensional view that does not do justice to the complexity of students' social and achievement strivings in the school setting.

THREE TRADITIONS OF SOCIAL GOAL RESEARCH

Kiefer and Ryan (2008) highlighted that research on social goals within educational psychology has evolved along three primary lines: the goal content, the social–academic goal, and social achievement goal tradition. In the following section, we discuss each of these perspectives, outline their historical roots, and synthesize key empirical contributions from these bodies of work. These three traditions are summarized in Table 8.1.

TABLE 8.1 Classification of the Various Social Goal Examples

Publication	Social Goal	Definition	Sample Item
Goal Content Approach			
Wentzel (1994)	Prosocial goal	"Students efforts to share and to help peers with social problems and efforts to share and help classmates with academic problems" (Wentzel, 1994, p. 175)	How often do you try to help kids when they have a problem?
	Social responsibility goal	"How often students try to keep promises and commitments made to peers and to follow classroom rules" (Wentzel, 1994, p. 175).	How often do you try to do what your teacher asks you to do?
Social Academic Goal Approach			
Dowson and McInerney (2004)	Social affiliation	"Wanting to achieve to enhance a sense of belonging to a group" (Dowson & McInerney, 2004, p. 295)	I want to do well at school so that I can feel close to my group of friends.
	Social approval	"Wanting to achieve to gain the approval of peers, teachers, and/or parents" (p. 296)	I try to do well at school to please my teachers.
	Social concern	"Wanting to achieve academically to be able to assist others in their academic or personal development" (p. 296)	I do my best at school so that I can give my friends help with their schoolwork
	Social responsibility	"Wanting to achieve to maintain interpersonal commitments, meet social role obligations, or follow social and moral rules" (p. 296)	I want to do well at school to show that I am being a responsible student.
	Social status	"Wanting to attain wealth and/or position in school and/or later life" (p. 297)	I do well at school so that I can get a high-paying job later on.
Social Achievement Goal Approach			
Ryan and Shim (2006)	Social development	"Concerns a focus on developing social competence… learning new things, growth, and improvement. Success would be judged by whether one is improving social skills, deepening the quality of relationships, or developing one's social life in general" (Ryan & Shim, 2006, p. 1247)	"I feel successful when I learn something new about how I relate to other people.

TABLE 8.1 Classification of the Various Social Goal Examples (Continued)

Publication	Social Goal	Definition	Sample Item
	Social demonstration approach	"Focus on demonstrating social competence and gaining from others positive judgments that one is socially desirable" (Ryan & Shim, 2006, p. 1247)	"It is important to me to have cool friends."
	Social demonstration avoidance	"Focus is on avoiding doing something that would incur negative judgments from others and indicate social undesirability" (Ryan & Shim, 2006, p. 1247)	I try not to goof up when I am out with people.

Tradition 1: Goal Content Approach

The goal content approach was the earliest social goal framework to gain recognition in the academic literature (Wentzel, 1993, 2021). Within this tradition, social goals are understood as the pursuit of specific social outcomes within the classroom context (Wentzel et al., 2018). Scholars working in this area conceptualize goals as "cognitive representations of what it is an individual is trying to achieve in a given situation" (Wentzel, 2000, pp. 105–106). When applied to social goals, the desired outcomes often include behaviors such as acting prosocially or demonstrating social responsibility in educational settings (OECD, 2023).

Wentzel (1989, 1993, 1994, 1998) pioneered the goal content approach. She focused mostly on two types of social goals: social responsibility and prosocial goals. Social responsibility goals (e.g., How often do you try to do what your teacher asks you to?) are defined as students' willingness to meet social demands or expectations, while prosocial goals (e.g., How often do you try to share what you've learned with your classmates?) are defined as students' willingness to share and help peers.

Tradition 2: Social-Academic Goal Approach

The social–academic goal perspective rose to prominence following the influential work of Urdan and Maehr (1995), who advocated for placing social goals on the same conceptual level as achievement goals. While achievement goals typically emphasize competence-based reasons for engaging in academic tasks, they posited that social goals reflect the pursuit of academic activities for socially driven reasons. This approach, described by Kiefer et al. (2008) as a "hybrid of social-academic goals" (p. 417), explores how students aim for academic success to fulfill various social motives (Cheng & Lam, 2013; King et al., 2013; Wang et al., 2019). It assumes a hierarchical structure of goals, where academic achievement functions as a means to attain broader, socially oriented objectives.

Dowson and McInerney (2001, 2003, 2004) carried out the most extensive empirical work on social-academic goals. Using a blend of quantitative and qualitative approaches, they identified five types of social-academic goals that students typically pursue: *social affiliation* (wanting to achieve in school in order to enhance a sense of belonging, e.g., "I want to do well in school so that I can feel close to my group of friends."), *social approval* (wanting to achieve in school in order to gain the approval of parents and teachers, e.g., "I try to do well at school to please my teachers."), *social concern* (wanting to achieve in school in order to help others, e.g., "I want to do well at school so that I can help other students with their work."), *social responsibility* (wanting to achieve in school in order to follow moral norms, e.g., "I want to do good schoolwork because other people expect it of me."), and *social status* (wanting to achieve in school in order to attain status, e.g., "I do good schoolwork so that I can get a good job in the future.").

Tradition 3: Social Achievement Goal Approach

The social achievement goal approach, developed by Ryan et al. (2008), is the most recent strand in the social goal literature. This framework focuses on how students define social competence and establish the standards for attaining it (Goagoses et al., 2021; Kamari et al., 2021; Liem, 2016). Within this tradition, students' socially oriented aims are referred to as *social achievement goals*, which have been categorized into three types: social development goals, which emphasize enhancing social competence (e.g., "I like it when I learn better ways to get along with friends."); social demonstration-approach goals, which involve efforts to showcase social competence and gain social approval (e.g., "It is important to me that other kids think I am popular."); and social demonstration-avoidance goals, which reflect the desire to avoid being perceived as socially incompetent (e.g., "When I am with other kids I don't want to be made fun of.").

POTENTIAL SYNERGIES AMONG THE THREE RESEARCH TRADITIONS

The three social goal traditions have proceeded in parallel with little crossover of ideas. Although developing an integrated framework that could synthesize these different theoretical traditions is beyond the scope of this chapter, perhaps one possible way to understand their interrelationships is through the goal complex approach (Liem & Senko, 2022; Senko et al., 2023). The key idea behind the goal complex approach is that lower-order goals could serve the function of fulfilling a higher-order goal.

The social-academic goal tradition, for example, can be understood as a specific type of goal complex where students pursue lower-order academic goals to achieve a higher-order social outcome. A student might, for example, strive to outperform others (performance-approach academic goal) in order to earn the approval of parents (social-approval) (Meurlin & Senko, 2025).

A goal complex approach can also include social achievement goal under its umbrella. For example, a student could strive to outperform peers (performance-approach academic goal) or gain social prestige among peers (social demonstration approach goal). The goal content approach could also be integrated into the goal complex approach. For example, a student might want to pursue the goal of improving her skills relative to her self-set standards (mastery-approach goal) in order to meet interpersonal commitments to her teachers (social responsibility goal).

The goal complex approach suggests that it is important to understand the effects of both the higher-order and lower-order goals (Liem & Senko, 2022). By attending to how goals cluster, interact, and serve higher-order motives, researchers can better understand the social needs that drive student motivation. The goal complex work is a promising avenue for future research but is still in its early stages. More research is needed to understand these dynamics (Liem & Senko, 2022; Liem et al., 2025; Meurlin & Senko, 2025; Tan et al., 2022).

A WORKING DEFINITION OF SOCIAL GOALS

Having reviewed how different scholars have conceptualized social goals, we now offer our own working definition. Goals in general have been described as internal representations of desired end states (Austin & Vancouver, 1996). More specifically, social goals have been characterized as "goals whose content encompasses the social aspects of the classroom" (Murphy & Alexander, 2000, p. 28). While informative, these definitions remain somewhat broad and would benefit from greater conceptual clarity. In this paper, we adopt a more refined definition following Elliot (2005), framing social goals as "cognitive representations of a desired future outcome related to the social aspects of the school setting."

We break this working definition into several components. The first part of the definition is that social goals are *cognitive representations*. As such, it shares many of the same features as other knowledge structures (Shah & Kruglanski, 2003). This cognitive representation definition therefore excludes constructs such as temperament, personality dispositions, and underlying motives (need for affiliation, need for power, fear of failure) which are more affect-based and dispositional (Elliot, 2005). Goals are more appropriately viewed as cognitive constructs representing areas in life toward which a person directs his or her energies (Elliot, 2021).

The second part of the definition–“desired future outcome”–pertains to the future-oriented nature of social goal striving. Social goals focus on future possibilities that are used to guide present behavior. This future may be something currently present that one is committed to keep or get rid of, or something currently absent that one is committed to get or prevent (Elliot, 2006).

The third part of the definition pertains to the object of the goal, which is the focal part of regulation. For social goals, we define the object in relation to outcomes related to the *social aspects of the school setting.* By social aspects, we mean that persons in the school context (e.g., parents, teachers, peers, classmates, peer group) form the focal object of social goals. The social-oriented nature of the focal object is what distinguishes social goals from other nonsocial goals. For example, goals that are purely oriented on one’s personal task competence (e.g., mastery goal) or goals that do not have an external social referent (e.g., work avoidance goal which pertains to wanting to avoid effort as much as possible) are not included in our social goal definition.

In distinguishing social goals from other types of goals, it is useful to perform a thought experiment. If a certain goal can be pursued even without the presence (real or imagined) of significant others, then it cannot be considered a social goal. For example, the goal of wanting to develop one’s math skills relative to self-set standards (mastery approach goal) or the goal of trying to avoid as much homework as possible (work avoidance goal) could be pursued (arguably) even without making explicit reference to other persons. However, social goals by their very nature involve the *social aspects* of the school environment and thus only make sense in relation to other people. The social goal of trying to gain the approval of teachers by finishing one’s homework (social approval goal), for example, does not make sense unless there is a teacher whom one wants to please.

We also wanted to confine the parameters of social goals to those that are relevant to the school setting. Social goals can also be pursued outside the school context. For example, Méndez-Giménez et al. (2018) has done much work on social goals in the sports context, while Girme et al. (2016) have explored social goals in various social settings such as the romantic context. We do not include these other types of social goals in our review and restrict ourselves to social goals that operate in the school domain given our focal interest on education-related outcomes.

Critiquing the Three Social Goal Research Traditions Using Our Definition

We now review the three social goal research traditions in relation to our working definition of social goals as "cognitive representations of a desired future outcome related to the social aspects of the school setting." The first part of the definition is that social goals are *cognitive representations*. All the three social goal research traditions fit in with our criteria of social goals as "cognitive representations." The three social goal traditions have measured social goals using self-reports and not projective techniques or other implicit measures. This indicates implicit acknowledgment that social goals as cognitive representations are partially accessible to our conscious minds.

The second part of the definition is that social goals are focused on a *desired future outcome*. While all three social goal traditions acknowledge that goals are future-oriented, not all of them explicitly operationalize goals as future-focused. For example, a sample item measuring Wentzel's (1994) prosocial goal pursuit is "How often do you try to help kids when they have a problem?" For social responsibility goals, a sample item is, "How often do you try to do what your teacher wants you to do?" These items make students' sample their past behaviors. Wentzel infers goal pursuit from these items that focus on past behaviors.

While past actions do give us much information about the goals that one pursues (a student who frequently helps others in the past seems to be logically pursuing prosocial goals), a probably better operationalization would be to ask students more directly about what they want to achieve in the future. A better item perhaps might be "I want to help my classmates when they have problems."

Dowson and McInerney's (2004) social-academic goals reflect the future orientation much more clearly. They ask questions such as, "I want to do well at school so I can feel close to my group of friends" (social affiliation goal) and "I want to do well in school to show that I am being a responsible student" (social responsibility goal). The use of the word "want" focuses on the future-oriented goal striving.

Ryan and Shim's (2006) operationalization of social achievement goals is not explicitly focused on the future either. Some of the items they used to measure social achievement goals pertain more to affect (e.g., "I *feel* successful when I learn something new about how I relate to other people;" social development goal) and value (e.g., "It is *important* to me to have cool friends."). Better alternatives might be to say, "I am striving to learn something new about how I relate to other people" and "My goal is to have cool friends."

Many of the existing goal research in the educational psychology literature has used goal items that do not explicitly focus on the future as well.

Items related to past behaviors, affect, and value have been frequently used. This goes back to a longstanding debate among goal researchers whether a broader conceptualization of goals as orientations (Ames, 1992) or whether a narrower conceptualization of goals is more appropriate (Elliot, 2005). We favor a narrower and more precise conceptualization of goals given that a broad conceptualization may hinder us from teasing out social goals from their relevant antecedents and consequences. Greater theoretical precision could be achieved if we make the operationalizations of social goals more closely aligned to the way goals are theoretically defined in the literature as focusing on the attainment of desired future outcomes.

The third component of our definition is that social goals are related to the *social aspects of the school setting.* Wentzel's (1994) social goals are pursued in relation to one's teachers and classmates. Dowson and McInerney's (2004) social-academic goals are targeted towards one's parents, teachers, and peers. Both social goal traditions fit within the parameters of our definition as relevant to the social aspects of school. The "social" in Ryan and Shim's (2006) social achievement goal approach is somewhat broader than our conceptualization. Social achievement goals could be pursued across different domains (at work, in school, in sports, etc.). In most of the existing studies, Ryan and Shim (2006) used student samples and the referent was one's peers or classmates in school. For example, when asking students to answer the item "It is important for me to have cool friends" (social demonstration approach goal), the "friends" in the item are clearly one's classmates. "This puts social achievement goals within our definition as related to social aspects of the school setting." However, one can easily imagine these social achievement goals to be pursued in nonschool settings as well.

Perhaps, one may ask what the advantages are of adopting a more constrained definition of social goals? First, a narrower definition will help us tease out social goal constructs from their consequences as well as their antecedents. For example, if social goal items include affect or emotions, then we do not know whether particular emotions actually ensue from particular types of social goals because they are confounded in the measures of goals. A more constrained definition allows us to map the nomological network of social goals more clearly. Second, a more precise definition allows us to closely align our theoretical constructs with the way we operationalize them. This is especially important in psychological research where we measure abstract concepts and not physical entities. Measurement is a key issue and fuzzy operationalizations decrease the theoretical precision of psychological knowledge that is accrued through research. Third, a more precise definition allows us to address the problems of an "overextended construct" which becomes a kitchen sink category such that it loses any meaningful theoretical value.

We are certainly aware that our definition of social goals may meet disagreement from other researchers. This is inevitable in a field where goals in general have been defined and operationalized in such a variety of ways, and where social goals have also suffered from the same fragmentation. However, we think that our definition offers a useful starting point to move the conversation on social goals forward.

CONCEPTUAL FRAMEWORK: ANTECEDENTS, CONSEQUENCES, AND MODERATORS OF SOCIAL GOALS

In order to give conceptual coherence to the vast array of studies on social goals housed under the three social goal research traditions, we organized them using a tentative conceptual framework presented in Fig. 8.1. The conceptual framework is organized according to three broad divisions: antecedents, consequences, and moderators of social goals.

A caveat, however, is in order. Much of the existing research on social goals has relied on correlational and cross-sectional studies (e.g., Kiefer et al., 2008; King & McInerney, 2019a; Wentzel, 2021). Therefore, much of what we know is more suggestive than conclusive. Social goal researchers

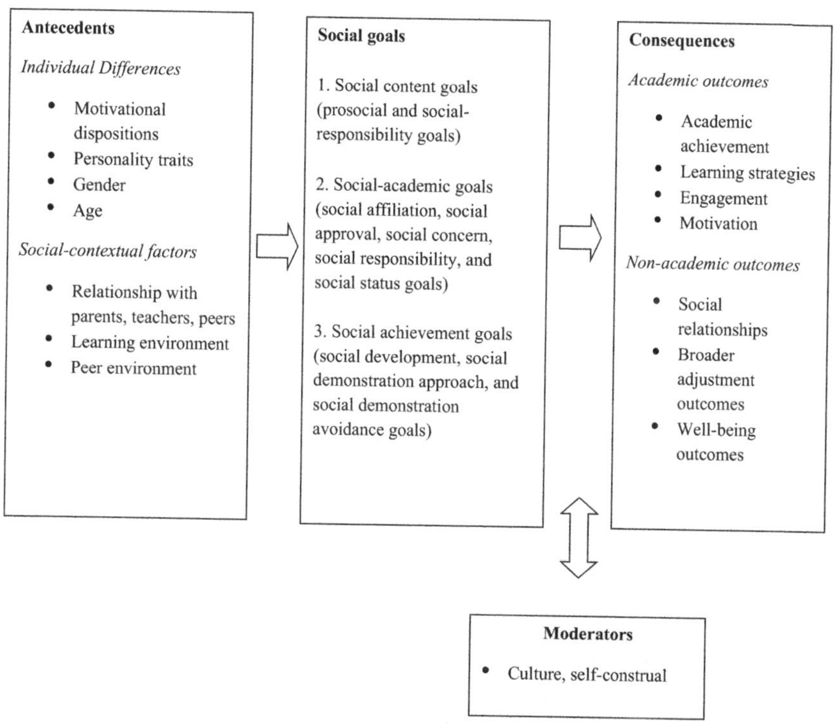

Fig. 8.1. A Conceptual Model of the Antecedents, Consequences, and Moderators of Social Goals.

still lack solid empirical knowledge about precise causal mechanisms regarding the relationships among antecedents and consequences of social goals. Ultimately, whether the variables we included in the conceptual framework serve as antecedents, consequences, or correlates of social goals is an issue that needs not be totally resolved here. Undoubtedly, over time there is some amount of reciprocal causation between social goals and many of these variables. For the present purposes, however, this classification scheme provides a useful heuristic for understanding social goals and for organizing the fragmented literature on social goals.

Fig. 8.1 presents the proposed framework. The variables listed in the conceptual framework are not meant to be exhaustive. The aim is to give a broad overview of the linkages established in existing social goal research and allude to other possible linkages that researchers could consider in future research.

Antecedents of Social Goals

Our survey of the empirical literature has shown that few studies have investigated possible antecedents of social goals. Consistent with the theorizing on goals, we argue that social goals are rooted in both individual difference variables and social-contextual factors.

Individual Differences

(a) Motivational dispositions. Early theorizing has portrayed goals as concrete representations of more abstract motivational dispositions (Cattell, 1967; McClelland, 1987). Motivational dispositions are usually considered as distal antecedents while goals are considered as proximal antecedents of key psychological outcomes.

Researchers have shown the linkage between motivational dispositions such as need for achievement and fear of failure to achievement goals (Elliot et al., 1997). It is also possible that social goals draw motivational energy from basic motivational dispositions. A good candidate would be the need for affiliation (Kordik et al., 2012). Individual differences in the need for affiliation may lead to differences in the strength of social goal adoption, with individuals having a stronger need for affiliation endorsing social goals to a greater extent (Rybnicek et al., 2019).

(b) Personality traits. Personality traits have been linked to achievement goal endorsement (Bipp et al., 2008). For example, trait conscientiousness has been found to be positively related to mastery-approach goals and openness to experience and negatively related to neuroticism. Performance avoidance goals are positively related to neuroticism and negatively related to extraversion and openness. Extending these findings to the social goal

literature, researchers could also look at how social goals are associated with personality traits. For example, we speculate that social demonstration avoidance goals investigated by Ryan and Shim (2006) might be positively correlated with neuroticism and negatively correlated with extraversion. This is because research has shown extraverted individuals to have more rewarding social interactions, while neuroticism has been linked to anxiety in various social situations (McCrae & John, 1992).

Social development goals, on the other hand, might be positively related to extraversion, agreeableness, and openness. Social concern goals (Dowson & McInerney, 2001) and prosocial goals (Wentzel, 1994) may be positively associated with agreeableness and extraversion and negatively associated with neuroticism. Social responsibility goals investigated by Wentzel (1994) and Dowson and McInerney (2004), on the other hand, might be positively linked to conscientiousness given that conscientious individuals are more likely to follow rules and social norms. These speculations await further empirical testing.

Social-Contextual Factors

Aside from individual difference antecedents, social goals can also be influenced by several social-contextual factors. In this section, we focus on the possible roles of social relationships and the learning environment on students' social goal pursuit.

(a) Parents. Parents are likely to be a potent influence on students' social goal adoption. Research in achievement goal theory has shown that students are strongly influenced by their parents' mastery or performance goal emphases (Friedel et al., 2007; Gutman, 2006). Similarly, although we know of no existing study that has tried to examine the linkage between parents' social goals and students' social goals, it is highly possible that students would be influenced by their parents' social goal emphasis as well. There is a large social psychology literature showing that people automatically pursue goals that are emphasized by people close to them (Shah & Devine, 2003). For instance, parental expectations have been shown to influence adolescents' goal setting and pursuit (Massey et al., 2008), and goals set by significant others can influence an individual's own goal setting and pursuit (Milyavskaya et al., 2018).

Parenting practices might also have direct implications for social goal research. One such practice would be parental involvement which could be seen in terms of joining teacher-parent conferences, helping children with homework, and attending children's extracurricular activities. Studies have shown that higher levels of parental involvement are associated with greater achievement (Boonk et al., 2018; Ogg & Anthony, 2020; Wilder, 2014). These parenting practices could have an impact on students' social goal pursuit. As Spera (2005, p. 128) noted, "Interacting and becoming involved with their children's life on a daily basis is a way parents can socialize their children." Thus, it is possible that parents who are involved in their children's daily life are more likely to facilitate the adoption of adaptive types of social goals. For example, one could expect children who have experienced high levels of parental involvement to adopt prosocial and social responsibility goals more strongly compared to those whose parents remain distant from their daily lives (Barger et al., 2019; Wilder, 2023).

Parenting style is also a crucial factor in student motivation and achievement. Numerous studies have found that authoritative parenting style (characterized by high levels of warmth and structure) facilitates higher academic outcomes (Carolan & Wasserman, 2015; Chan & Koo, 2011; Steinberg et al., 1992). Children of authoritative parents were more prosocial and achievement-oriented compared to those whose parents were not authoritative, and they are also more likely to internalize the values of their parents. Though we are not aware of any study that has directly examined the link between parenting style and social goals, one could expect adaptive types of social goals (e.g., prosocial goals, social responsibility goals, social development goals, social concern goals) to be associated with authoritative parenting styles.

(b) Teachers. Studies have shown that students' social goals are closely related to their relationships with their teachers. Self-determination theory has focused on the contrast between teachers who employ autonomy-supportive and those who employ controlling strategies (Reeve, 2009). Teachers who are autonomy supportive are focused on identifying and nurturing students' inner motivational resources, and frequently engage in providing informative feedback, listening to student input, giving students opportunities to choose what to work on and how to complete their tasks, and designing optimally challenging tasks. On the other hand, controlling teachers pressure students to think, feel, and behave in a certain way. Controlling practices include imposing strict deadlines, issuing controlling statements (e.g., "You ought to do it this way."), using threats to demand compliance, and prohibiting students from stating their own opinions (Reeve, 2009).

Research has shown that autonomy supportive instructional practices may help students internalize the values that are endorsed by the school and the teacher. Thus, it is reasonable to assume that students who perceive their teachers as autonomy supportive may endorse social goals such as prosocial and social responsibility goals, which are highly valued by adults. They are also less likely to engage in other types of social goals which are not endorsed by the teachers (e.g., such as pursuing social intimacy goals with nonachieving peers or pursuing status goals among nonachieving peers).

Aside from autonomy-support, there has also been a lot of research on the importance of feeling connected with the teachers (Granziera et al.,

2022; Martin et al., 2024). Research has shown that students who have warm and caring teachers have higher levels of psychological well-being (Tian et al., 2013). However, when students feel that the teacher or the school context does not fulfill their basic psychological needs, they may tend to devalue the norms of the school. This might be particularly relevant in the case of social-academic goals. When students adopt social-academic goals, they strive to do well in school due to social reasons which may include obtaining the teacher's approval (social approval goals) or being socially responsible (social responsibility goals). However, if they feel that teachers are not able to fulfill their needs for relatedness, they may look to other sources of social fulfillment.

(c) Peers. The peer group becomes a significant context for development during the adolescent stage (Brown et al., 2004). Researchers have shown that high school students spend more time with their peers (29%) which is almost twice as much as the time they spend with adults such as parents or teachers (15%) (Csikszentmihalyi et al., 1977). Friendships become characterized by increasing levels of intimacy and empathy during the adolescent stage. Thus, it is not surprising to find that friends resemble each other in a wide range of characteristics. This phenomenon has been termed as homophily (Brechwald & Prinstein, 2011).

Homophily may develop through two different mechanisms: selection and socialization. Selection pertains to the process whereby individuals select friends who are similar to themselves in key characteristics. Thus, it is possible to find that friends with similar social goals may affiliate with each other. On the other hand, socialization pertains to the process whereby friends become more similar to each other across time. This socialization effect has been observed for a wide range of characteristics, motivational beliefs, and behaviors (Brechwald & Prinstein, 2011; Kindermann, 2007). It is plausible to assume that the process of socialization might help friends converge in their level of social goal endorsement as well (King & Mendoza, 2021). It is also possible that friends who initially differ in their social goals may become more similar to each other after some time. This socialization effect may be accounted for by processes such as information exchange, peer modeling, and social reinforcement of peer norms (King, 2020; King & Mendoza, 2020).

Information exchange occurs when discussions among peers present students with new perspectives or ideas. When friends interact with each other and exchange information about their goals, they may also influence each other (Chiu & Chow, 2015). For example, two friends may talk about the importance of following school rules, and in the end may influence each other toward endorsing social responsibility goals more strongly.

Peer modeling refers to changes in cognitions or behaviors that result from observation of others. There has been a plethora of research on the crucial role of modeling in socializing academic beliefs and values (Musser et al., 2022; Usher & Pajares, 2008). Researchers have found that students who were exposed to coping models (peer models who initially demonstrated difficulty with a task but later succeeded in it) developed higher levels of self-efficacy beliefs (Schunk & Zimmerman, 1996). Similarly, when students see their friends adopting a certain type of social goals, they may also endorse this social goal more strongly.

Social reinforcement of peer norms is manifested when behaviors endorsed by peers become more strongly endorsed by the individual (Mertens et al., 2021). Conversely, beliefs and behaviors that are devalued by peers become more devalued by the individual as well. This can occur through a variety of indirect processes such as through gossiping, teasing, and humor (Goddard, 2018; Mertens et al., 2021). For example, if a student is in a peer group wherein peers frequently tease and laugh at other students who are obedient to the teachers (those who pursue social responsibility goals) then that student's endorsement of social responsibility goal is likely to decrease as well.

(d) Learning environment. Features of the learning environment may also influence the types of goals that students pursue. The transition from elementary to middle school is considered a stressful event in adolescents' life (Lovette-Wilson et al., 2022; Pajares & Graham, 1999) and may make certain types of social goals especially salient. In elementary schools, students usually stay with the same teacher all day, while in middle schools they get to interact with more teachers at shorter time spans. Moreover, students' transition to middle school also coincides with the onset of adolescence during which peers become more focal (Lam et al., 2014). Research has shown that during adolescence peers become a significant source of feedback for one's identity and self-evaluation, also known as reflected appraisal (Hergovich et al., 2002; Yue et al., 2021). Related to this, social goals related to attaining peer approval (social demonstration goals) or building relationships with peers (social affiliation goals) may increase in salience compared to those aimed at acquiring teacher approval. This dovetails with evidence showing that adolescent students place an increasingly high value on what their peers think of them (Ryan, 2001; Yue et al., 2022).

Another feature of the learning environment would be the use of collaborative or peer-mediated learning methods which may foster the development of goals related to building bonds among fellow learners (e.g., social affiliation, social development) (Johnson & Johnson, 2009). When cooperative learning is enacted, success in schoolwork is usually redefined from being an individualistic enterprise to a group endeavor. Some researchers suggest that collaborative learning activities are especially helpful in aligning social goals and academic goals. Phelan and her colleagues (Phelan et al., 1991, 1994) found that those who had difficulty coordinating social and academic pursuits achieved at higher levels in classrooms that used collaborative learning strategies. One could imagine that when students engage in collaborative learning, their academic goal of doing well in school and their social goals of feeling close to others can be accomplished at the same time (Juvonen & Wentzel, 1996; Loes, 2022). When students only engage in individual work, their social goals may be frustrated. As Martin and Dowson (2009, p. 330) wrote, "When the need for belongingness is fulfilled, this fulfillment produces positive emotional responses. In the academic domain, these responses are said to drive students' achievement behaviors to challenge, self-regulation, participation, and strategy use." Thus, the use of collaborative learning strategies which can help fulfill social needs may be especially useful for harnessing the power of social goals in order to optimize learning outcomes.

To summarize, there are strong theoretical reasons to suppose that relationships with parents, teachers, and peers as well as specific features of the learning environment have a key influence on students' social goals irrespective of the specific operational definition of the social goal. Although these assumptions are speculative, we have proposed specific theoretical mechanisms (e.g., parenting style, parental involvement, teacher autonomy-support, peer selection, peer socialization, goal alignment) that describe how particular antecedents may influence social goal pursuit.

Consequences of Social Goals

Having provided an overview of the potential influences on social goals, we now move to the consequences of pursuing social goals. For the sake of simplicity, we group them into two types of outcomes: academic-related and nonacademic related. Academic outcomes pertain to variables that are directly related to the learning such as academic achievement, learning strategies, academic motivation, engagement, and other indices of school functioning.

The second set of outcomes pertain to broader adjustment outcomes such as well-being, social competence, and socio-emotional outcomes. The boundary between these two sets of outcomes is fluid given that both sets of variables undeniably influence each other (Seligman et al., 2009). However, for the purposes of the current paper we thought it useful to differentiate between these two for the sake of clearer exposition. Compared to research on the antecedents of social goals, relatively much more work has been undertaken on the consequences of social goals. Thus, we are able to cite specific social goal studies in this section compared to the earlier one.

Social Goals and Academic Outcomes

Much research on social goals has been focused on mapping out its relationship to various types of academic outcomes. Social goal researchers from the goal content, social-academic, and social achievement goal traditions have contributed to advancing our knowledge on this front.

We first review research on the goal content perspective. In her early work, Wentzel (1991) found that students who endorsed social responsibility goals tended to perform better academically, with this relationship partially explained by their responsible behavior. Later, Wentzel (1996) showed that a combined measure of prosocial and social responsibility goals significantly predicted students' effort in English classes—even after accounting for traditional academic motivation variables. When mastery and performance goals, intrinsic value, and self-efficacy were included in the regression alongside social goals, only social goals emerged as significant predictors of effort in English. In addition to predicting effort, social goals were also positively linked to other motivational constructs such as self-efficacy, intrinsic value, and mastery goals. Notably, social goals predicted not only concurrent English grades but also English performance two years later.

Research has shown that social-academic goals are significantly linked to important academic outcomes. King, McInerney, and Watkins (2012) examined different forms of social-academic goals among secondary school students and found that these goals were significant positive predictors of behavioral, emotional, and cognitive engagement—even when mastery and performance goals were statistically controlled. Specifically, social concern, social responsibility, and social status goals emerged as strong predictors of student engagement (see also King et al., 2017). Similarly, Wolters et al. (2014) studied adolescent students and reported that social responsibility, social approval, and social affiliation goals were positively associated with intrinsic motivation, perceived importance of school, and the perceived utility of education. There are other studies that found some social goals as negatively associated with academic outcomes. For example, pursuing popularity as a social status goal is negatively associated with Grade Point Average (GPA) and may increase the risk of academic maladjustment among young individuals (Dawes, 2017).

There are fewer studies on the links between social achievement goals and academic outcomes. This probably reflects the newness of the social achievement goal approach and also the fact that most social achievement goal researchers were more interested in socio-emotional rather than academic outcomes (e.g., Jeanne Horst et al., 2007; Kuroda & Sakurai, 2011; Mouratidis & Sideridis, 2009; Shim, Cho, & Wang, 2013). The few existing studies, however, do show some evidence that social development goals are associated with more adaptive outcomes compared to social demonstration approach goals (Madjar et al., 2019). Social demonstration avoidance goals seem to have a weaker relationship with academic outcomes.

For example, Liem (2016) found that social development goals were positively associated with self-regulated learning and cooperative learning, while social demonstration approach goals were negatively related to academic effort and persistence. Social demonstration avoidance goals did not significantly predict achievement or effort. Mouratidis and Michou (2011) documented that social development goals were associated with more positive and less negative emotions in class. However, social demonstration approach goals were more highly associated with negative emotions such as anger, anxiety, boredom, and hopelessness. Social demonstration avoidance goals were not significantly associated with negative emotions in class.

Social Goals and Nonacademic Outcomes

Social goals may exert an especially powerful influence on well-being and socio-emotional adjustment. They may be even more important predictors of these outcomes compared to achievement goals given that well-being is closely tied to the quality of social relationships (Goswami, 2011; King, 2015; Lam, 2019).

Using a goal content approach, Anderman (1999) found that social relationship goals ("I want to be part of things that other students are doing in school") and social responsibility ("I try to do what my teacher asks me to do.") were positively associated with positive affect, while social status goals ("It's important for me to belong to the popular group at school.") were positively associated with negative affect. In another study, Wentzel (1994) found that prosocial goals were positively associated with peer acceptance, while social responsibility goals were positively associated with teacher acceptance.

Only a few studies have investigated the relationship of social-academic goals to nonacademic outcomes (King, 2016). For example, Ouano and Punugu (2012) examined the relationship between social-academic goals and life satisfaction and found that social affiliation, social approval, social concern, social responsibility, and social status goals were highly correlated with students' life satisfaction. King (2016) examined the association between social-academic goals and well-being. He found that social concern goals positively predicted better well-being as indexed by higher levels of self-esteem, life satisfaction, and positive affect. The other types of social-academic goals mostly had nonsignificant relationships with the well-being outcomes.

With regard to social achievement goals, research indicates that social development goals are linked to positive psychological adjustment and well-being, whereas social demonstration-avoidance goals tend to predict negative psychological outcomes. For instance, Shin and Ryan (2012) found that students who endorsed social development goals were more likely to exhibit prosocial behavior and higher levels of social competence. In contrast, those who pursued social demonstration-avoidance goals displayed greater tendencies toward aggression, social anxiety, and internalizing symptoms. The pattern for social demonstration-approach goals was more complex, as these goals were associated with both adaptive outcomes (e.g., social competence, popularity) and maladaptive outcomes (e.g., aggressive or socially anxious behaviors).

Social achievement goals have also been found to be related to students' emotional experiences (Bross et al., 2024; Shim, Wang, & Cassady, 2013). Students who pursued social development goals were more likely to experience positive emotions such as love and joy and less likely to experience negative emotions such as fear, anger, shame, and sadness. Conversely, those who pursued social demonstration avoidance goals were more likely to experience negative emotions such as fear, shame, and sadness, and less likely to experience positive emotions such as joy. Social demonstration approach goals were not significantly correlated with most of the emotions measured.

Social development goals have been found to be positively related to social self-efficacy (Shim & Finch, 2014). Social demonstration approach and social demonstration avoidance goals were both strongly correlated with social worry. Aside from social-achievement goal researchers, those who conduct research using the goal content and social-academic goal approaches have also conducted preliminary studies on the relationship between social goals and adjustment outcomes. For example, using the goal content approach, Wentzel et al. (2007) found that a composite score of prosocial and social responsibility goals were positively correlated with empathy and perspective-taking. Prosocial goals were positively correlated with prosocial behavior (Canevello & Crocker, 2020; Gęsiarz & Crockett, 2015; Wentzel et al., 2004).

Social Goal Moderators

While most of the research on social goals has focused on direct effects, it is also possible that certain variables would moderate the relationship between social goals and various outcomes. In this paper, we focus on the possible moderating role of culture and self-construal.

The cultural context may modify the relationship between social goals and how they are associated with outcome variables. Cultures vary systematically in the extent to which individuals are considered as autonomous or as deeply embedded in various social groups (Schwartz, 1992, 2004). In individualistic cultures, people are relatively free to express their personal preferences, opinions, and feelings and are able to emphasize their individual uniqueness, which makes independent self-construals more salient. On the other hand, in collectivist societies, individuals are socialized to conform to group norms and are expected to follow their social role obligations (Ding et al., 2024; Kyriacou, 2016). Hence, interdependent self-construals are more salient (Giacomin et al., 2020; Krys et al., 2022; Li et al., 2024; Smith & Bond, 2019).

Self-construals may moderate the impact of social goals on various educational outcomes. Especially pertinent would be the moderating effects of self-construal on social-academic goals (wanting to study for social reasons). Urdan and Maehr (1995) argued that for those with an interdependent self-construal, social-academic goals may be more internalized and pursued in a more autonomous manner compared to those with a more salient independent self-construal. A person with an interdependent self-construal sees himself/herself not as a separate entity but as tightly connected with significant others. Therefore, studying for the sake of others may be more internalized.

Correlational studies provide indirect support for this assumption. King et al. (2010, 2012a, 2014) carried out research on social-academic goals in the collectivist Chinese and Philippine contexts. They found that the different types of social goals were positive predictors of key learning outcomes. They concluded that in collectivist contexts, the effects of social goals may be more positive than what may have been found in Western settings. Bernardo (2008) found that striving to live up to parental and teacher expectations (akin to social approval goal) was positively associated with GPA among Filipino students. Cheng and Lam (2013) provided direct evidence for this showing that the pursuit of social approval goals was only detrimental for those with independent and not interdependent self-construal. To summarize, a whole host of individual differences and social-contextual factors have been found to be possible antecedents of social goals. In terms of the outcomes, we denote that social goals can affect both academic and nonacademic outcomes. While most of the existing literature has focused on direct effects, we also noted that the effects of social goals may be moderated by factors such as culture and self-construal among others.

DIRECTIONS FOR FUTURE RESEARCH

Given the relative dearth of research on social goals compared to the more mature achievement goal literature, we ask a few key questions that await further research:

1. How Do Social Goals Change Across Time?

Much of the existing social goal research is cross-sectional in nature. However, school motivation is not static but develops over time. For example, researchers have found that school motivation declines as students move from earlier grades to higher grades (Anderman, 1999; Balfanz et al., 2007; Cohen et al., 2023; Garon-Carrier et al., 2016). The declining levels of motivation have been attributed by some researchers to the stresses of puberty that adolescent students face as well as to the lack of fit between the psychological needs of adolescents and the affordances of the school environment (e.g. Eccles et al., 1993; Steidtmann et al., 2022).

Regardless of what causes the motivational decline, this decline seems to be widespread across cultures (e.g., Wang & Pomerantz, 2009) and has been documented for a wide range of motivational constructs (Blossfeld et al., 2024; Morton et al., 2024; Schweder & Raufelder, 2022; Van de gaer et al., 2009; Wild et al., 2024). It is possible that certain types of social goals may also decline. Pomerantz et al.'s (2011) study provides indirect evidence for this possibility. They found that adolescent students' sense of responsibility toward their parents declined during the seventh and eighth grades, at least for the American students. Although not directly assessing social goals, the decline in sense of responsibility may also be reflective of a decline in students' pursuit of social responsibility goals in the academic setting. Studies that show increases in delinquent behavior across the adolescent years also seem to provide partial support for the assumption that adaptive types of social goals may decline as students get older (Compas et al., 1995; Shek & Lin, 2016).

Not all social goals, however, may decline during adolescence. It is possible that social demonstration approach and social demonstration avoidance goals may increase in salience during the adolescent years given the heightened concern of adolescents toward how their peers view them at this age (LaFontana & Cillessen, 2010). Moreover, these particular social goals may also spike during transitions such as the transition from elementary to middle school or from high school to university given that students must renegotiate their identities when they enter a new context (Bellmore et al., 2011). Throughout different developmental stages, the meaning of different types of social goals may also vary. For example, in primary school, social responsibility goals may just pertain to following what the teacher says (e.g., not cheating, not talking to one's seatmates, finishing one's homework.). However, when students are in the university, social responsibility may take on a somewhat different meaning. Aside from following norms set up by the teacher, it may also involve more abstract moral commitments that could transcend or take precedence over the rules that the teacher has set in class.

To date, we still lack knowledge about the developmental trends associated with social goals. However, there are compelling theoretical reasons to assume that the developmental trajectories of different types of social goals will vary. Empirical studies are needed to give psychologists a more nuanced and detailed understanding of how social goals change across time.

2. What Roles Do Culture and Context Play in Social Goal Pursuit?

Culture and context have been found to influence a wide range of psychological processes. They also exert a large influence on determining which goals are important and which ones are not (Guo et al., 2022; Schwartz, 1992). For example, in individualist cultures more independent types of goals such as goals for self-determination and agency are more highly valued. In collectivist cultures, on the other hand, goals for conformity and belongingness may be more salient (Huppert et al., 2019; Liem & Elliot, 2018; Schwartz, 2004; Vishkin et al., 2023).

In light of this, it is plausible that cultural context shapes the kinds of social goals students prioritize in educational settings. Scholars in cross-cultural psychology suggest that social goals may hold greater importance in collectivist cultures, where interdependent views of the self are more common (Cheng & Lam, 2013; Senko et al., 2023; King, McInerney, & Watkins, 2012; King & McInerney, 2019; King et al., 2014). Individuals from collectivist societies are more likely to define themselves in relation to others, which may lead them to endorse social goals more strongly than those from individualist cultures. If this is the case, then social goal research may hold particular global relevance, especially given that the majority of the world's population resides within collectivist cultural frameworks (Hofstede, 2001).

3. Should Social Goals Be Bifurcated Into Their Approach Avoidance Dimensions?

Achievement goal theory, which focuses on mastery and performance, has advanced significantly by distinguishing between performance-approach and performance-avoidance goals (Linnenbrink-Garcia et al., 2012). Other developments in the theory have also emphasized the importance of differentiating mastery goals into mastery-approach and mastery-avoidance goals (Elliot & Murayama, 2008). Earlier research that failed to make these distinctions often resulted in conceptual ambiguity and inconsistent empirical findings. Perhaps, social goals could also benefit from incorporating these approach-avoidance distinctions.

Thus far, only studies that use the social achievement goal approach as well as a few other scattered studies have systematically included approach and avoidance dimensions of social goals. The majority of existing social goal studies only focus on approach forms of goals (e.g., Dowson & McInerney, 2004; Wentzel, 1994). Other studies have aggregated both approach and avoidance items (e.g., Miller et al., 1996) into an overall scale. Future studies may need to systematically incorporate the approach-avoidance distinction in their research.

4. What Happens When There Is Conflict Among Multiple Social and Nonsocial Goals?

Despite the acknowledgment that multiple-goal pursuit is the norm, and not the exception, educational psychologists have rarely examined what happens when multiple goals are in conflict (Boudreaux & Ozer, 2013). Research has shown that 47% of individuals regularly fail to enact their goals thereby demonstrating the pervasiveness of goal conflict (Sheeran, 2002). How will a student decide to allocate his time for example when the social goal of hanging out with friends (social intimacy goal) conflicts with the goal of mastering the material (mastery approach goal)?

Learners often find themselves in situations where various motivational tendencies conflict with each other (Brassler et al., 2016). Research on motivational conflict in the educational setting has been pioneered by M. Hofer and his colleagues (Hofer, 2007; Hofer et al., 2011). They mostly focused on situations wherein students are torn between leisure and study. Though they did not frame their research in terms of social goals, the academic-leisure choices could easily be rephrased in goal terminology as a conflict between different types of goals. Future research on social goals should account for how individuals would choose among competing goals and how, and why they allocate their resources as a result of this choice.

Applying this paradigm to the realm of social goals, researchers can explicitly measure goal conflict by asking participants to rate the relative salience of different goals. Making multiple social (and academic) goals salient at the point of measurement can facilitate a more accurate prediction of what students will actually do. For example, one can envision researchers asking participants to answer how important it was for them to (a) spend time with their peers (social affiliation goal) or (b) to spend time doing one's homework (mastery approach goal) and examine how individuals will allocate their resources to one or another type of goal.

5. Can We Design Intervention Programs to Develop Adaptive Types of Social Goals?

If social goals are to have a practical impact on students' lives, researchers need to design interventions that systematically encourage adaptive types of social goals and at the same time decrease the pursuit of maladaptive social goals. Correlational studies have shown that they are strongly related to the social context (Dawes, 2017; King & Ganotice, 2014; Spera & Wentzel, 2003). Hence, changing aspects of the social context may lead to subsequent changes in social goals. Moreover, brief experimental procedures have also been shown to be successful in modifying students' social goal pursuit (Cheng & Lam, 2013). These studies provide evidence for the malleability of social goals. Achievement goal researchers have designed successful interventions for encouraging the more adaptive mastery goals over the less adaptive performance goals in classroom settings (e.g., Bardach et al., 2020; O' Keefe et al., 2013). Perhaps, social goal researchers can take a cue from these intervention studies and design optimal learning environments that facilitate the pursuit of adaptive social goals.

6. What Other Outcomes Can Social Goals Account For?

Social goal research can become most useful if it can present a set of unique processes and outcomes most (or more) reliably explained or predicted by social (than academic) goals. Introducing such processes and outcomes will help establish social goals as independent predictors in their own right, rather than subsidiary predictors to academic goals of important student outcomes.

In the section on the antecedents and consequences of social goals, we elaborated on the academic and nonacademic outcomes that researchers have examined in relation to social goals. However, there are many other types of outcomes that could be investigated. Psychological adjustment, nature of peer relations, task-related interaction, and school affect, for example, are good candidates given their close association with interpersonal relationships. Future researchers can map out the consequences of social goals by focusing on a wider range of outcomes that are theoretically related to social goal pursuit.

7. What Other Methodological Approaches Can We Use?

Despite valuable insights generated by existing research, much of the work on social goals relies heavily on cross-sectional and correlational methodologies. While these designs are useful for identifying associations among constructs, they limit our ability to draw conclusions about developmental change, causality, or the mechanisms by which social goals influence academic and socio-emotional outcomes. To move the field forward, future studies should adopt more diverse approaches.

Specifically, longitudinal designs are needed to trace how students' social goals evolve over time and to examine the directionality of relationships between goals and outcomes such as well-being, peer relationships, and achievement motivation (e.g., King & McInerney, 2019a). In addition, experimental or intervention-based studies could test the malleability of social goals and evaluate the effectiveness of strategies aimed at promoting adaptive goals (e.g., emphasizing prosocial or social concern goals in classroom settings). Experience sampling methods or daily diary studies may also offer rich insights into the moment-to-moment activation of social goals in real-life contexts, capturing their dynamic nature. Lastly, mixed-methods and qualitative approaches (e.g., interviews and narrative analyses) can deepen our understanding of how students from diverse backgrounds interpret, prioritize, and act on different social goals. Such approaches would not only strengthen the ecological validity of findings but also ensure that future models of social goals are grounded in the lived experiences of students themselves.

8. How do digital technologies and AI shape students' social goals?

Despite the rapid digital transformation in education, the role of technology—and increasingly, artificial intelligence (AI)—in shaping students' social goals remains significantly underexplored. Most existing research assumes face-to-face interactions, overlooking how online, hybrid, and AI-mediated environments could shape students' social goals.

In online learning, visibility, peer interaction, and feedback mechanisms are altered. There is potential for increasing social demonstration goals (e.g., wanting to be seen as competent in online discussions), while decreasing opportunities for the pursuit of other social goals that require interpersonal connection (e.g., social affiliation goals). Conversely, collaborative AI tools that facilitate group activities, peer feedback, or team-based problem solving can strengthen students' orientation toward mutual support and shared success, thereby encouraging more positive forms of social goals such as social affiliation, concern, and responsibility goals.

To remain theoretically and practically relevant, social goal research must address how both digital platforms and AI tools mediate students' interpersonal motivations. Key design features—such as algorithmic visibility, AI-generated feedback, and digital anonymity—may influence how students set, pursue, and interpret social goals. Cultural norms around technology use may further moderate these effects. Future studies should investigate how these emerging tools reshape students' social goals. Understanding the interplay between AI, technology, and social goals will be critical for designing inclusive and socially supportive learning environments.

PRACTICAL IMPLICATIONS

Social goal research has practical implications for educators seeking to cultivate more inclusive, motivating, and relationally supportive school environments. Recognizing that students are driven not only by academic goals but also by diverse social goals suggests that learning environments must account for students' social motivation as central, not peripheral, to educational success.

Educators can use these insights to create classroom climates that validate and nurture a broader spectrum of social goals. For example, teachers can explicitly acknowledge and reward behaviors aligned with prosocial goals, social responsibility, and social development goals. They can also reframe classroom participation and group work to de-emphasize social comparison and social demonstration approach and social demonstration avoidance goals, while emphasizing collaboration and positive peer relationships.

Schools can also consider designing activities that cultivate both academic and adaptive social goals, reflecting prosocial values (e.g., community service and experiential learning activities), and cultivating school cultures that celebrate social responsibility and interpersonal relationships. Group portfolios, peer feedback, and team-based formative assessments can be used to document growth in social responsibility and interpersonal skills, offering a more holistic picture of student development.

Incorporating social goal research into everyday pedagogical practices also requires a shift in how student success is defined and measured. Traditionally, academic achievement and individual performance have dominated definitions of success, often reinforcing competitive classroom norms. However, by broadening success criteria to include social aspects of schooling, such as cooperation, peer support, and empathy, teachers can promote environments where students feel recognized not only for what they achieve individually, but also for how they contribute to the larger group and the community (Chen et al., 2025; Wang et al., 2024).

CONCLUSION

Social goals are an important part of students' lives and educational psychologists should turn their attention to this powerful yet neglected construct. In this chapter, we surveyed the three research traditions on social goals, proffered a working definition of social goals, and proposed a conceptual framework for identifying antecedents, consequences, and moderators of social goal pursuit. Given that social goal research is still in its early stages, many questions remain unanswered. We suggested future research directions that could move social goal research forward. We end the chapter with some applied implications, and encourage educators to consider the potential ways that social goals could inform their educational practice.

REFERENCES

Ames, C. (1992). Classrooms: Goals, structures, and student motivation. *Journal of Educational Psychology, 84*(3), 261–271. https://doi.org/10.1037/0022-0663.84.3.261

Anderman, L. H. (1999). Classroom goal orientation, school belonging and social goals as predictors of students' positive and negative affect following the transition to middle school. *Journal of Research & Development in Education, 32*(2), 89–103.

Austin, J. T., & Vancouver, J. B. (1996). Goal constructs in psychology: Structure, process, and content. *Psychological Bulletin, 120*(3), 338–375. https://doi.org/10.1037/0033-2909.120.3.338

Balfanz, R., Herzog, L., & MacIver, D. J. (2007). Preventing student disengagement and keeping students on the graduation path in urban middle-grades schools: Early identification and effective interventions. *Educational Psychologist, 42*(4), 223–235. https://doi.org/10.1080/00461520701621079

Bardach, L., Daumiller, M., & Lüftenegger, M. (2023). Multiple social and academic achievement goals: Students' goal profiles and their linkages. *The Journal of Experimental Education, 91*(4), 655–675. https://doi.org/10.1080/00220973.2022.2081959

Bardach, L., Oczlon, S., Pietschnig, J., Lüftenegger, M., Kendeou, P., & Graham, S. (2020). Has achievement goal theory been right? A meta-analysis of the relation between goal structures and personal achievement goals. *Journal of Educational Psychology, 112*(6), 1197–1220. https://doi.org/10.1037/edu0000419

Barger, M. M., Kim, E. M., Kuncel, N. R., & Pomerantz, E. M. (2019). The relation between parents' involvement in children's schooling and children's adjustment: A meta-analysis. *Psychological Bulletin, 145*(9), 855–890. https://doi.org/10.1037/bul0000201

Bellmore, A., Villarreal, V. M., & Ho, A. Y. (2011). Staying cool across the first year of middle school. *Journal of Youth and Adolescence, 40*(7), 776–785. https://doi.org/10.1007/s10964-010-9590-x

Bernardo, A. B. I. (2008). Individual and social dimensions of Filipino students' achievement goals. *International Journal of Psychology, 43*(5), 886–891. https://doi.org/10.1080/00207590701837834

Bernardo, A. B. I., Salanga, G. C., & Aguas, K. M. (2008). Filipino adolescent students' conceptions of learning goals. In G. A. D. Liem, D. M. McInerney, & O.-S. Tan (Eds.), *What the West can learn from the East: Asian perspectives on the psychology of learning and motivation* (pp. 169–190). Charlotte Information Age Publishing.

Bipp, T., Steinmayr, R., & Spinath, B. (2008). Personality and achievement motivation: Relationship among big five domain and facet scales, achievement goals, and intelligence. *Personality and Individual Differences, 44*(7), 1454–1464. https://doi.org/10.1016/j.paid.2008.01.001

Blossfeld, H.-P., Artelt, C., von Maurice, J., Rossbach, H.-G., & Weinert, S. (2024). Competence, motivation and interest development between primary school and tertiary education—A summary of findings from the BiKS-8-18 study. In *Educational processes, decisions, and the development of competencies from early preschool age to adolescence* (Vol. *16*). Springer Vieweg. in Springer Fachmedien Wiesbaden GmbH.

Boonk, L., Gijselaers, H. J. M., Ritzen, H., & Brand-Gruwel, S. (2018). A review of the relationship between parental involvement indicators and academic achievement. *Educational Research Review, 24*, 10–30. https://doi.org/10.1016/j.edurev.2018.02.001

Boudreaux, M. J., & Ozer, D. J. (2013). Goal conflict, goal striving, and psychological well-being. *Motivation and Emotion, 37*(3), 433–443. https://doi.org/10.1007/s11031-012-9333-2

Brassler, N. K., Grund, A., Hilckmann, K., & Fries, S. (2016). Impairments in learning due to motivational conflict: Situation really matters. *Educational Psychology, 36*(7), 1323–1336. https://doi.org/10.1080/01443410.2015.1113235

Brechwald, W. A., & Prinstein, M. J. (2011). Beyond homophily: A decade of advances in understanding peer influence processes. *Journal of Research on Adolescence, 21*(1), 166–179. https://doi.org/10.1111/j.1532-7795.2010.00721.x

Bross, T., Nett, U. E., & Daumiller, M. (2024). Interrelations among achievement goals and achievement emotions: A meta-analytic examination. *Educational Psychology Review, 36*(3), 98. https://doi.org/10.1007/s10648-024-09931-9

Brown, B. B., Lerner, R. M., & Steinberg, L. (2004). Adolescents' relationships with peers. In *Handbook of adolescent psychology* (pp. 363–394). John Wiley & Sons, Inc. https://doi.org/10.1002/9780471726746.ch12

Canevello, A., & Crocker, J. (2020). Prosocial orientations: Distinguishing compassionate goals from other constructs. *Frontiers in Psychology, 11*, 538165. https://doi.org/10.3389/fpsyg.2020.538165

Carolan, B. V., & Wasserman, S. J. (2015). Does parenting style matter? Concerted cultivation, educational expectations, and the transmission of educational advantage. *Sociological Perspectives, 58*(2), 168–186. https://doi.org/10.1177/0731121414562967

Cattell, R. B. (1967). *Personality and motivation: Structure and measurement.* Yonkers-on-Hudson, NY: World Book Company.

Chan, T. W., & Koo, A. (2011). Parenting style and youth outcomes in the UK. *European Sociological Review, 27*(3), 385–399. https://doi.org/10.1093/esr/jcq013

Chang, W. C., & Wong, K. (2008). Socially oriented achievement goals of Chinese university students in Singapore: Structure and relationships with achievement motives, goals and affective outcomes. *International Journal of Psychology, 43*(5), 880–885. https://doi.org/10.1080/00207590701836398

Chen, Y., Li, J., Chui, H., & King, R. B. (2025). Peer cooperation and competition are both positively linked with mastery-approach goals: An achievement goal perspective. *British Journal of Educational Psychology, 95*(4), 941–961.

Cheng, R. W., & Lam, S. (2013). The interaction between social goals and self-construal on achievement motivation. *Contemporary Educational Psychology, 38*(2), 136–148. https://doi.org/10.1016/j.cedpsych.2013.01.001

Chiu, M. M., & Chow, B. W. Y. (2015). Classmate characteristics and student achievement in 33 countries: Classmates' past achievement, family socioeconomic status, educational resources, and attitudes toward reading. *Journal of Educational Psychology, 107*(1), 152.

Cohen, R., Katz, I., Aelterman, N., & Vansteenkiste, M. (2023). Understanding shifts in students' academic motivation across a school year: The role of teachers' motivating styles and need-based experiences. *European Journal of Psychology of Education, 38*, 963–988. https://doi.org/10.1007/s10212-022-00635-8

Compas, B. E., Hinden, B. R., & Gerhardt, C. A. (1995). Adolescent development: Pathways and processes of risk and resilience. *Annual Review of Psychology, 46*(1), 265–293. https://doi.org/10.1146/annurev.ps.46.020195.001405

Csikszentmihalyi, M., Larson, R., & Prescott, S. (1977). The ecology of adolescent activity and experience. *Journal of Youth and Adolescence, 6*(3), 281–294. https://doi.org/10.1007/BF02138940

Dawes, M. (2017). Early adolescents' social goals and school adjustment. *Social Psychology of Education, 20*(2), 299–328. https://doi.org/10.1007/s11218-017-9380-3

Ding, X., Zhong, X., Kang, T., Wang, Y., & Li, J. (2024). Individualism vs. collectivism: Influences on attitudes in China toward the search for meaning in life. *Current Psychology, 43*(16), 14738–14750. https://doi.org/10.1007/s12144-023-05482-4

Dowson, M., & McInerney, D. M. (2001). Psychological parameters of students' social and work avoidance goals: A qualitative investigation. *Journal of Educational Psychology, 93*(1), 35–42. https://doi.org/10.1037/0022-0663.93.1.35

Dowson, M., & McInerney, D. M. (2003). What do students say about their motivational goals?: Towards a more complex and dynamic perspective on student motivation. *Contemporary Educational Psychology, 28*(1), 91–113. https://doi.org/10.1016/S0361-476X(02)00010-3

Dowson, M., & McInerney, D. M. (2004). The development and validation of the goal orientation and learning strategies survey (Goals-S). *Educational and Psychological Measurement, 64*(2), 290–310. https://doi.org/10.1177/0013164403251335

Eccles, J. S., Midgley, C., Wigfield, A., Buchanan, C. M., Reuman, D., Flanagan, C., & Mac Iver, D. (1993). Development during adolescence: The impact of stage-environment fit on young adolescents' experiences in schools and in families. *American Psychologist, 48*(2), 90–101. https://doi.org/10.1037/0003-066X.48.2.90

Elliot, A. J. (2005). A conceptual history of the achievement goal construct. In A. J. Elliot & C. S. Dweck (Eds.), *Handbook of competence and motivation* (pp. 52–72). Guilford Press.

Elliot, A. J. (2006). The hierarchical model of approach-avoidance motivation. *Motivation and Emotion, 30*(2), 111–116. https://doi.org/10.1007/s11031-006-9028-7

Elliot, A. J. (2021). Chapter Four: Self-efficacy and human motivation. In *Advances in motivation science* (Vol. *8*). Elsevier Science & Technology.

Elliot, A. J., Church, M. A., & Geen, R. (1997). A hierarchical model of approach and avoidance achievement motivation. *Journal of Personality and Social Psychology, 72*(1), 218–232. https://doi.org/10.1037/0022-3514.72.1.218

Elliot, A. J., & Murayama, K. (2008). On the measurement of achievement goals: critique, illustration, and application. *Journal of Educational Psychology, 100*(3), 613.

Elliot, A. J., & Sommet, N. (2023). Integration in the achievement motivation literature and the hierarchical model of achievement motivation. *Educational Psychology Review, 35*(3), 77.

Friedel, J. M., Cortina, K. S., Turner, J. C., & Midgley, C. (2007). Achievement goals, efficacy beliefs and coping strategies in mathematics: The roles of perceived parent and teacher goal emphases. *Contemporary Educational Psychology, 32*(3), 434–458. https://doi.org/10.1016/j.cedpsych.2006.10.009

Garon-Carrier, G., Boivin, M., Guay, F., Kovas, Y., Dionne, G., Lemelin, J.-P., Séguin, J. R., Vitaro, F., & Tremblay, R. E. (2016). Intrinsic motivation and achievement in mathematics in elementary school: A longitudinal investigation of their association. *Child Development, 87*(1), 165–175. https://doi.org/10.1111/cdev.12458

Gęsiarz, F., & Crockett, M. J. (2015). Goal-directed, habitual and pavlovian prosocial behavior. *Frontiers in Behavioral Neuroscience, 9*, 135. https://doi.org/10.3389/fnbeh.2015.00135

Giacomin, M., Jordan, C. H., Shackelford, T. K., & Zeigler-Hill, V. (2020). Interdependent and independent self-construal. In *In encyclopedia of personality and individual differences* (pp. 2319–2325). Springer International Publishing. https://doi.org/10.1007/978-3-319-24612-3_1136

Girme, Y. U., Overall, N. C., Faingataa, S., & Sibley, C. G. (2016). Happily single: The link between relationship status and well-being depends on avoidance and approach social goals. *Social Psychological and Personality Science, 7*(2), 122–130. https://doi.org/10.1177/1948550615599828

Goagoses, N., & Eilts, J. (2024). Exploring social goal orientations, self-perceptions and popularity with students attending regular and special education schools. *Journal of Community & Applied Social Psychology, 34*(5), e2888. https://doi.org/10.1002/casp.2888

Goagoses, N., Itenge, H., Winschiers-Theophilus, H., & Koglin, U. (2021). The influence of social achievement goals on academic engagement: A cross-sectional survey in a Namibian primary school. *South African Journal of Psychology, 51*(3), 356–368. https://doi.org/10.1177/0081246320957291

Goddard, C. (2018). "Joking, kidding, teasing": Slippery categories for cross-cultural comparison but key words for understanding Anglo conversational humor. *Intercultural Pragmatics, 15*(4), 487–514. https://doi.org/10.1515/ip-2018-0017

Goswami, H. (2011). Social relationships and children's subjective well-being. *Social Indicators Research, 107*(3), 575–588. https://doi.org/10.1007/s11205-011-9864-z

Granziera, H., Liem, G. A. D., Chong, W. H., Martin, A. J., Collie, R. J., Bishop, M., & Tynan, L. (2022). The role of teachers' instrumental and emotional support in students' academic buoyancy, engagement, and academic skills: A study of high school and elementary school students in different national contexts. *Learning and Instruction, 80*, 101619. https://doi.org/10.1016/j.learninstruc.2022.101619

Guo, M., Hu, X., & Leung, F. K. S. (2022). Culture, goal orientations, and mathematics achievement among Chinese students. *International Journal of Science and Mathematics Education, 20*(6), 1225–1245. https://doi.org/10.1007/s10763-021-10202-0

Gutman, L. M. (2006). How student and parent goal orientations and classroom goal structures influence the math achievement of African Americans during the high school transition. *Contemporary Educational Psychology, 31*(1), 44–63. https://doi.org/10.1016/j.cedpsych.2005.01.004

Hergovich, A., Sirsch, U., & Felinger, M. (2002). Self-appraisals, actual appraisals and reflected appraisals of preadolescent children. *Social Behavior and Personality, 30*(6), 603–611. https://doi.org/10.2224/sbp.2002.30.6.603

Hofer, M. (2007). Goal conflicts and self-regulation: A new look at pupils' off-task behaviour in the classroom. *Educational Research Review, 2*(1), 28–38. https://doi.org/10.1016/j.edurev.2007.02.002

Hofer, M., Kuhnle, C., Kilian, B., Marta, E., & Fries, S. (2011). Motivational interference in school-leisure conflict and learning outcomes: The differential effects of two value conceptions. *Learning and Instruction, 21*(3), 301–316. https://doi.org/10.1016/j.learninstruc.2010.02.009

Hofstede, G. (2001). *Culture's consequences: Comparing values, behaviors, institutions, and organizations across nations.* Sage.

Hofverberg, A., Eklöf, H., & Knekta, E. (2024). Stability and change in associations between social responsibility goals, achievement, and psychosomatic problems. *Scandinavian Journal of Educational Research*, 1–17. https://doi.org/10.1080/00313831.2024.2419070

Huppert, E., Cowell, J. M., Cheng, Y., Contreras-Ibáñez, C., Gomez-Sicard, N., Gonzalez-Gadea, M. L., Huepe, D., Ibanez, A., Lee, K., Mahasneh, R., Malcolm-Smith, S., Salas, N., Selcuk, B., Tungodden, B., Wong, A., Zhou, X., & Decety, J. (2019). The development of children's preferences for equality and equity across 13 individualistic and collectivist cultures. *Developmental Science, 22*(2), e12729. https://doi.org/10.1111/desc.12729

Jeanne Horst, S., Finney, S. J., & Barron, K. E. (2007). Moving beyond academic achievement goal measures: A study of social achievement goals. *Contemporary Educational Psychology, 32*(4), 667–698. https://doi.org/10.1016/j.cedpsych.2006.10.011

Johnson, D. W., & Johnson, R. T. (2009). An educational psychology success story: Social interdependence theory and cooperative learning. *Educational Researcher, 38*(5), 365–379. https://doi.org/10.3102/0013189X09339057

Juvonen, J., & Wentzel, K. R. (1996). *Social motivation: Understanding children's school adjustment.* Cambridge University Press.

Kamari, S., Fouladchang, M., Khormaei, F., & Jowkar, B. (2021). Social achievement goals and academic engagement: The mediating role of academic and social positive emotions. *Iranian Journal of Psychiatry and Behavioral Sciences, 15*(3). https://doi.org/10.5812/ijpbs.110241

Kiefer, S. M., & Ryan, A. M. (2008). Striving for social dominance over peers: The implications for academic adjustment during early adolescence. *Journal of Educational Psychology, 100*(2), 417–428. https://doi.org/10.1037/0022-0663.100.2.417

Kiefer, S. M., Ryan, A. M., & Harris, K. R. (2008). Striving for social dominance over peers: The implications for academic adjustment during early adolescence. *Journal of Educational Psychology, 100*(2), 417–428. https://doi.org/10.1037/0022-0663.100.2.417

Kim, Y., Yu, S. L., Wolters, C. A., & Anderman, E. M. (2021). Academic, social, and well-being goals in the classroom: The dynamic interplay between multiple goals and self-regulatory processes. *Contemporary Educational Psychology, 67*, 102018. https://doi.org/10.1016/j.cedpsych.2021.102018

Kindermann, T. A. (2007). Effects of naturally existing peer groups on changes in academic engagement in a cohort of sixth graders. *Child Development, 78*(4), 1186–1203. https://doi.org/10.1111/j.1467-8624.2007.01060.x

King, R. B. (2015). Sense of relatedness boosts engagement, achievement, and well-being: A latent growth model study. *Contemporary Educational Psychology, 42*, 26–38. https://doi.org/10.1016/j.cedpsych.2015.04.002

King, R. B. (2016). Social goals and well-being. *The Journal of Experimental Education, 85*(1), 107–125. https://doi.org/10.1080/00220973.2015.1111853

King, R. B. (2020). Mindsets are contagious: The social contagion of implicit theories of intelligence among classmates. *British Journal of Educational Psychology, 90*(2), 349–363. https://doi.org/10.1111/bjep.12285

King, R. B., & Ganotice, F. A. (2014). What's happening to our boys? A personal investment analysis of gender differences in student motivation. *The Asia-Pacific Education Researcher, 23*(1), 151–157. https://doi.org/10.1007/s40299-013-0127-4

King, R. B., Ganotice, F. A., & Watkins, D. A. (2012). Cross-cultural validation of the inventory of school motivation (ISM) in the Asian setting: Hong Kong and the Philippines. *Child Indicators Research, 5*(1), 135–153. https://doi.org/10.1007/s12187-011-9117-3

King, R. B., Ganotice, F. A., & Watkins, D. A. (2014). A cross-cultural analysis of achievement and social goals among Chinese and Filipino students. *Social Psychology of Education, 17*(3), 439–455. https://doi.org/10.1007/s11218-014-9251-0

King, R. B., Luo, Y., & Xie, M. (2024). Good begets good: The role of helping others on engagement and achievement among university students. *Research in Higher Education, 65*(5), 989–1006. https://doi.org/10.1007/s11162-023-09768-1

King, R. B., & McInerney, D. M. (2019a). Family-support goals drive engagement and achievement in a collectivist context: Integrating etic and emic approaches in goal research. *Contemporary Educational Psychology, 58,* 338–353. https://doi.org/10.1016/j.cedpsych.2019.04.003

King, R. B., & McInerney, D. M. (2019b). Social goals. In M. H. Jones (Ed.), *Social goals in the classroom: Findings on student motivation and peer relations.* Routledge.

King, R. B., McInerney, D. M., & Nasser, R. (2017). Different goals for different folks: A cross-cultural study of achievement goals across nine cultures. *Social Psychology of Education, 20,* 619–642.

King, R. B., McInerney, D. M., & Watkins, D. A. (2010). Can social goals enrich our understanding of students' motivational goals? *Journal of Psychology in Chinese Societies, 11*(2), 1–16.

King, R. B., McInerney, D. M., & Watkins, D. A. (2012). Studying for the sake of others: The role of social goals on academic engagement. *Educational Psychology, 32*(6), 749–776. https://doi.org/10.1080/01443410.2012.730479

King, R. B., McInerney, D. M., & Watkins, D. A. (2013). Examining the role of social goals in school: A study in two collectivist cultures. *European Journal of Psychology of Education, 28*(4), 1505–1523. https://doi.org/10.1007/s10212-013-0179-0

King, R. B., & Mendoza, N. B. (2020). Achievement goal contagion: Mastery and performance goals spread among classmates. *Social Psychology of Education, 23*(3), 795–814. https://doi.org/10.1007/s11218-020-09559-x

King, R. B., & Mendoza, N. B. (2021). The social contagion of students' social goals and its influence on engagement in school. *Learning and Individual Differences, 88,* 102004. https://doi.org/10.1016/j.lindif.2021.102004

Kordik, A., Eska, K., & Schultheiss, O. C. (2012). Implicit need for affiliation is associated with increased corrugator activity in a non-positive, but not in a positive social interaction. *Journal of Research in Personality, 46*(5), 604–608. https://doi.org/10.1016/j.jrp.2012.05.006

Krys, K., Vignoles, V. L., de Almeida, I., & Uchida, Y. (2022). Outside the "cultural binary": Understanding why Latin American collectivist societies foster independent selves. *Perspectives on Psychological Science, 17*(4), 1166–1187. https://doi.org/10.1177/17456916211029632

Kuroda, Y., & Sakurai, S. (2011). Social goal orientations, interpersonal stress, and depressive symptoms among early adolescents in Japan: A test of the diathesis-stress model using the trichotomous framework of social goal orientations. *The Journal of Early Adolescence, 31*(2), 300–322. https://doi.org/10.1177/0272431610363158

Kyriacou, A. P. (2016). Individualism–collectivism, governance and economic development. *European Journal of Political Economy, 42,* 91–104. https://doi.org/10.1016/j.ejpoleco.2015.11.005

LaFontana, K. M., & Cillessen, A. H. N. (2010). Developmental changes in the priority of perceived status in childhood and adolescence. *Social Development, 19*(1), 130–147. https://doi.org/10.1111/j.1467-9507.2008.00522.x

Lam, B. (2019). Well-being, psychological adjustments and effective social support giving. In *Social support, well-being, and teacher development* (pp. 85–133). Springer Singapore Pte. Limited. https://doi.org/10.1007/978-981-13-3577-8_3

Lam, C. B., McHale, S. M., & Crouter, A. C. (2014). Time with peers from middle childhood to late adolescence: Developmental course and adjustment correlates. *Child Development, 85*(4), 1677–1693. https://doi.org/10.1111/cdev.12235

Li, K., Wang, F., & Pi, Z. (2024). Culture and self-construal in the age of globalization: An empirical inquiry based on multiple approaches. *Frontiers in Psychology, 15*, 1353898. https://doi.org/10.3389/fpsyg.2024.1353898

Liem, G. A. D. (2016). Academic and social achievement goals: Their additive, interactive, and specialized effects on school functioning. *British Journal of Educational Psychology, 86*(1), 37–56. https://doi.org/10.1111/bjep.12085

Liem, G. A. D., Chan, M., Senko, C., Lerdpornkulrat, T., & Poondej, C. (2025). Do reasons behind striving to do better than others differ in degree, kind, or both? A person-centred analysis of performance-approach goal complexes. *Motivation and Emotion*, 1–16.

Liem, G. A. D., & Elliot, A. J. (2018). *Sociocultural influences on achievement goal adoption and regulation* (pp. 41–68). Information Age Publishing.

Liem, G. A. D., & Senko, C. (2022). Goal complexes: A new approach to studying the coordination, consequences, and social contexts of pursuing multiple goals. *Educational Psychology Review, 34*(4), 2167–2195. https://doi.org/10.1007/s10648-022-09701-5

Linnenbrink-Garcia, L., Middleton, M. J., Ciani, K. D., Easter, M. A., O'Keefe, P. A., & Zusho, A. (2012). The strength of the relation between performance-approach and performance-avoidance goal orientations: Theoretical, methodological, and instructional implications. *Educational Psychologist, 47*(4), 281–301. https://doi.org/10.1080/00461520.2012.722515

Loes, C. N. (2022). The effect of collaborative learning on academic motivation. *Teaching and Learning Inquiry, 10*, 1–17. https://doi.org/10.20343/teachlearninqu.10.4

Lovette-Wilson, C., Orange, A., & Corrales, A. (2022). Factors influencing student transition from elementary to middle school. *Educational Studies, 48*(3), 424–441. https://doi.org/10.1080/03055698.2020.1767039

Madjar, N., North, E. A., & Karakus, M. (2019). The mediating role of perceived peer motivational climate between classroom mastery goal structure and social goal orientations. *Learning and Individual Differences, 73*, 112–123. https://doi.org/10.1016/j.lindif.2019.05.009

Martin, A. J., Collie, R. J., Stephan, M., Flesken, A., Halcrow, F., & McCourt, B. (2024). The role of teaching support in assisting students' transition to high school. *Learning and Individual Differences, 109*, 102382. https://doi.org/10.1016/j.lindif.2023.102382

Martin, A. J., & Dowson, M. (2009). Interpersonal relationships, motivation, engagement, and achievement: Yields for theory, current issues, and educational practice. *Review of Educational Research, 79*(1), 327–365. https://doi.org/10.3102/0034654308325583

Massey, E. K., Gebhardt, W. A., & Garnefski, N. (2008). Adolescent goal content and pursuit: A review of the literature from the past 16 years. *Developmental Review, 28*(4), 421–460. https://doi.org/10.1016/j.dr.2008.03.002

McClelland, D. C. (1987). *Human motivation.* Cambridge University Press.

McCrae, R. R., & John, O. P. (1992). An introduction to the five-factor model and its applications. *Journal of Personality, 60*(2), 175–215. https://doi.org/10.1111/j.1467-6494.1992.tb00970.x

Méndez-Giménez, A., Cecchini-Estrada, J. A., & Fernández-Río, J. (2018). A multi-theoretical approach of the students' motivational profiles in physical education: Achievement and social goals. *Psicothema, 30*(4), 401–407. https://doi.org/10.7334/psicothema2018.88

Mertens, E. C. A., Deković, M., Van Londen, M., & Reitz, E. (2021). The role of classmates' modeling and reinforcement in adolescents' perceived classroom peer context. *Journal of Youth and Adolescence, 50*(2), 260–270. https://doi.org/10.1007/s10964-020-01325-8

Meurlin, R. T., & Senko, C. (2025). Whom are you trying to impress? Pursuing performance goals for parents, teachers, or classmates. *Journal of Educational Psychology, 117*(4), 663–678.

Miller, R. B., Greene, B. A., Montalvo, G. P., Ravindran, B., & Nichols, J. D. (1996). Engagement in academic work: The role of learning goals, future consequences, pleasing others, and perceived ability. *Contemporary Educational Psychology, 21*(4), 388–422. https://doi.org/10.1006/ceps.1996.0028

Milyavskaya, M., Werner, K. M., & Drapeau, M. (2018). Goal pursuit: Current state of affairs and directions for future research. *Canadian Psychology/Psychologie Canadienne, 59*(2), 163–175. https://doi.org/10.1037/cap0000147

Morton, L. B., Caughy, M., & Koss, K. J. (2024). School racial composition and changes in Black children's academic engagement and motivation during late elementary school. *Journal of Child and Family Studies, 33*(6), 2028–2041. https://doi.org/10.1007/s10826-024-02853-8

Mouratidis, A., & Michou, A. (2011). Self-determined motivation and social achievement goals in children's emotions. *Educational Psychology, 31*(1), 67–86. https://doi.org/10.1080/01443410.2010.518595

Mouratidis, A. A., & Sideridis, G. D. (2009). On social achievement goals: Their relations with peer acceptance, classroom belongingness, and perceptions of loneliness. *The Journal of Experimental Education, 77*(3), 285–308. https://doi.org/10.3200/JEXE.77.3.285-308

Murphy, P. K., & Alexander, P. A. (2000). A motivated exploration of motivation terminology. *Contemporary Educational Psychology, 25*(1), 3–53. https://doi.org/10.1006/ceps.1999.1019

Musser, L., Shalaby, M., Lehman, M., & Olympia, R. P. (2022). The impact of role models, mentors, and heroes on academic and social outcomes in adolescents. *Cureus, 14*(7), e27349. https://doi.org/10.7759/cureus.27349

OECD. (2023). *Education at a glance 2023: OECD indicators.* OECD Publishing. https://doi.org/10.1787/e13bef63-en

Ogg, J., & Anthony, C. J. (2020). Process and context: Longitudinal effects of the interactions between parental involvement, parental warmth, and SES on academic achievement. *Journal of School Psychology, 78*, 96–114. https://doi.org/10.1016/j.jsp.2019.11.004

O'Keefe, P. A., Ben-Eliyahu, A., & Linnenbrink-Garcia, L. (2013). Shaping achievement goal orientations in a mastery-structured environment and concomitant changes in related contingencies of self-worth. *Motivation and Emotion, 37*(1), 50–64. https://doi.org/10.1007/s11031-012-9293-6

Ouano, J. A., & Punugu, J. N. (2012). Social goals of Filipino adolescents: Do they contribute to student life satisfaction? *International Journal of Research Studies in Psychology, 1*(3), 43–51. https://doi.org/10.5861/ijrsp.2012.296

Pajares, F., & Graham, L. (1999). Self-efficacy, motivation constructs, and mathematics performance of entering middle school students. *Contemporary Educational Psychology, 24*(2), 124–139. https://doi.org/10.1006/ceps.1998.0991

Phelan, P., Davidson, A. L., & Cao, H. T. (1991). Students' multiple worlds: Negotiating the boundaries of family, peer, and school cultures. *Anthropology & Education Quarterly, 22*(3), 224–250. https://doi.org/10.1525/aeq.1991.22.3.05x1051k

Phelan, P., Yu, H. C., & Davidson, A. L. (1994). Navigating the psychosocial pressures of adolescence: The voices and experiences of high school youth. *American Educational Research Journal, 31*(2), 415–447. https://doi.org/10.3102/00028312031002415

Pintrich, P. R. (1994). Continuities and discontinuities: Future directions for research in educational psychology. *Educational Psychologist, 29*(3), 137–148. https://doi.org/10.1207/s15326985ep2903_3

Pomerantz, E. M., Qin, L., Wang, Q., & Chen, H. (2011). Changes in early adolescents' sense of responsibility to their parents in the United States and China: Implications for academic functioning. *Child Development, 82*(4), 1136–1151. https://doi.org/10.1111/j.1467-8624.2011.01588.x

Reeve, J. (2009). Why teachers adopt a controlling motivating style toward students and how they can become more autonomy supportive. *Educational Psychologist, 44*(3), 159–175. https://doi.org/10.1080/00461520903028990

Ryan, A. M. (2001). The peer group as a context for the development of young adolescent motivation and achievement. *Child Development, 72*(4), 1135–1150. https://doi.org/10.1111/1467-8624.00338

Ryan, A. M., & Shim, S. S. (2006). Social achievement goals: The nature and consequences of different orientations toward social competence. *Personality and Social Psychology Bulletin, 32*(9), 1246–1263. https://doi.org/10.1177/0146167206289345

Ryan, A. M., Shim, S. S., & Harris, K. R. (2008). An exploration of young adolescents' social achievement goals and social adjustment in middle school. *Journal of Educational Psychology, 100*(3), 672–687. https://doi.org/10.1037/0022-0663.100.3.672

Rybnicek, R., Bergner, S., & Gutschelhofer, A. (2019). How individual needs influence motivation effects: A neuroscientific study on McClelland's need theory. *Review of Managerial Science, 13*(2), 443–482. https://doi.org/10.1007/s11846-017-0252-1

Schunk, D. H., & Zimmerman, B. J. (1996). Modeling and self-efficacy influences on children's development of self-regulation. In *In social motivation* (pp. 154–180). Cambridge University Press. https://doi.org/10.1017/CBO9780511571190.009

Schwartz, S. H. (1992). Universals in the content and structure of values: Theoretical advances and empirical tests in 20 countries. *Advances in Experimental Social Psychology, 25*, 1–65. https://doi.org/10.1016/S0065-2601(08)60281-6

Schwartz, S. H. (2004). Mapping and interpreting cultural differences around the world. In H. Vinken, J. Soeters, & P. Ester (Eds.), *Comparing cultures: Dimensions of culture in a comparative perspective* (pp. 43–73). Brill.

Schweder, S., & Raufelder, D. (2022). Students' interest and self-efficacy and the impact of changing learning environments. *Contemporary Educational Psychology, 70*, 102082. https://doi.org/10.1016/j.cedpsych.2022.102082

Seligman, M. E. P., Ernst, R. M., Gillham, J., Reivich, K., & Linkins, M. (2009). Positive education: Positive psychology and classroom interventions. *Oxford Review of Education, 35*(3), 293–311. https://doi.org/10.1080/03054980902934563

Senko, C., Liem, G. A. D., Lerdpornkulrat, T., & Poondej, C. (2023). Why do students strive to outperform classmates? Unpacking their reasons for pursuing performance goals. *Contemporary Educational Psychology, 73*, 102178. https://doi.org/10.1016/j.cedpsych.2023.102178

Shah, J., & Devine, P. (2003). Automatic for the people: How representations of significant others implicitly affect goal pursuit. *Journal of Personality and Social Psychology, 84*(4), 661–681. https://doi.org/10.1037/0022-3514.84.4.661

Shah, J. Y., & Kruglanski, A. W. (2003). When opportunity knocks: Bottom-up priming of goals by means and its effects on self-regulation. *Journal of Personality and Social Psychology, 84*(6), 1109–1122. https://doi.org/10.1037/0022-3514.84.6.1109

Sheeran, P. (2002). Intention-behavior relations: A conceptual and empirical review. *European Review of Social Psychology, 12*(1), 1–36. https://doi.org/10.1080/14792772143000003

Shek, D. T. L., & Lin, L. (2016). What predicts adolescent delinquent behavior in Hong Kong? A longitudinal study of personal and family factors. *Social Indicators Research, 129*(3), 1291–1318. https://doi.org/10.1007/s11205-015-1170-8

Shim, S. S., Cho, Y., Helsper, C. A., Kiefer, S. M., & Wang, C. (2024). How do social achievement goals affect early adolescents' academic engagement? The role of feeling stressed and lonely. *The Journal of Early Adolescence*. https://doi.org/10.1177/02724316241273409

Shim, S. S., Cho, Y., & Wang, C. (2013). Classroom goal structures, social achievement goals, and adjustment in middle school. *Learning and Instruction, 23*, 69–77. https://doi.org/10.1016/j.learninstruc.2012.05.008

Shim, S. S., & Finch, W. H. (2014). Academic and social achievement goals and early adolescents' adjustment: A latent class approach. *Learning and Individual Differences, 30*, 98–105. https://doi.org/10.1016/j.lindif.2013.10.015

Shim, S. S., Wang, C., & Cassady, J. C. (2013). Emotional well-being: The role of social achievement goals and self-esteem. *Personality and Individual Differences, 55*(7), 840–845. https://doi.org/10.1016/j.paid.2013.07.004

Shin, H., & Ryan, A. M. (2012). How do young adolescents cope with social problems? An examination of social goals, coping with friends, and social adjustment. *The Journal of Early Adolescence, 32*(6), 851–875. https://doi.org/10.1177/0272431611429944

Smith, P. B., & Bond, M. H. (2019). Cultures and persons: Characterizing national and other types of cultural difference can also aid our understanding and prediction of individual variability. *Frontiers in Psychology, 10,* 2689. https://doi.org/10.3389/fpsyg.2019.02689

Spera, C. (2005). A review of the relationship among parenting practices, parenting styles, and adolescent school achievement. *Educational Psychology Review, 17*(2), 125–146. https://doi.org/10.1007/s10648-005-3950-1

Spera, C., & Wentzel, K. R. (2003). Congruence between students' and teachers' goals: Implications for social and academic motivation. *International Journal of Educational Research, 39*(4), 395–413. https://doi.org/10.1016/j.ijer.2004.06.006

Steidtmann, L., Kleickmann, T., & Steffensky, M. (2023). Declining interest in science in lower secondary school classes: Quasi-experimental and longitudinal evidence on the role of teaching and teaching quality. *Journal of Research in Science Teaching, 60*(1), 164–195.

Steinberg, L., Lamborn, S. D., Dornbusch, S. M., & Darling, N. (1992). Impact of parenting practices on adolescent achievement: Authoritative parenting, school involvement, and encouragement to succeed. *Child Development, 63*(5), 1266–1281. https://doi.org/10.1111/j.1467-8624.1992.tb01694.x

Tan, S. H., Liem, G. A. D., Ramos III, R. L., Elliot, A. J., Nie, Y., & Pang, J. S. (2022). Goal complexes: Integrating achievement goals as standards and self-attributed motives as reasons underlying goal pursuit. *Social Psychology of Education, 25*(4), 845–880.

Tian, L., Liu, B., Huang, S., & Huebner, E. S. (2013). Perceived social support and school well-being among Chinese early and middle adolescents: The mediational role of self-esteem. *Social Indicators Research, 113*(3), 991–1008. https://doi.org/10.1007/s11205-012-0123-8

Trinidad, J. E., Raz, M. D., & Magsalin, I. M. (2023). "More than professional skills:" Student perspectives on higher education's purpose. *Teaching in Higher Education, 28*(6), 1380–1394. https://doi.org/10.1080/13562517.2021.1891043

Urdan, T., & Maehr, M. L. (1995). Beyond a two-goal theory of motivation and achievement: A case for social goals. *Review of Educational Research, 65*(3), 213–243.

Usher, E. L., & Pajares, F. (2008). Sources of self-efficacy in school: Critical review of the literature and future directions. *Review of Educational Research, 78*(4), 751–796. https://doi.org/10.3102/0034654308321456

Van de gaer, E., De Fraine, B., Pustjens, H., Van Damme, J., De Munter, A., & Onghena, P. (2009). School effects on the development of motivation toward learning tasks and the development of academic self-concept in secondary education: A multivariate latent growth curve approach. *School Effectiveness and School Improvement, 20*(2), 235–253. https://doi.org/10.1080/09243450902883920

Vishkin, A., Kitayama, S., Berg, M. K., Diener, E., Gross-Manos, D., Ben-Arieh, A., Tamir, M., & Leach, C. W. (2023). Adherence to emotion norms is greater in individualist cultures than in collectivist cultures. *Journal of Personality and Social Psychology, 124*(6), 1256–1276. https://doi.org/10.1037/pspi0000409

Wang, F., King, R. B., & Zeng, L. M. (2024). Cooperative school climates are positively linked with socio-emotional skills: A Cross-National Study. *British Journal of Educational Psychology, 94*(2), 622–641.

Wang, J., King, R. B., & Rao, N. (2019). The role of social-academic goals in Chinese students' self-regulated learning. *European Journal of Psychology of Education, 34*(3), 579–600. https://doi.org/10.1007/s10212-018-0404-y

Wang, Q., & Pomerantz, E. M. (2009). The motivational landscape of early adolescence in the United States and China: A longitudinal investigation. *Child Development, 80*(4), 1272–1287. https://doi.org/10.1111/j.1467-8624.2009.01331.x

Wentzel, K. R. (1989). Adolescent classroom goals, standards for performance, and academic achievement: An interactionist perspective. *Journal of Educational Psychology, 81*(2), 131–142. https://doi.org/10.1037/0022-0663.81.2.131

Wentzel, K. R. (1991). Relations between social competence and academic achievement in early adolescence. *Child Development, 62*(5), 1066–1078. https://doi.org/10.2307/1131152

Wentzel, K. R. (1993). Motivation and achievement in early adolescence: The role of multiple classroom goals. *The Journal of Early Adolescence, 13*(1), 4–20. https://doi.org/10.1177/0272431693013001001

Wentzel, K. R. (1994). Relations of social goal pursuit to social acceptance, classroom behavior, and perceived social support. *Journal of Educational Psychology, 86*(2), 173–182. https://doi.org/10.1037/0022-0663.86.2.173

Wentzel, K. R. (1996). Social and academic motivation in middle school: Concurrent and long-term relations to academic effort. *The Journal of Early Adolescence, 16*(4), 390–406. https://doi.org/10.1177/0272431696016004002

Wentzel, K. R. (1998). Social relationships and motivation in middle school: The role of parents, teachers, and peers. *Journal of Educational Psychology, 90*(2), 202–209. https://doi.org/10.1037/0022-0663.90.2.202

Wentzel, K. R. (2000). What is it that I'm trying to achieve? Classroom goals from a content perspective. *Contemporary Educational Psychology, 25*(1), 105–115. https://doi.org/10.1006/ceps.1999.1021

Wentzel, K. R. (2021). Motivational decision-making in achievement settings: A competence-in-context approach. *Advances in Motivation Science, 8*, 245–284. https://doi.org/10.1016/bs.adms.2020.06.002

Wentzel, K. R., Barry, C. M., Caldwell, K. A., & Harris, K. R. (2004). Friendships in middle school: Influences on motivation and school adjustment. *Journal of Educational Psychology, 96*(2), 195–203. https://doi.org/10.1037/0022-0663.96.2.195

Wentzel, K. R., Filisetti, L., & Looney, L. (2007). Adolescent prosocial behavior: The role of self-processes and contextual cues. *Child Development, 78*(3), 895–910. https://doi.org/10.1111/j.1467-8624.2007.01039.x

Wentzel, K. R., Muenks, K., McNeish, D., Russell, S., & Graham, S. (2018). Emotional support, social goals, and classroom behavior: A multilevel, multisite study. *Journal of Educational Psychology, 110*(5), 611–627. https://doi.org/10.1037/edu0000239

Wild, S., Rahn, S., & Meyer, T. (2024). Factors mitigating the decline of motivation during the first academic year: A latent change score analysis. *Motivation and Emotion, 48*(1), 36–50. https://doi.org/10.1007/s11031-023-10050-1

Wilder, S. (2014). Effects of parental involvement on academic achievement: A meta-synthesis. *Educational Review, 66*(3), 377–397. https://doi.org/10.1080/00131911.2013.780009

Wilder, S. (2023). Effects of parental involvement on academic achievement: A meta-synthesis. In J. E. Martin, M. Bowl, & G. Banks (Eds.), *Mapping the field* (pp. 137–157). Routledge.

Wolters, C. A., Denton, C. A., York, M. J., & Francis, D. J. (2014). Adolescents' motivation for reading: Group differences and relation to standardized achievement. *Reading and Writing, 27*(3), 503–533. https://doi.org/10.1007/s11145-013-9454-3

Yue, C., Long, Y., Ou, K., Dong, X., & Cao, F. (2022). Influence of peers' actual appraisals on moral self-representations of Chinese adolescents. *Frontiers in Psychology, 13*, 995206. https://doi.org/10.3389/fpsyg.2022.995206

Yue, C., Long, Y., Yang, Z., Xiao, Q., & Pan, W. (2021). The influence of actual appraisals of peers on self-appraisals of personality traits for Chinese late adolescents: The mediating effect of reflected appraisals. *Frontiers in Psychology, 12*, 687482. https://doi.org/10.3389/fpsyg.2021.687482

SECTION 3

APPLIED PERSPECTIVES ON SELF RESEARCH

CHAPTER 9

A MULTILEVEL ANALYSIS UNRAVELING CONTRAST EFFECTS IN PERCEIVED BULLYING VICTIMIZATION

Luyang Guo
University of Macau, China

Herbert W. Marsh
Australian Catholic University, Australia

Kit-Tai Hau
The Chinese University of Hong Kong, Hong Kong

ABSTRACT

Would schools or countries with higher safety risks desensitize students and diminish their perception of bullying? This study explored the relationship between bullying, safety risks, and the contrast effect using data from the Programme for International Student Assessment (PISA) 2022 survey. Multilevel regression analyses were conducted to examine students' perceptions of being bullied in general, being bullied relationally, and being bullied physically/verbally and the relationship with safety risks at the student (L1), school (L2), and country (L3) levels. The study examined whether students in schools and countries with higher safety risks would perceive lower levels of bullying victimisation, as predicted by the frame-of-reference theory.

The Self in Context, pages 301–323

doi:10.1108/978-1-80686-869-820261009

Results indicated clear contrast effects at school and country levels, with students experiencing more safety risks perceiving less bullying victimisation. This finding highlights the importance of context in shaping students' perceptions of bullying victimisation and suggests that contextual factors influence how bullying is experienced and reported.

Keywords: Bullying victimization; safety risks; contrast effects; multilevel modeling; PISA

Large-scale questionnaire surveys are often celebrated for their ability to compare students from diverse backgrounds and cultural contexts. However, the objectivity of students' self-reported ratings in such surveys has been a topic of considerable debate (Linzarini & Catarino da Silva, 2024). Among the criticisms, the influence of reference frame effects has emerged as one of the key issues. The reference frame effect suggests that individuals' perceptions are often influenced by their surrounding context, leading to either contrast or assimilation. This phenomenon has been widely studied, notably in research on the Big-Fish-Little-Pond Effect (BFLPE), which hypothesizes that students' self-concepts are higher when surrounded by lower-performing peers (Marsh et al., 2004, 2015; Marsh & Hau, 2004).

Extending the BFLPE framework, the present study explored the impact of contrast effects on students' perceptions of bullying. Specifically, we aimed to investigate whether students' subjective ratings of bullying would be higher when their schools or countries contain more safety risks. This question gains further relevance when considering seemingly paradoxical findings (OECD, 2019a). For instance, economies with high levels of safety risks may report lower levels of school bullying just because they may perceive this violence as normal. To effectively intervene and reduce bullying behaviors, it is crucial to comprehend how safety risks at the school or country level influence students' perceptions of bullying prevalence.

BULLYING IN EDUCATIONAL SETTINGS

Bullying has long been recognised as a pervasive issue in schools worldwide, with significant implications for students' mental health, academic achievement, and overall well-being. Defined as repeated aggressive behavior involving an imbalance of power (Olweus, 1993), bullying can manifest in various forms, including physical, verbal, and relational aggression (Marsh, Guo, et al., 2023). The consequences of bullying are far-reaching, leading to both short- and long-term psychological issues such as anxiety, depression, and social withdrawal (Marsh et al., 2016; Wang et al., 2020).

Given the profound effects of bullying on youth, understanding its causes and consequences has become a central focus in educational research.

In recent decades, increasing attention has been devoted to understanding the broader environmental and contextual factors contributing to bullying. Research has demonstrated that school climate, peer dynamics, and teacher-student relationships play pivotal roles in both the prevalence and perception of bullying (Espelage & Swearer, 2003; Parada et al., 2005). Schools with positive climates, where students feel supported by their peers and teachers, tend to report lower rates of bullying and related behaviors (Cheon et al., 2023; Glew et al., 2005; Reeve, Cheon, & Marsh, 2023). In contrast, schools characterized by hostility, poor peer relationships, and teacher neglect experience higher instances of bullying (Reeve, Jang, et al., 2023; Thapa et al., 2013).

At the international level, large-scale assessments such as the Program for International Student Assessment (PISA) and the Trends in International Mathematics and Science Study (TIMSS) have contributed substantially to our understanding of bullying across different countries. These studies provide comparative insights into the prevalence of bullying and its relation to educational outcomes, offering data on both cognitive and non-cognitive factors (OECD, 2019a). While cognitive outcomes such as math and reading scores are critical, the inclusion of psychosocial indicators like bullying allows for a more comprehensive understanding of student well-being in schools (Lerner et al., 2021).

Moreover, International assessments have highlighted the role of cultural and societal norms in shaping bullying behaviors and perceptions. In some cultures, bullying may be perceived as a "normal" part of growing up, while in others, it may be viewed as a severe violation of social norms (Smith et al., 2016). These cultural differences are essential for developing effective, context-specific anti-bullying interventions. Understanding how cultural contexts influence perceptions of bullying is critical for both researchers and practitioners aiming to reduce bullying globally.

CONTRAST EFFECTS IN BULLYING

While much of the literature on bullying focuses on individual factors such as personality traits, peer influence, and family background, recent studies have shifted toward understanding the environmental and contextual effects of bullying. A key theoretical framework guiding this shift is the frame-of-reference theory, which posits that students' perceptions of their experiences are shaped by the broader environment in which they occur (Marsh et al., 2001; Marsh & Hau, 2004). According to this theory, individuals evaluate their experiences relative to those of others in their immediate environment. In the context of bullying, this implies that students in environments with higher levels of bullying or safety risks may perceive victimisation as less severe compared to students in safer environments due to a contrast effect influenced by their reference frame.

This effect is particularly relevant in international assessments like PISA, which provide data from diverse educational settings across multiple countries (Marsh et al., 2015). Self-reported questionnaire data have long been scrutinized for biases that compromise their objectivity. As Linzarini and Catarino da Silva (2024, p. 10) note, "self-reports suffer from significant levels of biases and limitations, including social desirability bias, immediacy bias, acquiescence bias, memory bias, and reference bias." Among these, the reference frame effect is particularly pertinent to this study, as it highlights how individuals' perceptions are influenced by their immediate environment, potentially leading to distortions in their responses. However, in traditional contextual effects like the BFLPE the focus is on self-perceptions rather than objective indicators (Marsh et al., 2015). Thus, for example, academic self-concept is not intended to be a proxy for actual achievement. But instead, it is an indicator of self-perceptions. In this respect, academic self-concept is a biased perspective of objective achievement, but also objective achievement is a biased indicator of self-perceptions. This distinction is critical in the evaluation of self-reported bullying.

Bullying perception provides a compelling lens through which to examine reference frame effects. For instance, PISA 2018 data reveal that the United States, a country with relatively frequent incidents of school violence, reported only 10% of students as being frequently bullied (OECD, 2019b). In contrast, regions with lower school safety risks, such as Hong Kong, Macau, and Singapore, reported higher percentages of frequently bullied students (13%, 11%, and 10%, respectively). These findings suggest the presence of a frame-of-reference effect, wherein students' perceptions of bullying are shaped by the relative safety or risk levels of their environments.

It is important to clarify that these findings do not imply a direct negative relationship between safety risks and bullying prevalence. Rather, they underscore the potential for contrast effects arising from environmental reference frames to influence students' subjective perceptions. In contexts with higher perceived safety risks, students may develop a heightened tolerance for certain behaviors, leading them to perceive bullying as less severe or even normal. Conversely, in safer environments, students may be more sensitive to negative behaviors, perceiving them as more severe. This contrast effect can operate at both the school and country levels, making it essential to explore how these contextual factors shape students' perceptions of bullying.

Several studies have applied frame-of-reference theory to investigate the role of school and country-level factors in influencing students' self-reports of bullying. For example, Chen et al. (2020) found that students in schools with positive climates tended to perceive their victimisation experiences as more severe compared to those in less supportive environments. At the national level, research has shown that students in countries with larger economic disparities reported higher rates of bullying (Elgar et al., 2015). However, the contrast effect of country-level safety risks on students' reported severity of bullying has not been thoroughly examined. The present study, therefore, builds on this body of work by examining whether contrast effects are observable in students' perceptions of bullying victimisation and safety risks across different school and country contexts using PISA 2022 data. By analyzing multilevel data, the study aims to provide a nuanced understanding of how environmental factors at the school (Level 2) and country (Level 3) levels shape students' perceptions of victimisation.

BULLYING, SOCIOECONOMIC STATUS, AND ACADEMIC ACHIEVEMENT

Bullying does not occur in isolation but interacts with various demographic factors, including socioeconomic status (SES) and academic achievement. Numerous studies have shown that students from lower SES backgrounds are more likely to be victims of bullying, likely due to their perceived vulnerability and limited access to social and economic resources (Hosozawa et al., 2021). Schools in disadvantaged areas often lack the social support and resources necessary to create a safe and positive school climate, further contributing to higher rates of bullying (Jansen et al., 2012).

Interestingly, some studies have found that students from higher SES backgrounds also report higher levels of bullying, particularly cyberbullying (Wang et al., 2009). This may be due to higher internet access and social interaction among wealthier students, as well as a lower tolerance for negative behaviors such as bullying. However, the association between SES and bullying remains complex, with effect sizes varying across studies depending on the specific measures of SES and the type of bullying examined (Tippett & Wolke, 2014).

The interaction between academic achievement and bullying is similarly complex. Research suggests that both low- and high-achieving boys are more likely to be bullied than girls and average achievers (Bergold et al., 2020; Lehman, 2015). This pattern may be due to the perceived inferiority of low-performing students and the unmasculine stereotype associated with high engagement and achievement in school. Additionally, bullying victimisation has been shown to negatively affect academic achievement in global adolescents (Ozyildirim & Karadağ, 2024). These patterns highlight the need for anti-bullying interventions that account for the unique social dynamics in different educational contexts.

The PISA dataset is particularly valuable for studying these relations. It includes detailed information on verbal, physical, and relational bullying and background factors such as academic achievement and SES, allowing researchers to explore how these factors intersect with different aspects of bullying and potential contrast effects. This study aims to contribute to this growing body of research by examining how SES and academic achievement influence students' perceptions of bullying victimisation and safety risks across country, school, and student levels.

MULTILEVEL ANALYSIS OF BULLYING

In bullying research, one of the significant challenges is accounting for the multilevel nature of data. Bullying is not just a result of individual behaviors; it is heavily influenced by broader environmental factors at both the school and societal levels (Marsh, Guo, et al., 2023). Multilevel modeling has emerged as a critical tool for disentangling these influences by allowing researchers to explore how factors at various levels—such as student characteristics, school climate, and country-level policies—interact to shape students' experiences with bullying (Marsh et al., 2023). This approach is essential in educational research, where students are nested within schools, and schools are further nested within national systems, making it necessary to consider these hierarchical structures.

The power of multilevel analysis lies in its ability to explore cross-level interactions and contextual effects, which are often missed in traditional single-level analyses (Raudenbush & Bryk, 2002). For example, the relationship between a student's SES and bullying victimisation may be influenced by the broader school environment, such as whether the school fosters a positive climate or struggles with safety issues. Similarly, national-level factors, such as economic disparities or societal attitudes toward violence, can shape how students perceive and respond to bullying behaviors. Multilevel modeling allows researchers to examine these complex cross-level relationships and better understand how individual experiences of bullying are embedded within broader social contexts (Marsh et al., 2015). By controlling for shared variance within groups (e.g., students within the same school), multilevel models also enhance the reliability of findings, ensuring that the effects of higher-level factors are accurately captured.

This study makes a valuable contribution by applying multilevel regression analysis to investigate the contrast effect in bullying victimisation across student, school, and country levels. Using data from the PISA 2022 survey, the study explored how school and national safety risks influence students' perceptions of bullying victimisation. By integrating individual-level factors with contextual influences, this research highlighted the importance of addressing both school and societal-level variables in anti-bullying interventions. The findings underscored the need for policies responsive to the specific educational contexts in which bullying occurs, offering insights for developing targeted strategies to reduce bullying behaviors in schools worldwide.

THE PRESENT STUDY

Building on existing research, this study aimed to investigate whether contrast effects are evident in students' perceptions of bullying victimisation and safety risks across different school (Level 2) and country (Level 3) contexts, utilizing data from the PISA 2022 assessment. The primary objective was to provide a nuanced understanding of how school and country-level environmental factors shape students' perceptions of bullying. Specifically, the study hypothesized that students in schools or countries with higher levels of safety risks would report lower perceived bullying victimisation due to the contrast effect. This hypothesis posited that in environments where safety risks were more prevalent, students might perceive bullying as less severe than other, more immediate threats. By examining these dynamics, the study sought to contribute to a deeper understanding of how contextual factors shaped students' experiences and perceptions of bullying.

METHOD

This study employed multilevel regression analyses to investigate the relationship between bullying, safety risks, and the potential existence of contrast effects in students' perceptions across three levels: student (L1), school (L2), and country (L3). We focused on three key dependent variables: general bullying victimisation, relational bullying victimisation, and physical/verbal bullying victimisation. The primary objective was to determine whether students in schools or countries with higher incidences of safety risks would report lower perceptions of bullying victimisation, consistent with the frame-of-reference theory (Marsh et al., 2015).

Participants

The dataset utilized for this study was drawn from the PISA 2022 survey, which provided comprehensive data on students' experiences with bullying and safety risks in schools. PISA 2022 covers 81 countries and economies and measures both cognitive outcomes (e.g., reading, math, and science scores) and non-cognitive factors, such as student self-reports on school climate, safety risk, and bullying victimisation. For the purposes of this study, we focused on gender, SES, academic achievement, and safety risks that are directly related to bullying.

Measures

Dependent Variables

PISA included a general bullying victimization scale consisting of nine items (Cronbach's $\alpha = 0.813$). An exploratory factor analysis indicated two distinct subscales, with one item overlapping both. The first subscale measured *relational bullying* (e.g., social exclusion, rumor-spreading; 3 items; $\alpha = 0.635$). It included the following items: *"Other students left me out of things on purpose," "Other students made fun of me,"* and *"Other students spread nasty rumors about me."*

The second subscale measured *physical/verbal bullying* (e.g., hitting, name-calling; 5 items; $\alpha = 0.757$). This subscale included the items: *"I was threatened by other students," "Other students took away or destroyed things that belonged to me," "I got hit or pushed around by other students," "I was in a physical fight on school property,"* and *"I gave money to someone at school because they threatened me."* One additional item, *"I stayed home from school because I felt unsafe,"* was included in the general bullying scale but did not load exclusively onto either subscale.

All items were self-reported by students using a four-point Likert scale (ranging from "Never or almost never" to "Once a week or more") as part of the PISA questionnaire.

Independent Variables

Perceived safety risks were measured at the student level and subsequently aggregated to the school and country levels. This construct was assessed using a five-item dichotomous scale (yes or no responses), with internal consistency reliability Cronbach's α 0.669. The items included: "Our school was vandalised," "I witnessed a fight on school property in which someone got hurt," "I saw gangs in school," "I heard a student threaten to hurt another student," and "I saw a student carrying a gun or knife at school." These items captured students' perceptions of safety risks within their school environment, providing a basis for examining the influence of safety risks on bullying victimisation at multiple levels.

Control Variables

We included several covariates to control for other relevant factors that affect bullying and safety perceptions. These included *academic achievement* (measured by students' PISA test scores in reading, math, and science) and *socioeconomic status* (SES; represented by the PISA index of economic, social, and cultural status [ESCS]). *Gender* was also included as a control variable at the student level, given the well-documented gender differences in bullying behaviors and victimisation (Bergold et al., 2020; Cosma et al., 2022).

Data Analyses

Multilevel regression modeling was chosen as the appropriate analytic technique due to the nested nature of the data, where students (L1) are nested within schools (L2), which are further nested within countries (L3). This hierarchical structure allowed us to account for the shared variance at each level while testing the contrast effect.

The models were estimated separately for the three dependent variables—general bullying victimisation, relational bullying victimisation, and physical/verbal bullying victimisation—to evaluate the impact of safety risks at each level (individual, school, and country). Safety risks were included in the analysis with both raw effects and contextual effects being assessed. The raw effect captured the direct association between safety risks and students' perceptions of bullying at the individual level (L1). In contrast, the contextual effect isolated the additional influence of safety risks at higher levels (school and country) by comparing the raw effects across levels. Specifically, contextual effects at L3 (country) were calculated by subtracting the L2 (school) raw beta values from the L3 values. While contextual effects at L2 were derived by subtracting L1 (student) raw betas from L2 values (Marsh et al., 2012). This approach allowed for a clearer distinction between individual-level perceptions and the broader environmental influences of schools and countries.

The contrast effect mechanism, as examined in this study, raises important questions about whether it reflects genuine perception shifts, normalization of bullying, or underreporting in high-risk environments. For instance, students in schools or countries with higher safety risks may perceive bullying as less severe relative to other, more immediate threats, leading to a genuine shift in perception where bullying is viewed as a lesser concern. Alternatively, the contrast effect could indicate a normalization of bullying in high-risk contexts, where frequent exposure to safety risks desensitizes students to bullying behaviors, making them less likely to recognize or report such incidents. Finally, the contrast effect might also reflect underreporting due to fear, stigma, or a lack of trust in reporting mechanisms, particularly in environments where safety risks are prevalent. By isolating contextual effects, this study aimed to disentangle these potential mechanisms and provided a more nuanced understanding of how environmental factors shaped students' perceptions of bullying.

Model Specification

Separate multilevel models were run for each dependent variable, examining both the raw and contextual effects of safety risks. Specifically, we tested whether safety risks at the student, school, and country levels predicted bullying victimisation ratings and whether contextual effects at the school and country levels influenced students' perceptions of bullying victimisation beyond individual-level safety risks. Gender, SES, and academic achievement were included as control variables in each model to account for individual differences in bullying perceptions and experiences.

RESULTS

Descriptive and Demographic Background

As expected, the constructs of general, relational, verbal/physical bullying victimisation and perceived safety risks were significantly correlated yet distinct within each school (ranging from 0.26 to 0.87, Table 9.1). The moderate correlations indicate that while related, the constructs capture distinct aspects of the school environment, justifying the appropriateness of separate analyses in this study. These variables are also context-dependent, reinforcing the necessity of examining their contextual effects.

At the student level, several noteworthy patterns emerged when examining the demographic variables (Table 9.2). Low-achieving students perceiving higher level of safety risks were more likely to report general bullying victimisation. Specifically, girls experienced more relational bullying, and advantaged boys reported more physical/verbal bullying victimisation.

At the school level, students in lower academic achievement, higher SES, and greater safety risk schools reported higher levels of relational, physical/verbal, and general bullying victimisation.

At the country level, neither academic achievement (e.g., national average scores) nor economic status (e.g., national average SES) had a significant impact on reported physical/verbal or general bullying victimisation. In contrast, countries with higher average academic achievement and lower economic status were more likely to report relational bullying.

Contrast Effects

Our central research question focused on the presence of contrast effects: whether students in schools or countries with more safety risks would perceive less bullying victimisation (Table 9.2). Firstly, the Intra-Class Correlation (ICC) of reported bullying was shown at Levels 2 and 3, warranting

TABLE 9.1 Correlation and Descriptives of Examined Variables at the Student Level.

	1	2	3	4	5	6	Mean	*SD*
1 Female gender	-						0.50	0.50
2 SES	−0.01	-					−0.16	1.08
3 Student achievement	0.03	0.49	-				461.13	96.89
4 Safety risks	−0.12	−0.01	−0.16	-			0.04	1.02
5 General bully	−0.04	−0.02	−0.10	0.33	-		−0.24	1.04
6 Relational bully	0.01	−0.02	−0.08	0.26	0.87	-	1.41	0.60
7 Physical/ verbal bully	−0.13	−0.05	−0.20	0.33	0.71	0.56	1.18	0.44

Notes: SD = Standard deviation; SES = Socioeconomic status.

TABLE 9.2 Contrast Effect of Students' Perceived Bullying Victimisation and Safety Risks.

	General Bully				Relational Bully				Physical/Verbal Bully			
	St.β	Raw β	Cont Eff	*SE*	St.β	Raw β	Cont Eff	*SE*	St.β	Raw β	Cont Eff	*SE*
Female	0.007	0.013		0.02	0.050c	0.101c		0.02	−0.092c	−0.184c		0.01
Academic	−0.054c	−0.078c		0.01	−0.044c	−0.066c		0.01	−0.120c	−0.178c		0.01
SES	0.007	0.009		0.01	−0.003	−0.005		0.01	0.021b	0.030b		0.01
Safe Risk	0.307c	0.335c		0.01	0.246c	0.274c		0.01	0.314c	0.346c		0.01
$R^2_{Student}$	0.100				0.065				0.134			
Sch Aca	−0.326c	−0.085c	−0.007	0.01	−0.303c	−0.063c	0.003	0.01	−0.554c	−0.172c	0.006	0.01
Sch SES	0.163c	0.040c	0.031	0.01	0.142a	0.028b	0.033	0.01	0.203c	0.059c	0.029	0.01
Sch Risk	0.626c	0.122c	−0.213	0.01	0.574c	0.089c	−0.185	0.01	0.513c	0.119c	−0.227	0.01
R^2_{School}	0.563				0.479				0.625			
ICC_{School}	0.039				0.027				0.061			
CNT Aca	0.341	0.052	0.137	0.03	0.532a	0.067a	0.130	0.02	−0.301	−0.038	0.134	0.02
CNT SES	−0.381	−0.059	−0.099	0.05	−0.519a	−0.065a	−0.093	0.03	−0.138	−0.018	−0.077	0.05
CNT Risk	0.245	0.038	−0.084	0.04	0.264	0.033	−0.056	0.03	0.032	0.004	−0.115	0.03
$R^2_{Country}$	0.103				0.156				0.184			
$ICC_{Country}$	0.025				0.016				0.020			

Notes: St. = Standardised; ICC = Intraclass correlations; Cont Eff = Contextual effect (Higher-level raw β—lower-level raw β); *SE* = Standard error; SES = Socioeconomic status; Sch = School; CNT = Country; Aca = Academic achievement.

the importance of examining the contextual effect of perceived bullying victimisation.

At the School Level

The results supported the existence of a contrast effect at the school level. Specifically, students in schools with higher levels of safety risks reported less general [contextual effect = *(L2, 0.122)—(L1, 0.335)* = −0.213], relational (−0.185), and physical/verbal bullying (−0.227), confirming the hypothesis that increased exposure to violence would lead to desensitization.

At the Country Level

The contrast effects at the country level were less prominent but consistent with those at the school level. Students in countries with higher levels of safety risks reported lower levels of general [contextual effect = *(L3, 0.038)—(L2, 0.122)* = −0.084], relational (−0.056), and physical/verbal bullying (−0.115), consistent with the hypothesis that the broader national context of safety risks might desensitize how students perceive bullying victimisation. When we used 2**SE* (standard error) as the threshold for significance, the contrast effect of safety risks on perceived physical/verbal bullying victimisation was significant at both the school and country levels.

Summary of Findings

Overall, the study found strong support for the contrast effect at the school and country levels, that perceived higher safety risks reduced students' reporting of bullying victimisation, especially physical/verbal bullying. These findings have important implications for understanding how context shapes students' experiences with bullying victimisation and how interventions might be tailored to address these differences across countries and school environments.

DISCUSSION

Bullying has long been central to scholarly debates because of its serious implications for students' physical, psychological, and mental health. The current study adds to this literature by examining the complex interactions between bullying, safety risks, and contrast effects, offering new insights into how individual-, school-, and country-level factors influence students' perceptions of bullying and safety. Leveraging the comprehensive PISA 2022 dataset, which includes data from 81 educational systems, and employing multilevel modeling, this study disentangles the layered influences that shape students' victimisation experiences. By integrating both micro-level (student) and macro-level (school and country) factors, this research illuminates the diverse ways environmental contexts shape how bullying is perceived and experienced.

Consistent with past research, boys were found to be more frequently involved in physical bullying as both perpetrators and victims (Kennedy, 2020). Lower-achieving students reported higher levels of both physical and relational bullying victimisation, likely reflecting their vulnerability in academic settings (Woods & Walke, 2004). Interestingly, however, contrary to the common view that lower SES students are more likely to be bullied (Tippett & Wolke, 2014), this study found that students from higher SES backgrounds also reported elevated levels of physical/verbal victimisation. This finding may be partly explained by the intolerance these students have toward unsafe school environments and the disruptive behaviors of their peers, leading to heightened reporting. Additionally, the competitive and hierarchical social structures in wealthier schools may exacerbate relational forms of bullying, such as exclusion and rumor-spreading. These patterns underline the importance of understanding bullying as a multidimensional issue shaped by a complex interplay of social hierarchies and academic achievement.

At the school level, lower academic achievement and advantaged SES background are associated with increased bullying behaviors, suggesting that students in underperforming schools may be more prone to engage in or experience bullying. While economic and educational indicators did not reach statistical significance at the country level, likely due to sample size limitations. The raw effects indicate that country-level bullying and safety risks influence students' perceptions, which was particularly evident for physical/verbal bullying. Physical/verbal bullying appears to be more sensitive to environmental factors than relational bullying. The results highlight the importance of considering both school and national contexts in developing interventions, as these broader environments shape students' experiences with bullying in meaningful ways.

Contrast Effect on Bullying Perceptions

A key contribution of this study lies in its exploration of the contrast effect on bullying perceptions across varying school and national contexts. Grounded in frame-of-reference theory, which posits that individuals' perceptions of their experiences are shaped by the surrounding environment (Marsh et al., 2023), this research investigates how students in schools or countries with higher levels of safety risks or violence may perceive bullying behaviors as less severe compared to their peers in safer environments. The contrast effect was examined at both the school (Level 2) and country

(Level 3) levels, offering a comprehensive understanding of how contextual factors influence students' perceptions of bullying victimisation.

The findings confirm the presence of contrast effects across all three forms of bullying—general, relational, and physical/verbal—supporting the hypothesis that broader school and national contexts of risk significantly shape students' perceptions. In environments where safety risks are prevalent, students may become desensitized to bullying, perceiving it as a less severe issue relative to more immediate threats to their safety. This desensitization suggests that students in high-risk contexts may develop a heightened tolerance for bullying behaviors, leading to lower perceived severity. These results provide critical insights into how national-level factors, such as societal norms and safety conditions, influence students' perceptions of school violence. Importantly, they underscore the necessity of tailoring anti-bullying programs to specific cultural and societal contexts, as a one-size-fits-all approach may fail to address the unique dynamics of different environments.

The observed contrast effects align with prior research indicating that unsafe school environments often exacerbate bullying behaviors (Glew et al., 2008). This relationship highlights the interconnectedness of bullying and safety risks, suggesting that a hostile or unsafe school climate can amplify physical and verbal bullying while simultaneously distorting students' perceptions of safety. Consequently, these findings emphasize the importance of school-level interventions aimed at improving safety and fostering a positive school climate. By addressing the root causes of safety risks and creating a supportive environment, schools can mitigate both the prevalence of bullying and its perceived severity, ultimately enhancing students' overall well-being.

The Role of Relational and Physical/Verbal Bullying

This study also adds to the literature by distinguishing between relational and physical/verbal bullying, showing that the former is more sensitive to environmental contexts. Relational bullying, including behaviors such as exclusion and rumor-spreading, was more likely to be downplayed by students in schools and countries with higher safety risks. This suggests that relational bullying, which is often less overt, may be more susceptible to being overlooked or minimized in environments where more visible safety concerns dominate students' attention. Conversely, physical and verbal bullying, which are more overt and objectively harmful, were less influenced by environmental factors, suggesting that these forms of bullying maintain their perceived severity across different contexts.

This distinction has significant implications for how bullying can be addressed in schools. Relational bullying, which includes behaviors such as exclusion, rumor-spreading, and social manipulation, is often harder to detect and can have long-lasting psychological effects on victims (Hymel & Swearer, 2015). Therefore, anti-bullying programs should place greater emphasis on identifying and addressing general and relational bullying, particularly in school environments where safety risks are moderate. Schools should provide students with the guidance and support they need to recognize and report relational bullying, as well as promote a culture of inclusion and respect.

The implications for anti-bullying interventions are significant. Schools need to place a greater emphasis on detecting and addressing physical and verbal bullying, particularly in environments where safety risks are prevalent. Because physical and verbal bullying can have long-lasting psychological effects and is harder to change than relational bullying (Hymel & Swearer, 2015), schools must create support systems that encourage students to recognize and report these behaviors. At the same time, relational bullying should not be neglected. Although these forms of bullying were less sensitive to environmental context, they still have profound negative impacts on students' well-being and academic performance (Woods & Walke, 2004). Anti-bullying programs must continue to focus on conflict resolution training, peer mediation, and promoting positive behaviors to reduce these types of bullying in schools (Kennedy, 2020; Smith, 2016). For effective verbal bullying interventions, follow-ups on incidents, record-keeping, and peer support are crucial (Smith et al., 2008).

Implications for Anti-Bullying Interventions

The findings of this study carry significant implications for the design and implementation of anti-bullying interventions, underscoring the need for nuanced, context-specific strategies that account for the complex interplay of individual, school, and country-level factors. The presence of contrast effects at both the school and country levels highlights the critical role of environmental safety risks in shaping students' perceptions of bullying. This suggests that anti-bullying policies must extend beyond individual schools to consider broader societal and cultural contexts, ensuring interventions are tailored to the unique challenges and dynamics of different environments.

Addressing Contrast Effects in High-Risk Environments

In schools and countries with high levels of safety risks, students may downplay the severity of bullying, perceiving it as less significant compared to other immediate threats. This desensitization poses a challenge for anti-bullying efforts, as students in these contexts may be less likely to recognize or report bullying behaviors. To counteract this, interventions in high-risk environments should prioritize raising awareness about the harmful effects of bullying and equipping students with the tools to identify and report such behaviors. Educational campaigns could emphasize that bullying, while perhaps less visible than other safety risks, has profound and lasting impacts on mental health and well-being. Additionally, improving overall school and national safety—through measures such as enhanced security protocols, conflict resolution training, and community engagement—could create a safer environment that reduces both bullying and students' tolerance for it.

Tailoring Interventions to Different Forms of Bullying

The study's distinction between relational and physical/verbal bullying highlights the need for targeted approaches to address these distinct forms of victimisation. Relational bullying, which is more subjective, may be overlooked in environments where safety risks dominate students' attention. Interventions should therefore focus on fostering a culture of inclusion and respect, teaching students to recognize subtle forms of relational bullying, such as exclusion and rumor-spreading, and encouraging them to report such behaviors. Peer mediation programs and social-emotional learning (SEL) curricula can be particularly effective in addressing relational bullying by promoting empathy, communication skills, and conflict resolution.

In contrast, physical and verbal bullying, which are more overt and less influenced by environmental factors, require clear, consistent enforcement of anti-bullying policies. Schools should establish robust reporting mechanisms, ensure timely follow-ups on incidents, and provide support for victims. Programs that promote positive peer interactions and bystander intervention can also help reduce physical and verbal bullying by empowering students to stand up against such behaviors.

Creating Safe and Supportive School Climates

The study's findings reinforce the importance of fostering safe and supportive school environments as a foundational strategy for reducing bullying. Schools with higher safety risks reported elevated levels of physical and verbal bullying, suggesting that unsafe environments exacerbate these behaviors. To address this, schools should prioritize improving teacher-student relationships, promoting positive peer interactions, and implementing clear, enforceable anti-bullying policies. Restorative practices, which focus on repairing harm and building relationships rather than punitive measures, can also contribute to a more positive school climate (Gaffney et al., 2021). Additionally, schools should provide training for teachers and staff to recognize and respond effectively to bullying incidents, ensuring that all members of the school community are equipped to create a safe and inclusive environment.

Targeting Vulnerable Student Populations

The demographic findings of this study reveal that certain groups—such as boys, students from higher socioeconomic backgrounds, and low-achieving students—are more vulnerable to bullying victimisation. Anti-bullying interventions should therefore be tailored to address the specific needs of these populations. For example, programs targeting boys could focus on reducing physical bullying and promoting positive masculinity, while interventions for low-achieving students might aim to enhance academic self-esteem and resilience (Dietrich & Ferguson, 2020). Students from higher socioeconomic backgrounds, who may experience relational bullying due to competitive social hierarchies, could benefit from programs that emphasize cooperation, empathy, and conflict resolution. By addressing the unique vulnerabilities of these groups, interventions can more effectively reduce bullying and its negative impacts.

Integrating School and National-Level Strategies

The study's multilevel analysis underscores the importance of integrating school and national-level strategies to combat bullying. At the national level, policymakers should consider how broader societal factors, such as economic disparities and cultural norms, influence bullying behaviors and perceptions. National campaigns to raise awareness about bullying, coupled with funding for school-based interventions, can create a cohesive approach to addressing this issue. Additionally, governments should prioritize improving overall safety and security, as these efforts can have a positive spillover effect on school climates and students' perceptions of bullying (Smith et al., 2008).

LIMITATIONS

While this study provides valuable insights into the multilevel dynamics of bullying, it is important to acknowledge several limitations that warrant consideration. First, the cross-country comparisons in this study are constrained by variations in cultural norms and reporting practices, which may influence how students perceive and report bullying. For instance, cultural attitudes toward bullying, tolerance for certain behaviors, and societal expectations around reporting victimisation can vary significantly across countries, potentially affecting the reliability and comparability of self-reported data. These cultural differences complicate efforts to draw universal conclusions and highlight the need for culturally sensitive interpretations of the findings.

Second, the study's reliance on self-reported measures of "perceived safety" and "perceived bullying" introduces potential confounding in the frame-of-reference effects. Unlike traditional contextual studies that use more objective measures (e.g., academic achievement or SES), perceptions of safety and bullying are inherently subjective and influenced by individual and environmental factors. This subjectivity makes it challenging to disentangle the extent to which students' perceptions are shaped by actual safety risks versus their personal interpretations of those risks. Future research should aim to incorporate more objective measures of safety and bullying to better distinguish between perceived and actual contextual influences.

Additionally, while this study focused on relational and physical/verbal bullying, it did not explore other forms of bullying, such as cyberbullying, which may be influenced by different contextual factors. Given the growing prevalence of cyberbullying in the digital age, understanding how environmental and cultural factors shape students' experiences with online bullying is a critical area for future research. Investigating these dynamics could provide a more comprehensive understanding of bullying in contemporary educational settings.

Finally, the cross-sectional design of this study limits the ability to draw causal inferences or track changes in students' perceptions over time. Longitudinal research is needed to explore how students' perceptions of bullying and safety risks evolve throughout their academic careers and how these changes are influenced by shifts in school and national contexts. Such studies would offer deeper insights into the long-term impacts of bullying and inform the development of interventions that address both immediate and enduring needs.

CONCLUSIONS

In conclusion, this study highlights the complex interactions between individual, school, and country-level factors in shaping students' perceptions of bullying victimisation and safety risks. The findings provide strong evidence for the contrast effect at both the school and country levels, suggesting that students in schools and countries with higher safety risks are more likely to downplay bullying behaviors, especially physical/verbal ones. These results have significant implications for educators and policymakers working to combat bullying in schools. Effective anti-bullying programs must be tailored to the specific needs of each context, considering both school and national-level factors. By addressing the broader societal influences on bullying behaviors and creating safe, supportive school environments, we can work toward reducing the prevalence of bullying and improving the well-being of students worldwide.

REFERENCES

Bergold, S., Kasper, D., Wendt, H., & Steinmayr, R. (2020). Being bullied at school: The case of high-achieving boys. *Social Psychology of Education, 23*(2), 315–338. https://doi.org/10.1007/s11218-019-09539-w

Chen, C., Yang, C., Chan, M., & Jimerson, S. R. (2020). Association between school climate and bullying victimisation: Advancing integrated perspectives from parents and cross-country comparisons. *School Psychologist, 35*(5), 311–320. https://doi.org/10.1037/spq0000405

Cheon, S. H., Reeve, J., Marsh, H. W., & Jang, H. (2023). Cluster randomized control trial to reduce peer victimisation: An autonomy-supportive teaching intervention changes the classroom ethos to support defending bystanders. *American Psychologist, 78*(6), 1–15. https://doi.org/10.1037/amp0001048

Cosma, A., Bjereld, Y., Elgar, F. J., Richardson, C., Bilz, L., Craig, W., Augustine, L., Molcho, M., Malinowska-Cieślik, M., & Walsh, S. D. (2022). Gender differences in bullying reflect societal gender inequality: A multilevel study with adolescents in 46 countries. *Journal of Adolescent Health, 71*(5), 601–608. https://doi.org/10.1016/j.jadohealth.2022.05.015

Dietrich, L., & Ferguson, R. F. (2020). Why stigmatized adolescents bully more: The role of self-esteem and academic-status insecurity. *International Journal of Adolescence and Youth, 25*(1), 305–318. https://doi.org/10.1080/02673843.2019.1622582

Elgar, F. J., McKinnon, B., Walsh, S. D., Freeman, J., D. Donnelly, P., de Matos, M. G., Gariepy, G., Aleman-Diaz, A. Y., Pickett, W., Molcho, M., & Currie, C. (2015). Structural determinants of youth bullying and fighting in 79 countries. *Journal of Adolescent Health, 57*(6), 643–650. https://doi.org/10.1016/j.jadohealth.2015.08.007

Espelage, D. L., & Swearer, S. M. (2003). Research on school bullying and victimisation: What have we learned and where do we go from here? *School Psychology Review, 32*(3), 365–383. https://doi.org/10.1080/02796015.2003.12086206

Gaffney, H., Ttofi, M. M., & Farrington, D. P. (2021). What works in anti-bullying programs? Analysis of effective intervention components. *Journal of School Psychology, 85*, 37–56. https://doi.org/10.1016/j.jsp.2020.12.002

Glew, G. M., Fan, M.-Y., Katon, W., & Rivara, F. P. (2008). Bullying and school safety. *The Journal of Pediatrics, 152*(1), 123–128.e1. https://doi.org/10.1016/j.jpeds.2007.05.045

Glew, G. M., Fan, M.-Y., Katon, W., Rivara, F. P., & Kernic, M. A. (2005). Bullying, psychosocial adjustment, and academic performance in elementary school. *Archives of Pediatrics & Adolescent Medicine, 159*(11), 1026. https://doi.org/10.1001/archpedi.159.11.1026

Hosozawa, M., Bann, D., Fink, E., Elsden, E., Baba, S., Iso, H., & Patalay, P. (2021). Bullying victimisation in adolescence: Prevalence and inequalities by gender, socioeconomic status and academic performance across 71 countries. *eClinicalMedicine, 41*, 101142. https://doi.org/10.1016/j.eclinm.2021.101142

Hymel, S., & Swearer, S. M. (2015). Four decades of research on school bullying: An introduction. *American Psychologist, 70*(4), 293–299. https://doi.org/10.1037/a0038928

Jansen, P. W., Verlinden, M., Berkel, A. D., Mieloo, C., van der Ende, J., Veenstra, R., Verhulst, F. C., Jansen, W., & Tiemeier, H. (2012). Prevalence of bullying and victimisation among children in early elementary school: Do family and school neighbourhood socioeconomic status matter? *BMC Public Health, 12*(1), 494. https://doi.org/10.1186/1471-2458-12-494

Kennedy, R. S. (2020). Gender differences in outcomes of bullying prevention programs: A meta-analysis. *Children and Youth Services Review, 119*, 105506. https://doi.org/10.1016/j.childyouth.2020.105506

Lehman, B. (2015). Physical and nonphysical bullying victimisation of academically oriented students: The role of gender and school type. *American Journal of Education, 122*(1), 133–159. https://doi.org/10.1086/683294

Lerner, R. M., Lerner, J. v., Murry, V. M., Smith, E. P., Bowers, E. P., Geldhof, G. J., & Buckingham, M. H. (2021). Positive youth development in 2020: Theory, research, programs, and the promotion of social justice. *Journal of Research on Adolescence, 31*(4), 1114–1134. https://doi.org/10.1111/jora.12609

Linzarini, A., & Catarino da Silva, D. (2024). *Innovative tools for the direct assessment of social and emotional skills* OECD Education Working Papers, No. 316. OECD Publishing. https://doi.org/10.1787/eed9bb04-en

Marsh, H. W., Abduljabbar, A. S., Morin, A. J. S., Parker, P., Abdelfattah, F., Nagengast, B., & Abu-Hilal, M. M. (2015). The big-fish-little-pond effect: Generalizability of social comparison processes over two age cohorts from Western, Asian, and Middle Eastern Islamic countries. *Journal of Educational Psychology, 107*(1), 258–271. https://doi.org/10.1037/a0037485

Marsh, H. W., Craven, R. G., & Parker, P. D. (2016). Temporal ordering effects of adolescent depression, relational aggression, and victimisation over six waves: Fully latent reciprocal effects models. *Developmental Psychology, 52*(12), 1994–2009. https://doi.org/10.1037/dev0000216

Marsh, H. W., Guo, J., Parker, P. D., & Pekrun, R. (2023). Peer victimisation: An integrative review and cross-national test of a tripartite model. *Educational Psychology Review, 35*, 46. https://doi.org/10.1007/s10648-023-09765-x

Marsh, H. W., & Hau, K.-T. (2004). Explaining paradoxical relations between academic self-concepts and achievements: Cross-cultural generalizability of the internal/external frame of reference predictions across 26 countries. *Journal of EducationalPsychology, 96*(1),56–67.https://doi.org/10.1037/0022-0663.96.1.56

Marsh, H. W., Lüdtke, O., Nagengast, B., Trautwein, U., Morin, A. J. S., Abduljabbar, A. S., & Köller, O. (2012). Classroom climate and contextual effects: Conceptual and methodological issues in the evaluation of group-level effects. *Educational Psychologist, 47*(2), 106–124. https://doi.org/10.1080/00461520.2012.670488

Marsh, H. W., Parada, R. H., & Craven, R. G. (2004). In the looking glass: A reciprocal effects model elucidating the complex nature of bullying, psychological determinants, and the central role of self-concept. In P. R. Smith & K. A. Kelly (Eds.), *Bullying in schools: How successful can interventions be?* (pp. 63–98). Elsevier. https://doi.org/10.1016/B978-012617955-2/50009-6

Marsh, H. W., Parada, R. H., & Yeung, A. S. (2001). Aggressive school troublemakers and victims: A longitudinal model examining the pivotal role of self-concept. *Journal of Educational Psychology, 93*(2), 411–419. https://doi.org/10.1037/0022-0663.93.2.411

Marsh, H. W., Reeve, J., Guo, J., Pekrun, R., Parada, R. H., Parker, P. D., Basarkod, G., Craven, R., Jang, H.-R., Dicke, T., Ciarrochi, J., Sahdra, B. K., Devine, E. K., & Cheon, S. H. (2023). Overcoming limitations in peer-victimisation research that impede successful intervention: Challenges and new directions. *Perspectives on Psychological Science, 18*(4), 812–828.

OECD. (2019a). *PISA 2018 assessment and analytical framework*. OECD Publishing. https://doi.org/10.1787/b25efab8-en

OECD. (2019b). *PISA 2018 results (volume I): What students know and can Do*. OECD Publishing.

Olweus, D. (1993). *Bullying at school: What we know and what we can do*. Blackwell Publishing.

Ozyildirim, G., & Karadağ, E. (2024). The effect of peer bullying on academic achievement: A meta-analysis study related to results of TIMSS and PIRLS. *Psychology in the Schools, 61*(5), 2185–2203. https://doi.org/10.1002/pits.23159

Parada, R. H., Marsh, H. W., Craven, R., & Papworth, B. A. (2005). Bullying in schools: What can we glean from self-concept theory? In Australian Association for Research in Education 2005 conference papers Australian Association for Research in Education.

Raudenbush, S. W., & Bryk, A. S. (2002). *Hierarchical linear models: Applications and data analysis methods* (2nd.). Sage Publications.

Reeve, J., Cheon, S. H., & Marsh, H. W. (2023a). Autonomy-supportive teaching enhances prosocial and reduces antisocial behavior via classroom climate and psychological needs: A multilevel randomized control intervention. *Journal of Sport & Exercise Psychology, 45*(1), 26–40. https://doi.org/10.1123/jsep.2022-0071

Reeve, J., Jang, H., Cheon, S. H., & Marsh, H. W. (2023b). Extending self-determination theory's dual-process model to a new tripartite model to explain diminished functioning. *Motivation and Emotion, 47*(5), 691–710. https://doi.org/10.1007/s11031-023-10019-0

Smith, P. K. (2016). Bullying: Definition, types, causes, consequences and intervention. *Social and Personality Psychology Compass, 10*(9), 519–532. https://doi.org/10.1111/spc3.12266

Smith, P. K., Kwak, K., & Toda, Y. (2016). *School bullying in different cultures: Eastern and Western perspectives*. Cambridge University Press.

Smith, P. K., Smith, C., Osborn, R., & Samara, M. (2008). A content analysis of school anti-bullying policies: Progress and limitations. *Educational Psychology in Practice, 24*(1), 1–12. https://doi.org/10.1080/02667360701661165

Thapa, A., Cohen, J., Guffey, S., & Higgins-D'Alessandro, A. (2013). A review of school climate research. *Review of Educational Research, 83*(3), 357–385. https://doi.org/10.3102/0034654313483907

Tippett, N., & Wolke, D. (2014). Socioeconomic status and bullying: A meta-analysis. *American Journal of Public Health, 104*(6), e48–e59. https://doi.org/10.2105/AJPH.2014.301960

Wang, G.-F., Han, A.-Z., Zhang, G.-B., Xu, N., Xie, G.-D., Chen, L.-R., Yuan, M.-Y., & Su, P.-Y. (2020). Sensitive periods for the effect of bullying victimisation on suicidal behaviours among university students in China: The roles of timing and chronicity. *Journal of Affective Disorders, 268*, 12–19. https://doi.org/10.1016/j.jad.2020.02.049

Wang, J., Iannotti, R. J., & Nansel, T. R. (2009). School bullying among adolescents in the United States: Physical, verbal, relational, and cyber. *Journal of Adolescent Health, 45*(4), 368–375. https://doi.org/10.1016/j.jadohealth.2009.03.021

Woods, S., & Wolke, D. (2004). Direct and relational bullying among primary school children and academic achievement. *Journal of School Psychology, 42*(2), 135–155. https://doi.org/10.1016/j.jsp.2003.12.002

CHAPTER 10

FACTORS INFLUENCING TEACHERS' MOTIVATING STYLES IN SINGAPORE: A WHOLE SCHOOL APPROACH

Chee Keng John Wang
National Institute of Education, Singapore

Woon Chia Liu
Nanyang Technological University, Singapore

Leng Chee Kong
Nanyang Technological University, Singapore

Li Lian Chua
Nanyang Technological University, Singapore

Ying Hwa Kee
Nanyang Technological University, Singapore

Betsy Ng
Nanyang Technological University, Singapore

Johnmarshall Reeve
Australian Catholic University, Australia

The Self in Context, pages 325–362

doi:10.1108/978-1-80686-869-820261010

ABSTRACT

In recent years, Singapore's education system has received international recognition due to our students continued and sustained high performance in internationally benchmarked tests of student achievement. Despite the stellar achievements, there are concerns that our students may be too focused on academic grades, and not enjoying their learning. To promote joy of learning and student engagement, we need to focus on teachers who are at the frontline of our education system and the environment that they are in. Teachers matter and they can create classroom climate that facilitates student growth and engagement, or one that thwarts student motivation and enjoyment. Grounded in a self-determination theory framework, this chapter examines the factors influencing teachers' motivating style and the effectiveness of an autonomy-supportive intervention offered to secondary school teachers and their students in Singapore. In the first part of the chapter, the extent to which school-related factors (factors from above), the teacher-related factor (factor from within) and student-related factors (factor from below) influence teachers' motivating style will be examined. In the second part, the chapter will present the effect of an autonomy-supportive intervention program on teachers and students. Data were collected via questionnaires and in-depth interviews from both the teachers and students' perspectives. We provide and overview of a whole school approach in motivating teachers and students.

Keywords: Self-determination theory; teacher motivating styles; school factors; teacher factors; student factors

Singapore's education system has garnered international recognition due to its students' consistent high performance in internationally benchmarked assessments such as the Trends in Mathematics and Science Study (TIMSS), the Progress in International Reading Literacy Study, (PIRLS) and Progress for International Student Assessment (PISA). In the 2022 results for PISA, Singapore's secondary students demonstrated a strong ability to apply thinking and reasoning skills in solving real-world problems (Organisation for Economic Co-operation and Development (OECD), 2023). In addition, 87% of the students (OECD average: 75%) reported that their teachers are interested in their well-being, which is a testament to the commitment of Singapore teachers in nurturing their students with heart and purpose (Ministry of Education, 2023). To a large extent, Singapore's success in education is attributed to its teacher education and development (e.g., Liu, 2022; Loh & Hu, 2019).

One of the most significant developments in Singapore's teacher education and development is the launch of the Singapore Teaching Practice

(STP) in 2017 (MOE, 2024). The STP is a model that makes explicit how effective teaching and learning are achieved in schools (Liu & Lim, 2018). It is anchored on the notion that teaching is a profession. There are three key components of the STP: (1) The Singapore Curriculum Philosophy articulates the beliefs about teaching, learning, and students' roles as learners; (2) Pedagogical Practices are key teaching processes that guide teaching actions; and (3) The Knowledge Bases inform practice and consist of subject matter, goals, and theories related to learners, learning, and teaching. Within the Knowledge Bases, Self-Determination Theory (SDT, Ryan & Deci, 2017) has been included as a theoretical framework to understand student learning and teacher practices. The STP was developed with practitioners in mind and is informed by local and international research providing the evidence base (e.g., Liu et al., 2014, 2016; Ng et al., 2015; Wang et al., 2017). Alongside with the launch of the STP, a master document on Motivation and a factsheet on motivation were shared with all schools in Singapore. These two documents focus on motivation from SDT's perspective, emphasizing that teachers can motivate their students using an autonomy-supportive motivating style. Singapore is probably the first country in the world to include SDT on a system level in its continuum of teacher education. After the launch of STP and the release of the documents on motivation, professional development sessions and workshops have been conducted for teachers regularly over the last few years.

Despite the push for an autonomy-supportive motivating style in teaching, there are concerns that not all teachers adopt this approach or are actively practising the approach. There is a need to identify the factors that influence teachers' motivating styles. The purpose of this chapter is to provide an overview of the theoretical framework of SDT and examine the factors that influence teachers' motivating styles in the classroom from a whole school perspective.

SELF-DETERMINATION THEORY

SDT is a key explanatory framework for understanding volitional behaviors (Deci & Ryan, 1985a, 1991; Ryan, 2023). Considering that our focus is on empowering teachers and developing autonomous learners, SDT offers great promise due to its emphasis on the different types of motivation with varying degree of self-determination, and its focus on basic psychological needs that are essential for growth and psychological health (Deci &Ryan, 2000).

SDT differentiates among four main types of behavioral regulation, each with different degrees of self-determined motivation (Ryan & Deci, 2000; Ryan & Deci, 2020). Intrinsic motivation represents the most desirable level of motivation and is thought to exist when an individual chooses to engage in an activity for its own sake, whether for interest, enjoyment or the opportunity to learn (Vallerand et al., 1992). Identified regulation refers to a more self-determined form of extrinsic motivation, describing behaviors where a person acts according to one's choice or values. Introjected regulation represents behaviors that are internally controlled or self-imposed and are performed out of guilt avoidance or ego enhancement. External regulation represents the least autonomous kind of motivated behaviors, where actions are controlled by external means, such as rewards or external authority.

According to SDT, human beings have three innate psychological needs: the need for autonomy, competence and relatedness, which are crucial for psychological growth and personal well-being. Autonomy refers to being self-initiating and taking ownership of one's behavior (Deci et al., 1991; Ryan & Deci, 2020). Competence involves experiencing optimal self-proficiency (Deci & Ryan, 1985a), while relatedness refers to the feeling of being close to and belonging to a social group (Ryan, 1993). Research has shown that high satisfaction of these needs facilitates autonomous motivation and is associated with positive affective and behavioral outcomes (e.g., Reeve et al., 2002; Ryan & Deci, 2020; Tsai et al., 2008). In contrast, low satisfaction of these needs thwarts autonomous motivation and is linked to negative outcomes (Reis et al., 2000; Ryan & Deci, 2020; Sheldon et al., 2001; Skinner & Edge, 2002).

Using SDT as the underpinning theoretical framework will help us understand how we can better support teachers by satisfying their basic psychological needs, thereby facilitating positive teacher outcomes such as autonomous motivation and an autonomy supportive motivational style. Teachers with an autonomy-supportive motivational style can, in turn, create an environment that promotes student autonomous motivation, well-being and growth.

TEACHER'S MOTIVATING STYLES

Teachers have always played a crucial role in the classroom. They engage directly with their students and structure the classroom environment from which these students come to learn every day. Their motivating styles can affect students' motivation, learning, emotions, and performance (e.g., Deci & Ryan, 1987; Reeve, 2016; Reeve & Cheon, 2021; Wang et al., 2016). A teacher's autonomy-supportive style has been found to be associated with a wide range of important student benefits, while a teacher's controlling or pressuring style is associated with various significant student costs (e.g., Cheon et al., 2014; Reeve & Cheon, 2021; Reeve et al., 1999; Reeve & Jang, 2006).

From SDT's perspective, teachers possess two types of motivating styles: autonomy supportive and controlling (Deci et al., 1981; Reeve, 2009). Autonomy support refers to the involvement and support one person provides to another's state of inner volition to act, which drives behavior (Reeve & Jang, 2006). It involves delivering instruction through an interpersonal tone of support and understanding that appreciates, supports, and vitalizes students' inner motivational resources, such as their intrinsic motivation and sense of personal causation (Assor et al., 2002; Reeve, 2016). Implicitly, during instruction, the teacher communicates to the students, "I am your ally; I am here to support you in learning; I am here to help you improve; I am here to assist you." This tone is conveyed through acts of instruction such as adopting the students' perspective, creating opportunities for student input and initiative, teaching in students' preferred ways, and acknowledging and accepting expressions of negative affect (Reeve, 2009).

Teacher controlling style is characterized by delivering instruction through an interpersonal tone of pressure, indicating that students should (or even must) think, feel, perform, and behave in a teacher-prescribed way (Assor et al., 2005; Reeve, 2009). Implicitly, the teacher communicates to the students, "I am your boss; I am here to watch you; I am here to socialize you; I am here to change you." This tone is conveyed through the use of directives, commands, and pressuring language ("you have to") and extrinsic incentives for desired behaviors and signs of achievement, such as a correct answer or a high test score.

As opposites, autonomy support and controlling represent a single bipolar continuum for conceptualizing the quality of a teacher's motivating style toward students (Deci et al., 1981). These two motivating styles are important because they predict both students' and teachers' classroom functioning and outcomes (see Cheon et al., 2014; Cheon & Reeve, 2015; Reeve & Cheon, 2021; Vansteenkiste et al., 2005). For example, Reeve and Cheon (2021) found that autonomy-supportive motivating style predicted greater teaching skill, teaching efficacy and stronger beliefs about autonomy-supporting teaching among teachers. The benefits to students include need satisfaction, intrinsic motivation, internalization as well as achievement grades (e.g., Black & Deci, 2000; de Charms, 1976; Flink et al., 1990; Vansteenkiste et al., 2004; Wang et al., 2016). Perhaps more importantly, carefully designed, theory-based interventions have been shown to help teachers become more autonomy supportive; therefore, we know that the autonomy-supportive motivating style is malleable or trainable (Cheon et al., 2018).

Table 10.1 provides the definition, enabling conditions and instructional behaviors associated with each style (Reeve, 2016).

It should be noted that effective teacher-focused interventions have been developed and implemented using other theoretical orientations, such as self-efficacy, mastery goal climate (i.e., achievement goals), goal-setting

TABLE 10.1 Definition, Enabling Conditions and Instructional Behaviors Associated With Autonomy Support and Controlling Motivating Styles.

Autonomy Support	Controlling
Definition Interpersonal sentiment and behavior teachers provide during instruction to identify, nurture, and develop students' inner motivational resources.	*Definition* Interpersonal sentiment and behavior teachers provide during instruction to pressure students to think, feel, or behave in a specific way.
Enabling conditions • Adopt the students' perspective. • Welcome students' thoughts, feelings, and actions. • Support students' motivational development and capacity for autonomous self-regulation.	*Enabling conditions* • Adopt the teacher's perspective. • Intrude into students' thoughts, feelings, or actions. • Pressure students to think, feel, or behave in a specific way.
Instructional behaviors • Take Students' perspective. • Vitalize inner motivational resources. • Provide explanatory rationales. • Use non-pressuring informational language. • Acknowledge and accept negative affect. • Display patience for self-paced learning.	*Instructional behaviors* • Adopt only the teacher's perspective. • Use environmental sources of motivation. • Directives without explanations. • Rely on pressuring language. • Counter and try to change expressions of resistance and negative affect. • Impatiently intrude on student's workspace.

theory, value interventions (i.e., Expectancy × Value theory), self-regulation, and motivational resilience. Nonetheless, a meta-analysis of all educational interventions showed that those based on SDT (e.g., an autonomy-supportive intervention) produced the strongest effect sizes (Lazowski & Hulleman, 2016). Moreover, an intervention that increases students' psychological needs also enhances the motivations emphasized by these other theoretical orientations, including self-efficacy and mastery goals (similar to competence), goal setting (i.e., promotion of intrinsic goals), value (similar to autonomy, particularly in terms of internalization of values), self-regulation (i.e., autonomous self-regulation), and resilience (similar to engagement) (Reeve et al., 2004; Cheon et al., 2018; Cheon, Reeve, & Song, 2016)

Research has shown that a number of factors influence teachers toward a more autonomy-supportive or a more controlling motivating style (e.g., Pelletier et al., 2002; Reeve, 2009). These influential factors can be categorized as "factors from above" (e.g., principals, school climate, and social contextual performance pressures; Taylor et al., 2009), "factors from within" (e.g., teachers' need satisfaction, teachers' causality orientation; Reeve et al., 1999;

Taylor et al., 2008), and "factors from below" (e.g., students' in-class displays of motivation, engagement, and prosocial behavior; Jang et al., 2016).

FACTORS FROM ABOVE

The principal's leadership style is one of the "factors from above" in shaping teachers' motivating style. Effective principals focus on (1) local and national standards that serve as benchmark expectations for excellent classroom performance and (2) strategies for how to meet and exceed these standards (DiPaola & Hoy, 2012). Through the supervisory process, principals communicate to teachers what the standards are, and they provide the support teachers need to build their professional capacity to meet those standards. Leadership occurs when a principal inspires and motivates teachers to invest their efforts in a cause—such as exceeding educational standards (Eyal & Roth, 2011). But there are different types of leadership, only some of which promote constructive outcomes, such as a positive school climate, staff morale, effective classroom practices, teachers' job satisfaction, and students' learning and achievement (Freiberg, 1998; Leithwood et al., 2008; Leithwood & Jantzi, 2006).

The most prominent difference in leadership styles is the distinction between transformational and transactional (Bass & Avolio, 1994). Transformational leadership is a style in which a principal (the leader) seeks to inspire teachers (followers) by promoting their strengths, listening to their concerns, focusing on their needs, and mobilizing their sense of purpose (Eyal & Roth, 2011; Judge & Piccolo, 2004; Leithwood & Jantzi, 2006). Specifically, transformational leadership is characterized by five leadership behaviors, including idealized influence attributes, idealized influence behaviors, inspirational motivation, intellectual stimulation, and individualized consideration (Avolio et al., 1999). Recently, Wang and his colleagues (Wang et al., 2023) re-examined the Multifactor Leadership Questionnaire (Avolio & Bass, 2004) and added contingent rewards as a new factor under transformative leadership. Following research in organization and educational settings (Gagné & Deci, 2005; Sheldon et al., 2003; Wang et al., 2023) and considering the six day-to-day behaviors that define transformational leadership style, we predicted transformational leadership will support teachers' autonomy-supportive motivating style.

In contrast, transactional leadership is a style in which the principal (the leader) uses directives and close supervision to gain teachers' (followers') compliance to leader-prescribed behaviors, standards, and outcomes (Judge & Piccolo, 2004). It is based on gaining followers' adherence to organizational rules and policies (Bass & Avolio, 1994), and is characterized by active monitoring and a clear emphasis on securing followers' compliance with the leader and organisational rules (Yukl, 2002). Because of these pressuring (rather than supportive) behaviors, we expected transactional leadership style to predict indicators of teachers' ineffective functioning, such as teachers' controlling motivating style (e.g., Deci et al., 1982; Eyal & Roth, 2011; Flink et al., 1990; Gagné & Deci, 2005; Leithwood et al., 2007; Pelletier et al., 2002; Sheldon et al., 2003). In Wang et al.'s study (2023), management by exception (passive), which exemplifies the traits of passive leaders who only act when expectations are not met, and laissez-faire emerged as a separate category of leadership style termed non-leadership. Although this form of leadership may give teachers a high degree of freedom, it may lead to a lack of direction and support, thus decreasing motivation for adopting an autonomy-supportive motivating style, which is a more challenging style for inexperienced teachers (Judge & Piccolo, 2004; Robert & Vandenberghe, 2021). Thus, non-leadership may predict both autonomy-supportive and controlling styles. In addition to school principals, the immediate supervisors' leadership styles may influence teachers' motivating style. Therefore, this study examines leadership styles at both levels (Lee & Nie, 2016).

A substantial body of work exists to show that school leadership plays a significant role in structuring a positive school climate (e.g., Kelley et al., 2005) and affecting teacher motivation (e.g., Bennell & Akyeampong, 2007), and that positive school climates are associated with improvements in staff performance, morale, and student achievement (e.g., Freiberg, 1998). Nonetheless, much less is known about the factors that facilitate teachers' motivating style. A positive school climate should positively predict an autonomy-supportive style and negatively predict controlling style.

Apart from leadership style, school-related factors such as teaching evaluations, time constraint, and pressure from the school administration to conform to certain teaching strategies had also been found to influence teachers' use of motivational strategies (e.g., Taylor et al., 2009). Perceived job pressure should negatively predict autonomy-support and positively predict controlling style.

FACTORS FROM WITHIN

For "factors from within," there is evidence to suggest that the psychological need satisfaction of teachers may influence the learning climate they create for their students or the strategies they use. For example, Taylor et al. (2008) found that when teachers' needs were fulfilled, they were more likely to understand their students, provide them with help, and offer meaningful rationale and choice. In other words, the more self-determined teachers feel, the more likely they are to create a self-determined learning climate for their students. Additionally, teachers with autonomous motivation were found to be more likely to adopt student-centered or productive teaching styles, whereas teachers with non-autonomous motivation were found to be more teacher-centered or utilized reproductive teaching styles (Hein et al., 2012).

According to SDT, personal disposition can also play a key role in predicting teachers' use of motivational strategies, particularly autonomy support (Taylor et al., 2008). More specifically, Deci and Ryan (1985) posited that individuals have a disposition toward autonomy, termed autonomous causality orientation, which varies among individuals. Causality orientations are motivational orientations that refer to the way people orient themselves to an environment and regulate their behavior as a result, or the extent to which they are self-determined across various settings. A high autonomous causality orientation would translate into a generalized tendency to pursue opportunities for the sake of self-determination. Research evidence supports this postulation (Reeve et al., 2018). Essentially, it is hypothesized that teachers with a high autonomous causality orientation will display more autonomy support, while controlling orientation will positively predict controlling style.

Teachers' intrinsic and extrinsic instructional goals may also play a crucial role in shaping their motivating style (Jang & Reeve, 2021). Intrinsic instructional goals focus on building classroom instruction to promote students' personal growth (pursue interest, dreams, and positive self-development) and relationship growth (pursue students' closer relationships and contribute to a more prosocial goals). Extrinsic instructional goals prioritize extrinsic achievements, such as high scores or assured success (pursue social compliments, approval, status). It has been found that teachers with intrinsic instructional goals are more likely to adopt autonomy-supportive motivating style (Jang & Reeve, 2021).

Teaching efficacy reflects a teacher's belief in his or her ability to achieve desired outcomes in student engagement and learning (Tschannen-Moran & Woolfolk Hoy, 2001). Teacher's self-efficacy has been found to be positively linked to the teacher's willingness to implement innovative instructional strategies, including autonomy-supportive teaching (Lauermann & Berger, 2021). Teacher's self-efficacy plays an important role in influencing a teacher's behavior and wellbeing (Schwarzer & Hallum, 2008).

FACTORS FROM BELOW

Finally, with respect to "factors from below," there is evidence to suggest that teachers' behavior depends on their students' motivation, abilities, behaviors and personal characteristics (e.g., Pelletier & Vallerand, 1996; Skinner & Belmont, 1993; Taylor et al., 2009). For example, Pelletier and Vallerand (1996) found that when teachers perceived their students to have low motivation or low engagement, they were more likely to adopt controlling motivating style (Pelletier & Vallerand, 1996; Reeve, 2016). In this study, we included teachers' perception of students' motivation, prosocial behavior and engagement as three factors from below.

PURPOSES OF STUDY

There are studies that examine relations between teacher motivating styles and student outcomes (e.g., How & Wang, 2016; Reeve et al., 2018; Wang et al., 2016). Likewise, a substantial body of work shows that school leadership plays a significant role in structuring a positive school climate (e.g., Kelley et al., 2005) and affecting teacher motivation (e.g., Bennell & Akyeampong, 2007). Furthermore, positive school climates are associated with improvements in staff performance, morale, and student achievement (e.g., Freiberg, 1998). Nonetheless, much less is known about the combination of factors that facilitate teachers' motivating styles. In an attempt to fill the empirical gap, this study adopts a whole school perspective and examines the relations between factors from above (e.g., principal leaderhship style, reporting office leadership style, school climate, perceived professional pressure), factors from within (e.g., causal orientation, goals, teacher efficacy, needs satisfaction and frustration, and motivation to teach) and factors from below (e.g., perceived students' motivation, engagement, prosocial behavior). The following research questions guide the study:

- What are the significant predictors from factors from above (e.g., principal leadership style, reporting office leadership style, school climate, perceived professional pressure) that contribute to teachers' adoption of an autonomy-supportive versus controlling motivating style?
- What are the significant predictors from factors from within (e.g., causal orientation, goals, teacher efficacy, needs satisfaction and frustration, and motivation to teach) that contribute to teachers' adoption of an autonomy-supportive versus controlling motivating style?
- What are the significant predictors from factors from below (e.g., perceived students' motivation, engagement, prosocial behavior) that contribute to teachers' adoption of an autonomy-supportive versus controlling motivating style?
- What are the contributions of factors from above and factors from below, beyond factors from within, in predicting autonomy-supportive versus controlling motivating style?

METHODS

Participants

A total of 872 teachers from 20 secondary schools in Singapore were recruited. Among them, there were 322 male teachers (36.9%) and 481 female teachers (55.2%) with 69 missing data (7.9%). These teachers taught a variety of subjects, ranging from languages to physical education. The teachers were in service from less than 1 year to 44 years (Mean = 12.88, SD = 8.50 years).

Procedure

Before the study, ethical approval was sought from the university Ethical Review Board's (IRB-2020-02-17, IRB-2020-02-017-01 and IRB-2020-02-017-02). After receiving approval, we obtained permission from the MOE and the principals of the schools to collect data from their teachers. Arrangements for data collection were made with schools that agreed to take part. Before responding to the questionnaires, participants were informed about the nature of the research and that their participation in the study was voluntary and they could withdraw at any time. In addition, the participants were assured that their confidentiality would be maintained. The participants took about 30 minutes to complete the questionnaire.

Measures

Autonomy-Supportive and Controlling Motivating Styles

We assessed teachers' motivating styles with the Situations in Schools questionnaire (SIS; Aelterman et al., 2019). The SIS presents 12 daily classroom situations that deal with different aspects of the daily teaching situation (e.g., "It is time for students to practice what they have learned. You…"). For each situation, four different teaching behaviors are offered (using a 7-point Likert scale of *1= Strongly Disagree to 7 = Strongly Agree*), we only used two teaching behaviors, one of which correspond to an autonomy-supportive style (e.g., "Ask students which type of practice problems they may want to work on the most.") and one of which corresponds to a controlling style (e.g., "I need you to work harder—now!"). Scores from the 12 response options representing each scale are averaged to create the autonomy-supportive motivating style and the controlling motivating style scores.

Leadership Style

Principal and reporting officer's leadership styles (as perceived by teachers) were measured by the revised Multifactor Leadership Questionnaire (MLQ; Wang et al., 2023). The revised MLQ used two 7-point Likert scales (1 = *Strongly Disagree* to 7 = *Strongly Agree*), one for principal and one for reporting officer. Twenty-one items assess the six components of transformation leadership style, which includes idealized attributes (3 items), idealized behaviors (4 items), inspirational motivation (4 items), intellectual stimulation (4 items), individual consideration (3 items), and contingent rewards (3 items) (e.g., "My principal/reporting officer is one who focuses on teachers' strengths"). Three items assess transactional leadership style (e.g., "My principal/reporting officer is one who focuses on teachers' mistakes"). Seven items assessed non-leadership which includes management-by-exception (passive)(3 items) and laissez-faire (4 items; e.g., "my principal/reporting officer avoids getting involved when important issues arise"). The measurement model had nine first-order factors and three second-order factors.

School Climate

We assessed teachers' perception of the school climate with the revised School Level Environment Questionnaire (Johnson et al., 2007), which used a 7-point Likert scale from 1 *(Strongly Disagree)* to 7 *(Strongly Agree)* to assess five dimensions of school climate: collaboration (3 items, e.g., "There is good communication among teachers"); student relations (4 items, e.g., "Most students are helpful and cooperative with teachers"); school resources (2 items, e.g., "The school library has sufficient resources and materials"); decision making (3 items, e.g., "Teachers are frequently asked to participate in decisions"); and instructional innovation (3 items, e.g. "Teachers are innovative"). The five factors were represented by one higher order factor.

Perceived Professional Pressures

Teachers' perceived job pressure were measured using the 10-item measure from Taylor et al.'s study (2008). There were three subscales: time constraints (e.g., "I am sometimes rushing to complete my lessons"), administrative pressures ("I wish I could teach in certain ways, but school policy does not allow it"), and external evaluation (e.g., "I am held responsible for student performance standards"). The scale used a 7-point Likert scale (1 = *Strongly Disagree* to 7 = *Strongly Agree).*

Psychological Need Satisfaction and Frustration During Teaching

We assessed teachers' need satisfaction and need frustration with the 24-item Basic Psychological Need Satisfaction and Frustration Scale

(BPNSFS; Chen et al., 2015). Using a 7-point Likert response scale (1 = *Strongly Disagree*, 7 = *Strongly Agree*), the BPNSFS offers six four-item scales to assess teachers' satisfaction of autonomy (e.g., "I feel a sense of choice and freedom in how I teach."), competence (e.g., "I feel capable when I am teaching."), and relatedness (e.g., "I feel close and connected to my students during my teaching."), as well as teachers' frustration of autonomy (e.g., "I feel forced to do many things I wouldn't choose to do."), competence (e.g., "When I teach, I feel insecure about my abilities."), and relatedness (e.g., "I feel that my relationships with students are superficial."). The three satisfaction scales were averaged into an overall need satisfaction score and the three frustration scales into a need frustration score.

Teaching Efficacy

To assess teaching efficacy, the widely-used short form of the Teachers' Sense of Efficacy Scale (TSES; Tschannen-Moran & Woolfolk Hoy, 2001) was used. The 12-item TSES assesses three aspects of teaching efficacy—namely, teaching efficacy for instructional strategies scale (4 items, e.g., "How much can you do to provide an alternative explanation when students are confused?"), teaching efficacy for student engagement scale (4 items, e.g., "How much can you do to motivate students who show low interest in school work?"), and teaching efficacy for classroom management scale (4 items, e.g., "How much can you do to calm a student who is disruptive or noisy?"). We used a 7-point Likert response scale (1 = *Strongly Disagree*, 7 = *Strongly Agree*), and scores from the three scales were averaged to create an overall score.

Motivation to Teach

To assess the autonomous and controlled motivations to teach, we used the 16-item Perceived Locus of Causality (PLOC; Goudas et al., 1994; Wang et al., 2019) scale. The PLOC scale features four four-item scales to assess intrinsic motivation, identified regulation, introjected regulation, and extrinsic regulation. Two scales are conceptualized as autonomous types of teaching motivation, including intrinsic motivation (e.g., "The reason I choose to teach is because I enjoy it.") and identified regulation (e.g., "The reason I choose to teach is because it is important."), while two scales are conceptualized as controlling types of teaching motivation, including introjected regulation (e.g., "The reason I choose to teach is, because if I didn't, I would feel guilty about myself.") and external regulation (e.g., "The reason I choose to teach is because it allows me to earn money."). A 1-7 response scale was used (1 = *Strongly Disagree*; 7 = *Strongly Agree*) and the scores on the intrinsic motivation and identified regulation scales are averaged into the autonomous motivation to teach score while scores on the introjected regulation and external regulation scales were averaged into the controlled motivation to teach (Vansteenkiste et al., 2009).

Intrinsic and Extrinsic Instructional Goals

To assess intrinsic and extrinsic instructional goals, teachers were asked to complete the 16-item Goal Content Questionnaire (GCQ; Sebire et al., 2008). The GCQ used a 1–7 response scale (1 = *Strongly Disagree*, 7 = *Strongly Agree*) to assess four instructional goals (4 items each, skill development, social affiliation, image, and social recognition), the first two of which were scored as intrinsic goals and the last two of which were scored as extrinsic goals (Sheldon & Kasser, 1998). The GCQ begins with the stem, "Please indicate to what extent these goals are important for you while teaching," to assess the skill development (e.g., "To acquire new teaching skills") social affiliation (e.g., "To form close bonds with my students"), image (e.g., "To be professional so to look expert to others"), and social recognition (e.g., "To be socially respected by others") goals.

Causality Orientations

To assess the autonomous and control causality orientations, teachers were asked to complete the Causality Orientations Scale (COS; Deci &Ryan, 1985b). The COS presents teachers with a series of 12 vignettes (short stories, such as "You are embarking on a new career. The most important consideration is likely to be":) that offer responses (scores on a 1–7 response scale; 1 = *Strongly Disagree* and 7 = *Strongly Agree*) that express either an autonomy (e.g., "how interested you are in that kind of work") and a control (e.g., "whether there are good possibilities for advancement") causality orientation. Impersonal orientation subscale was excluded from the current study.

Perceptions of Students' Motivation, Engagement/Disengagement, and Prosocial/Antisocial Behavior

Teachers were provided with six separate class lists that include the names of all the students in the class. Using a 10-point rating scale (1 = *Strongly Disagree*, 10 = *Strongly Agree*), teachers responded to a single item question (1 question per class list) to rate each student on his or her semester-long autonomous motivation ("is motivated by interest and curiosity"), controlled motivation ("is motivated by directives and grades"), engagement ("high effort, positive emotion, proactive participation, sophisticated learning strategies"), disengagement ("low effort, negative emotion, passive, superficial learning strategies"), prosocial behavior ("encourages, helps classmates"), and antisocial behavior ("verbally abuses, hurts classmates").

Data Analyses

In the first step, the factor structures of the measures described above were tested using confirmatory factor analysis (CFA). Secondly, the internal reliability coefficients and descriptive statistics were calculated. Thirdly, the correlation matrix between motivating styles and factors from the three levels were computed. In the main analysis, we conducted six multiple regressions to examine the predictors of the two motivating styles across the three levels. This was done to assess the predictive power of each factor. In the final step, we performed a hierarchical multiple regression, entering factors from within in the first step, followed by factors from above in the second step, and factors from below in the final step to examine the relative contributions of the different factors in predicting motivating styles. The order was decided by the results of the previous multiple regressions.

RESULTS

Table 10.2 shows the results of the CFAs of each of the measures. The fit indices of most measures were satisfactory, except for causality orientation. The reliability of all the measures were acceptable (see Table 10.3). In terms of teaching styles, the participants reported higher autonomy-supportive style than controlling style. For the factors from above, transformative leadership style of the principals and reporting officers were more prominent than their transactional and non-leadership styles. The school climate was generally positive, but the participants reported moderately perceived high pressure regarding time and evaluation. In the factors from within, participants reported high autonomous orientation, intrinsic instructional goals, autonomous motivation to teach, and need satisfaction. The teachers perceived their students to exhibit high levels of autonomous motivation, controlled motivation, engagement, and prosocial behaviors.

The associations between motivating styles and factors from above are shown in Table 10.4. Autonomy-supportive motivating style was positively related to transformative leadership and a positive school climate. The controlling motivating style was positively associated with transactional and non-leadership styles, perceived job pressure and negatively associated with a positive school climate. In terms of factors from within, autonomy-supportive style was positively correlated with autonomous orientation, intrinsic and extrinsic instructional goals, autonomous motivation to teach, need satisfaction, and teaching efficacy. On the other hand, controlling motivating style was negatively correlated with autonomous orientation, intrinsic instructional goals, autonomous motivation to teach, and teaching efficacy, but positively related to controlled orientation, extrinsic instructional goals, controlled motivation to teach (see Table 10.5).

In term of relations between motivating style and factors from below, autonomy-supportive motivating style was positively related to student engagement, autonomous motivation and prosocial behavior and negatively related to student disengagement. Controlling motivating style was positively related to student disengagement and antisocial behavior but negatively related to student autonomous motivation and antisocial behavior (see Table 10.6).

TABLE 10.2 Results of the CFAs for Measures.

Model	Scaled χ^2	df	NNFI	CFI	IFI	RMSEA (CI)
Situations in Schools	736.17	365	0.907	0.916	0.917	0.035 (0.031, 0.039)
MLQ (Principal)	924.98	418	0.931	0.938	0.938	0.042 (0.039, 0.046)
MLQ (RO)	97,668	417	0.932	0.939	0.939	0.042 (0.038, 0.045)
School Climate	410.60	171	0.939	0.950	0.951	0.041(0.036, 0.046)
Perceived Job Pressure	126.21	32	0.942	0.959	0.959	0.059 (0.048, 0.070)
Causality Orientation	571.81	239	0.872	0.889	0.891	0.041 (0.037, 0.045)
Instructional Goals	406.40	97	0.920	0.935	0.936	0.061 (0.055, 0.067)
Psychological Needs	386.74	67	0.883	0.914	0.914	0.075 (0.058, 0.082)
Motivation to Teach	631.51	237	0.939	0.948	0.948	0.045 (0.040, 0.049)
Teacher Efficacy	210.20	45	0.932	0.954	0.954	0.066 (0.057, 0.075)

Note: NNFI = Non-Norm Fit Index, CFI = Comparative Fit Index, IFI = Incremental Fit Index, RMSEA = Root Mean Square Error of Approximation, CI = 90% Confidence Interval.

TABLE 10.3 Internal Reliability Coefficients and Descriptive Statistics of the Key Variables.

Variables	α	Min	Max	Mean	SD
Autonomy-Supportive Style	0.82	2.35	5.00	3.65	0.47
Controlling Style	0.84	1.00	4.64	2.52	0.56
P Transformative	0.71–0.85	1.19	5.00	3.72	0.66
P Transactional	0.73	1.00	5.00	2.81	0.87
P Non-Leadership	0.78–0.82	1.00	4.71	1.87	0.75
RO Transformative	0.71–0.86	1.19	5.00	3.75	0.70
RO Transactional	0.71	1.00	5.00	2.74	0.87
RO Non-Leadership	0.79	1.00	4.86	1.83	0.75
School Climate	0.88	1.88	5.00	3.62	0.48
Time Pressure	0.77	1.00	5.00	3.16	0.86
Evaluation Pressure	0.81	1.00	5.00	3.33	0.87
Authority Pressure	0.74	1.00	5.00	2.45	0.93
Autonomous Orientation	0.78	2.67	5.00	4.03	0.43
Control Orientation	0.69	1.08	5.00	2.86	0.53
Intrinsic Teaching Goals	0.86	2.50	5.00	4.30	0.50
Extrinsic Teaching Goals	0.82	1.00	5.00	3.03	0.72
T. Autonomous Motivation	0.86	1.17	5.00	3.91	0.66
T. Controlled Motivation	0.80	1.00	5.00	2.37	0.76
Need Satisfaction	0.78–0.88	2.00	5.00	3.82	0.52
Need Frustration	0.81–0.85	1.00	5.00	2.39	0.63
Teacher Efficacy	0.90	2.00	5.00	3.69	0.50
S. Engagement	-	1.00	10.00	6.18	1.74
S. Disengagement	-	1.00	10.00	4.48	2.08
S. Autonomous Motivation	-	1.00	10.00	6.88	1.75
S. Controlled Motivation	-	1.00	10.00	7.40	1.64
S. Prosocial Behavior	-	2.00	10.00	6.80	1.49
S. Antisocial Behavior	-	1.00	10.00	2.99	1.97

Note: P = Principal, RO = Reporting Officer, T = Teacher, S = Student.

TABLE 10.4 Correlation Coefficients of Motivating Styles and Factors From Above.

Variables	1	2	3	4	5	6	7	8	9	10	11
1. Autonomy-Supportive Style	1.00										
2. Controlling Style	−0.11**	1.00									
3. P Transformative	0.26**	−0.07*	1.00								
4. P Transactional	−0.04	0.18**	−0.30**	1.00							
5. P Non-Leadership	−0.16**	0.22**	−0.63**	0.41**	1.00						
6. RO Transformative	0.21**	−0.01	0.60**	−0.16**	−0.42**	1.00					
7. RO Transactional	0.02	0.19**	−0.11**	0.70**	0.30**	−0.22**	1.00				
8. RO Non-Leadership	−0.08*	0.18**	−0.41**	0.28**	0.69**	−0.68**	0.32**	1.00			
9. School Climate	0.30**	−0.19**	0.56**	−0.31**	−0.50**	0.49**	−0.23**	−0.48**	1.00		
10. Time Pressure	−0.02	0.16**	−0.10**	0.15**	0.15**	−0.08*	0.15**	0.16**	−0.19**	1.00	
11. Evaluation Pressure	−0.06	0.25**	−0.20**	0.34**	0.23**	−0.16**	0.33**	0.18**	−0.37**	0.37**	1.00
12. Authority Pressure	−0.02	0.25**	−0.31**	0.27**	0.35**	−0.21**	0.24**	0.25**	−0.29**	0.29**	0.46**

Note: * $p < 0.05$, ** $p < 0.01$. P = Principal, RO = Reporting Officer.

TABLE 10.5 Correlation Coefficients of Motivating Styles and Factors From Within.

Factors from within	1	2	3	4	5	6	7	8	9	10
1. Autonomy-Supportive Style	1.00									
2. Controlling Style	−0.11**	1.00								
3. Autonomous Orientation	0.44**	−0.20	1.00							
4. Control Orientation	0.01	0.51**	0.03	1.00						
5. Intrinsic Teaching Goals	0.49**	−0.22**	0.48**	−0.13**	1.00					
6. Extrinsic Teaching Goals	0.16**	0.31**	0.11**	0.35**	0.13**	1.00				
7. T. Autonomous Motivation	0.48**	−0.13**	0.34**	−0.08*	0.56**	0.25**	1.00			
8. T. Controlled Motivation	0.02	0.37**	−0.14**	0.40**	−0.14**	0.49**	0.10**	1.00		
9. Need Satisfaction	0.32**	−0.18**	0.30**	−0.12**	0.41**	0.08*	0.44**	−0.11**	1.00	
10. Need Frustration	−0.18**	0.28**	−0.20**	0.29**	−0.29**	0.07*	−0.27**	0.25**	−0.60**	1.00
11. T. Efficacy	0.51**	−0.10**	0.30**	0.01	0.43**	0.14**	0.43**	−0.01	0.46**	−0.25**

Note: $^{*}p < 0.05$, $^{**}p < 0.01$. T = Teacher.

TABLE 10.6 Correlation Coefficients of Motivating Styles and Factors From Below.

Factors from Below	1	2	3	4	5	6	7
1. Autonomy-Supportive Style	1.00						
2. Controlling Style	−0.11**	1.00					
3. S. Engagement	0.23**	−0.07*	1.00				
4. S. Disengagement	−0.12**	0.13**	−0.67**	1.00			
5. S. Autonomous Motivation	0.26**	−0.12**	0.64**	−0.45**	1.00		
6. S. Controlled Motivation	0.19**	−0.06	0.56**	−0.35**	0.48**	1.00	
7. S. Prosocial Behavior	0.27**	−0.12**	0.49**	−0.37**	0.38**	0.32**	1.00
8. S. Antisocial Behavior	−0.09*	0.16**	−0.36**	0.46**	−0.26**	−0.28**	−0.34**

Note: *$p < 0.05$, **$p < 0.01$. S = Student.

Motivating Styles and Factors From Above

The results of the two regressions predicting motivating styles with factors from above showed that while the principal's non-leadership was a significant negative predictor of autonomy-supportive style, school climate was a positive significant predictor. Interestingly, reporting officers' transformative leadership and non-leadership and authority pressure, were positive predictors of both autonomy-supportive and controlling motivating styles (see Table 10.7). The models accounted for 14% to 15 % of variance in controlling and autonomy-supportive motivating styles, respectively.

Motivating Styles and Factors From Within

In predicting teachers' autonomy-supportive style by factors from within, the results of the regressions revealed that teachers' autonomous causality orientation, intrinsic instructional goals, autonomous motivation to teach, and teaching efficacy positively predicted autonomy-supportive style (R^2 = 0.41, $F(9, 850) = 66.23$, $p < 0.001$) (Table 10.8).

On the other hand, teachers' controlling style was positively predicted by control orientation, extrinsic instructional goals, controlled motivation to teach, need frustration and negatively predicted by autonomous orientation (see Table 10.8). Factors from within accounted for 36%–41% of variance in motivating styles respectively.

Motivating Styles and Factors From Below

Table 10.9 shows the results of regressions predicting motivating styles by factors from below. It was found that students' autonomous motivation and prosocial behavior positively predicted autonomy-supportive style (R^2 = 0.11, $F(6, 851) = 16.92$, $p < 0.001$). Students' anti-social behavior and engagement positively predicted teachers' controlling style, while students' autonomous motivation negatively predicted teachers' controlling style (R^2 = 0.04, $F\ (6, 851) = 6.06$, $p < 0.001$). Further stepwise regression was conducted to examine the relationship between engagement and controlling style, and it was confirmed that controlling style was positively predicted by antisocial behavior and negatively predicted by autonomous motivation.

Hierarchical Regressions

In the final analysis, the factors from within, factors from above, and factors from below were entered into the hierarchical regression in three blocks.

TABLE 10.7 Results of Multiple Regressions for Predictors of Motivating Styles With Factors From Above.

	Autonomy-Supportive Style				Controlling Style			
Variables	B	SE B	β	t	B	SE B	β	t
P Transformative	0.02	0.04	0.03	0.53	0.01	0.04	0.01	0.20
P Transactional	0.01	0.03	0.01	0.15	−0.02	0.03	−0.03	−0.56
P Non-Leadership	−0.11	0.04	−0.18*	−2.90	0.04	0.05	0.06	0.95
RO Transformative	0.14	0.04	0.21**	3.51	0.19	0.05	0.24**	4.02
RO Transactional	0.04	0.03	0.07	1.38	0.06	0.03	0.09	1.88
RO Non-Leadership	0.18	0.04	0.29**	4.49	0.14	0.05	0.19**	2.94
School Climate	0.30	0.04	0.31**	7.02	−0.08	0.05	−0.07	−1.52
Time Pressure	−0.01	0.02	−0.01	−0.25	0.02	0.02	0.04	1.04
Evaluation Pressure	−0.01	0.02	−0.01	−0.10	0.08	0.02	0.12**	3.05
Authority Pressure	0.07	0.02	0.14**	3.53	0.08	0.02	0.13**	3.35

Note: *$p < 0.05$, **$p < 0.01$. β = Standardized estimate.

TABLE 10.8 Results of Multiple Regressions for Predictors of Motivating Styles With Factors From Within.

	Autonomy-Supportive Style				Controlling Style			
Variables	B	SE B	β	t	B	SE B	β	t
Autonomous Orientation	0.23	0.03	0.21**	6.85	−0.21	0.04	−0.16**	−5.03
Control Orientation	0.01	0.03	0.01	0.26	0.42	0.03	0.40**	12.43
Intrinsic Teaching Goals	0.15	0.03	0.16**	4.40	−0.07	0.04	−0.06	−1.59
Extrinsic Teaching Goals	0.01	0.02	0.01	0.29	0.13	0.03	0.16**	4.82
T. Autonomous Motivation	0.15	0.02	0.20**	5.79	−0.03	0.03	−0.03	−0.91
T. Controlled Motivation	0.02	0.02	0.04	1.08	0.06	0.03	0.08*	2.39
Need Satisfaction	−0.03	0.03	−0.03	−0.83	0.02	0.04	0.01	0.37
Need Frustration	0.01	0.03	0.01	0.31	0.07	0.03	0.08*	2.22
T. Efficacy	0.29	0.03	0.30**	9.55	−0.03	0.04	−0.02	−0.67

Note: $^{*}p < 0.05$, $^{**}p < 0.01$. β = Standardized estimate.

TABLE 10.9 Results of Multiple Regressions for Predictors of Motivating Styles With Factors From Below.

	Autonomy-Supportive Style				Controlling Style			
Variables	B	SE B	β	t	B	SE B	β	t
S. Engagement	0.02	0.02	0.06	1.07	0.04	0.02	0.14^{*}	2.36
S. Disengagement	0.01	0.01	0.06	1.23	0.02	0 01	0.08	1.73
S. Autonomous Motivation	0.04	0.01	0.15^{**}	3.54	−0.04	0.01	-0.11^{*}	−2.55
S. Controlled Motivation	0.01	0.01	0.05	1.16	−0.01	0.01	−0.01	−0.06
S. Prosocial Behavior	0.06	0.01	0.20^{**}	5.32	−0.03	C.02	−0.07	−1.80
S. Antisocial Behavior	0.01	0.01	0.03	0.79	0.03	0.01	0.11^{**}	2.93

Note: $^{*}p < 0.05$, $^{**}p < 0.01$. β = Standardized estimate.

In predicting autonomy-supporting style, the factors from within (Step 1) predicted 41% of the variance in autonomy-supportive style ($R^2 = 0.41$, $F(9, 836) = 61.42$, $p < 0.001$), the factors from above predicted an additional 3% of variance in autonomy-supportive style ($R^2 = 0.44$, $F(10, 826) = 4.76$, $p < 0.001$), and in the third step, the factors from below predicted an additional 2% of variance in autonomy-supportive style ($R^2 = 0.46$, $F(6, 820) = 4.16$, $p < 0.001$).

In predicting teachers' controlling style, the factors from within (Step 1) predicted 36% of the variance in controlling style ($R^2 = 0.36$, $F(9, 836) = 51.45$, $p < 0.001$). In Step 2, the factors from above predicted an additional 2% of variance in controlling style ($R^2 = 0.38$, $F(10, 826) = 3.02$, $p < 0.001$), and in the third step, the factors from below predicted an additional 1% of variance in autonomy supportive style ($R^2 = 0.39$, $F(6, 820) = 2.56$, $p < 0.05$). Fig. 10.1 shows a summary of the results from the above regressions.

DISCUSSION

The purpose of this study was to adopt a whole school perspective and examine a combination of factors that influence teachers' motivating style. Specifically, this study took into account the wider school climate, professional pressure, and leadership practices, as well as student motivation, engagement and prosocial behaviors, rather than just looking at teacher factors in isolation. It examined the relations between factors from above, factors from within, and factors from below in predicting teachers' motivating styles. There are very few studies that have been conducted to examine factors from multiple levels that might influence teachers' motivating styles.

The results in general suggest that principals and reporting officers adopt a leadership style that was more transformative, and the school climate was generally positive. However, teachers reported moderately high perceived professional pressure in terms of time and evaluation. This is understandable, as parents and teachers in Singapore have traditionally place strong emphasis and expectations on high achievement standards for students, especially in STEM areas (Teo & Choy, 2021). Singapore's strong performance in international tests such as PISA and TIMSS over the years may also put pressure on the teachers to maintain their good work. Teachers' work performance is being appraised annually and they may perceive that they are being appraised based on their students' performance even though a range of other measures such as contribution to the character development of the students in their charge, their collaboration with parents and community groups, and their contribution to their colleagues and the school as a whole are included in performance appraisal (Liu, 2022).

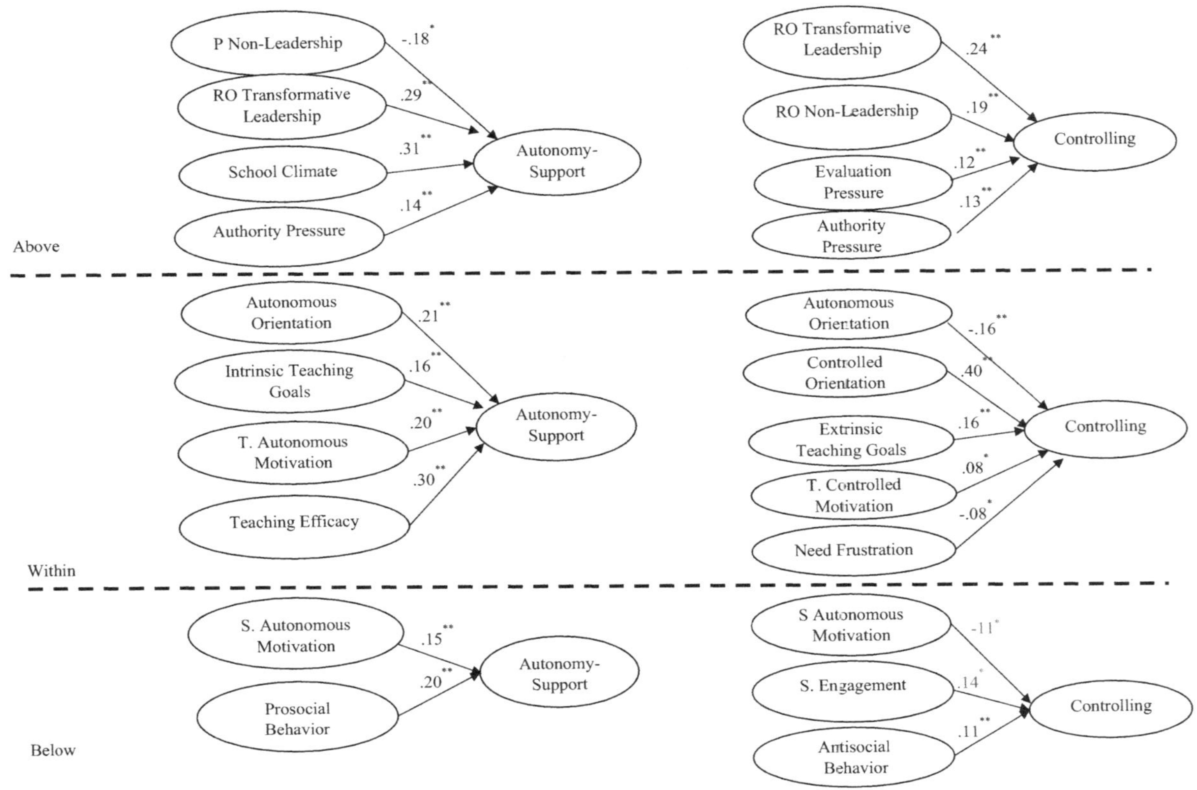

Fig. 10.1. Summary of Results in Predicting Motivating Styles.
Note: $*p < .05$, $**p < .01$, P = Principal, RO = Reporting Officer, T = Teacher, S = Student.

Among the factors from within, Singapore teachers exhibit high levels of autonomous orientation, intrinsic instructional goals, autonomous motivation to teach, and need satisfaction. The high level of intrinsic instructional goals of teachers is noteworthy and suggests that Singapore teachers, apart from wanting their students to do well academically, are focusing on promoting students' personal and relationship growth. This is in line with Singapore's Desired Outcomes of Education, launched in 2010, which highlighted the role of Singapore teachers in helping students develop into confident individuals, self-directed learners, active contributors, and concerned citizens (MOE, 2021).

Considering that teaching is seen as a career of choice by young people in Singapore (Liu, 2022), and altruistic and intrinsic reasons such as "making an impact" and "contributing to the future of the nation" are given by pre-service teachers as main reasons for choosing to teach (Low et al., 2017), it is not surprising that teachers have relatively high autonomous motivation to teach. Teachers are held in high regards in Singapore because they are trained and respected as professionals. The high quality of the teaching workforce in Singapore is attributed to a system that included multiple, coherent and complementary components associated with recruiting, developing, and retaining talented individuals within the teaching profession (see Liu, 2022 for details). Despite the rosy picture, there are challenges that Singapore needs to address such as high professional pressure, workload, and stress level.

It is encouraging that Singapore teachers have relatively high level of need satisfaction. Amongst the needs, autonomy, in particular, is an essential part of teachers developing feelings of competency, empowerment and professionalism (e.g., Paradis et al., 2018; Pearson & Moomaw, 2005). Autonomy is a matter of degree because it is impossible to be completely free of external influences and pressures, and autonomous acts can be externally motivated if the "self" endorses the external suggestions or prescriptions (Ryan & Deci, 2006). For teachers, external influences and pressures may be bureaucratic structures, national curriculum, test-based accountability, competition among schools, centrally prescribed pedagogies, which teachers may decide to endorse or ignore to differing degrees. Singapore teachers do not have full autonomy over curriculum and assessment because there is a national curriculum and national examinations. Nonetheless, they are encouraged to make pedagogical decisions to best help their students learn. The current result suggests that Singapore teachers largely accept the external influences and pressures. However, if too many demands are imposed on teachers, it will affect their perceived level of autonomy (e.g., Pelletier & Sharp, 2009; Prichard & Moore, 2016), and may in turn undermine their sense of professionalism (Perryman et al., 2011).

From the factors from above, it appears that principals' leadership style is not a major influence on teachers' motivating styles, though principals' non-leadership was found to negatively predict autonomy-support style. However, principals play an important role in shaping the school climate (Bennell & Akyeampong, 2007; Kelley et al., 2005), and a positive school climate is a key predictor of an autonomy-supportive motivating style. The transformative and non-leadership styles of direct reporting officers, along with the pressure from authority, were positive predictors of both autonomy-supportive and controlling motivating styles. This suggests that teachers should not feel pressured to adopt autonomy-supportive motivating style. Reporting officers need to use an autonomy-supportive approach to encourage teachers to adopt the style willingly; otherwise, transformative leaders may be seen as pseudo-transformational, that is, the leaders whose intentions are self-serving (Bass & Steidlmeier, 1999) which could negatively impact their followers.

Of the three levels, factors from within accounted for the highest amount of variance in predicting teachers' motivating style. Teachers' autonomy-supporting style was predicted by autonomous causality orientation, intrinsic instructional goals, autonomous motivation to teach, and teaching efficacy. Conversely, a controlling style was predicted by control orientation, extrinsic instructional goals, controlled motivation to teach, and need frustration. All the predictors were consistent with the literature, except for need satisfaction. It is possible that autonomous motivation is the product of need satisfaction, thus having a strong predictive power on autonomy-supportive style (Vallerand & Losier, 1999).

From the factors from below, autonomous motivation and prosocial behavior positively predicted autonomy-supportive style and autonomous motivation negatively predicted and antisocial behavior positively predicted controlling style.

The results of the hierarchical regression offer an interesting perspective in the adoption of motivating style. The factors from within accounted for the highest variance in motivating style. After controlling for the factors from within, factors from above and factors from below only accounted for a small additional variance (from 1% to 3%). This suggests that factors from above and factors from below may influence teachers' motivating styles indirectly through the factors from within. For instance, a positive school climate can enhance teachers' intrinsic instructional goals, motivation to teach, and teaching efficacy, thus encouraging them to adopt an autonomy-supportive motivating style. This demonstrates that factors from above and factors from below still play a meaningful role in shaping teachers' motivating style.

This study offers important implications. Firstly, it suggests that for recruitment, it is important to select teacher candidates who have an autonomous motivation to teach and see teaching as a profession that is meaningful. Singapore seems to have done well in her recruitment process by using a multi-pronged approach involving tools such as entrance proficiency tests, classroom simulations, and importantly, interviews with experienced educators and school leaders. During interviews, aspiring teacher candidates must convince the interview panel that they have the passion and interest in educating children, and the right attitudes and values to be a good teacher (Liu, 2022).

Although "motivation to teach" can be influenced by personal experiences and beliefs, autonomous motivation to teach is likely to be facilitated in an education system where teachers are empowered and believe that they have significant influence on the lives of children. This appears to be the case in Singapore where teachers are seen as being in a profession that has significant influence on the lives of children (Sim, 2012), and are lauded as custodians of societal values (Tan et al., 2012).

From another perspective, it is preferred to select teacher candidates with a more autonomous causality disposition for the teaching profession. Previous studies have established a strong relationship between personality and teachers' motivating styles (Reeve et al., 2018), showing that teachers with high autonomous causality orientation are more likely to adopt autonomy-supportive motivating style.

Secondly, school leaders, including reporting officers, can play key roles in facilitating teachers' adoption of autonomy-supportive motivating style. They can do that by fostering a positive and autonomy-supportive school climate and reducing teachers' perceived job pressure. Although causality orientation is relatively enduring, teachers can develop stronger autonomy orientations if their needs are satisfied, and they are in school environments that are autonomy supportive. It is plausible that Singapore's inclusion of the SDT within the STP framework, along with the emphasis on student and teacher motivation at a system level, has contributed to raising such awareness among school leaders and middle management.

Thirdly, strong teacher preparation is crucial since it is a key dimension in building teaching efficacy and improving teacher quality (e.g., Darling-Hammond, 2000; OECD, 2005). Likewise, professional development has been found to support capacity building, and to bring about curriculum and pedagogic reforms (Bautista et al., 2015). Singapore, like other top performing education systems in the world, has a system that includes coherent and complementary components associated with recruiting, developing, and retaining talented teachers (Darling-Hammond, 2017; Liu, 2022). In addition, Singapore has a policy provision for teacher professional development. Specifically, teachers are entitled to 100 hours of professional development per year. It is not compulsory to complete the 100 hours, but most teachers take advantage of them (Wong, 2013). Teachers are given time off and are fully subsidized by the MOE for professional development (Churchill & Wang, 2014).

Fourthly, research has demonstrated that teachers can learn to be more autonomy-supportive in their teaching by going through training like the

Autonomy-supportive intervention programme (ASIP) created by Reeve and his colleagues (Cheon et al., 2018; Reeve, 2016).

LIMITATIONS

There are a few limitations of this study. Firstly, as a cross-sectional study using questionnaires, the factors from above, within, and below were pre-determined by the researchers, potentially omitting other factors that may influence teachers' motivating styles that are not included in this study. Future studies should consider using qualitative methods to gain deeper insights into the factors not assessed through surveys. Secondly, since measurements were taken at a single time point, causality cannot be inferred. An experimental design would be more suitable for testing causality. Thirdly, the study did not consider variables such as gender, age and teaching experience, which could potentially impact teachers' adoption of an autonomy-supportive style. Future studies should include these factors in their analysis.

CONCLUSION

In conclusion, this research highlights the significant role that factors from within play in shaping teachers' motivating styles, with predictors such as autonomous causality orientation, intrinsic instructional goals, and teaching efficacy emerging as key determinants of an autonomy-supportive approach. The findings suggest that while factors from above and below contribute to teachers' motivating styles, their impact is largely indirect through factors from within. Although factors from above and below accounted for only a small percentage of the variance in teacher motivating styles, their influence remains important, underscoring the complex interplay between various levels of influence in educational settings. This study reinforces the need for a whole school approach to understanding and enhancing teachers' motivating styles, considering both the internal factors of teachers and the broader contextual factors that can support or undermine these motivations. It also highlights the importance of a holistic approach to teacher recruitment, preparation, and professional development to nurture autonomy-supportive educators.

Singapore's education system offers valuable insights in this regard, with its rigorous recruitment process, emphasis on professional growth, and policies that empower teachers. By fostering a positive school climate, ensuring strong teacher preparation, and providing ongoing professional development, education systems can create conditions that enable teachers to develop and sustain an autonomy-supportive motivating style. Future research could explore how these findings translate across different educational contexts.

ACKNOWLEDGMENTS

This study was funded by Singapore Ministry of Education (MOE) under the Education Research Funding Programme (OER 12/19 LWC) and administered by National Institute of Education (NIE), Nanyang Technological University, Singapore. Any opinions, findings, and conclusions or recommendations expressed in this material are those of the authors and do not necessarily reflect the views of the Singapore MOE and NIE.

REFERENCES

Aelterman, N., Vansteenkiste, M., Haerens, L., Soenens, B., Fontaine, J. R. J., & Reeve, J. (2019). Toward an integrative and fine-grained insight in motivating and demotivating teaching styles: The merits of a circumplex approach. *Journal of Educational Psychology, 111*(3), 497–521. https://doi.org/10.1037/edu0000293

Assor, A., Kaplan, H., Kanat-Maymon, Y., & Roth, G. (2005). Directly controlling teacher behaviours as predictors of poor motivation and engagement in girls and boys: The role of anger and anxiety. *Learning and Instruction, 15*(5), 397–413. https://doi.org/10.1016/j.learninstruc.2005.07.008

Assor, A., Kaplan, H., & Roth, G. (2002). Choice is good, but relevance is excellent: Autonomy-enhancing and suppressing teacher behaviours predicting students' engagement in schoolwork. *British Journal of Educational Psychology, 72*(2), 261–278. https://doi.org/10.1348/000709902158883

Avolio, B. J., & Bass, B. M. (2004). *Multifactor leadership questionnaire. Manual and sampler set: Multifactor leadership questionnaire, manual and sample set* (3rd ed.). Mind Garden.

Avolio, B. J., Bass, B. M., & Jung, D. I. (1999). Re-examining the components of transformational and transactional leadership using the multifactor leadership. *Journal of Occupational and Organizational Psychology, 72*(4), 441–462. https://doi.org/10.1348/096317999166789

Bass, B. M., & Avolio, B. J. (1994). *Improving organizational effectiveness through transformational leadership.* Sage.

Bass, B. M., & Steidlmeier, P. (1999). Ethics, character, and authentic transformational leadership behaviour. *The Leadership Quarterly, 10*(2), 181–217. https://doi.org/10.1016/S1048-9843(99)00016-8

Bautista, A., Wong, J., & Gopinathan, S. (2015). Teacher professional development in Singapore: Depicting the landscape. *Psychology, Society, & Education, 7*(3), 311–326.

Bennell, P., & Akyeampong, K. (2007). *Teacher motivation in sub-Saharan Africa and south Asia.* DFID.

Black, A. E., & Deci, E. L. (2000). The effects of instructors' autonomy support and students' autonomous motivation on learning organic chemistry: A self-determination theory perspective. *Science Education, 84*(6), 740–756. https://doi.org/10.1002/1098-237X(200011)84:6<740::AID-SCE4>3.0.CO;2-3

Chen, B., Vansteenkiste, M., Beyers, W., Boone, L., Deci, E. L., & et al. (2015). Basic psychological need satisfaction, need frustration, and need strength across four cultures. *Motivation and Emotion, 39,* 216–236.

Cheon, S. H., & Reeve, J. (2015). A classroom-based intervention to help teachers decrease students' amotivation. *Contemporary Educational Psychology, 40,* 99–111. https://doi.org/10.1016/j.cedpsych.2014.06.004

Cheon, S. H., Reeve, J., Lee, Y., & Lee, J. (2018). Why autonomy-supportive interventions work: Explaining the professional development of teachers' motivating style. *Teaching and Teacher Education, 69,* 43–51.

Cheon, S. H., Reeve, J., & Song, Y. G. (2016). A teacher-focused intervention to decrease PE students' amotivation by increasing need satisfaction and decreasing need frustration. *Journal of Sport & Exercise Psychology, 38,* 217–235.

Cheon, S. H., Reeve, J., & Song, Y. -G. (2019). Recommending goals and supporting needs: An intervention to help physical education teachers communicate their expectations while supporting students' psychological needs. *Psychology of Sport and Exercise, 41,* 107–118. https://doi.org/10.1016/j.psychsport.2018.12.008

Cheon, S. H., Reeve, J., Yu, T. H., & Jang, H. R. (2014). The teacher benefits from giving autonomy support during physical education instruction. *Journal of Sport & Exercise Psychology, 36*(4), 331–346. https://doi.org/10.1123/jsep.2013-0231

Churchill, D., & Wang, T. (2014). Teacher's use of iPads in higher education. *Educational Media International, 51*(3), 214–225. https://doi.org/10.1080/09523987.2014.968444

Darling-Hammond, L. (2000). Teacher quality and student achievement: A review of state policy. *Education Policy Analysis Archives, 8,* 1. https://doi.org/10.14507/epaa.v8n1.2000

Darling-Hammond, L. (2017). Teacher education around the world: What can we learn from international practice? *European Journal of Teacher Education, 40*(3), 291–309. https://doi.org/10.1080/02619768.2017.1315399

deCharms, R. (1976). *Enhancing motivation: Change in the classroom.* Irvington.

Deci, E. L., & Ryan, R. M. (1985a). *Intrinsic motivation and self-determination in human behaviour.* Plenum Press.

Deci, E. L., & Ryan, R. M. (1985b). The general causality orientations scale: Self-determination in personality. *Journal of Research in Personality, 19,* 109–134. https://doi.org/10.1016/0092-6566(85)90023-6

Deci, E. L., & Ryan, R. M. (1987). The support of autonomy and the control of behaviour. *Journal of Personality and Social Psychology, 53*(6), 1024–1037.

Deci, E. L., & Ryan, R. M. (1991). A motivational approach to self: Integration in personality. In R. A. Dienstbier (Ed.), *Nebraska symposium on motivation* (pp. 237–288). University of Nebraska Press.

Deci, E. L., & Ryan, R. M. (2000). The 'what' and 'why' of goal pursuits: Human needs and the self-determination of behaviour. *Psychological Inquiry, 11,* 227–268. https://doi.org/10.1207/S15327965PLI1104_01

Deci, E. L., Schwartz, A. J., Sheinman, L., & Ryan, R. M. (1981). An instrument to assess adults' orientations toward control versus autonomy with children:

Reflections on intrinsic motivation and perceived competence. *Journal of Educational Psychology, 73*, 642–650.

Deci, E. L., Spiegel, N. H., Ryan, R. M., Koestner, R., & Kauffman, M. (1982). Effects of performance standards on teaching styles: Behaviour of controlling teachers. *Journal of Educational Psychology, 74*(6), 852–859.

Deci, E. L., Vallerand, R. J., Pelletier, L. G., & Ryan, R. M. (1991). Motivation and education: The self-determination perspective. *Educational Psychologist, 26*, 325–346. https://doi.org/10.1080/00461520.1991.9653137

DiPaola, M. F., & Hoy, W. K. (2012). *Principals improving instruction: Supervision, evaluation, and professional development.* Information Age Publishing.

Eyal, O., & Roth, G. (2011). Principals' leadership and teachers' motivation: Self-determination theory analysis. *Journal of Educational Administration, 49*(3), 256–275.

Flink, C., Boggiano, A. K., & Barrett, M. (1990). Controlling teaching strategies: Undermining children's self-determination and performance. *Journal of Personality and Social Psychology, 59*, 916–924. https://doi.org/10.1037/0022-3514.59.5.916

Freiberg, H. J. (1998). Measuring school climate: Let me count the ways. *Educational Leadership, 56*(1), 22–26.

Gagné, M., & Deci, E. L. (2005). Self-determination theory and work motivation. *Journal of Organizational Behaviour, 26*(4), 331–362.

Goudas, M., Biddle, S., & Fox, K. (1994). Perceived locus of causality, goal orientations, and perceived competence in school physical education classes. *British Journal of Educational Psychology, 64*, 453–463.

Hein, V., Ries, F., Pires, F., Caune, A., Heszteráné, E. J., Emeljanovas, A., & Valantiniene, I. (2012). The relationship between teaching styles and motivation to teach among physical education teachers. *Journal of Sports Science and Medicine, 11*(1), 123–130.

How, Y. M., & Wang, C. K. J. (2016). Creating an autonomy-supportive physical education (PE) learning environment. In W. C. Liu, J. C. K. Wang, & R. M. Ryan (Eds.), *Building autonomous learners: Perspectives from research and practice using self-determination theory* (pp. 207–225). Springer.

Jang, H., Kim, E. J., & Reeve, J. (2016). Why students become more engaged or more disengaged during the semester: A self-determination theory dual-process model. *Learning and Instruction, 43*, 27–38. https://doi.org/10.1016/j.learninstruc.2016.01.002

Jang, H., & Reeve, J. (2021). Intrinsic instructional goal adoption increases autonomy-supportive teaching: A randomized control trial and intervention. *Learning and Instruction, 73*, 101515. https://doi.org/10.1016/j.learninstruc.2020.101415

Johnson, B., Stevens, J. J., & Zvoch, K. (2007). Teachers' perceptions of school climate: A validity study of scores from the revised school level environment questionnaire. *Educational and Psychological Measurement, 67*, 833–844.

Judge, T. A., & Piccolo, R. F. (2004). Transformational and transactional leadership: A meta-analytic test of their relative validity. *Journal of Applied Psychology, 89*, 755–768.

Kelley, R. C., Thornton, B., & Daugherty, R. (2005). Relationships between measures of leadership and school climate. *Educational and Psychological Measurement, 126*(1), 17–25.

Lauermann, F., & Berger, J. (2021). Linking teacher self-efficacy and responsibility with teachers' self-reported and student-reported motivating styles and student engagement. *Learning and Instruction*, 101441. https://doi.org/10.1016/j.learninstruc.2020.101441

Lazowski, R. A., & Hulleman, C. S. (2016). Motivation interventions in education: A meta-analytic review. *Review of Educational Research, 86*, 602–640.

Lee, A. N., & Nie, Y. (2016). Teachers' perceptions of school leader empowering behaviours on psychological empowerment: A moderated path analysis. *New Waves Educational Research & Development, 19*(2), 36–58.

Leithwood, K., Harris, A., & Hopkins, D. (2008). Seven strong claims about successful school leadership. *School Leadership & Management, 28*(1), 27–42.

Leithwood, K., & Jantzi, D. (2006). Transformational school leadership for large-scale reform: Effects on students, teachers, and their classroom practices. *School Effectiveness and School Improvement, 17*(2), 201–227.

Leithwood, K., Mascall, B., Strauss, T., Sacks, R., Memon, N., & Yashkina, A. (2007). Distributing leadership to make schools smarter: Taking the ego out of the system. *Leadership and Policy in Schools, 6*(1), 37–67.

Liu, W. C. (2022). *Singapore's approach to developing teachers: Hindsight, insight, and foresight.* Routledge.

Liu, W. C., & Lim, Y. C. (2018). Understanding teaching, learning and learners: The Singapore teaching practice. In W. C. Liu, C. Koh, D. Choy, & J. Tay-Lim (Eds.), *Understanding teaching, learning and learners: A guide for Singapore teachers* (pp. 1–23). Cengage Learning Asia.

Liu, W. C., Wang, C. K. J., Kee, Y. H., Koh, C., Lim, B. S., & Chua, L. (2014). College students' motivation and learning strategies profiles and academic achievement: A self-determination theory approach. *Educational Psychology, 34*(3), 338–353.

Liu, W. C., Wang, J. C. K., & Ryan, R. M. (2016). *Building autonomous learners: Perspectives from research and practice using self-determination theory.* Springer.

Loh, J., & Hu, G. (2019). *Teacher education in Singapore. Oxford research encyclopedia of education.* Oxford University Press.

Low, E. L., Ng, P. T., Hui, C., & Cai, L. (2017). Teaching as a career choice: Triggers and drivers. *Australian Journal of Teacher Education, 42*(2), 28–46. https://doi.org/10.14221/ajte.2017v42n2.3

Ministry of Education. (2021). *Desired outcomes of education: Find out what you child will be learning in each key stage of their education.* https://www.moe.gov.sg/education-in-sg/desired-outcomes

Ministry of Education. (2023). *Singapore's strong showing in PISA 2022 afirms resilience of education system through COVID-19 pandemic.* https://www.moe.gov.sg/news/press-releases/20231205-singapore-strong-showing-in-pisa-2022-affirms-resilience-of-education-system-through-covid-19-pandemic

Ministry of Education. (2024). *The Singapore teaching practice.* https://academyofsingaporeteachers.moe.edu.sg/professional-excellence/the-singapore-teaching-practice

Ng, B., Liu, W. C., & Wang, C. K. J. (2015). A preliminary examination of teachers' and students' perspectives on autonomy-supportive instructional behaviors. *Qualitative Research in Education, 4*(2), 192–221. https://doi.org/10.17583/qre.2015.1463

Organisation for Economic Co-operation and Development (OECD). (2005). *Teachers matter. Attracting, developing and retaining effective teachers.* OECD Publishing. https://doi.org/10.1787/9789264018044-en

Organisation for Economic Co-operation and Development (OECD). (2023). *PISA 2022 results (volume I): The state of learning and equity in education.* https://www.oecd.org/en/publications/pisa-2022-results-volume-i_53f23881-en/full-report/the-state-of-learning-and-equity-in-education-in-2022_e65c570e.html

Paradis, A., Lutovac, S., Jokikokko, K., & Kaasila, R. (2018). Canadian and Finnish upper-secondary school mathematics teachers' perceptions of autonomy. *Pedagogy, Culture & Society, 26*(3), 381–396. https://doi.org/10.1080/14681366.2017.1407957

Pearson, L. C., & Moomaw, W. (2005). The relationship between teacher autonomy and stress, work satisfaction, empowerment, and professionalism. *Educational Research Quarterly, 29,* 38–54. https://files.eric.ed.gov/fulltext/EJ718115.pdf

Pelletier, L. G., Séguin-Lévesque, C., & Legault, L. (2002). Pressure from above and pressure from below as determinants of teachers' motivation and teaching behaviours. *Journal of Educational Psychology, 94*(1), 186–196. https://doi.org/10.1037/0022-0663.94.1.186

Pelletier, L. G., & Sharp, E. C. (2009). Administrative pressures and teachers' interpersonal behaviour in the classroom. *School Field, 7*(2), 174–183. https://doi.org/10.1177/1477878509104322

Pelletier, L. G., & Vallerand, R. J. (1996). Supervisors' beliefs and subordinates' intrinsic motivation: A behavioural confirmation analysis. *Journal of Personality and Social Psychology, 71,* 331–341. https://doi.org/10.1037/0022-3514.71.2.331

Perryman, J., Ball, S., Maguire, M., & Braun, A. (2011). Life in the pressure cooker – School league tables and English and Mathematics teachers' responses to accountability in a results-driven era. *British Journal of Educational Studies, 59*(2), 179–195. https://doi.org/10.1080/00071005.2011.578568

Prichard, C., & Moore, J. (2016). The balance of teacher autonomy and top-down coordination in ESOL programs. *Tesol Quarterly, 50*(1), 190–201. https://doi.org/10.1002/tesq.278

Reeve, J. (2009). Why teachers adopt a controlling motivating style toward students and how they can become more autonomy supportive. *Educational Psychologist, 44,* 159–175. https://doi.org/10.1080/00461520903028990

Reeve, J. (2016). Autonomy-supportive teaching: What it is, how to do it. In W. C. Liu, J. C. K. Wang, & R. M. Ryan (Eds.), *Building autonomous learners: Perspectives from research and practice using self-determination theory* (pp. 129–152). Springer.

Reeve, J., Bolt, E., & Cai, Y. (1999). Autonomy-supportive teachers: How they teach and motivate students. *Journal of Educational Psychology, 91,* 537–548.

Reeve, J., & Cheon, S. H. (2021). Autonomy-supportive teaching: Its malleability, benefits, and potential to improve educational practice. *Educational Psychologist, 56*(1), 54–77. https://doi.org/10.1080/00461520.2020.1862657

Reeve, J., & Jang, H. (2006). What teachers say and do to support students' autonomy during a learning activity. *Journal of Educational Psychology, 98*, 209–218.

Reeve, J., Jang, H., Hardre, P., & Omura, M. (2002). Providing a rationale in an autonomy-supportive way as a strategy to motivate others during an uninteresting activity. *Motivation and Emotion, 26*, 183–207.

Reeve, J., Jang, H., Carrell, D., Jeon, S., & Barch, J. (2004). Enhancing students' engagement by increasing teachers' autonomy support. *Motivation and Emotion, 28*, 147–169. https://doi.org/10.1023/B:MOEM.0000032312.95499.6f

Reeve, J., Jang, H., & Jang, H. (2018). Personality-based antecedents of teachers' autonomy-supportive and controlling motivating styles. *Learning and Individual Differences, 62*, 12–22. https://doi.org/10.1016/j.lindif.2018.01.001

Reis, H. T., Sheldon, K. M., Gable, S. L., Roscoe, J., & Ryan, R. M. (2000). Daily well-being: The role of autonomy, competence, and relatedness. *Personality and Social Psychology Bulletin, 26*, 419–435.

Robert, V., & Vandenberghe, C. (2021). Laissez-faire leadership and affective commitment: The roles of leader-member exchange and subordinate relational self-concept. *Journal of Business and Psychology, 36*, 533–551. https://doi.org/10.1007/s10869-020-09700-9

Ryan, R. M. (1993). Agency and organisation: Intrinsic motivation, autonomy and the self in psychological development. In J. Jacobs (Ed.), *Nebraska symposium on motivation: Developmental perspectives on motivation* (pp. 1–56). University of Nebraska Press.

Ryan, R. M. (2023). *The Oxford handbook of self-determination theory (Oxford library of psychology series)*. Oxford University Press.

Ryan, R. M., & Deci, E. L. (2000). Intrinsic and extrinsic motivations: Classic definitions and new directions. *Contemporary Educational Psychology, 25*, 54–67. https://doi.org/10.1006/ceps.1999.1020

Ryan, R. M., & Deci, E. L. (2006). Self-regulation and the problem of human autonomy: Does psychology need choice, self-determination, and will? *Journal of Personality, 74*, 1557–1586. https://doi.org/10.1111/j.1467-6494.2006.00420.x

Ryan, R. M., & Deci, E. L. (2017). *Self-determination theory: Basic psychological needs in motivation, development, and wellness*. The Guilford Press.

Ryan, R. M., & Deci, E. L. (2020). Intrinsic and extrinsic motivation from a self-determination theory perspective: Definitions, theory, practices, and future directions. *Contemporary Educational Psychology, 61*, 101860. https://doi.org/10.1016/j.cedpsych.2020.101860

Schwarzer, R., & Hallum, S. (2008). Perceived teacher self-efficacy as a predictor of job stress and burnout. *Applied Psychology: An International Review, 57*, 152–171. https://doi.org/10.1111/j.1464-0597.2008.00359.x

Sebire, S., Standage, M., & Vansteenkiste, M. (2008). Development and validation of the goal content for exercise questionnaire. *Journal of Sport & Exercise Psychology, 30*, 353–377.

Sheldon, K. M., Elliot, A. J., Kim, Y., & Kasser, T. (2001). What is satisfying about satisfying events? Testing 10 candidate psychological needs. *Journal of Personality and Social Psychology, 80*(2), 325–339.

Sheldon, K. M., & Kasser, T. (1998). Pursuing personal goals: Skills enable progress, but not all progress is beneficial. *Personality and Social Psychology Bulletin, 24*(12), 1319–1331. https://doi.org/10.1177/01461672982412006

Sheldon, K. M., Turban, D. B., Brown, K. G., Barrick, M. R., & Judge, T. A. (2003). Applying self-determination theory to organizational research. *Research in Personnel and Human Resources Management, 22*, 357–394.

Sim, A. (2012). *Speech by Ms Sim Ann, senior parliamentary secretary, Ministry of Education and Ministry of Law at the NIE teachers' investiture ceremony at 9.30am on Wednesday, 11 July 2012, at the Nanyang auditorium, Nanyang Technological University.* https://www.yumpu.com/en/document/view/38145573/speech-by-senior-parliamentary-secretary-ministry-of-law-and-

Skinner, E., & Edge, K. (2002). Self-determination, coping, and development. In E. L. Deci & R. M. Ryan (Eds.), *Handbook of self-determination research* (pp. 297–337). University of Rochester Press.

Skinner, E. A., & Belmont, M. J. (1993). Motivation in the classroom: Reciprocal effects of teacher behaviour and student engagement across the school year. *Journal of Educational Psychology, 85*(4), 571–581.

Tan, O. S., Liu, W. C., & Low, E. L. (2012). Educational reforms and teacher education innovations in Singapore. In O. S. Tan (Ed.), *Teacher education frontiers: International perspectives on policy and practice for building new teacher competencies* (pp. 71–91). Cengage Learning Asia Pte Ltd.

Taylor, I. M., Ntoumanis, N., & Smith, B. (2009). The social context as a determinant of teacher motivational strategies in physical education. *Psychology of Sport and Exercise, 10*, 235–243. https://doi.org/10.1016/j.psychsport.2008.09.002

Taylor, I. M., Ntoumanis, N., & Standage, M. (2008). A self-determination theory approach to understanding the antecedents of teachers' motivational strategies in physical education. *Journal of Sport & Exercise Psychology, 30*(1), 75–94. https://doi.org/10.1123/jsep.30.1.75

Teo, T. W., & Choy, B. H. (2021). STEM education in Singapore. In O. S. Tan, E. L. Low, E. G. Tay, & Y. K. Yan (Eds.), *Singapore math and science education innovation: Beyond PISA* (pp. 43–59). Springer.

Tsai, Y., Kunter, M., Lüdtke, O., Trautwein, U., & Ryan, R. M. (2008). What makes lessons interesting? The role of situational and individual factors in three school subjects. *Journal of Educational Psychology, 100*, 460–472.

Tschannen-Moran, M., & Woolfolk Hoy, A. (2001). Teacher efficacy: Capturing an elusive construct. *Teaching and Teacher Education, 17*(7), 783–805. https://doi.org/10.1016/S0742-051X(01)00036-1

Vallerand, R. J., & Losier, G. F. (1999). An integrative analysis of intrinsic and extrinsic motivation in sport. *Journal of Applied Sport Psychology, 11*, 142–169.

Vallerand, R. J., Pelletier, L. G., Blais, M. R., Briere, N. M., Senecal, C., & Vallieres, E. F. (1992). The academic motivation scale: A measure of intrinsic, extrinsic, and amotivation in education. *Educational and Psychological Measurement, 52*, 1003–1017. https://doi.org/10.1177/0013164492052004025

Vansteenkiste, M., Sierens, E., Soenens, B., Luyckx, K., & Lens, W. (2009). Motivational profiles from a self-determination perspective: The quality of motivation matters. *Journal of Educational Psychology, 101*, 671–688. https://doi.org/10.1037/a0015083

Vansteenkiste, M., Simons, J., Lens, W., Sheldon, K. M., & Deci, E. L. (2004). Motivating learning, performance, and persistence: The synergistic role of intrinsic goals and autonomy support. *Journal of Personality and Social Psychology, 87*, 246–260. https://doi.org/10.1037/0022-3514.87.2.246

Vansteenkiste, M., Simons, J., Lens, W., Soenens, B., & Matos, L. (2005). Examining the motivational impact of intrinsic versus extrinsic goal framing and autonomy-supportive versus internally controlling communication style on early adolescents' academic achievement. *Child Development, 2*, 483–501.

Wang, C. K. J., Liu, W. C., Kee, Y. H., & Chian, L. K. (2019). Competence, autonomy, and relatedness in the classroom: Understanding students' motivational processes using the self-determination theory. *Heliyon, 5*(7), e1983. https://doi.org/10.1016/j.heliyon.2019.e01983

Wang, C. K. J., Liu, W. C., Nie, Y., Chye, S., Liem, G. A., Lim, B. S. C., Tay, E. G., Chiu, C., & Hong, Y. (2017). Latent profile analysis of students' motivation and outcomes in Mathematics: An organismic integration theory perspective. *Heliyon, 3*(5), e00308. https://doi.org/10.1016/j.heliyon.2017.e00308

Wang, C. K. J., Ng, B. L. L., Liu, W. C., & Ryan, R. M. (2016). Can being autonomy-supportive in teaching improve students' self-regulation and performance? In W. C. Liu, J. C. K. Wang, & R. M. Ryan (Eds.), *Building autonomous learners: Perspectives from research and practice using self-determination theory* (pp. 227–243). Springer.

Wang, J. C. K., Liu, W. C., Kee, Y. H., Ng, B., Chua, L., & Hu, L. (2023). Measuring educational leadership in Singapore: Re-examining the psychometric properties of the multifactor leadership questionnaire. *Frontiers in Psychology, 14*, 1280038. https://doi.org/10.3389/fpsyg.2023.1280038

Wong, K. Y. (2013). Diverse pathways for life-long teacher professional development. In *Paper presented at the International Science, Mathematics and Technology Education Conference (ISMTEC 2013)*, Bangkok, Thailand.

Yukl, G. A. (2002). *Leadership in organizations* (5th ed.). Prentice Hall.

CHAPTER 11

UNDERSTANDING UNIVERSITY STUDENTS' DEPRESSION AND ANXIETY FROM A SELF-DETERMINATION THEORY PERSPECTIVE: INDIVIDUAL, CONTEXTUAL, AND SOCIOCULTURAL SHIFTS

Frédéric Guay
University of Laval, Canada

William Gilbert
Université de Sherbrooke, Canada

Julien S. Bureau
Université Laval, Canada

The Self in Context, pages 363–398

Published under exclusive licence by Emerald Publishing Limited
doi:10.1108/978-1-80686-869-820261011

ABSTRACT

University students are under pressure. What are the factors responsible for what some call a "psychological distress epidemic"? In this chapter, we analyze various factors linked to students' experience of emotional challenges such as recurrent anxiety and depression symptoms during their studies. While individual factors like genetic predisposition, coping strategies, and cognitive assessment play a role in mental health, focusing solely on these factors may not provide a comprehensive understanding of students' well-being. Exploring contextual and sociocultural elements as well as how these elements have evolved in higher education in the last decades could offer insights into why this generation of students faces particularly high levels of anxiety. Using the self-determination theory as a framework for interpretation, we look at what changed, for better or for worse, in students' pathways in the higher education landscape. In particular, societal shifts toward inclusion, but also increased competitiveness and reduced alternatives may explain why students today are faced with challenges in meeting their psychological needs and experiencing positive mental states.

Keywords: Depression; anxiety; basic psychological needs; self-determination theory; higher education

College and university[1] students typically fall within the age range of 18–29 years, a developmental period called emerging adulthood (Arnett et al., 2014). This period is characterized by substantial changes as individuals transition from late adolescence into adulthood, a period of high autonomy and responsibility. Changes in this period generally include moving away from parents' home, gaining greater financial autonomy, developing more intimate relationships with significant others and pursuing a meaningful educational endeavor. In this chapter, we focus our attention on young adults who attend university given that this period is associated with peaks in stress (Pitt et al., 2018), which can lead to the onset or worsening of mental health issues such as depression and anxiety.

The prevalence of depression and anxiety among university students is notably high. A meta-analysis conducted by Li et al. (2022), which encompassed 64 international studies involving over 100,000 individuals, found that the rates of depression and anxiety symptoms among university students were 33.6% and 39%, respectively. Moreover, Satinsky et al. (2021) reported significant levels of clinically relevant symptoms of anxiety and depression among Ph.D. students, with 24% exhibiting depression and 17% displaying anxiety. These percentages underscore that depression and anxiety are prevalent among both undergraduate and graduate students. In addition, it appears that the prevalence of these mental health issues is much higher among students than in the general population (Sharp & Theiler, 2018). For instance, a survey by Evans et al. (2018) indicated that graduate students are over six times more likely to experience depression and anxiety than the general population. Specifically, 41% of graduate students exhibited moderate to severe anxiety, in stark contrast to only 6% of the general population. This survey also revealed that 39% of graduate students fell within the moderate to severe range for depression, compared to 6% of the general population.

Given the high prevalence of mental health issues among students, it is not surprising that depression and anxiety symptoms have become the main reason students seek mental health support within post-secondary institutions (Center for Collegiate Mental Health, 2017). This requires the mobilization of an increasing number of resources to deliver appropriate students' support services, especially considering that these symptoms can significantly alter students' academic functioning and quality of life (Ribeiro et al., 2018). More broadly, emerging adulthood is a critical period for mental health intervention, and timely treatment is essential as it can prevent the deterioration of depression and anxiety symptoms into more severe disorders with longer-lasting consequences and a grimmer prognosis (Schulenberg et al., 2004). Without surprise, the scientific community has shown considerable interest in the phenomenon of students' mental health. In fact, research focusing on mental health and well-being among university students has seen consistent growth since 1975 (Hernandez-Torrano et al., 2020).

In this chapter, we analyze various factors linked to students' experience of emotional challenges such as recurrent depression and anxiety symptoms during their studies. Although individual factors like genetic predispositions, gender, personality, and coping strategies play a role in depression and anxiety, exploring how contextual and sociocultural elements have evolved in the last decades could offer insights into why current generations of students face particularly high levels of anxiety and depression. Societal shifts such as the rise of digital media, but also increased competitiveness, reduced alternatives in the labor market, and global environmental and political instability may explain why today's students struggle with their mental health. We selected these individual, interpersonal, contextual, and societal shift factors because anxiety and depression among university students arise from a complex interplay of personal vulnerabilities (e.g., coping strategies), social dynamics (e.g., peer and family support), institutional pressures (e.g., academic demands), and broader societal changes (e.g., economic instability). Understanding these multi-level influences allows for a more comprehensive approach to prevention and intervention, addressing both proximal and distal determinants of student mental health. Using self-determination theory (SDT) as a framework for interpretation, we explain why some individual and contextual factors as well as societal shifts are linked to symptoms of depression and anxiety.

ANXIETY AND DEPRESSION AMONG UNIVERSITY STUDENTS

Anxiety and depressive disorders both belong to the broader category of internalizing disorders and often cooccur. A worldwide survey reported that 45.7% of individuals with lifetime major depressive disorder had a lifetime history of one or more anxiety disorder (Kessler et al., 2015). According to the DSM-5, depression and anxiety both involve a constellation of symptoms. For *depression*, the most important ones are depressed mood and diminished interest or pleasure in all, or almost all, activities. Along with these symptoms, individuals may experience significant weight loss or gain, a decrease or increase in appetite, a slowing down of thought and a reduction of physical movement, fatigue or loss of energy, feelings of worthlessness or inappropriate guilt, diminished ability to think or concentrate, indecisiveness, and recurrent thoughts of death. For *anxiety*, the most important symptom is excessive worry, which encompasses a plurality of concerns that are difficult to manage. This is often accompanied by other symptoms such as restlessness, fatigue, difficulty concentrating, irritability, muscle tension, and sleep disturbances.

Aside from the fact that these emotional states are experienced negatively by most individuals, they also have the potential to significantly alter university students' functioning. Indeed, depression and anxiety are integral components of a broader phenomenon known as psychological distress (Drapeau et al., 2012). Numerous studies have shown that psychological distress can profoundly hinder students' learning and academic performance, both directly and by prompting risk behaviors compromising their health and overall functioning (Sharp & Theiler, 2018). More specifically, students grappling with mental health issues tend to be more frequently absent (Bruffaerts et al., 2018; Hysenbegasi et al., 2005) and are at a higher risk of prematurely discontinuing their studies (Eisenberg et al., 2009), which subsequently hampers their socio-professional integration (Xin et al., 2010). Moreover, a study conducted by BlackDeer et al. (2021) revealed that students diagnosed with depression and anxiety who remain untreated for their symptoms tend to have lower GPAs compared to those who receive appropriate treatment. These findings are particularly noteworthy, as they indicate that with timely intervention, students receiving appropriate help regarding their symptoms of depression and anxiety can perform better than their counterparts, and potentially achieve academic outcomes that are comparable to those of students without these symptoms.

In addition, research indicates that students experiencing psychological distress are more susceptible to developing low self-esteem (Gilbert et al., 2024) and suicidal thoughts and behaviors (Tang et al., 2018). They are also more likely to engage in substance use, including alcohol and cannabis

(Gilbert, Bureau, et al., 2023; Lechner et al., 2020; Tian et al., 2021), exhibit low levels of physical activity (Gilbert, Demanins, et al., 2023; Knowlden et al., 2016), and adopt unhealthy dietary habits (Deasy et al., 2014; Gilbert, Demanins, et al., 2023; Peltzer & Pengpid, 2017). These have detrimental consequences that are well documented for students' learning capacities and academic success (Burrows et al., 2017; Curcio et al., 2006; Whatnall et al., 2022).

Contrary to expectations, a study conducted by Cvetkovski and Mackinnon (2018) reveals that university students experiencing psychological distress, characterized by symptoms of depression and anxiety, exhibited lower dropout rates and higher completion rates by their fourth academic year compared to their peers without psychological distress. These findings are intriguing, as they would indicate that although psychological distress can negatively impact a student's overall educational experience, it may not be as detrimental to academic progress as assumed. If replicated, this unexpected outcome could indicate a strong desire for achievement among those reporting high levels of psychological distress, suggesting that these challenges have the potential to be somewhat functional to a highly demanding environment, and provides hope that, for the majority, they could be relatively transient. This may be highly dependent on the proximal causes for which these symptoms are developed. Either way, even an intense drive to excel could lead to adverse consequences, including suicidal thoughts, substance abuse, low physical activity levels, and unhealthy dietary habits. Overall, one can expect even high-achieving students who experience depression and anxiety symptoms to still face significant negative repercussions in their academic and personal lives.

INDIVIDUAL DETERMINANTS OF DEPRESSION AND ANXIETY

According to Wittenborn et al. (2020), depression and anxiety involve a complex interplay between biological, psychological, social, and environmental factors. For example, distorted thinking, excessive stress, and maladaptive coping strategies can contribute to these two internalized problems. Consequently, the specific etiology of depression and anxiety can vary significantly from one individual to another. For instance, a student's depression may stem from a breakup with a loved one, while for another person these symptoms might stem from dysfunctional routines and exacerbated by academic failures. In this section, we will explore the most common individuals' determinants associated with both internalized disorders. It is important to note, however, that the determinants of depression and anxiety share considerable overlap in the ways they combine to produce symptoms of depression and anxiety, but also in the way one determinant (e.g., genetic) may share action mechanisms with another one (e.g., gender differences).

Genetics Factors

Anxiety and depressive disorders demonstrate a moderate heritability rate of roughly 40%, with research suggesting a shared genetic vulnerability among these internalizing problems (Kalin, 2020). For instance, Thorp et al. (2021) examined the genetic underpinnings of symptoms associated with depression and anxiety. Through a comprehensive analysis of the data, these researchers discovered that the symptoms of depression and anxiety are phenotypes of two distinct yet closely related genetic groups. This classification facilitated an investigation into the associated genes. They identified 89 genetic variants linked to depression and 102 associated with anxiety, each located within specific genomic regions. Upon validating these findings in a separate extensive cohort of nearly 1.9 million individuals, a significant majority of the results were corroborated. The results clearly indicate that genetic connections exist between depression and anxiety, while also highlighting their unique characteristics. However, whether the presence of these emotional states in one individual is associated with genetic components does not seem to have important implications in terms of intervention strategies, as evidenced by a meta-analysis indicating that genetic variations across patients do not influence the efficacy of cognitive behavioral therapy in the treatment of anxiety disorders (Schiele et al., 2021).

Gender Differences

It is commonly observed that women suffer more from anxiety and depression symptoms than men (Li et al., 2022). Compared to men, women are twice as likely to be affected by anxiety, including the various associated comorbidities such as agoraphobia (2 times higher than men), specific phobias including fear of animals (2.4 times higher), panic attacks (2.5 times higher), social anxiety (2.0 times higher) and generalized anxiety (2.1 times; Hallers-Haalboom et al., 2020). Several factors have been mentioned in the literature to explain such differences, including genetic and environmental factors. The role of these different factors can be better understood based on stress-vulnerability models (Ingram & Luxton, 2005). More precisely, people are said to have individual predispositions that lead them to experience more psychological distress when faced with different stressors. For example, Hallers-Haalboom et al. (2020) note that women are biologically more sensitive to stress, probably because such a mechanism has proved useful for their role in the survival of offspring. Psychologically, women would perceive symptoms of psychological distress as more unpleasant and develop hypersensitivity or fear of such symptoms (Carpenter et al., 2022). Furthermore, women, compared to men, are more likely to abnegate their need for autonomy to please others (Nsair & Piszczek, 2021), which would contribute to generating more anxiety. In other words, by making more compromises than men to preserve the well-being of important ones, women would unfortunately experience more psychological distress. Specifically, research shows that women have greater concerns about relationships, which is linked to depression (see Wittenborn et al., 2020). Moreover, gender roles play a part in the etiology of anxiety and depression. Research has shown that higher masculinity in men and women predicted lower anxiety and depressive symptoms among students. In contrast, higher feminity in men and women was associated with higher anxiety and depressive symptoms (Arcand et al., 2020). Finally, women are more likely to have experienced traumatic events in their childhood, which would also explain why they experience more anxiety and depression later as these events are known as triggers for psychological distress later in life (Knipscheer et al., 2020).

Neuroticism

Neuroticism is a personality trait associated with a heightened propensity to experience negative emotions and to interpret stressful situations in an exaggerated manner. This trait poses a significant risk for the persistence of internalizing symptoms (Prince et al., 2021; Williams et al., 2020). Neuroticism is correlated with several clinically relevant traits, including anxiety sensitivity, intolerance of uncertainty, perfectionism, and experiential avoidance (Naragon-Gainey & Watson, 2018). Negative emotions such as depression, fear, anxiety, and hostility are often considered facets of neuroticism. However, neuroticism does not always directly cause emotional disorders. Instead, it interacts with various stressors to shape emotional responses. For instance, many individuals may encounter a stressful situation that leads to a panic attack, but not all will develop a panic disorder. According to the model of functional mechanisms (Barlow et al., 2021), a negative emotional reaction following a stressful event can precipitate an emotional disorder in individuals with high levels of neuroticism. This occurs because they perceive the situation as uncontrollable and react adversely to their emotional experiences. Conversely, individuals with low levels of neuroticism tend to view negative emotions as acceptable, controllable, and tolerable, which helps prevent the onset of emotional disorders. Moreover, it has been found that neuroticism has long-lasting effects on anxiety and depression, even when researchers adjusted for baseline symptoms and psychiatric history (Jeronimus et al., 2016).

Coping

Coping is a set of cognitive and behavioral strategies mobilized by people in response to a stressful event or demand (Stephenson & DeLongis, 2020). In some models, notably that of Lazarus and Folkman (1984), it is assumed that coping with various demands (1) is an interactive process between an individual and their environment, (2) involves managing the demands placed on a person, (3) requires an assessment of the situation and available resources, and finally (4) involves cognitive and behavioral processes to minimize demands. The cognitive and behavioral processes in this last step are represented by different types of coping strategies that may vary in their effectiveness. Lazarus and Folkman (1984) identified two main categories of coping strategies: problem-focused and emotion-focused. Problem-focused strategies involve trying to change the reality of a stressful situation. This can be done by gathering details or learning skills that might help address the problem, organizing tasks to reduce stress from competing demands and seeking instrumental social support. Emotion-focused strategies involve managing the emotions associated with stress without changing the stressful event. These strategies involve seeking emotional and social support from friends or family, engaging in positive reinterpretation, using relaxation techniques, or relying on distraction, denial or avoidance (Biggs, Brough, & Drummond, 2023).

To date, multiple meta-analyses demonstrated that some coping strategies, including negative emotional-focused strategies such as avoidance and mental/behavioral disengagement, are more consistently associated with depression and anxiety symptoms (e.g., Cheng et al., 2023; Groth et al., 2019; Kato, 2015; Penley et al., 2002). This suggests that individuals may engage in a variety of coping strategies that are not effective in managing the demands they face and, therefore, hinder their adjustment and well-being. Accordingly, many researchers and clinicians now agree that, beyond the type of coping strategies used (whether problem-focused or emotion-focused), the key factor is an individual's ability to flexibly select strategies that best meet the unique demands of each situation (Stephenson & DeLongis, 2020). In other words, individuals who consistently and rigidly rely on the same coping strategies, regardless of the context, are more at risk of developing mental health issues.

Summary of Individual Determinants

Anxiety and depression symptoms and disorders are associated with individual vulnerabilities that university students may have limited control over, such as gender, the neurotic personality trait, and genetic predispositions. These factors significantly increase the risk of experiencing internalized problems among students. Conversely, students possess greater control over the coping strategies they employ to manage their stress. It is important to note that these individual risk factors are not exhaustive. Other factors exist such as anxiety sensitivity, intolerance of uncertainty, and perfectionism. For the sake of conciseness, we have not reviewed them.

Furthermore, individual characteristics interact with environmental influences, which can exacerbate symptoms of anxiety and depression. The following section will elaborate on these factors.

ENVIRONMENTAL FACTORS LINKED TO STUDENTS' ANXIETY AND DEPRESSION

Family

The relationship between family dynamics and internalized disorders among university students has been extensively studied. For instance, positive family communication and a cohesive-flexible family structure are correlated with lower levels of anxiety and depression (Berryhill et al., 2018). Furthermore, a supportive family environment during the COVID-19 pandemic, characterized by adaptation and stability, was inversely related to depression, anxiety, and stress (Revollar et al., 2023). Family social support is a significant predictor of reduced anxiety and depressive symptoms (Romero et al., 2015). Additionally, family-related factors such as parental education are negatively linked with levels of depression, anxiety, and stress in students (Gilbert, Demanins, et al., 2023; Haq et al., 2018). Thus, it is evident that family dynamics play a crucial role in the mental health of university students. Poor family functioning and lack of support are associated with increased anxiety and depression, whereas positive family interactions and support can help alleviate these mental health challenges. These findings highlight the necessity of considering family-related factors in interventions aimed at enhancing the mental well-being of university students, as well as targeting students with a chaotic familial background for preventive interventions such as support groups.

Peers

High-quality peer relationships are linked to reduced levels of anxiety and depression among university students. For instance, a study conducted by Swenson et al. (2008) evaluated the importance of the closeness of peer relationships with both high school and university friends, examining various adjustment outcomes such as academic performance, social integration, emotional well-being, and institutional attachment among first-year university students. The findings indicate that maintaining a close relationship with a high school friend is advantageous during the initial weeks of the university transition. However, as the semester progresses, the benefits of forming close relationships with new university friends become more pronounced. Furthermore, multiple dimensions of adolescents' social relationships significantly influence feelings of anxiety and depression. Specifically, associations with different peer groups (both high and low status), positive attributes within best friendships, and the presence of a dating relationship have been found to mitigate feelings of social anxiety (Greca & Harrison, 2005). Conversely, experiences of relational victimization and negative interactions within best friendships are predictive of heightened social anxiety. This could be particularly the case for subgroups of boys that adhere to ideals of physical toughness, which have shown to lower self-esteem (Santos et al., 2013). In terms of depression, as with anxiety, affiliation with a high-status peer group offers some protective effects, while relational victimization and negative dynamics in best friendships and romantic relationships are correlated with increased depressive symptoms (Greca & Harrison, 2005). Moreover, a randomized controlled study by Harra and Vargas (2023) involving a small sample of undergraduate students exhibiting moderate symptoms of anxiety or depression ($n = 32$) demonstrated that participation in a mentorship program (the help of another student to face university challenges) significantly reduced depressive symptoms over time.

Professors and University Programs

Although numerous studies, literature reviews, and book chapters examine factors contributing to student anxiety and stress, as well as potential interventions, many of these works overlook the role of professors (Di Placito-De Rango, 2018). Yet, existing literature indicates that clear instructions and positive feedback from professors can significantly reduce student anxiety (Gilbert et al., 2021). Conversely, a professor's haste to teach knowledge may result in a loss of control, fostering feelings of helplessness and anxiety among students. Additionally, high expectations from teachers regarding student performance can diminish motivation and increase anxiety levels (Goetz et al., 2013). In fact, academic assessments of knowledge are often associated with substantial stress, which can provoke anxious responses that adversely affect student success. A meta-analysis has identified anxiety as a significant barrier to working memory, consequently impairing performance across various tasks (Moran, 2016). Recently, Hsu and Goldsmith (2021) introduced five evidence-based strategies that educators can adopt to help reduce students' anxiety:

- First, recognize the mental health issues that young adults encounter. This involves understanding the underlying challenges and knowing how and when to direct students to campus resources when necessary.
- Second, build trust with students. This can be achieved by learning their names through methods like name tags and using appropriate humor to create a welcoming classroom environment.

- Third, promote individual autonomy. Be mindful of stress-inducing learning strategies, such as cold calling. To help alleviate anxiety, thoughtfully organize groups or allow students to select their own, fostering an inclusive classroom where everyone is treated fairly, avoiding microaggressions and stereotype threats.
- Fourth, address test anxiety. Consider incorporating alternative assessments to decrease the reliance on high-stakes testing and its accompanying stress. Adjust exam formats to lower anxiety levels and implement interventions, such as encouraging students to write about their anxiety, to enhance their performance.
- Fifth, encourage effective learning strategies. Promote strong learning techniques and a growth mindset so that students understand they could improve.

Moreover, the *program* in which students are enrolled significantly influences their mental health. Unlike high school, where program selection is limited primarily to specific courses, the educational path becomes far more differentiated at the university levels. Indeed, post-secondary students face the challenge to match program choice with core aspects of their identity. Moreover, the experience within different programs can vary considerably. Some programs provide a wider array of electives, diverse internship opportunities, and enhanced chances for interaction with the faculty members. Gilbert et al. (2021; 2023a) posited that programs designed to help fulfill students' psychological needs for autonomy, competence, and relatedness are most likely to foster positive mental health outcomes among young people. Students who perceive their programs to offer on-topic and relevant course lists and offer opportunities to get to know the academic staff report lower levels of anxiety and depression. Conversely, students who perceive their program as unjustly prescriptive and inflexible, as well as providing heavy workload that hampers other facets of their life such as socializing are more prone to experiencing anxiety and depression. Importantly, the workload associated with study programs also emerged as a significant risk factor for anxiety and depression among university students (Mofatteh, 2021).

Summary of Environmental Factors

This brief overview suggests that parents, peers, professors, and university programs can significantly influence the symptoms of anxiety and depression in students. Positive classroom environments, supportive relationships with parents and friends, and participation in nurturing university programs appear to serve as protective factors against these mental health challenges. However, although these elements are important, there are also macro-level factors that may hinder or intensify these symptoms. Below, we will examine some of these additional influences.

SOCIETAL SHIFTS LINKED TO STUDENTS' ANXIETY AND DEPRESSION

Data from the National Survey on Drug Use and Health (NSDUH), an annual survey examining substance use and mental health in the United States, indicated that the prevalence of anxiety among American adults rose from 5.12% in 2008 to 6.68% in 2018. An analysis by age group revealed a particularly significant increase among respondents aged between 18 and 25, with rates climbing from 7.97% to 14.66%. This rise was more pronounced than in the other age groups (Goodwin et al., 2020). Moreover, in Norway, a study revealed a significant increase in psychological distress among adolescents and young adults, while depressive symptoms declined in older adults (Krokstad et al., 2022).

These statistics are intriguing because if psychological distress was mainly the product of individual differences—in terms of genetics, coping strategies, or neuroticism—along with contextual influences such as relationships with peers and teachers, we would expect mean anxiety and depression levels in all age groups to remain relatively stable over decades rather than increase. Thus, societal shifts might explain this increase, especially for individuals aged between 18 and 25 years old. According to Seligman (1990), several aspects of modern life have eroded traditional sources of well-being, leading to greater feelings of helplessness and dissatisfaction. For instance, as modernity has progressed, urbanization, mobility, and technological advances have reduced close social connections, leading to more isolation and loneliness (Chen et al., 2022). Moreover, modern societies place a high value on individual achievement, independence, and self-reliance. While these values can promote personal freedom, they can also create pressure to succeed, especially for young adults who are still gathering the building blocks of their adult life, which may come with immense pressure and dread. The very high amount of uncertainty for their future that university students face in changing times may be particularly strong contributing factors to stress, anxiety, and feelings of inadequacy. Below we review a portion of the empirical work based on some of these societal shifts.

Social Media and Technology

Children, adolescents, and young adults are growing up in an increasingly digitalized society, where social media and technology play a central role in their daily lives. Constant exposure to idealized representations of life and success on social media can foster social comparison, which may lead to feelings of inadequacy and low self-esteem, potentially increasing internalized symptoms. A recent scoping review indicated that social media usage exceeding three hours per day is linked to higher levels of anxiety and depression (Hilty et al., 2023). Moreover, passive browsing on social media is associated with greater risks of anxiety and depression compared to purposeful, positive, and active engagement. Although the direction of effects is unknown, passive browsing as a coping strategy for existing distress symptoms could be part of a vicious circle that triggers more negative adjustment. Notably, girls and young women are particularly vulnerable to the negative psychological effects of social media (Hilty et al., 2023). However, males with emotional dysregulation are likely to be more problematically engaged in Internet use than females (Gioia et al., 2021). The overuse of technology has also been linked to disrupted sleep and stress, which can subsequently lead to anxiety and depression (Hussain & Griffiths, 2021).

Loneliness and Social Isolation

Despite their greater online connectivity compared to older adults, Beam and Kim (2020) highlighted that loneliness—the overwhelming uncomfortable feeling of disconnection from others—is particularly prevalent among young adults. Recent evidence even suggests that feelings of loneliness are on the rise among younger populations, particularly those suffering from psychological distress (Achterbergh et al., 2020; Alam et al., 2024). Numerous factors related to social media could explain this phenomenon, including the replacement of nurturing, face-to-face interactions with superficial relationships online, as well as a decline in the development of social skills (e.g., reading body language, engaging in small talk, handling social conflicts).

Regardless of the reasons, loneliness has serious consequences, including an increased risk of depression, weakened immunity, chronic illness, mortality, and even premature death (Infurna et al., 2024). In their systematic review, Mann et al. (2022) found that loneliness can precipitate mental health issues among students, including depression. A comprehensive study involving 308,849 participants with various ages monitored over an average of 7.5 years, revealed that individuals with strong social relationships have a 50% greater likelihood of survival than those with weak or insufficient social connections (Holt-Lunstad et al., 2010). This effect is comparable to the benefits of quitting smoking and surpasses many well-known mortality risk factors, such as obesity and physical inactivity. Notably, the consistency of this association across various demographics—including age, sex, initial health status, and cause of death—regardless of the follow-up period suggests that the relationship between social connections and mortality is reproduced in various populations. Therefore, efforts to mitigate these risks should not be confined to specific subgroups, such as the elderly.

Pressure to Achieve

In today's hypercompetitive environment, individuals may perceive a significant pressure to succeed, excel, and continually improve—a phenomenon termed socially prescribed perfectionism (Curran & Hill, 2019). This trait dimension encapsulates the belief that others impose perfectionistic expectations on oneself, indicating that such demands are perceived to stem from external sources. The research conducted by Curran and Hill (2019) revealed a linear increase in the mean levels of various dimensions of trait perfectionism over time, highlighting the escalating pressures faced by contemporary late adolescents and emerging adults. Notably, the most pronounced increase was observed in socially prescribed perfectionism, with statistical analyses indicating a 32% rise in this dimension from 1989 to 2017. According to Flett et al. (2022), the effects of socially prescribed perfectionism on individuals are unequivocal. Meta-analyses have established significant correlations between socially prescribed perfectionism and adverse outcomes, including suicidal ideation, burnout, and various health issues (Limburg et al., 2017). For example, a meta-analysis by Smith et al. (2017) revealed that perfectionistic concerns (like socially prescribed perfectionism) were the predominant factor in predicting psychopathology.

Lifestyle Factors

Modern lifestyles can contribute to mental health struggles. Sedentary behavior, poor nutrition, and lack of sleep all negatively impact emotional well-being (Skrove et al., 2013). For example, data from the Youth Risk Behavior Surveillance System (YRBSS) and other national surveys, as well as longitudinal studies in transportation, education, social media, and recreational sectors, showed evidence of significant changes: Active commuting, high school physical education, and outdoor play (in 3- to 12-year olds) declined over periods. Thus, technological and societal changes have impacted the types of physical activities performed by US youth (Bassett et al., 2015). This is not without consequence for young adults' mental health. Indeed, sedentary behavior is a risk factor for increased anxiety and depression symptoms in adults. Replacing sedentary behavior with moderate-to-vigorous activity may reduce mental health risks (Kandola et al., 2021).

Economic Pressure and Job Insecurity

Long-term employment has increasingly become a rarity, with job opportunities often being temporary or contract-based (Sparks et al., 2001). These shifts have contributed to a heightened sense of job insecurity among the global workforce (Scott, 2004). The fast-paced economy, rising living costs, and job insecurity can create chronic stress, particularly among younger generations who often struggle to afford necessities such as housing, food, and health care (Martinez et al., 2021). Indeed, it appears that perceived job insecurity leads to stronger turnover intention among younger employees compared to older ones (Cheng & Chan, 2008). Moreover, in a meta-analysis, Kim and von DemKnesebeck (2015) revealed that job insecurity and unemployment were significantly related to a higher risk of depressive symptoms, especially for younger respondents (<40 years).

During times of few economic opportunities, the pressures of financial instability and job insecurity often reach their peak. Research indicated a significant correlation between economic recessions and heightened incidences of depressive symptoms, self-harming behaviors, and suicide, both during and after these downturns (Guerra & Eboreime, 2021). Notably, following the 2008 global financial crisis, many developed nations experienced an uptick in the prevalence of depressive symptoms and disorders. This period also saw a marked increase in the utilization of mental health care services for individuals experiencing depressive symptoms (Guerra & Eboreime, 2021). Concerns about economic stability can create a sense of uncertainty about the future, which can be particularly durable and stressful for young adults who are navigating major life decisions and transitions.

Global Issues and Uncertainty

The world now faces significant challenges, including climate change, armed conflicts, and the lingering effects of the COVID-19 pandemic. These global issues have created in many a sense of uncertainty about the future, helplessness, and dread, contributing to psychological distress among younger populations. In terms of climate change, a literature review conducted by Brophy et al. (2022) revealed that young adults experience significant eco-anxiety related to the current and future consequences of climate change. This eco-anxiety, in addition to the few significant global actions taken to limit the consequences of climate change, can lead to more serious mental health issues, including depression, anxiety, and intense emotion responses such as sadness, anger, and fear. Youth from vulnerable communities, such as Indigenous populations or those with strong connections to the land, are particularly susceptible to the emotional impacts of climate change.

With regards to armed conflict, a study conducted by Riad et al. (2022) examined the mental health implications of the Russian-Ukrainian War, which started in 2022, on young adults in Central Europe, with a particular focus on Czech University students. Utilizing standardized assessment tools, the research found that over one third of participants displayed moderate to severe symptoms of anxiety and depression. Notably, female participants and those who frequently consumed news through social media reported elevated levels of these mental health issues. The findings underscore the necessity of acknowledging the psychological impact of such armed conflicts on young adults and advocate for targeted interventions aimed at high-risk groups.

The COVID-19 pandemic has significantly increased levels of anxiety, depression, and other stress-related symptoms due to factors like self-isolation, lockdowns, unemployment, and economic uncertainty. Specifically, it appears that the publication of daily COVID-19 infection rates and reductions in human mobility, were associated with an increased prevalence of major depressive and anxiety disorders. Females and younger age groups were also more affected by the pandemic than males and older age groups. Overall, it appears that in 2020, the pandemic was responsible for 53.2 million cases of major depressive disorder and 76.2 million cases of anxiety disorders (Santomauro et al., 2021).

Moreover, the COVID-19 pandemic had significant repercussions in the field of education, particularly by disrupting teaching and learning due to the abrupt transition to online instruction. Many teachers were unprepared for this shift, lacking both the technical skills and familiarity with evidence-based online teaching methods (Middleton, 2020). As a result, the quality and time of instruction during the pandemic varied widely, from minimal adaptations to highly innovative approaches. This disruption in instructional quality and time, combined with social isolation and many other lost opportunities for personal and professional development, negatively impacted the socio-emotional growth of many emerging adults (Crăciun, 2024). Among these consequences is a decline in social skills (Hussong et al., 2021), which may further contribute to the mental health issues currently observed among this population.

Summary of Societal Shifts

The rapid advancement of technology has ushered in the digital age, presenting remarkable opportunities alongside unforeseen challenges. Although social media facilitates global connectivity, it also cultivates an environment with constant comparison and unrealistic expectations. This virtual landscape can sometimes eclipse genuine interpersonal interactions, resulting in heightened feelings of isolation and inadequacy. Furthermore, individuals are increasingly grappling with loneliness, economic pressures, and job insecurity, which intensify the demand for academic and professional success. In this competitive climate, students often face overwhelming expectations from themselves, their families, and society at large.

The relentless pursuit of perfection, or even the impression that one needs to go above their capabilities only to fit in society, can result in significant stress and burnout. Additionally, we are currently navigating a landscape marked by uncertainty, characterized by accelerating outcomes of climate change and armed conflicts worldwide, as well as the lingering effects of the COVID-19 pandemic. Despite all these massive societal changes, it is important to also consider that higher prevalence of psychological distress symptoms could be partly explained by the fact that anxiety and depression are less stigmatized nowadays than in previous eras, thereby leading young adults to feel more comfortable to disclose their psychological distress in surveys. Although reduced stigma may account for part of the recent increase in the prevalence of anxiety and depression in young adults, it is certainly not the sole contributing factor. It is crucial to acknowledge the many challenges this population faces and to cultivate environments where students feel safe, supported, and empowered to seek assistance when necessary. This principle forms the foundation of SDT, which seeks to address issues associated with suboptimal contexts and societal changes that adversely affect human well-being.

SDT AS AN INTEGRATIVE FRAMEWORK TO UNDERSTAND ANXIETY AND DEPRESSION

SDT explains human well-being and motivation by viewing individuals as proactive agents. It posits that people naturally seek growth and new experiences but require supportive environments to flourish and thrive. Unfortunately, many social contexts, like universities, can hinder these tendencies, leading to disengagement and ill-being. SDT highlights the interaction between individuals and their environments in shaping adjustment. The theory includes mini theories that address various aspects of motivation and personality, with this chapter focusing on types of motivation and basic psychological needs.

Autonomous Versus Controlled Motivations

Students have various motivations for engaging in schoolwork. According to SDT, these underlying reasons are crucial as they lead to differing outcomes. It is possible to identify different types of motivation based on their level of self-determination—that is, how much a behavior truly originates from the individual or the "self." Some motivations are autonomous, while others are controlled. Intrinsic motivation is characterized by performing an activity for its inherent enjoyment and satisfaction (Ryan & Deci, 2000). In contrast, extrinsic motivation involves engaging in an activity for instrumental reasons rather than its inherent qualities. SDT identifies various categories of reasons that may regulate behavior within extrinsic motivation, also called regulations or forms of extrinsic motivation, which vary in their levels of self-determination or autonomy: external regulation, introjected regulation, identified regulation, and integrated regulation (Ryan & Deci, 2000). External and introjected regulations are considered controlled motivations, while identified and integrated regulations are autonomous motivations, more akin in their outcomes to intrinsic motivation. Thus, SDT recognizes that some extrinsic motivations can be volitional, meaning that students who lack intrinsic motivation for a subject may still achieve positive cognitive, emotional, and behavioral outcomes if these extrinsic motivations align with their sense of self or core values.

External regulation occurs when a behavior is driven by the desire for rewards or the avoidance of punishment. For example, students motivated to take science courses to secure a car offered contingently by their parents are considered externally motivated. Introjected regulation refers to behaviors performed due to internal pressures like guilt or obligation; individuals acknowledge the reasons for their actions but do so in a controlled manner. An example of introjected regulation is students attending school to prove their worth or comply with cultural expectations. Identified regulation arises when individuals recognize the importance of a behavior and personally align with the reasons for their actions. For instance, some students might not enjoy biology but recognize its importance for pursuing a career they are passionate about. Integrated regulation occurs when identified regulation aligns very well with personal values and needs, making the behavior a core part of one's identity. This requires individuals to have a coherent sense of self (Deci et al., 1996), allowing them to connect the significance of a behavior with other aspects of their lives. An example of integrated regulation is when students consider that studying their major aligns with how they see their current and future self, and fully integrate it as part of their identity. Recent systematic reviews and meta-analyses suggest that intrinsic motivation and integrated regulation share conceptual traits that make them challenging to distinguish empirically (Howard et al., 2017; Vasconcellos et al., 2020).

In SDT, motivation types exist along a continuum of self-determination that reflects the quality of motivation rather than its intensity (Bureau et al., 2023). Motivation types are expected to correlate in a quasi-simplex manner, with stronger positive correlations among adjacent motivations compared to distant ones. For example, identified regulation and intrinsic motivation should show a positive and moderate correlation, stronger than that between intrinsic motivation and introjected regulation. Previous research has supported this autonomy continuum (Guay et al., 2016; Otis et al., 2005; Ryan & Connell, 1989). Furthermore, this continuum also illustrates how different motivation types influence various educational outcomes. The more autonomous the motivation, the more positive the outcomes for students.

Howard et al. (2021) conducted a meta-analysis encompassing 344 samples with over 200,000 students from various countries. The results revealed that intrinsic motivation correlates with student success and well-being, while identified regulation is particularly linked to persistence. Introjected regulation showed a positive correlation with persistence and performance goals but also with indicators of anxiety. Conversely, external regulation did not correlate with performance or persistence but was associated with lower well-being. This meta-analysis was conducted globally, without considering university students in a more detailed way. However, recent research findings show that autonomous motivation among university students relates negatively to depression (Leow et al., 2016; Pineda et al., 2024).

In sum, the more students find interest and value in learning activities, the more likely they are to achieve positive educational outcomes. Relying on contingent rewards or punishments as motivational strategies appears ineffective in fostering student engagement and adjustment.

Basic Psychological Needs

To understand why some students are autonomously motivated while others are driven by controlled reasons or have differing goals, SDT introduced the concept of basic psychological needs. This theory identifies three fundamental psychological needs: competence, autonomy, and relatedness (Ryan & Deci, 2017). In SDT, these needs are viewed as universal rather than individual subjective differences. Consequently, SDT posits that (a) the extent to which individuals are healthy and effective hinges on the fulfillment of these needs; (b) the deprivation or active hindrance to the satisfaction of psychological needs leads to ill-being and mental health issues; and (c) these needs are essential across varying ages, genders, cultures, and socioeconomic backgrounds (Deci & Ryan, 2000, 2012). Thus, psychological needs are innate sources of satisfaction that encourage optimal functioning. While the satisfaction of these needs fosters autonomous motivation, their frustration can lead to controlled motivations. Focusing solely on needs satisfaction might overlook the detrimental effects of frustration, while focusing only on frustration might ignore the potential for growth through satisfaction (Jang et al., 2016). Accordingly, SDT postulates that the social context surrounding students plays a crucial role in meeting those needs as well as thwarting them (Campbell et al., 2018).

Competence. The need for competence is defined as the desire to effectively engage with one's environment (White, 1959). This need drives students to seek challenges slightly beyond their current abilities and to practice activities that enhance their skills. Importantly, it is not the level of ability a student achieves that matters, but rather the subjective experience of feeling competent. Given its direct connection to performance (Guay et al., 2003), satisfying this need has significant adaptive implications for students. Without the satisfaction of this need, students may be less inclined to pursue actions that help them overcome obstacles. For instance, Bureau et al.'s (2022) meta-analysis found that competence was the most important predictor of motivational outcomes across students from various age groups, and Guay et al. (2004) found that young adults who attained higher educational levels of education perceived themselves as more competent elementary school pupils a decade earlier. Thus, fulfilling the need for competence is crucial for optimal functioning in school settings.

Relatedness. The need for relatedness encompasses the necessity of forming close, secure emotional bonds with significant others and feeling part of a community (Ryan & Deci, 2017). This need helps explain why individuals have effective and harmonious interactions within their groups. Meeting the need for relatedness also enables students to develop their potential. For example, a talent for music may flourish in an environment where children feel supported by their parents, whereas conditional regard or emotionally distant parenting may hinder such potential (Roth & Assor, 2012).

Autonomy. The need for autonomy involves the necessity of experiencing choice, willingness, and volition in one's actions. Students who feel a sense of autonomy act in ways that align with their interests and values (Deci et al., 2013). This need is intricately linked to the "self," which serves as the active center for integration, initiation, and spontaneous engagement within social contexts. In SDT, this integrative process is central to the self, incorporating new functions, values, experiences, and inclinations (Ryan & Deci, 2017). When students receive support for their autonomy, they exhibit greater volition in their behaviors (Guay & Vallerand, 1996) and thoroughly internalize educational aspects that allow them to voluntarily embrace school demands and expectations. In SDT, autonomy is not synonymous with independence; individuals can be autonomously dependent on others, and autonomy is not a developmental stage but an essential aspect of life from beginning to end. Furthermore, autonomy is not equivalent to a detachment from significant relationships; numerous studies have shown that feeling accepted and connected to others enhances one's sense of autonomy (e.g., Guay et al., 2008).

Sheldon and Krieger (2007) examined the satisfaction of the three psychological needs among university law students. Law students were selected because law school is an exceptionally stressful experience. Their findings indicate that enrollment in a law school predicted diminishing levels of students' satisfaction of their psychological needs and overall well-being over the course of three years. Declines in autonomy, competence, and relatedness contributed to diminished well-being. Notably, perceived autonomy support from faculty members alleviated these declines, resulting in improved well-being. Furthermore, institutional differences were found to influence outcomes, with more controlling educational settings exacerbating negative effects. Similarly, need frustration as well as perceived need thwarting from faculty members and peers were linked to higher levels of anxiety and depression among undergraduate students (Gilbert et al., 2021; 2023a).

Basic Psychological Needs and Positive Psychology

It is essential to recognize that SDT was not specifically developed to address anxiety and depression. Rather, it aligns with the principles of the positive psychology movement, emphasizing wellness as a lifestyle in which one's human capacities are fully realized and utilized. Just as physical health relies on certain fundamental needs, psychological wellness also requires specific nutrients. According to SDT, these nutrients are the three psychological needs—competence, relatedness, and autonomy—which are viewed as crucial for well-being and optimal functioning. A primary focus of SDT is to promote the satisfaction of these essential psychological needs to foster vitality and overall wellness. The theory suggests that individuals are most engaged, thriving, and fully functional in environments that allow them to fulfill or contribute to fulfilling these needs (Ryan & Deci, 2010). Consequently, when individuals experience a state of wellness, the likelihood of developing severe and recurrent symptoms of depression and anxiety should be significantly reduced. Within the context of SDT, anxiety and depression are regarded as critical indicators that individuals have deficits in the fulfillment of their psychological needs (Vansteenkiste & Ryan, 2013).

USING SDT TO UNDERSTAND THE EFFECTS OF INDIVIDUAL, CONTEXTUAL, AND SOCIETAL FACTORS ON STUDENTS' ANXIETY AND DEPRESSION

The model illustrated in Fig. 11.1 posits that individual characteristics, contextual factors, and societal shifts can significantly impede the satisfaction of students' psychological needs, potentially resulting in controlled regulations such as external or introjected motivation types, which may ultimately contribute to anxiety and depression. In essence, the identified factors can obstruct at least one of the needs outlined by the theory. Some factors may lead individuals to experience frustration regarding a single need, while others may affect all three needs simultaneously. As previously discussed, when one or more psychological needs are thwarted, students tend to exhibit

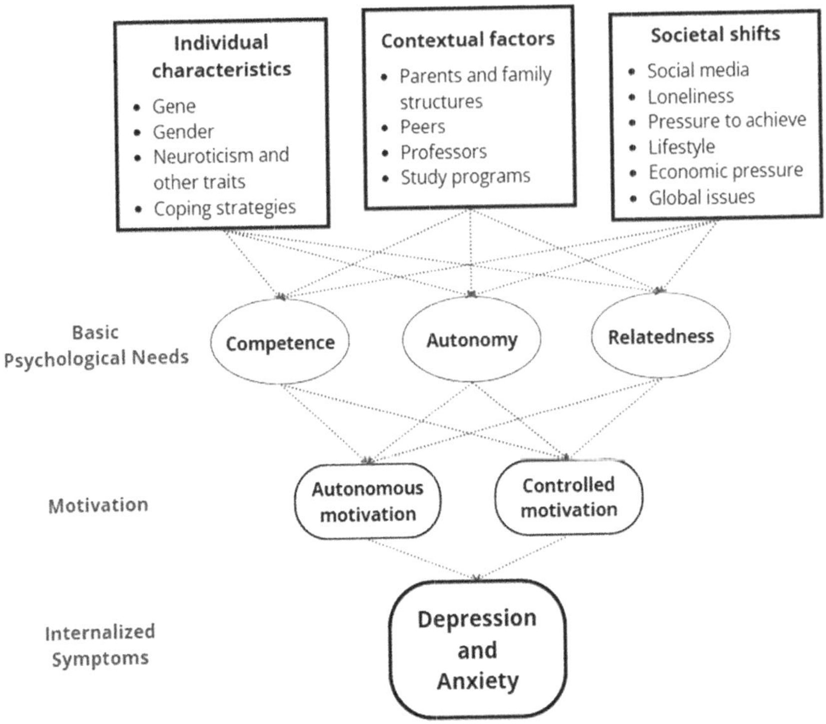

Fig. 11.1. A Model of University Students' Anxiety and Depression Based on SDT.

higher levels of controlled motivations in comparison to autonomous motivations. This experience of controlled motivations results from both internal and external pressures which can ultimately exacerbate symptoms of anxiety and depression. While it is not feasible to review all empirical studies related to the aforementioned factors, we will present selected research that has examined a few of these factors through the lens of SDT, namely neuroticism, peers and professors/program, and pressure to achieve.

Neuroticism

Van den Broeck et al. (2016) noted in their literature review that neuroticism negatively correlates with the satisfaction of the needs for autonomy, competence, and relatedness. However, the mechanisms linking neuroticism to these need-based experiences remain unclear. These mechanisms are likely varied, including the tendency to interpret stressful events more negatively. Individuals with high neuroticism may strongly believe they lack the resources to address such stressors effectively (thwarting their need for competence) and feel compelled or constrained to alleviate the debilitating and intolerable negative emotions resulting from stress (thwarting their need for autonomy). Furthermore, their ruminative thoughts, when expressed to others, may lead to a lack of perceived compassion and reduced social support (thwarting their need for relatedness). In contrast, individuals with low neuroticism tend to harbor more positive thoughts, believing they possess the inner resources to cope with stressors (fulfilling their need for competence). They often view the negative emotions arising from stressful events as normal, with the expectation that they can choose the best way to help these feelings subside over time (fulfilling their need for autonomy). Additionally, they actively seek appropriate help and do not perceive feedback from others as a threat to their relationships (fulfilling their need for relatedness).

Therefore, neuroticism constitutes a risk factor for the fulfillment of psychological needs. While genetic factors may contribute to the development of this personality trait, it is possible that parental discourse reinforcing the notion that all encountered stressors are dangerous further thwarts the psychological needs of children exposed to such beliefs. To ensure healthy functioning in the face of stressors, it is vital for parents to normalize certain stressors and assist their children in managing their negative emotions. Over time, this can significantly enhance young people's ability to proactively fulfill their own psychological needs (Laporte et al., 2021).

Peers/Professors/Programs

Gilbert, Bureau, et al. (2023) investigated whether the basic psychological needs for competence, autonomy, and relatedness serve as key mechanisms linking undergraduate students' educational experiences with their peers, professors, and study programs with various health-related outcomes, including anxiety and depression. The results from person-centered analyses revealed three distinct profiles of need satisfaction and frustration among students. Profile 1, labeled "High Need Satisfaction," included 25.04% of the sample and was characterized by above-average levels of need satisfaction and below-average levels of need frustration. Profile 2, labeled "Average Need Satisfaction," accounted for 45.34% of the sample and was defined by average levels of autonomy and competence satisfaction and frustration, alongside moderately high levels of relatedness satisfaction and moderately low levels of relatedness frustration. Lastly, Profile 3, labeled "Need Frustration," included 29.62% of the sample and featured above-average levels of need frustration coupled with below-average levels of need satisfaction. Within this profile, the need for competence was notably the most frustrated, followed by the needs for relatedness and autonomy. Overall, the findings indicated that the social and educational environments in college—specifically, the support received from peers and from different components of study programs—significantly predicted higher levels of need satisfaction (profile 1) and lower levels of need frustration (profile 3) among students. Furthermore, more adaptive profiles (1 and 2) of need satisfaction/frustration were associated with enhanced self-control, reduced anxiety and depression, and healthier lifestyle behaviors.

Overall, these results indicate that the educational context in which students engage in their studies has the potential to significantly alter their levels of anxiety and depression during their undergraduate experience. Environments that support students' needs for autonomy, competence, and relatedness are associated with reduced feelings of anxiety and depression. Conversely, contexts that frustrate these fundamental needs contribute to heightened emotional distress. This highlights the importance of creating supportive and nurturing academic environments where students feel empowered and connected. To do so, universities can implement strategies such as providing accessible mentorship programs, fostering inclusive communities, and encouraging open communication between students and faculty.

Pressure to Achieve

As previously discussed, there is a notable societal shift indicating that the current generation of students faces greater pressure to achieve than any prior generation. Not only that, but the perspective of "achieving" seems less likely for students of this generation than for those of previous ones. For instance, the concept of the American Dream—the belief that success can be attained through hard work and determination—is perceived as increasingly unattainable by younger Americans compared to their older counterparts (Borelli, 2024). This perception may be attributed to the prevailing social, economic, and political context in the United States, where well-paying jobs have become less common due to stagnant wages, the scarcity of middle-income positions, technological advancements, globalization, and the decline of labor unions. Such heightened competition can adversely affect individuals' psychological needs for autonomy and relatedness. For example, Kasser (2010) reviews various studies on capitalism and found that individuals believing in materialism, competition, and self-interest tend to experience greater pressure and coercion, thus thwarting their need for autonomy. This suggests that individuals struggle to fulfill their need for autonomy when they strongly endorse values inherent in capitalist ideology. Furthermore, concerning the need for relatedness, Gilbert et al. (2009) conducted a study involving participants diagnosed with depression. They found that when individuals feel insecure in their social environments, they may compare themselves to others, fostering a fear of rejection if they perceive themselves as inferior or subordinate. This dynamic can increase susceptibility to depression, anxiety, and stress.

Autonomous and Controlled Regulations and Their Linkages Anxiety and Depression

In the preceding section, we presented several examples derived from research findings that illustrate the connections between individual, contextual, and societal shifts and their impact on anxiety and depression. As illustrated in the model depicted in Fig. 11.1, the mechanisms underlying these effects are categorized into autonomous and controlled regulations. The detrimental influence of need thwarting on anxiety and depression can be attributed to students developing a greater reliance on controlled motivations in their academic pursuits. For instance, a meta-analysis conducted by Howard et al. (2021) identified a significant positive correlation between controlled motivations and symptoms of anxiety and depression, while revealing a negative correlation between autonomous motivation and these internalized conditions. This raises the question as to why these effects occur. Individuals behaving out of autonomous motivation have been shown to display less mental fatigue and high energy levels (Herlambang et al., 2021). Depression can also be viewed as an adaptation to conserve one's energy levels, which would support the idea that autonomous motivation reduces the likelihood of depression. Individuals behaving out of controlled regulation, on the other hand, are often motivated by the desire to attain or avoid some external contingencies and to evade negative emotions such as guilt, which can lead to feelings of helplessness and frustration. Students may experience continual pressure to meet external standards, resulting in chronic stress that contributes to increased anxiety symptoms. This type of motivation may also foster contingent self-esteem, wherein students strive to achieve specific outcomes deemed valuable by significant others, such as their parents and society at large. Consequently, these compounded external and internal pressures are likely to exacerbate symptoms of anxiety and depression.

CONCLUSION

In this chapter, we have delineated various individual, contextual, and societal factors associated with anxiety and depression, two widely recognized internalized disorders. We have provided a concise overview of SDT and analyzed several of these factors through its lens. Our primary conclusion is that these factors generally undermine the satisfaction of fundamental psychological needs for autonomy, competence, and relatedness. They also steer students from autonomous motivations and are likely to foster controlled forms of motivation in individuals' daily activities. When these activities are mostly governed by controlled motivations rather than autonomous ones, individuals are at a higher risk of experiencing anxiety and depression, as evidenced by recent meta-analytical findings (Howard et al., 2021).

Furthermore, SDT posits that the absence of anxiety and depression does not necessarily equate to a fulfilling life; rather, individuals must satisfy their psychological needs to achieve overall well-being. Notably, numerous intervention programs for schools have been established to promote these needs among pupils (Guay et al., 2016). However, similar interventions must be implemented at the university level. A broader reflection on the detrimental effects of societal shifts that have occurred over the past few decades is necessary to help university students better adapt to their academic life and beyond.

NOTE

1. Hereafter we only use university students to refer to students of both institutions.

REFERENCES

Achterbergh, L., Pitman, A., Birken, M., Pearce, E., Sno, H., & Johnson, S. (2020). The experience of loneliness among young people with depression: A qualitative meta-synthesis of the literature. *BMC Psychiatry, 20,* 1–23. https://doi.org/10.1186/s12888-020-02818-3

Alam, I., Khayri, E., Podger, T. A., Aspinall, C., Fuhrmann, D., & Lau, J. Y. (2024). A call for better research and resources for understanding and combatting youth loneliness: Integrating the perspectives of young people and researchers. *European Child & Adolescent Psychiatry, 33*(3), 939–942. https://doi.org/10.1007/s00787-022-02125-0

Arcand, M., Juster, R. P., Lupien, S. J., & Marin, M. F. (2020). Gender roles in relation to symptoms of anxiety and depression among students and workers. *Anxiety, Stress & Coping, 33*(6), 661–674. https://doi.org/10.1080/10615806.2020.1774560

Arnett, J. J., Žukauskienė, R., & Sugimura, K. (2014). The new life stage of emerging adulthood at ages 18–29 years: Implications for mental health. *The Lancet Psychiatry, 1*(7), 569–576. https://doi.org/10.1016/S2215-0366(14)00080-7

Barlow, D. H., Curreri, A. J., & Woodard, L. S. (2021). Neuroticism and disorders of emotion: A new synthesis. *Current Directions in Psychological Science, 30*(5), 410–417. https://doi.org/10.1177/09637214211030253

Bassett, D., John, D., Conger, S., Fitzhugh, E., & Coe, D. (2015). Trends in physical activity and sedentary behaviors of United States youth. *Journal of Physical Activity and Health, 12,* 1102–1111. https://doi.org/10.1123/jpah.2014-0050

Beam, C. R., & Kim, A. J. (2020). Psychological sequelae of social isolation and loneliness might be a larger problem in young adults than older adults. *Psychological Trauma. Theory, Research, Practice, and Policy, 12*(S1), S58. https://doi.org/10.1037/tra0000774

Berryhill, M., Harless, C., & Kean, P. (2018). College student cohesive-flexible family functioning and mental health. *The Family Journal, 26*, 422–432. https://doi.org/10.1177/1066480718807411

Biggs, A., Brough, P., & Drummond, S. (2023). Lazarus and Folkman's psychological stress and coping theory. In C. L. Cooper & J. Campbell Quick (Eds.), *The handbook of stress and health: A guide to research and practice* (pp. 351–364). Wiley.

BlackDeer, A., Patterson, D. S. W., Maguin, E., & Beeler-Stinn, S. (2021). Depression and anxiety among college students: Understanding the impact on grade average and differences in gender and ethnicity. *Journal of American College Health, 71*(4), 1091–1102. https://doi.org/10.1080/07448481.2021.1920954

Borelli, G. (2024, July 2). *Americans are split over the state of the American dream.* Pew Research Center. https://www.pewresearch.org/short-reads/2024/07/02/americans-are-split-over-the-state-of-the-american-dream/

Brophy, H., Olson, J., & Paul, P. (2022). Eco-anxiety in youth: An integrative literature review. *International Journal of Mental Health Nursing.* https://doi.org/10.1111/inm.13099

Bruffaerts, R., Mortier, P., Kiekens, G., Auerbach, R. P., Cuijpers, P., Demyttenaere, K., ..., & Kessler, R. C. (2018). Mental health problems in college freshmen: Prevalence and academic functioning. *Journal of Affective Disorders, 225*, 97–103. https://doi.org/10.1016/j.jad.2017.07.044

Bureau, J. S., Guay, F., Plamondon, A., Ratelle, C. F., Howard, J. L., & Gilbert, W. (2023). Empirical testing of an alternative modeling of the self-determination continuum. *Motivation and Emotion, 47*(1), 46–60. https://doi.org/10.1007/s11031-022-09976-9

Bureau, J. S., Howard, J. L., Chong, J. X., & Guay, F. (2022). Pathways to student motivation: A meta-analysis of antecedents of autonomous and controlled motivations. *Review of Educational Research, 92*(1), 46–72. https://doi.org/10.3102/00346543211042426

Burrows, T., Goldman, S., Pursey, K., & Lim, R. (2017). Is there an association between dietary intake and academic achievement: A systematic review. *Journal of Human Nutrition and Dietetics, 30*(2), 117–140. https://doi.org/10.1111/jhn.12407

Campbell, R., Boone, L., Vansteenkiste, M., & Soenens, B. (2018). Psychological need frustration as a transdiagnostic process in associations of self-critical perfectionism with depressive symptoms and eating pathology. *Journal of Clinical Psychology, 74*(10), 1775–1790. https://doi.org/10.1002/jclp.22628

Carpenter, J. K., Bragdon, L., & Pineles, S. L. (2022). Conditioned physiological reactivity and PTSD symptoms across the menstrual cycle: Anxiety sensitivity as a moderator. *Psychological Trauma. Theory, Research, Practice, and Policy, 14*(3), 453–461. https://doi.org/10.1037/tra0001129

Center for Collegiate Mental Health (CCMH). (2017). *Annual report.* Publication No. STA 18-166. https://ccmh.psu.edu/assets/docs/2017_CCMH_Report-1r4m88x.pdf

Chen, Y., Cowden, R. G., Fulks, J., Plake, J. F., & VanderWeele, T. J. (2022). National data on age gradients in well-being among US adults. *JAMA Psychiatry, 79*(10), 1046–1047. https://doi.org/10.1001/jamapsychiatry.2022.2473

Cheng, C., Ying, W. J., Ebrahimi, O. V., & Wong, K. F. E. (2023). Coping style and mental health amid the first wave of the COVID-19 pandemic: A culture-moderated meta-analysis of 44 nations. *Health Psychology Review, 18*(2), 141–164. https://doi.org/10.1080/17437199.2023.2175015

Cheng, G. H. L., & Chan, D. K. S. (2008). Who suffers more from job insecurity? A meta-analytic review. *Applied Psychology, 57*(2), 272–303. https://doi.org/10.1111/j.1464-0597.2007.00312.x

Crăciun, I. C. (2024). Learning from experience: Perceptions of socio-emotional development among German students during COVID-19. *Emerging Adulthood, 12*(3), 426–437. https://doi.org/10.1177/21676968231211961

Curcio, G., Ferrara, M., & De Gennaro, L. (2006). Sleep loss, learning capacity and academic performance. *Sleep Medicine Reviews, 10*(5), 323–337. https://doi.org/10.1016/j.smrv.2005.11.001

Curran, T., & Hill, A. P. (2019). Perfectionism is increasing over time: A meta-analysis of birth cohort differences from 1989 to 2016. *Psychological Bulletin, 145*(4), 410. https://doi.org/10.1037/bul0000138

Cvetkovski, A. F., & Mackinnon, A. J. (2018). Student psychological distress and degree dropout or completion: A discrete-time, competing risks survival analysis. *Higher Education Research and Development, 37*(3), 484–498. https://doi.org/10.1080/07294360.2017.1404557

Deasy, C., Coughlan, B., Pironom, J., Jourdan, D., & Mcnamara, P. M. (2014). Psychological distress and lifestyle of students: Implications for health promotion. *Health Promotion International, 30*(1), 77–87. https://doi.org/10.1093/heapro/dau086

Deci, E. L., & Ryan, R. M. (2000). The" what" and" why" of goal pursuits: Human needs and the self-determination of behavior. *Psychological Inquiry, 11*(4), 227–268. https://doi.org/10.1207/S15327965PLI1104_01

Deci, E. L., & Ryan, R. M. (2012). Motivation, personality, and development within embedded social contexts: An overview of self-determination theory. In R. M. Ryan (Ed.), *The Oxford handbook of human motivation* (pp. 85–107). Oxford University Press.

Deci, E. L., Ryan, R. M., & Guay, F. (2013). Self-determination theory and actualization of human potential. In D. M. McInerney, H. W. Marsh, R. G. Craven, & F. Guay (Eds.), *Theory driving research: New wave perspectives on self-processes and human development* (pp. 109–133). IAP Information Age Publishing.

Deci, E. L., Ryan, R. M., & Williams, G. C. (1996). Need satisfaction and the self-regulation of learning. *Learning and Individual Differences, 8*(3), 165–183. https://doi.org/10.1016/S1041-6080(96)90013-8

Di Placito-De Rango, M. L. (2018). Situating the post-secondary instructor in a supportive role for the mental health and well-being of students. *International Journal of Mental Health and Addiction, 16*, 284–290. https://doi.org/10.1007/s11469-017-9740-4

Drapeau, A., Marchand, A., & Beaulieu-Prévost, D. (2012). Epidemiology of psychological distress. In L. L'Abate (Ed.), *Mental illnesses-understanding, prediction and control* (pp. 105–134). IntechOpen.

Eisenberg, D., Golberstein, E., & Hunt, J. B. (2009). Mental health and academic success in college. *The B.E. Journal of Economic Analysis & Policy, 9*(1), 1–35. https://doi.org/10.2202/1935-1682.2191

Evans, T. M., Bira, L., Gastelum, J. B., Weiss, L. T., & Vanderford, N. L. (2018). Evidence for a mental health crisis in graduate education. *Nature Biotechnology, 36*(3), 282–284. https://doi.org/10.1038/nbt.4089

Flett, G. L., Hewitt, P. L., Nepon, T., Sherry, S. B., & Smith, M. (2022). The destructiveness and public health significance of socially prescribed perfectionism: A review, analysis, and conceptual extension. *Clinical Psychology Review, 93,* 102130. https://doi.org/10.1016/j.cpr.2022.102130

Gilbert, P., McEwan, K., Bellew, R., Mills, A., & Gale, C. (2009). The dark side of competition: How competitive behaviour and striving to avoid inferiority are linked to depression, anxiety, stress and self-harm. *Psychology and Psychotherapy, 82*(Pt 2), 123–136. https://doi.org/10.1348/147608308X379806

Gilbert, W., Bureau, J. S., Poellhuber, B., & Guay, F. (2021). Predicting college students' psychological distress through basic psychological need-relevant practices by teachers, peers, and the academic program. *Motivation and Emotion, 45*(4), 436–455. https://doi.org/10.1007/s11031-021-09892-4

Gilbert, W., Bureau, J. S., Poellhuber, B., & Guay, F. (2023a). Educational contexts that nurture students' psychological needs predict low distress and healthy lifestyle through facilitated self-control. *Current Psychology, 42*(33), 29661–29681. https://doi.org/10.1007/s12144-022-04019-5

Gilbert, W., Demanins, S. A., Bureau, J. S., Guay, F., & Morin, A. J. (2023b). On the nature, predictors, and outcomes of undergraduate students' psychological distress profiles. *Learning and Individual Differences, 108,* 102378. https://doi.org/10.1016/j.lindif.2023.102378

Gilbert, W., Eltanoukhi, R., Morin, A. J., & Salmela-Aro, K. (2024). Achievement goals as mediators of the links between self-esteem and depressive symptoms from mid-adolescence to early adulthood. *Journal of Youth and Adolescence,* 1–18. https://doi.org/10.1007/s10964-024-02045-z

Gioia, F., Rega, V., & Boursier, V. (2021). Problematic internet use and emotional dysregulation among young people: A literature review. *Clinical Neuropsychiatry, 18,* 41–54. https://doi.org/10.36131/cnfioritieditore20210104

Goetz, T., Lüdtke, O., Nett, U. E., Keller, M. M., & Lipnevich, A. A. (2013). Characteristics of teaching and students' emotions in the classroom: Investigating differences across domains. *Contemporary Educational Psychology, 38*(4), 383–394. https://doi.org/10.1016/j.cedpsych.2013.08.001

Goodwin, R. D., Weinberger, A. H., Kim, J. H., Wu, M., & Galea, S. (2020). Trends in anxiety among adults in the United States, 2008–2018: Rapid increases among young adults. *Journal of Psychiatric Research, 130,* 441–446. https://doi.org/10.1016/j.jpsychires.2020.08.014

Greca, A., & Harrison, H. (2005). Adolescent peer relations, friendships, and romantic relationships: Do they predict social anxiety and depression? *Journal of Clinical Child and Adolescent Psychology, 34,* 49–61. https://doi.org/10.1207/s15374424jccp3401_5

Groth, N., Schnyder, N., Kaess, M., Markovic, A., Rietschel, L., Ochsenbein, S., & Schultze-Lutter, F. (2019). Coping as a mediator between locus of control, competence beliefs, and mental health: A systematic review and structural equation modelling meta-analysis. *Behaviour Research and Therapy, 121*, 103442. https://doi.org/10.1016/j.brat.2019.103442

Guay, F., Larose, S., & Boivin, M. (2004). Academic self-concept and educational attainment level: A ten-year longitudinal study. *Self and Identity, 3*(1), 53–68. https://doi.org/10.1080/13576500342000040

Guay, F., Lessard, V., & Dubois, P. (2016). How can we create better learning contexts for children? Promoting students' autonomous motivation as a way to foster enhanced educational outcomes. In W. Liu, J. Wang, & R. Ryan (Eds.), *Building autonomous learners: Perspectives from research and practice using self-determination theory* (pp. 83–106). Springer.

Guay, F., Marsh, H. W., & Boivin, M. (2003). Academic self-concept and academic achievement: Developmental perspectives on their causal ordering. *Journal of Educational Psychology, 95*(1), 124–136. https://doi.org/10.1037/0022-0663.95.1.124

Guay, F., Marsh, H. W., Senécal, C., & Dowson, M. (2008). Representations of relatedness with parents and friends and autonomous academic motivation during the late adolescence–early adulthood period: Reciprocal or unidirectional effects? *British Journal of Educational Psychology, 78*(4), 621–637. https://doi.org/10.1348/000709908X280971

Guay, F., & Vallerand, R. J. (1996). Social context, student's motivation, and academic achievement: Toward a process model. *Social Psychology of Education, 1*(3), 211–233. https://doi.org/10.1007/BF02339891

Guerra, O., & Eboreime, E. (2021). The impact of economic recessions on depression, anxiety, and trauma-related disorders and illness outcomes—a scoping review. *Behavioral Sciences, 11*(9), 119. https://doi.org/10.3390/bs11090119

Hallers-Haalboom, E. T., Maas, J., Kunst, L. E., & Bekker, M. H. (2020). The role of sex and gender in anxiety disorders: Being scared "like a girl"? *Handbook of Clinical Neurology, 175*, 359–368. https://doi.org/10.1016/B978-0-444-64123-6.00024-2

Haq, M., Dar, I., Aslam, M., & Mahmood, Q. (2018). Psychometric study of depression, anxiety and stress among university students. *Journal of Public Health, 26*, 211–217. https://doi.org/10.1007/s10389-017-0856-6

Harra, R., & Vargas, I. (2023). A peer-based mentoring program for reducing anxiety and depression symptoms among college students: A preliminary study. *Journal of American College Health*, 1–8. https://doi.org/10.1080/07448481.2023.2172580

Herlambang, M. B., Cnossen, F., & Taatgen, N. A. (2021). The effects of intrinsic motivation on mental fatigue. *PLoS One, 16*(1), e0243754. https://doi.org/10.1371/journal.pone.0243754

Hernández-Torrano, D., Ibrayeva, L., Sparks, J., Lim, N., Clementi, A., Almukhambetova, A., ..., & Muratkyzy, A. (2020). Mental health and well-being of university students: A bibliometric mapping of the literature. *Frontiers in Psychology, 11*, 1226.

Hilty, D. M., Stubbe, D., McKean, A. J., Hoffman, P. E., Zalpuri, I., Myint, M. T., ..., & Li, S. T. T. (2023). A scoping review of social media in child, adolescents and young adults: Research findings in depression, anxiety and other clinical challenges. *BJPsych Open, 9*(5), e152. https://doi.org/10.1192/bjo.2023.523

Holt-Lunstad, J., Smith, T. B., & Layton, J. B. (2010). Social relationships and mortality risk: A meta-analytic review. *PLoS Medicine, 7*(7), e1000316. https://doi.org/10.1371/journal.pmed.1000316

Howard, J. L., Bureau, J. S., Guay, F., Chong, J. X., & Ryan, R. M. (2021). Student motivation and associated outcomes: A meta-analysis from self-determination theory. *Perspectives on Psychological Science, 16*(6), 1300–1323. https://doi.org/10.1177/1745691620966789

Howard, J. L., Gagné, M., & Bureau, J. S. (2017). Testing a continuum structure of self-determined motivation: A meta-analysis. *Psychological Bulletin, 143*(12), 1346–1377. https://doi.org/10.1037/bul0000125

Hsu, J. L., & Goldsmith, G. R. (2021). Instructor strategies to alleviate stress and anxiety among college and university STEM students. *CBE-Life Sciences Education, 20*(1), es1. https://doi.org/10.1187/cbe.20-08-0189

Hussain, Z., & Griffiths, M. D. (2021). The associations between problematic social networking site use and sleep quality, attention-deficit hyperactivity disorder, depression, anxiety and stress. *International Journal of Mental Health and Addiction, 19*(3), 686–700. https://doi.org/10.1007/s11469-019-00175-1

Hussong, A. M., Benner, A. D., Erdem, G., Lansford, J. E., Makila, L. M., & Petrie, R. C., & SRA COVID-19 Response Team. (2021). Adolescence amid a pandemic: Short and long-term implications. *Journal of Research on Adolescence, 31*(3), 820–835. https://doi.org/10.1111/jora.12671

Hysenbegasi, A., Hass, S. L., & Rowland, C. R. (2005). The impact of depression on the academic productivity of university students. *The Journal of Mental Health Policy and Economics, 8*(3), 145–151. PMID : 16278502.

Infurna, F. J., Dey, N. E., Gonzalez Avilés, T., Grimm, K. J., Lachman, M. E., & Gerstorf, D. (2024). Loneliness in midlife: Historical increases and elevated levels in the United States compared with Europe. *American Psychologist.* Advance online publication. https://doi.org/10.1037/amp0001322

Ingram, R. E., & Luxton, D. D. (2005). Vulnerability-stress models. In B. L. Hankin & J. R. Z. Abela (Eds.), *Development of psychopathology A vulnerability-stress perspective* (pp. 32–46). Sage publications.

Jang, H., Kim, E. J., & Reeve, J. (2016). Why students become more engaged or more disengaged during the semester: A self-determination theory dual-process model. *Learning and Instruction, 43*, 27–38. http://dx.doi.org/10.1016/j.learninstruc.2016.01.002

Jeronimus, B., Kotov, R., Riese, H., & Ormel, J. (2016). Neuroticism's prospective association with mental disorders halves after adjustment for baseline symptoms and psychiatric history, but the adjusted association hardly decays with time: A meta-analysis on 59 longitudinal/prospective studies with 443 313 participants. *Psychological Medicine, 46*, 2883–2906. https://doi.org/10.1017/S0033291716001653

Kalin, N. H. (2020). The critical relationship between anxiety and depression. *American Journal of Psychiatry, 177*(5), 365–367. https://doi.org/10.1176/appi.ajp.2020.20030305

Kandola, A. A., del Pozo Cruz, B., Osborn, D. P. J., Stubbs, B., Choi, K. W., & Hayes, J. F. (2021). Impact of replacing sedentary behaviour with other movement behaviours on depression and anxiety symptoms: A prospective cohort study in the UK Biobank. *BMC Medicine, 19,* 1–12. https://doi.org/10.1186/s12916-021-02007-3

Kasser, T. (2010). Capitalism and autonomy. In V. I. Chirkov, R. M. Ryan, & K. M. Sheldon (Eds.), *Human autonomy in cross-cultural context: Perspectives on the psychology of agency, freedom, and well-being* (pp. 191–206). Springer.

Kato, T. (2015). Frequently used coping scales: A meta-analysis. *Stress and Health, 31*(4), 315–323. https://doi.org/10.1002/smi.2557

Kessler, R. C., Sampson, N. A., Berglund, P., Gruber, M. J., Al-Hamzawi, A., Andrade, L., …, & Wilcox, M. A. (2015). Anxious and non-anxious major depressive disorder in the World Health Organization World Mental Health Surveys. *Epidemiology and Psychiatric Sciences, 24*(3), 210–226. https://doi.org/10.1017/S2045796015000189

Kim, T. J., & von Dem Knesebeck, O. (2015). Is an insecure job better for health than having no job at all? A systematic review of studies investigating the health-related risks of both job insecurity and unemployment. *BMC Public Health, 15,* 1–9. https://doi.org/10.1186/s12889-015-2313-1

Knipscheer, J., Sleijpen, M., Frank, L., de Graaf, R., Kleber, R., Ten Have, M., & Dückers, M. (2020). Prevalence of potentially traumatic events, other life events and subsequent reactions indicative for posttraumatic stress disorder in the Netherlands: A general population study based on the trauma screening questionnaire. *International Journal of Environmental Research and Public Health, 17*(5), 1725. https://doi.org/10.3390/ijerph17051725

Knowlden, A. P., Hackman, C. L., & Sharma, M. (2016). Lifestyle and mental health correlates of psychological distress in college students. *Health Education Journal, 75*(3), 370–382. https://doi.org/10.1177/0017896915589421

Krokstad, S., Weiss, D. A., Krokstad, M. A., Rangul, V., Kvaløy, K., Ingul, J. M., …, & Sund, E. R. (2022). Divergent decennial trends in mental health according to age reveal poorer mental health for young people: Repeated cross-sectional population-based surveys from the HUNT study, Norway. *BMJ Open, 12*(5), e057654. https://doi.org/10.1136/bmjopen-2021-057654

Laporte, N., Soenens, B., Brenning, K., & Vansteenkiste, M. (2021). Adolescents as active managers of their own psychological needs: The role of psychological need crafting in adolescents' mental health. *Journal of Adolescence, 88,* 67–83. https://doi.org/10.1016/j.adolescence.2021.02.004

Lazarus, R. S., & Folkman, S. (1984). *Stress, appraisal, and coping.* Springer publishing company.

Lechner, W. V., Laurene, K. R., Patel, S., Anderson, M., Grega, C., & Kenne, D. R. (2020). Changes in alcohol use as a function of psychological distress and social support following COVID-19 related university closings. *Addictive Behaviors, 110,* 106527. https://doi.org/10.1016/j.addbeh.2020.106527

Leow, K., Lee, M., & Lynch, M. F. (2016). Big five personality and depressive symptoms: A self-determination theory perspective on students' positive relationships with others. *Ideas and research you can use: VISTAS,* 2–11, 2016.

Li, W., Zhao, Z., Chen, D., Peng, Y., & Lu, Z. (2022). Prevalence and associated factors of depression and anxiety symptoms among college students: A systematic review and meta-analysis. *Journal of Child Psychology and Psychiatry, 63*(11), 1222–1230. https://doi.org/10.1111/jcpp.13606

Limburg, K., Watson, H. J., Hagger, M. S., & Egan, S. J. (2017). The relationship between perfectionism and psychopathology: A meta-analysis. *Journal of Clinical Psychology, 73*(10), 1301–1326. https://doi.org/10.1002/jclp.22435

Mann, F., Wang, J., Pearce, E., Ma, R., Schlief, M., Lloyd-Evans, B., ..., & Johnson, S. (2022). Loneliness and the onset of new mental health problems in the general population. *Social Psychiatry and Psychiatric Epidemiology, 57*(11), 2161–2178. https://doi.org/10.1007/s00127-022-02261-7

Martinez, S. M., Esaryk, E. E., Moffat, L., & Ritchie, L. (2021). Redefining basic needs for higher education: It's more than minimal food and housing according to California university students. *American Journal of Health Promotion, 35*(6), 818–834. https://doi.org/10.1177/0890117121992295

Middleton, K. V. (2020). The longer-term impact of COVID-19 on K–12 student learning and assessment. *Educational Measurement: Issues and Practice, 39*(3), 41–44. https://doi.org/10.1111/emip.12368

Mofatteh, M. (2021). Risk factors associated with stress, anxiety, and depression among university undergraduate students. *AIMS Public Health, 8*(1), 36. https://doi.org/10.3934/publichealth.2021004

Moran, T. P. (2016). Anxiety and working memory capacity: A meta-analysis and narrative review. *Psychological Bulletin, 142*(8), 831–864. https://doi.org/10.1037/bul0000051

Naragon-Gainey, K., & Watson, D. (2018). What lies beyond neuroticism? An examination of the unique contributions of social-cognitive vulnerabilities to internalizing disorders. *Assessment, 25*(2), 143–158. https://doi.org/10.1177/1073191116659741

Nsair, V., & Piszczek, M. (2021). Gender matters: The effects of gender and segmentation preferences on work-to-family conflict in family sacrifice climates. *Journal of Occupational and Organizational Psychology, 94*(3), 509–530. https://doi.org/10.1111/joop.12361

Otis, N., Grouzet, F. M., & Pelletier, L. G. (2005). Latent motivational change in an academic setting: A 3-year longitudinal study. *Journal of Educational Psychology, 97*(2), 170. https://doi.org/10.1037/0022-0663.97.2.170

Peltzer, K., & Pengpid, S. (2017). Loneliness: Its correlates and associations with health risk behaviours among university students in 25 countries. *Journal of Psychology in Africa, 27*(3), 247–255. https://doi.org/10.1080/14330237.2017.1321851

Penley, J. A., Tomaka, J., & Wiebe, J. S. (2002). The association of coping to physical and psychological health outcomes: A meta-analytic review. *Journal of Behavioral Medicine, 25*(6), 551–603. https://doi.org/10.1023/A:1020641400589

Pineda, D., Lozano-Jimenez, J. E., & Moreno-Murcia, J. A. (2024). Autonomy support in higher education: A key strategy for the well-being of university students. *F1000Research, 13*, 839.

Pitt, A., Oprescu, F., Tapia, G., & Gray, M. (2018). An exploratory study of students' weekly stress levels and sources of stress during the semester. *Active Learning in Higher Education, 19*, 61–75. https://doi.org/10.1177/1469787417731194

Prince, E. J., Siegel, D. J., Carroll, C. P., Sher, K. J., & Bienvenu, O. J. (2021). A longitudinal study of personality traits, anxiety, and depressive disorders in young adults. *Anxiety, Stress & Coping, 34*(3), 299–307. https://doi.org/10.1080/10615806.2020.1845431

Revollar, C., Yañez, G., & Sarmiento, P. (2023). Family social climate and anxiety, depression and stress in university students in times of covid-19. *Nursing & Care Open Access Journal.* https://doi.org/10.15406/ncoaj.2023.09.00260

Riad, A., Drobov, A., Krobot, M., Alkasaby, M., Peřina, A., & Košč, M. (2022). Mental health burden of the Russian–Ukrainian War 2022 (RUW-22): Anxiety and depression levels among young adults in central Europe. *International Journal of Environmental Research and Public Health, 19*(14), 8418. https://doi.org/10.3390/ijerph19148418

Ribeiro, I. J., Pereira, R., Freire, I. V., de Oliveira, B. G., Casotti, C. A., & Boery, E. N. (2018). Stress and quality of life among university students: A systematic literature review. *Health Professions Education, 4*(2), 70–77. https://doi.org/10.1016/j.hpe.2017.03.002

Romero, D., Riggs, S., & Ruggero, C. (2015). Coping, family social support, and psychological symptoms among student veterans. *Journal of Counseling Psychology, 62*(2), 242–252. https://doi.org/10.1037/cou0000061

Roth, G., & Assor, A. (2012). The costs of parental pressure to express emotions: Conditional regard and autonomy support as predictors of emotion regulation and intimacy. *Journal of Adolescence, 35*(4), 799–808. https://doi.org/10.1016/j.adolescence.2011.11.005

Ryan, R. M., & Connell, J. P. (1989). Perceived locus of causality and internalization: Examining reasons for acting in two domains. *Journal of Personality and Social Psychology, 57*(5), 749. https://doi.org/10.1037/0022-3514.57.5.749

Ryan, R. M., & Deci, E. L. (2000). Intrinsic and extrinsic motivations: Classic definitions and new directions. *Contemporary Educational Psychology, 25*(1), 54–67. https://doi.org/10.1006/ceps.1999.1020

Ryan, R. M., & Deci, E. L. (2010). A self-determination theory perspective on social, institutional, cultural, and economic supports for autonomy and their importance for well-being. In V. I. Chirkov, R. M. Ryan, & K. M. Sheldon (Eds.), *Human autonomy in cross-cultural context: Perspectives on the psychology of agency, freedom, and well-being* (pp. 45–64). Springer.

Ryan, R. M., & Deci, E. L. (2017). *Self-determination theory: Basic psychological needs in motivation, development, and wellness.* Guilford publications.

Santomauro, D. F., Herrera, A. M. M., Shadid, J., Zheng, P., Ashbaugh, C., Pigott, D. M., ..., & Ferrari, A. J. (2021). Global prevalence and burden of depressive and anxiety disorders in 204 countries and territories in 2020 due to the COVID-19 pandemic. *The Lancet, 398*(10312), 1700–1712. https://doi.org/10.1016/S0140-6736(21)02143-7

Santos, C. E., Galligan, K., Pahlke, E., & Fabes, R. A. (2013). Gender-typed behaviors, achievement, and adjustment among racially and ethnically diverse boys during early adolescence. *American Journal of Orthopsychiatry, 83*, 252.

Satinsky, E. N., Kimura, T., Kiang, M. V., Abebe, R., Cunningham, S., Lee, H., ..., & Tsai, A. C. (2021). Systematic review and meta-analysis of depression, anxiety, and suicidal ideation among Ph. D. students. *Scientific Reports, 11*(1), 14370. https://doi.org/10.1038/s41598-021-93687-7

Schiele, M. A., Reif, A., Lin, J., Alpers, G. W., Andersson, E., Andersson, G., ..., & Lueken, U. (2021). Therapygenetic effects of 5-HTTLPR on cognitive-behavioral therapy in anxiety disorders: A meta-analysis. *European Neuropsychopharmacology, 44*, 105–120. https://doi.org/10.1016/j.euroneuro.2021.01.004

Schulenberg, J. E., Sameroff, A. J., & Cicchetti, D. (2004). The transition to adulthood as a critical juncture in the course of psychopathology and mental health. *Development and Psychopathology, 16*(4), 799–806. https://doi.org/10.10170S0954579404040015

Scott, H. (2004). Reconceptualizing the nature and health consequences of work-related insecurity for the new economy: The decline of workers' power in the flexibility regime. *International Journal of Health Services, 34*, 143–153. https://doi.org/10.2190/WAM3-MNN2-6UNF-FDEX

Seligman, M. E. (1990). Why is there so much depression today? The waxing of the individual and the waning of the commons. In R. E. Ingram (Ed.), *Contemporary psychological approaches to depression: Theory, research, and treatment* (pp. 1–9). Springer US.

Sharp, J., & Theiler, S. (2018). A review of psychological distress among university students: Pervasiveness, implications and potential points of intervention. *International Journal for the Advancement of Counselling, 40*, 193–212. https://doi.org/10.1007/s10447-018-9321-7

Sheldon, K. M., & Krieger, L. S. (2007). Understanding the negative effects of legal education on law students: A longitudinal test of self-determination theory. *Personality and Social Psychology Bulletin, 33*(6), 883–897.

Skrove, M., Romundstad, P., & Indredavik, M. (2013). Resilience, lifestyle and symptoms of anxiety and depression in adolescence: The Young-HUNT study. *Social Psychiatry and Psychiatric Epidemiology, 48*, 407–416. https://doi.org/10.1007/s00127-012-0561-2

Smith, M. M., Vidovic, V., Sherry, S. B., & Saklofske, D. H. (2017). Self-oriented perfectionism and socially prescribed perfectionism add incrementally to the prediction of suicide ideation beyond hopelessness: A meta-analysis of 15 studies. In *Handbook of suicidal behaviour* (pp. 349–369). https://doi.org/10.1007/978-981-10-4816-6_19

Sparks, K., Faragher, B., & Cooper, C. L. (2001). Well-being and occupational health in the 21st century workplace. *Journal of Occupational and Organizational Psychology, 74*(4), 489–509. https://doi.org/10.1348/096317901167497

Stephenson, E., & DeLongis, A. (2020). Coping strategies. In K. Sweeny, M. L. Robbins, & L. M. Cohen (Eds.), *The Wiley encyclopedia of health psychology* (pp. 55–60). John Wiley & Sons Ltd.

Swenson, L., Nordstrom, A., & Hiester, M. (2008). The role of peer relationships in adjustment to college. *Journal of College Student Development, 49*(6), 551–567. https://doi.org/10.1353/CSD.0.0038

Tang, F., Byrne, M., & Qin, P. (2018). Psychological distress and risk for suicidal behavior among university students in contemporary China. *Journal of Affective Disorders, 228*, 101–108. https://doi.org/10.1016/j.jad.2017.12.005

Thorp, J. G., Campos, A. I., Grotzinger, A. D., Gerring, Z. F., An, J., Ong, J. S., ..., & Derks, E. M. (2021). Symptom-level modelling unravels the shared genetic architecture of anxiety and depression. *Nature Human Behaviour, 5*(10), 1432–1442. https://doi.org/10.1038/s41562-021-01094-9

Tian, S., Zhang, T., Chen, X., & Pan, C. (2021). Substance use and psychological distress among school-going adolescents in 41 low-income and middle-income countries. *Journal of Affective Disorders, 291*, 254–260. https://doi.org/10.1016/j.jad.2021.05.024

Van den Broeck, A., Ferris, D. L., Chang, C. -H., & Rosen, C. C. (2016). A review of self-determination theory's basic psychological needs at work. *Journal of Management, 42*, 1195–1229. https://doi.org/10.1177/0149206316632058

Vansteenkiste, M., & Ryan, R. M. (2013). On psychological growth and vulnerability: Basic psychological need satisfaction and need frustration as a unifying principle. *Journal of Psychotherapy Integration, 23*(3), 263–280. https://doi.org/10.1037/a0032359

Vasconcellos, D., Parker, P. D., Hilland, T., Cinelli, R., Owen, K. B., Kapsal, N., …, & Lonsdale, C. (2020). Self-determination theory applied to physical education: A systematic review and meta-analysis. *Journal of Educational Psychology, 112*(7), 1444–1469. https://doi.org/10.1037/edu0000420

Whatnall, M., Ashton, L., Patterson, A., Smith, J., Duncan, M., Burrows, T., Kay-Lambkin, F., & Hutchesson, M. (2024). Are health behaviors associated with academic performance among tertiary education students? A systematic review of cohort studies. *Journal of American College Health, 72*(3) 957–969. https://doi.org/10.1080/07448481.2022.2063024

White, R. W. (1959). Motivation reconsidered: The concept of competence. *Psychological Review, 66*(5), 297–333. https://doi.org/10.1037/h0040934

Williams, A. L., Craske, M. G., Mineka, S., & Zinbarg, R. E. (2020). Neuroticism and the longitudinal trajectories of anxiety and depressive symptoms in older adolescents. *Journal of Abnormal Psychology, 130*(2), 126. https://doi.org/10.1037/abn0000638

Wittenborn, A. K., Lachmar, E. M., Huerta, P., Mitchell, E. A., & Tseng, C. F. (2020). Global epidemiology, etiology, and treatment: Depressive and anxiety disorders across the lifespan. In K. S. Wampler, M. Rastogi, & R. Singh (Eds.). *The handbook of systemic family therapy* (Vol. 4, pp. 243–265). https://doi.org/10.1002/9781119438519.ch92

Xin, Z., Zhang, L., & Liu, D. (2010). Birth cohort changes of Chinese adolescents' anxiety: A cross-temporal meta-analysis, 1992–2005. *Personality and Individual Differences, 48*(2), 208–212. https://doi.org/10.1016/j.paid.2009.10.010

CHAPTER 12

A SET OF PROPOSITIONS ABOUT TEACHER SELF-CONCEPT[1]

John Hattie
University of Melbourne, Australia

Michael Witter
Australian Catholic University, Australia

ABSTRACT

This paper addresses the underexplored domain of teacher self-concept by introducing the ROPE model—a process-oriented framework that conceptualizes self-concept as a dynamic interplay of motivations, beliefs, and attributes. The proposal is that teacher self-concept is primarily driven by two core motivational strands: self-improving (seeking growth and feedback to enhance impact) and self-aligning (seeking confirmation and consistency with existing self-views). The ROPE model weaves together three levels—motivations (strands), beliefs (yarns), and attributes (fibers)—to illustrate how teachers form, maintain, and enact their professional identities. Part I outlines the theoretical foundations and structure of the ROPE model; Part II explores how self-improving and self-aligning orientations manifest in classroom practice, pedagogical choices, student engagement, and adaptability; and Part III discusses implications for teacher recruitment, professional development, performance appraisal, and future research.

Keywords: Teacher self-concept; ROPE model; motivation; beliefs; attributes

The Self in Context, pages 399–437

Published under exclusive licence by Emerald Publishing Limited
doi:10.1108/978-1-80686-869-820261012

Roche and Marsh (2000) argued that teacher self-concept shares common traits with the well-established student self-concept literature, including its multidimensionality, the process of self-perception compared to some frame of reference, and the development of self-concept as conditioned by feedback and experience - such that teachers become progressively more aware of their strengths and weaknesses over time, and are more likely to have self-concepts that align with external ratings and appraisal if they receive such feedback regularly. While a large literature exists on student self-concept, a surprisingly limited corpus of studies on teacher self-concept is available. To the best of our knowledge, there is no well-established equivalent model to the Shavelson et al. model of equivalent teacher model self-concept structure (Marsh & Shavelson, 1985; Marsh et al., 2019; Shavelson et al., 1976).

There is, however, a rich literature on teacher self-efficacy; nevertheless, critical distinctions exist between self-concept and self-efficacy (Hussain et al., 2022; Morris et al., 2017). Marsh et al. (2019) conducted the most extensive study to date that distinguishes between teacher self-concept and self-efficacy. While the two terms have much in common, self-concept is more descriptive, evaluative, and based on past accomplishments, whereas self-efficacy is constructed to be prospective (What can I do); and the presence of frame of reference effects (social and dimensional comparisons) influence self-concept but not self-efficacy.

Yeung et al. (2014) defined teacher self-concept as "teachers' self-perceptions of their own teaching effectiveness." Yeung et al. argued that these perceptions are influenced by whether teachers prioritize teaching or learning. This distinction led to a distinction between a teacher-centered and student-centered approach, with implications for student engagement and deep learning. They also emphasized the importance of teachers' beliefs, particularly their growth versus fixed mindsets, regarding students' capacity for learning. Using data from 208 teachers and an adapted version of the Marsh Self-Description Questionnaire (Marsh et al., 1983), they examined three key areas: the value teachers place on student engagement (Value), their beliefs about fixed ability (Beliefs), and their orientation (Student- or teacher-centered). Results indicated a positive relationship between self-concept and valuing of learning, a higher value placed on student engagement, and a negative relationship between valuing learning and fixed ability beliefs. They concluded that understanding teachers' self-concepts and value beliefs is essential for facilitating student learning.

Glotova and Wilhelm (2014) highlighted the critical influence of teachers' self-concept on various teaching dimensions. Teachers with high self-esteem demonstrated superior interpersonal and emotional skills, including adaptability, emotional regulation, conflict management, listening, and empathy. They engaged more effectively in dialog, motivated and inspired students, set strategic goals, and exhibited a growth-oriented mindset. In contrast, teachers with low self-esteem struggled with emotional control, communication, and flexibility, often reacting rather than proactively managing classroom situations. These findings underscore the pivotal role of self-concept in developing essential teaching competencies and enhancing overall classroom effectiveness. Similarly, Lohbeck et al. (2018) identified six dimensions of teachers' self-concepts—pedagogical skills, content knowledge, consulting, innovation, media use, and diagnostics—all of which were positively linked to teaching enjoyment and negatively correlated with anxiety and anger. Paulick et al. (2016) further examined the interplay between preservice teachers' professional knowledge and self-concept, arguing that pedagogical, psychological, and content knowledge domains significantly influence their teaching effectiveness. Lauermann and ten Hagen (2021) noted a significant research gap in the empirical study of teacher self-concept, particularly in its connection to student outcomes in primary and secondary classrooms. Synthesizing limited research, they claimed that teacher self-concept encompasses interpersonal skills (e.g., communication and empathy), emotional regulation, pedagogical expertise (e.g., diagnostics and innovation), and evaluative practices (e.g., goal setting and strategic thinking).

This paper presents a set of propositions about teachers' self-concept, drawing from social science research on the primary motivations behind self-perception (Swann & Buhrmester, 2015; Swann & Read, 1981; Swann et al., 1989), as well as evidence from studies within the teacher literature. However, all claims must be open to falsification, and there is a great need for empirical evaluation of the claims. The paper is divided into three parts. Part I reviews the existing literature on teacher self-concept, differentiates it from self-efficacy, and introduces the three levels of the ROPE model (motivations, Beliefs, and Attributes) as an alternative to structural self-concept models. Part II establishes differences between self-improvers, self-aligners, self-achievers, and self-sustainers based on beliefs and attributes. Part III discusses how the ROPE model can inform teacher recruitment, professional development, and performance appraisal while also identifying key research questions for further empirical validation. The paper concludes that fostering a self-improving orientation in teachers' self-concept—where feedback, adaptability, and learning and impact-centered approaches are prioritized—maximizes teacher effectiveness and student outcomes, making it a crucial area for future research and policy development.

PART I. A ROPE PROCESS MODEL OF TEACHER SELF-CONCEPT

A substantial body of research has explored the structure of self-concept, identifying numerous dimensions that shape an individual's understanding of themselves (Hattie, 1992; Marsh et al., 2002, 2012). However, fewer studies have explored the processes that link these dimensions to form a cohesive picture of a person's self-concept or predict how someone might respond based on their strengths across these dimensions (Hattie, 1992, 2004). By "processes," we refer to the psychological mechanisms and actions through which teachers strive to maintain or enhance their self-concept and self-esteem. These processes are dynamic, encompassing cognitive, emotional, and behavioral responses to external feedback, social interactions, and internal self-perceptions. They capture how teachers interpret, respond to, and integrate their experiences to align with their self-views or to enhance their sense of worth.

Unlike structural models (e.g., Marsh-Shavelson, & Yeung et al. model), which conceptualize self-concept as a top-down or bottom-up collection of dimensions (e.g., pedagogical skills, subject expertise, or interpersonal abilities), the ROPE model emphasizes processes—the motivations, beliefs, and attributes that shape how teachers interpret and respond to feedback, challenges, and student outcomes. This process-oriented approach acknowledges that self-concept is not a fixed entity but rather an ongoing, adaptive system, driven by four major motivational forces: self-improving (seeking growth and adaptation) and self-aligning (maintaining consistency and reinforcing existing beliefs), self-achieving (focusing on high performance and outcomes through structure, order, and consistency) and self-sustaining (maintaining wellbeing and protecting personal balance). By focusing on the flow of self-concept through interwoven fibers, yarns, and strands, the ROPE model more effectively captures the complex, situation-dependent nature of teaching, providing deeper insights into why some teachers adopt change and maximize student impact. In contrast, others resist innovation and focus on preserving established practices. This shift from a static structure to a dynamic process enables a more nuanced and actionable understanding of how teacher self-concept shapes classroom effectiveness, professional growth, and student success.

James (1890, p. 56) aptly observed that humans are "choosers," constantly seeking to impose order and coherence on the events they encounter. To survive and thrive, individuals must derive meaning from their experiences to understand and anticipate them, thereby exerting some control over the complexities of life. This involves making choices about how to interpret events, select courses of action, and evaluate outcomes. These choices shape not only how individuals process their experiences but also how they maintain a coherent sense of self and adapt to the demands of their environment.

The *first* premise of the "ROPE" model relates to the maxim by Wittgenstein (1958) that the strength in the ROPE "lies not in one fiber running throughout its length, but in the overlapping of many fibers" (Section 67). The *second* premise is that there are various "strands" of self-concept that serve as primary motives, leading to the invocation of situation-specific self-beliefs (or "yarns"), such as beliefs about education and those relating to personal agency and responsibility. In turn, these beliefs relate to various attributes ("fibers") that serve our self-motivations, thereby bringing meaning, predictability, or sense to our sense of self-concept and self-esteem. Hence, the ROPE model works in a series of interweaving threads to form fibers and strands, creating a sense of continuity within ourselves.

Hattie (1992, 2004) outlined a more generic ROPE model of self-concept. He outlined various self-strategies we use to protect, present, preserve, and promote our sense of self to "back ourselves," i.e., maintain a sense of self-esteem—or, to purloin Marsh's terms, to reflect glory about ourselves. The primary level was the motivations that influence the choice of strategies that are used to "negotiate demands in their environment, and these strategies in turn influence their behavior within this environment" (Buss & Cantor, 1989). Then, the more situation-specific orientations or dispositions that our overarching belief of self is somehow maintained (e.g., self-efficacy, performance vs learning strategies, personal control). The third level includes more specific strategies such as self-handicapping, setting low expectations, discounting or distorting, perfectionism, social comparison, and self-monitoring. Under the ROPE model, the process of integration stems from the interlinking of various strategies across the three levels. The Level One strategies are more enduring, whereas Level Three strategies are more dependent on time, situation, cost of processing and integrating, and whether the processing is private or public (For an example of a ROPE model in a different context, see Scarborough (2001) Reading ROPE model.)

Primary to this teacher self-concept ROPE model is that self-concept relates more to how we select, bias, and interpret the information we receive. It is neither a set of faculties nor subdimensions (as the Shavelson et al. model proclaims) but a set of strategies and processes akin to many overlapping fibers which form yarns and then into strands. The search should be for the flow, the directions, the degrees of overlap or integration, and the goals of the self that is then situationally invoked in a time, place, culture, and with others. Self-concept is more a part of goal-strivings than a set of dimensions.

There is a long history of seeking differing motivations to form self-concepts, although the terms and their definitions have slightly differed. Festinger (1954) introduced his social comparison theory, emphasizing that individuals compare themselves to others to evaluate their abilities and opinions. Festinger identified two motives: self-improvement, where individuals strive to grow or improve, and self-enhancement, where they seek to protect their self-esteem by favoring comparisons that cast them in a positive light. Swann (2012) used the terms "self-verification" or "motivation for consistency," as individuals seek feedback that aligns with their existing self-views, whether positive or negative, to maintain stability and coherence in their identity. In contrast to self-verifiers, self-enhancers are driven by a need to boost their self-esteem and project a favorable self-image, often prioritizing positive feedback and emotional gratification over accuracy.

Two of the motivations used in this chapter (self-enhancing and self-alignment) differ somewhat from Swann's notions of self-enhancement and self-verification. Swann sees self-enhancement as those who seek positive feedback to boost their self-esteem and maintain a positive image (and reject views not consistent with these beliefs), and self-verification as those who seek confirmation of their existing self-views because of their need for predictability and coherence. We use the notion of self-improvement as the claim that the primary motive is to receive feedback and construct situations where teachers can then improve their teaching mission. In contrast, we use self-aligners as those who seek to verify their current beliefs about themselves as effective teachers and align with their concepts of their "best" or "ideal" self.

Möller and Marsh (2013) expanded the understanding of comparison processes by introducing dimensional comparison theory. They showed how individuals compare social, temporal, and dimensional comparisons to self-evaluate, self-enhance, self-maintain, and self-improve. They noted that particular motivations for dimensional comparison may be triggered in different situations, and

> ...people need to compare their abilities in different domains to identify their strengths and weaknesses. Self-enhancement, self-maintenance, and self-improvement motivations may trigger dimensional comparisons when the affective quality of the target, as an aspect of the self under consideration, is negative rather than positive. Dimensional comparison with a better off domain may help enhance, compensate, or maintain self-worth and mood and improve achievement in the target domain. (p. 555)

Somewhat similarly, Ryan and Deci's (2017) self-determination theory highlights the interplay between self-growth and the need for affirmation and external validation, and Heine et al. (1999) showed significant cultural variations in privileging self-improvement (more so in Western cultures) or self-alignment (more so in Eastern countries; see below for more extensive description of aligners and improvers), but this often ignores the high variability within these cultures (Shulruf et al., 2011).

Fig. 12.1 illustrates the three major aspects of the ROPE model, which encompasses four primary self-motivations, various beliefs, and four sets of attributes that collectively form a teacher's self-concept. Each level is more differentiated and specific, and continuity of self-concept is provided by the various motivations that lead to the selection or invocation of situation-specific orientations, resulting in different self-strategies. The highest level identifies four major self-motivations: to self-improve (to seek evidence to improve), to self-align (to seek evidence to support and enhance our current beliefs about ourselves), to self-sustain (to minimize risk, maintain well-being, and preserve personal balance), and to self-achiever (to seek order, control, and consistency through structured routines and clear expectations). These influence our beliefs (the yarns) about our teaching and ourselves as

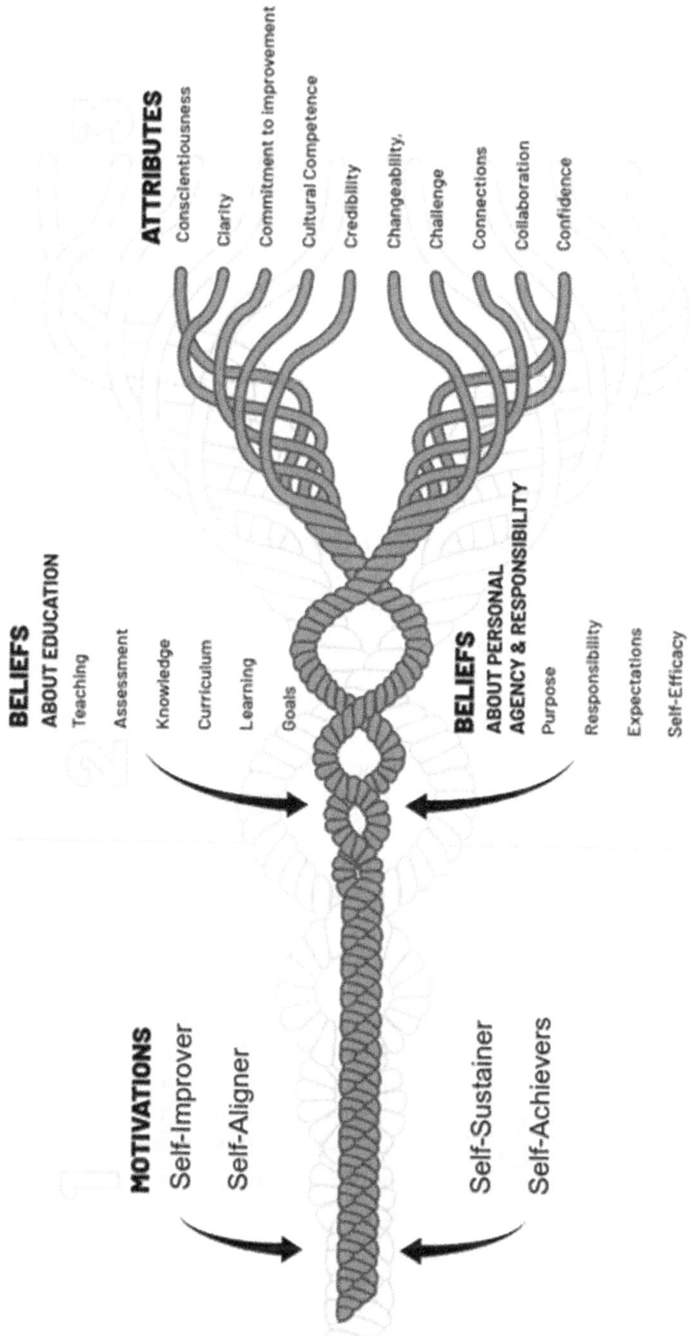

Fig. 12.1. An Illustrated ROPE Model of Teacher Self-Concept.

teachers. In turn, these beliefs influence the four sets of Attributes that shape how we think, make decisions, and interpret our impact on students (the fibers).

The attributes (fibers) are akin to Hidi and Renninger's (2006) notion of that which "triggers situational interest"; that is, the initial spark of curiosity or attention, often elicited by novel, surprising, or personally relevant stimuli. This phase is typically short-lived and externally driven, capturing an individual's immediate focus. The beliefs (yarns) are more akin to "maintained situational interest," which involves the subsequent phase where attention and engagement are sustained over a more extended period. This maintenance is facilitated by meaningful and relevant tasks that encourage deeper involvement. The progression from triggered to maintained interest is crucial for fostering deeper, more enduring forms of the teacher's self-concept. There is a hierarchy with strands at the top level, yarns in between, and fibers at the lowest level: Strands impact yarns, and yarns impact fibers.

The Primary Motives of Teacher Self-Concept

The argument is that teachers use a combination of four primary motivations—self-improving, self-aligning, self-achiever, or self-sustaining—to protect, present, preserve, and promote their sense of self when making social comparisons with others. While many teachers may have a dominant motivation, all have a profile across these four, and the primary motivation may change depending on the situation. These four primary motivations act as buffers against the constant inflow and outflow of information, defining teachers' orientations or dispositions and helping them deal with conflicting self-beliefs. Although situationally influenced, these motivations are enduring, providing consistency and predictability in managing self-concept and maintaining identity.

Self-improving assumes that teachers are highly motivated to increase their feelings of personal worth. Self-improvers project optimism about future outcomes, present themselves positively, and are strongly influenced by feedback—positive evaluations enhance their mood, while negative evaluations are interpreted as opportunities for improvement. Their motivation fosters emotional resilience, better coping strategies, and a proactive approach to goal pursuit. By prioritizing accuracy over positivity, they position themselves for long-term growth, improved problem-solving, and authentic relationships. They are more likely to accept and learn from negative feedback, enabling them to confront challenges realistically and seek practical solutions. In teaching, self-improvers are more likely to adopt a learning orientation, utilizing feedback to refine their teaching practices and enhance their impact on students. They are more willing to seek, accept, and address evidence about their effectiveness, whether it pertains to what they taught well, whom they taught effectively, or areas needing improvement. This reflective approach enhances their capacity to adapt and improve, ultimately benefiting students.

Self-aligning involves motives aimed at preserving firmly held self-views by seeking feedback that confirms existing self-perceptions, whether positive or negative. Self-aligners actively solicit feedback that aligns with their self-conceptions, paying closer attention to and recalling confirming feedback better. They regard such feedback as more accurate, credible, and diagnostic, attributing it to their dispositions. Moreover, they ensure others perceive them in ways consistent with their self-views, even if this means accepting critical or negative evaluations. Self-aligners value consistency and predictability in their self-conceptions, often gravitating toward relationships and environments that reinforce their identity. However, self-aligners may struggle with overconfidence, reject critical feedback, and miss opportunities for growth. Their reliance on positive feedback can make them emotionally vulnerable to criticism, limiting their ability to confront challenges realistically.

Self-achieving involves emphasizing accuracy and maintaining order, completing or "ticking off" tasks, meticulously planning lessons, monitoring progress and documenting achievement. These teachers prioritize control, routine and achievement in the classroom environment, providing clarity, maintaining student compliance and measuring outcomes. They strongly emphasize structured teaching, aligning with a preference for clarity and control. They see errors as disruptions or failures to be minimized, and strive for consistency and predictability in self-conceptions. They can be very sensitive to context, allowing them to deliver the curriculum most efficiently while maintaining order.

Self-sustaining involves a drive to manage energy and time effectively, ensuring personal balance and resilience by keeping things as simple as possible and sticking to tried-and-true methods. They prioritize avoiding perceived threats to their sense of self and overall well-being, and avoid risk by preferring safe tasks for themselves and their students to minimize failure. They tend to downplay, deflect, or dismiss criticism, seeking stability and coherence in their self-views, and finding comfort in familiar routines, while resisting changes that might disrupt their equilibrium. They often engage in self-handicapping, such as setting low goals or finding excuses in others or resources for potential failures, to protect against disappointment.

The first two motivations are more improvement and achievement driven (and aligners come close to improvers if the programs being implemented are similar, although aligners will more willingly adopt school-mandated programs even when they are less impactful). The second two motivations are more preservation and avoidance-driven. Self-aligners and self-achievers are more outward and externally focused, whereas self-improvers and self-sustainers are more inward and internally focused (Table 12.1).

TABLE 12.1 The Four Primary Motivations Classified by Two Drives and Two Foci.

	Outward/External Focus	Inward/Internal Focus
	Self-aligners	*Self-improver*
Improvement/ Achievement driven	Standard focused	Growth seeker
	Outcome-oriented	Adaptable
	Feedback confirming	Authentic confidence
	Structured communicator	Problem solver
	Rule follower	Learning oriented
	Risk adverse	Collaborator
	Self-achiever	*Self-sustainer*
Presentation/ Avoidance driven	Outcome driven	Workload manager
	Routine oriented	Stress avoidant
	External recognition seeking	Risk minimizing
	Error minimizing	Sensitive to criticism
	Predictability seeking	Preference for predictability
	Compliance focused	Low expectations

The primary difference lies in their motivational focus: Self-improvers prioritize emotional gratification, and maintaining a favorable self-image. These teachers are more likely to demonstrate high self-efficacy, reflective practice, and a learning orientation. These traits enable them to adapt and improve based on feedback, ultimately improving their teaching impact. Self-aligners prioritize accuracy, stability, and consistency. They seek feedback that aligns with their self-views, even if it is negative, to reinforce their identity and support personal growth. Teachers with a self-aligning orientation may focus more on external validation and performance, with less emphasis on continuous improvement. Self-achievers are more order-driven, preferring routines and structure. They are also outcome driven, both in terms of accomplishing tasks and achieving clear learning outcomes. Self-sustainers regard prioritizing their workload as manageable, aim to reduce stress for themselves and their students, minimize risk by providing work that is neither too difficult nor too challenging, and are sensitive if not defensive to criticism.

All four motivations employ a variety of self-strategies, but the self-improving motivation tends to foster a more enduring and transformative approach to teaching. While self-aligners may excel in maintaining emotional resilience and motivation, self-improvers are better equipped for long-term growth and authentic relationships with their students. In educational contexts, self-improvers are more likely to have a significant impact on students due to their willingness to accept and act upon critical feedback about their teaching effectiveness, and their orientation toward mastery over performance. Self-achievers may also be impactful teachers, given their emphasis on effective performance and demonstrating success in concrete terms, but their overemphasis on external outcomes may diminish their investment in relationships with students and make them more susceptible to stress or burnout if their achievement goals are not met. Self-achievers prefer the autonomy of their class, are less likely to be collaborative as they value their independence, and fit school mandates and policies into their existing ways of working, while appearing to be very compliance-oriented. Self-sustainers are excellent managers of their time, resources, and procedures, continually finding ways to balance their workload and personal well-being. They want "more of the same" as they believe their methods have continued to work and there is little reason to change them.

A fundamental premise is that self-improvers are more likely to have a higher impact on students, particularly as they are more adept at employing a more expansive repertoire of self-strategies to protect, present, preserve, and promote their sense of self. They are more likely to accept and integrate negative feedback as part of a broader, resilient self-conception, set high expectations and challenging goals that foster growth and learning (learning orientation), exhibit high personal control, relying less on external validation and more on intrinsic motivation, and engage in fewer avoidance strategies such as discounting or social comparison (see Caprara et al., 2006; Herman et al., 2018; Schwarzer & Hallum, 2008).

Self-aligners can have a similar high impact on students, provided the programs they implement are aligned with evidence-informed best practices. Such alignment reduces the discrimination between aligners and improvers, although aligners are more closely tied to covering the curriculum, as that is the system's mandate. They are less receptive to improvement once they have established a pattern of classroom interaction and practices than those who are improvers, and soon revert to preferring routines and risk-averse interactions.

Self-aligners and self-sustainers are more likely to engage in self-concept protection, relying on defensive and protective self-strategies to shield themselves from perceived threats to their sense of self. Their strategies are often geared toward self-protection rather than growth. Self-sustainers are more likely to engage in self-handicapping, such as setting low goals or creating excuses for potential failures, to protect against disappointment, exhibit a performance orientation, focusing on external validation rather than intrinsic learning, experience uncertain personal control, leading to reliance on external attributions for failures, use strategies like discounting, distortion, and high levels of social comparison to minimize the impact of negative feedback, and avoid risk and prefer safe tasks to prevent failure, which limits growth opportunities. These tendencies make them less likely to assimilate negative feedback into a cohesive self-view, instead of avoiding, distorting, or diminishing its importance (Bernichon et al., 2003).

While we argue that there are four primary motives, it is critical to note (as Möller & Marsh, 2013 did) that there can be occasions when a teacher, for example, who is predominantly a self-improver, moves more toward a self-aligning or self-achiever motive (e.g., when teaching out-of-field). There may be greater self-alignment in the earlier years of teaching, and a transition to a more self-improving concept of self with more experience (very few start as self-achievers or self-sustainers). Teachers may have a primary motivation in their professional teaching lives but not necessarily transfer this to their home, relationship, or leisure situations; or they might prioritize self-improving to maintain self-concept consistency but switch to self-aligning when it benefits their social standing or emotional well-being (and similarly a self-aligner may invoke self-improving motivations in some specific instances). Thus, these four primary motivations do not always dominate how we choose to act and think, but significantly influence our thoughts and actions. They are more guiding forces that provide an impetus for action but do not solely determine the outcomes; they form a profile, although one or two motivations may dominate. They serve as drivers and strivings rather than fixed ways of doing and thinking. There can be substantial within-person variability in our dominance of these four motivators, but one or the other tends to be prioritized, allowing us to identify teachers who are more self-improvers than others who are more self-aligners, self-sustainers, or self-achievers.

Across all the foci within this study, Table 12.2 highlights the differences between improvers, aligners, achievers, and sustainers.

Beliefs

Research on teacher beliefs emerged as early as the 1950s and has steadily become a significant topic in educational research. Fives and Buehl (2012) characterized teacher beliefs as filters, frames, and guides for teachers. Beliefs thus take on both a retrospective role in contributing to interpreting past experiences and a prospective role in influencing teachers' future personal actions. Fenstermacher (1978) argued that efforts to promote effective teaching were inextricably linked to teachers' beliefs, which he suggested were key mediators of instructional choices and actions. These notions of the relative stability of teachers' beliefs and their congruence with practice have become recurrent themes captured in seminal reviews on teacher beliefs research (see Basturkmen, 2012; Kagan, 1992; Pajares, 1992; Santos & Miguel, 2019), and more recent research extends this argument to suggest that teachers' beliefs mediate their effectiveness in the classroom (Sabarwal et al., 2022; Witter, 2023). A more nuanced view of the research suggests that beliefs are context-dependent, making them prone to instability and inconsistency in practice (Buehl & Beck, 2014; Fives & Buehl, 2012), yet there is a consensus that teachers' beliefs are a vital part of their identity, that is, their self-concept.

TABLE 12.2 Contrasting Self-Improving, Self-Aligning, Self-Achievers, and Self-Sustaining Teachers.

Dimension	Self-Improving Teachers	Self-Aligning Teachers	Self-Achieving Teachers	Self-Sustaining Teachers
Focus	Forward-looking, fostering growth and innovation	Stability, predictability, and maintaining consistent self-views	Order, structure, testing, and maintaining smooth classroom operation	Workload management, personal well-being, and preserving equilibrium
Cognitive strategies	Emphasize metacognitive and higher-order thinking skills	Focus on confirming existing beliefs, recalling confirming feedback, and reinforcing identity	Focus on accuracy, careful planning, monitoring, structured delivery, measuring clear outcomes	Simplify tasks, avoid challenging or risky learning situations, and minimize cognitive strain
Classroom environment	Dynamic and student-centered, encouraging engagement and exploration	Stable and consistent, maintaining teacher-defined norms	Orderly, tightly controlled, and highly structured	Predictable, low-stress, comfortable, and risk-averse
Adaptability	Highly adaptable; use feedback constructively to refine and improve practices	Adaptable mainly to maintain self-consistency; selectively adapt when aligned with self-views	Adaptable within fixed routines; sensitive to context but resistant to deeper change	Low adaptability; prefer familiar routines and resist change that threatens balance
Teaching approach	Focus on innovative, evidence-based, learner-centered approaches.	Emphasize methods that reinforce their established practices, often adopting school-endorsed programs if they align with their views	Highly structured lessons with emphasis on control, rules, and step-by-step methods	Low-risk, simplified teaching strategies focused on manageable tasks and reduced stress for the teacher and students
Goal setting	Set high expectations and challenging goals to foster deep learning and student growth	Set goals that confirm and maintain existing competence and reinforce stability	Set goals around clear, precise, and easily monitored outcomes	Set low or moderate goals focused on ease of achievement and minimizing workload or risk

(Continued)

TABLE 12.2 Contrasting Self-Improving, Self-Aligning, Self-Achievers, and Self-Sustaining Teachers. (Continued)

Dimension	Self-Improving Teachers	Self-Aligning Teachers	Self-Achieving Teachers	Self-Sustaining Teachers
View of errors	View errors as opportunities for learning and growth	Accept errors only when they can be interpreted as consistent with self-view	View errors as disruptions to be minimized; emphasize error prevention	Avoid situations where errors might occur; deflect, downplay, or excuse errors to maintain comfort and stability
Student engagement	Foster student-driven learning, collaboration, and exploration	Focus on predictable, teacher-managed engagement that reinforces classroom norms	Focus on compliance and task completion within structured lessons	Focus on maintaining calm, low-effort engagement that reduces stress for all
Use of feedback	Embrace feedback as a tool for reflection and continuous improvement	Use feedback primarily to confirm existing self-views; selectively internalize feedback	Use feedback for monitoring and validating order and achievement	Downplay or avoid critical feedback, and use much praise
Student-centered practices	Encourage autonomy and critical thinking through dynamic learning strategies	Focus on teacher authority while maintaining consistency with their self-view	Strongly teacher-centered; prioritize order, clarity, and teacher control	Minimize student demands; prioritize teacher comfort and predictable routines
Innovation	Regularly experiment with and adapt new strategies to enhance teaching effectiveness	Adopt innovations only if they align with their existing practices or reinforce their identity	Willing to adjust in service of greater efficiency or stronger demonstrable outcomes	Avoid innovation; prefer familiar methods and routines to preserve well-being and minimize disruption
Classroom climate	Growth-oriented, values curiosity and learning from mistakes	Stability-oriented, values consistency and predictability in self-identity and classroom dynamics	Order-focused, values rules, routines, and control	Low-stress, routine-based, values predictability and calm

TABLE 12.2 Contrasting Self-Improving, Self-Aligning, Self-Achievers, and Self-Sustaining Teachers. (Continued)

Dimension	Self-Improving Teachers	Self-Aligning Teachers	Self-Achieving Teachers	Self-Sustaining Teachers
Student outcomes	Foster deep understanding, critical thinking, and independent problem-solving	Focus on consistent performance and maintaining established standards	Ensure task completion, clear and measurable learning outcomes, and rule-following	Prioritize student well-being and task completion with minimal stress; often maintain surface-level learning
Overall impact	Cultivate an engaging, future-focused learning environment that promotes mastery and resilience	Create structured, predictable environments that reinforce their identity and maintain consistent outcomes	Deliver well-organized, compliant where students know expectations and produce tangible academic results, with possibly more emphasis on lower-order thinking.	Maintain calm, stable classrooms focused on efficiency, routine, and minimizing demands on teacher and students alike, often with limited growth focus

When viewed through a systems lens, beliefs can be understood as internalized networks of interconnected individual beliefs, including more dominant and established central beliefs alongside peripheral beliefs that may have less influence on teacher behavior (Mansour, 2009). However, there is a debate about the extent to which research in this area should focus on examining teachers' belief systems compared to isolated, specific beliefs (Fives & Buehl, 2012; Nespor, 1987; Pajares, 1992).

The premise of the ROPE model is that teacher beliefs are better viewed as larger systems, with four primary self-motives that drive teacher self-concept related to two major sets of teacher self-concept beliefs: Beliefs about education and Beliefs about personal agency and responsibility. Teachers' beliefs are appropriately viewed as overlapping and connected fibers, which work in tandem to lead teachers to bring meaning to particular situations, and also mediate the strategies that are selected and implemented in their work. Within the ROPE, it can be posited that a central part of teacher self-concept as a process is the formation of reciprocal relationships wherein teachers' beliefs inform their actions and experiences, but also their actions and experiences may inform their beliefs with through dynamic, complex, interactive processes (e.g., Bandura, 1997; Fives & Buehl, 2012).

Following the notion of central and peripheral beliefs, an important consideration for teacher self-concept is how to identify those particular teacher beliefs that are likely to play the most vital role in shaping their self-concept, particularly in relation to motivations for choosing beliefs related to self-improvement or self-alignment. Those beliefs relate to the most key practices and student outcomes. Most notably, this includes pedagogical beliefs related to teaching, assessment, curriculum, expectations, goals, models of learning, purposes for teaching, and self-efficacy or confidence to impact the learning lives of their students. We suggest 10 major beliefs, organized under two dimensions: beliefs about education and beliefs about personal agency and responsibility.

Beliefs About Education

Beliefs about education and teaching practices have been a subject of extensive research, with scholars identifying various frameworks to categorize these beliefs, ranging from broad dichotomies to more nuanced multidimensional models that reflect the complex nature of educational philosophies and approaches. We identified six major sets of beliefs about teaching, knowledge, assessment, curriculum, goals, and learning.

Teaching Beliefs

A common thread across many of these studies of beliefs about teaching is the dichotomous grouping of these beliefs into two broad categories: student-centered and teacher-centered (Fives et al., 2014). Kember (1997) suggested that teacher-centered beliefs about teaching view teaching as a content-oriented activity focused on imparting information and transmitting knowledge to students. Student-centered beliefs view teaching as a learning-oriented activity that facilitates understanding, conceptual change, and intellectual development. Although many have claimed that teachers' beliefs and practices are generalizable, these are not necessarily binary. Kember's model is highly consistent with the work of Collins and Pratt (2011), who identified five categories of teaching conceptions, from teacher to student-oriented. The first is transmission beliefs, which assume the teacher's responsibility is to present the content accurately and efficiently to learners, and it is the learners' responsibility to master that content. The second is apprenticeship beliefs, which assume that the teacher is a capable practitioner of what they teach and that the teacher should regularly demonstrate best practice, guiding students to take on more of the work gradually. The third is developmental beliefs, which assume that good teaching begins with learners' prior knowledge and a commitment to changing students' thinking by focusing on increasing complexity and deeper understanding of the content. The fourth is nurturing beliefs, which emphasize the need to respect the learner's self-concept and self-efficacy, and the importance of teachers caring deeply about their learners and supporting effort as much as achievement. This involves striking a balance between challenging students to do their best while still supporting and nurturing their efforts to be successful. The fifth conception category, social reform, emphasizes the pursuit of social change more than individual learning, the commitment to social issues and social change, and the need to ground teaching in communicating what changes must take place in society. Although Kember and Pratt's studies have primarily focused on university students, the model has also been supported in secondary school and cross-cultural settings studies (Chen et al., 2012; Fives et al., 2014).

Knowledge Beliefs

Teachers hold beliefs about the nature of knowledge—whether fixed or evolving, compartmentalized or integrated—about the process of knowing (how knowledge is validated), and about teaching knowledge (whether their role is to deliver knowledge or facilitate its discovery). These beliefs, including perspectives on constructivist versus transmissive approaches, significantly influence how teachers design lessons, engage with students, and perceive their own professional growth, ultimately shaping educational outcomes.

Shulman (1987) emphasized the specialized knowledge required for effective teaching, outlining several key domains. These include content knowledge (a deep understanding of the subject matter), pedagogical knowledge (expertise in teaching strategies, classroom management, and instructional methods), and pedagogical content knowledge (the ability to teach subject matter in ways that are comprehensible and meaningful to students). Additionally, Shulman highlighted curricular knowledge (understanding the structure, sequencing, and alignment of curriculum), knowledge of learners and their characteristics (awareness of students' developmental stages, needs, and backgrounds), knowledge of educational contexts (familiarity with the broader social, cultural, and institutional environment), and knowledge of educational goals, purposes, and values (understanding the ethical and philosophical aims of education). Together, these domains form a comprehensive framework for understanding the multifaceted expertise essential to effective teaching (see also Ball et al., 2008; Baumert & Kunter, 2013; Blömeke et al., 2015; Danielson, 2007; Darling-Hammond & Bransford, 2007; Mishra & Koehler, 2006; Verloop et al., 2001; Windschitl et al., 2011).

Assessment Beliefs

Brown (2008) argued that teachers' beliefs about assessment interact with other types of pedagogical beliefs and likely shape the variety of choices teachers make in the classroom, as well as their endorsement and use of different types of assessment evidence. Hattie and Brown (2011) similarly noted the vital role that assessment beliefs play in determining the extent to which teachers view themselves as evaluators of their impact and how they utilize assessment evidence to steer their teaching. Brown identified four key conceptions of assessment: (1) a belief that assessment is useful in improving teacher instruction and student learning by providing quality information for decision-making, (2) a belief that assessment is about accountability of students, (3) teachers or schools are made accountable through internal or external evaluations, and (4) assessment is irrelevant and/or potentially harmful to the work of teachers and lives of students.

Curriculum Beliefs

Cheung and Ng (2000) studied teachers' beliefs about the purpose of curriculum. They identified four major orientations: (1) a humanistic conception that advocates that the student is the center and source of all curriculum, (2) a social reconstructionist orientation that sees school and curriculum as a means by which we can direct social reform or change, (3) a technological orientation focused on finding efficient means of reaching planned learning objectives, often through the use of modern technology, and (4) an academic orientation aimed at developing students' rational thinking and inquiry skills. Cheung and Ng's (2000) measurement tool, aligned to these four orientations, suggests that many teachers possess pluralistic views about curriculum, simultaneously endorsing multiple orientations. Brown found that particular curriculum beliefs appeared to share elements of continuums identified in models of teaching and learning beliefs. For example, he found that technological beliefs aligned with elements of surface learning beliefs, while humanistic and academic beliefs aligned with deep learning beliefs.

Goal Beliefs

Another key type of motivational belief relates to teachers' goals. Butler (2007, 2014) argued that teachers are motivated to varying degrees by goals related to mastery (improving their skills and understanding), ability (demonstrating high or masking low ability), building relationships with students, and avoiding work. Studies have found correlations between teachers' mastery orientations and instructional emphasis on deep over surface learning (Butler, 2014; Retelsdorf et al., 2010).

Learning Beliefs

There are fewer studies of teachers' beliefs about how we learn. Marton and Säljö (1976) proposed a model of learning based on surface-to-deep learning (but never claimed that these are aligned with teacher and student orientations). Surface beliefs about learning are primarily characterized by a focus on reproducing knowledge and rote learning. Learning is distinguished by a "reproductive" conception of learning that focuses on recalling the details presented, with comparatively passive engagement. Deep conceptions of learning are characterized by deepening and expanding understanding, motivated by a genuine interest in content and an authentic satisfaction from engaging in learning, and learning was distinguished by a focus on finding the purpose of a text, drawing appropriate conclusions, and engaging actively with the content (Biggs, 1987; Biggs et al., 2001; Entwistle, 2007; Purdie & Hattie, 2002).

Biggs (1987) initially proposed three types of learning beliefs, which are reflected in particular motivations and self-reported strategies. Surface belief was characterized primarily by extrinsic motivators, such as the fear of failure, and strategies, including the reproduction of information and rote learning. The deep approach was characterized by intrinsic motivators, such as genuine interest in the content, a sense of satisfaction derived from studying, and strategies focused on maximizing meaning and expanding understanding. Biggs also identified a third approach, which is achieving, motivated by a desire to obtain the highest grades, with strategies focused on organizing time, working space, and investing in a manner that produces the best academic results.

Following the Biggs model, Purdie and Hattie (2002) identified six distinct types of learning beliefs that mapped against surface and deep learning factors. (1) Learning as increasing knowledge (accumulating facts, information, and content and a focus on memorization and recall); (2) Learning as memorizing (learning is seen as storing information for later use, such as in tests or exams, with an emphasizes rote learning without necessarily understanding the material); (3) Learning as acquiring facts, skills, and methods (involves acquiring practical skills, techniques, and specific methods to solve problems or accomplish tasks); (4) Learning as making sense or abstracting meaning (learning is seen as constructing meaning and understanding, rather than merely acquiring isolated pieces of information, and learners actively connect concepts to form a coherent understanding); (5) Learning as Interpreting and understanding reality (learning is about developing a deeper understanding of the world and making sense of one's experiences, and thus emphasizing critical thinking and reflection), and (6) Learning as changing as a person (learning is viewed as transformative, leading to personal growth and a change in the learner's perspective, behavior, or identity). They also noted a relationship between the number of different beliefs students held and their self-reported academic performance (the greater the number of conceptions, the higher the achievement).

Beliefs About Personal Agency and Responsibilities

A second major set of beliefs that significantly influences teachers' self-concept is that related to personal agency and responsibility. These beliefs encompass teachers' sense of purpose that drives them to enter and remain in the profession, their expectations about students' capabilities and potential, and their self-efficacy regarding their teaching abilities. Understanding these beliefs is crucial as they shape teachers' motivations, actions, and ultimately, their impact on student outcomes.

Purpose Beliefs

This belief is the core reason why teachers choose to enter and stay in the profession. Expectancy-value theory suggests that two key direct influences on motivation are expectancies (of success) and values, which also influence performance, effort, and persistence (Wigfield & Eccles, 2000). Watt and Richardson (2007, 2012) applied this theory to teacher motivation and purpose. Their "Factors Influencing teaching" model suggests that among the common values motivating teachers to choose teaching as a profession are "intrinsic value" (personal interest in teaching, passion for education, and a love for working with children or students), "personal utility value" (which includes job security, time for family, and job transferability), and "social utility value" (which consists of a desire to shape the future of children, enhance social equity, make a social contribution; Watt & Richardson, 2007, p. 176). They also consider the teacher's perceptions of task demand and task return, prior experience as a student, and whether becoming a teacher was a fallback career (cf. Bartanen et al., 2025).

Teachers who initially self-rated highly on social utility motivations were more likely to exhibit higher levels of persistence, which in turn predicted more positive expectations for students, stronger feelings of relatedness to students, and less likelihood of responding negatively to students' mistakes. On the other hand, those who considered teaching a fallback option had lower levels of planned career persistence, effort, leadership aspirations, and reported negative teaching behaviors due to lower persistence. Intrinsic value was so highly interrelated with social utility values and negatively correlated with fallback that it was excluded from the analysis (Watt & Richardson, 2014).

Responsibility Beliefs

Scriven (1994) outlined the duties of teachers, emphasizing the high levels of responsibility they bear for their profession. He noted that his list of duties was more extensive than they might typically do (based on a job analysis) and more about what they *ought* to be doing. He also outlined the quality standards of these duties (Acceptable, Good, and Excellent) and noted that the standards may be weighted differently for different contexts (The duties included subject matter knowledge, instructional competence, course construction and improvement skills, assessment competence, and professionalism.) Such responsibilities can be seen in many lists of professional standards and evaluation models. The key is that they are not merely lists of tasks, but duties, which imply a responsibility to accomplish them to a high standard (see also Priestley et al., 2015; Stengel, 2010). Within these responsibilities, there can be degrees of autonomy in how they are enacted. Thus, teachers do not have unchecked autonomy, as they work within system demands; nor do systems have unfettered control over teachers' performance of their duties, as this cannot only stifle creativity and adaptability but also lead to less effective progress by students. Trust, but verify; innovate, but do not abuse; innovate with integrity; and reinforce your efforts with evidence of their impact on students. Autonomy allows teachers to leverage their expertise, but it comes with the responsibility to their students, school leadership, system mandates, and community expectations. However, a key duty to note is that teachers must also be the critics and conscience of the educational experiences, duty expectations, policies, and future.

While all four motivation profiles acknowledge their professional responsibilities, they enact them in distinct ways, ranging from growth-oriented self-improvement to stability-seeking self-discipline and self-sustaining pragmatism, each influenced by their underlying motivational drives. Self-improvers see responsibility as an internal drive for personal and professional growth, proactively engaging in innovation, reflection, and professional learning to enhance their impact. Self-aligners prioritize external consistency, aligning their practices with school or system expectations to maintain stability and meet institutional goals, often focusing on compliance rather than deep change. In contrast, self-achievers emphasize responsibility through order, routine, and precision, focusing on fulfilling duties through structured, risk-averse approaches that maintain classroom control and instructional clarity. Self-sustainers frame responsibility around personal well-being and workload balance, aiming to meet expectations while preserving their energy and avoiding disruptive changes. While all teachers recognize their professional responsibilities, their motivations shape whether they pursue growth and innovation or prioritize stability, predictability, and self-preservation.

Expectation Beliefs

Teacher expectations for students are important beliefs that are likely to play a significant role in the development of a teacher's self-concept. Building on the seminal Pygmalion in the Classroom study by Rosenthal and Jacobson (1968), teacher expectation effects have consistently been recognized as influential in shaping teacher behavior and impacting student outcomes. While authors have suggested a range of magnitudes of the impact that teachers' beliefs have on student outcomes, ranging from small (Brophy, 1983; Jussim & Harber, 2005) to medium (Hattie, 2023), but more nuanced findings indicate that the effects of teachers are much higher and often large on vulnerable learners, such as those from low SES backgrounds, low-achieving students, or culturally and linguistically diverse students (Jussim & Eccles, 1992; Jussim et al., 1996; Rubie-Davies, 2014).

Rubie-Davies (2014, 2017) has demonstrated that teachers who have high expectations tend to have them for all their students with much success (d = 0.96). In contrast, those who have low expectations also tend to have them for all their students and are far from successful (d = 0.03). Rubie-Davies & Hattie, 2024) also showed the marked differences in the climate, actions, and behaviors in classes of high compared to low expectation teachers. High expectation teachers are more likely to facilitate positive and supportive classroom environments, more likely to engage all students in cognitively demanding teaching and learning, and more likely to persist and work with struggling learners, while low expectation teachers are more likely to stereotype low-expectancy students, engage them in surface learning experiences, use static differentiation strategies (like always placing low expectancy students in low ability groups), give up on struggling students, and less likely interact with or attempt to engage all learners equally (Inan-Kaya & Rubie-Davies, 2022; Rubie-Davies, 2014).

Self-Efficacy Beliefs

As noted above, the self-efficacy of teachers is arguably the most studied and well-established type of teacher belief (Tschannen-Moran et al., 1998; Hoy et al., 2009). Teachers' self-efficacy, defined as their confidence in their capabilities to teach and impact their students, is grounded in Bandura's (1997) social-cognitive theory of motivation. Two metaanalyses show the high relations between teachers self-efficacy and student outcomes: Klassen and Tze (2014), with $d = 0.28$, and Kim and Seo (2018) with $d = 0.20$, as well as self-efficacy relating to commitment to teaching (Chesnut & Burley, 2015), teacher resilience (Mu, 2024), job satisfaction (Kasalak & Dagyar, 2020) and avoidance of burnout (Shoji et al., 2016). Other studies show the positive impact of higher confidence on improved student motivation, engagement, and achievement, greater student self-efficacy and belief in their capabilities, and better classroom climate and reduced behavioral issues (de Ruig et al., 2024; Hettinger et al., 2024; Zee & Koomen, 2016).

Summary of Beliefs

Witter and Hattie (2024) examined the complex interactions among a wide range of teacher beliefs. Their study was based on the hypothesis that teachers' beliefs interact in ways consistent with existing literature on belief systems. They proposed that multiple distinct beliefs would likely correlate, allowing teachers to hold theoretically dichotomous beliefs. Additionally, they suggested that certain beliefs might be more dominant and central, while others would remain more peripheral. They also hypothesized that teacher beliefs factors could be reduced to "higher order" factors representing multiple correlated types of teacher beliefs defined by larger dimensions. An initial survey instrument was designed using prevalidated teacher beliefs scales broken into 43 specific factors nested within 11 teacher beliefs (e.g., including the 9 cited above). The survey was administered to 663 teachers (444 elementary and 167 high school teachers). Pedagogical beliefs measured included beliefs about teaching, learning, epistemology, curriculum, and assessment, while motivational beliefs measured included self-efficacy beliefs, goal orientation, sense of responsibility, and purposes for teaching. Teacher beliefs about students measured included teacher expectations, student-teacher relations, and beliefs about students' intelligence and effort.

They identified five higher-order factors. The first higher-order factor included beliefs focused on the purposes of social responsibility and the impact on learners, reflecting values and practices of deep and relationship-driven conceptions of teaching and learning, as well as mastery and relational goal orientations that emphasize self-improvement and connectedness with students. The second factor reflected a set of beliefs about learning, in particular fixed ability and surface learning beliefs. These beliefs reflected fixed-mindset characteristics about the self and students, low expectations for learners, surface conceptions of teaching and learning, goal orientations focused on demonstrating ability rather than mastery, and work- and ability-avoidant behaviors. The third area comprised four distinct aspects of teacher personal responsibility and accountability, including responsibility for achievement, motivation, and teaching. The fourth combined self-efficacy and intrinsic drive beliefs about classroom management and instruction, with purposes for teaching based on perceived ability and genuine interest in teaching. Notably, self-efficacy and intrinsic motivation clustered together as a collective form of teacher motivation. This factor represents teacher confidence in managing the classroom and providing instruction, as well as intrinsic motivation. The fifth higher-order, pro-assessment beliefs included positive beliefs about assessment accountability for students and schools, assessment as a means to demonstrate learning, and using assessment for improvement.

The argument is that self-aligning teachers seek consistency between their existing self-concept and their experiences, as they strive for stability and coherence. They aim to align their beliefs and actions with their perceived identity, often focusing on reinforcing what they already believe about themselves as educators. Self-aligning teachers are likely to hold beliefs that validate their existing practices and perceptions, avoid significant changes to their established methods, and focus on interpreting past experiences to confirm their effectiveness and competency. They are more likely to adopt teacher-led or transmission-based teaching models that reinforce their role as the expert and authority, and may struggle to accept high levels of personal responsibility for teaching and learning. These teachers' high or low self-efficacy is tied heavily to maintaining and validating their existing practices.

Self-improving teachers are more open to feedback and willing to adapt and experiment with new strategies to improve their teaching effectiveness. They believe in their ability to improve student outcomes and in students' capacity for growth, fostering high expectations for all learners; hence, they are likely to adopt developmental, nurturing, or social reform-oriented teaching models, emphasizing collaboration, critical thinking, and student empowerment. These teachers frequently re-evaluate their practices and beliefs to align with evolving educational paradigms and research. Their self-efficacy is tied heavily to their intrinsic motivation and enjoyment of teaching, seeking mastery and innovation.

Self-achieving teachers value feedback as external recognition of their performance and accomplishments. They take personal responsibility for their teaching and outcomes, but may be more likely to focus high expectations on higher performing learners. Their focus on structure, routine, and control may correspond with beliefs about teaching that are more teacher-centered and focused on clear and straightforward measures of learning. These teachers are more performance versus mastery driven, and their high versus low sense of self-efficacy is tied heavily to the clear achievement of them and their students.

Self-sustaining teachers value feedback that supports and validates their existing expertise and wellbeing, but are less likely to see themselves as personally responsible for aspects of teaching and learning that conflict with their need for balance and risk minimization. These teachers' beliefs about teaching and learning emphasize comfort, low-stress, and reasonable expectations for students that may coincide with more superficial and simplistic pedagogical approaches and outcomes for learners. These teachers' high versus low sense of self-efficacy is filtered through sustainable practices and experiences; when they are able to maintain low-stress, comfortable classrooms and manage their responsibilities and activities with balance and self-care, they may experience higher levels of self-efficacy than when the opposite conditions are in place.

Attributes

Implicit in the above beliefs are various attributes of teachers. We identify 10 such attributes, primarily drawn from the higher effect sizes from a synthesis of over 400 influences on student achievement (Hattie, 2023). These include Confidence, Credibility, Clarity, Collaboration, Changeability, Connections, Challenge, Cultural competence, and Commitment to improvement. These attributes are not directly aligned with the Beliefs above, but they inform the formation of those beliefs.

Professional Attributes

(1) Conscientiousness, the bedrock of professional integrity, manifests in a teacher's meticulous preparation, consistent follow-through, and unwavering commitment to their students' success. A conscientious teacher demonstrates resilience in addressing challenges, attentiveness in crafting effective lesson plans, and adaptability in meeting the diverse needs of learners. This trait reflects diligence

and a profound sense of responsibility to nurture an environment where every student feels valued and supported.

(2) Clarity is crucial in helping students grasp complex concepts and expectations. A teacher with clarity can distill intricate ideas into digestible lessons, articulate constructive feedback, and set achievable goals.

(3) Commitment to Improvement. Effective teachers are lifelong learners who continuously seek professional growth through ongoing education, reflection, and collaboration. This mindset ensures they stay current with best practices and evolving educational trends.

(4) Cultural competence. Understanding and respecting cultural diversity is critical in today's globalized society. Culturally competent teachers incorporate inclusive practices, honor students' unique backgrounds, and teach in ways that affirm and celebrate diversity.

Adaptive Capacity

(5) Credibility (especially when aligned with confidence) is built on authentic, transparent, and ethical behavior. A credible teacher models consistency between words and actions, demonstrating moral and intellectual integrity that earns the respect of students, colleagues, and parents alike.

(6) hangeability: Adaptability is essential in a rapidly changing educational landscape. Teachers must be able to pivot their instructional strategies to meet the evolving needs of students, incorporate new technologies, and address unexpected challenges. Adaptable teachers create inclusive environments that respect diverse learning styles and foster student resilience.

(7) Challenge: Resilience. Teaching often involves navigating challenges stemming from student behavior, systemic constraints, or personal setbacks. Resilient teachers demonstrate perseverance, maintain a positive outlook, and model problem-solving skills for their students, fostering a culture of growth and persistence.

Relational Skills

(8) Connections: Empathy. Empathy allows teachers to understand and connect with students on a personal level, creating a safe and supportive learning environment. By recognizing and valuing the emotional and social dimensions of their students' experiences, empathetic teachers build stronger relationships that enhance engagement and motivation.

(9) Collaboration, meanwhile, enriches the educational ecosystem by leveraging the collective strengths of educators, parents, and the broader community. A collaborative teacher seeks to learn from peers, build partnerships with families, and engage students as

co-creators in their learning. These traits create a powerful synergy, fostering environments where knowledge thrives, relationships flourish, and aspirations are realized.

Personal Confidence

(10) Confidence stems from deep subject knowledge, pedagogical expertise, and the ability to adapt instructional strategies to dynamic classroom contexts. When teachers exude confidence, they inspire trust, encourage participation, and foster a culture of academic risk-taking among students.

Table 12.3 outlines the fundamental differences between these 10 attributes for self-improving and self-aligning teachers, reflecting their different motivational drivers and approaches to their teaching. Self-Improving teachers are deeply driven by their passion for personal and professional growth. They embrace feedback, seek collaboration, and continuously adapt their teaching to maximize student outcomes. Their high self-efficacy and resilience enable them to navigate challenges with optimism, fostering dynamic and student-centered classrooms that prioritize deep learning, innovation, and sustained improvement. Self-Aligning teachers are primarily motivated by the need for consistency, coherence, and validation of their established self-views. They are selectively adaptive, engaging in change only when it aligns with their personal identity or system mandates. These teachers maintain stable, predictable environments, with moderate collaboration and a strong preference for preserving their familiar practices and routines. Self-achieving teachers thrive on order, structure, precision and outcomes. They emphasize

TABLE 12.3 Fundamental Differences Between These 10 Attributes for Self-Improving, Self-Aligning, Self-Achieving, and Self-Sustaining Teachers.

Attribute	Self-Improving	Self-Aligning	Self-Achieving	Self-Sustaining
1. Conscientiousness	Variable, but driven by intrinsic purpose to grow; proactive, reflective, goal-seeking.	Variable, but geared toward maintaining consistency and system compliance.	Very high, with strong focus on meticulous planning, precision, and routine.	Moderate, focused on personal well-being, avoiding excessive workload.
2. Clarity	Uses clarity to promote deep learning and long-term growth; adjusts for impact.	Seeks clarity to confirm current practices and validate self-concept.	Prioritizes clarity to maintain control and produce evidence of achievement.	Maintains basic clarity to minimize stress, simplify tasks, and avoid risks.

(Continued)

TABLE 12.3 Fundamental Differences Between These 10 Attributes for Self-Improving, Self-Aligning, Self-Achieving, and Self-Sustaining Teachers. (Continued)

Attribute	Self-Improving	Self-Aligning	Self-Achieving	Self-Sustaining
3. Commitment to improvement	Central drive; embraces feedback, pursues continual personal/professional development.	Moderate; improves when aligned with current self-views or system demands.	Variable; focused on maintaining stability and minimizing disruptions, but may adapt to improve efficiency or outcomes.	Low; prefers familiar routines, avoids changes that threaten equilibrium.
4. Cultural competence	High; seeks to understand diverse learners to maximize growth potential.	Selective; values cultural elements only if they align with existing identity.	Low to moderate; emphasizes uniformity and traditional norms for predictability.	Variable; avoids complexity, may prefer culturally familiar or simple contexts.
5. Credibility	Built through openness, transparency, and demonstrated growth and results.	Built through maintaining predictable, consistent behaviors and conformity.	Built through strict adherence to routines, policies, and structured practices, as well as tangible results.	Built through reliability and avoidance of risks that could challenge status quo.
6. Changeability	Very high; thrives on adaptation and flexible thinking for continuous learning.	Moderate; changes cautiously, only within bounds of established identity.	Variable; avoids change except when required to maintain order or enhance efficiency.	Very low; resists change to protect personal balance and minimize stress.
7. Challenge (resilience)	High; embraces setbacks as learning opportunities; persists toward growth goals.	Moderate; resilient when experiences align with self-concept, otherwise vulnerable.	Moderate; resilience stems from structured predictability, but avoids deeper risks.	Low; avoids high-pressure challenges; prioritizes emotional stability and comfort.
8. Connections (empathy)	High; builds deep, authentic connections with students and colleagues.	Moderate; connects with those who affirm their self-views, selective empathy.	Low to moderate; focused on task completion and maintaining authority roles.	Moderate; maintains surface-level harmony, avoids emotionally taxing connections.

(Continued)

TABLE 12.3 Fundamental Differences Between These 10 Attributes for Self-Improving, Self-Aligning, Self-Achieving, and Self-Sustaining Teachers. (Continued)

Attribute	Self-Improving	Self-Aligning	Self-Achieving	Self-Sustaining
9. Collaboration	High; seeks input and feedback from others, values joint learning and co-creation.	Moderate; collaborates selectively to reinforce existing practices.	Low; prefers working independently within structured systems.	Low; limits collaboration to minimize additional workload or discomfort.
10. Confidence	Deep, intrinsic confidence rooted in self-efficacy and adaptive learning.	Conditional confidence based on external validation and self-consistency.	Task-specific confidence derived from control and accomplishment.	Defensive confidence; avoids situations that might challenge self-image.

tain a highly organized and predictable teaching environment. Self-Sustaining teachers prioritize maintaining personal well-being and a manageable workload. They tend to avoid risks, simplify tasks, and resist changes that could disrupt their sense of equilibrium. These teachers favor familiar methods and low-stress environments, seeking stability and comfort over deep professional growth or extensive student engagement.

PART II. HOW THE ROPE MODEL CAN RELATE TO DECISIONS ABOUT CLASSROOM PRACTICES

The claim is that there are four primary motivations for teacher self-concept: self-improving., self-aligning, self-achievers, and self-sustainers. These four distinct teacher self-motivations fundamentally shape how teachers view their approaches to classroom practices, student engagement, feedback, and professional growth. There are several ways in which self-improvers, self-aligners, self-achievers, and self-sustainers may differ in their classroom practices, each shaped by their core motivational focus: thinking, feedback, collaboration, inquiry, structure, goals, connections and climate.

In developing metacognitive and cognitive skills, self-improvers prioritize teaching students how to think deeply and reflectively, fostering higher-order reasoning, critical thinking, and problem-solving skills. They see themselves as deliberately guiding students through metacognitive strategies to build independent learning capacity. In contrast, self-aligners emphasize more surface-level skills that align with established routines, offering selective opportunities for problem-solving only when they fit comfortably within predictable structures. Self-achievers focus on procedural precision and basic skills, ensuring students master routines, limit errors, and produce clear results, which may or may not promote conceptual depth. Meanwhile, self-sustainers simplify the cognitive demands in their classrooms, favoring straightforward tasks that are easy for both teacher and students to manage, reducing the likelihood of stress or frustration.

Approaches to feedback also differ markedly. Self-improvers embrace feedback—both giving and receiving—as a central mechanism for growth and improvement. They explicitly teach students how to act on feedback and model openness to constructive critique. Self-aligners selectively use feedback, primarily to validate existing practices, often filtering or disregarding feedback that challenges their self-concept or routines. Self-achievers treat feedback as a corrective tool to maintain accuracy and compliance, emphasizing its role in keeping students geared toward performance outcomes rather than promoting reflection. Self-sustainers, on the other hand, tend to avoid critical feedback altogether, favoring praise and reassurance to preserve personal well-being and classroom harmony, viewing feedback as potentially destabilizing.

Collaborative and social learning also reveals clear contrasts. Self-improvers actively foster collaboration, encouraging peer learning, teamwork, and open dialog among students to build social engagement and deeper learning. In contrast, self-aligners prefer to rely on individual tasks and more structured forms of interaction, using group work only when it reinforces classroom predictability and confirms their teaching methods. Self-achievers minimize collaborative learning altogether, preferring controlled, individual activities that focus on compliance and accuracy, reducing potential disruptions. Similarly, self-sustainers may collaborate in support of wellbeing, self-care and workload reduction, but may otherwise tend to avoid group work, preferring solitary and low-pressure learning tasks that maintain calm and limit the complexity of social dynamics.

In terms of active and inquiry-based learning, self-improvers emphasize student-centered approaches that promote problem-solving, exploratory learning, and critical thinking, trusting students to take intellectual risks and valuing open-ended questions. Self-aligners prefer to maintain more traditional, teacher-directed instruction, cautiously avoiding approaches that might challenge classroom stability or introduce unpredictable outcomes. Self-achievers rely heavily on teacher-centered and tightly controlled lesson delivery which may limit opportunities for student-led inquiry or exploration. Self-sustainers are possibly the least likely to use inquiry-based approaches, opting instead for familiar, low-risk instructional methods that reduce uncertainty for themselves and their students.

When it comes to teaching, self-improvers skilfully blend a range of evidence-based instructional approaches, using scaffolding to ensure that students connect ideas and deepen their learning. Self-aligners favor structured, sequential lessons that ensure content is covered thoroughly and in an orderly fashion, focusing on clarity and routine. Self-achievers rely on tightly structured, step-by-step instructional methods, utilizing highly predictable lesson formats to maintain control, minimize classroom variability and produce clear evidence of learning on a frequent basis. Self-sustainers prefer instructional approaches that are simple and brief, intentionally designing lessons that are manageable and free from undue stress for teacher and students alike.

Goal setting and mastery expectations are another major point of difference. Self-improvers regularly set high but achievable goals focused on mastery over performance, encouraging students to persist through challenges and focus on deep learning and personal growth. Self-aligners set more cautious, predictable goals that align with maintaining consistency and ensure safe success without disturbing classroom routines. Self-achievers prefer precise, procedural goals that emphasize clear, demonstrable knowledge and skills, with an emphasize on performance and demonstrated ability over improvement and incremental growth. Self-sustainers, by contrast, set minimal and easily achievable goals aimed at reducing effort, minimizing risk, and maintaining emotional equilibrium for themselves and their students.

Finally, classroom climate and cultural norms diverge according to these motivations. Self-improvers cultivate environments where mistakes are normalized as learning opportunities, fostering resilience, curiosity, and a growth mindset among students. Self-aligners focus on maintaining calm, predictable classrooms where mistakes are cautiously managed, with an emphasis on avoiding disruptions rather than embracing errors as learning tools. Self-achievers operate highly controlled classrooms centered around task completion, rule enforcement, and minimizing mistakes, treating errors as disruptions that must be quickly corrected. Self-sustainers, in contrast, design low-pressure, emotionally safe classrooms where the primary objective is to minimize stress or the risk of failure, often by sidestepping challenging tasks and maintaining routines that foster emotional comfort.

PART III: IMPLICATIONS OF THE ROPE MODEL FOR PRACTICE

Teacher self-concept is critical to teaching effectiveness, student engagement, and classroom dynamics. The ROPE Model promotes that teachers' self-concept is a rich interweaving of motives, beliefs, and attributes. The most effective notions (i.e., the beliefs most aligned with higher impact on the learning lives of students) of teacher self-concept are associated with self-improvers; that is, teachers who seek feedback, even if negative, to improve their teaching. Such teachers are reflexive and improvement-oriented, engaging in high-impact strategies such as goal setting, having high expectations for all, and aiming to foster a culture where students feel invited to come and learn, and are taught to drive their own learning. Self-improvers excel in conflict management and adaptability, are empathetic and have high levels of communication skills, and are optimistic and solution-focused.

The claim is that both the various motivations relate to a particular form of thinking about themselves, which we term evaluative thinking (Archibald, 2024). Evaluative thinking involves critical thinking skills to analyze evidence, question assumptions, and accurately interpret the results from assessments (such as assignments and test scores) to inform the next steps in teaching. While all teachers can engage in evaluative thinking, their motivations shape how they apply it and the purposes it serves. Self-improvers embrace evaluative thinking as a tool for growth and adaptation, using assessment evidence to refine their teaching, challenge assumptions, and actively pursue strategies to improve student outcomes. They are highly responsive to evidence about both successes and shortcomings, seeing gaps as opportunities for targeted action. They can stand in their students' shoes and seek critique about their impact from colleagues. Self-aligners engage in evaluative thinking primarily to validate their existing practices and maintain consistency. They are more likely to interpret evidence in ways that confirm their current approach, sometimes rationalizing why learning did not occur rather than questioning their methods. Self-achievers use evaluative thinking in a rule-based, procedural way, focusing on whether students followed directions, mastered routines, or met specific behavioral and academic standards. Their evaluations tend to emphasize compliance and accuracy, with limited attention to deeper reflection or instructional change. Self-sustainers engage in evaluative thinking cautiously, primarily to ensure that classroom practices remain manageable and do not threaten their sense of equilibrium. They may selectively focus on evidence that reassures them their methods are effective enough, often avoiding complex analyses that might suggest the need for change. In this way, evaluative thinking is present across all four motivations, but its depth, flexibility, and purpose vary markedly, reflecting each teacher's underlying drive toward improvement, validation, control, or stability.

There are implications for education policy from this model of teacher self-concept. To maximize the probability of selection, those who are most likely to be motivated by self-enhancement may need to prioritize candidates based on their openness to feedback, willingness to reflect on practice, and adaptability. Initial courses can then focus on how to reflect critically on their instructional impact. Professional development should emphasize formative feedback, self-reflection, high expectations, adaptive expertise, and collective efficacy, rather than primarily reinforcing traditional teaching practices. There needs to be a focus on what teachers understand by their "impact", how they would provide evidence about this impact, and address the "Three Impact Questions" (What did I teach well? Who did I teach well? How much learning did I cause?). This focus should provide scaffolded pathways that progressively move teachers toward self-improvement strategies. Performance appraisal systems need to move from focusing on adherence to curriculum and policies to assessing the impact of teaching on student learning. Accountability systems could include evidence of improvements (e.g., progress toward achievement) as much as, if not more than, achievement status of the students, and value school and system cultures that foster innovation, risk-taking, and collective models of teachers critiquing and improving their practice to enhance the learning lives of students.

This ROPE model has focused on four major motivations that form a teacher's self-concept. While these can be core notions, we have noted that there can be situations where a predominantly self-improving teacher reverts to self-alignment (and vice versa). Additionally, we acknowledge other motivations, but claim they are not as dominant among teachers or are informed by the four primary motivations, such as self-assessment, self-consistency, self-protection, self-regulation, self-determination, self-comparison, and self-handicapping (Hattie, 2004). More empirical evidence and case studies are needed to test the propositions about these processes.

There can also be multiple paths to high self-concept and self-esteem. Within the ROPE model, teachers with dominance in each of four motivations can be said to have "high teacher self-concept." For example, self-improvers derive high self-esteem from their confidence, responsiveness, collaboration, conscientiousness, and the challenges they face in teaching, as well as from their improvement-oriented thinking, adaptive expertise, impact on students, and willingness to seek and act on evidence of areas needing growth. A self-aligner may experience high self-esteem when their teaching aligns with their firmly held self-views and external expectations; they may feel validated and proud to be recognized as effective deliverers of curriculum through teacher-led, structured approaches, finding satisfaction in clarity, predictability, and adherence to traditional transmission methods, which they regard as more effective and appropriate than student-led inquiry or innovative practice. A self-achiever can hold high self-esteem by valuing their role as a precise, orderly, and dependable professional—deriving satisfaction from maintaining classroom control, delivering structured lessons, consistently adhering to routines and expectations, and achieving clear positive outcomes with their students. They may take pride in their ability to uphold standards, minimize errors, and maintain a predictable and tightly managed teaching approach, regarding these as hallmarks of effective teaching. A self-sustainer can also perceive themselves as having high self-esteem by valuing their ability to maintain personal well-being, manage workloads effectively, and create a low-stress classroom environment. They may feel validated and effective when they can sustain a sense of calm, avoid unnecessary risks, and maintain a manageable, consistent teaching approach that meets expectations without overextending themselves. Thus, across all four profiles, teachers may report high or low self-esteem, depending on how well their dominant motivation aligns with their teaching reality and personal beliefs about effectiveness. Thus, all four motivations can be said to have lower or higher self-esteem (i.e., valuing their beliefs about themselves).

It must be reiterated that while this article draws from various sources, many of its claims remain hypothetical and require further research. Testing the ROPE model requires a combination of longitudinal, experimental, psychometric, and classroom-based research. By rigorously assessing how teacher self-concept develops, affects teaching effectiveness, and can be shaped by professional learning and policy, the education field can move toward evidence-based interventions that cultivate self-improving teachers—those most likely to drive student learning and success. Some key research questions include: How does a teacher's self-concept evolve across the four maturation stages over time? Over cultures? Over curricula domains? How can interventions designed to promote self-improvement shift teachers from toward a self-improving orientation? Can the ROPE model be operationalized into a reliable and valid measure of teacher self-concept? How are the classrooms and outcomes for students different across the four motivations? How do these teachers respond to different types of feedback? How do teachers' beliefs about learning, ability, and responsibility differ, and how does this affect student achievement? How do school leadership methods relate to the four motivations?

CONCLUSIONS

As noted at the outset, there is no extensive literature on teacher self-concepts; hence, this article aims to prompt, promote, and press for more investigations into how teachers perceive themselves. These self-concepts may change with experiences in the classroom, across levels of schooling, and possibly across different cultures, as well as between various curricula domains. The strong recommendation is to see teacher self-concept more as a series of ways of thinking, that is, how they process information based on such fundamental issues of self-improving and self-aligning.

The paper introduces the ROPE model of teacher self-concept, which departs from traditional hierarchical structural models by focusing on psychological processes and motivations. The ROPE model conceptualizes teacher self-concept as a dynamic and adaptive system, shaped by four primary motivational forces: self-improvement (teachers seeking growth and embracing feedback for continuous learning), self-aligning (teachers prioritizing stability and validation of their existing self-views), self-achieving (teachers emphasizing order, precision, adherence to routines, and production of clear outcomes), and self-sustaining (teachers focusing on maintaining personal well-being, emotional balance, and manageable workloads). The claim is that these motivations influence teachers' beliefs about education and personal agency, shaping their attributes and teaching behaviors. The model's implications for teacher recruitment, professional development, and evaluation highlight the need for further empirical validation to establish its predictive power for teaching effectiveness and student success.

NOTE

1. We thank Jens Moeller, Thorben Jansen, Luke Rowe, Lyn Sharratt, Ronnel King, and Herb Marsh for improvements to this chapter.

REFERENCES

Archibald, T. (2024). Evaluative thinking. In *Research handbook on program evaluation* (pp. 35–49). Edward Elgar Publishing.

Ball, D., Thames, M. H., & Phelps, G. (2008). Content knowledge for teaching: What makes it special? *Journal of Teacher Education, 59*(5), 389–407.

Bandura, A. (1997). *Self-efficacy: The exercise of control.* W. H. Freeman.

Bartanen, B., Kwok, A., Avitabile, A., & Kim, B. H. (2025). Why do you want to be a teacher? A natural language processing approach. *Educational Researcher, 54*(1), 7–20.

Basturkmen, H. (2012). Review of research into the correspondence between language teachers' stated beliefs and practices. *System, 40*(2), 282–295.

Baumert, J., & Kunter, M. (2013). The COACTIV model of teachers' professional competence. In *Cognitive activation in the mathematics classroom and professional competence of teachers: Results from the COACTIV project* (pp. 25–48). Springer US.

Bernichon, T., Cook, K. E., & Brown, J. D. (2003). Seeking self-evaluative feedback: The interactive role of global self-esteem and specific self-views. *Journal of Personality and Social Psychology, 84*, 194–204.

Biggs, J., Kember, D., & Leung, D. Y. (2001). The revised two-factor study process questionnaire: R-SPQ-2F. *British Journal of Educational Psychology, 71*(1), 133–149.

Biggs, J. B. (1987). *Student approaches to learning and studying. Research monograph.* Australian Council for Educational Research.

Blömeke, S., Gustafsson, J. E., & Shavelson, R. J. (2015). Approaches to competence measurement in higher education. *Zeitschrift für Psychologie, 223*, 3–13.

Brophy, J. E. (1983). Research on the self-fulfilling prophecy and teacher expectations. *Journal of Educational Psychology, 75*(5), 631.

Brown, G. T. (2008). *Conceptions of assessment: Understanding what assessment means to teachers and students.* Nova Science.

Buehl, M. M., & Beck, J. S. (2014). The relationship between teachers' beliefs and teachers' practices. In *International handbook of research on teachers' beliefs* (pp. 66–84). Routledge.

Buss, D. W., & Cantor, N. (1989). *Personality psychology: Recent trends and emerging directions*. Springer-Verlag.

Butler, R. (2007). Teachers' achievement goal orientations and associations with teachers' help seeking: Examination of a novel approach to teacher motivation. *Journal of Educational Psychology, 99*(2), 241.

Butler, R. (2014). What teachers want to achieve and why it matters: An achievement goal approach to teacher motivation. In P. W. Richarson, S. A. Karabenick, & H. M. G. Watt (Eds.), *Teacher motivation* (pp. 20–35). Routledge.

Caprara, G. V., Barbaranelli, C., Steca, P., & Malone, P. S. (2006). Teachers' self-efficacy beliefs as determinants of job satisfaction and students' academic achievement: A study at the school level. *Journal of School Psychology, 44*(6), 473–490.

Chen, J., Brown, G. T., Hattie, J. A., & Millward, P. (2012). Teachers' conceptions of excellent teaching and its relationships to self-reported teaching practices. *Teaching and Teacher Education, 28*(7), 936–947.

Chesnut, S. R., & Burley, H. (2015). Self-efficacy as a predictor of commitment to the teaching profession: A meta-analysis. *Educational Research Review, 15*, 1–16.

Cheung, D., & Ng, P. H. (2000). Science teachers' beliefs about curriculum design. *Research in Science Education, 30*, 357–375.

Collins, J. B., & Pratt, D. D. (2011). The teaching perspectives inventory at 10 years and 100,000 respondents: Reliability and validity of a teacher self-report inventory. *Adult Education Quarterly, 61*(4), 358–375.

Danielson, C. (2007). *Enhancing professional practice: A framework for teaching*. AsCD.

Darling-Hammond, L., & Bransford, J. (Eds.). (2007). *Preparing teachers for a changing world: What teachers should learn and be able to do*. John Wiley & Sons.

de Ruig, N. J., Zee, M., & de Jong, P. F. (2024, May). Understanding the interplay between teacher self-efficacy, teacher–student interactions, and students' self-regulated learning skills at different levels of classroom ecology. *Frontiers in Education, 9*, 1392907. Frontiers Media SA.

Entwistle, N. (2007). 1 Research into student learning and university teaching. In *BJEP monograph series II, number 4-student learning and university teaching* (Vol. *1*, pp. 1–18). British Psychological Society.

Fenstermacher, G. D. (1978). 4: A philosophical consideration of recent research on teacher effectiveness. *Review of Research in Education, 6*(1), 157–185.

Festinger, L. (1954). A theory of social comparison processes. *Human Relations, 7*(2), 117–140.

Fives, H., & Buehl, M. M. (2012). Spring cleaning for the "messy" construct of teachers' beliefs: What are they? Which have been examined? What can they tell us? In K. R. Harris, S. Graham, T. Urdan, S. Graham, J. M. Royer, & M. Zeidner (Eds.), *APA educational psychology handbook, individual differences and cultural and contextual factors* (Vol. *2*, pp. 471–499). American Psychological Association.

Fives, H., Lacatena, N., & Gerard, L. (2014). Teachers' beliefs about teaching (and learning). In *International handbook of research on teachers' beliefs* (pp. 249–265). Routledge.

Glotova, G., & Wilhelm, A. (2014). Teacher's self-concept and self-esteem in pedagogical communication. *Procedia-Social and Behavioral Sciences, 132*, 509–514.

Hattie, J. (2004, July). Models of self-concept that are neither top-down or bottom-up: The ROPE model of self-concept. In *Proceedings of the 3rd international biennial self research conference.*

Hattie, J. (2023). *Visible learning: The sequel: A synthesis of over 2,100 meta-analyses relating to achievement.* Routledge.

Hattie, J. A. (1992). *Self-concept.* Erlbaum.

Hattie, J. A., & Brown, G. T. L. (2011). Assessment and evaluation. In C. Rubie-Davies (Ed.), *Educational psychology: Concepts, research and challenges* (pp. 102–117). Routledge.

Heine, S. J., Lehman, D. R., Markus, H. R., & Kitayama, S. (1999). Is there a universal need for positive self-regard? *Psychological Review, 106*(4), 766.

Herman, K. C., Hickmon-Rosa, J., & Reinke, W. M. (2018). Empirically derived profiles of teacher stress, burnout, self-efficacy, and coping and associated student outcomes. *Journal of Positive Behavior Interventions, 20*(2), 90–100.

Hettinger, K., Lazarides, R., & Schiefele, U. (2024). Longitudinal relations between teacher self-efficacy and student motivation through matching characteristics of perceived teaching practice. *European Journal of Psychology of Education, 39*(2), 1299–1325.

Hidi, S., & Renninger, K. A. (2006). The four-phase model of interest development. *Educational Psychologist, 41*(2), 111–127.

Hoy, A. W., Hoy, W. K., & Davis, H. A. (2009). Teachers' self-efficacy beliefs. In *Handbook of motivation at school* (pp. 641–668). Routledge.

Hussain, M. S., Khan, S. A., & Bidar, M. C. (2022). Self-efficacy of teachers: A review of the literature. *Multi-Disciplinary Research Journal, 10*(1), 110–116.

Inan-Kaya, G., & Rubie-Davies, C. M. (2022). Teacher classroom interactions and behaviours: Indications of bias. *Learning and Instruction, 78*, 101516.

James, W. (1890). *The principles of psychology.* Henry Holt.

Jussim, L., Eccles, J., & Madon, S. (1996). Social perception, social stereotypes, and teacher expectations: Accuracy and the quest for the powerful self-fulfilling prophecy. *Advances in Experimental Social Psychology, 28*, 281–388. Academic Press.

Jussim, L., & Eccles, J. S. (1992). Teacher expectations: II. Construction and reflection of student achievement. *Journal of Personality and Social Psychology, 63*(6), 947.

Jussim, L., & Harber, K. D. (2005). Teacher expectations and self-fulfilling prophecies: Knowns and unknowns, resolved and unresolved controversies. *Personality and Social Psychology Review, 9*(2), 131–155.

Kagan, D. M. (1992). Implication of research on teacher belief. *Educational Psychologist, 27*(1), 65–90.

Kasalak, G., & Dagyar, M. (2020). The relationship between teacher self-efficacy and teacher job satisfaction: A meta-analysis of the teaching and learning international survey (TALIS). *Educational Sciences: Theory and Practice, 20*(3), 16–33.

Kember, D. (1997). A reconceptualisation of the research into university academics' conceptions of teaching. *Learning and Instruction, 7*(3), 255–275.

Kim, K. R., & Seo, E. H. (2018). The relationship between teacher efficacy and students' academic achievement: A meta-analysis. *Social Behavior and Personality: An International Journal, 46*(4), 529–540.

Klassen, R. M., & Tze, V. M. (2014). Teachers' self-efficacy, personality, and teaching effectiveness: A meta-analysis. *Educational Research Review, 12*, 59–76.

Lauermann, F., & ten Hagen, I. (2021). Do teachers' perceived teaching competence and self-efficacy affect students' academic outcomes? A closer look at student-reported classroom processes and outcomes. *Educational Psychologist, 56*(4), 265–282.

Lohbeck, A., Hagenauer, G., & Frenzel, A. C. (2018). Teachers' self-concepts and emotions: Conceptualization and relations. *Teaching and Teacher Education, 70*, 111–120.

Mansour, N. (2009). Science teachers' beliefs and practices: Issues, implications and research agenda. *International Journal of Environmental & Science Education, 4*(1), 25–48.

Marsh, H. W., Ellis, L. A., & Craven, R. G. (2002). How do preschool children feel about themselves? Unraveling measurement and multidimensional self-concept structure. *Developmental Psychology, 38*(3), 376.

Marsh, H. W., Pekrun, R., Parker, P. D., Murayama, K., Guo, J., Dicke, T., & Arens, A. K. (2019). The murky distinction between self-concept and self-efficacy: Beware of lurking jingle-jangle fallacies. *Journal of Educational Psychology, 111*(2), 331.

Marsh, H. W., Relich, J. D., & Smith, I. D. (1983). Self-concept: The construct validity of interpretations based upon the SDQ. *Journal of Personality and Social Psychology, 45*(1), 173–182.

Marsh, H. W., & Shavelson, R. (1985). Self-concept: Its multifaceted, hierarchical structure. *Educational Psychologist, 20*(3), 107–123.

Marsh, H. W., Xu, M., & Martin, A. J. (2012). Self-concept: A synergy of theory, method, and application. In K. Harris, S. Graham, & T. Urdan (Eds.), *APA educational psychology handbook*. American Psychological Association.

Marton, F., & Säljö, R. (1976). On qualitative differences in learning: I—outcome and process. *British Journal of Educational Psychology, 46*(1), 4–11.

Mishra, P., & Koehler, M. J. (2006). Technological pedagogical content knowledge: A framework for teacher knowledge. *Teachers College Record, 108*(6), 1017–1054.

Möller, J., & Marsh, H. W. (2013). Dimensional comparison theory. *Psychological Review, 120*(3), 544.

Morris, D. B., Usher, E. L., & Chen, J. A. (2017). Reconceptualizing the sources of teaching self-efficacy: A critical review of emerging literature. *Educational Psychology Review, 29*, 795–833.

Mu, G. M. (2024). A systematic literature review of building resilience for pre-service teachers. *International Journal of Educational Research, 128*, 102476.

Nespor, J. (1987). The role of beliefs in the practice of teaching. *Journal of Curriculum Studies, 19*(4), 317–328.

Pajares, M. F. (1992). Teachers' beliefs and educational research: Cleaning up a messy construct. *Review of Educational Research, 62*(3), 307–332.

Paulick, I., Großschedl, J., Harms, U., & Möller, J. (2016). Preservice teachers' professional knowledge and its relation to academic self-concept. *Journal of Teacher Education, 67*(3), 173–182.

Priestley, M., Biesta, G. J. J., & Robinson, S. (2015). Teacher agency: What is it and why does it matter?. In R. Kneyber & J. Evers (Eds.), *Flip the system: Changing education from the bottom up*. Routledge.

Purdie, N., & Hattie, J. (2002). Assessing students' conceptions of learning. *Australian Journal of Educational and Developmental Psychology, 2*, 17–32.

Retelsdorf, J., Butler, R., Streblow, L., & Schiefele, U. (2010). Teachers' goal orientations for teaching: Associations with instructional practices, interest in teaching, and burnout. *Learning and Instruction, 20*(1), 30–46.

Roche, L. A., & Marsh, H. W. (2000). Multiple dimensions of university teacher self-concept. *Instructional Science, 28*, 439–468.

Rosenthal, R., & Jacobson, L. (1968). *Pygmalion in the classroom*. Holt, Rinehart and Winston.

Rubie-Davies, C. (2014). *Becoming a high expectation teacher: Raising the bar*. Routledge.

Rubie-Davies, C. (2017). *Teacher expectations in education*. Routledge.

Rubie-Davies, C. M., & Hattie, J. A. (2024). The powerful impact of teacher expectations: A narrative review. *Journal of the Royal Society of New Zealand*, 1–29.

Ryan, R. M., & Deci, E. L. (2017). *Self-determination theory: Basic psychological needs in motivation, development, and wellness*. Guilford Press.

Sabarwal, S., Abu-Jawdeh, M., & Kapoor, R. (2022). Teacher beliefs: Why they matter and what they are. *The World Bank Research Observer, 37*(1), 73–106.

Santos, D., & Miguel, L. (2019). The relationship between teachers' beliefs, teachers' behaviors, and teachers' professional development: A literature review. *International Journal of Education and Practice, 7*(1), 10–18.

Scarborough, H. S. (2001). Connecting early language and literacy to later reading (dis)abilities: Evidence, theory, and practice. In S. Neuman & D. Dickinson (Eds.), *Handbook for research in early literacy* (pp. 97–110). Guilford Press.

Schwarzer, R., & Hallum, S. (2008). Perceived teacher self-efficacy as a predictor of job stress and burnout: Mediation analyses. *Applied Psychology, 57*, 152–171.

Scriven, M. (1994). Duties of the Teacher. *Journal of Personnel Evaluation in Education, 8*(2), 151–184.

Shavelson, R. J., Hubner, J. J., & Stanton, G. C. (1976). Self-concept: Validation of construct interpretations. *Review of Educational Research, 46*(3), 407–441.

Shoji, K., Cieslak, R., Smoktunowicz, E., Rogala, A., Benight, C. C., & Luszczynska, A. (2016). Associations between job burnout and self-efficacy: A meta-analysis. *Anxiety, Stress & Coping, 29*(4), 367–386.

Shulman, L. (1987). Knowledge and teaching: Foundations of the new reform. *Harvard Educational Review, 57*(1), 1–23.

Shulruf, B., Hattie, J., & Dixon, R. (2011). Intertwinement of individualist and collectivist attributes and response sets. *Journal of Social, Evolutionary, and Cultural Psychology, 5*(1), 51.

Stengel, B. S. (2010). Autonomy? Or responsibility? *Educational Theory, 60*(1), 19–28.

Swann, W. B. Jr. (2012). Self-verification theory. In V. Zeigler-Hill & T. K. Shackelford (Eds.), *Encyclopedia of personality and individual differences* (pp. 1–9).

Swann, W. B. Jr., & Buhrmester, M. D. (2015). Identity fusion. *Current Directions in Psychological Science, 24*(1), 52–57.

Swann, W. B. Jr., Pelham, B. W., & Krull, D. S. (1989). Agreeable fancy or disagreeable truth? How people reconcile their self-enhancement and self-verification needs. *Journal of Personality and Social Psychology, 57*, 782–791.

Swann, W. B. Jr., & Read, S. J. (1981). Self-verification processes: How we sustain our self-conceptions. *Journal of Experimental Social Psychology, 17*(4), 351–372.

Tschannen-Moran, M., Hoy, A. W., & Hoy, W. K. (1998). Teacher efficacy: Its meaning and measure. *Review of Educational Research, 68*(2), 202–248.
Verloop, N., Van Driel, J., & Meijer, P. (2001). Teacher knowledge and the knowledge base of teaching. *International Journal of Educational Research, 35*(5), 441–461.
Watt, H. M., & Richardson, P. W. (2007). Motivational factors influencing teaching as a career choice: Development and validation of the FIT-Choice scale. *The Journal of Experimental Education, 75*(3), 167–202.
Watt, H. M., & Richardson, P. W. (2012). An introduction to teaching motivations in different countries: Comparisons using the FIT-Choice scale. *Asia-Pacific Journal of Teacher Education, 40*(3), 185–197.
Watt, H. M., & Richardson, P. W. (2014). A motivational analysis of teachers' beliefs. In *International handbook of research on teachers' beliefs* (pp. 191–211). Routledge.
Wigfield, A., & Eccles, J. S. (2000). Expectancy–value theory of achievement motivation. *Contemporary Educational Psychology, 25*(1), 68–81.
Windschitl, M., Thompson, J., & Braaten, M. (2011). Ambitious pedagogy by novice teachers: Who benefits from tool-supported collaborative inquiry into practice and why? *Teachers College Record, 113*(7), 1311–1360.
Witter, M. (2023). *Examining multiple dimensions of teacher quality. Doctoral dissertation.* University of Melbourne.
Witter, M., & Hattie, J. (2024). Can teacher quality be profiled? A cluster analysis of teachers' beliefs, practices and students' perceptions of effectiveness. *British Educational Research Journal, 50*(2), 653–675.
Wittgenstein, L. (1958). *Philosophical investigations.* G. E. M. Anscombe, Trans. (3rd ed.). Macmillan.
Yeung, A. S., Craven, R. G., & Kaur, G. (2014). Teachers' self-concept and valuing of learning: Relations with teaching approaches and beliefs about students. *Asia-Pacific Journal of Teacher Education, 42*(3), 305–320.
Zee, M., & Koomen, H. M. (2016). Teacher self-efficacy and its effects on classroom processes, student academic adjustment, and teacher well-being: A synthesis of 40 years of research. *Review of Educational Research, 86*(4), 981–1015.

CHAPTER 13

UNDERSTANDING MOTIVATION ACROSS CULTURES: DENNIS MCINERNEY'S ENDURING LEGACY

Ronnel B. King
The Chinese University of Hong Kong, Hong Kong

Herbert W. Marsh
Australian Catholic University, Australia

Rhonda G. Craven
Australian Catholic University, Australia

Theresa Dicke
Australian Catholic University, Australia

Frédéric Guay
University of Laval, Canada

The Self in Context, pages 439–445

Published under exclusive licence by Emerald Publishing Limited
doi:10.1108/978-1-80686-869-820261013

ABSTRACT

This chapter honors the lasting impact of Dennis M. McInerney, to whom this volume is dedicated. It highlights his significant scholarly contributions and features tributes from colleagues and friends whose lives were profoundly influenced by him. Some of the verbatim reflections presented in this chapter build on responses originally sent to the *AERA 2022 SSRL Times Magazine* (Whitehead et al., 2022) and a tribute written by Bembenutty et al. (2022) published in *Educational Psychology Review* (2022). We acknowledge these sources at the outset of the chapter and include a formal reference to ensure that proper credit is given to the contributing authors and their institutions.

This volume is dedicated to the memory of Dennis Michael McInerney, a pioneering scholar and an extraordinary human being whose life and work left an indelible mark on the field of educational psychology. In preparing this tribute, we also draw on earlier published reflections and memorial pieces that documented Dennis McInerney's scholarly and personal influence (Bembenutty et al., 2023; Whitehead et al., 2022). Throughout history, educational psychology has been shaped by creative thinkers who redirected the field in new and meaningful ways. Dennis was one of those rare visionaries. He was most renowned for his sociocultural approaches to motivation and learning, challenging us to look beyond narrow, parochial perspectives and engage with the wider, more diverse world. True to this conviction, he made a second home in Asia, where he built a flourishing career in Singapore and Hong Kong, mentoring a new generation of scholars and helping transform institutions into research-intensive universities.

Dennis' academic legacy is vast. He authored widely used textbooks, nearly 200 research articles, and edited landmark series on motivation and self-research. He urged us to rethink the dominance of Western theories by balancing etic (universal) and emic (culture-specific) approaches, showing us that cultural "differences" were not errors to be corrected but insights into human diversity. His work illuminated how family, peers, teachers, and cultural context shape motivation and achievement, with a deep commitment to equity, especially for Indigenous and underrepresented students. He was fearless in questioning conventions, whether methodological orthodoxy or theoretical assumptions, and his intellectual courage opened new paths for the field.

But beyond his scholarship, Dennis was a man of uncommon warmth, generosity, and joy. He touched countless lives—not just through his ideas, but through his friendship, mentorship, and sheer zest for life.

We the editors of this volume recall our memories of Dennis.

Ronnel: *I learned as much from Dennis in the office as in the restaurants he loved. Dennis loved life, and his joie de vivre was contagious. He was a good role model for me, as he lived life to the fullest. Dennis was many things to me—a boss, a mentor, a travel partner, a drinking buddy, and a beloved friend. Most of all, he was my 师父 (Shifu), a Chinese term usually translated to "master." However, the most accurate translation would be a teacher (shi) and a father (fu). He was a teacher and father to me in the truest sense of the word. His presence has much enriched my life.*

Herbert: *Dennis was a wonderful colleague. Professionally, I could always count on Dennis to provide an alternative perspective when I needed it. But my fondest memories are the many social occasions we shared. Dennis was a party animal who loved life and was great fun to be with. His wicked sense of humor has always brought a smile to my face, even when directed at me. And sometimes, I brought out the devil in Dennis. I will greatly miss him, as we all will.*

Rhonda: *What a terrible loss for Dennis' family, friends, and indeed, the world. Dennis was not only a stellar academic but an extraordinary human being who devoted his life to enriching and transforming the lives of children and communities across the globe. He believed deeply in the power of education to unlock human potential and continued advancing knowledge long after retirement. A trailblazer in motivation theory, he was also among the first non-Indigenous scholars to champion the rights, recognition, and self-determination of Indigenous peoples worldwide.*

Beyond his scholarship, Dennis was a loyal friend—wise, generous, and full of life. His humor, warmth, and irrepressible spirit made every gathering brighter. He lived life on his own terms: traveling the world, forging friendships, and sharing laughter and wine along the way. Dennis was an intergalactic superstar of humanity whose light will continue to inspire and guide all who had the privilege of knowing him.

Theresa: *Though my own interactions with Dennis were brief, his reputation as both a pioneering scholar and a generous colleague preceded him. His work exemplified a rare blend of theoretical sophistication and cultural sensitivity, continually reminding us to consider how context and culture shape motivation and learning. Dennis's commitment to inclusive, globally minded research has profoundly influenced how we understand and support diverse learners and teachers. His intellectual legacy continues to guide our thinking and connect scholars across continent— a lasting testament to the breadth and humanity of his vision."*

Frédéric: *I first met Dennis at the Self Conference in 2004, held at the Max Planck Institute in Berlin. During a conversation about my plans to spend a sabbatical at the Self Research Center in Sydney, he immediately put me at ease. His warmth, openness, and genuine interest in my aspirations gave me a profound sense of encouragement and made the prospect of working at the Center, alongside my family, even more appealing.*

Later, I had the privilege of collaborating with him on editing a book for the series International Advances in Self Research, an experience that remains among the most enriching of my career. He also invited me to write a commentary for a special issue on culture and motivation in the British Journal of Educational Psychology. This was my first experience contributing to such a prestigious publication, and once again, his mentorship proved invaluable. His guidance was marked by generosity, patience, and a rare blend of intellectual rigor and humility. He never imposed; he always invited dialog. His subtle, warm sense of humor brought lightness to even the most demanding moments. Beyond his profound contributions to educational psychology, it was his humanity that left the deepest impression on me. His legacy continues to inspire me and countless others.

Other colleagues and friends recall how their lives have been touched by Dennis.

- *Dennis McInerney exemplified the art of embracing both difference and shared humanity. He moved effortlessly between his independent and interdependent selves—assertive in his scholarly vision yet always attuned to others' perspectives. With humility, warmth, and deep respect, he valued cultural nuance while remaining grounded and inclusive in his interactions across cultures. Dennis showed us what it means to be both true to oneself and deeply connected to others. That is what we aspire to become—not only as scholars, but as human beings. I will always cherish his presence in my life and the lasting example he set for us all* –Gregory Arief Liem
- *I first met Professor Dennis McInerney in the early 1990s while working with Professor Herbert Marsh in Sydney. Dennis was an inspiring and generous scholar whose enthusiasm for educational psychology was infectious. His textbooks became classics in Australia, reflecting his unique ability to enliven theory with the personal stories of the scholars behind it. When he later moved to Hong Kong, he quickly developed a deep affection for the city, speaking fluent Cantonese and engaging warmly with local colleagues. Dennis's remarkable scholarship, collegiality, and humanity left*

a lasting legacy in educational psychology and in the hearts of those who knew him. –Kit Tai Hau

- *While his scholarly achievements are widely celebrated, those who knew Dennis remember him most fondly for his personal warmth, humility, and generosity of spirit. I recall meeting him for the first time at the National Institute of Education, Nanyang Technological University, in Singapore, where he was on study leave. In his office stood a display of his many books—13 at the time. I remarked, "Wow, you've written thirteen academic books in motivation and school psychology. That is truly remarkable!" He smiled and replied cheerfully, "Oh, now it's fifteen. The books were sold faster than I could write." That moment captured the essence of Denni — accomplished yet modest, always good-humored, and deeply human. Professor McInerney was esteemed not only as a scholar of international standing but also as a mentor, colleague, and friend. He was unfailingly considerate, kind-hearted, and wise—a person who, in true Australian fashion, would "bend over backwards" to help others. Whether through his constructive feedback on a student's work, his thoughtful guidance to junior colleagues, or his ever-present encouragement, he embodied the spirit of collegiality and mentorship that defines the very best of academia.* –Magdalena Mok
- *One of my most significant memories is my very first encounter with him in San Antonio, which left me with the impression of a true human being who is natural, down to earth, with big smiles and laughter. Dennis was genuinely concerned about the development of younger researchers across cultures and sacrificed his time to offer the needed support. I hope to practice what I learned from my mentor and friend.* –Aloy Anyichie
- *In my work, Dennis has been a great mentor. He has helped me review numerous proposals I have drafted and provided the most valuable feedback to me to improve them. He knew that as a junior researcher, I was often worried about proposals, publications research, and almost every aspect of the academic job, so he generously shared his experiences and gave advice, and never forgot to encourage me. Dennis is not only a good teacher and mentor, but most importantly, he has also been an excellent family friend. I still remember hanging out in Chicago and New York for dinners and chats. He played with my little boy, who, by that time, was only two years old. He gave us advice about how to raise that little boy. After I had settled down in Hong Kong, we regularly hung out with other friends for dinners, talking about things happening in our lives and jobs. Whenever we saw him, he showed us his brightest side; he would share many happy things and tell many jokes, and then everybody laughed. This time has become my best memory. Unfortunately, we have lost this great teacher, mentor, and friend, who has been our inspiration and role model throughout the past years. We will miss him and cherish all the great memories with him.* –Hui Wang

- *Dennis lived a happy, full life—I am sure of that. He was a genuinely nurturing supervisor who valued the life and well-being of everyone. At the same time, Dennis set high standards in his professional work. He knew how to enjoy a social life. Regularly after work, he would make it a point to invite friends and colleagues for social gatherings. All enjoyed the time spent together, and Dennis shared many exciting stories and wisdom. He will be dearly missed.* –Fred Ganotice
- *I am honored to be Dennis' only and last doctoral student at the Education University of Hong Kong. I still vividly remember that when I first met him in his office in 2009, he was very serious and gave me a long reference list, including his books and journal articles. He guided me through my doctoral journey. I learned the foundation of research from him, who helped me revise my dissertation. I especially appreciated the tremendous support he gave me while I was writing my dissertation and grieving the loss of my father at the same time. Not only was Dennis a great scholar, doing research and teaching with great passion and perseverance, but he was also a role model and caring teacher. He was very positive and always encouraged me, guiding me on my career path. I will always apply my knowledge to supervise my students.* –Grace Chao
- *In times when I felt rejected and discouraged, Dennis was there to passionately share words of encouragement, which enhanced my eagerness to improve my research program. In our mentoring sessions throughout these years, he was a great source of delightful, humorous, and inspirational lessons not only about strengthening research impacts and improving teaching effectiveness but also about prioritizing positivity in life, such as traveling, playing mahjong, cooking, and baking. These fantastic memories have made me realize that striving for professional growth is not an excuse for not living life to the fullest.* –Jesus Datu
- *Dennis' generosity and wisdom have brought invaluable mental resources to my academic career. Under Dennis' mentorship, I had the great honor to co-author with him two articles; one appeared in Learning and Individual Differences and the other in the Journal of Experimental Education, both addressing developmental issues of metacognitive strategy use and the impact on language learning achievement. Dennis' generously left his academic heritage with us by sharing his data with junior scholars in Hong Kong. His legacy became an inspiration for me.* –Yuyang Cai
- *I first met Dennis in the mid-1970s. At that time I was impressed by his research into the cognitive abilities of Australian aboriginals. Later, his development of the Inventory of School Motivation helped us obtain a research grant. This allowed us to explore the impact of changes to the educational system on the enthusiasm for learning of Hong Kong students. Rest in Peace my friend.*—David Watkins
- *"Larger than life, Dennis guaranteed fun in every gathering."* –Andrew Martin

- *"The most gregarious, generous, and down-to-earth academic I had ever met. He focused less on the work and more on the people."* –Nathan Hall
- *"The first thing I noticed about you was your energy. While you've taken that energy with you, you left a little of it behind for us."* –Anthony Dillon
- *"His joie de vivre was infectious… the world feels less bright without him."* –Helen Watt
- *Thank God Dennis and I had 17 quality years together. It was my honor to be able to share every single happiness and sadness with Dennis. I will miss him. I will always hold onto the amazing memories we shared. Goodbye Dennis. I know we only let go of your body, but your love will be with me, with us and our families forever. You are leaving behind a legacy of kindness, compassion, and generosity.* –Hing Tung Tsang, Patrick

There are many others whose lives Dennis touched. We celebrate Dennis not only for his distinguished scholarship but also for his human spirit. His theoretical brilliance, intellectual courage, and care for others—especially those from marginalized communities—will continue to inspire future generations. For those of us who knew him, his greatest gift was simple but profound: he made life richer, brighter, and more meaningful.

With gratitude and love, we honor the remarkable life of Dennis Michael McInerney through this volume.

REFERENCES

Bembenutty, H., Liem, G. A. D., Allen, K. A., King, R. B., Martin, A. J., Marsh, H. W., …, & Datu, J. A. D. (2023). Culture, motivation, self-regulation, and the impactful work of Dennis M. McInerney. *Educational Psychology Review, 35*(1), 28.

Whitehead, A., Bembenutty, H., & Murphy, P. F. (Eds.) (2022, September), *Times magazine* (Vol. 5, p. 7). Dennis McInerney.

Printed and bound by CPI Group (UK) Ltd, Croydon, CR0 4YY
21/09/2026
14966034-0008